PIONEER OF
MEXICAN-AMERICAN
CIVIL RIGHTS

ALONSO S. PERALES

PIONEER OF
MEXICAN-AMERICAN
CIVIL RIGHTS

ALONSO S. PERALES

CYNTHIA E. OROZCO

Arte Público Press
Houston, Texas

Pioneer of Mexican-American Civil Rights: Alonso S. Perales is made possible in part through a grant from the Summerlee Foundation. We are grateful for their support.

Recovering the past, creating the future

Arte Público Press
University of Houston
4902 Gulf Fwy, Bldg 19, Rm 100
Houston, Texas 77204-2004

Cover design by Mora Des!gn

♾ The paper used in this publication meets the requirements of the American National Standard for Information Sciences—Permanence of Paper for Printed Library Materials, ANSI Z39.48-1984.

20 21 22 23   4 3 2 1

Dedicated to Adela Sloss-Vento

Table of Contents

Acknowledgements ix
List of Abbreviations xiii
Foreword by Honorable Julián Castro xv
Introduction: Forgotten, Remembered, Attacked xvii

PART I: ACROSS TIME

Chapter 1
The Mexican Colony in San Antonio and South Texas,
1910-1960 3

Chapter 2
Early Family Life in Alice, Texas 17

Chapter 3
World War I in San Antonio, Texas 31

Chapter 4
Education in Washington, DC 39

Chapter 5
Organizing in San Antonio and the Lower Rio Grande
Valley, 1920s 47

Chapter 6
Harlingen, Texas Convention Excludes Mexicans, 1927 54

Chapter 7
Founding of the Latin American Citizens (LAC) in the
Valley, 1927..61

Chapter 8
Founding of the League of United Latin American Citizens
(LULAC) in Corpus Christi, 1929 70

Chapter 9
The LULAC Constitution, 1929 74

Chapter 10
Perales and LULAC, 1930-1960 85

Chapter 11
   Activist, 1930s 116

Chapter 12
   Activist, 1940s 126

Chapter 13
   Activist, 1950s 143

PART II: PUBLIC IMPACT

Chapter 14
   Attorney 163

Chapter 15
   Politico 187

Chapter 16
   Public Intellectual 216

Chapter 17
   US Diplomat in Latin America 240

PART III: PRIVATE LIFE

Chapter 18
   Religion 263

Chapter 19
   Character 271

Chapter 20
   Family 290

Chapter 21
   Friends and Adversaries 304

Chapter 22
   Health and Death 326

PART IV: PERALES ON TRIAL

Chapter 23
   In Defense of Perales in Latino History 337

Chapter 24
   Conclusion 369

Selected Bibliography 372
Timeline: Life of Alonso S. Perales 383
Notes 389

Acknowledgements

I thank Dr. Nicolás Kanellos, Dr. Gabriela Baeza Ventura and Dr. Carolina Villarroel of Arte Público Press for asking me to write Alonso S. Perales' biography. Historian F. Arturo Rosales experienced an untimely death in 2016 while researching and writing his book on Perales which he began in 2009. He had written six chapters, all about the era before 1920, and three from which I garnered information.[1] His chapters on Perales' life in Alice, Texas; the Perales brothers' participation in World War I; and early family life proved useful. My book *No Mexicans, Women or Dogs: The Rise of the Mexican American Civil Rights Movement* and Jose Ramírez' book on World War I identified the significance of the war on Perales. Fortunately, I had already spent forty years studying the Mexican-American civil rights movement in Texas, especially LULAC, so Perales was familiar to me.

This effort would have been considerably more difficult without three books already written on Perales. In 1977 elder civil rights leader Adela Sloss-Vento wrote his biography. She was Perales' ally, a major activist from 1927 to 1990 and became an acquaintance of mine in 1978. After Perales died in 1960 she spent decades trying to get the public and LULAC to recognize Perales' legacy. Her quest is revealed in my book *Agent of Change* published in January 2020.

Historian Richard A. Garcia's book on San Antonio in the 1930s provided the first insight into Perales' ideology and offered significant detail about the city's Mexican origin populace. Thirdly, in 2012 Arte Público Press published conference papers about Perales organized by the University of Houston's Recovering the US Hispanic Literary Heritage Program and attorney/scholar Michael A. Olivas. Numerous scholars contributed original essays on Perales including Olivas,

Benjamín Márquez, Joseph Orbock Medina, Lupe S. Salinas, Aaron E. Sánchez, George A. Martínez, Mario T. García, Virginia Marie Raymond, Norma Adelfa Moulton, Donna M. Kabalen de Bichara, F. Arturo Rosales; and Emilio Zamora. It is rare when a Chicana scholar can benefit from insight from other Latino scholars on a biography. Contributors tackled Perales from the vantage point of specific disciplines and topics. Salinas and Olivas addressed him as an attorney. García saw Perales as a political Catholic. Zamora showed Perales' work in international diplomacy while Raymond revealed Perales' anti-communist ideology and his criticism of the Catholic Church. Medina raised issues about a singular vision of Mexican-American civil rights; Sánchez addressed issues of citizenship and belonging. Literary scholar Moulton focused on letters written by ordinary people victimized by racial discrimination. Kabalen de Bichara focused on Perales' letters and one of his books and his deconstructed sytems of thought while Martínez addressed Perales' anti-racism work from a critical race perspective. My contribution to Olivas' book detailed Perales' LULAC work in the 1930s and an expanded version appears here in chapter 11.

I thank a number of archives and libraries including Special Collections, M.D. Anderson Library at the University of Houston where the Perales papers are housed; University of Texas at Austin Dolph Briscoe Center for American History; Nettie Lee Benson Latin American Collection at the University of Texas at Austin; James Jernigan Library at Texas A&M University in Kingsville; Cushing Library at Texas A&M University at College Station; Institute of Texan Cultures of San Antonio; Center for Southwest Research at the University of New Mexico; Bancroft Library at the University of California at Berkeley; Chicano Studies Research Center at UCLA; and the National Archives in Washington, DC. The Texana Room in the San Antonio Public Library also proved useful. Graduate student Manny Grajales helped with research at Texas A&M University in College Station. At the University of Houston I thank Christian Kelleher, Lisa Cruces and Imelda Cervantes.

At the Benson I thank University of Texas Mexican American Library Program librarians Roberto Urzúa, Elvira Chavaria (who built

the foundation of the LULAC Archive), Gilda Baeza and Margo Gutiérrez, all now retired but who laid the foundation of archives so LULAC
research was possible. Both Chavaria and Gutiérrez tried to acquire the
Perales papers for UT Austin. I also thank the Benson staff who provided friendship over decades: Wanda, Ann, Carmen and Mike, all retired.

My journey as a young historian began at age 20 as a sophomore
in a class with Victor Nelson Cisneros when I wrote a thirty-page
research paper with ninety-nine footnotes. I especially thank the
belated Adela Sloss-Vento of Edinburg who shared her papers with
me in 1979 when I was a young historian. Likewise, she contacted
Marta Pérez Perales so she might permit me use her husband's papers
in 1979 from which I wrote my senior honors thesis completed in
1980. This allowed me to detail Perales' activities in the 1920s. In
2009 the University of Houston obtained the Perales papers. Dr.
Arnoldo Carlos Vento kindly shared the Sloss-Vento papers located in
Austin from 2012 to 2016. Historian J. Gilberto Quezada and Elaine
Ayala of the *San Antonio Express* also assisted.

The following institutions provided research and travel support:
Arte Público Press, Eastern New Mexico University, Ruidoso and
Eastern New Mexico University, Portales. I also thank work-study student Paula Gómez. Halen Anderson proved a skillful assistant and I
thank Teresa Palomo Acosta and Judge Lupe Salinas for their insight
on several chapters. Marta and Raimundo Perales, children of Perales,
also helped as did niece Araceli Pérez Davis and Blanca E. Perales.

Finally, I would like to thank my family. My mother, Aurora E.
Orozco was a Dreamer in the 1920s, community leader, LULACer,
writer and orator. I also thank my father Primitivo, a Mexican immi-
grant bootmaker. My sister Meta Orozco shared her home with me in
Houston while sister Sylvia Orozco, the founder and director of
Mexic-Arte museum, did so in Austin. I also thank husband Leo
Martínez. Finally, I thank son Lucky, a wonderful dog and family
member, always allowed and cherished.

Ruidoso, New Mexico C.E.O.
Fall 2021

List of Abbreviations

ACSSP American Council of Spanish-Speaking Persons (Southwest & Chicago)

AFL American Federation of Labor (national)

AGIF American G.I. Forum (national)

AHA Alianza Hispano Americana (national)

ANMA Associacion Nacional Mexico Americana (New Mexico)

CCC Civilian Conservation Corps (national)

CIO Congress of Industrial Organization (national)

CSO Community Service Organization (California, Arizona)

FEPC Federal Employment Practices Commission (national)

GGL Good Government League (San Antonio)

GNC Good Neighbor Commission (Texas)

LAC Latin American Citizens League (South Texas, especially the Valley)

LULAC League of United Latin American Citizens (national)

MALDEF Mexican American Legal Defense and Education Fund (national)

MAYO Mexican American Youth Organization (Texas)

OKA Order Knights of America (San Antonio)

OSA Order Sons of America (San Antonio and South Texas)

OST Order Sons of Texas (San Antonio)

PAPA Pan American Progressive Association (San Antonio)

PASSO Political Association of Spanish Speaking Organization (Southwest)

PART Pan American Round Table (Texas)

RUP Raza Unida Party (Texas, New Mexico, Midwest)

SIL School Improvement League (San Antonio)

TFW Texas Farm Workers (Texas)

UFW United Farm Workers (national)

WPA Works Progress Administration (national)

Foreword

Nearly a decade ago, when the United Census Bureau announced the findings of its latest decennial count, many Americans greeted the news of explosive growth within the Latino community with concern and curiosity. What would the "Hispanicization" of our country mean for America's future? What, they wondered, were Latinos all about? For those who still wonder—or who simply want to better understand how the promise of America moves from a dream nearer to reality— the story of Alonso S. Perales is a must read. Born just before the turn of the 20th century and orphaned at age six, Perales lived a hard-scrabble life as a young man in the small town of Alice, Texas, before serving in the United States Army during World War I, graduating from college and law school, pushing for civil rights as a lawyer and activist, and authoring books and opinion columns. Indeed, Perales demonstrated the very values that propelled our democracy forward: love of country, a willingness to work hard, and commitment to equality and the rule of law.

Few have done as much as Perales to make the promise of America real for Mexican-Americans. He understood the power of community-building and the urgency of pushing his fellow Americans to work toward justice for all, so that our nation could one day live up to its highest ideals. As principal founder of the League of United Latin American Citizens (LULAC) and its third president, Perales created and helped build an organization nearly unmatched in its advocacy for Mexican-American and broader Latino advancement across generations. Perales was foundational to Latino civil rights in San Antonio, Texas, and the United States. As Latinos seeking the American Dream confronted one hurdle after another, from segregation and disenfranchisement to economic injustice and nativist immigration laws, LULAC stood at the vanguard of empowerment, as it does today.

In many ways, Perales exemplified the best of service to others. He was also human—and a politician—and therefore flawed and complex. Historian Cynthia E. Orozco compellingly explores Perales' life in full, to take the measure of a man whose life's work added up to hard-won progress for the Mexican-American community he so loved and dedicated his life to fighting for.

Tucked below the headlines of the 2010 census was another figure. Almost a quarter of children under eighteen in our country are Latino. America's destiny and the destiny of the Latino community have never been more intertwined. Fortunately, generations of Latinos stand on Perales' shoulders: young men and women who've earned a higher education, served our country overseas, started their own businesses, shepherded scientific breakthroughs, and broken barriers at city halls, state capitols and in the halls of Congress.

One January day in the not too distant future, a Latino or Latina will be sworn in as President of the United States. That moment will not only make history, it will also be a moment of celebration, and a time to give thanks to so many pioneers who helped bring it to fruition. May Alonso S. Perales's name be spoken that day.

Julián Castro
Former Secretary of Housing and Urban Development
June 2020

Introduction

The Defender of La Raza
Five decades of a vibrant voice
In Texas courts you hear
And before Congress resonates constantly
Wants to defend huge freedoms
Against unfair bigots
That impurgatory of people's rights
His harmony and bravery breaks union
The voice proclaims the fraternity
To all the men of America
That happiness can be wrought
Of the righteousness of Homer's justice
On the lips of Alonso S. Perales
Against the treacherous nestling malice
In the calling voice lights
Of equity in the Mexican soul
That with skillful alacrity defends
The Indo-Hispano-American Raza.[1]

Prof. Manuel Urbina, San Antonio

This book argues that Alonso S. Perales was one of the most significant Latinos in the United States leaving a civic, political, educational and intellectual legacy unmatched by few others. He was an elite but a man of his own making. As a civil rights activist, he founded the League of United Latin American Citizens (LULAC) in 1929, not only one of the oldest Latino civic associations in the United States but one of the most effective. In civic engagement, no one matches his call for the racial uplift of La Raza. In politics, he helped initiate serious efforts at political empowerment of Mexican Americans and Latinos through the voting box in the 1930s long before Willie Veslásquez did so in San Antonio, Texas in the 1970s. Perales sought to pass Texas state and federal legislation banning racial discrimination. He collaborated with Senator Dennis Chávez as the lone Latino in Congress in the 1940s, and pressed for the Federal Employment Practices Commission (FEPC), a federal employment anti-discrimination agency during World War II and before today's Equal Employment Opportunity Commission. He also helped elect Henry B. González as a Mexican American in the Texas legislature and who would become the first Tejano in Congress. In education, Perales fought for school desegregation across Texas and initiated a mass movement for more and better public schools for Mexican-descent people in San Antonio. As a public intellectual, he in effect defined "Mexican Americanism," an emerging identity and political philosophy, spreading and living this ideology for over four decades.

Perales' history pertains to Latinos, not just people of Mexican descent. He did so as a US diplomat in Latin America; as a civil rights activist fighting discrimination against Latinos and Latin Americans in the United States; and also by serving Nicaraguan Americans as a Consul General for Nicaragua in the United States in the 1940s and 50s. Perales may have been the first Latino diplomat in US history. Few Latinos had connections to Latin American politics and policies, outside of their respective home countries if born outside of the United States.

There was no other more significant Mexican American in the United States in the twentieth century than Alonso S. Perales. His daughter noted, "He had a vision; he had a dream. I want to say he was like Martin Luther King—but he preceded Martin Luther King."[2] Wife Marta noted "Lider nació, y nada pudo contener su marcha, por que los hombres que nacen para eso, vienen al mundo uno cada siglo."[3] (He was born a leader and nothing could stop his march because he was born for this. Leaders come around once a century.)

His contemporary Professor Benjamin Cuellar Sr. called him, "El Paladín de la Raza" (The Knight of la Raza).[4]

Historian Emilio Zamora also spoke to his historical significance: "I honestly believe that Perales is the most important Mexican-American leader of the 20th century" and also calling him "the most active proponent of civil rights legislation for Mexicans living within the United States.[5] Historian Joseph Orbock Medina noted, "Perales rightfully occupies a prominent place in Mexican-American history as perhaps the foremost proponent of Latino racial pride."[6] Judge/scholar Lupe Salinas concluded, "All Latinos, not just Mexican-descent persons, owe Alonso S. Perales, this illustrious person, an incredible and immeasurable appreciation for making life a better one for Latinos in the United States."[7] This is not an overstatement since Perales founded LULAC, the most important Latino civil rights organization in the 20th century. He was its principal founder and intellectual father.[8] This book will also show that Perales was a "transformative, controversial, and complex" man as several scholars have commented.[9]

Forgotten

Despite these characterizations, Perales has largely been forgotten. He was praised and honored a few times during his lifetime. Co-activist Adela Sloss-Vento of San Juan and Edinburg, Texas, a woman, recognized his genius during his lifetime and without her we would have known little about him. Yet, he was also publicly criticized. He was attacked not only by white racists but also by Mexican journalists in Texas and Mexican-American civic leaders and allies who disagreed with his ideas or methods. After his death in 1960 he was unknown to Chicano movement activists of the late 1960s and maligned by Chicano historians as late as the 2010s.

Perales was born in 1898 and died in 1960. He was an attorney, US diplomat, public intellectual, the principal founder of LULAC, and major civil rights leader. He died before LULAC had a permanent national office and before the field of Chicano history in the academy existed. In 1960 there were likely two professionally trained Mexican-American historians in the United States. Dr. Ernesto Galarza and historian Dr. Carlos E. Castañeda of the University of Texas at Austin was Perales' co-activist and best friend but, unfortunately, died in 1958 before Perales passed.

Forgotten and Remembered

Let us briefly examine how Perales was appreciated over the decades. He congratulated the editors of San Antonio's new children's monthly magazine *Alma Latina* and subsequently in April 1932, this LULAC monthly publication "for the interests of the Latin American children," featured his picture on the cover.[10] *LULAC News* reported on Perales in "Who's Who in the Lulac" (Aug. 1931) and "S.A. Club Banquets Brother Perales" (January 1933). A poem in his honor also appeared in May 1934. Sloss-Vento recognized Perales' significance as early as the 1930s.[11] She penned "The League of United Latin Americans by Its Founder, Attorney Alonso S. Perales" for *La Prensa*, the only statewide Spanish-language newspaper in Texas and wrote a similar essay for *LULAC News*.[12] She had begun her activism in 1927 when she graduated from Pharr-San Juan High as a twenty-six year old and introduced herself to Perales.[13]

Perales himself sought to document his contributions to the League and tell his version of LULAC's founding in volume two of *En Defensa de Mi Raza* in 1937. Ben Garza, the first national president of LULAC, died in 1937 and as a result the League began to reflect on its history and founders. Despite this documentation Garza would be called the "Father of LULAC," even being referred to as such by LULAC co-founder M.C. Gonzales, one of eleven key founders.[14] It is not clear if he gave Garza this title to spite Perales or to honor the deceased Garza.

When Perales published his book *En Defensa de Mi Raza* he included writing by other activists, intellectuals, and friends. Castañeda noted, "Atty. Alonso S. Perales rightfully can be called the defender of our Race. He has not been the only one, but among those who in the last years have been disturbed by serious problems, no one has done more than he."[15] Castañeda also referred to his "vision of a prophet."[16]

In the 1940s a few community members acknowledged Perales. A *calavera*, a Day of the Dead poem, was written about him; it read:

From the beginning
A symbol of correction
with powerful words
said with conviction
A Tejano patriot
who defended the Mexicano
in any given moment
He was a mover and man of ideas
A powerful man, a 100%
in the court, in a fight.[17]

Perales was the subject of other lauding *calaveras* in this decade.[18]

In the 1950s Perales received his proudest accolade, a merit of achievement from Spain. News magazine *Revista Latino-Americano* of Mission, Texas dedicated an entire issue to him including essays by co-activists Sloss-Vento and J. Luz Sáenz. Sáenz referred to him as a "gladiator."[19] Sloss-Vento also penned an article to *La Prensa* of San Antonio in March 1952 about the award and his "noble struggle."[20] Likewise, in 1952 he was named Outstanding Latin American in Texas by the University of Texas Latino Student Alba Club, advised by both Castañeda and Dr. George I. Sánchez.[21] Perales received yet another award from Spain in 1952 as "Titular Member of the Institute of Hispanic Culture."[22]

Finally, in 1960 as another decade passed, San Antonio LULAC also honored him, months before he died in May. In San Antonio in 1960 Fort Worth rancher/oilman Jack Danciger said, "I hope the people of San Antonio will in the near future set aside one day at 'La Villita' to honor his name."[23] The *Encyclopedia of American Biography* contacted wife Marta Perales but no article resulted.[24] Downtown LULAC Council No. 363 also honored him at its founders' banquet in 1962.[25]

When Perales' body was moved to Alice, Texas *La Verdad* journalist Santos de la Paz of Corpus Christi proposed "Perales Park" "with gardens, playground equipment for children, benches for the repose of visitors, and most important, in the middle of it, a monument in memory of such a great defender and excelling Mexican-American."[26] He said, "we should go ahead with the idea of donating one, but one in honor of this town's son who brought great honor to it with his many merits." Sloss-Vento, probably added the additional thought on the park: ". . . such a great defender and excelling Mexican-American. . . this dream can and should become a reality."[27] Though Perales' compadre Fortino Treviño and his wife reported over $2,200 collected, it never transpired.[28] In 1969 Alice resident Rafael Treviño and twenty others tried to get Alice High named after the hometown boy but others, mostly European Americans, sought to honor writer J. Frank Dobie instead and the school board simply decided on Alice High.[29] The board, probably Anglo-dominant, ignored the petition with 3,000 signatures.[30] San Antonio LULAC, and especially Luis Alvarado (a son-in-law of Perales' co-activist Sáenz) of Council 2, also sought to bring attetion to Perales throughout the years.[31]

By the 1970s few had ever heard of Perales.[32] In 1974, the persistent Sloss-Vento brought his name to the attention of national LULAC but without success.[33] Marta Perales wrote national LULAC president about "a room full of manuscripts of a lifetime dedication."[34] IMAGE, a San Antonio Mexican-American organization, honored Perales that year and Arno Press with its Chicano historian editorial board reissued his book *Are We Good Neighbors?*[35] In 1975 San Antonio Chicano activists discovered Perales' legacy; *Chicano Times* wrote a short biographical article based on talks with wife Marta titled "Who Was Alonso Perales?"[36] The *Times* noted "the verifiable treasure of old newspapers, clippings, letters and other documentation, even tapes of the work that occupied Mr. Perales' lifetime work."[37] In 1977 school leaders inaugurated the Alonso S. Perales School on the West side in San Antonio with Congressman Henry B. González as keynote speaker. Nephew Dr. Alonso M. Perales wrote a short bio for the program which noted "Mexican American children and youth of this country who will soon become adults, and as they witness our efforts, will ask us for an accounting of our labor for the Mexican American cause."[38] At the dedication ceremony, Perales' fellow LULAC Council 16 member from the 1930s Charles Albidress Sr. said, "Many of you here today are wondering who the late Alonso S. Perales was and why he is being honored here today."[39]

Across the decades Sloss-Vento made the most effort to acknowledge Perales' legacy. In 1977 she self-published the biography *Alonso S. Perales: His Struggle for the Rights of Mexican-Americans.* Unfortunately, because she wrote outside of traditional academic history circles and because she was an elder woman, her book did not have the impact it should have; today World Catalog.org shows only forty-six libraries own a copy.[40] She sought to establish that Perales and not Ben Garza was the true founder of LULAC.[41]

I heard of Perales in 1978 when I was a sophomore at the University of Texas at Austin (UTA) and wrote a research paper. My topic was the origins of LULAC. UTA libraries had Perales' books and even more fortuitous, I was fortunate to be a work/study student at the Center for Mexican American Studies where Dr. Arnoldo Vento, son of Sloss-Vento, learned of my work. He told me about his mother's book. She allowed me to visit and use her archives in Edinburg, Texas. She urged me to visit Perales' wife hoping that I could give Perales and co-activists Sáenz and J.T. Canales their due as other LULAC founders. She wrote a letter of introduction for me and Marta Perales accepted my request to visit. She was friendly and gracious, and gave me access to Perales' papers located in the house. (Other archives were located in the garage.) In 1980 I completed my senior honors thesis, using Perales'1920s documents as well as Sloss-Vento's.[42] When I attended the national LULAC conference in Houston in 1979, the League's 50th anniversary, much more was made of first president Ben Garza than Perales, the second president. Most were unaware that Garza was the first president only because Perales orchestrated this choice.[43]

Perales was largely forgotten in the 1980s but saw sporadic recognition in the 1990s. In 1989 historian Richard A. Garcia revived Perales when he wrote the insightful *Rise of the Mexican American Middle Class* about San Antonio; it was the first to place Perales in historical context though without access to Perales' papers. In 1990 Marta Perales sought and received recognition for her husband at the national LULAC convention in Albuquerque which I attended. In the early 1990s as a UCLA graduate student writing my dissertation and as Research Associate for the *New Handbook of Texas* I wrote a short bio about Perales for the Texas encyclopedia which was published in 1996.[44] In 1994 Erasmo Figueroa of San Antonio tried to create a LULAC Scholarship Foundation in Perales' honor.[45] And in 1999 Perales was honored during LULAC Week in Alice.[46]

In 2000 Araceli Pérez Davis, Marta Perales' niece, resurrected Perales in *El Mesteño*, a popular South Texas history and culture magazine.[47] In 2003 Josh Gottheimer included him in *Ripples of Hope: Great American Civil Right Speeches* but the same year the *San Antonio News* reported "Unsung Hero of Civil Rights 'Father of LULAC' a Fading Memory."[48] In 2003 reporter Hector Saldaña noted, "Perales' story rests in dozens of moldy boxes once coveted by his widow, a high-strung former opera singer who in later years vacillated between guarding that packaged legacy and threatening to burn the entire lot, says Perales' nephew."[49] A Texas Historical marker was erected in Jim Wells county in 2003.[50] In 2008 historian Mario T. García addressed Perales as a Catholic.[51]

In 2009 after Marta Perales' death, the Perales' children finally chose to place the Perales papers with the US Hispanic Literary Heritage Program at the University of Houston and have now been available to scholars. The Program organized a Perales conference and Michael A. Olivas, scholar and attorney, edited the conference volume. My chapter noted, "The year is 2012 and we still know little about Alonso S. Perales, activist, civil rights leader, lawyer, US diplomat, author, columnist, orator, teacher, publisher, and translator. Historians and political scientists have overlooked, minimized, and misunderstood him despite the fact that he was one of the most important

Mexican American activists/public intellectuals in the United States in the 20th century."[52]

Perales was well aware of his own significance and prized his archives. On his death bed he cried worrying about his papers and legacy. His books, *En Defensa de Mi Raza* (1936-37) and *Are We Good Neighbors?* (1948) might have kept his memory alive but they were self-published in limited editions. Perales had reason to cry. In 1960 mainstream libraries neglected Mexican-American history, including elites. Even in the 1970s no one was preserving LULAC materials even though it was a middle-class organization and most of its documents in English. It was not until 1980 that LULAC national president Ruben Bonilla created the LULAC Archive at the University of Texas at Austin.

Several historians and librarians tried to get the Perales papers into a profesional repository before 2009.[53] Chicano academics and librarians tried to get the Perales family to donate/sell the papers in the early 1970s. In 1972 Professor Jose Limón of UTA inquired about the papers suggesting they "will eventually result in a published biography of the life of Alonso S. Perales."[54] Perhaps Marta did not respond because in 1970 her lawyer sent Manuel Bernal of San Antonio a demand letter asking for "all of the literary material and tapes that were intrusted (sic) to you by Mrs. Alonzo S. Perales."[55] A 1979 letter by Professor Donna R. Tobias said that she understood the collection was going to UTA.[56] In 1981 Elvira Chavaria, Mexican-American Studies librarian at the UTA Benson Latin American Collection, wrote the Perales family about the papers.[57] In 1982 historian Mario T. García also wrote Marta Perales. In 1988 UTA's Benson's Margo Gutiérrez, tried to get the archives informing widow Perales that the Dr. Carlos E. Castañeda and Dr. George I. Sánchez papers were at UTA.[58] In 2001 Gutiérrez noted, "they [the papers] have suffered severe deterioration due to pests, humidity, dust, etc." And that the "bulk of the papes are in a garage that has no doors and is exposed to the elements, in crushed cardboard boxes with no or ill-fitting lids. . . . It's a crying shame."[59]

In 2002 national LULAC held its annual convention in San Antonio where I ran into Perales' daughter, Marta Perales Carrizales. She visited the LULAC history booth organized by Benny Martínez of Goliad. I introduced myself, noting that I had visited her mother and the archives in the late 70s. She gasped, "¡La niña, la niña. Eres la niña!" (The girl. The girl. You are that girl!) (Indeed, I was a young woman scholar in the making). She suggested I visit with her and brother Raimundo at the family home. I advised the family that their father's papers belonged in a professional archive and suggested they request immediate archival processing and a public conference.

Unfortunately, some materials deterioriated or were lost since wife Marta did not release the papers during her lifetime of ninety-nine years. For instance, the tapes alluded to by *Chicano Times* in 1975 did not survive. There are no sound recordings in the collection though Perales was an orator and radio guest. Sloss-Vento even bought him a tape-recorder so he could document his speeches. Moreover, the Perales family allowed San Antonio-newspaperman, printer and activist Rómulo Munguía to sift through materials to decide what to remove.

Munguía was an advocate for Mexican-descent workers; in the late 30s he changed a Catholic newspaper to become a pro-worker, pro-union paper with the subtitle "La Voz: Periódico de Justicia y Accion Social."[60] And his daughter Mary had married Perales' adopted son Raimundo.

The University of Texas Press published my book *No Mexicans, Women or Dogs Allowed, The Rise of the Mexican American Civil Rights Movement* in 2009 where I detailed the rise of LULAC referring to it as part of a broader social movement that started independently of Perales'actions. I detailed the work of Perales and ten other founders.

Once the University of Houston's Recovery Program obtained the archive, over 11,000 items (not pages) had to be organized and processed into fourteen boxes. Olivas and the Program organized a public conference with an edited volume, *In Defense of My People, Alonso S. Perales and the Development of Mexican-American Public Intellectuals*, published.[61] Scholar George A. Martinez noted Perales' lack of name recognition by the general public. He wrote, "For some reason, Alonso S. Perales has not achieved the fame of other Mexican Americans who have been important in the effort to secure the rights of Mexican Americans."[62] Ironically, attorney Gus Garcia, one of Perales' protégées, has received more acclaim from the general public, though this can in part be attributed to a Supreme Court win as well as the fact that he was a tragic figure as an alcoholic dying on a park bench.[63]

Brandon Mila's master's thesis in history on Perales in 2013 also helped highlight Perales' contributions. He was the first scholar independent of the conference to assess Perales' early life and also revised some of my findings in *No Mexicans*.[64] In 2015 historian Richard A. Garcia dared to write that "Alonso S. Perales was the most famous American of Mexican descent from the 1920s until his death in 1960."[65] While he is still not "famous," he was most important along with US Senator Dennis Chávez once called "the lone voice for Mexican rights in Washington between the 1930s and 1950s."[66] (Chávez and Congressman Antonio Fernández were both New Mexican LULACers.) Another sign of the lack of recognition for Perales was San Antonio's city tricentennial celebration and publications in 2018 when I was still the only person pronouncing his name.[67]

Attacked

Despite Perales' numerous contributions he was criticized by Mexicans in the United States, Mexican Americans, and Euro Texans. A light criticism appeared as early as 1931 when a LULAC poem called him a "regular Cotorra" (female parrot.)[68] He was also attacked by the entire political spectrum—conservatives, liberals and radicals. Mexican journalist Carlos Basañez Rocha of the Lower Rio Grande Valley in Texas called him a racist and a false prophet in the 1920s.[69] San Antonio communist labor organizer Emma Tenayuca of the 1930s told me he was a "nut." And in the 1950s Dr. George I. Sánchez called him "a pathetic figure, a psycho-neurotic with delusions of grandeur."[70] A comical poster of "Sharyland" (between Mission and McAllen, Texas) in the 1950s also mocked Perales likely because he supported conservative Allan Shivers for governor and not liberal Ralph Yarborough.[71] A flyer titled "Ya Llegó el Circo Perales" (The Perales Circus has arrived) and signed "The Committee" was perhaps the lowest assault towards him because of his pro-Shivers sentiment, likely a flyer produced by media-savvy Ed Idar Jr. of the American G.I. Forum, another Mexican-American civil rights organization.[72] The poster mocked "Clown Perales" for supporting state representative Allan Shivers for governor and allegedly "speaking against the idea of the Mexican-Texans be given representation."[73] His wife Marta wrote that there were "Judases of our own descent. Those who were envious of him made his life much harder and more difficult."[74]

Perales was also attacked by Euro-Texans, blacklisted and spied on by the US government. In the 1940s Euro-Texan congressman/mayor Maury Maverick called Perales an "agitator by trade."[75] In the 1940s during World War II he was also spied upon by the federal government likely because he and LULAC representatives had regular contact with the Mexican government during the war.[76] He was also attacked by William Blocker, US Consul in Reynosa. He was black-balled from obtaining employment in the US government or military during this war and in the 1950s he was labeled a communist.[77]

After his death in the 1960s, Chicano scholars across the decades also criticized Perales. In the 1970s they criticized LULAC (and by extension, Perales) charging it with assimilation, middle-class bias and anti-Mexican sentiment.[78] Judge/scholar Lupe Salinas noted anti-LULAC analysis prevalent in Chicano history suggesting that LULAC had "malevolent goals; having middle class objectives and overlooking the needs of the Mexican American workers; seeking assimilation into the United States mainstream at the expense of their Mexican background; claiming to be white at the expense of African Americans; and possessing an anti-Mexican immigrant sentiment." In the 2000s LULAC (and Perales) were charged with conservative principles as well. Likewise, I pointed to LULAC and Perales' exclusion of women from 1929 to 1933 and its marginalization of women in separate ladies chapters from 1933 to 1970.[79]

In the midst of these charges, still other scholars began to provide more nuanced analyses. They typically used LULAC archives, other sources and/or read LULAC sources more carefully. These historians incuded Richard A. Garcia, Mario T. García, Arnoldo de León, Guadalupe San Miguel, Thomas Kreneck, Craig Kaplowitz, Emilio Zamora, Thomas Guglielmo, Matthew Gritter and Gabriela González.

Terminology

This book will make extended use of racial/ethnic terminology. The question of identity is key to this study and readers must understand the politics of naming before proceeding.

Identities, both by insiders and outsiders, are important. This study mentions how outsiders named the Mexican-origin community through racial formation and racialization, two concepts critical in understanding racial identity. Scholars Michael Omi and Howard Winant define "racial formation" as the "process by which social, economic, and political forces determine the content and importance of racial categories, and by which they are in turn shaped by racial meanings."[80]

In the 1920s when Perales was a young adult, "whites," "Mexicans," "México Texanos," "Americans" and "La Raza" were common identities. The 1920s witnessed a new era in how the Mexican-origin people were being imagined, defined and constructed both by whites and on their own. The meaning of "Mexican" in the United States changed from the 1910s to the 1920s with a "Mexican race" being constructed and becoming synonymous with immigrant. After the 1920s the dominant community continued to call all of La Raza "Mexican" despite citizenship or class. During World War II the term "Latin American" began to appear to describe Mexican-descent people in the United States and by the late 1960s the term "Mexican American" appeared in US discourse to describe United States citizens of Mexican descent. Perales used all these terms with pride.

Racialization, "the extension of racial meaning to a previously racially unclassified relationship, social practice, or group," is another important concept used here.[81] Understanding the use of "Mexican" as a racialized imaginary in the United States is key to this study. As the "Mexican race" and "Mexicans" were being defined in a different way, a new paradigm—the "Mexican problem"—emerged. The LULAC organization and Perales' life project was a response to the "the Mexican problem"—a paradigm EuroAmericans created to racialize and subordinate La Raza. Hereafter, when this study employs the term "Mexican" in quotes it is to denote racialization—racist and essentialized EuroAmerican perceptions of La Raza. The labeling of La Raza as a homogeneous Mexican problem was synonymous with EuroAmericans' appropriation of "Americanness" for themselves. The early 1910s saw the dominant society defining "American" in a typically WASP way. Mexican immigrants were also part of this racialization.

The 1920s saw this community referred to as "illegal aliens" and the 1950s saw reference to "wetbacks," undocumented Mexican immigrants but which was also used pejoratively to the entire Mexican-descent community in the United States.

This book gives attention to how insiders (the Mexican descent community) named and defined themselves through self-identity, class formation, community formation, nationalism and citizenship. Self-reference and identity are both historically specific, reflecting a particular times in history. Variables of citizenship, class, birthplace, residence, language use, education and color influenced ethnic, racial and national identity. Social, cultural, political and ideological differences existed within the Mexican-origin community.[82] Gender also impacted identity within the Raza community.

While acknowledging the multiplicity and impermanency of identities, this study uses specific terms in specific ways. This research rejects the labeling of the entire community as "Mexican" or "Mexican American." I use "Mexican origin" and "Mexican descent" to denote a "common" group distinct from EuroAmericans. "EuroAmerican" will also be used and is synonymous with "white" and "American." Mexican will designate those born in Mexico, whose life experience was largely there, and who were citizens there. "Mexican" in quotes will designate the racialized imaginary.

Mexican Americans and Hybridity

The term "Mexican American" hardly existed in public discourse in the 1920s or 1930s and would only become mainstream in the late 60s. Still, its emergence represented a shift from a Spanish to an English cultural milieu and a shift by Mexican Americans in Texas from a regional identity to a national identity.[83] Mexican Americans had been citizens of the United States since 1848, but not until the twentieth century would a significant sector become true hybrids—Mexican and American. Public schools and military service fostered a hybridity now more American. The Mexican-American male middle class of the 1920s of which Perales was a major leader was the first truly bilingual, bicultural sector and which consciously asserted citizenship and membership in the United States.

The hybrid Mexican American was constructed by European Americans, Mexican Americans and Mexicans. The dominant society's evolving, shifting and contradictory relationship with La Raza included segregation and assimilation. European Americans fostered assimilation through the Americanization movement and English-only. On the other hand, European Americans also hindered incorporation of La Raza. Whites made La Raza an "other" by institutionalizing racial segregation, constructing the "Mexican problem" and establishing the Border Patrol in 1924. They also racialized La Raza by re-emphasizing the construct called the "Mexican race." Likewise, they homogenized La Raza by failing to acknowledge citizenship within the Mexican origin community, calling all of La Raza "Mexican." "Mexican" was part of the dominant society's racial discourse used to disempower; it was synonymous with "alien," "wetback," "non-citizen" and "un-American."

Racial formation also evolved in contradictory ways. While the dominant society fostered Mexican Americanization, European Americans also created a shifting, complex and contradictory racial imaginary. In 1920 the US census included La Raza as white but by 1930 it referred to the "Mexican race" for the first time, excluding La Raza from the category of "white."

At the same time, Mexican Americans played an active role in forming this "new race" of Mexican Americans. They helped form this "race," not biologically, but by constructing this identity and politic in a relational way with European Americans and Mexicans from Mexico as major points of reference. Both European Americans and Mexicans resisted change and were uncomfortable with this new development. Mexican immigrants complained when Mexican Americans began to emerge as a new sector within La Raza.

Mexican Americans embraced this new ethnic/national identity. "Mexican American" was not yet part of European American discourse; whites did not invent or promote the term. Middle-class Mexican Americans believed it accurately described their hybridity. As Latino scholar Félix Padilla has noted, "ethnic identity is not fixed and can constitute a strategy to attain the needs and wants of the group."[84] Indeed, Mexican Americans believed it necessary to affirm their Americanness by acknowledging US citizenship. They believed it moved European Americans away from racialization practices.

Those claiming this new identity, like Perales, challenged the binary, either/or identities of "Americans" versus "Mexicans." Activists sought to broaden and complicate these narrow categories so as to demand acceptance and respect for hybridity. Mexican Americans sought respect and acceptance of their difference from Mexicans in the United States. There was no one Mexican culture in the country. They tried to convince Mexicans in the United States that the empowerment of La Raza was connected to citizenship. Both European Americans and Mexican nationalists in the United States would be slow to accept plurality and difference.

"Mexican Americanization was well under way in Mexican communities by the end of the 1920s," historian Aaron E. Sánchez has observed.[85] Mexican Americans were neither Mexican nor American; they did not fit into narrow social constructions of "Mexican" or "American." At the same time, they were both American and Mexican. Keen to this peculiar condition emerging in the 1920s were several scholars: anthropologist Manuel Gamio of Mexico, political scientist Oliver Douglas Weeks; and economist Paul S. Taylor. Gamio

conducted ethnographic work in Texas in the 1920s. His "Relaciones
entre Mexicanos, México-Texanos y Americanos" (Relations between
Mexicans, México Texanos, and Americans) is the best discussion of
the topic.[86] Weeks wrote of the Mexican Americanization of politics
evident in the founding of LULAC. Paul S. Taylor's study of the Corpus Christi region showed, "the term Mexican-American is as yet little used . . . conscious of their American citizenship."[87] He added, "I
have employed it here, however to denote a small but significant
group in south Texas, which, as its members have become conscious
of their American citizenship, has assumed this name."[88] Hybridity
was part of the group identity of Mexican Americans. The impact of
public schooling on La Raza was recognized by *La Crónica* newspaper in Laredo as early as 1911, if not earlier. The paper explained that
Spanish proficiency was declining.[89] Educator William John Knox of
San Antonio also saw hybridity through the English language, the
public school and skilled occupations.[90]

Mexican Americans, hybrids, decided they could use US citizenship as strategy in the empowerment of La Raza. Perales was the first
to truly articulate this plan.

La Raza

La Raza was a popular self-referent in the 1920s. The term "La
Raza" first appeared in the United States in the 1850s but was popularized with the publication of José Vasconcelos' *La Raza Cósmica* in
1925 in Mexico, a book about that nation's racial mixture. The idea of
La Raza was based on common culture based on language, religion
and customs, real or imagined. In Texas, immigration from Mexico
strengthened this cultural base.[91]

Scholar Frances Jerome Woods explained use of La Raza in San
Antonio in the 1940s. She wrote as "a generic denomination by which
he [or she] includes all Mexicans regardless of class differences or
place of birth. This ethnic consciousness becomes intensified in those
who live in a predominately Anglo or non-Latin society that regards
Mexicans as culturally different, and for the most part, socially inferior. Sociologically, therefore, recognizable physical or cultural char-

acteristics do not per se indicate membership in an ethnic group. It is rather the identification of self with the group or the 'we-feeling' that is significant."[92] She added, "Pride in La Raza, which has persisted over generations, is at the basis of ethnic activities sponsored by Mexican leaders."[93] The term's use declined in the 1950s, perhaps due to more evident cultural differences between Mexican Americans and Mexicans, at least in Texas.

La Raza was an oppressed people within the United States but could also refer to "the people" in Mexico or other Latin American countries as well. Acknowledging its prevalent use in the early 20th century, historian Elliot Young has argued that La Raza was an idealized concept and not a homogeneous community with one vision since class was a major contradiction within it.

However, La Raza was an "imagined community" and useful transnational concept in which citizenship, class and gender differences were subordinate. Perales used it to refer to a community based on race and transnationalism across the US and Mexico border and even Latin America. For Perales, referring to La Raza was a way to speak of both Mexican Americans, Mexicans and Latinos. It was a way to ignore citizenship much like European Americans did. Perales referred to La Raza but also made distinctions by citizenship between Mexicans and Mexican Americans. Yet, Perales argued that those who were US citizens should claim the United States as their home and those without US citizenship still had rights here.

Latin Americans

"Latin American" is another key term used here. Due to the US Good Neighbor Policy of the 1930s the group reference "Latin American" becan to emerge in the 1930s and was popular in the 1940s and 1950s. In the 1920s the United States continued its tradition of "Pan-Americanism," better and friendly relations with Latin America though meek. In the 1930s President Franklin Delano Roosevelt created the Good Neighbor Policy with Latin America and saw more Americans referring to Latinos in the United States as Latin Americans. It was used to mean the same as "Hispanic" or "Latino" today, both specific to the United States or to peoples in the Américas. "Latina" or "Latino," used to encompass all Hispanic peoples in the United States, became common in the 1980s though Perales occasionally used the term in the 1920s. "Chicana" or "Chicano" refers to the post-1963 Mexican-American people in the United States as reflective of the social movement called the Chicano movement which lasted until the late 1970s. Perales died in 1960 before the Chicano movement. "Tejano" refers to Mexican Americans in Texas.

Book Organization

This book is organized into four parts. Part I "Across Time" (chapters 1-13) is organized chronologically. Chapter 1 describes the Mexican colony of South Texas and especially San Antonio from 1910-1960. Most attention is given to the 1910-1930 period to explain conditions Perales began with. Later, other chapters address the 1930s, 40s, and 50s. Chapter 2 discusses Perales' early family life in Alice, Texas. Chapter 3 addresses his role in World War I. Chapter 4 focuses on Perales in the 1920s as he began his civil rights and public intellectual activism to combat the "Mexican problem." Chapter 5 deals with San Antonio's Mexican-American civil rights organizing which Perales sought to influence as well as his lecture tour through South Texas.

Chapter 6 touches on the Harlingen Convention of 1927 at which Perales and others addressed whether Mexican citizens should be permitted to join a new association. Chapter 7 examines the formation of the Latin American Citizens League (LAC) in the Valley. Chapter 8 summarizes Perales' role in founding LULAC in 1929. Chapter 9 examines the original LULAC constitution written in 1929 of which Perales played a role. Chapter 10 addresses his relations with LULAC from 1929 to 1960 as well as the persistence of the League. Chapters 11, 12 and 13 emphasize Perales' wide-ranging activism across the 1930s, 40s and 50s.

Part II "Public Impact" (chapters 14-17) addresses Perales' influence through various personas. Chapter 14 examines Perales as an attorney; Chapter 15 discusses him as a politico; and Chapter 16 treats him as a public intellectual as he sought to place Latinos in US public consciousness.[94] Chapter 17 deals with Perales as a Pan-American ideologue in the United States as well as his diplomat work in Latin America. His role as Consul General for Nicaragua in the United States is also mentioned.

Part III "Private Lives" (chapters 18-22) examines Perales' private life. Chapter 18 looks at his religious sentiment while Chapter 19 seeks to delve into his character. Chapter 20 focuses on his family life, wife/widow Marta and nephew Dr. Alonso M. Perales. Chapter 21 investigates his friendships and adversaries while chapter 22 looks at his health and death.

Part IV "Perales on Trial" (chapters 23-24) weighs how several generations of historians and political scientists have interpreted Perales' and LULAC's role in Latino and Latina history especially in regard to race, class, citizenship, and gender. It also unveils Perales' and LULAC's contributions. Chapter 24 concludes with my thoughts on Perales' legacy.

PIONEER OF
MEXICAN-AMERICAN
CIVIL RIGHTS

ALONSO S. PERALES

PART I
Across Time

CHAPTER 1

The Mexican Colony in San Antonio and South Texas, 1910–1960

Alonso S. Perales' story begins in South Texas where he helped initiate the Mexican-American civil rights movement in Texas. The rise of cities, factories and agribusiness altered South Texas in the 1910s and 20s. A major wave of Mexican immigrants changed the racial landscape. The 1930s brought the Great Depression including deportation and repatriation while World War II saw more employment, new issues of employment discrimination and more immigration.

Perales grew up in South Texas, especially in Alice and San Antonio, a distinctive economic, political, racial and cultural province. This chapter addresses the status of the Mexican-origin community in South Texas especially urban San Antonio, rural Alice and the Lower Rio Grande Valley (hereafter, the Valley), an agricultural region, from 1910 to 1960. The Mexican-American male middle class arose in the 1920s amidst heightened racial violence and segregation. The Mexican immigrant population expanded in the 1910s, 20s and during the US/Mexico Bracero program from 1942 to 1964. Therefore, Perales had to operate in both a Mexican-American and Mexican context within Texas.

Perales' life project was to indeed "redeem La Raza" in South Texas and the United States as historian Gabriela González has suggested. In addition to issues mentioned above, there were other attacks on La Raza. She wrote, "Redeeming la Raza was about discrediting the 'Mexican problem' narrative or racial scripts that informed fear-based exclusionary movements whose prominent and loud voices included nativists calling for immigration restriction,

3

eugenicists clamoring for racial purity, social scientists providing the intellectual justifications politicians needed to institutionalize racism, white supremacists building an extensive Jim Crow southern society, and working-class ethnics claiming whiteness and adopting racist attitudes toward groups in even more precarious positions than their own."[1] Perales had his work cut out for him.

South Texas

North of the Rio Grande River, south of San Antonio and east of the Gulf of Mexico lies South Texas which includes San Antonio, Corpus Christi, Laredo, towns like Alice and the Valley.[2] Native Americans made their homelands here though Spain colonized this area as its far northern frontier with missions, pueblos/villas, ranchos and presidios. South Texas became the major home for the Texas Mexican-descent populace.

In 1821 Mexico took over the area and after Texas independence, the Texas republic controlled the area. Texas joined the United States in 1845. Even after the US-Mexican war of 1846-1848 most Mexican Americans considered Mexico their homeland. Only a few, especially politicians and veterans, connected to US politics with some participating in this nation's Civil War. After 1870, the South Texas economy changed once the railroad reached San Antonio and Alice.

Although most residents were US citizens, they continued to refer to themselves as "Mexicans," "México Texanos" and members of "La Raza." Intellectual José Vasconcelos of Mexico, author of *La Raza Cósmica* (The Cosmic Race), popularized "La Raza" which emphasized Spanish-indigenous mixture and it would remain popular in the United States until after World War II. "Mexican American" was rarely used until the 1960s. Waves of Mexican immigrants added additional layers of Mexicanness in the 1910s, 20s and 50s.[3]

San Antonio

When Perales left Alice, Texas he moved to San Antonio, the largest city in Texas in the 1910s. It surpassed Houston, Austin or Dallas in the 1920s and its residents were the wealthiest in the state as well. The "Metropolis of the Southwest," it was the "financial, educational, cultural, and recreational capital of South Texas as well as its wholesale distributing and retail trading center."[4] World War I also fostered urbanization with improved transportation especially highways and railroads. Petrochemical and communication industries boomed. The city developed a military infrastructure with bases like Sam Houston, and it also served as a labor distribution point for La Raza migrating across the United States. Railroad yards, packing plants, garment factories as well as the retail trade, construction and service industry needed Mexican labor. By the 1930s the brewing, pecan shelling, light manufacturing and meatpacking had expanded.[5] The 1940s saw greater expansion of the military industrial complex with Kelly base, offering more employment and higher wages.

San Antonio's population grew from 53,321 in 1900 to 231,542 in 1930. Between 1890 and 1900, it had the most Mexican-origin people in the nation. In 1910 La Raza numbered 29,480 and 82,373 (35%) in 1930. From 1910 to 1930, some 25,000 political refugees escaped Mexico due to the Mexican Revolution; this group included political thinkers and intellectuals. Exiled political refugees became intellectuals and advocates for the community. So by 1930 there were more Mexican-descent people here than in any other US city. In 1940 La Raza population was 253,854; 408,442 in 1950; and 587,718 in 1960, 41.5% of the populace.

Perales was aware of this significant demographic base. Four waves of Mexican immigrants arrived: upper-class political exiles in the 1900s, workers in the 1920s and religious exiles due to the Cristero revolt in the late 20s, and later, *braceros* in the 40s and 50s. San Antonio was reMexicanized. By 1960, the Mexican-descent community constituted 41% of the population, whites 51.6%.[6] Historian Rodolfo Acuña noted that San Antonio "in 1960 was unquestionably the most important Texas city for Mexican-Americans because by 1960 there were 217,688 Mexican-Americans in the city that was second and third generation, and only 30,299 that were first generation. In fact, San Antonio with its West side contained 17.2% of the 1,417,810 Mexican-Americans in the state of Texas."[7]

The Lower Rio Grande Valley

South of San Antonio and south of Corpus Christi lies the Valley, an agricultural heartland spanning a million acres. Perales spent time here from the mid-1920s to 1930. The Valley witnessed development, commercial agriculture and European American contact after the railroad arrived in 1904. Agribusiness made the Valley the state's most productive agricultural region with Mexican-origin families who prepared the land and picked crops. New towns emerged by 1930. These included Brownsville (population 22,000), Harlingen (14,000), San Benito (12,500), McAllen (10,000), Edinburg (7,000), Mission (6,500), Mercedes (7,000), Weslaco (7,000) and Donna (6,000). By 1929, three-fourths of the Valley residents lived in towns over 2,500.

Race relations and culture changed. Midwesterners moved into the Valley and Mexicans and Mexican-Americans worked as their farmworkers. Yet, a small Mexican-American middle class was emerging—it was this middle class that Perales saw as the human capital for Mexican-American activism. By the 1940s and 50s agribusiness had established extreme labor exploitation of both Mexican *braceros* and unauthorized immigrants spurred on by the Bracero program, an agreement between the United States and Mexico permitting the labor into the United States from 1942 to 1964.

Alice

Perales' hometown of Alice was sixty miles west of Corpus Christi; he lived here until around 1915. Though the railroad reached Alice in 1883 the town was not incorporated until 1904 with 887 residents. Some 1,180 people lived there in 1920 and oil led to 4,239 by 1931. In 1940, the population was 7,792; 16,414 in 1950; and 20,861 by 1960. By 1930 65% of the county was of Mexican-descent.[8]

Racially segregated neighborhoods existed for white, "Mexicans," and African Americans there. About 10% of Alice's population was African American and their children attended the segregated Adams Elementary School.[9] Perales saw this segregation and exclusion of African Americans and it is here that he likely came to believe that African Americans were inferior to both whites and Mexican-descent people.

Demographic Change in South Texas

Mexican immigration impacted South Texas. By 1930 15% of immigrants were Mexican, up 1% from 1900. US immigration laws in 1917, 1921 and 1924 permitted some Mexican workers into the nation. Numerical restrictions were placed on Mexican immigrants for the first time by the 1924 law. Also around the early 1920s, the derogatory term "wetback" began appearing though it would not become commonplace until the 40s and 50s.[10]

The US Border Patrol, founded in 1924, also fostered an "alien" status and facilitated deportation. During the first half of 1929, over 2,600 Mexicans were deported from Brownsville, Mercedes and Hidalgo, Valley towns. The United States now made a distinction between Mexican Americans and immigrants. This led Perales to vehemently claim US citizenship.

The Mexican Immigrant Middle Class

Most immigrants lacked a profession or skills and upon their arrival added to the already poor Mexican-descent working class. Yet, the immigrant population was significant and included people with wealth or middle-class status. A small number of middle- and even upper-class political refugees found a haven in San Antonio, South Texas and border towns where they became business owners. The families of Francisco I. Madero, Venustiano Carranza and Francisco "Pancho" Villa, all key and prominent families associated with the Mexican Revolution, moved to San Antonio with women performing philanthropic work.[11] Ignacio and Alicia E. Lozano, exiles, established the first statewide Spanish-language newspaper in Texas, *La Prensa*, in San Antonio in 1913. Leonides González, a mayor from a silver-mining community brought his family and became a business manager for *La Prensa*; he was the father of future Henry B. González, US Congressman.[12] Likewise, José Rómulo and Carolina Munguía arrived in the 1920s; their grandson Henry Cisneros became the mayor of San Antonio in the 1970s.

La Prensa existed into the 1960s and was not only the major daily in San Antonio but for the state. It provided the dominant thinking for the Mexican-descent community, espousing mostly Mexican nationalism. It advocated for Mexican and Latin American culture (not US culture); advocacy for all Mexicans (including Mexican Americans); non-stereotypical behavior (laziness, thievery); and parenting emphasizing virtue and hard work. It rejected US culture and Mexican Americanness. However, one historian's recent research suggests that during and after World War I that *La Prensa* shifted more attention to the United States than Mexico.[13] Perales asserted Mexican Americanness as a contemporary identity and LULAC "oriented Mexicans toward a future in the United States, as Mexican Americans."[14] *La Prensa* slowly conceded to Mexican Americanness and Mexican Americanism when in 1941 it published bilingually in part. Still, Spanish remained immigrants' dominant language; their children would become bilingual if in school.

Mexican professionals and the middle class were articulate and nationalistic toward Mexico. Mexican intellectuals in San Antonio included Lic. Querido Moheno, Lic. Rene Capistrán de Garza and Nemesio García Naranjo. This sector forced Perales to speak loudly — he had to compete with Mexican nationalists (Mexicanists) in Texas for the soul and future of Texas.

The Working Class

As agribusiness and industrialization increased so did the Mexican-origin working class. Wages were determined by race, gender, age, language and citizenship. Indeed, in 1930 half of Mexican-origin workers labored as farmworkers. Steady or permanent jobs were not always available. Wages were even lower in the Valley, sometimes a fraction of the cost of living. Indeed, the Valley experienced semi-colonial wages similar to ex-slaves in the Reconstruction South.

Most Mexican-descent women were not employed and instead, tended their homes. Heteropatriarchal ideology suggested women marry and raise children. Perales' mother was a homemaker and so, he also felt that women's primary place was the home. In 1930, most worked as domestics and farmworkers. In San Antonio, they also found employment in the garment, candy and cigar factories; few were clerks or in trades or professions. Retail shops in downtown San Antonio refused to hire Mexican-descent clerks. Mexican-descent children had to work since few women worked for wages and wages were low. This working class lacked adequate housing, clothing and food; few owned telephones and washing machines. For instance, in San Antonio only 600 Raza households owned a telephone in the mid-1920s. On the eve of the Great Depression most of La Raza were poor joining many other families throughout the United States in this status. Most would remain members of the working class from 1930 to 1960. Low wages, dual wages based on race and gender and lack of promotion would be serious issues, not to mention the Great Depression.

The Mexican-American Middle Class

Nonetheless, a small Mexican-American middle class rose in the 1920s. Education, bilingualism, maleness and a Mexican immigrant clientele made this possible. It was made of small businessmen, skilled workers and professionals. One historian has estimated the middle class as 5,000 out of 80,000 members of La Raza around 1930. A 1924 directory named 600 businessmen and skilled laborers yet few were doctors or lawyers; Perales would become the second or third Mexican-American lawyer in Texas.

Since Perales resided in San Antonio after the mid-1910s, he was able to assess La Raza's progress. Around 1930 he said there had been improvement in the last ten years pointing to its cultural clubs, civic and fraternal clubs, recreation clubs and commercial groups.[15] And by the late 1930s, he noted, "The Mexican colony of San Antonio is more advanced than the Mexican colony twenty years ago."[16] By the 1940s, Mexican Americans had their own Pan American Optimist Club, a charitable club assisting its working class.

There was not an independent Mexican-American female middle-class sector before the 1970s. Some women worked in family businesses though most middle-class Mexican-descent women were clerks. Teaching was another virtually closed occupation though Ester Pérez Carbajal excelled at Main High School. There was a Spanish Speaking Parent Teachers Association (PTA) in the late 20s to the early 40s but white women's middle-class clubs still excluded them. (Perales' wife Marta did not have a paid career. She accessed most of her status through her husband's work and activities.)

Racial Violence

Racial violence was commonplace. Whites saw persons of Mexican descent as "Mexicans," commonly referred to them as "Meskins," "Messcans" or "greasers" and were often treated similarly despite citizenship, class, language and region. In 1920, the US census considered La Raza "white" but by 1930 designated as "Mexican" suggesting a racial downgrade. Whites appropriated the term "American" for themselves.

Middle-class Mexican Americans began to use "Mexican American" in the 1920s. LULAC founder J.T. Canales testified before the US Senate in 1930 and he had to define "Mexican American" for them. LULAC founder J. Luz Sáenz wrote *Los México Americanos en la Gran Guerra (Mexican Americans in the Great War)* in the early 1930s.

Most of the racial violence against La Raza was in the 1910s and especially during the South Texas conflict of 1915 connected to the Plan de San Diego, Texas. The Texas Rangers instigated state-sanctioned racial violence in the 1910s so J.T. Canales of Cameron County, the lone Mexican-American state representative in the House, filed charges against them. Perhaps Canales' attention to this wanton violence led Mexican Americans in San Antonio to organize in 1920.

The Ku Klux Klan (KKK) also inflicted hatred. Reactivated after World War I, they added La Raza as a target, likely motivated by increased Mexican immigration. The year 1920 saw 450,000 members but down to 780 by 1930. Five hundred Klansmen called San Antonio their home. Their signs banned "Mexicans" in the Valley and border towns too. After World War I, they lynched three Mexican Americans.

Despite the Klan's presence, racial violence against La Raza decreased in the 1920s. Most of this violence occurred from 1910 to 1918.[17] Historians have identified 282 lynchings of "Mexicans" between 1889 and the 1920s. Anywhere between 300 to 5,000 persons of Mexican-origin were murdered, some lynched, between 1915-1917 during the South Texas conflict. North of San Antonio and west of

Dallas in the town of Ranger, whites ran some 600 Mexican-descent persons out of the oil rich town around 1921.[18] In 1922 the *New York Times* wrote, "The killing of Mexicans [in the United States] without provocation is so common as to pass almost unnoticed."[19] Elias Villarreal Zarate was lynched in 1922 in Weslaco in the Valley and Perales protested this event.[20] Historians Webb and Carrigan claim whites lynched 600 Mexican-descent people in Texas before 1928.[21] The 1930s and beyond did not witness another lynching of a person of Mexican-descent in Texas. La Raza found little recourse.

Racial Segregation

Racial segregation increased and was further institutionalized in the 1920s, even for those claiming Canary Island descent in San Antonio. When the Texas state constitution was rewritten during Reconstruction, it did not mention "Mexicans"—only "whites" and "colored." Nonetheless, a tripartite segregated school system arose by the 1890s.

Perhaps the first kind of segregation to develop was in housing leading to barrios and *colonias*. San Antonio's West side became a Mexican quarter. Racial covenants in real estate prevented buying homes or land outside the barrios. In the 1920s Perales denounced the McAllen Real Estate Board and the Delta Development Company because of discriminatory housing practices.[22] He and attorney Carlos Cadena filed a lawsuit against racial covenants in real estate in San Antonio in 1947.

Numerous public facilities were also segregated. The types of facilities varied widely: restaurants, hotels, swimming pools, churches and cemeteries. M.C. Gonzales, a LULAC founder, remembered the "No Mexicans Allowed" signs all from El Paso to Brownsville as well as the "Little Mexicos."[23] Signs stated, "No Mexicans Allowed," "Whites Only," "For Whites" and "For Mexicans," and "No Mexicans, Negroes or Dogs Allowed" from the 1910s to the late 1960s. In 1945, after Sergeant Macario García was denied service, attorney and LULAC member of Houston, John J. Herrera, noted signs read, "Mexicans served in Rear" in restaurants.[24] A 1948 sign read, "Mexicans will not Be Served Inside" and "This Park is for Whites, Mexicans Keep Out."[25] Perales saw these places as "public properties and we taxpayer citizens have as much right to the use of same, without being subjected to humiliations, as anyone else."[26]

Despite middle-class status, light skin or proficiency in English, prejudice was the order of the day. For instance, whites called millionaire and state representative J.T. Canales "the greaser from Brownsville" during a legislative session. Racial segregation was a major issue through the late 60s. It smacked at the dignity of all persons of Mexican descent even the educated or financial elite.

Education

After 1876, school segregation increased even though it was initially targeted at African Americans. Separate schools or school buildings were built for "Mexicans." The 1920s saw more "Mexican" schools and by 1942 there were 122 in fifty-nine counties.

Early San Antonio did not have segregated schools though in the 1910s residential segregation effectively created Mexican schools in San Antonio. Most of the students at Navarro, González, Ruiz, Johnson and Barclay were "Mexican." In 1927 San Antonio was "the only city of any size in Texas, outside of the border cities of Eagle Pass and Laredo, that [which] permits the Mexicans to attend school with the native white American children in the elementary grades."[27] Overt attempts to segregate Mexican children in South San Antonio were made in 1930.

Segregated schools were physically inferior, understaffed and lacked resources. A 1929 Texas school report noted, "In some instances segregation has been used for the purpose of giving the Mexican children a shorter school year, inferior buildings and equipment, and poorly paid teachers."[28] The 1920s saw La Raza insist on more classrooms, better-constructed schools and more schools. Perales noted, "The general tendency of our Anglo American co-citizens is to educate the Mexican children in huts and jacales while for Anglo American children they build magnificent brick buildings. There are towns in Texas where our Mexican children can't attend a high school because they are not permitted."[29] Beginning in the 1930s activists like Perales called for bond elections for more and better schools.

The Mexican-origin student population increased over time. In the early 20s only half of all Mexican-origin Texas children attended school with most finishing less than four years of schooling. In 1922 in San Antonio Mexican-descent children were less than 2% but 15% in 1928. In 1920 only 250 members of La Raza were in San Antonio high schools.[30] This became the first generation of bilingual and bicultural Mexican Americans. Many were placed in vocational training and girls were trained for housewifery; high school graduation was rare.

College graduates were also rare. In 1930 less than 200 out of 38,000 went to Texas colleges and 34 were from Mexico—Mexican Americans comprised less than 1 percent of all college students. Six times as many African Americans attended college in Texas in 1930 because of historically Black colleges. In 1928-29, there were fifty-seven Spanish-surname undergraduates at the University of Texas at Austin, thirty from the Valley. In 1946, only 114 Latinos attended UT Austin.[31] In 1933, fifty attended the Arts and Industries College in Kingsville. As late as 1942 Ruth L. Martinez of Claremont College in California called any Mexican/Mexican American in the United States "unusual" upon completion of high school or junior college.[32]

Graduate students and faculty were also rare. In the late 1920s Carlos E. Castañeda, born in Tamaulipas, raised in Brownsville, and a Mexican citizen until 1936, was a graduate student at the University of Texas, Austin; later as professor he became Perales' best friend. Castañeda may have been the only Raza professor in the state of Texas in 1930. Jovita González of Roma obtained her masters there in 1932. As a Mexican-American woman González was not sought after and especially in the years of the Depression, employed women were expected to defer their jobs to husbands and men. No Mexican-American woman would join the University of Texas Austin faculty until the 1940s. Dr. George I. Sánchez of New Mexico, who was a graduate student there in the 1930s, joined the UT faculty in the Education Department in the early 1940s and remained there into the 1970s. He became a national president of LULAC in the early 1940s.

Despite racism and neglect, the Mexican-origin community sought education and racial uplift by establishing classes, schools, libraries, bookstores and publishing houses. The tradition of private "escuelitas" (little schools) was common.[33] Alice, Texas had two private Mexican schools in 1899 and Perales benefitted from its teachers and students.

Lack of Political Power

Around 1900 most Mexican Americans were not engaged in politics. Exclusionary practices, political intimidation, voter alienation and ignorance were common. Mexicans living in Texas became US citizens in 1845. Fewer Mexican Americans served as elected officials after 1900 and were almost non-existent at the state level. J.T. Canales was the only Mexican-American state representative from 1905 to 1910 and 1917 to 1920. Augustín Celaya followed from1933 to 1941. Carlos Bee, an American raised in Mexico, served from 1914 to 1919 and Henry B. González of San Antonio joined the state legislature in 1956. Irma Rangel of Kingsville became the first Mexican-American woman state legislator in the 1970s.

Political representation varied by county and locale. In 1929 in San Antonio sheriff Alfonso Newton Jr. was the only Mexican American elected to a city or county office.[34] Political machines existed in San Antonio by the 1890s and the illiterate and Spanish-speakers were allowed to vote. Texas began a poll tax after 1902 and machines paid poll taxes, paid later by workers. Some were offered petty jobs or paid a dollar.

Mexican citizens in Texas could vote from 1887 to 1927. The state constitution of 1887 let Mexican male nationals vote if they stated future plans to naturalize. This especially helped the state Democratic machine from the 1880s to 1920. In San Antonio, Progressives called The Better Government ended this practice. Perales commented: "In some towns the system is well organized and in others it is not, but there is no room for doubt that this new bossism prevails regularly."[35] White Valley newcomers "condemned the Mexican-Americans as an ignorant people who were unfit to have a vote."[36] In 1917 Spanish and German interpreters were also terminated.

Use of the white primary varied by date and locale. It did *not* take shape in South Texas from the 1880s to the 1920s. However, in the mid-1920s it was put into practice in some counties. The Democratic Party needed more Mexican-American votes so in 1932 Mexicans were considered "whites" in the primary.[37] In 1944, African Americans challenged the legality of the white primary as it applied to them and won their case.

Assuming most voters were middle class, this group exercised an independent vote. In 1928, 50,000 persons in Bexar county paid their poll tax. Of these 5,000 were Mexican-Americans. Perales would seek to promote independent payment of the poll tax by Mexican-Americans to foster empowerment.

Most Mexican-American women remained outside of electoral politics during the 1920s. A few middle-class Mexican-American women voted. In the 1930s Adela H. Jaime, secretary of the women's club Minerva in 1919 and 1927 mutualista auxiliary Benovelencia Feminina president worked with politician Maury Maverick.[38] Mrs. Ruben Lozano, wife of lawyer Ruben Lozano, also headed a political club in San Antonio.[39] Mexican-American women in the Valley also organized a political club in the early 1930s.

But no Mexican-American woman held public office in Bexar County in the 1920s.[40] In contrast, it was typical for white women to serve as county assessors. It was not until 1954 that Texas women could serve on juries. The League of Women Voters, the Federation of Business and Professional Women's Clubs and other women's clubs did not admit Mexican-American women.

Perales promoted payment of the poll tax, independent Mexican-American partisan activity outside of the white controlled Democrat or Republican parties, voter turnout and Mexican-American candidates. In San Antonio Mexican-American voter turnout started to matter more by early 1940s. The Latin American Democrats organized in the 1940s.[41] Mexican-American voter turnout was 55.7% in 1948; 68.7% in 1956; and 87.1% in 1964 in San Antonio.[42] Perales played a major role in this change. Today's Southwest Voter Registration and Education Project in San Antonio established in 1974 by Willie Velásquez, the oldest and largest non-partisan voter registration project for Latinos, followed the work of Perales and LULAC in the 1930s. The era of no person of Mexican-descent holding statewide office ended when Governor John Connally appointed Roy Barrera as secretary of state in 1960.[43]

Conclusion

South Texas developed a new Mexican-American male middle class of which Perales was a part. It served the new wave of Mexican immigrants. Mexican-American business in the finance, industrial, transportation or communications sectors did not exist. Small businesses serving the barrios were numerous but few were professionals or educated. This community lived in an era of "Americans" over "Mexicans," "whites" over "Mexicans" and "coloreds" and other people of color and "American citizens" over "aliens" or "non-citizens," men over women, the middle class over the working class, and English-speakers over Spanish-speakers.

Education was largely inaccessible to La Raza. High school graduation was rare and college the exception. Perales' access was unusual. This access was even more rare for women.

Population change, especially due to Mexican immigration, brought forth new race relations. Whites responded with segregation in a new racial order. They also imagined "Mexicans" as "other." Perales rejected "otherness," feeling American like most whites.

Despite racial animosity, Americanization and assimilation increased due to public schools and culturally Mexican Americans emerged as a hybrid people. Yet, color, physical attributes, accents and the Spanish surname still marked "Mexican" bodies. Perales' color cast him as "Mexican."

An active, strong independent Mexican-American voter group, cognizant of the new social, political and economic order began to emerge and mobilize. They sought to change the political landscape with Mexican-American voter turnout, the election of a few Mexican Americans and less overt racism.

This context gave rise to Perales' activism and his drive for "redeeming La Raza" in the late 1910s and 20s. It also gave birth to a parallel development, the formation of the civil rights organization, the Order Sons of America in San Antonio in 1921.

CHAPTER 2
Early Family Life in Alice, Texas

Alonso S. Perales was shaped by local, state, national and global developments but his formation took place in little Alice, Texas. He had life-changing, detrimental events occur in his family while living in Alice. But he also had significant educational opportunities there. After Perales finished his schooling in rural Alice he moved to San Antonio where he found extensive career opportunities. This chapter surveys Perales' family life in Alice south of San Antonio. Second, it explains how and why Alice provided important educational opportunities. One of these opportunities was access to Spanish proficiency. Third, it covers Perales' training at a business college in San Antonio. Fourth, his early white-collar employment in San Antonio, the Mexican capital of Texas and the United States at the time, is covered. Lastly, the chapter focuses on the Americanization movement (not to be confused with the general pattern of assimilation), an ideological current in the United States in the mid to late 1910s which impacted Perales' intellectual formation and which became the focus of the first newspaper essay he wrote.

Family

Perales was born to Susanna Sandoval and Nicolás Perales on October 17, 1898. Father Nicolás Perales was born in Potrerillos, Nuevo León south of Hidalgo County in the Lower Rio Grande Valley; he was a shoe and bootmaker.[1] His mother was from Roma, Texas. Siblings included the following in order: (unidentified name of brother), Francisca, Rosa, Nicolasa, Emilio and Luis. Brother Luis was born in

Mexico. So, Perales' father and his brother were born in Mexico. This mixed-citizenship family background contributed to Perales' understanding of both Mexican and Mexican-American perspectives. Perales' father also had a child named Zeferino before he married Susanna.[2] Perales maintained some contact with Zeferino because in 1937 Zeferino helped sell Perales' book.[3]

Tragedy struck the family repeatedly. In 1904 one of Alonso's brothers died and while burying him, Alonso's father had a heart attack and also died; Perales was six.[4] Sra. Perales made *empanadas* (filled sweet bread) and the Perales children "put them into a type of wagon walking the 'caliche' streets all around the town to sell them."[5] He also joined his brothers selling tamales his mother made after his father died.[6] This would be the beginning of Perales' work. Then in 1910 mother Susanna died of tuberculosis when Perales was twelve.[7] A relative took the girls to the Corpus Christi area but had no room for the boys. Young Perales slept under a porch.

Young friend Fortino Treviño convinced his family to take him in. Young Perales left the family house on Flores Street in 1910 to live with the barber Cresencio Treviño whose house stood a block away on Chaparral Street. The Treviño home in Alice proved advantageous. Perales moved in with Eugenia Naranjo and husband Cresencio, a barber and according to fellow Alice resident J. Luz Sáenz "well respected in our community."[8] The family had three children including Fortino.[9] Sáenz said Fortino was one of the few Mexican-descent boys who "among the very few who never allowed Anglo students to humiliate him."[10] Fortino fought in World War I and sent all his earnings to his father for a better barber shop.[11] Likewise, he would become a long-term friend of Perales and a LULAC member as noted in chapter 21.

Sister Nicolasa died in 1919 and two years later sister Francisca died in 1921. So, Alonso suffered five deaths within two decades. Alonso might have become a broken, homeless, depressed alcoholic or wayward boy. Perhaps the charitable and loving Treviño family saved him. And/or perhaps Perales' Christian upbringing saved him. Perales was raised with high morals. Perhaps community members took special care of young Alonso because of these tragedies.

While in Alice, Perales developed both a strong work-ethic and ambition. He picked cotton in elementary school, laid railroad ties and lubricated locomotive wheels, hot and difficult work in the South Texas sun and work typically done by persons of Mexican descent and African Americans.[12] According to Perales' daughter in 2019, "Treviño also told us that together they would be in the fields picking cotton under the hot Texas sun. At the end of the furrow they would stop for a moment to cool off. Daddy would look at the torn and bleeding fingers of his hands. He would tell all who would listen, "¡Miren cómo están nuestras manos! Tenemos que estudiar y aprender."[13] (Look at our hands! We have to study and get educated.) He learned of the life of the working class first-hand. According to relatives he spoke all of his life of the personal abhorrence that he had for manual labor.[14] And "he grew his fingernails long, clean, and manicured as an emblem," a relative added.[15] Because his father was a shoemaker, he also knew that the life of artisans was easier. Since his mother was a homemaker he came to believe a woman's place was the home caring for the family. This would have a profound influence on how he saw women's role in civic society.

Alice

While Perales had numerous deaths in the family, he was also impacted by positive acquaintances and opportunities that Alice, Texas permitted. Nineteenth-century businessman Trinidad Salazar indirectly influenced him. In 1888 Salazar was a passenger on the first San Antonio and Aransas Pass Railway train that arrived at the town site that became Alice. He bought merchandise in San Antonio and sold it from a cart. By 1890 his store became the largest general-merchandise business between Corpus Christi and Laredo, including a mortuary and locally processed leather goods like shoes.[16] Salazar employed Perales' father. Young Perales would have likely seen Salazar's entrepreneurship before he died in 1921.

Despite its rural character, Alice proved to be a most excellent environment for young Perales. Although small, it fostered Perales' intellectual growth. Alice grew from 2,136 in 1910 to 3,500 in 1914 to 7,792 in 1940. The public schools were cruel to Mexican-descent children. The Spanish language had been excluded from school curriculum since the nineteenth century so Spanish-speakers had to sink or swim in an English-only environment. Most teachers were racist; the curriculum was without attention to Mexican-American history; and Mexican-descent students were not encouraged to advance in their studies. According to LULAC co-founder Sáenz, an Alice teacher complained that "if I had known that I was going to teach English to the Mexicans I would not have come from so far away."[17] However, Sáenz also encountered supportive white high school teachers Nat and Alice Benton. Sáenz graduated from high school in 1908 when Perales was ten.[18] Perales attended grade schools in Alice from 1905 to 1912 but did not graduate from high school. Dr. Carlos E. Castañeda noted, "Since very young he was forced to struggle for the right of his existence and to educate himself."[19] According to Perales' widow years later, he "became sensitive to the issue when he was exposed to discrimination in school."[20] Still, Perales learned how to speak English and that would prove a major asset throughout his life; most members of the Mexican-descent community could only speak Spanish.

Besides access to at least a seventh-grade education where Perales learned English, he may have also attended a private Mexican school there. A few educated Mexican-descent people opened small private schools (*escuelitas*) to teach Mexican history, Spanish and fostered pride in Mexicanness. Before 1920 there were at least two Mexican private schools in Alice, one by Eulalio Velásquez and the other by Pablo Pérez. These schools "provided instruction in Spanish and taught Mexican history and culture by choice, and not merely as a response to school segregation and exclusion."[21] Pérez taught arithmetic, language arts, literature and Mexican history.[22]

Newspaperman and teacher Eulalio Velásquez likely influenced young Perales though the Perales archive provides no documentation. According to Rosales' research Velásquez was Perales' instructor.[23] Born in San Pedro de Roma (now Ciudad Miguel Alemán), Tamaulipas, Mexico in 1868, Velásquez married Balbina Gongora from Roma, Texas in 1895. An 1890 graduate of Baylor University School of Business where he studied agriculture, Velásquez became a publisher and accountant. He lived in Laredo.[24] The Velásquez moved to Alice in

1903 and published *El Cosmopolita*, the first Spanish-language newspaper there and which lasted ten years. The newspaper featured articles on business, economics, agriculture, health and the arts. In 1903 Velásquez constructed a two-story building for *El Cosmopolita* and a private co-ed elementary day school in Spanish and night classes on agriculture and business. It had a library which Velásquez shared with non-students as well.[25] Perales would have seen the newspaper and seen adults reading it and may have used the library. *El Sol,* another newspaper, existed there too. Before Perales left the town a third paper, *El Latino Americano*, arose in 1914 with Amado Gutiérrez as its director. There were also two English-language newspapers, the *Alice Echo* and *Alice News*. Newspapers would have been especially important since Alice had no public library until 1935.[26]

Velásquez offered adult night courses. He was also an accountant to several businesses and helped organize *fiestas patrias* (Mexican patriotic festivities).[27] A strong advocate of historical literacy of Mexico, that passion rubbed off on young Mexican-descent children. In 1906 he published "Escuelas Mexicanas en Texas, artículos publicados en *El Cosmopolita*," a rebuttal to the Alice newspaper *El Sol* which "claimed that independent Mexican schools were not preparing Mexican youth for life in the United States."[28] This was likely a discussion about Mexicanist versus Mexican-Americanist tendencies that Perales would address twenty years later. Perhaps orphan Perales attended Velásquez' classes for free or at a discounted rate.

Velásquez taught student Sáenz pride in Mexican history, heritage and culture. Historian Emilio Zamora noted "Sáenz's vast cultural repertoire" particularly his "command of history and literature."[29] Zamora added, "I am not surprised by his mastery of the Spanish language and Mexican history and culture [. . .] I have credited his good schooling and mentoring in Alice, along with his studious nature and determined personality, to explain his analytical skills and self-assuredness."[30] During Sáenz' stint as a World War I soldier he wrote Velásquez from France, "I write to you as someone who has always been concerned about our people's well-being."[31]

Contact with Velásquez or enrollment in Mexican private schools served to develop racial pride in Sáenz and likely Perales and a knowledge base that latter-day reformers especially post-1929 and pre-1970 civil rights activists would lack. Historian Ignacio M. García noted, "Unlike the older generation who extolled their Mexican and Spanish heroes, and to a lesser extent the great Indian civilizations of Mexico, as well as some of the original Mexican-American elites, the new reformers [post-WWII civil rights activists] could go back no further than World War II."[32] In other words, after WWII as more Mexican Americans attended more years in US schools they were becoming Americanized since they had little access to Mexican history and Spanish. Indeed, few *escuelitas* survived the Depression.

In 1914 Velásquez and his family moved to Kingsville. There he published his "A la memoria del ilustre ciudadano Presidente Benito Juárez: Documentos oficiales, oración fúnebre, poesías, pensamientos, etc., relativos a la vida del Benemérito de las Américas" from the press or newspaper called *El Popular*.[33] He was even involved in the Plan de San Diego event of 1915 described in chapter 1. He was arrested as a co-conspirator in a plot to renew raids. The Plan was supposedly hatched by José Morín, a former supporter of Pancho Villa and Victoriano Ponce, a Kingsville, Texas baker. After the intercession of a Mexican-American pastor and Euro-Texan lawyer Thomas Hook, Velázquez who professed his innocence, was released. Perales' brothers, Emilio and Luis, helped obtain his release from jail in 1916.[34] So he was likely a family friend. Velásquez then moved to Eagle Pass on the Mexican border where he published another weekly newspaper until 1920. Eventually he returned to Mexico to the city of Chihuahua where in partnership with his older sons he opened a publishing house. They continued to publish in Mexico, in Querétaro and then in Orizaba, Veracruz where he died on September 18, 1941. In the late 1930s Perales reestablished contact with him. Velásquez wrote Perales to congratulate him on his 1937 book.[35]

A third person who may have influenced Alonso was a son of Pablo Pérez, another proprietor of a private Mexican school. Pablo Pérez was a founder of San Diego, Texas but moved to Alice, Texas where he became wealthy.[36] A fourth person who may have influenced young Perales was Elena Zamora. Sáenz and perhaps Perales benefitted from teachers like Zamora.[37] She arrived in Alice in 1903, taught in Alice for several years and served as principal.[38] She taught Mexican heritage and folklore and instilled a love of Mexican culture in J. Frank Dobie who would later become a Southwest folklorist and professor. [39] By the 1920s Alice had a small Mexican-American middle class. In the 1910s Salazar and Velásquez were there. In the 20s Franco Pérez had a real estate and life insurance business while Pablo Pérez and Elena Zamora were respected teachers.[40] Alonso saw the spectrum of class differences—entrepreneurs, members of the middle class, artisans, laborers and farmworkers. He would have also seen educational differences from the well-educated Velásquez to illiterates who could neither read nor write in English or Spanish.

Spanish Proficiency

One of the most important skills Perales developed in Alice was Spanish proficiency which he could not learn in the Alice public schools. Like other Mexican-origin children he benefitted from Spanish-speaking parents. However, it was his contact with the Spanish-language press and intellectuals like Velásquez or Pérez which impressed on him the significance of reading, writing and speaking Spanish fluently. A latter Euro-Texan boss in San Antonio took note of Perales' unique bilingual status for his generation in the 1920s, "Contrary to the rule [at least in San Antonio], he also is educated in his native language, Spanish."[41] Despite his training in Spanish, he still felt his Spanish was not perfect. Indeed, when materials needed to be translated into Spanish for some 1927 civil rights materials, he asked newspaperman Eduardo Idar of Laredo to put into "perfect Spanish."[42] Perales had profound respect for the Spanish language because it was part of what constituted Latino/Latin American culture. (Perales also took a French class in 1929, so he understood the value of being multilingual not just bilingual. Perhaps French involvement in World War I motivated him to do so.)[43] His Spanish proficiency would be an asset not just for his volunteer work in the Spanish-speaking community in the United States but also for the US government for his paid diplomatic career in Latin America.

Draughon's Business College, San Antonio

Perales left Alice for San Antonio to advance his education and career opportunities. In 1912 brothers Emilio and Luis moved likely to Kingsville but both ended up in San Antonio.[44] With both his parents deceased, at age 15 young man Perales ventured 128 miles away to San Antonio to join brother Luis. Not only was San Antonio the largest city in Texas before 1930, it was also the "Tejano capital" and/or "the capital of the Mexico that lies within the United States."[45] San Antonio in the mid-1910s was an industrializing city with segregated Mexican, African American and white sides of town, German Americans being a notable ethnicity there. The North side consisted of the Euro-Texan elite; the South side, lower and middle-class whites; the East side, African American; and West side was Mexican descent.[46] On the north section of the West side was Prospect Hill, an enclave for the emerging Mexican-descent middle class.[47] The wealthiest Mexicans lived on San Pedro St. out of the West side.[48] The Perales brothers lived at 122 South Street on the West side.

Perales enrolled at Draughon's School of Business and which provided training to work and operate in a more literate, bureaucratic and business English-speaking world. Draughon's had thirty schools in Southern and Western states by 1921. He worked in the day and attended class at night.[49] In 1915 Draughon's offered banking spelling, shorthand, penmanship, bookkeeping, typewriting, punctuation, letter writing, commercial law, business English and rapid calculation.[50] Perales took a business course which included stenography, typewriting, applied business English, letter writing and spelling.[51] He attended from April to November 1915. J.B. Andrews, one of his employers, would later say that he was a "first class stenographer, very efficient on the typewriter and he has a perfect knowledge of English."[52] Perales could type forty to sixty words a minute and could take 80 to 100 words in dictation.[53] Perales called his schooling there "business training."[54] Prospective teachers also took classes at business schools like Draughon. According to historian Zamora, "Many would-be teachers like Sáenz attended business schools in preparation for classroom work since few university teacher-training programs existed at the time. Once they finished their business school instruction and secured a job with a school, they often attended teacher-training institutes organized by experienced teachers to ensure that the novices learned the trade."[55]

Perales made a few friends at the school. He met Filiberto Galván and Pablo González, son of Dr. Domingo González, a San Antonio physician, both of San Antonio. Later, in 1927 Galván was involved with Perales' civil rights activism in Edinburg.[56] Then Galván moved to Houston where he became an administrator for a steamship company in Galveston. It is unknown if Galván was involved in Houston LULAC. However, at least on one occasion Galván met Perales and his wife in the city as they traveled through Houston on their way to New Orleans and to Latin America. González was not involved in 1920s Mexican-American civil rights activism but joined LULAC Council 16 in San Antonio in the 1930s and also became an attorney.

White-Collar Employment

Schooled in business and administrative know-how at Draughon's Perales began his career in white-collar work leaving the working class for good. Around November 1915 he took his first professional job with a calendar firm as a stenographer and translator.[57] Alonso then worked at the L. Frank Saddlery Company, a "leading business house of the city."[58] Here he became Assistant Export Manager, Shoe Findings Department and worked as a stenographer where he did Spanish translation and stenography in English.[59] A photo documents the company's Mexican saddle makers. Its export business was tied to Mexico. Perales' father's trade as a shoemaker/bootmaker made this a fit. He made $75 a month here for two years from November 1915 to April 1918.[60] Perales then took a better job with more pay; upward mobility would become his typical pattern. The company later became the Straus-Frank Company and by 1924 it had representatives in Mexico, Cuba and Puerto Rico. It had shifted from supporting the cattle business to providing supplies for cars. It sold saddles, harnesses, collars, awning covers and car seats for cars.[61] This job mattered even after Perales left because he obtained good reference letters from Euro-Texan businessmen.

In April 1918 Perales worked for the US Postal Censorship Office earning $111 monthly.[62] This job was connected to World War I which began in Europe in 1914. He likely reviewed Spanish-language newspapers for pro-German and anti-American sentiment and also worked there as a stenographer until October 1918.[63] This job would have made him even more aware of the significance of newspapers as opinion-making. It would have also made him conscious of ideological argumentation on political issues.

In April 1918 the Mexican Gulf Oil company in Tampico, Mexico offered Perales a position as a stenographer and he applied for a passport. He had no qualms about moving to Mexico because it was not foreign to him because he grew up along the Texas Mexican borderlands/*frontera* in South Texas.

Besides advancing his education and career, Perales was already networking with journalists of the Spanish-language press. In May 1918 *La Prensa* of San Antonio reported on a trip he made to Kingsville.[64] In 1918 *El Latino Americano* of Alice also wrote about him.[65] Perales was already keen to the idea of the press reporting on his activities—he knew he was unusual. From 1918 on Perales learned how to access the press, using it to his advantage. However, to the US government he was an ordinary man and like thousands of other men was drafted into World War I which the United States entered in 1917.

The Americanization Movement

After Perales' stint in the war (discussed in chapter 3) he began his "career" as a public intellectual. Assuming he had been reading newspapers for years, especially *La Prensa* of San Antonio, his literacy was high. The first article he wrote was "Como Inculcar Americanismo en este País" (How to Inculcate Americanization in this Nation) for *La Evolución* of Laredo, a newspaper run by the Idar family.[66] Perhaps he wrote for this newspaper because he may have met editor Clemente Idar of Laredo who was an activist and advocate for Mexican-descent involvement in the war and whose family had organized a major anti-lynching convention in 1911 in Laredo. Perhaps he came across one of the Idars' newspapers as a censor of anti-American or pro-German sentiment during the war.

Perales' first essay was a response to an article by Nathaniel M. Washer, chairman of the Bexar County Board of Americanization, titled "Sowing Americanism to Raise Better Citizens" in the *San Antonio Express*. Perales referenced Mexican-American veterans who had just returned from World War I and were denied restaurant service due to their race, one of who was Sáenz. The article mentioned his letter to Washer. (It would be common for Perales to publicize his private letters.) He told Washer that he was an American of Mexican descent. He then cited a few specific incidents of racial segregation in Alice and San Antonio. He noted, "All these injustices have been committed by people with a horrible as well as by an intellectual point of view. In these cases, should be applied individually and not collectively, as typically happens based on a person's merits and not the members of a race."[67] Perales also published this essay in *La Época* of San Antonio and *La República* of El Paso.[68] He was already striving for more than local impact. With this published article near the turn of the new decade, the 1920s, Perales mapped out his future as social critic, public intellectual, anti-racist and defender of La Raza.

It is no accident that the first topic Perales addressed was Americanization and racial discrimination. Emerging around 1914, the Americanization movement defined US society in the 1910s and 20s as well as helping to mold a Mexican-American identity. It should not be confused with the daily assimilation process already occurring in US society. Rather, it was a social movement beginning in the mid-1910s and died in the early 1920s. A response to "too much" non-European immigration, the movement labeled immigrants a "social problem," promoted English-only and advanced so-called "Americanism." It defined an "American" as a patriotic English-speaking Anglo-Saxon in the United States. Four million immigrants who spoke a language other than English were a considered a threat.[69] All Mexican-descent people in the United States were targets of its reform if not its exclusion.

Although proponents defined "Americanization" vaguely, its efforts were widespread. They advocated the superiority of the English language, patriotism, citizenship and antiradicalism. The movement highlighted US patriotism and citizenship. It stressed civic participation but was xenophobic. Settlement homes, women's clubs, churches, schools, industrial plants, labor unions and chambers of commerce advanced it. In San Antonio the Christian Woman's Board of Missions of the Disciples of Christ opened the Mexican Christian Institute in 1913. Bilingual Mexican-Americans Micaela Tafolla and Clara Cantú at the YWCA's International House and National Catholic Community House witnessed their institutions work toward this effort. In the Rio Grande Valley, home economics clubs reached out to Mexican-descent homemakers to teach home economics "American-style."[70] Local defense councils created during World War I also advanced the cause.[71] In 1920 Washington, DC's International Reform Bureau studied how to Americanize Mexicans, and Texas schools expanded these initiatives.

Federal and state laws also promoted Americanization. The federal Espionage Act of 1917 and Sedition law of 1918 promoted loyalty to the federal government. Likewise, the Texas legislature passed the Hobby Loyalty Act in 1917 to "ferret out Mexican propaganda, pro-Germanism, anti-Americanism, and to assist in winning the war."[72] During World War I, Texas also made criticism of the US government, its flag, its officers, its uniform or questioning US participation in the war punishable by fine and imprisonment.[73]

The movement promoted English as the nation's official language. Fifteen states passed laws requiring English as the sole language of instruction in the 1920s,[74] and Texas prohibited German and Spanish in public schools. Annie Webb Blanton, Texas superintendent of public schools, sought to enforce English-only. She wrote, "If you desire to be one with us, stay, and we welcome you, but if you wish to preserve, in our state, the language and custom of another land, you have no right to do this . . . You must go back to the country which you prize so highly."[75] The Texas state legislature banned the teaching of Spanish during World War I and only World War II and concerns about the US's Good Neighbor policy ended the ban in 1941.

While mostly racist notions of "Americanization" were promoted, Perales accepted only some of its tenets. He believed in full participation in US society but did not believe in "losing" Mexican culture or

Spanish. He was patriotic toward the United States and La Raza. He did not believe in English-only as most proponents of Americanization did. He was fully bilingual, bicultural and bi-literate in English and Spanish. He exemplified a new, emerging Mexican-American identity and culture, a hybrid created from Mexican and US traditions. Few in his generation had excellent Spanish and English literacy skills.

Conclusion

While Perales' formative years were rural, he grew up in the surprisingly intellectually and culturally rich environment of Alice, Texas. Spanish-language newspapers and *escuelitas* existed there. While he did not graduate from Alice High, he obtained the maximum education possible there and left town speaking perfect English. Likewise, while he may have been subjected to subtractive schooling in the Alice public schools where English-only existed and where only European American history was taught, he benefitted directly or indirectly from town intellectuals, the bilingual and bicultural Eulalio Velásquez and Pablo Pérez. He learned Mexico's history and pride in Mexicanness. He may have also been influenced by principal and teacher Elena Zamora. His ability in the Spanish language, moreover, was good or excellent.

Perales experienced working-class life first hand since his father was an artisan and his mother, a homemaker. And he would have known about the lives of laborers, the bulk of the population, since he himself experienced work in the fields and on the tracks, earning low wages from hard, hot labor. Yet, Perales had numerous exemplary role models with middle-class standing: entrepreneurs, newspapermen, an accountant and teachers. LULAC co-founder M.C. Gonzales noted the influence of Alice on Perales: "Little did the world know when you were born in Alice, Texas, that that humble town had produced the outstanding leader of the Latin race over a period of two decades."[76] Assessing Alice's influence on a young man is difficult but what is known is that Perales left the town bright, optimistic, hardworking and literate in two cultures and languages.

Perales moved to San Antonio for educational and career opportunities. Working in the day and studying at night, he attended a business college where he learned white-collar skills and perfected his ability in stenography and business training. Likewise, he sought career mobility with each new job, earning more each time and expanding his repertoire of white-collar skills. He also learned the value of networking and using the press to his advantage; he was learning to be a master of the media. He was already energetic, ambitious and community-minded.

Perales was impacted by national ideological developments in the United States, the Americanization movement, a racist and xenophobic movement which narrowly defined US citizenship. But as a critical thinker, Perales only accepted some of its tenets, especially US patriotism, and not its racist ideas. Right after Perales exited the US army in World War I he began his work as a public intellectual in the US and Spanish-language press asserting Mexican-Americans' citizenship in the United States and the humanity of Mexicans in the United States.

Perales acknowledged his own Mexican Americanness and the hybridity of who and what Mexican Americans were. Mexican Americans were still connected to Mexico through family, heritage and language. His own family included Mexican citizens. Moreover, it was Mexican Americans and Mexicans in the United States that he cared about, not Mexicans in Mexico. His heritage was Mexican and American but Mexico was not his homeland. And unlike most of La Raza, *both* his Spanish and English were good to excellent—he was unusual. Most Mexican Americans and Mexicans could not speak or write in English.

In 1920 Perales was only twenty-two years old but well-prepared to be a life-long critic of US racism and a crusader for La Raza.

CHAPTER 3

World War I in San Antonio, Texas

World War I (WWI) was a defining event for both the United States and Alonso S. Perales. Historian F. Arturo Rosales observed that World War I was "an unexpected window of opportunity to fulfill the portly ambition of Mexican Americanism—to show they [Mexican Americans] deserved full citizenship."[1] Both Mexicans and Mexican Americans were impacted by the war and participated in the war effort. This chapter first introduces World War I. Second, it looks at Mexican and Mexican-American men in the war and its impact on them. It investigates the question of La Raza's loyalty and citizenship as it related to the war. Third, it examines Perales' and his brothers' experience in the war as well as that of a few of Perales' friends who joined him fighting for civil rights after 1920.

World War I

This global conflict started in 1914 but the United States officially entered in 1917. Some 24 million US citizens and noncitizens (unauthorized immigrants) registered for the US draft.[2] A million Texas men were drafted including 80,000 Mexican-descent residents and 30,000 additional Spanish-surnamed men.[3]

This horrific war witnessed the new technology of tanks, machine guns, poison gas and rat-infested trenches. In fall 1917 the average life expectancy of a private on the Western Front was thirty to fifty days.[4] It is no wonder soldier J. Luz Sáenz of Alice, Texas and later a friend to Perales wrote about "going to the slaughter" though he still volunteered.[5] Some 5,000 Texans died in the war including Mexicans

31

and Mexicans Americans. The United States readily allowed Mexicans to fight this war despite lacking US citizenship.

San Antonio, Texas saw the physical manifestation of the war as it became a major military installation site. In 1916 Kelly Field at Fort Sam Houston was built. Following a year later were Brooks Field, Camp Travis, Camp Bullis and Camp Stanley in Leon Springs in northern San Antonio.[6] San Antonio would host six US army installations, giving the city a military-like outlook and make it one of the most militarized cities in the world.[7] The city likewise saw US nationalism as a major ideological force there; Mexican Americans would increasingly express US patriotism here.

World War I and Mexican-Descent Men

World War I had a tremendous impact on Mexican-descent people in the United States.[8] Mexican Americans had participated in the US Civil War, Spanish-American War and Filipino-American War of 1903 but World War I proved to be one in which a major shift in identity occurred. It highlighted citizenship and led veterans to ask why they were treated like second-class citizens when they returned to racial segregation practices in the United States.

In 1917 the draft began with the government requiring young men to register. Likewise, "foreigners" also had to register stating their nationality.

The war introduced questions about citizenship. Many Mexican Americans were unsure of their citizenship status. From 1836 to 1848 the citizenship of those living in the Nueces strip south of Corpus Christi and north of the Rio Grande was unclear. Adding still more confusion were changes in Mexico's laws. The 1917 Mexican constitution recognized Mexican Americans as Mexican citizens if one of the parents was born in Mexico.[9] Further complicating the issue was the fact that "declarants," immigrants who had already applied for US citizenship, could be drafted if from war-neutral countries like Mexico.[10] Citizenship laws were unknown, misunderstood and confusing.

Loyalty to one nation or multiple nations was another issue that the war exaggerated. Were Mexican Americans in Texas loyal to the United States? Or were they loyal to Mexico? Loyalty questions were especially applied to Spanish-language and other non-English (foreign) language newspapers. After the Espionage Act was passed in 1917 newspapers critical of the US government or sympathetic to the Allies, were deemed illegal. Newspaperman Clemente Idar of Laredo and young Perales monitored Spanish-language newspapers.[11] In May 1918 Perales' censor work at the U.S. Postal Service paid him $115 a month. [12] Likewise, the Trading with the Enemy Act was also passed in 1917 and El Paso's *La República* was shut down. San Antonio's *La Prensa*, while initially neutral, changed its tune and lauded Raza soldiers' patriotism to the United States.[13]

La Raza responded to the call to war in different ways. Draft dodgers fled to Mexico. In 1916, 38,000 left to Mexico and 93,000 did so in 1917. Some 3,000 Mexican-descent people abandoned Mission, Texas to Mexico during the war.[14] Texas Rangers' cooperation with draft boards also caused apprehension. Leaders like J.T. Canales and Clemente Idar gave "loyalty speeches" to encourage Mexican-American residents in South Texas to do their part. Still others did not register since they did not consider themselves US citizens.

Others readily registered. LULAC founder J. Luz Sáenz volunteered. Felipe García of Duval County volunteered and would become a life-long friend of Perales after settling in Mission, Texas. He wrote the US government to "request permission to organize the young men into Spanish-speaking companies" but the government did not accept volunteer units.[15] He was later drafted or volunteered and was stationed at Camp Travis in Austin.[16]

Mexican-descent men also had to address stereotypes of male cowardice.[17] A 1918 *San Antonio Express* subheading read: "Not a Man of Latin Blood Can Be Located to Fight for America."[18]

Mexican-descent men served the war in numerous ways. Some were chief registrants, clerks and interpreters for the draft.[19] Clemente Idar worked as an informant for the Justice department.[20] Adina de Zavala, the daughter of Lorenzo de Zavala, served as state treasurer of the Council of National Defense.[21] At least three Mexican Americans served as officers.[22] Sáenz applied for officer training school twice but was denied without explanation.[23]

Some veterans helped establish the Order Sons of America (OSA) in 1921 and LULAC in 1929. M.C. Gonzales of San Antonio and Perales, Sáenz and Fortino Treviño, all from Alice, were activist veterans. Gonzales worked as an interpreter for the military attaché at the US embassy in France and Spain while OSA Corpus Christi president Ben Garza served in the shipyards.

Military service had a major impact on Mexican-origin veterans. José Manuel Escajeda of El Paso also went on to become El Paso National Bank's vice president of Latin American Affairs.[24] But most encountered racism upon their return. Mexican nationals who served in the war found third-class citizenship.

The Perales Brothers and the Draft

Three Perales boys registered for the draft. Emilio, Alonso's older brother, registered in 1917 when he was 25 but he was not drafted because he was married with children.[25] Perales' other older brother Luis registered for the draft in 1917 at the age of 20 when he was working in the Kingsville railroad roundhouse. He declared Alice, Texas as his place of birth on his registration but he also revealed having enrolled as a Mexican citizen with the Mexican Consul in Brownsville. Luis may have registered as a Mexican citizen in May 1917 to avoid the draft. Luis' border crossing documents in 1924 and 1936 maintained by the United States noted the state of Coahuila in Mexico as his birthplace. Later in 1940 when he lived in Laredo his citizenship was challenged. By then brother Alonso was an attorney and helped Luis obtain a Texas birth certificate based on oral references instead of written documents. He was likely born in Mexico but had lived so many years in Texas that culturally he was more of a Mexican American; Perales knew how to obtain a desired outcome for his brother. Even the fluidity of identity/birthplace/citizenship existed in the Perales' family.

Alonso was also drafted—he did not volunteer. In April 1918 he applied for a passport to travel to Tampico, Tamaulipas to work as a stenographer for the Mexican Gulf Oil Company but the draft interrupted his career.[26] A notice arrived in October 1918 and he received orders to report to Fort Sam Houston in San Antonio. He immediately applied for appointment as an army field clerk for which he received $1,200.[27] After soliciting recommendations from previous employers assuring he had competency in shorthand and typing, the army sent him to the Southern Division's Camp Stanley in Fort Sam Houston. There he trained as an army field clerk, a rank equivalent to a warrant officer today and a position given to enlisted personnel with special skills.[28] These skills prevented him from seeing combat.

Perales was stationed at the Headquarters Cavalry Officers' Training School in Camp Stanley in San Antonio where he was army field clerk under the Adjutant General. Unlike other LULAC co-founders Sáenz and M.C. Gonzales, Perales did not go overseas; he spent his entire enlistment in San Antonio. On November 29, 1918, the War Department issued orders commanding he and army clerk Charles Yonge report to Governor's Island in New York and wait transport to France.[29] However, neither had to comply—the war was winding down. Another reason Perales did not have to report to Camp Stanley on December 24 was that the post was so crowded that Perales was provided with a stipend to live off the camp. A family crisis also intervened. Perales' sister Nicolasa died in 1919.[30] On December 27, 1919 Perales appealed to his commander and he was discharged from Fort Sam Houston on January 6, 1920.[31] He received his Honorable Discharge certificate on January 6, 1920 indicating that he served as an army field clerk, received a Victory Medal but saw "no battles, engagements, skirmishes" and no overseas service and a $60 service bonus.[32] Moreover, Perales obtained two glowing letters of recommendation from Fort Sam Houston officers that day.[33] The war was over; Perales was alive and had a bright future.

With the war over by mid-January 1920 Perales was on his way to a successful civilian life. On January 2, 1920, Perales received a telegram that he had been recommended to work with the Department of Commerce's Bureau of Standards Division in Washington, DC as a stenographer and typist with a salary of $90 a month but up to $120 a few months later.

After WWI, Perales began contemplating the need for Mexican-American civil rights activism. Once the war was over, Mexican-descent soldiers felt they had served their country. Some gave their lives and others risked theirs. But in Texas while the war did divert negative attention from Mexican-origin people to Germans and German Americans, anti-Mexican sentiment did not cease.[34] Racism against La Raza was common so World War I veterans took action. According to Perales' autobiographical essay on the origins of LULAC in his book *En Defensa de Mi Raza* in 1937, he began contemplating activism in 1919. He discussed the idea with Pablo González and Filiberto Galván, Draughon school classmates. He began with a 1919 letter to the press. He said a hotel did not permit "Mexicans" despite their citizenship even a teacher (likely J. Luz Sáenz) who had already been hired by the local school.[35] He considered racist incidents "counterproductive to Americanization efforts."

Perales' Co-Activists in WWI: J. Luz Sáenz, M.C. Gonzales and Fortino Treviño

After the war, Perales' life would be intertwined with other Mexican-American veterans, especially J. Luz Sáenz of Alice; M.C. Gonzales of San Antonio; and Fortino Treviño of Alice.[36] To fully understand Perales, let us examine the lives of Sáenz and Gonzales. (Treviño, one of his best friends, will be discussed in chapter 21.)

J. Luz Sáenz of Alice was one of the most important Mexican Americans in World War I and became one of Perales' closest friends. Born in 1888 to Rosalío Sáenz and Cristina Hernández in Realitos, Duval County, Texas near Alice, J. Luz was one of eight children. The Sáenz family moved to Alice in 1900, and there, J. Luz graduated from high school in 1908. He also interacted with teachers Velásquez and Pérez. Ten years older than Perales, he became Perales' lifelong friend and co-activist from the 1920s on. Sáenz became a teacher after attending a business college in San Antonio. He obtained his teacher's certificate and began his lifelong career as an educator in and out of the classroom. He married María Petra Esparza in 1917; they had nine children.

Unlike Perales, Sáenz volunteered for military duty. He served with the 360th Regiment Infantry of the 90th Division from Texas and was stationed in France and occupied Germany. While serving, he kept notes, letters, newspaper articles and a diary and also mailed letters and notes to his family. He published his diary *Los México-Americanos en la Gran Guerra y su contingente en pro de la democracia, la humanidad, y la justicia* (Mexican Americans in the Great War and its contingent for democracy, humanity, and justice) in 1933. It included comments critical of the US government and US society though it also revealed his patriotism toward the United States. For instance, in August 1918 he wrote: "To Our Government: Our sacrifice in battle is the ultimate act of protest against a determined group of petty citizens who have never been able to rid themselves of their racial prejudice against our people."[37]

Like Perales, Sáenz did not have to endure trench warfare because he was also a clerk typist. But he was shipped to Europe, was always close to the front lines and witnessed first-hand the horrors of war. After the war, he and Luis Rodríguez of the Sociedad de la Unión, the largest *mutualista* in San Antonio, envisioned a monument on Main Plaza and even succeeded in getting Mayor C.M. Chamber's promise to erect it. Sáenz published his book calling for the memorial but it was never built. Under M.C. Gonzales' presidency of LULAC the fund that the organization devoted to this cause was shifted to Latino scholarships. Sáenz' book proved the only monument to Raza WWI veterans.

M.C. Gonzales was another Mexican American who fought in World War I and would be tied to Perales the rest of their lives. After obtaining a certificate from Nixon-Clay Business School in Austin he became a law clerk at the age of sixteen. He worked for the district judge of Hidalgo County, as chief clerk at the capitol in Austin and then as a secretary for the Patterson and Love law firm in Austin. During the war Gonzales served as secretary and interpreter to the military attaché at the US Embassy in Spain and France from 1918 to 1919.[38]

Gonzales showed an early interest in civil and labor rights in 1917. While at the Austin Patterson and Love firm, he became a secretary in the founding of La Liga Protectora Mexicana (Mexican Protective League). The FBI investigated this organization during the war.[39] After the war in 1921 he helped organize the Asociación Jurídica Mexicana (a legal assistance organization) which provided legal advice to tenant farmers. Also, in the early 1920s Gonzales joined others, some of who were also veterans, in the Order Sons of America, the first Mexican-American civil rights group founded in San Antonio in 1921. He would also become a LULAC co-founder.

Conclusion

World War I bolstered nationalism in US society and in residents like Perales, J. Luz Sáenz, and M.C. Gonzales. It was a defining event in the history of Mexican-descent men in Texas fostering and cementing a Mexican-American consciousness for the first time. Indeed, soldiering and veteran status provided an important aspect of identity formation in the making of the Mexican-American male middle class for which Perales would become a major voice. Latinas did not have this experience.

Perales did not volunteer to fight in World War I as did Sáenz. Perales enhanced his clerical skills during the war but did not experience travel to Europe or across the United States.[40] Other veterans like Sáenz and M.C. Gonzales broadened their worldview with travel to Europe. Veteran status became another reason Perales would fight for first-class citizenship. As stated by historian Nicholas Villanueva, "Mexican American veterans returned from the war with a new hope for civility in Texas."[41] However, Perales was emboldened by the insult of second-class citizenship of Mexican-descent soldiers who were allowed in the battlefields but not in restaurants and whose children were segregated in schools.

The war bolstered US patriotism among Mexican-American veterans. This loyalty to the United States would at times seem hyperbolic. However, in the shadow of the war; in the context of treatment as second-class citizenship; and in the shadow of being seen as hyphenated Americans, this patriotism made sense to veterans like Perales. Moreover, given the fact that they were ethnics in the United States marked by non-white color, it was up to them to assert their US citizenship.

CHAPTER 4
Education in Washington, DC

The 1910s provided Perales a junior high education and business skills though he saw further maturation in education, intellect and experience as an adult in the 1920s. This chapter unveils Perales' life in the early 20s in Washington, DC. Here he partook of white-collar employment, finished high school, obtained a college education and studied law. He became a young intellectual here. Secondly, it also shows Perales as a young master of the media, learning how to use newspapers to promote himself and his ideas.

Working and Studying in Washington, DC

A 1920 Alice Spanish-language newspaper announced Perales' departure to Washington, "Para Washington"[1] (To Washington). No document suggests why he decided to move there. However, he took a civil service exam and was appointed to a position in Washington, DC.[2] Perhaps Perales wanted to learn how politics worked and decided to move to the pinnacle of power. Perhaps this is where he was offered a good job. An ambitious, skilled twenty-two-year-old Perales began to carve out his future in Washington, DC.

Washington, DC did not have a sizeable Latino population around 1920. Scholar Enrique S. Puma noted, "With the exception of foreign diplomats, a few professionals, and *políticos* who lived in the city during political transitions, and the occasional public intellectual, Latinos tended to congregate in nearby cities such as Philadelphia and New York, where the economic and cultural ties with their home countries had been solidified since the early days of the nineteenth century."[3]

Which public intellectual Puma referred to is unknown—perhaps Perales met that man. It is also likely that young, curious, mobile and ambitious Perales traveled to both Philadelphia and New York with its Puerto Rican and other Latino populace. Moreover, it was here in DC that Perales further developed both his Latino and Latin American consciousness. He likely met a few Latinos during World War I; there were few in San Antonio. However, in DC he would have met Latinos as well as elite Latin Americans from different countries in government positions.

Perales lived in DC from 1920 to 1924 but was intermittedly there until 1932. In 1920 he joined the US Bureau of Standards, a division of the Department of Commerce, as stenographer and clerk making $1,400 plus a bonus.[4] This was a step up from his $1,200 annual salary as an army field clerk.[5] In 1923 he sought a job closer to his apartment since the "downtown bureau" was far and "causes me to squander one hour daily on the street cars . . ."[6] So Perales had an urbane existence in DC traveling across the city. By March 1923 he accepted a position as Spanish-English stenographer with the Inter American High Commission, making $1,500.[7] He took a civil service exam and was then appointed to this position.[8]

Luckily for Perales, he traveled to DC with his soul mate. He met Marta Engracia Peña Pérez of Rio Grande City of South Texas while in San Antonio and she joined him in DC in late1922.[9] Marta, a bright and self-determined young woman, had attended college at Our Lady of the Lake in San Antonio but soon found a niche for herself in DC as a newlywed. While she did not work outside the home, she made social opportunities for herself. She wrote sisters Hilda and Lola, "I am having a better time because I have more friends and Chito [Perales] has more time to take me to visit them and if he doesn't take me I go on my own and that way I have someone to talk [to]. A young lady who I like a lot. I also like to go downstairs to talk to her. She is real nice. I just look at our mail box downstairs and she sends [sent] them to me via the servants."[10] It is unknown who the servants worked for. Marta would have spent most of her time alone since husband Perales worked and went to college at night. Perhaps she spent her time socializing, reading, singing and listening to music. A photo shows her with friend Mrs. Keething in DC.[11] On occasion the couple also hosted guests in their apartment such as a Colonel Kreger who dined with them at their home.

Perales accessed the education, clubs and opportunities available to him. He typically worked in the day and attended school at night. While he worked at the Department of Commerce he enrolled in Preparatory School, a YMCA-sponsored institution conducted by the Department of Education from January 1920 to June 1921. There he earned 15½ credits, enough to provide him with the equivalent of a high school diploma. He also took English, English Literature, Public Speaking, Latin, Spanish (credit with exam), American History, English History, Medieval-Modern History, Physiology, Algebra, Plane Geometry and received credit for his study at Draughon's.[12] These classes likely gave him a broader world view. His early knowledge of Spanish likely helped him improve his writing and speaking abilities while his public speaking class would help him develop as an orator.

In fall 1921 Perales attended the Junior College Department of Columbia University (also known as the Columbian College at George Washington University) from September 1921 to July 1922.[13] By 1922 he was connected to the Department of Arts and Sciences at George Washington University, a Jesuit college.[14] There he studied English Rhetoric, Political Science, Economics and Spanish (credit with exam). He also took Psychology and Logic but a new job in the West Indies interrupted this course work and he did not finish. He graduated from the School of Economics and Government at National University.[15] Perales was already beginning to conduct diplomatic work for the United States in Latin America for which he would have a career throughout most of the 1920s.

By 1923 Perales was at Columbia University (February to June 1923) where he took Psychology with the university president. During those same months he studied at Georgetown University Law School where he took Real Property, Domestic Relations, Sales, Bailments and Criminal Procedure. From June 1923 to June 1925 he also studied law "under the tutorship of Judge W.S. Anthony, Assistant District Attorney of San Antonio.[16] There he studied Corporations,

Torts, Pleading, Evidence, Criminal Law and Procedure, Real Property and Equity, and Pleading and Practice.[17]
In 1925 he took his bar exam but noted that he was working in a
lawyer's office for the past six months before doing so, likely J.B.
Anthony's.[18] By September 1925 he had obtained his law license to
practice law in Texas.[19] He received his LLB from the National University School of Law in 1926.[20] (National University School of Law
merged into the George Washington School of Law in 1954.[21]) In fall
1929 Perales attended the National University School of Economics
and Government. He enrolled in Biological Science, Comparative
Government, Economics, Federal Trade Commission, French, Psychology and Sociology.[22] By 1930 he was perhaps the most-educated
Mexican American in the United States.

While Perales learned much about England, US history and US
law in his studies, he did not have an opportunity to study Mexican
American, Mexican or Latin American Studies outside of his Spanish
classes. When that opportunity presented itself in San Antonio in the
1940s, he took advantage of it. In 1944 he studied the History of Art in
Mexico, Mexican History, Mexican Literature, Spanish, Mexico's
Problems and InterAmerican Relations at the newly opened Universidad Nacional Autónoma de México (UNAM) in San Antonio for
which he received a certificate.[23] This was fortuitous for Perales
because this was the only place in the United States that the Mexican
college opened a branch.

While in college Perales participated in student organizations
thereby giving him a basis from which to understand how organizations could advance particular interests. There is no evidence that
Perales belonged to any organizations before he arrived in DC. He
joined Club Español for which he gave a lecture about President
Álvaro Obregón of Mexico; he also recited poetry and played the part
of the prince in the play "Cinderella."[24] He also joined the Free Lance
club. By 1927 he was writing about the significance of organization
in an essay called "Organization" for *La Prensa* of San Antonio.[25]
Shortly after LULAC was founded in 1929 he wrote co-founder J.T.
Canales, the "League must be an Organization of the members, for the
members, and by the members."[26] He believed in the empowerment

of members, not just strong leadership. Later in 1934 in "Las Sociedades Como Medio de Progreso," (Organizations as a Means of Progress) in *En Defensa de Mi Raza*, he wrote, "Communities that lack cultural, commercial, civic and social organizations and have to depend entirely on the government for their development are generally the most backward communities in the world."[27] Perales saw organizations as key to human progress.

Perales' work experience and education helped to form a self-confident and ambitious man. Applying for a job in 1923 he wrote, "Allow me to state, in this connection, that I am thoroughly experienced in secretarial, stenographic and general office work."[28] Another 1923 letter stated, "I am therefore taking the liberty of addressing you to inquire as to whether you could transfer me to a higher paying position in some other Department."[29] Perales believed he deserved better and more and asked for it.

Master of the Media

Before Perales returned to Texas he had already learned the art of controlling the message, self-promotion and promotion of collective action through newspapers. Perales must have begun to recognize the significance of the newspaper early on; there is no evidence he took a communications or media class. Newspapers covered Perales' activities including his social visits beginning in 1918 and his departure for Washington, DC, the activity of a 22-year-old though a unique one. Newspapers did not seek this info out—Perales fed them his news. For instance, his college graduation photo appeared in *Las Noticias* of Laredo, Texas, a newspaper affiliated with the Idar family.[30] In 1923 *El Fronterizo* in Texas reported that Perales was going to write some pro-Raza essays—even his intention made news.[31] Moreover, when Perales returned to Texas in 1924 newspaper *El Nacional* of San Antonio summarized his history and resumé including a complete list of his diplomatic endeavors, a list of all his publications and activism to date, and a photo.[32] *El Centro del Valle* newspaper of Mercedes, Texas reported his visit to its office.[34]

When Perales joined the J.T. Canales law firm in McAllen in 1927 he once again used the newspaper as a tool. He informed the

McAllen Daily Press of his move reading, "Alonso Perales Locating Here." It noted "he is only 27 years of age and has attained prominence as a statesman" and "Perales is well known to the people of the Valley because of his numerous articles appearing in Valley papers."[34] In July 1927 a newspaper article read, "My Projects for the Immediate Future" by Perales.[35] *Diógenes* of McAllen included an article about him with the subtitle "Brilliant Career."[36] Newspapers were already using adjectives to describe Perales.

Even more telling of Perales' savvy media relations and promotion of collective action were his 1927 comments to civil rights activist Eduardo Idar of Laredo with regards to which newspapers to send news about the Mexican-American civil rights group they were forming. He advised newspaperman Idar, "Allow me to suggest that a statement be prepared in English announcing the formal installation of the Laredo council, and send it to the following newspapers: *Brownsville Herald, Edinburg Valley Review, Mission Times, Harlingen Star, San Antonio Express, SA Evening News, SA Light, Austin American, Houston Chronicle, Houston Post, Dallas News, Fort Worth Starr-Telegram, CC Caller, Mercedes Tribune, Mercedes News Item, Falfurrias Facts, Alice _____* (his blank), and *McAllen Monitor.* That is what we did when we installed the Brownsville Council. The idea, of course, is to advertise our League as widely as possible."[37] Perales sought to inform non-Mexican-origin people of La Raza's activities and civic work. He not only understood that news should be sent to newspapers, he suggested it be sent to numerous newspapers, sent to newspapers in English, and he knew the names of almost all the English-language newspapers throughout South Texas and beyond.

Perales did not just inform the media of his own actions; even before he returned to Texas he was already evolving into a public intellectual. Perales might have stayed in Washington, DC but he realized he could have a greater impact in Texas and it was his and Marta's home. There was one major national problem for Perales after he finished his education and it manifested itself nowhere more than Texas—the "Mexican problem."[38] (Imagine Perales' life had there been no problem.) Before Perales became the major founder of

LULAC in 1929, he was already protesting against the US' "Mexican problem." He did so as a public intellectual, an intelligent and insightful social critic.

Perales began his anti-racist crusade in 1919. On February 17, 1920, he wrote "Americanism and the Americanized Mexican."[39] In 1921 he wrote "Protesta Contra lo Aseverado por James E. Ferguson" (Protest Against What James E. Ferguson Stated) which he later published in his book *En Defensa de Mi Raza*.[40] In 1921 *El Imparcial de Texas* (San Antonio), reported, "Un Americano sale a la Defensa de los Mexicanos" (An American Defends Mexicans). The essay noted Perales' response to the *Ferguson Forum* and called him "un amante de la justicia" (one who appreciates justice). And the paper added, "He makes all Mexicans and those that love Mexico thank him."[41] In 1923 he wrote an editorial criticizing racial real estate covenants in San Antonio.[42] On August 20, 1923, he wrote the essay, "La ignorancia como causa de los prejuicios raciales" (Ignorance as a cause of racial prejudice).[43] In October 1923 he wrote "El Problema de los México-Americanos."[44] So before Perales returned to Texas, he was already addressing Mexican-American issues and tackling the "Mexican problem" as a public intellectual.

The Perales moved to Texas in 1924 but were in Washington intermittently. In 1921 they lived at 800 21st St Northwest and in 1926, for example, they lived at 900 19th St. in the Northwest part of the city in an apartment.[45]

Conclusion

Perales spent the early 1920s in Washington, DC initially as a stenographer. This white-collar experience allowed him not only to finish high school and obtain a college education, it allowed him to become an intellectual. Not stopping with his undergraduate degree, he took on legal training for a career as a lawyer. His stenography, Spanish and legal training prepared him for a career as a diplomat in Latin America in the mid-1920s and early 1930s.

Perales was a self-made man because he valued upward mobility, sought out skills and studied to achieve his goals. He worked in the day and studied at night. Perales matured into an intellectual in the education-rich and politics-rich environment of Washington, DC. He also learned the power of organizations belonging to several student organizations including a Spanish club. Young wife Marta accompanied him to DC and provided support.

Perales actively and successfully used the newspaper to promote himself and his work and was becoming a master of the media submitting personal achievements to newspapers. Perales was not a narcissist—he was simply letting others know that he was accomplished, a feat few Mexican Americans could even dream of and much less acquire. Moreover, this "self-promotion" was part of his strategy of Mexican-American empowerment. It was good publicity for La Raza showing non-Raza that they were a capable people if given opportunity.

Perales' most excellent educational training authorized him for future endeavors: to conduct diplomatic work for the US government beginning in 1922; to become an attorney; to become a public intellectual. Later, he would begin a civil rights campaign in the Valley in South Texas in 1924, join a law firm, organize a major civil rights conference in Harlingen, Texas in 1927, and establish LULAC in 1929. He took on a herculean project in the 1920s—solving the "Mexican problem" by eradicating Texas racism against Mexican-descent people.

CHAPTER 5

Organizing in San Antonio and the Lower Rio Grande Valley, 1920s

The first Mexican-American civil rights organization was founded in San Antonio in 1921 though Perales was not a member. This chapter highlights Raza organizations in the United States, Texas and San Antonio in the 1920s and with which Perales was dissatisfied. These included the Order Sons of America (OSA), El Club Protector México Texano (Texas Mexican Protective Club), Order Sons of Texas (OST) and Order Knights of America (OKA).[1] It reveals Perales' opinions of these associations, especially the OSA, the only one which expanded further south into South Texas outside of San Antonio. Secondly, the chapter describes Perales' efforts along with that of fellow Alice native and World War I veteran J. Luz Sáenz in a 1924 speaking tour to prepare Mexican-American men south of San Antonio in the Rio Grande Valley for civil rights activism there.

National and Texas Civil Rights Efforts

Only one national Mexican-American organization existed in 1920. Founded in Arizona in the 1880s and which expanded throughout the Southwest, the Alianza Hispano Americana was a mutual aid association. Given the overwhelmingly working-class nature of the Mexican-descent community in the United States, perhaps no national association could emerge until the 1920s. Moreover, necessary national transportation (highways) and communication systems (telephones) were not in place until after World War I. Still, money was needed to organize and this was easier as a Mexican-American middle class began to emerge.

In Texas there were a few similar groups organized on behalf of La Raza. Mason chapters existed in San Antonio, Corpus Christi and Laredo while there were twenty-four chapters of the Orden Caballeros de Honor (Order Knights of Honor) in Texas in 1911. The Woodmen of the World (W.O.W.) (known as Los Leñadores del Mundo or Los Hacheros), offered sickness and burial insurance benefits.

Earlier organizations and movements in Texas tried to organize La Raza regardless of citizenship. These included the Gregorio Cortez defense network in 1901, the Agrupación Protectora Mexicana (Mexican Protective Association) in 1911, the Primer Congreso Mexicanista (First Mexicanist Congress) in 1911 and the Liga Protectora Mexicana (Mexican Protective League) in the late 1910s. None of these organizations survived. However, several key leaders emerged from these efforts including J. Luz Sáenz from the Cortez efforts and Agrupación; the Idar family of Laredo from the Congreso efforts; and M.C. Gonzales from the Liga Protectora. Likewise, they would also be joined by the only Mexican-American state legislator J.T. Canales who waged an investigation against the Texas Rangers in 1919.

Dating back to the mid-nineteenth century, *mutualistas* (mutual aid societies) proved the most important organizations in San Antonio and the state. *Mutualista* tenets included fraternity, Mexican nationalism and self-help. About 100 organizations existed in Texas around 1900.[2] Both Mexicans and Mexican Americans could join. Their civil rights issues were often referred to as "defense" or "protection" and they typically worked with the Mexican consulate; some were like trade unions. In 1926 nine of these groups formed an alliance, La Alianza de Sociedades Mutualistas but it did not survive. San Antonio had twenty-five *mutualistas* with 10,000 members from 1915 to 1930.

By the 1920s the Mexican government began to involve itself in the organizational life of its people living in the United States. Since over one million Mexicans immigrated to the United States, Mexico organized offices called consulates with an official representative of the Mexican government. The Consulates organized gender-segregated associations, Comisiones Honoríficas (Honorific Commissions) for men and Cruz Azul Brigadas (Blue Cross Brigades) for women. Fifty-two Brigades and thirty-five Comisiones existed in Texas.

San Antonio Civil Rights Organizations, 1920

The first Mexican-origin civil rights organization was the Order Sons of America. It was formed before Perales began his civil rights activism and when he was living in Washington, DC. Since he chose not to join its efforts after he moved to Texas, this merits some discussion. In 1920 and 1921, eight friends barbecued at Lorenzo Morales' ranch near Helotes, northwest of San Antonio. The group included John C. Solís, a 20-year-old wholesaler. He and several others were World War I veterans. Solís would prove to be the most consistent key leader and activist after 1920. Ramón H. Carvajal Jr., a well-read barber; Santiago (James) G. Tafolla Sr., District Clerk in the Criminal Court and Feliciano G. Flores, a deputy sheriff, also got involved. Also assisting was Eleuterio Escobar Jr., a salesman for Fox Photo Company, and a veteran. Tafolla Sr., better educated and more influential, presided.

Over 150 men attended the first meeting and they selected the name "Order Sons of America" or "Orden Hijos de América" (hereafter OSA), "America" a reference to the United States in 1921. It did not appeal to Mexican nationalism. Its purpose was to "work for the intellectual and social progress of the Spanish-speaking community residing in the United States" and made reference to the US constitution.[3] It referred to the development of its members but was not a mutualista.

The authors of the 45-page constitution were Clemente Idar of Laredo, Tafolla Sr. and Carvajal Jr. Idar was an American Federation of Labor (AFL) organizer.[4] The constitution contained aspects of a mutualista, a civic association, political group and a labor organization. The OSA was aware of its own place in history, stating it sought to "turn the tide of events" based on the "duties, rights, and prerogatives as citizens of the United States.[5]

The Orden based its membership on citizenship, class and gender, excluding Mexicans and women though ladies' auxiliaries were allowed. Membership ranged between 50 and 250. It lobbied Governor Miriam Ferguson to pardon Sabas Castillo for an alleged crime, and held public events on constitutional rights and voting.

Perales did not join the OSA. He was in Washington where he worked with the Department of Commerce but he kept informed of San Antonio activism.[6] Friends sent him news clippings about the OSA.[7] The OSA split into the Order Sons of Texas, El Club Protector México Texano and the Order Knights of America, all in San Antonio. This fracturing led Perales to believe that the OSA had serious leadership and constitution issues.

Other Civil Rights Associations in San Antonio

El Club Protector México Texano was established in 1921 to address suffrage, citizenship and rights. Solís and M.C. Gonzales joined. Feliciano Flores organized the Order Sons of Texas (OST), the second group that left the OSA. Perales returned to San Antonio in June 1923 and joined the group but did not believe it adequate and thought it was the president's political instrument. This was the first evidence of his contact with any of these San Antonio associations.[8] Back and forth to Washington, DC in July 1924 Perales spoke at the OST's first anniversary, stressing veteran status and US citizenship. He said, "These men of Mexican descent marched to the battlefields and exposed their lives in defense of the flag with stars and stripes. Those men who were lucky enough to return with their lives, returned to see the antipathy that the Americans had for them. It [The hatred] had persisted for almost a century and increased day by day even though at the same time they had been predisposed 'to be or not to be' [US citizens]."[9] He found the OST lacking.

Order Sons of America Expands to Corpus Christi

The OSA expanded south of San Antonio into South Texas in Pearsall and Somerset by 1923. J.T. Canales also gave talks in the Valley in 1925.[10] Corpus Christi, Alice, Kingsville, Beeville and Uvalde also formed councils though Corpus Christi proved the most important. John Solís of San Antonio moved to Corpus Christi to re-organize the OSA Corpus Council in 1924. Its membership ranged from 20 to 250.

Corpus fought segregation at a swimming pool, beach and in its local jury system. On December 1, 1925, it sent the court a petition from "citizens and taxpayers of Mexican extraction."[11] It was not able to desegregate the Corpus Christi school system's four white elementary schools. La Raza had a "Mexican" school, a two-story frame building. So they received a new building, the Chester L. Heath School. The Corpus Christi chapter founded OSA councils in Alice, Beeville, Kingsville and Uvalde. The Alice council's membership averaged between thirteen and twenty-nine. Perales was likely aware that the OSA reached his hometown.

San Antonio's Order Knights of America

While Corpus proceeded with success, San Antonio's OSA fractured again. The Order Knights of America (OKA) was the third splinter group. The Club Protector fell apart and left some OSA members—especially Solís and Gonzales further alienated. They disliked Tafolla's and Flores' involvement in politics and because Tafolla kept the presidency. Perales would also take exception to this control.

The OKA included members of the "Mexican Race" and sought "progress and general advancement as such citizens and inhabitants of the United States of America."[12] Perhaps the inclusion of Mexicans was due to Gonzales' official ties to the Mexican consulate as well as a belief that middle-class Mexican males could uplift the race. About fifty men attended meetings. Carbajal served as president. The OKA distributed 1,500 free monthly bilingual news magazines addressing socio-economic conditions, legal issues and tenant farmers.

Perales also found the OKA inadequate and did not join. Another possible criticism was that according to J.T. Canales, the OKA was more of a ritualistic society; he said it was "a secret society with a ritual somewhat similar to the Masons."[13] But it in fact publicized its meetings.

Perales and Sáenz' Talks in the Valley, 1924

Since Perales was dissatisfied with the OKA, OSA, Club Protectora and OST, he decided to begin to plant the seeds for an alternative organization. He believed in rotating leadership and did not like OSA state president James Tafolla's meddling in politics. He wanted more effective leadership and perhaps for the president to be more of a public intellectual. So along with J. Luz Sáenz, they initiated civil rights activism in the Lower Rio Grande Valley south of Corpus Christi. They announced a series of talks advocating for the need to organize; they visited Corpus Christi, Kingsville, Falfurrias, Edinburg, Mission and Rio Grande City. Perales prepared a form letter to "Sr. Don _____" to inform society leaders of the tour.[14] Spanish-language newspapers such as *El Monitor* of Falfurrias and flyers promoted it.

Perales' intentions were made clear at a Kingsville talk. Rio Grande City newspapers *El Independiente* and *El Fronterizo* reported on this event. He made a distinction between the future of both Mexicans and Mexican Americans perhaps signaling for the first time that La Raza's civic associations should pay attention to citizenship. He advised Mexicans to keep their nationality, but he asked Mexican Americans to get involved and vote. He addressed the issue of possible naturalization by Mexican immigrants. He must have done so because to begin to argue for naturalization would have been unpopular and would have had overwhelming opposition, especially from the Mexican-owned and Mexican-run press inside of Texas.

The Alice natives also advocated for a united effort to uplift through education and voting. Perales stated that education "facilitates economic progress and from economic progress, social evolution results" adding "The vote is our voice in government."[15]

After the lecture tour Perales was in and out of Texas. In 1927 Perales established his practice in the Valley at the law office of Canales & McKay in the Nasser Building in McAllen.[16] Canales helped the young attorney get started and Perales issued a press statement noting he would be in his law office in McAllen and Rio Grande City by July 15, 1927.[17] Also that month he announced a statewide effort composed of Mexican Americans for the betterment of Mexican Americans "en lo particular y de la raza Mexicana en general."[18] (specifically Mexican Americans and the Mexican people in general.) So in 1927 he had continued to address the interests and needs of two distinctive groups, Mexican Americans and Mexicans.

Conclusion

In 1920 Perales recognized that there was no major Mexican-American civil rights organization anywhere in the country although San Antonio had the largest Mexican populace in the United States. In 1921 activists organized the Order Sons of America in San Antonio initiating the Mexican-American civil rights movement. By 1923 Perales was investigating the strengths and weaknesses of the OSA and splinter groups. He found them lacking either because of the president's extensive power, the president's involvement with politics; and, in the case of the OSA, too much control by the San Antonio organization; and their inclusion of Mexican immigrants and/or excessive rituals.

And while the OSA had already embarked on expansion further into South Texas, especially Corpus Christi and Alice, Perales and J. Luz Sáenz extended civil rights activism into the Rio Grande Valley for the first time. They initiated a lecture tour addressing the needs of La Raza. Settling into his law practice in McAllen in July 1927 Perales' next step was to call a conference to address which of the organizations should take the lead and whether or not Mexican citizens should be allowed. The next phase of this civil rights saga would take place not in San Antonio which had been the heart of Mexican-American civil rights organizing but in Harlingen, Texas in the Valley where Perales had settled.

CHAPTER 6
Harlingen, Texas Convention Excludes Mexicans, 1927

This chapter discusses Perales' role in calling a major convention of Mexican-descent men in Harlingen, Texas.[1] First, it shows his initial call for the convention and his role at the meeting. Second, it reveals newspaper accounts of the event reporting the exclusion of Mexican citizens. Third, Perales' response to critics of the exclusion is unveiled. Fourth, the chapter analyzes Perales' treatises explaining the divergence of the future of Mexican Americans and Mexicans in the United States, one of his most important acts as a public intellectual. Finally, the chapter mentions Mexican-American M.C. Gonzales' role at the convention. Gonzales would become a lifelong co-activist of Perales.

Calling the Convention

In 1927, Perales and allies called a major South Texas civil rights conference. On July 2, 1927, he told *El Fronterizo* of Del Rio he was concerned with the betterment of Mexican Americans "en lo particular y de la raza Mexicana en general"[2] (especially Mexican Americans and the Mexican people in general). The citizenship issue was the most important convention business though not planned that way. Perales, J. Luz Sáenz, J.T. Canales and several other men established a provisional "Pro-Raza" committee in July 1927 with Perales as president. The committee's name was ambiguous; it may have suggested both Mexican Americans and Mexicans would be included. One committee member called the group "la Asociación Pro-Patria" (the Pro-Fatherland Association) with members from the Valley. Perhaps some interpreted the "fatherland" to be Mexico.

Perales must have contemplated what it may have meant if he/they had publicized the convention for Mexican Americans only. Perhaps he believed it political suicide. Mexicans owned and ran numerous newspapers, including the influential statewide-newspaper *La Prensa*. Mexican journalists were influential in their communities; Perales did not need journalists or community intellectuals as enemies before the convention. And had Perales argued for the naturalization of Mexican immigrants in the 1920s he would have embarked on a massive mission with overwhelming opposition, especially from the Mexican-owned and Mexican-run press. Recent Mexican emigres were numerous, some highly educated and vocal nationalists. Many expected to move back to Mexico although most never did. Had Perales suggested a Mexican American only event he would have been called "agringado," "vendido" or elitist. As historian Aaron E. Sánchez has stated, "In the ideological world of México de afuera, U.S.-Mexicans were the lowest form of traitors and renegades."[3] The Spanish-language press probably would have retaliated. Would *La Prensa* of San Antonio have continued to provide Perales access to its newspaper as a guest writer? Would Perales have endangered his activist career early on?

The Committee was of two opinions with one group wanting an organization of Mexican descent while the other wanted only Mexican Americans. Perales favored separate organizations based on citizenship but said a conference should determine that. Correspondence from Perales to director of *México en el Valle* newspaper of Mission Carlos Basañez Rocha three days before the event shows Perales wanted a Mexican-American association though he said both groups would decide. The convention would also decide which organization would lead the effort.

Yet, on August 5, *La Prensa*, the statewide-newspaper announced a Mexican-American membership before the meeting; perhaps Perales contacted this paper or wrote the article. Newspapers were already providing contradictory reports of the forthcoming event. All men were invited; women were not.

One newspaper reported on the agenda: selecting the board of directors, constitution, citizenship, headquarters, the Supreme Council, the incorporating organization and dues. The conference program cited these issues as questions.

Carlos Basáñez Rocha, director of *México en el Valle* in Mission, wrote Perales about the citizenship question. Perales told him that the organizers sought an organization that would uplift Mexican Americans and Mexicans, when possible. He also said it would be composed of men who were leaders but that conventioneers would decide on the citizenship issue. Both *México en el Valle* and *El Comercio* of Harlingen, apparently Mexican-owned newspapers, foresaw conflict due to Perales' position. Imagining a united Raza, M. Flores Villar of *El Comercio* suggested that Perales and several committee members had bad intentions.

Just how many attended the Harlingen convention is unclear though *La Prensa* reported 200 delegates. No major Mexican-only organizations such as the Comisiones Honoríficos, which the Mexican consulate had formed, were named as attendees. Perales and Sáenz were elected president and secretary, respectively, allowing Perales considerable control. Attendees allowed all in attendance to vote which made Mexicans more numerous. However, apparently the Committee or Perales selected conference speakers in advance, so Mexican Americans still had an upper hand. Perales, brothers Clemente and Eduardo Idar of Laredo, and Canales spoke and argued for a Mexican American only organization. They sought to preserve their organizational vision. The OKA and the Corpus Christi OSA foresaw the possibility that Mexican Americans might be fewer at the convention and had devised a plan in case the vote did not go in their favor. No minutes of the convention are found among secretary Sáenz' papers but apparently no Mexicans spoke from the likely podium.

What is clear is that attendees with a pro-Mexican inclusion vision walked out of the Harlingen Convention.

Convention Reports in the Press

Reports of the convention appeared in both English-language and Spanish-language papers. Perhaps Perales or Canales submitted news to the English-language papers. It is unlikely that a Mexican American worked at these newspapers or that a European American attended, understood Spanish and reported on the event. The *Mission Enterprise* reported that the meeting was reorganized after Mexicans left. It reported that Mexicans walked out as perhaps some Mexican Americans did.

The *McAllen Daily Press'* article looks like Perales' wording; the last paragraph read: "This organization movement has aroused a great deal of interest among the Spanish-speaking inhabitants of Texas and has made American citizens of Mexican-descent more determined than ever to educate and organize themselves and to vote intelligently to the end that they may become better citizens and enjoy to the fullest exten (sic) the blessings of liberty and civilization."[4]

The Spanish-language press gave both Mexican-American and Mexican perspectives. Perales wrote Canales on September 1, 1927, noting he had taken his advice—he sent "Aclaración al Margen de la Convención" (Clarification with regards to the Convention) to newspapers though also signed by Clemente Idar and Sáenz.[5] The language in this report looks similar to the English-language Mission newspaper so perhaps Perales or Canales wrote both. A professional reporter would not comment on "brilliant" deliberations or an "unjust" attitude. Perales wrote Canales that he thought he heard Canales refer to Mexicans sympathetically as "poor destitutes," perhaps the cause of the walkout.

México en el Valle was especially critical of Perales. Basañez Rocha of *México* said there were voting irregularities and that Perales offered mixed messages about citizenship. It is true that the initial call referred to "Pro-Raza" though Mexican Americans could be pro-Raza on their own. Basañez Rocha also said that Federico Johnson of Mercedes, F. Sánchez Hernández and M.C. Gonzales agreed with *México en el Valle's* accounts of the proceedings.[6]

Perales responded to Basañez Rocha through a letter and he also told Sáenz exactly how to respond to Basañez Rocha. He also mentioned the possibility of charging him with libel or possibly have him deported. Perales did not like public criticism and felt strongly against those who disagreed with him. He also wrote Canales about attacks on the Brownsville native.

Perales responded to Mexican critics. He wrote a series of essays in September 1927 entitled "La Evolución de la Raza Mexicana" (The Evolution of the Mexican Race) in *La Prensa* arguing that the evolution of Mexican Americans and Mexicans in the United States differed. He did not foresee other future waves of immigration and did not consider families with mixed citizenship such as his own. Perales wrote that he had intended to form a strong Mexican-American organization at Harlingen. Indeed, the Harlingen Convention succeeding in founding the new Latin American Citizens League (LAC). The McAllen chapter of LAC also responded to attacks on Perales. McAllen LAC president Deodoro Guerra suggested Mexican citizen "aliens" might be deported. Perales may have also written Guerra's letter.

Perales' Essay on the Mexican Exclusion

The Harlingen exclusion of Mexicans was apparently quite controversial because Perales explained it in the press for several years. In September 1927 he wrote the two-part essay "La Evolución de la Raza Mexicana" and in February 1929 he wrote "La Unificación de los México Americanos" (The Unification of Mexican Americans), shortly after LULAC's founding.

Perales argued that Mexican Americans were privileged by their US citizenship; that each group was defined by either US or Mexican nationalism; that conflict would erupt between the two inside one organization; that voting was critical to Mexican-American empowerment of which Mexican nationals could not participate.

Regardless of any suggestions Mexican Americans had, no Mexican statewide organization formed. Perhaps this leadership lacked statewide reach or it could have been that this leadership was focused on Mexico's politics and returning to "*la patria*," the motherland/fatherland. The Mexican community in Texas also suffered from severe class differences, as well as ideological differences toward Mexico's politics. The Mexican consulate was unable to make more of the Comisiones Honoríficas and Cruz Azul associations. Mexican women were also unable to step forward to provide this potential leadership.

Historian F. Arturo Rosales raised another question: Were Mexicans excluded to silence Mexican nationalist elites and intellectuals out of the organization so as to prevent disagreement and discord? He suggested, "A tentative assessment is that Alonso S. Perales and his colleagues had these Mexicans in mind more than the working class immigrants when they wanted to prohibit Mexican nationals from joining LULAC."[7] Perales did not directly attack, contradict or respond to these elites and intellectuals like Nemesio García Naranjo. Instead, he offered an alternative voice and the political strategy of Mexican Americanism.

Perales and emerging organizations would not abandon Mexicans in the United States. "The day the Mexican-American betters his own conditions and finds himself in a position to make full use of his rights of citizenship, that day he will be able to aid [all of] the Mexican citizens [in the United States] in securing what is due him and to help him assure himself of his own welfare, justice, and happiness."[8]

M.C. Gonzales' Role at the Harlingen Convention

After Harlingen, there was also discussion as to M.C. Gonzales' position on the citizenship question. Gonzales' was a major leader in the OSA and OKA but was also employed by the Mexican Consulate in San Antonio by 1927. Perales believed Consul Alejandro Carrillo had "sent" Gonzales as his representative to the conference.

Perales also believed that Gonzales favored an organization of Mexican Americans and Mexicans and supported Basañez Rocha. He expressed this in a note to San Antonio OSA members as well as Clemente Idar and warned them of his "future dealings with M.C. Gonzales."[9] Although conflict with Gonzales would continue across the decades, Perales was astute enough to work side by side with him in similar pursuits.

Conclusion

Alonso S. Perales was the major organizer of the Harlingen Convention. He wanted to organize Mexican Americans only but he said democracy should rule. Early news reports noted that a Mexican-American organization was in the making though Mexicans were also invited. Perales and other Mexican-American leaders controlled the event. As a master of the media, Perales also sought to control reports of the conference in the press. It appears that he wrote several news reports of the event himself. He also penned some "clarifications" about the exclusion of Mexicans. Perales understood that the controversy was not over and the La Raza public had to be convinced of the appropriateness of the exclusion. As both a master of the media and public intellectual, in a series of articles, Perales explained how the political future of Mexican Americans was diverging from that of Mexicans in the United States.

The convention highlighted emerging conflict between M.C. Gonzales and Perales. While they were just beginning a long-term relationship lasting decades, tension would characterize their relationship as seen in chapter 21 on friends and frenemies.

Perales would now begin his campaign for Raza rights and continued to call Mexican citizens "hermanos de raza" (racial brethren) the rest of his life.[10] Sisters would join efforts later.

CHAPTER 7

Founding of the Latin American Citizens League (LAC) in the Valley, 1927

No unifying organization resulted from the Harlingen, Texas convention so Perales had not yet achieved his goal of male Mexican-American unification. The Order Sons of America (OSA), the Order Sons of Texas (OST) and the Order Knights of America (OKA) failed to merge there. Instead, a new association was formed. This chapter reports on Perales' role in founding this new Valley organization in 1927. After Harlingen "settled" the citizenship question, the Latin American Citizens League (hereafter written as LAC and not to be confused with LULAC formed two years later) was founded at that conference.[1] Second, this chapter examines Perales' role in the naming of the new association and its expansion throughout the Valley, Laredo, and Zapata, Texas. Third, it also examines the OKA's role in facilitating a merger.

LAC's Constitution

Since activists did not incorporate themselves into the OSA, they established another organization at Harlingen. On August 26, 1927, Perales asked OSA president James T. Tafolla Sr. for his cooperation stating, "[W]e shall discard the idea of joining it and instead will at once select a name for our own organization."[2]

The new organization's name was important because Perales wanted ed potential members to know that only Latinos (who were US citizens) were permitted. It was briefly called "Latin American Citizens,"

"Mexican American Citizens League" and "League of Latin American Citizens of the Valley." Perales was the first to use "Latin American" and "Citizens" in the name of a civil rights organization. Perales' work as a diplomat since 1922 likely influenced the use of "Latin American." On October 31 Perales wrote Canales, "By the way, what about changing its name once more and making it read: League of American Citizens of Latin Descent. It is longer, but much clearer. All ambiguities incident to the term 'Latin-American' are thus eliminated."[3] Perales also referred to the "League of American Citizens of Latin Descent."[4] Its 1928 organizational manual read "League of Latin American Citizens." (They did not use an acronym; LAC will be used hereafter.) McAllen served as headquarters.[5]

LAC's constitution was prepared by Eduardo Idar with oversight by Perales and Canales.[6] In an undated document Perales made substantive suggestions on how to improve the OSA's fifty-four-page constitution. He suggested two major revisions: First, "The entire membership shall consist wholly of American citizens of Mexican or Spanish descent."[7] This showed he was already thinking beyond Mexican Americans and/or was aware of San Antonio's Canary Islanders who claimed Spanish descent and perhaps other Latinos as well. The second suggested revision was that "No person shall be eligible for active membership who holds a public office. Such person, however, shall be eligible for honorary membership." Excluding elected officials was a way to keep politics out of the association.[8]

In September 1927 Perales was still considering cooperating with the OSA. Canales and Eduardo Idar studied the OSA constitution with advice from the OSA in Corpus Christi. Ben Garza wrote Perales of two concerns. Corpus Christi questioned provision 2 on why the headquarters would follow the president's residency. Corpus members also asked why the organization would not allow elected officials and seek to elect some of its own. Garza wrote, "As you know our main things (sic) that we are working for, they only can be reach (sic) through politics, therefore the more of our own men we can put in public offices the quicker we can accomplish them." Garza added, ". . . but what we are trying to do know (sic) is, to have some kind of representation in our City or County affairs, so we can get what is coming to us, it is our duty to do it, as Citizens and tax payers of our respective city."[9] Given the history of political bossism in Texas and given Tafolla's alleged penchant for political meddling, Perales did not want elected officials in LULAC. On the other hand, Garza addressed political empowerment by electing Latinos into office.

In October 1927 Perales wrote Canales suggesting they adopt a draft by Idar since both of them were busy. By late October 1927 Perales felt the pressure to have a constitution in place. He wrote Canales, "I feel very much inclined to adopt the draft submitted by Eduardo Idar" and that it should be published in English and Spanish.[10]

On November 2 calling Idar's draft "temporary," Perales wrote, "Therefore, I locked myself behind doors to-day [sic] and examined your draft very carefully and made several changes."[11] On November 4 Perales wrote Idar that Canales was too busy to draft the temporary constitution. He said he was "sending you herewith the draft prepared by you and revised by me in order that you may proceed to put it in printed form" and he suggested the name "League of American Citizens of Latin Descent." While adding suggestions he enumerated what he believed "the main features of our Organization are that we shall have a President General, two permanent delegates from each Council to attend the annual convention with instructions to act, Headquarters will be wherever to President General may happen to reside, no person who holds a public office shall be eligible for active membership; and there will be several ways of calling a Convention; that is to say, the President General may call it when he deems it necessary, or the two local councils can petition him to call a convention. These special features make our League very different from the Order Sons of America. These are essential safeguards and we must have them, even if because of same the Sons of America should not want to join forces with us."[12]

On November 9 Canales wrote Perales, "I have looked over the outline of the constitution which you sent me on November 2nd and by inserting the form of application which we have adopted here and the oath for members and for the officers you will have a very good constitution which can serve us for the present and I am in favor of having it printed as soon as possible."[13] As a printer, Idar was authorized to print it for use by its ten councils.[14] Written in Spanish, it was titled "Constitución y Leyes de la Liga de Ciudadanos Americanos de Origen Latino."[15] Canales prepared the oath and application forms.[16] On November 19 Idar suggested that Canales, Perales, Tafolla Sr., Garza and he "get together to study a new constitution and by-laws for both organizations."[17] There was no further discussion about the making of the constitution.

The Perales papers include LAC's constitution.[18] The original twelve aims and objectives follow:

1. To develop within the members of our race, the best, purest and most perfect type of a true and loyal citizen of the United States of America.

2. To uproot from our political body all attempts and tendencies to establish racial, religious or social distinctions between our citizens and partners in opposition to the true spirit of Democracy and that contradict our Constitution and Laws.

3. To use all legal means at our fingertips to ensure that all citizens in our country enjoy equal rights; that the equal protection of the laws of this country be extended to them and that they be granted equal opportunities and privileges.

4. That the acquisition of the English language, our country's official language, is necessary to enjoy all our rights and privileges, in that sense we declare that it's the official language of this organization and we demand, at the same time, that we learn it, speak it and teach it to our children.

5. We solemnly declare once and for all, that we honor and respect our racial origin, and take pride in it.

6. Each of us has equal responsibility to our Institution, to which we voluntarily swear subordination and obedience.

7. The League of Latin American Citizens of Latin Origin is not a political club; but, as conscious citizens, we will participate in local, state and national political rallies, under a collective interest, disregarding and abjuring once and for all, any personal commitment that is not in harmony with these principles.

8. We will use our vote and influence to support the political success of individuals who through actions demonstrate respect and consideration for our people.

9. We extol as leaders those who among us through their integrity and culture demonstrate they are capable of leadership and guidance.

10. We will maintain means of publicity to share these principles, to extend branches of our organization and to consolidate it.

11. We will oppose any radical, violent manifestation that creates conflicts and disrupts the peace and tranquility of the country.

12. We will encourage the creation of educational institutions for American citizens of Latin origin, and we will support our existing ones.[19]

In February 1928 Canales printed more copies of the LAC constitution as well as the manual, two separate documents. He wrote Perales who was in Cuba on a diplomatic mission, "Our League of LA Citizens is getting on very nicely. I have obtained the consent of the Councils to print 500 copies of the constitution you outlined with a few changes suggested by me and 1000 copies of a Manual for use in services which I have prepared myself."[20] Canales developed the membership questionnaire which asked about citizenship and voting qualifications and which required the signature of two members in good standing.[21] This questionnaire was part of the Manual. The LAC constitution was in place in 1928 and was used to write LULAC's constitution in 1929.[22]

Canales also printed copies of the "Manual for use by the League of Latin American Citizens" which he wrote on his own.[23] The bilingual Manual included patriotic US songs and rituals in English; a standard meeting agenda; "Objetos y Fines de la LACL" (Objectives and Aims); and "Código" (Code). This code would later be called the LULAC Code though it was the LAC Code and Idar has been credited as its author. The objectives and aims now numbered twenty-one goals.[24]

LAC differed from the OSA and its splinter groups. In 1937, Perales wrote that the OSA, OST and OKA "NO CORRESPONDÍAN

CON EL IDEAL QUE NOSOTROS NOS HABÍAMOS FORMA-
DO." [Emphasis his] ("They didn't correspond to the goals we
had.")[25] "We" referred to Perales and possibly his friends Pablo
Gonzálcz and Filiberto Galván and/or J. Luz Sáenz. Apparently the
ideal was to have a Mexican-American-only organization, a rotating
presidency, the elimination of mutual aid tenets and a more activist
orientation.

LAC chapters

LAC councils were established in Harlingen, Brownsville, Mercedes, Weslaco, Mission, Edinburg, La Grulla, Encino and Peñitas in
the Valley. Councils were also created in Laredo and Zapata, border
towns as well as Gulf and La Salle in Matagorda County outside of
South Texas.[26] Membership varied between 30 and 100 as in Laredo
where the Idar brothers played a key role.[27]

McAllen organized the first chapter.[28] Minutes show Perales as
the chair of the state organizing committee; McAllen president as
Deodoro Guerra; and membership varying from members to seventy-
three.[29] Among Perales' notes is a "Program for Meeting of League of
Latin-American Citizens" with possible "Arbitration, Propaganda,
Programs, Interior Relations, and Foreign Relations" committees.[30]
Note that LAC would deal with US domestic issues and foreign issues
as well. Moreover, Perales was continuing to think of "propaganda."
Another meeting note shows officers included chairs to committees
on arbitration, propaganda, interior relations and foreign relations.[31]
By December 1927 there was talk of an annual convention and
Perales was to serve as President General until then.[32]

LAC did not allow women or Mexican nationals. Adela Sloss of
San Juan in the Valley, a high school graduate, asked Perales about his
activism but he did not suggest she join. This was a men-only organization.

On diplomatic assignment for the US government, Perales left the
United States to Cuba in January 1928 but returned in February leav-
ing Canales in charge. This departure could have appeared like
Perales was merely initiating an effort and not following through.
Indeed, Ben Garza of Corpus Christi warned Perales, "Your departure

to foreign countries is a handicap that you to (sic) provide for" though still complimenting him for the "racial revolution" he had begun.[33] Perales wrote Canales about the murder of two Mexicans and wounding of a third near Stanton, Texas around December 22. In January Perales told Canales, "I am strongly in favor of having our League, as a whole go on record as protesting emphatically and demanding that the guilty parties be given the punishment they deserve. It will be a big boost for our League."[34] In the meantime Perales maintained relations with Garza of Corpus Christi while he was juggling US diplomatic appointments especially in Managua, Nicaragua.

Perales wrote Garza comparing La Raza in the United States and Nicaraguans, giving us insight into both his US bias and camaraderie with Latin Americans. He wrote, "Mexican-American[s] have accomplished nothing" and that "our Mexican districts in the United States are just as filthy and backward as Managua" and asked, "What are we Mexican-Americans going to do about the matter?" He said a "strong, powerful organization composed of and led by intelligent, energetic, progressive, honest and unselfish Mexican-Americans" was needed to counter this problem.[35]

Merging LAC, OSA and OKA

In late 1928, Perales initiated unification efforts. With Perales in and out of the United States, unity talks and correspondence were initiated by Corpus Christi OSA, OKA, Sáenz and Perales; they discussed a merger, future leadership and a name. Santiago Tafolla Sr. of the San Antonio OSA wanted the name "Order Sons of America." While he obstructed the merger, Perales was trying to accomplish his goal. He had several major philosophical differences with the OSA which he shared with Eduardo Idar: "These special features make our League very different from the Order Sons of America. These are essential safeguards and we must have them, even if because of time the Sons of America should not want to join forces with us."[36] While the OSA and Perales' proposed group had the same goals, Perales refrained from attacking Tafolla Sr. personally.

By November 1928 Perales refused to join with the San Antonio OSA. Idar suggested Canales serve as General President and Perales and Tafolla Sr., Honorary Presidents. Both Perales and Canales did not favor the OSA's leader or constitution and found the group ineffective.[37] Additionally, Perales felt he knew what was best for Mexican Americans. According to Idar, Tafolla Sr. thought Perales was too young to be president.[38]

Plans for a merger by thirteen LAC councils, at least four active OSA chapters and the OKA slowed down. Moreover, Perales was in Washington, DC, Cuba, and Nicaragua most of 1928.[39] Perales then planned another way to merge: by including the Corpus Christi OSA and OKA in LAC. In April Perales began courting OSA Corpus president Garza, even suggesting that he could be LAC president. This support by Perales of Garza for president contrasted his thinking earlier because a year earlier on October 31, 1927, Perales wrote Canales, "Mr. Canales, I have already launched the movement to make you our first President General."[40]

The next year on February 7, 1929, Perales attended a Corpus Christi OSA meeting where it was "agreed right there to sever their connection with the Order Sons of America."[41] Perales believed the groups would merge with LAC leading the effort. By Feb. 8, 1929, Perales was in Rio Grande City.[42] According to Perales' version of the founding of LAC which appeared in *En Defensa de Mi Raza* in 1937, Perales convinced the reluctant Canales of the merger.[43] Perales' vision was in the works.

Conclusion

Perales, Canales, Eduardo Idar and J. Luz Sáenz led Mexican American civil rights organizing in the Valley in South Texas and founded the Latin American Citizens (LAC) there as well as in Laredo, Zapata, Gulf and La Salle. It was the first Mexican-American civil rights organization in deep South Texas, the Valley. But Perales had grander visions beyond the Valley. Although existing associations did not unite at Harlingen in 1927, Perales pushed for the merger of major South Texas Mexican-American civil rights organizations—a smaller man would have been satisfied with creating a new association that he could control. Perales orchestrated the merger of LAC, OSA chapters (except San Antonio) and Order Knights of America (OKA). In organizational negotiations Perales made sure that LAC—not the OSA—took leadership.

The OSA had led the initial Mexican-American civil rights campaign in Texas but Perales highlighted its limitations—its president was allegedly self-interested; the constitution gave San Antonio too much control; and the OSA had already splintered in San Antonio. LAC was LULAC's precursor. Its ideology was expressed in a detailed constitution with twelve aims and purposes, a code and a manual. The constitution was largely written by Eduardo Idar with oversight by Perales and Canales. Canales would later prepare the manual and include twenty-one goals.

Perales' tenacity allowed him to consolidate his vision. He became LAC's state organizer. While Idar initially suggested Canales as statewide president (instead of Perales or Tafolla Sr.) for the future association merged from the OSA, OKA and LAC, Perales offered the compromise candidate Ben Garza.

LAC continued the tradition of homosociality, men organizing with men; Perales' vision did not include women.

CHAPTER 8

Founding of the League of United Latin American Citizens (LULAC) in Corpus Christi, 1929

Two years after founding the Latin American Citizens (LAC) in the Valley in 1927, Perales would found the League of United Latin American Citizens (LULAC) in Corpus Christi in 1929.[1] This chapter addresses the founding event in which Alonso S. Perales played a key role as an organizer, speaker and ideologue in February 1929. Moreover, this chapter shows he played a major role in selecting LULAC's future leadership and defining its principles.

About 175 persons attended the Corpus Christi convention where LAC, the Order Knights of America (OKA), and the chapter of the Order Sons of America (OSA) merged to create LULAC. The San Antonio OSA did not join. They met at Salón Obreros y Obreras (Working Men and Women's Hall). Fortunately, details of the event were recorded by convention observer and political scientist Oliver Douglas Weeks, a colleague of Dr. Carlos E. Castañeda of the University of Texas at Austin. Castañeda had contacted J.T. Canales of LAC about the event and likely arranged his attendance.

Perales made decisions about the presidency and secretary before the convention began. Among his papers is "Program for To-day's (sic) Meeting" in which he had already decided who would speak and who would be selected. In this program note he wrote that he "Will make a motion that Mr. Ben Garza be elected the Permanent Chairman of this Conference and that Lic. Gonzalez be made Permanent Secretary." Like the Harlingen convention, Perales would typically plan out desired outcomes; he wanted to control this situation though not democratic. Charismatic Garza would be the compromise president (not Tafolla Sr., not M.C. Gonzales, not J.T. Canales, and not Perales).[2] He also wrote in his plans "During the discussion Mr. Perales will be recognized by the Chairman."[3] Ben Garza called the meeting to order and was selected presiding officer. Conventioneers chose M.C. Gonzales secretary. Proceedings were conducted in both English and Spanish.

Those speaking for unity included the following in this order: Perales, Sáenz, Eulalio Marín, Canales and Gonzales. Tafolla Sr. attended the event but it is likely that Perales made sure he did not get the floor.

Perales addressed the convention first. He said, "Never as now will we have a better opportunity of uniting ourselves and in a harmonious union of force and patriotism to claim our rights and prerogatives which [sic] will be the only things that we will bequeath to our children." He declared, "I vote for unification" to which there was prolonged applause.[4] This was the most important applause he would receive in his lifetime; he had succeeded in convincing members of other associations that a new organization—LULAC—was needed.

A commission composed of two representatives from each merging organization was established to select a name and "basis of operation."[5] It included Perales and Canales (LAC); Mauro Machado and John Solís (OKA); Eulalio Marín and Andrés De Luna (ex-Corpus Christi OSA); and Fortino Treviño (Alice OSA). Perales and Canales had the opportunity to further position themselves to define the new organization's tenets.

A document in the Perales archive reports on "principles" that commission members agreed upon. Apparently Perales and Canales, both lawyers, arrived at the gathering with LAC's constitution and its aims and principles in their Manual. The Manual's Aims and Principles were presented to the group; only aim 7 which stated "We will create mutual protection fund for the defense in court, education, and our own culture" was deleted.

The commission also agreed on the following:

*The Committee agrees that only American citizens shall be members.

*The Committee accepted the "Foreword" proposed by Mr. Solis. The same is attached hereto.

*We recommend that the following be the organization's permanent name: United Latin American Citizens.

*We recommend that the following shall be the aims and principles of the League which, in due time, shall be translated into English.

*We further recommend that an Executive Board consisting of the following persons be appointed as the temporary Executive Council of this new organization.

Ben Garza, President
M.C. Gonzales, SA
J.T. Canales of Brownsville
Prof. J. Luz Sáenz, McAllen.[6]

Take note that Perales did not work to make himself the leader or even a member of the board of directors. Note that Garza was given leadership. Gonzales, a lawyer and the most elite leader from San Antonio, was not made the first president and San Antonio's influence was lessened. The influence of Canales and Sáenz of LAC was eminent.

The commission recommended the name "United Latin-American Citizens" (ULAC); membership confined to United States citizens; a constitutional convention in Corpus Christi on May 19; English as its official language (although LAC's constitution was presented here in Spanish); and twenty-one principles.[7] The principles would be translated to English later. Finally, the committee also recommended the OKA's foreword in its constitution be accepted.

The commission recommended the following temporary executive officers: President Ben Garza; Secretary M.C. Gonzales; and Trustees Canales and Sáenz. *El Paladín* became the official newspaper and Corpus Christi temporary headquarters. A constitutional convention was set for May 19, 1929. Members of ULAC left the meeting united. (To avoid confusion I will refer to ULAC as LULAC from hereafter though the name was not officially changed until May 1929.)

Perales was pleased with the event. His letter to OKA member Eleuterio Escobar stated, ". . . it was a complete success, and that our new Organization, the United Latin American Citizens, comprises a considerable number of our very best Mexican-American citizens. My understanding is that it is not a purely political club but an Organization that will earnestly endeavor to promote *all phases* of our evolution."[8]

Conclusion

Perales attended the founding convention of LULAC in Corpus Christi in February 1929 but had already made major decisions beforehand. He orchestrated the selection of its first officers with Ben Garza of Corpus Christi as president. He also likely planned the selection of the convention commission which would agree on the principles set forth by his team. LAC leaders Perales, J.T. Canales and Eduardo Idar arrived with the 1928 LAC constitution and manual in hand which included these principles. San Antonio OSA president Santiago Tafolla Sr. and the San Antonio OSA were marginalized with Perales and the new LULAC organization surpassing and replacing them.

Perales was only 31 years old and he had reached his most important lifetime accomplishment—the founding of LULAC. He could not foresee that LULAC would become the most critical Latino civil rights organization of the twentieth century.

CHAPTER 9
The LULAC Constitution, 1929

The most important LULAC photo shows ninety-seven men attending the May 1929 constitutional convention. The photo was likely taken by Professor Oliver Douglas Weeks of the University of Texas who Dr. Carlos Castañeda had introduced to J.T. Canales through correspondence.[1] LULAC held its constitutional convention in Corpus Christi, Texas. This chapter first reviews events at the LULAC constitutional convention at which Perales was absent. He did not attend because he was fulfilling diplomatic activities for the United States. Second, it analyzes Perales' role in the making of the LULAC constitution. Third, it focuses on LULAC's aims and principles, its major premises. Fourth, it explains Perales' critique of the 1922 Order Sons of America (OSA) constitution. Finally, the LULAC code is outlined, a key philosophical document.

LULAC's Constitutional Convention, May 1929

In February, the new organization founded in Corpus Christi was the United Latin American Citizens (ULAC) but the May convention changed the name to League of United Latin American Citizens (LULAC). Its first officers were Ben Garza, president; M.C. Gonzales, vice-president; Andrés de Luna, secretary; and Louis Wilmot, treasurer. As prescribed by the constitution, the secretary and treasurer automatically came from the president's hometown. Laredo was chosen as the 1930 convention site.

The most important work in writing the LULAC constitution occurred before the February convention. The Latin American Citizens (LAC) constitution had been completed and printed a year earlier. At the February 1929 convention J.T. Canales served as chair of the constitutional committee with members De Luna and Eulalio Marín of the Corpus Christi OSA; Fortino Treviño of the Alice OSA; Mauro Machado and John Solís of the Order Knights of America (OKA) and Perales of Latin American Citizens (LAC). A constitutional committee was also appointed to work after the February meeting. It consisted of two representatives from each delegation present; among them were Canales, M.C. Gonzales, John Solís, Eulalio Marín, Eduardo Idar, Andrés De Luna, Joe Stillman and J. Luz Sáenz.

The committee that organized the May constitutional convention included LULAC President Ben Garza, Secretary De Luna, and Stillman, all of Corpus. About 150 persons met on May 18 and 19, 1929 at Salón Ignacio Allende. The business meeting was attended by ninety-seven men including fifty-four delegates. Conventioneers readjourned on Sunday morning for a session conducted in Spanish. LULAC asked Prof. Carlos E. Castañeda to address the gathering even though he was a Mexican citizen; his paper, "The Mexicans' Right to Public Education" was read.

President Ben Garza appointed a committee to develop council by-laws and rituals. The first and most complete local Rules of Order and By-Laws in the Perales collection is a bound thirty-page document and is signed by J. Luz Sáenz (chair), Eulalio Marín and De Luna, Committee on Constitution, By-Laws and Rules of Order[2] though according to the 1940 essay in *LULAC News*, Clemente Idar wrote these local rituals.

LULAC made Perales honorary president at the May 1929 constitutional convention. According to historian J. Gilberto Quezada, "Alonso S. Perales sent a congratulatory telegram wishing them good luck, which was read into the minutes. Before the convention ended, all the attendees concurred unanimously to bestow on Attorney Alonso S. Perales, 'the name of Honorary President, which was immediately communicated to him by telegram.'"[3] The rights or obligations of an honorary president were not outlined.[4]

LULAC's Constitution

Most of the LULAC constitution was written before the May convention since it had already been hashed out by LAC leaders Idar, Canales, and Perales. LULAC was based on LAC though LAC likely used the OSA constitution largely influenced by Clemente Idar.

Canales chaired the constitutional committee in Corpus Christi in May 1929.[5] One of the most important features of the constitution was its now twenty-five aims and principles. In 1953 Canales claimed he wrote the first four "aims and principles" and Eduardo Idar, the other twenty-one.[6] Canales probably wrote the first six aims because these all, with the exception of aim 4, begin with "To." Those following, with the exception of aim 10, 12 and 13 begin with "We." In a two-page summary of LULAC's history by Canales he said, "the first, or original constitution, which was written entirely by me, incorporating the aims and purposes . . . ."[7] Canales' version changed over the years.[8] It is clear that Canales was the author of most of the LULAC constitution but at various junctures Eduardo Idar, Perales and Sáenz have also been named co-authors of the aims and principles.

A complete copy of the final 1929 LULAC constitution does not exist in the Perales archive. Political scientist Oliver Douglas Weeks obtained a copy of the document in February 1929. I have located one draft of the LULAC constitution among Adela Sloss-Vento's papers,[9] prepared before May 1929. While there is no date on the document, it is dated by the fact that it includes reference to Corpus Christi as the place where the first annual convention would be thereby suggesting it was written after Garza was selected LULAC president in February 1929. Six pages long, it contains five articles on organizational name; membership; supreme council; local councils; and twenty-five aims and purposes. Members had to be US citizens and no elected or appointed official was allowed.

Attorney Canales had an understanding of organizational protocol and legalese, allowing him to prepare the final LULAC constitution. The fourteen-page constitution had a foreword and nine articles.[10] Article 1 addressed name; Article II aims and purposes; Article III membership including a questionnaire; Article IV the supreme council; Article V local councils; Article VI (no title) addressed saluting the flag, dues and cause for expulsion; Article VII motto and oath of officers and members; Article VIII removal and impeachment of officers; Article IX amendments to this constitution. Canales—not Perales—authored most of the constitution.

LULAC Constitution's Aims & Principles

Perhaps the most important part of the LULAC constitution was Article II, its aims and principles. Perales' handwriting, notations, and suggested revisions can be found on several versions of the aims and principles, one in the Perales archive and another in the Adela Sloss-Vento papers.

The LAC constitution had twenty-one principles though principles 1, 2, 3 and 4 of the LULAC constitution were new. The new principles addressed citizenship, discrimination, equal rights and English as the "official language of our country." These four principles are the ones that Canales claimed he wrote.

The LULAC aims and principles follow:

1. To develop within the members of our race the best, purest and most perfect type of a true and loyal citizen of the United States of America.
2. To eradicate from our body politic all intents and tendencies to establish discriminations among our fellow-citizens on account of race, religion or social position as being contrary to the true spirit of Democracy, our Constitution and Laws.
3. To use all the legal means at our command to the end that citizens in our country may enjoy equal rights, the equal protection of the laws of the land and equal opportunities and privileges.
4. The acquisition of the English language, which is the official language of our country, being necessary for the enjoyment of our rights and privileges, we declare it to be the official language of this Organization, and we pledge ourselves to learn and speak and teach the same to our children.

5. To define with absolute and unmistakable clearness our unquestionable loyalty to the ideals, principles and citizenship of the United States of America.

6. To assume complete responsibility for the education of our children as to their rights and duties and the language and customs of this country; the latter, in so far as they may be good customs.

7. We solemnly declare once and for all to maintain a sincere and respectful reverence for our racial origin of which we are proud.

8. Secretly and openly, by all lawful means at our command, we shall assist in the education and guidance of Latin Americans and we shall protect and defend their lives and interest whenever necessary.

9. We shall destroy any attempt to create racial prejudices against our people, and any infamous stigma which may be cast upon them, and we shall demand for them the respect and prerogatives which the Constitution grants to us all.

10. Each of us considers himself with equal responsibilities in our organization, to which we voluntarily swear subordination and obedience.

11. We shall create a fund for our mutual protection, for the defense of those of us who may be unjustly persecuted and for the education and culture of our people.

12. This Organization is not a political club, but as citizens we shall participate in all local, state and national political contests. However, in doing so we shall ever bear in mind the general welfare of our people, and we disregard and abjure once for all any personal obligation which is not in harmony with these principles.

13. With our vote and influence we shall endeavor to place in public office men who show by their deeds, respect and consideration for our people.

14. We shall select as our leaders those among us who demonstrate, by their integrity and culture, that they are capable of guiding and directing us properly.

15. We shall maintain publicity means for the diffusion of these principles and for the expansion and consolidation of this organization.
16. We shall pay our poll tax as well as that of members of our families in order that we may enjoy our rights fully.
17. We shall diffuse our ideals by means of the press, lectures and pamphlets.
18. We shall oppose any radical and violent demonstration which may tend to create conflicts and disturb the peace and tranquility of our country.
19. We shall have mutual respect for our religious views and we shall never refer to them in our institutions.
20. We shall encourage the creation of educational institutions for Latin Americans and we shall lend our support to those already in existence.
21. We shall endeavor to secure equal representation for our people on juries and in the administration of Governmental affairs.
22. We shall denounce every act of peonage and mistreatment as well as the employment of our minor children, of scholastic age.
23. We shall resist and attack energetically all machinations tending to prevent our social and political unification.
24. We shall oppose any tendency to separate our children in the schools of this country.
25. We shall maintain statistics which will guide our people with respect to working and living conditions and agricultural and commercial activities in the various parts of our country.[11]

Replacing the OSA Constitution

The LULAC constitution replaced what Perales believed were problems with the Order Sons of America. He suggested adding provisions electing the president general at the annual convention; headquarters at the president's city or town; convention delegates; the exclusion of elected officials from active membership; and membership only for US citizens of Mexican or Spanish descent.[12] He also called for change in regards to officers and permanent committees.[13]

The LULAC constitution made all councils equally important and did not permit geographical/regional supremacy or centralization. Perales did not want San Antonio to dominate the new civic association. Perales also targeted the article that stipulated that the President of the United States and governors of the states where the OSA existed would be ex-officios. He believed this homage excessive, especially since they were elected officials. LULAC allowed elected officials to be passive members who could speak at meetings but could not vote.[14] This would prevent political bossism. He also sought to omit provisions that protested work on Sunday, promises of finding employment for members and offering assistance and protection to sick members, the latter two *mutualista* tenets. LULAC also got rid of references to Mexican citizens or residents. One way the Mexican male middle class would still be included was a provision under membership: "Any person of distinction, or who has rendered distinguished service to the organization" could be an honorary member.[15] (Dr. Carlos E. Castañeda fit this category.) Perales translated the LULAC constitution into English in the 1930s.[16]

The constitution contained several aims and articles written in language which largely excluded women. Aim 10 noted LULAC would place men in public office. Absent in the League's aims was any mention of the particular subordination that Mexican-origin women faced such as the fact that Texas women (including Mexican-American women) were prohibited from jury service. (This changed in 1954.) No allusion was made to ending gender discrimination. The 1922 OSA constitution permitted "men, local ladies' auxiliaries, and youth councils."[17] Clemente Idar is likely responsible for the potential inclusion of "ladies" in that constitution. His sister and co-activist Jovita Idar was a feminist. But no OSA men or any women organized any ladies auxiliaries. The LULAC constitution abolished references to ladies' auxiliaries and no specific reference to women as members was made. Clearly, the working class, the less educated and women were not allowed in early LULAC.

Perales, Canales and LULAC underestimated Mexican-American women's potential and undermined Mexican-American empowerment by excluding women. Women's suffrage had passed in 1920 and they failed to see Mexican-American women as voters and political leaders. Perales did not typically refer to Mexican-American women voters and he argued, instead, that they should work in Parent Teacher organizations or join the League of Women Voters.[18] After women began to join LULAC as auxiliary members in the early 1930s, Perales seems to have acknowledged women's civic potential. He wrote Canales and Canales responded, "I believe that you are correct with reference to the fact that under our constitution both males and females can become active members of a council. I am glad that I had this foresight when I wrote that article of the constitution not limiting the members to male persons."[19] This issue arose when two LULAC men from Edinburg called for women's chapters. Canales went on to say that LULAC's supreme council (national board) should address the question of separate chapters for men and women. Ladies LULAC, segregated chapters, were permitted in 1933.

With the formation of LULAC and the demise of the OSA which lasted from 1921 to 1929, five ideological shifts were enacted by Perales and the founding of LULAC: A shift from (1) from a working-class to a middle-class ideology; (2) from a *mutualista* orientation to an organization of Mexican-American professionals, small businessmen and skilled laborers; (3) from a subtle emphasis on US citizenship to an organization stressing US citizenship; (4) from a Mexican identity to an emerging Mexican-American identity; and (5) from the conscious inclusion of women in community organization to their unconscious exclusion in political organization. While the OSA constitution largely reflected labor organizer Clemente Idar's ideology in 1922, LULAC reflected the influence of a more mature Eduardo Idar (his brother) in 1929, Perales, and Canales. It incorporated a response to changes in immigration law, especially the 1924 immigration law and the creation of the Border Patrol, giving Mexican Americans more privilege than Mexicans.

The LULAC Code

According to a 1940 *LULAC News* essay Eduardo Idar wrote what is now referred to the "LULAC Code." Co-founder J.T. Canales credited Perales with either writing the LULAC Code or with Perales furnishing it to him.[20] This Code first appeared in LAC's printed Manual in 1928; no copy has been found in the Perales archive. It follows:

> Respect your citizenship and preserve it; honor your country, maintain its traditions in the spirit of its citizens; and embody yourself into its culture and civilization.
>
> Love the men of your race, be proud of your origin and maintain it immaculate, respect your glorious past, and help to defend the rights of your own people;
>
> Learn how to fulfill your duties before you learn how to claim your rights; educate yourself and make yourself worthy; and stand high in the light of your own deeds; you must always be loyal and courageous;
>
> Filled with optimism, make yourself sociable, upright, judicious, and above all things be sober and collected in your habits, cautious in your actions and sparing in your speech.
>
> Study the past of your own, and the country to which you owe your allegiance, learn how to master with parity the two most essential languages—English and Spanish;
>
> Always be honorable and high minded; learn how to be self-reliant upon your own qualifications and resources;
>
> Believe in God, love humanity and rely upon the framework of human progress, slow, unequivocal, and firm;
>
> In war serve your country, in peace your convictions; discern, investigate, mediate, and think, study, at all times be honest and generous.
>
> Let your firmest purpose be that of helping to see that each new generation of your own shall be of a youth more efficient and capable and in this let your own children be included."[21]

Historian Gabriela González suggests that "it contained the major principles of the Mexican American political mindset" providing a map on how to redeem La Raza.[22] The Code was also Perales' moral and political philosophy. He believed in citizenship and civic activism. He did all he could for self-improvement before he asked the dominant society to end its racism. Perales was honorable as individuals should be. As a Christian, Perales had faith and believed in good will. Perales had learned his history—American, Mexican and Mexican American. And Perales believed in progress, made possible by each generation.

Conclusion

While Clemente Idar was likely the major author of the OSA constitution, Perales was LULAC's intellectual architect and Canales and Perales, its organizational architects. It was Perales who pushed for an organization different than the OSA. Eduardo Idar, Perales, Canales and J. Luz Sáenz were the major authors of LAC's aims and principles. LAC's constitution written by Eduardo Idar, Perales and Canales served as the basis of the LULAC constitution. Perales served on the constitutional committee at the February 1929 founding convention along with chair Canales. However, Perales did not attend the LULAC constitutional convention. It was Canales who wrote the bulk of the LULAC constitution.

LULAC eliminated OSA tenets which hindered the organization's growth and success. LULAC allowed for rotating leadership, removed control from San Antonio, ensured no politicians could influence the new association from inside and removed mutual aid principles. Perales achieved his vision.

LULAC's aims and principles were its guiding ideology. It was the first major assertion of "Mexican Americanism" in action in an organization. LULAC would prove a successful and permanent institution because it had specific, well thought out ideological principles and became a practical, functioning association, especially courtesy of Canales. Eduardo Idar's LULAC Code provided a strong moral guide.

Unfortunately, Canales, Perales and LULAC also contributed to the political marginalization of Mexican-descent women. The League was not yet able to conceptualize equal opportunity for women in the 1920s or in the decades to come. Sure enough, Mexican-American women would insert themselves into LULAC circles, first forming ladies' auxiliaries, and then, once permitted, Ladies LULAC after 1933. Both Canales and Perales welcomed women into the LULAC fold.

CHAPTER 10
Perales and LULAC, 1930-1960

As the major founder of LULAC, Perales was invested in the organization, especially its first decade. Had Perales and others foreseen the Great Depression perhaps they would not have established the League. The Depression was in full force only months after its founding; financial hardship should have doomed LULAC but it survived and became the most important Latino civil rights organization in the United States. This chapter analyzes its growth and reception before 1960. Second, it addresses LULAC's finances in the Depression. Thirdly, it discusses Perales and LULAC's role in a Congressional testimony on Mexican immigration in 1930. Fourthly, Perales' national presidency (1930 to 1931) is discussed. Fifth, his role as a LULAC member from 1931 to 1940 is evaluated. Sixth, his role in LULAC Council 2 is included. Seventh, Perales' role in founding LULAC San Antonio LULAC Council 16 is presented. Eighth, conflict between Council 2 and Council 16 is introduced. Ninth, Perales' ties to LULAC after 1940 is studied. Finally, LULAC's persistence is analyzed.

LULAC's Initial Reception and Growth

The most important man responsible for founding LULAC—Alonso S. Perales—attended its founding convention in February 1929, but no photo documents that event. However, a photo was taken of the constitutional convention in May 1929, perhaps by Professor Oliver Douglas Weeks, but Perales was absent from that event. Ironically, his absence from that photo foreshadowed how he would be forgotten.

Women were also absent from the photo. Mexican-origin women received the League with open arms though LULAC did not ask them to join until 1933. In June 1929 LULAC held a mini-convention in McAllen (probably the Supreme Council's meeting) and according to *El Paladín* of Corpus Christi there was in attendance "a large number of women for whom the convention was a matter of great interest."[1] In November 1929 the Alpha Club of Corpus Christi organized the Agrupación Filantrópica de Damas (Women's Philanthropic Group) to raise Christmas funds for children. They held a joint planning meeting with LULAC Council No. 1 at the home of Ofelia and Louis Wilmot. In late November the two groups co-sponsored a carnival, a dinner dance with a raffle on December 5 and a concert at the Junior High on December 15, raising over $400.[2]

While some European Americans attacked the League, some Mexican citizens in Texas criticized it.[3] Economist Paul S. Taylor's interview with a Corpus Christi LULAC member reported the following:

> The average non-political American of Latin descent calls us [the members of LULAC] "renegade." He says, "you are Mexicans, not Americans." Mexican citizens even in their press attack us. We are called renegade and anti-Mexicans. We call them visitors. They tell us, who are trying to tell them [Mexicans in Texas] to be more loyal to the United States. "But your forefathers are all of Mexican origin and you should continue to be Mexican." We say he is a visitor and none of his business.[4]

LULAC member Cástulo Gutiérrez of Del Rio responded to Mexican criticism in an essay entitled "Para los que no conocen nuestra institución" published in the local *El Popular:*

> The objective of the American league is not to Americanize the Mexican, much less to banish the Spanish language as

has wrongfully been disclosed. The Mexican American who does not become a citizen will remain the conquered one. I believe that after they have children here they will be severed from the political machine of this country, thinking they can unite in body and soul to Mexico.[5]

He added, "it is precious [for Mexican Americans] to incorporate their soul and spirit in Mexican things, but not their body. This is impossible without living in Mexico or better said, ceasing to live in the United States."[6] He referred to Mexican Americans, Mexicans in the United States and Mexicans in Mexico as a family.[7] What benefitted the Mexican American "would also bring benefits to the Mexican citizen, who are our fathers, grandparents, and friends," he concluded.[8] Gutiérrez voiced LULAC thought.

Criticism of LULAC led Perales to write the seven-part essay "La Unificación de los México-Americanos" (Mexican American Unity) which *La Prensa* published from September 4 through September 10, 1929.[9] It is significant that Perales referred to the unity of Mexican Americans—not La Raza. He reiterated that LULAC was not founded to Americanize Mexican citizens in Texas; he stressed that its goal was not to separate itself from Mexicans. Moreover, the progress of Mexicans in the United States would occur when Mexican Americans were able to help newly arrived immigrants.[10] Regardless of criticism, the League prospered. The creation of the monthly news magazine *LULAC News* in 1931 facilitated communications.

Some localities readily embraced LULAC. By April 1929 thirteen councils existed including Alice, Brownsville, Corpus Christi, Encino, La Grulla, San Antonio and McAllen.[11] And by May Robstown, Falfurrias and Edinburg had joined.[12] By December 1932 LULAC had twenty-nine councils.[13]

By 1936 Perales referred to LULAC as a national organization.[14] The Order Sons of America had been envisioned as a national organization, but it spread only to a few towns outside of San Antonio and never reached the Valley. LULAC was first planted in New Mexico in 1934 and by 1938 national LULAC had a New Mexican president.[15] On the eve of United States' entrance into World War II, LULAC was national with chapters firmly rooted in Texas and New Mexico and with chapters in Colorado, Arizona and California. California chapters appeared briefly in Los Angeles and Sacramento.[16] A Washington, DC council also existed briefly. Chapters outside of Texas made it "Southwestern" and the DC chapter also made it national.

LULAC and the Depression

Perales and others founded LULAC in February 1929 months before the Depression. Not only would LULAC address racial subordination, racial segregation and disempowerment, it would attempt to fight these ills when LULAC members themselves were financially challenged. Middle-class Mexican-American professionals hardly existed but there were plenty small business people in many Texas towns and cities. Even Mexican Chamber of Commerce associations were few and underdeveloped; in fact, San Antonio's was founded around the same time as LULAC in 1928 while Corpus Christi and Dallas founded theirs in the 1930s. Still, there was no Texas state Mexican or Mexican-American Chamber of Commerce until 1975.[17] Moreover, the middle class contracted during the Depression. According to one source the "Mexican merchant class shrunk by over 500 percent between 1924 and 1939."[18] Even though LULAC members were middle class, they too were impacted by the Depression.

LULAC survived on a shoe-string budget. It could not afford a central administrative office in any city, state or in the nation in the 1930s. Nor could LULAC afford a travel, phone or secretarial budget. There was no endowment, no corporate donors or white liberals funding the League in the 1930s. Government grants did not exist and LULAC had no major fundraising events in the 1930s. LULAC survived only because it had rotating officers at the state level and men and later women who could pay their own way. LULAC fully funded itself with membership costs and fundraisers. Likewise, it survived because once it initiated its monthly magazine *LULAC News* in 1931, different LULAC chapters paid for its publication by selling ads to local Mexican-origin businesses.

Despite funding issues LULAC expanded between 1929 and 1940 though simultaneously contracting. Some councils would fold while others were formed and then dormant councils would also be revived—this is the constant cycle in the League. According to LULAC co-founder Canales, over 1000 attended the first anniversary celebration with nineteen councils present.[19] In 1930, 800 attended the second national convention in Alice, Texas and in 1931, 1,000.[20] These were Texas conventions as no other state had LULAC in the early 1930s. In May 1932 there were 24 local LULAC councils and 29 by December.[21] Later in 1932 there were 37 councils.[22] In May 1933, 23 of 45 councils were present at the state convention with 500 in attendance. By 1940 LULAC had established over 100 men's councils and over 20 ladies' councils.[23] In the late 40s there were over 150 councils throughout the nation.[24]

Perales' archive reveals the League's financial challenges during the 1930s. It was expensive to work for the cause. Membership was $20.00 annually. Other expenses including funding the *LULAC News* at a suggested magazine cost of $1.00 a month; publishing it cost $25.00 monthly.[25] It was difficult to publish monthly.[26] A thousand copies were printed in May 1932.[27] In November 1934 a one-page mimeograph constituted the *LULAC News*.[28] When LULAC national president Mauro Machado's administration (1934-35) published several *LULAC News* monthlies in 1934, Perales called this one of his outstanding accomplishments.[29]

LULAC News was only one expense. Other expenses included desegregation legal work; a World War I veterans' memorial; a college scholarship fund; special regional, state and national conventions; and out of town organizing efforts. Perales himself told a friend he may not have the $20.00 needed to attend the 1934 national convention.[30] Moreover, travel expenses included gas, car repairs, lodging and meals. San Antonio LULAC Council 2 acted as the "Flying Squadron," its members spread LULAC to surrounding towns on the weekends.[31] Being a good LULAC member also required payment of one's poll tax. In short, keeping LULAC active cost money every month for each member.

Perales' papers contain scattered references to fundraising difficulties. LULAC sought to fund World War I veteran J. Luz Sáenz' effort to build a monument to veterans in San Antonio but could not afford to continue to raise monies for the project. Instead, this money was transferred to funding desegregation efforts in Mission and Del Rio under the M.C. Gonzales administration (1931-32).[32] Despite the Depression each LULAC council was to raise $45.00 by October 1, 1931 for "school defense."[33] Likewise, money was moved again to pay for college scholarships. National President J.T. Canales (1932-33) asked the Hebbronville LULAC council to raise money for four or five scholarships.[34]

Perales' papers also show that sometimes LULAC councils folded because members could not afford dues. In May 1933, Perales told a LULAC council, "Due to the Depression it looks like we are all victims of it" and he advised a council to tell LULAC national, "We haven't paid our dues because we don't have any money. But the torch of LULAC is still lit."[35] Perales did not chastise or pity them. Likewise, Canales wrote LULAC national president M.C. Gonzales in 1932, "I doubt however whether the Penitas, La Grulla and McAllen councils can be re-organized for the reason that the people haven't got any money. . ." [36] In fact, keeping a LULAC council alive during the 1930s meant success. San Antonio's Council 2, for instance, never folded but Council 16 of Crystal City did. It disbanded for sixteen months due to "acute conditions" but reorganized in July 1931.[37] But then it folded again. So, when Perales founded a second LULAC council in San Antonio, he used the number 16 from this defunct chapter. LULAC called these "inactive," "dormant" or "dead" councils and the Depression often explained their demise in the 30s.

Perales' Congressional Testimony, 1930

Around 1930 an immigration restrictionist named John Box of Texas introduced the Box bill in Congress. Recall that the 1924 immigration law was the first to restrict immigration from the Western Hemisphere. Also note that the US Border Patrol had been created in 1924. Several LULAC leaders including Perales as honorary president testified as an early attempt to assert LULAC's significance and to provide a Mexican-American voice on the issue.[38] Up to this point as an organization LULAC had not yet discussed immigration policy. This was their first attempt to assert Mexican-American perspectives into national policy discussions. The Mission, Texas LULAC council raised funds to send Perales to Washington.[39] There is no evidence LULAC or LULAC President Ben Garza asked Perales and J.T. Canales to appear as through a formal decision by officers or a vote.

Perales and Canales attended to counter racist charges made by the American Federation of Labor whose representatives testified that Mexican immigrants were "an inferior and degenerate race incapable of being assimilated." Canales wrote that they went "to refute these untrue and unjust charges which reflects upon the honor and integrity of our race."[40] At the hearing, Canales stated, "We are not against anything that is just and right, that would take into consideration that local conditions and apply common sense to them."[41]

Opening his statement, Perales said, "I want to state that I am not here to oppose the Box bill or the Johnson bill or any other bill, but to promote the welfare of Texas—of the American people."[42] He went on to protest, "I do wish to refer to the statements made by some sponsor of this quota bill, to the effect that the Mexican people is (sic) an inferior and degenerate race."[43] He added, "The charge is also made that Mexicans ought to be restricted because they do not become American citizens. I am one of the founders of what is known in Texas as the League of United Latin American Citizens."[44] He suggested that there were loyal Mexican Americans like LULAC and that the interests of Americans should be considered first.[45] He added, "Being a Mexican by blood, and being just as proud of my racial extraction as I am of my American citizenship, I feel it my duty to deny most emphatically that the Mexican race is inferior to any other race . . ." In 1937, however, Perales would later write that he had opposed a proposed quota by the Box bill.[46]

Perales sought to defend the dignity of the Mexican people. When Congressman Green asked him, "I would like to ask the gentleman if he believes we should have any restrictions on immigration from Mexico into the United States?" Perales responded, "Yes; if you can prove that these Mexicans come in here to compete with American citizens." So he did privilege US citizens over Mexican immigrants. Yet, he continued to denounce rationales of "racial inferiority" and "racial degeneracy."

Reports of Perales' testimony at Congress typically identified him as pro-Raza. A *La Prensa* newspaper read "Elogios al Lic. A. Perales Por La Labor Desarrollada en Pro De La Raza Mexicana" (Praise for Attorney A. Perales for his pro-Raza Work) which included a copy of LULAC President Ben Garza's letter to Congressman John N. Garner and Garner's response to Garza.[47] Perales probably wrote this letter for Garza. For some reason Garza did not testify despite the newspaper article "Ben Garza Goes to Washington to Aid in Fight on Immigration Bills."[48]

Perales would continue to address immigration across the decades. He testified in 1939 before the House Committee on Immigration[49] and was vocal on the entrance of *braceros,* authorized Mexican immigrants from 1942 to 1964 and argued against their exploitation.

Perales as National LULAC President, 1930-1931

Because of conflict over Perales' testimony before Congress in 1930, Perales ran into conflict with several other LULAC leaders and vowed to quit LULAC.[50] But he did not. He even became national president months later. Serving as the second national president from May 1930 to May 1931, Perales had a successful and productive national administration.[51]

National LULAC included the president general, vice-president, secretary, treasurer and, for the first time, a Board of Trustees. During Perales' administration, E.E. Peña of San Diego, Texas served as vice-president while the secretary and treasurer Andrés De Luna and Luis Wilmot of Corpus Christi continued in the same role from the previous administration. The Board included Perales, De Luna, Wilmot and past president Garza, J. Luz Sáenz, J.T. Canales and M.C. Gonzales.

President Perales was most active. During his tenure he: 1) gave twenty-one lectures to LULAC councils; 2) gave twenty-five other lectures to other groups; 3) helped the Mission and Del Rio School Defense Committee raise funds to fight school segregation; 4) translated the LULAC constitution into Spanish; and 5) kept in close contact with the various councils of the League and offered many valuable suggestions and good advice.[52] He facilitated LULAC's continued expansion in South Texas. He "laid the foundation for new councils in Houston, Raymondville, Mercedes, Guerra, Hebbronville, San Juan, Kingsville, Rivera and Salinera."[53] Likewise, he corresponded with others in Gulf, San Angelo and Wharton, all outside of South Texas.[54] When he left the presidency twenty-four active councils were intact.[55] Making contact with members and councils helped keep councils alive. Of all these councils Houston proved to be the most persistent.

Perales' presidency had no budget. "Of all the Councils visited Del Rio was the only one that defrayed my expenses," he wrote, "and I accepted only at the urgent insistence of the members of said Council. All the work was done by me free of charge with greatest pleasure."[56] He used any and all means to educate and inspire members and the Spanish-reading public. His goal as president was to "keep up the spirit of the membership by sending them lectures, etc. once a week or at least twice a month."[57]

His administration embraced both the English and Spanish languages although LULAC's constitution authorized English as its official language. Just a month before a LULAC circular was passed allowing local LULAC councils to speak Spanish due to attendance by some newspapermen.[58] There is no evidence that any LULACer complained of the use of the Spanish language since most LULAC members were Spanish-dominant or bilingual. Spanish would reach a broader audience, an audience not always literate in English. In doing so, Perales acknowledged that many LULAC members and potential LULAC members were Spanish-dominant. He did not believe in English-only and did not privilege the English language. Likewise, he used Spanish-language radio.[59] In 1934 LULAC also published bilingual citizenship manuals.[60] These manuals helped Mexican immigrants become US citizens; indeed, LULAC did not "abandon" Mexican immigrants.

Perales succeeding in keeping *LULAC News* alive. In May 1932 he noted, "I have plenty of material for the May issue of *LULAC News* and we can have the same printed immediately after you arrive here." He then suggested to Canales that Director of Publicity F. Valencia would censor material under Gonzales or John Solís' authority.[61] Here we see Perales had conflict with both Gonzales and Solís of Council 2 of San Antonio.

Despite all of his work, Perales noted there was indeed an "erroneous impression in the minds of some of my fellow-members that during my incumbency I did nothing for the League." Who stated this is unknown. Because of this impression, he wrote a memo documenting his efforts. Likewise, a friend (likely Canales) wrote about his contributions in "Some of the things Alonso S. Perales has done for the League of United Latin American Citizens."[62] Perhaps members' criticism or lack of faith was because Perales spent six months out of the country while president—he was still a US diplomat. In fact, shortly after Perales' presidency in early summer he had to travel to Nicaragua in December 1932.[63] Moreover, *LULAC News* did not report all of Perales' activities and La Raza continued to experience racial/class/ gender subordination despite his good deeds.

Desegregating schools was a priority for LULAC and Perales. Roberto Austin of Mission, Texas in the Valley wrote him about problems there. So, by January 11, 1931 Perales had established a Pro-Defense School Children group there which he headed and for which he prepared a petition.[64] Perales and F.G. Garza of McAllen served as attorneys for the Mission school issue.[65]

Perales and LULAC were silent on issues of the deportation of Mexican-descent people, an action by the US government during the early years of the Depression. LULAC national president M.C. Gonzales referred to repatriation in one issue of *LULAC News* in November 1931.[66] Most deportations occurred outside of San Antonio in rural communities and in some towns where there was no LULAC. According to one historian, deportation is "a topic which historians today see as one of the major victimization episodes regarding Mexicans in the United States. This could possibly support the allegation by some historians that Mexican-American leadership held an anti-Mexican immigrant bias. But rather, Perales often would express concern about the treatment of Mexican immigrants."[67] Still, Perales did not address the topic in his writings. Both Mexicans and Mexican Americans were indiscriminately impacted though more of these efforts occurred in California and the Midwest.

Perales seems to have been so concerned with local LULAC's survival that he did not spend time attempting to inform the dominant society about LULAC. There is no evidence that he wrote any articles for any local, state or national newspaper in English during his tenure. Nor did he write any memorandum to all LULAC councils as did later LULAC president Frank Galván of El Paso about a US census reclassification from "Mexican" to "colored"; Perales, however, did write for *LULAC News*.

Perales as LULAC Member, 1931-1937

Although Perales' presidency ended in May 1931, he continued to work with LULAC in various offices and capacities. He was a Board of Trustee member from 1931-1937.[68] During the M.C. Gonzales administration (May 1931-May 1932), he was involved with the Special convention held in Nov. 1931 in San Antonio addressing the Del Rio segregation case and scholarship guidelines.[69] Indeed in 1932 Perales wrote a LULAC member that it was "bad precedent" to allow a San Antonio LULACer to be national president.[70] Perales then planned the Canales presidency, nominating him and lobbying for his support through letters to different councils.[71] He hoped Canales would accept the nomination and was "certain he will accept it rather than see our league meet with disaster."[72] Canales won and as president hoped for fifty councils by 1933.[73] During Canales' presidency (May 1932-May 1933) Perales served as "Special Organizer" and had the "authority to organize new councils where no councils existed" and also re-organized inactive councils in McAllen, Penitas, Kingsville, Alice and Laredo.[74] In June 1932, Perales chaired the Educational Committee which gave five $100.00 scholarships to Latino college students.[75] LULAC did not favor Mexican Americans over Latinos. Perales also presided over the special Del Rio convention.[76] He also continued to support *LULAC News*; one of his May 1932 notes read, "I will gather all the material for the May issues and we shall have it printed immediately after we confer with you."[77]

During the Mauro Machado presidency (1933-1934), the fifth president, Perales also "issued several circulars and bulletins to the Councils and had (sic) same published in the newspapers."[78] And he served as Organizer General and Inspector General. [79] In April 1934 Perales appeared in a photo taken as a LULAC member at a special convention in San Antonio.[80] In 1935 Perales addressed the Houston national convention; reportedly 4,000 attended the Houston City Auditorium social that evening.[81] Under the Frank J. Galván Jr. presidency (1935-36) Perales acted as inspector general.[82] By 1937 there was a Legislative Committee, chaired by Canales and with six others including Perales.[83]

Canales' and Perales' activist agenda were similar. After Canales' presidency (May 1932 to May 1933), Canales issued a "Program of Activities Recommended by the retiring Pres. General to local councils." He suggested: "1) the investigation of schools; 2) health; 3) PTA noting LULAC "should encourage each Latin-American mother to be a member of said association"; 4) hospitals; 5) red-light districts; and 6) school attendance.[84] Perales' priorities were the same. In 1934 Perales recommended these activities: 1) "schools/sanitation/mental retarded? /playground"; 2) health and tuberculosis; 3) PTA, encouraging "each Latin-American mother to be a member of said Association"; 4) hospital; 5) red light district; 6) school attendance; 7) Boy Scouts; and 8) Lecture: civic/hygiene/disease."[85] They believed that the schooling mattered most and health key especially given the preponderance of tuberculosis. (Note the belief that women belonged in the PTA and that Girl Scouts were not organized.) The red-light district issue would be taken up by the League of Loyal Americans, another group Perales formed in the late 1930s.[86] (See chapter 15 on politics.)

During the Mauro Machado presidency (1933-1934) Perales also "issued several circulars and bulletins to the Councils and had (sic) same published in the newspapers"[87] and he served as Organizer General and Inspector General.[88] Apparently, there was financial mismanagement or embezzlement under the Machado administration.[89] Perales was not happy with Machado noting, "We will never stop blaming Canales and [MC] Gonzales for having wished him upon us."[90] In 1935 Perales also addressed the Houston national convention.[91]

Under the El Pasoan Frank Galván presidency (1936-37) Perales acted as Inspector General.[92] By 1937, there was a Legislative Committee, chaired by Canales and with six others including Perales.[93] By 1937 Perales, by now a delegate of LULAC Council 16, began to address national US legislation at the national conventions; these resolutions addressed support for the Black-Connery bill for minimum wage/maximum work hours and prohibited child labor. National LULAC also proposed support for the Wagner-Steagall bill for better housing for the poor. [94] National LULAC also supported the McComrach bill which warned against the "evils in Communism, fascism and any other 'isms' not in harmony with our form of government and our American institutions."[95]

The 1937 national convention was Perales' last. It was President Galván (1936-1937) who made the key decision to disallow dual councils, two chapters in one town or city. (Perales founded Council 16 in San Antonio though the city had Council 2.) Even so, in 1938 during the Ramón Longoria of Harlingen presidency (1937-38) Perales served as an attorney for Hondo LULAC council 37 addressing inadequate school facilities.[96] Thereafter Perales' name faded from official LULAC documents.

Perales in San Antonio LULAC Council 2

Besides his national presidency and various positions at the national level, Perales was also active at the local level in San Antonio. When LULAC was founded in 1929, members of the Order Sons of America and Order Knights of America merged to form LULAC Council 2 in San Antonio. Council 2 presidents in the 1930s included M.C. Gonzales, John Solís, Tomás A. Garza, Carlos A. Ramírez, Adolph A. Garza, Jake Rodríguez and Severino Martínez though its key leaders included M.C. Gonzales, John Solís and Machado. Perales' disagreements with Gonzales would impact his work in LULAC and led to a separate council in San Antonio. There was already a history of conflict with Gonzales. First, they had differing positions on the question of whether Mexican citizens should be admitted to the civil rights organization at the Harlingen convention. Secondly, they also disagreed as to whether Perales and Canales should have testified before a Congressional immigration hearing in 1930 on behalf of LULAC.[97] Thirdly, Perales did not agree with some of Council 2's activities. After a few years as a member of Council 2, Perales charged its members with inappropriate activity in electoral politics. Yet Perales believed, "We must play an independent role in politics without allegiance to a single party or faction."[98] Without Council 2 archives it is difficult to tell if some of its members acted on behalf of individual interests or if an individual saw their own influence as synonymous with La Raza's interests.

Perales also conflicted with Gonzales and other Council 2 members on a fourth issue: national LULAC leadership. For instance, in April 14, 1932 Gonzales and Tomás F. Garza sent a "Dear LULAC Brother" letter in support of John Solís' bid for national presidency.[99] Apparently Perales did not believe Solís capable of leading LULAC, perhaps because he had not finished high school, lacked written skills or because he was friends with Gonzales or sided with Gonzales. (Perales seemed to have been concerned with presidents' and other members' writing skills. In a letter to Canales around 1930 he suggested national president Ben Garza get a stenographer, probably because he had limited writing skills.)[100] Or perhaps Perales was concerned with Solís' resignation as Gonzales' secretary during Gonzales' national administration.[101] Perales was also concerned with San Antonio's domination of the presidency as had been the case with Tafolla in the OSA. Nonetheless, Solís never became national president.

Another sign of conflict was evident when Perales referred to Gonzales, Solís and Machado as the "San Antonio gang" in his correspondence. He noted that *LULAC News* director Felipe Valencia "admitted to me this morning that he was with the San Antonio gang" and that the bunch would instruct Valencia what to publish.[102] Perales advised Canales not to appoint the gang to his presidential staff. Because of this tension, Perales founded a second LULAC men's council in San Antonio arguing that LULAC councils in Edinburg and Mission had already established a precedent for a second chapter in each town. Perhaps he felt Council 2 did not welcome him, noting, "donde una puerta se cierra otra se abre" (When one door closes another opens.)[103] Moreover, he wrote that "friendly, constructive competition" was healthy as evident in the example of the American Legion.

A controversy emerged over the question of whether San Antonio needed or should have two councils. National President Canales asked Solís, Machado and Adolfo Garza to invite potential members to join Council 2, but Solís asked them not to join a rival council.[104] At first Perales conceded to Canales but later wrote, "[let me] remind you that there are about 90,000 Mexicans in this city and our League should aid to serve the whole community. To do this, the number of LULAC members in this city must be increased."[105] Potential members (of a second council) "are not the type that can be herded or controlled," he argued. "See what they can do and if not, I shall insist that you authorize me to install a new council in San Antonio." Perales' personality was to insist on an action he believed correct. Almost a year later Canales wrote Perales, noting "Watch closely what the disturbing element of the San Antonio council, to-wit: Juan C. Solís and M.C. Gonzales are going to do."[106] This time Canales conceded to Perales and mentioned the possibility of a new council. But Canales still tried to prevent the birth of the second council remaining independent in thought and action from Perales, before and after Council 16 was ultimately created.

In a transcript of a memorandum, Perales explained that Council 2 was "compose[d] chiefly of young Hispanic-American lawyers employed either at the Court House or at the City Hall . . . Interests and activities centered principally around the objective of keeping their own jobs and helping other members of Council No. 2 secure political positions. This group did little or nothing to further the real aims and purposes of the [LULAC] Organization." Gonzales was a lawyer as was Adolph Garza but there were not more. In contrast, he said Council 16 consisted of "**independent** (emphasis his) business and professional men."[107] This conflict between Perales and Gonzales (or Council 16 and Council 2) should not be construed as an inactive Council 2. According to Gonzales, its activities included 1) public school segregation; 2) no jury service for Mexican Americans; 3) segregated public accommodations; 4) racial covenants in real estate; and 5) voting rights.[108] But perhaps Perales wanted more and better committee work tackling these problems, more independent thinkers and a more educated middle class. A list of committees under Council 2 has not been located but it is likely they had fewer committees though more members. Perales believed the power of LULAC lay in committees. He wrote Antonia Gómez in 1933: "The success of our labors depends largely upon how diligently, actively, and enthusiastically the standing committees work." [109] In November 1933 he wrote about Council 16, "We meet regularly on Wednesday evening. I wish every Council would become active, but it is difficult mainly because we lack the necessary leadership in some communities."[110]

According to historian Laura Cannon in 1938 Council 2 was quite active. Its efforts included a poll tax campaign, support for a local school bond issue, campaigning for US Representative Maury Maverick, a benefit show, support of pecan shellers and sending six cars full of LULACers to the El Paso national convention, and succeeding in winning the bid to host the 1939 national convention.[111]

Perales also felt individual interests and egos were another problem. He wrote LULAC member Eleuterio Escobar, "The major obstacle seems to be to satisfy ambitions of popularity and notoriety of a few individuals. In order to do this so we have to suppress or at the very least control that of others."[112] Perhaps it was hard for Perales to "submit" and/o resist the opportunity to lead given his talents. He seemed to have strong ideas of what he believed an active, activist LULAC council should be.

Perales in San Antonio LULAC Council 16, 1933-1937

Perales founded Council 16 to allow himself more influence in local LULAC, to encourage more and better activism and to enhance LULAC's work in San Antonio. As noted, Council 16 originally belonged to Crystal City.[113] Perales enlightened skeptics about the prospects of a second chapter; he wrote, "This council does not propose to antagonize or obstruct the efforts of any other Council, but rather seeks to cooperate in the realization of this work," noting that 95% of its membership were new to LULAC.[114] For Perales, the purpose of a second San Antonio council was to improve the membership of Council 2; to increase activities; to be more proactive and more professional; and to locate men free of political bossism and obligations to city hall."[115]

Perales did not found the council because of egotism or a desire to preside—in fact, he was never its president. When the council was founded around March 18, 1933, the first president was Pablo G. González, a brother of folklorist Jovita González, classmate at Draughon's business school and lawyer. Latter presidents included Dr. Orlando Gerodetti (1934); Matias Trub (1935) and Charles Albidress Sr. (1936).[116] According to Eleuterio Escobar, Council 16 was organized by Perales, P.G. Gonzalez, Mauro Machado and others.[117] (I have found no evidence Machado was involved.)

However, the formation of the council was also about his tension with M.C. Gonzales. Around January 1934 Gonzales visited Perales to talk about this competition and Perales jotted down the following: "That he wanted my assurance that I would not accept either the temporary or permanent chairmanship of the organization," and "the idea being not to make it appear that I or he were leaders in this movement" and "that if his group were not treated fairly, they would form another organization."[118]

The council resolved to address the eight issues LULAC President Canales had outlined: public schools (mental retardation, playgrounds); health conditions (tuberculosis); PTA (encourage Latin American mothers to join); hospital conditions; red-light districts; school attendance; boy scouts; and lectures (civics, hygiene, disease).[119]

Council 16 had numerous committees: education, school facilities, boy scouts, judiciary auxiliary, health, housing, recreational centers, poll tax, justice, Latin-American cadets, Pro-Plaza Típica Mexicana and Children's Protective League, perhaps more committees than Council 2.[120] Other years it also had sports, entertainment, beautiful yards, social hygiene, wage scale, social justice, legislative and Texas Centennial committees.[121] A 1934 document also reveals its concerns: 1) investigate every Latin American child to see if retarded; existence of playgrounds; make sure they are sanitary; work with school boards to improve conditions; 2) health; cooperate with county and city units and State Tuberculosis Association; 3) cooperate with PTAs and encourage Latin American mothers to join; 4) urge city and county commission to improve hospital conditions; 5) crusades against red light district near schools; 6) work with school board to promote attendance and organize PTAs with Latin American parents; 7) boy scouts; and 8) lectures on civics, hygiene and disease prevention.[122] Education and health were priorities.

The size and class composition of Council 16 made it different from Council 2. The latter had about 130 members while Council 16 had 35 members.[123] A "List of Approved Prospective Members" for Council 16 included Eleuterio Escobar Jr., Dr. [Delgado], Dr. H.N. González, Henry Guerra, Juvencio Idar (relative of the Idar family of Laredo) and Carlos Cadena, a young man in his 20s, who would become an attorney and argue before the Supreme Court in the 1950s.[124] So both a smaller organization as well as more educated professionals could make a difference, Perales believed. By the 1940s someone compared the differences between Council 16 and Council 2 as the difference between huaraches (poor's sandals in Mexico) vs. "patent-leather or silk-stocking."[125]

Perales not only founded Council 16 but was also an extremely active member. He chaired the education, pro-justice and Mexican plaza típica committees and was a member of school facilities, recreation centers and poll tax committees.[126] The poll tax committee published an eight-page newspaper "Actualidad" annually with 10,000 copies.[127] In honor of the Texas Centennial, Council 16 sought to make a Mexican plaza on the West side to represent the state's Spanish colonial past and foster San Antonio tourism.[128] It sought to show pride in redeveloping part of the West side with a potential $400,000 in federal funds. But it was never built and nor was the history archive to preserve Spanish colonial history that teacher Ester Pérez Carvajal sought ever created.[129]

Council 16 had great success in addressing insufficient schools on the West side and South side and birthed the School Improvement League, a new organization focusing on more and better schools through the 1950s. Council 16 first opened night schools with free books for adults with classes from 4 to 9 pm. This occurred while Perales chaired the education committee.[130] It also initiated a "Survey made by the Committee on Public School Buildings and Recreational Facilities of the LULAC" on September 27, 1934.[131] The council's stationary read, "The League of United Latin-American Citizens Asks for More and Better Schools for the Western Section of the City."[132] It cooperated with Council 2 on this issue and also garnered the support of fifty Raza organizations.[133] Later this effort took on a life and organization of its own as the Liga Defensa Pro-Escolar (School Defense League and later called the School Improvement League), headed by LULAC member Eleuterio Escobar and it became a mass movement.[134] State Superintendent of Schools L.A. Woods wrote Escobar around 1934, "Please be advised that it has come to me that you have two councils in your territory which represent the United Latin-American citizens. It seems that these two councils are at cross purposes."[135] What these possible different approaches were is unknown.

LULAC brought attention to racist school practices. It wrote the San Antonio ISD board that there were twenty-eight schools which spent $2,470,628 on their students and eleven schools on the West side which spent $1,350,959. But in these eleven schools there were 12,334 students and eighty-four more rooms were needed.[136]

Council 16 also addressed racial classification by the US census. The issue was addressed in El Paso. A resolution was introduced by Charles Albidress Sr. of Council 16 and Charles A. Ramírez of Council 2 at the national convention but likely written by Perales "to send a copy of this resolution to the Honorable Maury Maverick, with the request that he be good enough to take this matter up immediately with the Bureau of the Census with a view of having persons of Mexican or Spanish extraction definitely and permanently classified as whites and not as of color."[137]

Registrars of Vital Statistics in San Antonio, Houston, Dallas and Fort Worth "had, for some time, been classifying Mexicans as colored in rendering their vital statistics reports to the Census Bureau of the U.S. Department of Commerce. Naturally, a very vigorous protest has been registered by our people through the entire State of Texas" and Perales said "white" included Mexicans.[138] Perales explicitly noted that his call for an appropriate racial classification was not about shame in being Mexican. "We are very proud of our racial extraction and we did not wish to convey the impression that we are ashamed to be called

Mexicans."[139] In 1936, national LULAC President Galván wrote a letter to all LULAC councils noting, "There is no question in my mind but that the Census Bureau of the Department of Commerce has insulted our race in classifying us as colored in their statistics reports."[140] Perales did not consider whiteness superior to Mexicanness but like most members of La Raza he believed Mexicanness superior to Blackness. Racism against persons of Mexican descent emanated from both Mexico and the United States. LULAC worked successfully with Mexican consuls, the US State Department, and local, state and federal officials to obtain a change in racial classification.[141]

Council 16 also addressed pending state and national legislation. It addressed equitable funding for equal educational facilities, urging state legislators that a rider be attached to the next appropriation bill.[142] At the 1937 convention Perales presented a host of resolutions, some addressing support for various bills in Congress. He believed LULAC could not stand on the sidelines while significant legislation was being promoted. So he introduced five resolutions related to federal legislation. Resolution 2 supported the Black-Connery bill for minimum wage and maximum hours for child labor and prohibition of child-labor produced goods across interstate lines.[143] He wrote, "We Mexican Americans who truly wish our people to progress should immediately support this legislation. We should realize that as long as our people are paid less than a living wage which would allow them to live as human beings, we cannot progress."[144] Resolution 3 sought to limit child labor under age 18. The LULAC national convention approved the resolutions but M.C. Gonzales voiced opposition.[145] It is unclear if he did so because Perales presented them or because Gonzales may have interpreted the resolutions as an entrance into partisan politics which was contrary to the 1929 constitution. But Perales saw these bills as pro-Raza. Resolutions passed in 1937 constituted LULAC's continuation of earlier 1930 efforts to address national policy. Historian Craig Kaplowitz has stated, "Overall, LULAC became part of the New Deal coalition, supporting its bills and efforts."[146]

Council 16 also took part in the Flying Squadron, efforts begun by Council 2 to establish more LULAC councils in the state. They worked to organize LULAC in New Braunfels, Seguin and San Marcos in spring 1938.[147] Past Council 16 president Charles Albidress Sr. wrote, "We would travel at approximately 30 miles speed every week in our old autos from San Antonio to Laredo, Austin, Del Rio, Corpus Christi, Eagle Pass and points between condemning discrimination in our public schools. Many times we hold meetings with school officials, other community leaders, and yes, held citizens' rallies in the barrios to educate and give moral support to our Mexican-American brethren."[148] It helped Ozuna LULAC Council 28 and the Ozuna Latin American Parent-Teacher Association as well as Hondo, Alice, Sabinal, Millett and Melvin with school issues.[149]

Council 16 and Perales also addressed inadequate housing.[150] Its housing committee sought to "replace all unsanitary shacks and corrals in the western section of the city with houses fit for human habitation."[151] One other issue they addressed was racial violence. In 1936 they protested the dragging of three young Mexican-origin men by someone driving a car.[152]

Council 16 also dealt with low wages but in a middle-class way. Council 16 established a Wage Scale committee. Along with Ladies LULAC Council 12 of San Antonio they sent 160 letters to employees to persuade them to pay a living wage noting it is "absolutely indispensable that he receive (receives) for his services a wage that will permit him to maintain a human standard of living." Perales naïvely believed, "Industrial leaders and businessmen and others persons who employ Latin Americans will increase their wages."[153] But just like white legislators would not end racism due to white interests, business owners would not raise employee wages due to class interests. Organizations like LULAC were needed; unions were also necessary.

Conflict between LULAC Council 2 and Council 16

Even with separate chapters, conflict between Council 2 and Council 16 continued. They especially disagreed about future national LULAC leadership. Perales warned Canales, "get ready for a big fight to prevent Council No. 2 from getting the President General next May."[154] In a letter to Dr. Carlos E. Castañeda, Perales noted that Canales and Gonzales wanted Ermilio Lozano as President for 1934-35 while Perales and Council 16 supported Pablo G. González.[155] While noting González' inexperience, Perales told Canales he would train Pablo and that he was trying to "safeguard the interests of the League. That's all."[156] Perales wrote, "I am seriously considering Mr. Pablo G. Gonzalez for the presidency . . . he can appoint Mr. Gregorio R. Salinas, Secretary and Mr. George D. Vann, Treasurer."[157] Perales believed he knew which leaders the League needed though González was from San Antonio.

Upset with Council 16, in 1937 some members of Council 2 decided to act against Perales' council. Council 2 and Council 1 (Corpus Christi) introduced a resolution at the national convention to force Council 16 to merge with Council 2. Resolution 8 asked the national president to order a merger when two councils existed in one city; he was to do so within 30 days. M.C. Gonzales, Leo Durán (Council 1), and two others who introduced the resolution said there was a "strong impression upon the Anglo-Saxon public that a division of opinion, animosity, hatred, and social feeling exist between the two" and that Council 16 looked down on Council 2 due to its "poor and humble members."[158] Perales disagreed. Council 16 responded to this suggested merger by putting down the national president. On May 22, 1937, Council 16 sent out a form letter about President Ramón Longoria of Harlingen; it read: "Anyone can be President General even if he has not worked on behalf of our race or our League and even if he has only been a member a few days."[159]

Perales explained convention actions in a letter to Castañeda.[160] He wrote, "Well, Sir, the Principal Founder of the League of United Latin American Citizens—yours truly—has been 'kicked' out; in fact, the entire Council 16 suffered the same fate." Here Perales acknowledged his role as key founder. Council 16 was asked to merge with Council 2 within thirty days. The vote on the issue was 22 for and 22 against the merger with the El Paso council and specifically Frank

Galván casting the deciding vote on the last day as the LULAC national president.

A July 1937 *LULAC News* unsigned editorial "An Amendment or Resolution?" addressed the issue. Some Council 16 members believed the merger issue should have been a constitutional amendment and not a resolution. In August 2, 1937 the new National President Ramón L. Longoria wrote Council 16 noting they had not abided by official LULAC decisions and that their charter was to be surrendered.[161]

In August 1937 the controversy continued. San Antonian Jacob Rodríguez, likely a Council 2 member, responded to an essay in Perales' recently released *En Defensa de Mi Raza* where he said, "the only one opposed to his Resolutions was Bro. Manuel C. Gonzalez, and that in order to better voice his opposition that he asked for the use of the amplifying system up on the stage." He went on to say, "The ONLY opposition that Bro. Gonzalez offered the Resolutions presented by Bro. Perales was his objection to the HEADING of said resolutions, and he, through that same amplifying system that Bro. Perales refers to, made a motion that said Resolutions be adopted, and this motion carried AFTER Bro. Perales AGREED to ALLOW the HEADINGS of his Resolutions to BE CHANGED! AND THAT'S THE TRUTH!!"[162]

By October 1937, Canales entered the fray by penning an essay, "The Right of LULAC Councils to Secede and Form a Rival Organization." He argued for unity but also concluded that a council was a legal entity worthy of preservation; moreover, he added that the resolution introduced should not have been retroactive. He then called for a special convention.[163] By February 1938, some LULAC councils realized it was a mistake to force Council 16 to merge and a new resolution followed. But the new resolution failed—Council 16 was not re-instated.[164] Despite this attempted reversal, Council 16 was permanently voted out of existence. Perales reported the events as follows: "The President General of the League then ordered Council No. 16 to surrender its charter, which it did."[165] One letter suggests that Perales got pushed out and noted that some LULAC members were not happy about a Perales-less LULAC. "Bear in mind that our race will be much stronger if we all belong to LULAC instead of having two Leagues for the same purpose," another said, adding, "You are a glorious leader of our race."[166]

By 1939, personality differences were so prominent in LULAC moving an anonymous member to write "Machine Politics and Methods in LULAC" for *LULAC News* for the August issue.[167] In 1934 Perales told H.H. Contreras, his brother-in-law, that "delegates, with few exceptions, do not take trouble to think." He added, "elect a man who is qualified in every respect."[168] In 1937 Adolfo de la Garza, LULAC Mission council president in the Valley, noted the problem of electing friends and trading promises.[169] Perales also noted these problems in 1937.[170] Perales disappeared from the LULAC membership by the summer of 1937 when he did not join Council No. 2. He held no LULAC office between 1937 and 1938 and he was not a speaker at the June 1939 national convention.[171] A man of principles, Perales refused to join Council 2.

Decades later, in 1960, Canales explained Perales' departure from LULAC: "Unfortunately, Mr. Perales disagreed with some members of said Council and left Council 2 soon after he had served as the Second President General. When I became President General in 1932, I established Council No. 16, organized by Perales, Dr. H.N. Gonzales and other intellectuals to cure this disagreement, but it was fought by Council No. 2 and eventually wiped out and so Perales ceased to be an active member of the League. Luz Saens [sic] had, or left after this incident."[172]

While it may appear that Perales was booted out of LULAC, it would be more appropriate to see his actions as secession. Moreover, Perales took this political *movida* (move) and created a new opportunity. Shortly after he exited LULAC, he established yet another civic organization—the League of Loyal Americans (Loyals) which had three chapters in San Antonio by 1937. Once again, Perales showed that he did not seek to be **the** leader or the one and only leader. He wanted to be influential and was happy with more activist groups; he would not let LULAC stand in his way.

The Loyals were created "To develop within the members of the Hispanic-American Race loyal and progressive citizens of the United

States of America; to uphold and defend our American form of Government and our American Institutions; to take an active interest in the civic, social and moral welfare of the community . . ." By 1939, Council 16 had officially died but the Loyals were "now known as Council 16 of The League of Loyal Americans."[173] The Loyals are addressed in chapter 13.

Perales and LULAC after 1937

At some point Perales became a life member of LULAC or at least he said so once.[174] While Perales was not a LULAC member in the 1940s the organization would continue to serve the Latino community. A historian noted, "With the exception of LULAC and the NAACP, few organizations in Texas rallied to the cause of Mexican and black workers."[175] LULAC also played a role in the California 1948 *Mendez vs. Westminster* case which desegregated state schools.[176] In 1949 attorney and LULAC member Gus Garcia called LULAC a "mere skeleton" "with no national leadership, no national newsletter, and no national consensus."[177] But there were national leaders, *LULAC News* still existed, and LULAC included numerous voices. While Dr. George I. Sánchez, past national LULAC president in the early 1940s, called LULAC an "amateurish operation" in 1953, it still achieved numerous successes. Critics often wanted more and better from the volunteer organization of colonized Mexican Americans, even its own members and leaders.

Perales did not write a summation of his time in LULAC but left scattered memories in various letters and they were not typically positive. In 1954 he likened conflict between communists and US Senator Joe McCarthy to him and LULAC. "It reminds me of the fights we used to have in LULAC organization. The envious ones would oppose whatever resolution Perales presented just because it was Perales."[178] But he was exaggerating. In 1957 around the League's anniversary in February the *San Antonio Light* stated "LULAC Job Praised." "The Lulacs are doing top job in the education field in Texas, according to Alonso Perales."[179]

Perales also reflected on LULAC in May 1958. Perales and Canales saw one another in April and that prompted this reflection from Canales: "The people for whose rights you were fighting became indifferent toward their true friends and the champions of their civic rights. Eventually, you were paid for your noble efforts by being thrown out; or maybe by compelling you to leave the League— the Instrument you had created. In other words, you were paid by ingratitude. I became interested and joined said organization because of my admiration for you and Prof. Sáenz."[180] He wrote, "regardless of what may have happened in the growth and development of Lulac the fact remains that you, Professor Sáenz and I were the principal founders of Lulac in Harlingen, Texas, in the year, 1927, and were very much present when the amalgamation [sic] of organizations took place in Corpus Christi in the year 1929, and no one can erase those facts and take away from us the satisfaction of having founded an organization that has enabled our people to march forward in the evolution of this great nation of ours and to acquire due respect and recognition as first-class citizens of the United States of America."[181] Here, Canales also credited Perales and Sáenz as major founders.

Perales' last thoughts on LULAC appeared in January 1960. In a letter to Canales he noted: "It seems that the LULAC organization has recognized its BIG blunder and want[s] to right things. Before their next annual Convention [,] they are celebrating its twentieth {fortieth} anniversary and they want you to be their honor guest of honor and keynote speaker; then at their annual convention they want to right things. I am inclined to go along with them and trust you will see your way clear to do likewise. After all, we are the real founders of the League and they know it and they now want to acknowledge it publically."[182] So at least before Perales died, he felt LULAC was acknowledging him. It appears that the groundwork to recognize Perales laid by San Antonio LULAC leader Luis Alvarado, son-in-law of J. Luz Sáenz, was beginning to pay off.

Perales may have also been slighted by LULAC because besides his friend Dr. Carlos E. Castañeda there was only one other trained Mexican-American historian in the country and no LULAC historian. After first national president Ben Garza died, misinformation about the League's history began to appear. Perales tried to set the record straight in his book *En Defensa de Mi Raza* in 1937, but a dedicated historian was needed. Moreover, in 1940 *LULAC News* began to include sporadic information about LULAC's origins and its history. The February 1940 *News*, sponsored by Corpus Christi council, included the first attempt. Likely written by Andrés De Luna, it was Corpus Christi-centered and did not properly situate the Order Sons of America of San Antonio or Perales' role.[183] A 1955 article by George J. Garza, LULAC member, also slighted Perales' significance.[184] A factually correct history could not yet be written without numerous archives in libraries.

LULAC's Persistence after Perales' Departure

Despite Perales' exit from LULAC and despite his death in 1960, LULAC persisted. In 1937 the *Brownsville Herald* wrote that it "appeared to be predestined for failure because of its almost impossibly high aims."[185] Again, in 1932 there were 46 councils and 100 by 1940.[186] Jacob Rodríguez of San Antonio formed California's first council in 1933 in Sacramento.[187] The League never ceased existing though individual local councils would come and go as would individual members. Even Council 1 was briefly disorganized on March 16, 1933. Rural councils—especially lacking a middle-class, educated persons or financially independent businesspeople—would come and go. One such council was Council 100 in Cuero, Texas, my hometown. Founded in 1940, it was hailed as a great landmark for the League though most councils preceding it had died. Cuero lasted only briefly. It reappeared in the 1970s and then died thereafter a few years. It has not reappeared again. By 1948 there were 151 councils in the United States, mostly in the Southwest.[188]

Councils experienced a revival after World War II and veterans were among the new members. The conflict between councils 2 and 16 had been forgotten and Perales was active in the Loyals. In January 1948 in San Antonio LULAC had 230 members and then 75 more members joined in May.[189] Meetings were said to start at 8 pm and end around eleven and included "knock-down and drag out battles." Council 2 had ten committees.[190]

LULAC expanded to New Mexico in the mid-1930s. Thereafter "state organizers" began to appear.[191] M.G. Gameros was state organizer for California in 1937-38. In 1938 A.P. Deus was state organizer for Colorado. Then by 1940 "regional governors" appeared with Arturo C. González of Del Rio organizing in Arizona. By 1955 chapters existed in Texas, New Mexico, Arizona, California and Colorado and chapters had in existed in Washington, DC, the East Coast and Chicago.[192] By 1956 regional governors existed for Iowa, Illinois and Wisconsin. In 1958 Michigan and Minnesota were added. In 1959-1960 on the eve of Perales' death about 340 chapters existed. But that year only 75 chapters were listed on the national roster. A year later there were 111 chapters. In 1961 LULAC spread "from the Wilmington harbor on the West Coast to the New York harbor on the East Coast."[193] In 1964 258 councils disappeared; 142 were listed on the roster but only were 98 in good standing.[194] By 1979 LULAC existed in 33 states.[195]

LULAC's tenuous status was addressed in 1949 by Dr. George I. Sánchez who had served as national president in the early 1940s. In a letter to the ACLU seeking possible monies for stabilization, he wrote, "The League has counsels [councils] in all the Southwestern states, but is still poorly organized and weak. This is due primarily to the lack of full-time leadership, of which in turn is due to financial resources. The League is ready and willing to move along any lines which look towards liberalism in general and the improvement of Spanish-speaking peoples in particular."[196] In 1953 he also wrote LULAC national president John Herrera, "The LULAC mountain [lion] mightily . . . and, except on very rare occasions, gives birth to a mouse."[197] While critical of LULAC he was himself a LULAC national president. Historians have also assumed that LULAC in the pre-Chicano movement era was destined for the dust bin. One historian incorrectly surmised the following: "Indeed, by 1960, some leaders of LULAC were prepared to disband the organization, convinced that the combination of court victories, the dismantling of formal segregation, and economic improvement meant their job was done."[198]

LULAC survived amid persistent racism, political threats, government surveillance and lack of funding.[199] In 1981 historian Rudy Acuña finally conceded that, "It survived in the most hostile of environments and kept Chicano issues at the forefront."[200] Indeed,

LULAC survived because of continued resistance to racism. While Perales and LULAC sought to help in the US WWII war effort, the US federal government feared their ties to Mexico. The United States was not sure if Mexico was pro-Allied or pro-Axis. Historian Carlos Blanton noted, "To exert pressure on civil rights, they enlisted a foreign government—and a not always friendly one at that—in the middle of a terrible conflict [World War II]. This had the potential to expose them to the kinds of attacks that could destroy lives and careers. . . LULAC, during the Second World War, acting on complaints made by the entire Chicana/o community, no matter how small the place or unknown *la gente.*"[201]

LULAC's persistence also needs to be juxtaposed with other Latino civil rights groups. The Alianza de Hispano Americana, founded in Arizona in the 1890s, became a more overt civil rights group in the 1950s but did not survive. The Congreso de Habla Española, especially strong in California, of the 1930s and 40s and the 1950s Asociación Nacional México-Americana, especially in New Mexico, were "short-lived forays" since both tried to "broaden the civil rights agenda to include working-class issues. Because of the vigorous anti-socialist atmosphere in the United States, these groups found it very difficult to survive.[202] In Texas a Confederation of Mutualistas existed but did not survive. In Chicago Mexican-descent people founded La Confederación de Sociedades Mexicanas de los Estados Unidos de América in 1925. It started with thirty-five mutual aid societies but was unable to become a national or permanent society.[203]

LULAC's liberalism also helps explain its persistence. Historian Richard A. Garcia astutely noted that LULAC sought a "liberal American public collectivity" but a private Mexican self for the individual.[204] While LULAC had both Democrats and Republicans as its national leadership, it was/is fundamentally "liberal."

Despite LULAC's liberal and patriotic bent, it was nonetheless a target of government surveillance. Government surveillance apparently began after the Spanish Civil War in 1936. In 1940 a New Orleans report noted LULAC members meeting with the Mexican consul and that "LULACS were being financed by the Mexican government through its consular service in the United States." A Denver report noted a suspicious Antonito, Colorado LULAC chapter. They were wary of membership fees crossing state lines and "because Mexicans generally are unreliable and untrustworthy." This report was sent to the El Paso office some twenty years later in 1961. Moreover, a 1941 file notes there was "some indication that it may have been used for communistic purposes in the Rio Grande Valley of Texas." Scholar José Angel Gutiérrez noted that during the early 50s the FBI was focused on "1) The lobbying role against the 'bracero' program; 2) The legal challenges in the state and federal courts against the school segregation of students of Mexican ancestry; and 3) The efforts to place LULAC members on selective service boards across the Southwest."[205]

Perales was also investigated. A 1942 FBI report noted, "The Committee of 100, a purely political organization, composed of Americans of Mexican descent and Alonso S. Perales, Attorney at Law, 714 Gunter Building, San Antonio, is its chairman."[206]

Conclusion

LULAC was founded on the eve of the Great Depression, this nation's most challenging economic collapse. Despite numerous obstacles, the League expanded rapidly in Texas with 100 councils by 1940. It also expanded across the Southwest before the end of World War II and into the East Coast and Midwest before 1960. Lacking permanent funding, a permanent office and suffering the demise of hundreds of local councils over the years, it survived because LULAC's ideology and constitution were well thought out—liberal and pragmatic, not radical or communist.

Perales sought to direct LULAC's early course but did not try to control it. He orchestrated the selection of several national presidents in the 1930s including Ben Garza, himself, and Canales. Perales was an effective national president keeping councils alive by maintaining communication. After his presidency, he joined LULAC Council 2 but founded Council 16, also in San Antonio, due to leadership differences.

Although Perales officially exited LULAC in 1938 this chapter confirms what historian Richard A. Garcia stated in 1991: "Perales mirrored LULAC and the organization mirrored him."[207] After quitting LULAC, Perales continued to aid the organization and found other associations with similar principles. He never "quit" LULAC. Without Perales there would be no LULAC.

CHAPTER 11
Activist, 1930s

The 1930s was a difficult era in the United States for all including Mexicans and Mexican Americans. The early 1930s saw the
deportation of several thousand Mexicans and Mexican Americans
from Texas back to Mexico and nationally, some half a million.[1] In
San Antonio hundreds of men and twenty-five women had been
deported by 1939.[2] Texas was also a major point of departure for Mid-
western Mexican-descent people leaving the United States. Other
Mexicans and Mexican Americans voluntarily returned to Mexico to
avert poverty and heightened anti-Mexican-descent sentiment. Most
New Deal federal job programs discriminated against Mexican Americans. Segregation, including in public schools, as well as the racist
administration of justice continued though lynching of persons of
Mexican-descent subsided in Texas.

The 1930s were a challenge. There was no minimum wage, unem-
ployment benefits, social security, medicare, medicaid, aid to dependent children or small business loans. Veterans' benefits were minimal.
Minimum wage laws passed in 1938 and that meant an increase of .25
cents an hour but did not include domestics (mostly women) and farmworkers (mostly people of color). Pecan shellers earned $1.29 a week.[3]
Nor was there any financial aid for college students and scholarships
were rare. Most of La Raza was not even completing high school.

Some 90,000 to 100,000 persons of Mexican descent lived in San
Antonio during the Depression. By 1930 La Raza worked in railroad
yards, packing plants, military bases, garment factories, service establishments, retail trade, construction and an informal market. Most of

La Raza was working class and many undocumented. Political, educational and social conditions were poor. San Antonio had a political machine dependent on Mexican-American and African American voters but with no people of color on the city council or county commission between 1930 and 1940.[4] Around 1940 only 9% of the city's high school graduates were of Mexican descent.[5] In 1932 Perales reported only 9 of 350 college students in the city were Spanish-surnamed including Catholic colleges such as St. Mary's and Our Lady of the Lake.[6] Housing conditions were dismal; tuberculosis and intestinal disease were major causes of death.[7]

This decade would see Perales not only fully occupied with LULAC—not always as an official LULAC member—but in numerous other endeavors. This chapter first deals with his efforts in education to improve San Antonio schools through LULAC Council 16 and then through the School Improvement League (SIL). Second, it covers Perales' work in fostering federal New Deal housing programs in San Antonio. Third, Perales' role in the Pecan Sheller's strike in San Antonio in 1938 is highlighted; it was the largest strike in the city's history and one of the largest in the United States during the Depression. Finally, Perales' volunteer work to improve the health of La Raza is discussed, particularly his fight against tuberculosis.

LULAC Council 16 and the School Improvement League in San Antonio, 1934

Education was a major issue for Perales and LULAC. The August 1931 *LULAC News* stated, "Educate the children of Mexican extraction and [we/you] will have a new generation that will measure [up] to the requirements of American standards."[8] In 1932 another LULAC member lamented, "THERE ARE 100,000 MEXICAN CHILDREN, CITIZENS OF TEXAS, NOT IN SCHOOL!"[9] As chapter 8 showed LULAC Council 16 of San Antonio also initiated the effort that would become a mass movement in San Antonio—the effort to build and improve schools serving La Raza. West side schools had 12,334 students and eleven schools while the non-West side had 12,224 students in twenty-eight schools. And 286 teachers taught in Mexican schools with 339 in white schools. Some $24.50

was spent per student on the West side but $35.96 for others. There was overcrowding, inferior buildings, insufficient schools and racist appropriation of school funding.[10]

Council 16 formed a committee giving attention to inferior schools. Member Eleuterio Escobar headed Council 16's Schools and Playground Committee in 1933 whose goal was to "ensure that children West Side children had safe playgrounds, cafeterias, and schools comparable to those in other sections of the city."[11] The committee "sought to see physical improvements in the 'Mexican schools,' fewer students per classroom, and the elimination of half-day classes due to overcrowding on the West Side."[12] It also sought more teachers, cafeteria space and playgrounds. In September 1934 it issued a survey of the public school buildings and recreational facilities.[13] This Council 16 effort morphed into a separate organization called the School Improvement League (SIL) with seventy-three partner organizations representing 75,000 persons in the 1930s. In 1934 SIL published *El Defensor de la Juventud* (The Children's Defender) and in the 40s, *ABC Journal*.

Escobar was associated with civil rights activism since the early 1920s. He was a World War I veteran and opened a furniture store in San Antonio. He witnessed conflict between Santiago Tafolla Sr. and Feliciano Flores at an Order Sons of America meeting in the early 1920s. In 1927 as a member of the Order Knights of America he attended the Harlingen Convention. Though he only had a third-grade education he "had an almost perfect command of the English language."[14] In 1936 he founded the International Leather and Importing Company, acquired real estate and donated a six-acre farm for a playground.[15] He also helped finance future attorney Gus Garcia's education.[16]

The SIL was active from 1933 to 1941 dying because of US entrance into World War II and Escobar's family concerns. Between 1937 and 1947 no school was built on the West side although the population there had increased significantly. School conditions were the worst at Edgewood. At Edgewood the school population boomed from 1939 to 1949 from 1,586 students to 6,000. In 1949, 2,400 students attended seventy classrooms in half-day sessions. A Congressional committee noted, it was "the worst we had encountered in any school district."[17] For instance, in 1947 Jefferson High on the North side of the city had thirty-three acres while Sidney Lanier on the Westside had two and half.[18]

In 1947 the SIL was reactivated and Escobar rejoined. In 1947 it petitioned the school board for six to eight new elementary schools, a junior high, a senior high and a vocational school. The group took photographs as evidence for their case; one of Escobar's most useful photos was a Sidney Lanier student playing the clarinet on a commode since there was no band hall.[19] SIL supported the election of then-attorney Gus Garcia to the school board. In 1948 they helped obtain $250,000 improvements at Sidney Lanier.[20] With help from the new Mexican-American civic organization Pan American Progressive Association (PAPA), they also got $20,000 a year for West side schools.[21] The 1949 federal Gilmer-Aikin educational funding bill also helped. Finally, in 1950 the group supported a $9.3 million bond issue for school construction.

While Escobar took the reins of SIL, Perales continued to be involved in these school issues. In October 1951 ex-congressman and ex-mayor Maury Maverick made an appointment with the San Antonio school board for Dr. Carlos E. Castañeda, Escobar, Perales, Rev. Isaac S. Lugo and others. The group met in Perales' office before they met with the board.[22] SIL would later disband around 1956. Another victory for the SIL was the founding of the Eleuterio Escobar School with twenty-six rooms at a cost of $350,000.[23] While Escobar had a school named for him while alive, Perales would not see this for himself though it was Perales' Council 16 that attacked deficient schools and became a mass movement and longterm effort to improve and construct schools for the Mexican-descent on the West and South sides of San Antonio.

New Deal programs, 1935

San Antonio was residentially segregated with whites on the north side; African Americans on the east; and Mexican-descent people on the west side.[24] San Antonio's West side with some 100,000 Mexican-descent residents was considered one of the worst slums in the world.[25] A 1930s study showed 14,700 Mexican-origin families living in substandard housing.[26] The San Antonio Housing Authority noted that 90% of West side housing fell below standards. Housing consisted of "floorless shacks, which rented for two to eight dollars per month and were crowded together on every lot; houses without plumbing, sewer connections, and most of them without electric lights. Outside the houses there were usually no sidewalks—streets were not paved and outdoor toilets were only a few feet from the houses."[27] There were also shacks without toilets and running water that rented for 50 cents a week.[28] Affordable and adequate housing for persons of Mexican descent in San Antonio was lacking. LULAC Council 16 had a housing committee in 1933 and on which Perales served.[29] Its housing committee sought to "replace all unsanitary shacks and corrals in the western section of the city with houses fit for human habitation."[30] Council 16 and Perales helped Father Carmelo Tranchesse obtain a federal housing project.[31]

According to wife Marta Perales, Alonso wrote President Franklin D. Roosevelt about dilapidated housing in San Antonio.[32] First Lady Eleanor Roosevelt visited San Antonio and the Alazan-Apache courts for the Mexican-descent and Victoria Courts for African Americans were built.[33] In 1937 at the LULAC Houston National Convention Perales wrote a resolution to promote the Wagner-Steagall Act to support low-income public housing. The Act passed.[34] Federal slum clearance also meant more residents moved to the West side. The San Antonio Housing Authority was finally created in 1937.[35]

In 1939 Perales wrote US Senator Morris Sheppard about federal support to "build these sanitary and modern dwellings so greatly needed by our less fortunate people of this city. No doubt you are aware of the fact that according to official statistics, more people die of tuberculosis in San Antonio than in any other city in the United States. Inadequate housing is responsible for it to a great degree." He also informed him that some property owners did not want to sell to end the "Slum Clearance Project."[36] Indeed, a document by the Committee on Housing for Bexar County noticed the following problems: vermin-infested, disease-infected; insufficient water supply; inadequate toilet accommodations; defective plumbing, poor ventilation, fire hazard, unclean surroundings; and drainage."[37]

Perales also addressed racial segregation in New Deal programs.[38] In 1935 friend and LULAC member Dr. Castañeda informed him that the Federal Relief Administration Program (FERA) (1933 to 1935 before the WPA) was establishing five camps for young women ages 16-25 of which San Antonio was to receive one for whites and another for Mexicans. The YWCA, YMCA and International Institute favored the camps even if segregated.[39] Perales argued even if fifty Mexican girls had to lose jobs it was better to insist on one integrated camp.[40] He saw these camps as a potential crack in segregationist practices and policies.

Pecan Shellers' Strikes, 1938

In the 1930s there were thousands of strikes for fair employment and better wages across the United States. Mexican-descent women were especially active in cigar, garment and pecan-shelling strikes in Texas and especially San Antonio. Between 10,000 and 20,000 shellers worked in the city making $1 or $2 a week.[41] There were several strikes in the pecan-shelling industry but the most important one occurred in 1938 since it was the city's first major labor-management dispute and because the strike was successful.[42] Not only was the Depression in full force, Mexican-descent women were readily exploited.[43] Moreover, San Antonio was in the Deep South, the "least industrialized and least unionized part of the country."[44] Various unions of pecan shellers began to strike in 1934; one led by Magdaleno Rodríguez had 10,000 members.[45]

The 1938 Pecan Shellers strike was one of the largest strikes in the United States during the Depression.[46] In 1936 the Southern Pecan Shelling Company's sales totaled $3 million while a pecan sheller typically made $1.56 for 64 hours or $1.16 per week or 5 cents an hour.[47] The Catholic Church, LULAC Council 2 and the Mexican Chamber of Commerce initially opposed the strike.[48] But according to historian Laura Cannon, "Midway through the strike, these groups changed their position and started supporting the workers."[49]

The Mexican Chamber of Commerce, the Loyals affiliated with Perales and LULAC Council 2 asked leader strike Donald Henderson to sign a statement that he was not a Communist Party member and believed in American institutions and when he refused to sign they called for his removal as strike leader.[50] The Loyals protested to the mayor and voted to support the strike if Communist leadership by Emma Tenayuca[51] and the Workers' Alliance was eliminated.[52] LULAC Council 2 president Pablo Meza argued at a state commission hearing that Henderson was a communist.[53] Industrialist Julius Seligman did grant the Loyals and the Mexican Chamber permission to audit his books and accounts to assess a possible pay increase and this idea was presented at a strikers meeting.[54] Rejecting the offer, workers eventually won union recognition, a closed shop, a checkoff system and a grievance committee but ultimately the profit-driven business shifted to mechanization.[55]

Perales did not believe in radical labor unions or strikes though they were another essential kind of resistance to ethnic, gender and labor discrimination. San Antonio had about ten communist unions in the late 1930s.[56] In 1938 Perales wrote in Rómulo Munguía's *El Pueblo*: "There should be no support or voting for radical labor unions; pecan shellers' strikes; or Communist, Socialist, or Nazi leadership; and no membership in any organizations with Communist affiliations, such as the Congress of Industrial Organizations and the Worker's Alliance of America (Emma Tenayuca was a member)."[57] A year later, Perales wrote that he "bitterly opposed to the policy of any organization, regardless of its kind of character, that admits communists, nazists (sic) or fascists in their ranks" and not just those in the CIO.[58]

Historian Zaragoza Vargas has criticized LULAC's response to the strike. He wrote, "The Mexican consul's office did nothing on behalf of the striking women cigar workers. Nor did LULAC; its members were likely shamefaced about the unruly actions of the striking Tejanas, but they also stayed out of the fray for fear of the wrath of the Anglo power structure."[59] But as shown in my *No Mexicans* book and this book LULAC was all about tearing down the "wrath of the Anglo power structure." Additionally, as Zaragoza Vargas added, "The timid and relatively weak middle-class Mexican American establishment was represented by the conservative League of United Latin American Citizens. This self-serving, 'loyal and patriotic' Mexican American organization sympathized with the pecan shellers' deplorable working conditions and dismal wages but, along with the Mexican Chamber of Commerce and the Catholic archbishop of San Antonio, condemned the strike because of its Red leadership. LULAC unfortunately supported the repatriation campaigns by the U.S. Border Patrol and called for the suppression of the pecan shellers' strike by the police."[60] But there is no evidence of LULAC supporting any repatriation or deportation campaigns or calls for police suppression. And LULAC was far from "self-serving." While Perales believed workers should speak to employers, he did not advocate for unionization. As president of the "Comision Pro-Aumento de Jornales de la Liga de Ciudadanos Unidos" (Commission for Wage Increases, League of United Citizens, Council 16), he spoke to the Mexican Protestant Workers' Association suggesting workers' children finish school, join the Boy Scouts and adults attend night school. Perales also said workers could only afford $5 a month rent and he noted "the situation of our people is critical that they be paid the value of their work."[61] Indeed in 1939 housing authorities estimated that 45% of the Mexican community earned less than $555 a year and 75% earned less than $950 annually.[62]

In 1939 Emma Tenayuca, a communist and Pecan Shellers leader, wrote a mixed review of LULAC. On the negative side she wrote, "In the past, its viewpoint was colored by the outlook of petty-bourgeois native born, who seek escape from general oppression that has been the lot of the Mexican people as a whole. It meant an attempt to achieve Americanization, while barring the still non-naturalized foreign-born from membership. It resulted in the glorification of the English language and Anglo-American culture to the extent of prohibiting Spanish within the local societies." But she and husband Homer Brooks also praised LULAC in their essay titled "The Mexican Question": "In Texas they have led successful struggles against segregation in public schools, parks, etc., not only in behalf of American citizens, but of all Mexicans . . . [T]his important organization of the Mexican middle class will play an increasing role in the general movement for Mexican rights."[63] Note that they said "Mexican rights" and not "Mexican American only rights."

Liberal LULAC proved more successful than the radical Communist Party. Texas had about a thousand Communists in the late 30s, many of Mexican descent.[64] In the 1940s sociologist Sister Woods interviewed a Mexican lawyer who said the following about communism among La Raza: "The average Mexican is only vaguely acquainted with the Communist movement, and there is little likeli-

hood that Communism will ever make inroads into the masses of the
Mexican population, provided we continue to make at least some
progress along the lines of social and economic betterment. Our religion is still very influential . . . and we owe much to it in the rejection
of the spread of Communism among the Mexicans—only a noisy
demagogue during a period where hungry people here, like hungry
people everywhere, were grabbing at straws."[65] Communism was not
popular among La Raza though they were supportive of direct action
through strikes, especially during the Depression.

Fighting Tuberculosis

Disease was a major problem in San Antonio in the 1930s. Tuberculosis and intestinal disease caused death and in 1937 there were 310
Mexican deaths among 100,000 Mexicans; 138 for African Americans
and 56 for Euro-Texans in the city.[66] In the late 40s it had the highest
tuberculosis rate in the country for cities over 100,000 persons.[67] It
was exacerbated by poor housing and overcrowding in homes; Father
Carmelo Tranchesse noted, "it is not unusual in San Antonio to find
Mexican families of from four to ten persons living in a one room
shack."[68] While Mexican-descent women played a key role in creating
a Mexican health clinic as early as 1925 and another in the 1930s
known as Clínica de la Beneficencia Mexicana, it was not enough.[69]
From 1933 to 1949, Perales was involved in anti-tuberculosis
efforts,[70] his mother and sister died from tuberculosis so the cause
was personal. Perales was a member of the Bexar County Tuberculosis Association in 1933.[71] LULAC Council 16 worked with the Texas
Tuberculosis Society (TTS) and in 1933 three members were physi-
cians.[72] In 1934, it organized the First Latin-American Health Week
in coordination with R.C. Ortega, TTS' director of the Mexican
Health Service.[73] Perales chaired a session at Sidney Lanier High with
LULAC members Dr. H.N. Gonzales and Dr. O.F. Gerodetti and Ortega.[74] Two years later, in 1936, Perales publicized a Harlingen convention of the Texas State Anti-tuberculosis Association in *La Prensa*.[75] From 1933 to 1940 he worked with the Tuberculosis Control
Council.[76] Around 1941 Perales and others were discussing the creation of a specialized tuberculosis hospital for the city.[77] Perales also

joined the San Antonio Health Board in the mid-30s. In June 1940 he quit this board and the advisory board drafting a city manager charter because campaign promises had not been kept.[78]

Conclusion

Despite the Depression and personal financial challenges, Perales contributed to important developments in San Antonio in the 1930s. He founded LULAC Council 16 which led to the formation of the School Improvement League led by Eleuterio Escobar from the mid-30s into the 1950s. Activist Demetrio Rodríguez would take up the issue of unequal public school funding in San Antonio in the 1980s.[79] Perales also helped establish federal housing units in San Antonio, though segregated, and fought against racially segregated federal work camps for women. He also fought the tuberculosis crisis among La Raza in San Antonio.

Perales did not support the Pecan Shellers' Strike of 1938 which included the communist leadership of Emma Tenayuca. However, once LULAC and the Loyals of which Perales was a leader were assured of the removal of communist leadership, they supported the strike. Unfortunately, mechanization led to the decline of the industry in the city. While Perales supported both a minimum wage and a fair living wage, he did not support strikes and he abhorred communists. The Mexican-origin people's education, housing and health improved due to the work of Perales, LULAC and the School Improvement League in San Antonio in the 1930s.

CHAPTER 12
Activist, 1940s

The 1940s were largely defined by World War II which began in 1939. The US entered the war in 1941 and the war ended in 1945. The war introduced three major issues for Mexican-descent people and Latinos: 1) the treatment of Latino soldiers; 2) the Bracero Program (1942-1964), an international agreement between the US and Mexico which authorized a labor program sending Mexican immigrant workers to fulfill US employers' needs due to labor shortages; and 3) the Federal Employment Practices Commission (FEPC), a new federal agency created to oversee the elimination of race discrimination in employment by the federal government or federal government contractors so US efforts in the war could run smoothly.

Mexican-descent people experienced the same patterns with working-class and middle-class Mexican Americans obtaining little racial equality or class mobility.[1] For instance, Malcolm Ross of the American Civil Liberties Union (ACLU) noted that lawyers, businessmen and Mexican consuls were turned down from entering public places due to race though noting fair-skinned people like Dr. Carlos E. Castañeda could pass.[2] Yet, even Castañeda's letters to Perales reveal that he experienced racism and anti-Catholic sentiment in the University of Texas Austin History Department. (See Chapter 20.)

During the 1940s Perales continued his efforts at the local level in San Antonio but expanded his antidiscrimination efforts at the state, national and international levels, often intertwined. This chapter first documents Alonso S. Perales' attempts to seek government employment for himself during the war. Second, it shows Perales played a major role in getting the state of Texas banned from obtaining *braceros* under the Bracero Program involving negotiations with the state of Texas and Mexico. Third, at the national level, Perales advocated for the first federal antidiscrimination agency, the Federal Employment Practices Commission (FEPC) which began modern civil rights policy since the end of US Reconstruction in 1877. The FEPC was a precursor to the Equal Employment Opportunity Commission (EEOC). Fourth, the chapter reveals Perales' work for desegregationist state legislation in Texas leveraging the US Good Neighbor policy which began in 1933 under President Franklin Delano Roosevelt. Fifth, at the local level, Perales took up volunteer work with the Pan American Optimist Club which directly aided working-class Mexican-descent children.

Perales witnessed two broad civic and political developments which led to greater success in the post-1945 years. LULAC surged after World War II. Moreover, in Texas and the nation, a new Mexican-American civil rights organization joined LULAC and the Loyals— the American GI Forum. Physician Dr. Héctor P. García, a member of LULAC Council 1 of Corpus Christi and its veteran committee, founded this veterans' national association which spread throughout Texas, the Southwest and the Midwest. Its overt connection to veteran status helped Latinos since they were appealing to whites' conscience based on US patriotism. A second development was a key electoral win by attorney Gus García to the San Antonio school board in 1948. This political advancement signaled to Mexican Americans that a Mexican American could be elected in San Antonio and beyond.

Perales' Potential Employment Opportunities during World War II

World War II created potential professional opportunities for Perales as well as a new terrain for the old issue of racism. Perales thought the war might provide employment. Indeed, he was a veteran, a diplomat with significant experience, and a seasoned bilingual attorney. Perales believed "my age, education, training, and experience" made him an ideal candidate for the US Air Corps.[3] Had he been a European American and had he not been an activist, he may have been offered numerous jobs.

Perales began his quest for a professional position related to the war in December 1941. In April 1942 he sent a letter to retired Major General Arthur W. Brown noting his age, training and experience.[4] In May 1942 he wrote friend Dr. Carlos E. Castañeda, "But somehow we have not been able to impress our Government with our potential usefulness due to our Hispanic background." He added, "Our government is losing time, as the Germans, Italians, and Japanese have been very active in Hispanic America [and] have made deep inroads into the souls and hearts of some of those peoples. Who could counteract said activities better than an American citizen of Hispanic descent?"[5] Axis powers were attempting to woe Latin American nations on their side and against the United States. Also that month he also wrote Captain C.F. Detweiler of the US Air Corps that he could be of service "in combating fifth column and espionage activities in Hispanic America."[6]

Apparently by July 1942 Perales considered "service either in the army or in the diplomatic services."[7] That month he applied to the Board of Economic Warfare under the Department of State for a position as Officer in the Foreign Service Auxiliary since he had heard it had selected four whites, one Latin American and a Syrian-American from San Antonio and Laredo.[8] He wrote friend Castañeda with the list of men selected to go to Montevideo, Uruguay, Mexico City, Guatemala City and Bogota, Columbia. Perales added, "They seem to be selecting men who have not only a good education but also a good economic background. It is the policy the regular Foreign Service has pursued for years, as you know. Well, you and I do not have the money, but we certainly can deliver the goods and make friends for our Nation."[9] He believed class background counted and he knew race mattered. He also tried to get an appointment as an officer in the US army, preferably in the Military Intelligence Dept. and hopefully in Argentina but was unsuccessful.[10]

In August Perales applied to serve as a Foreign Services Auxiliary officer.[11] By August 1942 Major General Arthur W. Brown reminded Perales that his possible assistance was limited since he was retired and told him to get a strong letter of support from a member of Congress.[12] Perales informed him that he had applied to the Judge Advocate General of the Army for an appointment especially since the local draft boards were inducting married men.[13] By September Perales resigned to feeling that military intelligence "does not seem to be interested in me." And ". . . as I might be inducted as a private most any time now."[14] Brown informed him that 15,000 applications had been received for seventy-five jobs.[15]

Perales feared being drafted again. Indeed, in August 1942 the *San Antonio Light* reported that married men who had no children were being inducted; Perales said "This means I am apt to be called most any time."[16] In September Perales wrote Brown, "I might be inducted as a private most any time now."[17] Perhaps Perales feared the battle lines and likely felt he had more to offer the United States than just his body. By September 1942 Perales was seeking a position as head of the Spanish-language division in a war agency. He preferred to "join the Army as an officer" but was willing to "grab the next best post offered" which would be "much better than being a buck private." He added, "The outcome of our [a reference to Hispanics] efforts to obtain recognition in the matter of responsible appointments is most disheartening."[18]

By October Perales noted the placement of Spanish-speaking attorneys for these jobs but only one who was a US citizen. He noted, "It seems that we just simply are not wanted in high positons."[19] As historian Carlos Blanton noted about Dr. George I. Sánchez, "he experienced the limits of civic participation in that the nation he loved was not willing to lay aside racism in order to achieve wartime unity."[20] Perales hoped that he and Castañeda would be offered important positions but they were men of color.

In October 1942 Perales took a medical exam and received bad news. His blood pressure was 175 and he disqualified himself. He was also told he was colorblind and needed some dental work.[21] Finally, that month Perales had an interview with the US Navy, but his blood pressure was at 175 and he was rejected.[22] This was likely his first knowledge of his poor health.

Perales, however, likely did not receive a post because of his activism. Historian Arturo F. Rosales noted that in November 1942

US Consulate William H. Blocker was asked to conduct a study of the extent of race discrimination against Mexican Americans. Perales and others provided him fodder. Rosales concluded, "But perhaps unbeknownst to Perales, Blocker quickly identified him as a mettlesome troublemaker in more than one piece of correspondence in the files of his confidential report. This probably led to Perales not receiving a commission in the military which he strenuously sought."[23]

Perales not only sought opportunity for himself during the war but also for La Raza. He hoped that war-time participation this time [after World War I] might finally make a difference in improving race relations. In 1944 he wrote, "Our hope is that when our brothers return from the warfront that they will find if not a more truly democratic Texas at least a political climate much healthier than when they left to go to war." He called for equality: "Equal in the trenches, but also equal in the factories, in the stores, in the schools, in the churches, in the restaurants, in the barbershops, in the theatres, and everywhere else."[24]

The war and its anti-Nazi, anti-fascist ideology gave cause for yet another reason to fight racial discrimination. Perales frequently voiced anti-fascist sentiment during the war. He said during a radio interview, "We have but one heart and that belongs not to Hitler, Mussolini or Stalin, but to the United States of America."[25] Perales and the Committee of 100 appealed to Mexico's "Comité Mexicano Contra el Racismo." He explained in the Comité's newsletter *Fraternidad* in December 1944, "Because any discriminatory act based on racial difference today represents important support for the common enemy against the entire civilized world: Nazi fascism." He called for an end to differential treatment towards a José Pérez versus a Joe Smith.[26]

While Perales expressed pride in the participation of Latino soldiers in the war he also posed several critical questions. His 1947 book included "Citations to the Congressional Medal of Honor for Six Latin Americans of the State of Texas," noting the work of José M. López, Macario García, Cleto L. Rodríguez, Lucian Adams, Silvestre S. Herrera and Alejandro R. Ruiz.[27] He also included newspaper articles listing the killed, wounded, missing and prisoners of wars. Perales asked why Latinos were over-represented among the dead, decades before Chicano Vietnam protestors. Perales of The Committee of One Hundred wrote two US House of Representatives from Texas with the statement, "Please ascertain from our War Department why is it that from fifty percent to seventy-five percent of the casualties from South Texas are soldiers of Mexican descent."[28]

Bracero Program

Perales opposed the Bracero Program, and in 1947, wrote US Commissioner of Immigration Watson Miller noting that *braceros* undercut Mexican-American workers' wages and, consequently, were forced into the migrant labor stream.[29] At its 1942 national convention LULAC argued for the end of the Bracero Program "because of the fact that the conditions complain in said Resolution [of 1942] still exist, and the same exploitation, discrimination, and segregation is still being practiced against the Mexican people in Texas."[30] After the war ended and into the 50s the program continued. In 1958 LULAC also argued that it "destroyed the bargaining power for better wages of our American citizens of Mexican descent."[31] Perales, like LULAC, was concerned with labor exploitation of both Mexican and Mexican Americans.

Perhaps Perales' most significant role at the international level was his work with Mexico in banning the entrance of Mexican *bracero* workers into Texas as historian Emilio Zamora has shown.

Although the United States had the upper hand over Mexico in *bracero* negotiations, another international agreement between the two countries gave Mexico a little more ability to exert authority over all persons of Mexican-descent in the United States. The Consular Agreement of 1942 permitted Mexican consulates to protect the rights of Mexican citizens before federal, state and local authorities.[32] So Perales used this leverage to inform both US federal officials and Mexican politicians of racism in Texas. This led to the temporary banning of *braceros* into Texas. But agribusiness was stronger and they were re-admitted.

Federal Employment Practices Commission

In June 1941 responding to pressure by African American leaders A. Phillip Randolph and Walter White who threatened public demonstrations, President Franklin D. Roosevelt issued an executive order to combat discrimination in wartime industries, government employment and unions and created the Federal Employment Practices Committee (FEPC). At the Congressional level in the early 1940s was one person of color in the Senate, New Mexican Dennis Chávez and two non-whites in the House of Representatives, two African American men.[33] (Chávez won since Hispanos constituted 39% of the state population and there was less racial discrimination in New Mexico against Hispanos.)[34] Chávez became a key advocate for FEPC.

Political scientist Matthew Gritter noted, "The existence of the FEPC provided a new option for Mexican American civil rights leaders eager for remedies that could improve opportunities for members of their community."[35] In the 1940s Perales was active on the issue of employment discrimination, especially racially defined jobs and dual wages that paid whites one wage and Mexican-descent people another. He wrote that economic discrimination included: "1) refusal to hire; 2) refusal to train; 3) refusal to upgrade; and 4) payments of lower wages."[36] In Perales' own words against "economic discrimination": "He is refused employment. He is denied an opportunity to acquire higher knowledge, and secure better positions. He is refused promotions on the basis of seniority and qualifications. He is paid smaller wages than the Anglo-Saxon for the same kind of work."[37] FEPC determined that oil-refining and shipbuilding industries in Texas and copper-mining businesses in Arizona and New Mexico were especially culpable of racist hiring and promotion practices against African Americans, Mexican-descent workers and Native Americans.

From 1941 to 1946, Congress passed legislation with funding for this law. Gritter noted that Mexican-American activists welcomed FEPC because "the Texas Good Neighbor Commission was not seen as useful by the leaders . . ."[38] The Texas Good Neighbor Commission (GNC) had no funding nor enforcement powers and operated from token racial goodwill toward La Raza. It also specifically excluded attention to African Americans.

Senator Chávez played a pivotal role in supporting FEPC which would address racism against Latinos in Texas, New Mexico, Arizona, California, Illinois and Louisiana. Chávez was well aware of employment discrimination in New Mexico. For instance, Julián A. Hernández of Santa Fe wrote him about racism in Los Alamos, home to the center which developed the atomic bomb, "They tell you that over fifty percent of the employees are Spanish-American, but those fifty percent are mostly laborers and the ones that have office jobs do not rate the pay standards of an Anglo. Little by little they are forcing the Spanish people to resign by some way or another and employing Anglos from outside."[39] Likewise, Dr. Carlos E. Castañeda reported on racist hiring and wages in Silver City in Southern New Mexico noting that Kennecott Copper Corporation, American Smelting and Refining Company, Peru Mining Company, Empire Zinc Mining Company, Black Hawk Mining Company, US Smelter and Mining Company and Asarco Mining Company all discriminated against Mexican-descent workers and Native Americans through improper classification, refusal to upgrade and differential wage scales.[40] Senator Chávez and the Union of Mine, Mill and Smelter Workers asked the FEPC to address differential treatment of Mexican-descent miners.[41]

One of the most propitious developments for Latinos was the hiring of LULAC member Dr. Carlos E. Castañeda as an FEPC regional director. According to Castañeda, less than 5% of the Mexican-descent population worked in war and essential industries and those employed here were restricted to unskilled labor jobs regardless of ability, training or qualifications.[42] Castañeda worked with FEPC from 1943 and 1944, taking official leave from the University of Texas at Austin's History Department. Castañeda suggested three or four field examiners for San Antonio, Houston, El Paso, Albuquerque and New Orleans.[43] Later, Castañeda became a Special Assistant to the Chairman for Latin American Problems for FEPC.[44]

Castañeda noted, "In the oil, aircraft and mining industries, in the numerous military installations, in the munitions [ammunitions] factories and shipyards, and in the public utility corporations, such as gas, light, and transportation companies, their employment has been limited and their opportunities for advancement restricted."[45] *LULAC News* reported specific incidents of employment discrimination in its November 1941 and January 1942 issues.[46]

Latino civil rights leaders from across the Southwest were involved in FEPC efforts. They included Eduardo Quevedo, Samuel Paz, Ignacio López and Dr. Ernesto Galarza of California.[47] The most important Latinos in this effort, however, were Dr. Carlos E. Castañeda, Perales, Dr. George I. Sánchez, and M.C. Gonzales in conjunction with Senator Dennis Chávez. According to historian Félix Almaráz, Sánchez informed many of the director positions and field investigators in Dallas, San Francisco and Denver though he did not inform Castañeda.[48]

FEPC created twelve regional offices to address workers' needs and scholars have shown that Tejanos and New Mexicans were better prepared, and more organized to address Latino workers' needs in their respective states. In California, Manuel Ruiz, Dr. Víctor Egas and Bert Corona argued their case but there FEPC mostly addressed African American needs even though the Latino population was larger.[49] In Texas, New Mexico and Louisiana 37% of the cases addressed Latinos while in California, Arizona and Nevada only 22% of the cases dealt with Latinos.[50] LULAC played a key role in Texas and New Mexico.

When World War II ended Latinos joined African Americans in arguing for a permanent FEPC. Historian Rosales noted that Perales corresponded with A. Phillip Randolph. He "sought to strategize with A. Phillip Randolph on how to pass the permanent FEPC bill by outlawing filibustering by opponents in Congress."[51] Perales stated, "A federal law is necessary in order to put an end to this painful situation immediately. The education program is useful, but it is very slow, and we have no time to lose."[52] Political scientist Gritter reported that Castañeda, Perales and past LULAC national president and educator George I. Sánchez "strung together a rationale for a permanent FEPC as it pertained specifically to people of Mexican origin" and that "committed civil rights leaders used available ideology to advance the interests and opportunities of their community."[53]

Perales testified before Congress at the Senate Education and Labor Committee on S.101 and S. 459 bills arguing for FEPC's extension. He said, "We, American citizens of Mexican extraction designated as Spanish-Americans, Latin-Americans, Mexican-Americans, some 3,000,000 in Texas and the Southwest find that our effort to eliminate discrimination by mutual cooperation and education have accomplished nothing. We are discriminated against more widely today than 24 years ago—socially, politically, economically, and educationally."[54] Perales also testified on March 12, 1945 along with Eduardo Quevado and Samuel Paz.[55] He also sent a statement or testified before the Senate Committee on Labor and Education on March 13, 1945; he said 10,000 were employed at Kelly Field, the San Antonio military base, but "our men of Mexican descent never could hold a position of a higher category than that of laborer or mechanic's helper."[56] Perales also wrote about Shell Oil Company's economic discrimination.[57]

Perales first contacted Senator Chávez in 1938 through a letter of introduction. Then in August 1944 Chávez wrote Perales as chair of the Committee of One Hundred, a spin-off of the Loyals, to endorse Senate Bill S2046 before his committee to argue for a permanent FEPC.[58] Chávez also sent the Committee of 100 a telegram asking for a representative to appear before an FEPC sub-committee on Sept. 6 or 7, 1944.[59]

But Southern Congressmen, Western Republicans and other racists prevented a permanent FEPC.[60] Chávez joined the coalition, the Committee for a Permanent FEPC (or National Council for a Permanent FEPC), as the only person from the Southwest but with a few New York Puerto Ricans.[61] US Senators Tom Connally and Pappy O'Daniel of Texas as well as Governor Coke Stevenson were against the FEPC.[62] Southerners said it constituted "invasion of states' rights and would increase racial tension."[63] Perales wrote about this unfortunate stop in racial and economic progress for La Raza in the *Pan-American*, a news magazine begun by LULACer Jacob Rodríguez of San Antonio.[64]

Some politicians, especially Southerners and including Congressman Maury Maverick worked against the FEPC, probably unbeknownst to Mexican-American civil rights activists. Maverick, Chief Bureau of Governmental Requirements of the War Production Board, Division of Industry Operations, wrote Lawrence W. Cramer, Executive Secretary, President's Committee on FEPC the following: ". . . there is little discrimination . . . there is no economic discrimination against Latin-Americans hardly anywhere in Texas. . . . All Mexican racial agitators, pretty near, are in San Antonio. You will find there

Mr. Alonzo Perales, a lawyer and agitator by trade, who will bellow that the Mexicans are badly treated. Most of his instances, however, will be that somebody didn't speak politely to a Mexican at a skating rink or something of that kind." Maverick also suggested Cramer speak to M.C. Gonzales of the Mexican consulate and Ignacio Lozano, the publisher of *La Prensa*, a well-educated and intelligent Mexican.[65] Maverick lied and/or saw the scenario through white eyes, aligning himself with racist practices, suggesting Texas did not need FEPC, and maligned Perales. He probably belittled Perales because Perales was a great "racial agitator" and did not support his mayoral race in the late 1930s. Moreover, Gonzales and Lozano, would have reported racism just like Perales. Maverick changed over time and became more liberal against segregation and supportive of workers' causes, including some of Perales' causes.

FEPC, though short-lived, benefitted working men and women of African American, Latino- and Native American-descent though not Asian Americans. Community organizations like LULAC—and not just individuals—made the FEPC's more successful. Gritter showed "striking contrast in terms of resources and positive outcomes for people of Mexican origin" and "how community-based leadership has the potential to produce results."[66] FEPC produced more and better results in Texas because LULAC supported it there. FEPC director Dr. Castañeda summed up FEPC success for Latino workers: "throughout Texas, New Mexico, and Louisiana the shipyard, the airship factories, the oil industry, the mines, the munition [ammunition] factories, and the numerous military and naval installations slowly, reluctantly, and with much misgivings, began to give the Mexican-American a trial in semiskilled positions, and eventually in some skilled jobs."[67] He reported that even some large scale farm employers improved opportunities for their workers.[68] The National Council for a Permanent FEPC told San Antonio people of color they "must revert to the old sub-standard wages and discriminatory practices in employment."[69] FEPC was a precursor to the Equal Employment Opportunity Commission (EEOC) established in 1964 as part of the Civil Rights Act of 1964. While FEPC did not address gender discrimination or sectors outside of government/government-contracted industries it claimed some victories.[70]

Anti-Discrimination Bills in the Texas Legislature

Perales and allies sought state legislation to end discriminatory practices in 1941, 1943 and 1945. They sought this in the context of the Good Neighbor policy during World War II when the United States was wary of "international ramifications of domestic race problems."[71] Perales felt education was too slow and legislation necessary. This was a new strategy away from the local level of appealing to local whites' goodwill to be more inclusive, a strategy with mixed success. Perales wrote, "The Congress of the United States and the Texas Legislature should each pass an Anti-Race Hatred Law similar to the one now in force in the State of New Jersey, making it unlawful for any person to incite racial prejudice, by word or deed, against members of the Caucasian Race."[72] He wrote in *La Prensa*: "What we urgently need in Texas is a law by the Texas Legislature or the U.S. Congress that prohibits the humiliation of Mexicans in public establishments like restaurants, theaters, pools, etc. and a good concentration camp to put away for the duration of the war all the owners of such businesses as fifth-columnists, saboteurs of President Roosevelt's Good Neighbor Policy, and traitors to the Nation."[73] San Antonio politician Paul Kilday told Perales that the US Congress did not have the power to make an anti-discrimination law and suggested he propose a draft and strategy for "ensuring its compliance with the constitution."[74]

So in 1941 Perales and M.C. Gonzales sought an anti-discrimination bill through the state legislature. They approached San Antonio state representative Fagan Dickson to introduce a Racial Equality bill, House Bill 909. It read, "All persons of the Caucasian Race within the jurisdiction of the State are entitled to the full and equal accommodations, advantages, facilities, and privileges of all public place of business or amusement."[75] The bill was met with "laughs, murmurs of disapproval, and a few shouts of dissent."[76] Dickson advised Perales to write Undersecretary of State Sumner Welles, Secretary of State Cordell Hull and President Franklin D. Roosevelt to write Texas house committee members.[77] The bill was not voted on and died.

In 1941 Perales wrote Castañeda, "We succeeded in getting a rider thru at the last session, and now we have to request the present Legislators to be on the lookout and be sure to include the rider again when the appropriate bill comes up for consideration. The matter of a 'broad law' is the thing to aim out, of course, but I believe it would be rather difficult to have it passed. The Legislators from the districts where we are not liked would oppose such a law, I believe, and after that they would be so alert on the subject that not even a rider could get by without strenuous objection on their part." [78] The bill failed. Perales asked the governor to introduce the bill with a special session to no avail.[79]

House Bill 68, 1943

In January 1943 San Antonian Pat Dwyer introduced House bill 68 in the Texas House and Clem Fain introduced Senate Bill 203, two other antidiscrimination bills. Perales, Gonzales, Castañeda and Sánchez wrote letters.[80] Perales asked Castañeda to get behind House Bill 68 as the newly appointed director of the Committee on Inter-American Affairs. Perales noted, ". . . we are up against a tough fight. It will not be as easy as we had thought."[81] Perales and Gonzales testified before the Senate State Affairs Committee.[82] While 68 and 203 were rejected, a concession was won with a resolution. The Caucasian Race-Equal Privilege resolution stated "all persons of the Caucasian Race" were "entitled to equal accommodations" in "all public places of business and amusement" and suggested violators were "violating the good neighbor policy of our State." [83] Perales was disappointed as noted in his letter to Castañeda: "All the [Texas legislature] . . . did was to pass a resolution stating that they disapproved of racial discrimination in Texas, or words to that effect. This means that we did not get the law we wanted and which our nation needs in order to unite the people of the Americas. Needless to say I feel very much discouraged."[84] In February 1944 the Fourth Court of Civil Appeals in Texas ruled that the resolution had no legal teeth.[85]

Consequently, the Mexican government decided to take decisive action. It banned *braceros* (temporary authorized Mexican immigrant workers) from Texas in June 1943. Governor Coke Stevenson decided to protect Texas agribusiness and announced the Good Neighbor Policy of Texas as a concession and in August 1943 he created the Texas Good Neighbor Commission with six board members, including a few Mexican-American men, to investigate discrimination. In 1944 Perales of the Committee of 100 informed President Franklin Delano Roosevelt, "For the past four years we have been asking the Texas Legislature to pass a law forbidding the humiliation of Mexicans and Hispanic peoples generally in this State, but it has absolutely refused to do so." Likewise, LULAC Council 2 organized a meeting with the Council of Pan American Relations, the Mexican Businessmen's Association, Confederación de Latino Americanos, the Order Sons of America, Club Democrático and Defensor de Los Obreros, and wrote a resolution asking Texas Governor Coke R. Stevenson to pass a law to protect "people of Mexican extraction, whether they be citizens of Mexico or native American."[86]

Senate Bill 1 (Spears Bill), 1945

In January 1945 Texas State Senator J. Franklin Spears of San Antonio introduced yet another antidiscrimination bill. In Mexico the Comité Mexicano Contra el Racismo, an anti-racist group, saw the bill as a "transcontinental step."[87] An incident in Pecos, Texas in West Texas also brought international attention to the problem when the head of Mexico's Congress was denied admittance into a local restaurant. Perales' Committee of One Hundred and Loyals expressed embarrassment noting that the incident should "make every right thinking and fair-minded American blush with shame" and push for the Spears bill.[88]

Perales went as far as trying to convince the German-American community of the necessity of supporting the Spears bill.[89] He appealed to their respect for US soldiers and stated, "The question is what are we willing to do for them?" with "them" being a reference to Latino soldiers.[90] He identified Seguin legislator R.A. Weinert and New Braunfels's Frank B. Voight as opponents distinguishing themselves with "anti-Mexicanism."[91] LULAC sent 500 letters to the Women's Federation Clubs of Texas and 500 letters to the American Legion posts as well. Still, their efforts fell on deaf ears and proved futile.[92]

When the Spears bill was rejected a San Antonio newspaper sarcastically wrote, "Chiefly, the bill is designed to aid and please Mexican-Americans."[93] This was white consensus at the time. After the Spears bill's defeat, Perales said La Raza would have to wait until "the bad Texans are educated." And he also chastised Mexico, "the day that

Mexico decides to take the necessary action towards that end."[94] He did not hold his breath. Mexico also had little power over the United States though students at Puebla University protested the admission of US students into their college.[95] Despite legislative failure throughout the 1940s, Perales continued to fight for anti-racist legislation through his writing and correspondence.[96]

Pan American Optimist Club

Despite these setbacks, Perales continued to work at the local level. Without Perales as a member, LULAC continued to play an important role in San Antonio. In 1948 it ran a weekly radio program called "LULACs on the March."[97] In the 40s Perales was still involved with the Loyals. Besides the significant work Perales did in numerous organizations, two other groups he joined in the 1940s were the Pan American Progressive Association (PAPA) and the Pan American Optimist Club. Several other political organizations emerged in the 40s including the Fraternal Union of San Antonio, the Democratic Club-Fraternal Union and the Independent West Side Democratic Society of Bexar County.[98] The Centro Cívico Social, mostly focused on school facilities, was also formed in 1947.[99]

By 1943 there were enough middle-class businessmen that La Raza could exercise its civic virtue by uplifting others with charity through an Optimist Club. Optimism was its guiding philosophy but it promoted interest in "good government and civic affairs," patriotism, international friendship and global youth development.[100] While Euro-Texan Optimists members numbered 150 in San Antonio in the late 40s the Latin American Optimists had twenty members.[101] In February 1949 Perales invited Dr. Héctor Urrutia, Dr. Eduardo T. Jiménez, Dr. Juan Rivero, Dr. Leopoldo Lemus and Mr. Frank Gonzalez, all men, to join.[102] Meetings were held at the upscale Gunter Hotel.

In 1948 Perales presided over the Pan American Optimist Club.[103] Sociologist Sister Frances Woods who studied San Antonio ethnic leadership in the late 1940s considered the Optimists "the outstanding association with a single ethnic purpose" describing it as "primarily a business and social organization with a subsidiary welfare purpose-

'helping the boys.'"[104] Given its wealthier business and professional membership, the organization gave scholarships to Latino youth, purchased a tractor for the county home for boys and sponsored athletics and lectures. It sent 100 boys to camp at Kerrville one year, financed trips for Boy Scouts and donated to athletic events.[105] In 1947 it sent the Boy Scouts to Mexico City.[106] The Optimists helped boys more than girls. They played baseball with LULAC Council 2 with LULAC earning $900.[107] The organization also sponsored a Fiesta de la Raza at the Municipal Auditorium celebrating Columbus Day (*Día de la Raza*).[108] Optimists invited Castañeda to speak at its "Fiesta de la Raza."[109]

Like Perales, the Optimists were do-gooders. In 1948 it gave three university scholarships for students to attend Trinity University.[110] Funds were also given to the San Antonio Transit Company for a bus for underprivileged children at Collier School. A LULAC-Optimist baseball game earned $1651 and a 1949 financial statement showed $1733 from the LULAC v. Optimists game while $50 was donated for lighting for the House of Neighborly Service; $150 for furniture for the Newman Club, a Catholic group; San Fernando Cathedral gym, $215; and Christmas baskets for ninety-six "Poor Families."[111] Optimists also participated in a bike safety campaign on the radio.[112] Though Perales passed in 1960, in 1968 the Pan American Optimists were still involved in charity work and helped youth and community projects.[113]

Conclusion

World War II created both new opportunities and obstacles for Latinos and Perales. Perales sought high-level employment during World War II but was ignored and blocked because he was Latino and considered an agitator. Perales could have focused on his own upward mobility but spent little time on this effort. The war led to the arrival of thousands of Mexican *braceros* into Texas and the nation. Perales worked with LULAC and others to ban *braceros* into racist Texas towns because of low wages, racism and displacement of Tejano workers.

At the national level Perales saw the opportunity to support efforts by a federal agency banning employment discrimination against Mexican-descent people and Latinos. He cooperated with US Senator Dennis Chávez and Dr. Carlos E. Castañeda to work with the Federal Employment Practices Commission (FEPC) to promote Latino workers, especially men, in defense industry jobs. He testified before Congress reporting dual wages, lack of promotion opportunity and argued for a permanent FEPC agency. Later twenty-nine states passed fair employment legislation though Texas did not. In the 1960s, the Civil Rights Act of 1964 enacted FEPC's goal ending race discrimination in the workplace and institutionalizing the Equal Opportunity Commission.

At the state level Perales worked with other allies on several legislative bills to seek a Texas statewide antidiscrimination bill prohibiting discrimination against Latinos and the Texas Good Neighbor Commission (GNC) was created as a result. Realizing the political and financial weakness of the GNC, Perales also utilized affidavits by La Raza to the GNC. He and M.C. Gonzales forwarded these affidavits to the US State Department, thereby making them federal and therefore international complaints when made by Mexican citizens in the United States. Thus, he made racism an international affair with Mexico. This strategy helped to ban *braceros* coming into Texas temporarily.

Continuing his work at the local level, Perales also presided over the Pan American Optimist Club, another male club. Attending these meetings were likely a relief for Perales since its charitable projects benefitted the less privileged, especially Latino boys; they were less focused on uplifting young girls. The Optimists dealt with poverty resulting from racism and classism and allowed Perales and his comrades to help poor Raza directly. As a Christian, Perales could see and feel the immediate results of this charity. It took civic, political and financial muscle and effort by individuals to change the status of La Raza. Perales recognized that the problems of Latinos existed at all levels—international, national, state and local—and could be remedied; no effort was too small. Perales' belief in change permitted him to build a better future.

CHAPTER 13
Activist, 1950s

The 1950s saw Alonso S. Perales slow down due to his health and the adoption of three children. Perales had high blood pressure at least since 1942. The decade saw the continuation of racial segregation though important victories in school desegregation had been won. In employment, the 1950s witnessed the Bracero Program permitting exploitation of Mexican workers until 1964. In education, more Mexican Americans were graduating from high school and World War II veterans could now attend college for free. And in politics, more Mexican Americans were voting and a few more Mexican-American men were elected to office.

By the 1950s major Mexican-American civic organizations in San Antonio included LULAC, the American GI Forum (AGIF), Mexican Chamber of Commerce, School Improvement League (SIL), Pan American Progressive Association and Pan American Optimist Club.[1] Mexican organizations also existed such as the Sector Popular Cívico Mexicano, Agrupación de Ciudadanos en el Extranjero (ACME) and some *mutualistas*.[2] Women continued to belong to homosocial organizations like Ladies LULAC and women's clubs. Perales was not a member of LULAC, AGIF or SIL in the 1950s. His activism this decade intermixed with familiar organizations as well as several new local, state and national associations.

This chapter first looks at Perales' support of Henry B. González of San Antonio to the Texas legislature. Second, it focuses on his work for Spears bill, yet another Texas antidiscrimination attempt. Third, it covers his denouncement of a scholarly book about "wetbacks" he deemed racist and investigates his orchestration of a conference against the book in Mission, Texas. Fourth, it shows his support of the *Hernandez vs. State of Texas* case decided at the Supreme Court in 1954. Fifth, it covers Spain's acknowledgement of Perales' lifetime work through a prestigious award as well as his award from the University of Texas at Austin Latino student group, the Alba Club. Finally, it describes Perales' likely influence on Carlos Cansino of San Antonio who made an impact in the late 60s and 70s during the Chicano Movement. The Chicano Movement followed the Mexican-American civil rights movement that Perales helped to initiate in the 1920s; the Chicano Movement existed from 1963 to the late 1970s across the United States.

Support for Henry B. González

After World War II more Mexican Americans continued to organize in partisan ways, run for office and vote for Mexican-American candidates or candidates they believed pro-Raza. San Antonio saw the rise of the Loyal American Democrats, the Alamo Democrats and the West Side Voters League.[3] By 1948 attorney Gus Garcia had been elected to the school board and Mexican Americans in San Antonio gained more hope. García was the first on the school board but there were no Mexican Americans on city council. He followed Perales' unsuccessful attempt and probably Mexican Americans' realization that with more of their votes, a Mexican American could win in San Antonio.

In the 1950s several Mexican-American men ran for the state legislature. Before the 1950s only a few Mexican-Americans had served in the state legislature in the twentieth century: J.T. Canales, Carlos Bee (1915-1918) and Augustine Celaya (1933-1947).[4] Carlos Bee was born in Mexico and moved to San Antonio when he was five. It is unclear if he considered himself a Mexican American or could speak Spanish or aligned himself with La Raza. Celaya represented Cameron County (Brownsville) in the Texas legislature for several terms before an unsuccessful run for Congress.[5] In the 50s three attorneys, Henry B. González and Albert Peña Jr. of San Antonio and John

J. Herrera of Houston ran for the Texas legislature as did educator and LULAC-member Edmundo Mireles of Corpus, Raymond Donley of Austin and Ramón Guerra of McAllen.[6] Only González won. González was yet another person that Perales influenced and would not only become a Texas legislator but a US Congressman in the mid-60s.[7] Leonidas González, a past mayor in Mexico, an employee of *La Prensa* and Perales' friend, approached Perales after his son Henry "had been going all over town seeking employment." Perales "immediately got on the telephone and obtained an interview for him."[8]

Years later in 1950 Perales supported González for the state legislature. He sent out postcards to "Muy estimado amigo" (My dear friend) asking for a $10 donation.[9] Attorney Charles Albidress Jr., son of activist Charles, responded to his compadre with "I wish you lots of success in your fund raising."[10] A document also reads "Meeting of Business Men's Club for Henry Gonzales" with Albert Peña Jr. and Gus Garcia also present.[11] Perales was also heard on KIWW radio station proclaiming, "Not a single Mexican American should fail to vote for Henry B. González for the Texas legislature."[12] He said, "Siendo así es muy justo y muy necesario que tengamos Legisladores de linaje mexicano en dicha Legislatura, ya que siendo de nuestra estrirpe racial pondrán más empeño y se interesan más en que se hagan leyes que beneficien a TODOS los habitantes del Estado."[13] Perales' papers also include a list of contributors to the González campaign; a list of persons to whom postcards were sent including medical doctors; and another list of Latinos with phone numbers, likely voters.[14]

Mexican Americans who were Democrats forged the Loyal American Democrats in the city in 1952 in which Rómulo Munguía, Lalo Solís (brother of John Solís) and Peña Jr. played prominent roles. The white-controlled Good Government League (GGL) dominated San Antonio politics from 1954 to 1971. It included a committee of Mexican-descent people which operated as a West side GGL coalition of businessmen and professionals though associated with stockbroker Alfredo Vásquez originally of El Paso. They selected José Olivares for city council in 1955. Three Mexican Americans won city offices by 1956.[15] GGL worked against Henry B. González for Congress in 1961.[16]

The election of González as a state senator to the Texas legislature signaled a new day, one that Perales had sought for Mexican Americans since the 1920s. Perales wrote Carlos E. Castañeda, "P.S. I too am delighted that Henry Gonzalez was elected State Senator. Our golden dreams are beginning to become a reality, thanks to God."[17] A year later in 1957 Castañeda wrote Canales a similar note about Perales and González; he wrote, "Your work and that of Perales and other pioneers in behalf of equal rights for all have borne fruit and demonstrated by the brilliant filibuster staged by Henry B. González and Kazen. There are many other signs today that shows that our labors designed to train and give an opportunity to the best element of our Latin Americans were not in vain."[18]

González was the first Tejano state senator. "Kika" de la Garza of the Valley would join him in 1964. González would later become a US Congressman joining Antonio Fernández (1943-1957) and Joseph Montoya (1957-77) of New Mexico and Edward Roybal (1963-75) of California, the only Latinos in Congress before 1960 and in the 20th century. (Though Octavio Larrazolo originally of Mexico did serve in Congress representing New Mexico in the 1910s; and Dennis Chávez died in 1962.) González would protest the poll tax in Congress in 1964.[19] Times had changed; the days of no Tejanos on the San Antonio city council and in the Texas state legislature were over. Later, González starkly criticized the Chicano Movement organization Mexican American Youth Organization (MAYO), which he believed radical in post-60s era.[20]

Spears Bill, 1951

The 1940s saw no success by Mexican-American activists in getting the white state legislature to pass a Texas antidiscrimination bill in 1941, 1943 and 1945. By 1951 another bill was in the works, this one introduced by Texas State Senator J. Franklin Spears and which referred to "Mexican or Latin-American origin" and economic discrimination.[21] Perales wrote Dr. Castañeda, "Messrs. Gus Garcia, Carlos Cadena, and I got together and went over the Spears bill carefully and made some slight changes. The only major change was with reference to the peñalty. This time, instead of providing for a fine or a jail sentence, we decided to insert a civil damages clause to see if it would be easier to LULAC." He added, "If they approve [,] the Bill will be submitted in both houses at the request of both Organizations."[22] The organizations were LULAC and the American GI Forum.[23] Even though Perales was not a member of LULAC he continued to conduct its business. This bill did not pass and in 1951 there was not a single Mexican American, African American or person of color in the Texas state legislature—white racists were still the majority.

"Wetback" Pamphlet, 1951-52

A controversy started when Dr. George I. Sánchez commissioned a study by academics Lyle Saunders and Olen Leonard on unauthorized Mexican immigrants in the Lower Rio Grande Valley of Texas. The immigrants were not *braceros*.[24] In the early 50s a group of Mexican workers entered the United States without permission—this group was called "wetbacks," a derogatory name referring to immigrants crossing the Rio Grande River. The study was based on numerous sources including anonymous interviews. The title alone was racist though few protested the moniker.

The pamphlet—while not quite a book, it was larger than a booklet and critics referred to it as a "pamphlet"—infuriated Perales. He was upset at the racist stereotypes of the Mexican-descent people interviewees used. He had already spent three decades fighting against racialization. He wrote Dr. Sánchez, "The statements are unfair because they are untrue and cowardly because the names and addresses of the informants were not given. In my name and in the name of all my friends from the Lower Rio Grande Valley, we hereby demand that you finish [furnish] us at once the names and addresses of each and everyone [sic] of the persons quoted on pages 65-88 of said pamphlet."[24] Sánchez was irked at Perales' demand and responded with a curt letter. Canales wrote Perales on the issue on November 28, 1951: "heaps of insults were directed at us Americans of Mexican descent (at the Valley residents, particularly, but they hurt us all). Why did Dr. Sánchez approve of the publication of such tripe? Could it be because Dr. Sánchez felt that since the ones defamed and libeled were Mexican-Americans from Texas it did not affect him since he comes from New Mexico. Had I been in his shoes, I would have said, 'Go ahead and say what you will about the wetback, but leave out the Americans and permanent residents of Mexican descent.'"[25]

Canales sided with Perales and J. Luz Sáenz on this issue. In a letter, Perales said, "I resent this and I told Dr. Sánchez personally in Austin last July. Dr. Sánchez has acted very unwisely, to say the least. I am afraid that our mutual friend, Gus Garcia, has been contaminated by Dr. Sánchez. Keep this confidential but with your eyes open."[26]

Attorney Gus Garcia sided with Dr. Sánchez over the pamphlet. On December 6, 1951 García wrote Perales defending the publication, "I do not agree with you when you say that is cowardly because the authors do not give a source of quotes. If you will look into the ethics of social researchers you will learn that they, like us lawyers, have certain restrictions placed upon divulging information as to sources of material."[27]

On December 8, 1951 before the Forum's Texas state convention took place, Perales wrote Dr. Héctor García of the AGIF, "I sincerely hope also that your Organization will not, under any circumstances, give anyone a clean bill or OK in connection with the preparation and publication of said pamphlet. To do so would be to amount to placing the stamp of approval upon the utterance of those who stated in the pamphlet that nearly all Mexicans (regardless of citizenship and length of residence in the Valley) have syphilis, lice and are stupid and cowards. Sánchez never should have approved the pamphlet much less made possible its publication . . . it will place the Forum in a very bad light."[28] But the Texas AGIF approved the publication anyway.

On December 11, 1951 Perales was looking for litigants to file a lawsuit. He wrote Sáenz, "If 6 or 12 men of our race from the Valley would tighten their pants, they could file a lawsuit for half a million dollars for damages and harm against the University of Texas."[29] *La Verdad*'s editor Santos de la Paz of Corpus Christi released headlines attacking the pamphlet. He suggested "it was strictly written for Anglos" and that "the recipients were meticously [meticulously] selected" and that it reeked of communism.[30] De la Paz wrote that the public should be "asking [for] the immediate destitution of Sánchez from the University of Texas and from the state of Texas."[31] No one stepped forward and the idea of the lawsuit was dropped. In January 1952 National LULAC president George Garza wrote Sánchez, "We have heard by way of the 'grapevine' that some pressure was being brought to bear against you in connection with the release for publication of the information contained in the pamphlet . . ."[32] This threat explains Sánchez' failure to remain Perales' ally. Perales should not have suggested a possible lawsuit against the university because Sánchez might have lost his job and he was a national asset for Latinos. Perales also considered suing the University of Texas for libel.[33]

Canales also believed Dr. Sánchez wrong. He wrote nephew Dr. Hesiquio N. Gonzales of Houston, "If the people in San Antonio think that we have no right to criticize Dr. Sánchez when he does wrong, then there is no democracy in our organization and he is not considered a human being, but a god, and we do not entertain any such views of any human being! Dr. Sánchez never consulted us, or any of his friends, when he approved the Wetback pamphlet, unconditionally, and neither did the GI Forum, nor the LULAC Regional Convention."[34] The AGIF and the Texas Regional convention of LULAC held in Galveston on January 25-26 had approved the pamphlet.

The publication of this book with racist commentary changed Perales' future opportunities because he broke ties to activist Dr. George I. Sánchez. Perales distanced himself from him, becoming permanent adversaries, and shutting the door to all the national activities with which Sánchez was associated. Sánchez also disassociated himself from Perales; there is no evidence that the two worked together again. Perales also stopped working with Dr. Héctor P. García, major leader of the AGIF who supported Sánchez, and attorney Gus García. It did not help that a regional Texas LULAC convention also sided with Sánchez and that National LULAC president George Garza (1950-1952) was a student of Dr. Sánchez.

Response to the "Wetback" Pamphlet: Latin American Conference in Mission, Texas, 1952

On February 22, 1952 *La Verdad* condemned the publication paid for by University of Texas funds and, thus, taxpayers.[35] On March 9, 1952 a conference at Mission in the Valley was organized to respond to the pamphlet. While it is not clear who called it, Perales orchestrated some of the events from afar and in advance although he did not attend[36] possibly because he would have been called an outsider. This, too, was strategic to mask his role and enhance the appearance of the event as an enraged grassroots effort.

The public was invited to condemn the pamphlet. Santos de la Paz of *La Verdad* told Perales about Soledad T. Hernández, a woman who wanted to attend and visit radio stations to encourage others to go to the conference.[37] De la Paz told Sáenz that Hernández should contact Adela Sloss-Vento and Sra. Santos V. Lozano of Raymondville, Perales' sister-in-law to encourage women to talk about it with other women.

Perales also wrote Sloss-Vento, "I am not going . . . I think that the meeting should be the people from the Valley and no one else with the exception of Mr. De La Paz who should help under all circumstances . . . so they don't say we were were agitating from outside . . . My wish is that you, Prof. Sáenz and Mr. De La Paz work in perfect harmony before, during, and after the meeting.[38] In Perales' style he told others what to do. He also wrote Sáenz recommending, "Don't allow debates and don't let those from San Antonio and Corpus (the enemy camp) take the baton. Don't even let those speak. It would not surprise me if they brought Gus and others to spoil the meeting. . . . Don't allow debates over the pamphlet."[39] This attempt to silence was undemocratic on Perales' part. It was yet another example of his attempt to orchestrate a desired outcome.

The press was informed of the conference and journalists attended. We can be sure that Perales approached the press before the event because a pre-conference article referred to Perales as a knight (*paladín*).[40] Moreover, Perales made strategic contact beforehand with conference speakers including Canales, Sáenz and Dr. Castañeda. On May 1952 Perales wrote about Castañeda's speech there.[41] Sloss-Vento was either not invited to speak or declined the offer so she could record the event. She audio-taped the proceedings and gave them to Canales because they are now located in the Canales Papers at Texas A&M University in Kingsville. She was also likely the person who photographed the event; photos can be found in the Sáenz and Canales collections.

A conference report was written. The Committee report was signed by Santos de la Paz, chair and committee members Roberto E. Austin, Luis Alvarado and O.T. Salinas.[42] Austin was Perales' friend and Alvarado was J. Luz Sáenz' son-in-law. However, it is most likely that the report was written by Perales because he wrote Sáenz, "The authors of the resolutions are you and De La Paz. OK."[43] But Sáenz probably decided against this because his name failed to appear on the report. More evidence that it was Perales behind the conference report is a document in his papers called "Draft of Resolution Adopted by Leaders of the Latin American Citizenry of the Lower Rio Grande Valley" with some of his handwriting.[44]

A year after the conference, conflict between Perales and Dr. Sánchez over the pamphlet continued. In 1953 state legislator/ex-mayor Maury Maverick of San Antonio called a meeting of leaders Dr. Sánchez, Dr. Garcia, attorney/professor Carlos Cadena, attorney Gus Garcia, attorney M.C. Gonzales and Perales to discuss another anti-discrimination bill. Perales and Sánchez were still not speaking to one another. Maverick wrote Sánchez: "And if you don't meet with Alonzo (sic) Perales I am going to have you shot without right of trial by jury. This is the 'acid' test of friendship."[45] It is unknown if either or both attended—their alliance was over.

American Council on Spanish-Speaking Persons, 1941-1958, a Missed Opportunity for Perales

Despite some advances in the 1940s, by the 1950s not that much had changed for people of Mexican descent at the national level. According to historian Ignacio M. García there was not yet a "national voice," little "transcendence of regions and localities" and no head-quarters, funds and national magazine.[46]

Yet, there was one new national organization which waged new important and successful civil rights efforts not mentioned by García: the American Council of Spanish-Speaking Persons (ACSSP). The organization was largely the mastermind of Sánchez.

Indeed, in 1941 Dr. George I. Sánchez received significant funding from the Bunns, the first infusion of funding from white liberals. Scholar Nancy MacLean noted, "Where whites recognized the plight of Mexican America at all, they tended to treat it as a regional rather than a national concern, and one of little importance to others. Mexican Americans had no civil rights analogous to the NAACP supported by white liberals, or the Urban League funded by corporate contributions."[47] With these new funds, in 1943 Sánchez asked M.C. Gonzales to write hypothetical briefs on school segregation, real estate clauses, white man's primary and jury membership but sought to include Perales as well. He wrote, "I suggest that you may want to join with Mr. Perales in planning and writing these briefs."[48] Roger Baldwin of the American Civil Liberties Union (ACLU) also had ties with Dr. Sánchez and M.C. Gonzales but Perales was outside of this circle.[49]

Dr. Sánchez had considerable success in accessing funds which most Latinos would not begin to access until the late 60s and 70s. Sánchez worked with the liberal Robert C. Marshall Trust Fund of New York to fund national Latino efforts at racial justice. Its goal was to empower Mexican-descent peoples, Puerto Ricans and other Latinos. In 1952 Robert Baldwin, chair of the ACLU, contacted academic Lyle Saunders in New Mexico of the "Wetback" pamphlet fame and Saunders contacted Sánchez. The latter then organized a conference in El Paso, Texas.

The new organization received $53,000 over four years. It cooperated with LULAC in Texas; the Alianza Hispano Americana and Community Service Organization in Arizona; Community Councils in Colorado; and the Mexican American Council of Chicago.[50] The Sánchez-driven ACCSP proved to be important on the regional and national level though it did not include Perales. My *New Handbook of*

Texas article reported: "ACSPP gave grants-in-aid to fund specific cases, including a segregation case in Glendale, Arizona; Hernández v. State of Texas; the Anthony Ríos police brutality case in Los Angeles; the Robert Galvan alleged Communist alien deportation case in California; and the Winslow, Arizona swimming pool desegregation case." In Texas it helped desegregate Austin and Houston public housing and tended to school desegregation in Nixon, Carrizo Springs, Mathis and Driscoll.[51]

Numerous attorneys worked with the ACCSP but not Perales. These included Gus Garcia, M.C. Gonzales, Carlos Cadena, as well as John J. Herrera, Chris Alderete, James DeAnda, Albert Peña Jr., Richard M. Casillas, Carlos Castillón and A.L. Wirin of the Los Angeles ACLU.

Perales was not invited to participate in ACSSP efforts because of the Sánchez rift. Perales told Dr. Castañeda, "I see where Sánchez is the big shot of the American Council of Spanish-speaking people . . . Gustavo is general counsel . . . Those two always move together and with the eye on the ball."[52] He also publicly criticized Sánchez and the ACSSP for seeking $5 contributions suggesting that the monies might be used to finance copies of the Wetback pamphlet.[53] In my opinion, this was a cheap shot.

The ACSSP was largely funded by white liberals; Latinos were charged to financially sustain the ACSPP but did not do so or were unable to do so. Although one historian called it "left-leaning," its ideology and tactics were the same as LULAC's and Perales'.[54] Its office closed in 1956 and the association died by 1958.

Anglo-Latin Good Relations Committee

In the early 1950s Mexican American leaders were frustrated with the lack of success of the Texas Good Neighbor Commission addressed in Chapter 12 so they created the Human Relations Council (HRC). But by July 1951 Canales noted that HRC lacked funds to accomplish its goals.[55] That month Perales told Dr. Castañeda that Canales was forming yet another new organization in Alice. Perales said so approvingly, noting "it seems to me that the formation of a new organization is in order."[56] This was his way of lamenting the

HRC's failure as well as slighting LULAC and the AGIF, both of with which he was disappointed due to the Wetback pamphlet. Canales called Mexican-American leaders together on July 29, 1951 in Corpus Christi.

The HRC, the Texas Pro-Human Relations Fund Committee and the Latin American Convention of South Texas (the Mission conference leaders) merged on May 4, 1952.[57] Another name batted around was the Anglo-Latin Good Relations Committee.[58] Canales suggested to nephew Dr. Hesiquio N. González that Castañeda, Perales or Sáenz become the new chair.[59] But it appears that this suggestion for leadership was not heeded or possible; elder statesmen Castañeda, Perales and Sáenz wanted other new leaders.

Canales called for "modern progress" and the organizing group seems to have included Canales, Castañeda, Louis Wilmot of Corpus Christi LULAC, Ed Idar Jr. and Dr. Héctor P. García. (Wilmot had been with LULAC since the 1920s; Ed Idar Jr. was the son of Eduardo Idar, LULAC founder, AGIF leader and Sánchez ally.) Dr. Sánchez was probably not invited and Perales did not attend. Its goals were vague except uplifting of "Citizens of Latin American extraction of Texas."[60] Canales believed civil rights cases funding needs in Texas were imminent.

Canales was elected conference chair and he invited attorney Gus Garcia to provide the keynote. Garcia suggested there were already too many organizations but went on to say "many of whose leaders have grown indolent and sedentary—who assume stuffy poses and bask in the glory of lofty title, while the world around their ivory towers is on fire . . . I believe that it is high time you and I assumed our full responsibility. . . ."[61] These leaders conveniently went unnamed. Was this an attack on Perales? Perales was never an "ivory tower" resident—he had been in the political trenches since 1919. And one could argue that Garcia, an alcoholic and spendthrift, himself did not assume "full responsibility."

The Anglo-Latin Good Relations Committee's aims and purposes were threefold addressing better understanding; improving welfare of Mexican-descent citizens and residents; and providing financial aid for any organization or group of "citizens for defense and protection of the const. rights of all Americans."[62] The resulting organization's leadership included Dr. Hesquio González, Canales' nephew. But by the end of the year the association fell apart. Perhaps González lacked leadership skills or maybe the civic-minded Raza public believed LULAC and AGIF's efforts were being duplicated. Homosociality still prevented men from tapping into female leadership. So, another attempt died; LULAC and the AGIF continued; and Perales continued on his own path. One historian suggested this new organization was an attempt by LULAC leaders Canales, Sáenz and Perales to control civil rights activism.[63] But they were no longer LULAC members and simply tried new organizations, rejecting racism and acquiescence, and as now elders, obsolescence.[64] Nor was theirs an attempt to "rein in younger activists who had advocated liberal and sometimes confrontational strategies for success."[65] These elders continued to stand for social justice for La Raza.

The Hernández case at the US Supreme Court, 1954

In the early 1950s a major Texas case developed into a Supreme Court Case for which Perales played a minor role. And as will be shown in chapter 14, Cadena and lawyer Garcia were protégés of Perales.[66] Attorneys Carlos Cadena, Gus Garcia and John J. Herrera worked the case. According to Perales' daughter Marta, Perales and Canales wrote the briefs while historian Ignacio M. García credits Cadena with writing the briefs and Cadena and Gus Garcia making the opening arguments.[67] Cadena said he wrote the briefs.[68]

Numerous entities contributed funds including the ACSSP, LULAC and AGIF. According to historian Mario T. García some $3,000 was raised.[69] Cadena and Perales communicated about Canales' $900-check for Cadena and the case.[70] In 1991 Cadena recalled that LULAC Council 2 donated $900 for court costs and that he earned about $700 for his work. Cadena also noted, "And we collected $50 from Joe, and $25.00 from Pete . . ." suggesting everyday persons also contributed.[71] According to another source "San Antonio LULAC", likely Council 2 and the Ladies LULAC or male LULAC members' wives, held a tamalada with dancer Irma Rodríguez performing, Sylvia Acosta singing, and the Eugene Nolasco orchestra playing. Reportedly then LULAC and the Texas GI Forum raised $1,236 for the case.[72]

Accolades from Spain's Government and the University of Texas Austin Alba Club, 1952

Into the fourth decade of his activism, Perales received two significant awards from Spain as well as one from the Alba Club of the University of Texas at Austin, a Latino student group composed mostly of male veterans and some women.[73] Its sponsors were Drs. Sánchez and Castañeda and each year they honored a respected community member. Its awardees included Gus Garcia in 1952.

The event was held at Our Lady of the Lake University, a Catholic university in San Antonio, where wife Marta obtained her Bachelor of Arts. Perales wrote Sáenz, "Thanks to God that someone (even if far in Spain) had a kind word for those like you and I who have spent/wasted our lives combating injustices they have committed and keep committing against our Raza."[74] Perales knew it was not a waste. The *Revista Latino-Americana* of Mission, Texas edited by Gilberto Díaz devoted an entire issue to Perales' award including essays by Sáenz and Sloss-Vento.[75] Elisa G. de Longoria wrote Perales to congratulate him noting "as always you are our knight and liberator."[76] Unfortunately, Canales and Sloss-Vento could not attend.[77] Canales noted, "I regretted very much not to be in San Antonio to contribute with my presence to honor our mutual friend Perales. He certainly deserved the honor bestowed upon him and I wrote him a personal letter."[78] Perales also received a medal of rank of commander of the Spanish Order of Civil Merit from the Instituto de Cultural Hispánica de Madrid as a titular member on October 12, 1952.[79]

Influencing Carlos Cansino and his Impact on the Chicano Movement in New Mexico and the Midwest

Perales had an indirect influence on others including Carlos Cansino of San Antonio who became a Chicano militant in the 1960s.

Cansino had an erratic career-path and erratic educational path but was imbued with the spirit of Perales' resistance and brought new Chicano movement tactics to Mexican Americanism in Albuquerque, New Mexico.

Cansino, born in 1931, was a migrant worker and a combat medic in the Korea War.[80] He attended Fox Tech in 1953 and St. Mary's University in San Antonio and was active with the Catholic Youth Organization in 1953. He became a teacher at Edgewood School in San Antonio. When he studied at the University of New Mexico in Albuquerque as an older student in the 1990s he told me he admired Perales who he knew about while living in San Antonio. He moved to New Mexico and then worked at Sandia Base Hospital in Albuquerque. Later he worked in Kentucky and Germany.

In the mid-60s Cansino returned to Los Duranes, an Albuquerque barrio where he became president of Los Duranes Improvement Association. The association "carried signs asking for a new school, a better library, a new Spanish-speaking principal, a Head Start kindergarten program and a better school." When he moved back to San Antonio in 1969, he made a fiery speech at the Alamo on April 26. He also established *El Papel*, a Chicano newspaper. In 1975 he supervised migrant farmworkers at the Green Giant Canning Company in Montgomery, Minnesota. Worker demands there included meal tickets for each day not worked, a forty-hour work week, and immediate payment for transportation costs.

Cansino also made an impact in a school walkout at Washington Middle School in Albuquerque. They gave the school seventeen demands including "teachers who demonstrate prejudice against Mexican-Americans or Negroes will be fired;" "We demand a REAL bi-lingual, bicultural education"; "We demand a textbook and curriculum changes-to place emphasis on Mexican-American history [and] culture."[81] He was also familiar with the activities of the Alianza Mercedes which sought the return of Spanish/Mexican land grants to Hispanos of New Mexico.[82]

Cansino reported his guiding principles:

Know yourself and your forefathers, your history, and be proud that you are of Mexican descent.
Learn both good Spanish and good English.
Learn all you can about and from the gringo so you can beat him at his own game: competition.
Strive for equal position and pay with the gringo and take no less.
Strive for the unity of the Mexican and Spanish American in all the Southwest.
Do not criticize your own people, but direct criticisms or hostility where it should go in a positive and constructive way at the Anglo-Saxon.
Do not forget your people when you are emancipated financially; remember you are one of them.
Education is the key to success.[83]

These principles were based on the LULAC code written by Eduardo Idar. Cansino added "gringo" and "Spanish-American" popular in New Mexico but these principles were the same. The goals of Eduardo Idar, Perales, and Cansino were similar: Mexican American/Chicano empowerment.

Conclusion

Perales had numerous disappointments in the 1950s including: failure to obtain a state antidiscrimination law, the publication of a book he deemed racist but sanctioned by Dr. George I. Sánchez and lack of success in another statewide organization attempt (Anglo-Latin Good Relations Committee) outside of LULAC and the American GI Forum. Perales felt like the Wetback pamphlet re-inscribed the racial script of the "Mexican problem" that had existed since the 1920s. He and Dr. Sánchez developed a permanent rift so Perales was left out of Sánchez's national efforts with the American Council of

Spanish-Speaking Persons which proved successful in legal antidis-crimination work. Perales' health declined, his friend J. Luz Sáenz died and his best friend Dr. Carlos E. Castañeda also passed in 1958. But Perales also had reason to be pleased. On the national level the *Brown v. Topeka* school desegregation lawsuit was a victory not just for African Americans but also for La Raza. In Texas he saw schools like Mathis, Texas desegregated; he saw La Raza protest a book; he learned of ACSSP's victories; and he witnessed the election of Henry B. González to the Texas legislature, the first Mexican American there in over a decade. Moreover, the city of San Antonio passed a desegregation ordinance of city facilities.[84] He was also con-nected to the Carlos Cadena/Gus Garcia/John J. Herrera/LULAC and Forum victory at the Supreme Court. In his personal life he was like-ly happy with the addition of children to his family.

Most of Perales' efforts in this decade were at the local level. While he played an active role in the South Texas conference denouncing the "Wetback pamphlet," he did not take leadership of several emerging Texas organizations. Perales' foundational work in the 1950s had a lasting impact in creating the conditions which could allow for the Chicano movement which would emerge in Texas in 1963. Perales also influenced Carlos Cansino who became a figure of the Chicano movement in Albuquerque, New Mexico and in the Mid-west in the 60s and 70s.

Perales received recognition of his lifetime service in the 50s. These included awards from the Spanish government, the Spanish Institute and UT Austin's Alba Club. While racism and oppression were still the norm in the 1950s, there was a difference between 1950 and 1959. He witnessed progress and that is why in his February 1960 photo at the San Antonio anniversary event of LULAC's founding nearly forty years later, Perales was smiling.

PART II
Public Impact

CHAPTER 14
Attorney

This chapter surveys Alonso S. Perales' activities and activism as a lawyer across the decades. First, it covers his legal training. Second, it addresses his employment and private law practice from the mid-20s to 1960. Third, key legal cases in which he participated are discussed. Finally, it describes his mentorship and influence over younger Mexican-American lawyers Henry B. González, Gus Garcia and Carlos Cadena, all who became central to San Antonio politics. González became a US Congressman, García became the first Mexican American on the San Antonio school board and Cadena became an important lawyer arguing three cases before the Supreme Court. Perales also influenced Albert Peña Jr. of San Antonio who became the first Bexar County commissioner. He also mentored teenager Vilma Martínez, who became an attorney after Perales' death and is associated with women's rights and the Chicano movement of the post-1963 era. She joined the Mexican American Legal Defense Fund (MALDEF) and became a US ambassador to Argentina.

Legal Training

Perales began law school at George Washington University (GWU) in February 1923.[1] In 1923 in a newspaper essay he explained why he himself likely chose this profession. The essay called for more Mexican-American lawyers and noted "Mexican citizens have recourse because the diplomatic system of Mexico provided protection through the consuls but Mexican Americans in this atmosphere of racial discrimination do not. That is why we Mexicans need more lawyers from our community."[2] In June 1924 he applied for a license to practice law as did M.C. Gonzales of San Antonio joining some ninety people who applied to the State Board of Legal Examiners including a woman and an African American man.[3] Perales wrote H.C. Clamp on September 6, 1924 about failing the bar.[4] In October 1926 Perales wrote the GWU dean stating "I want to get an LL.B. degree from GWU."[5] He did so. Perales and Gonzales were the second and third Mexican-American lawyers in Texas, following J.T. Canales who obtained his law degree from the University of Michigan in 1898.[6]

In the early 1920s Perales apparently worked for several Euro-Texan lawyers in San Antonio. In February 1924 attorney Bat Corrigan wrote a letter on his behalf to the State Board of Legal Examiners.[7] In April 1925 Perales accepted a job offer from a San Antonio law firm likely with lawyer Minner.[8] And past employer J.B. Andrews of Frank Saddlery Company wrote Judge Wincheser Kelso that "because of certain conditions [Perales'] connections with a law firm in this city will be terminated."[9] What these "conditions" were he did not say. This was probably at the law firm attorney Anthony worked for. Carl C. Wurzbach also wrote a letter to the board on his behalf.[10] Perales took the bar exam in June 1925 and was admitted to the Texas Bar in September 1925.[11]

Employment and Private Practice

In the 1920s Canales of Brownsville, Texas was the only Mexican-American lawyer in Texas before Perales. Perales was fortunate because father-in-law Casimiro Pérez Alvarez was Canales' friend.[12] Perales asked Canales for advice after finishing law school in 1926, asking him where he should open his law practice. To practice civil and criminal law Perales needed experience, Canales bluntly informed him and he suggested he start at the bottom in a small town.[13] Canales also let him know that his diplomatic and international law experience would not help him get a job.[14] In 1927 Canales told him that he could be appointed as Rio Grande City's city attorney where Perales' wife was from; the town had recently been incorporated.[15] In November 1926 Perales told Canales that he was coming to Texas soon and that "I shall try to save some money for the starvation period."[16] Perales told him he preferred to work with an experienced lawyer and Canales told him he drove to Rio Grande City every week on business.[17]

By May 1, 1927 Perales was discussing the possibility of a shared office between Brownsville and Rio Grande City.[18] Finally settling in, Perales' first office in the Rio Grande Valley was part of the Canales and McKay law firm located in the Nasser Building in McAllen.[19] On August 11, 1927 *McAllen Daily Press* reported that Perales held a public meeting in town.[20] In 1928 Perales thought he might be named legal counsel, perhaps for Rio Grande City, and might earn $5000 a year but apparently that did not pan out.[21] Perales was in and out of the Valley still working on diplomatic missions for the US government until 1932.

While Perales could have worked as an attorney in Washington DC, he decided to make Texas his permanent home. Perales suggested to friend and activist Dr. Carlos E. Castañeda that Castañeda would "shine more at Texas U than in Washington and thus bring us more prestige as an ethnic group," suggesting that Perales believed he himself might make a greater impact in Texas. He added, "In Washington you would be one of many brilliant stars. Not so in Texas, where you are one of FEW brilliant stars."[22] In April 1929 after some more time in Washington DC, Perales noted his intention to establish a law office in Texas: "I am seriously considering returning to Texas upon the completion of my present assignment with a view of opening up a law office. I don't know where I shall establish my headquarters, but it may be San Antonio, Laredo or Corpus. It seems to me that San Antonio is a little crowded already with Latin-American lawyers and lawyers, who though not of Latin extraction, speak Spanish well enough to attract our people."[23] Maybe Perales wanted to be in a city rather than a town in the Valley. (Or maybe Perales saw more opportunities in the city, cosmopolitan city life or maybe he saw more oppression in the Valley? Or perhaps he wanted to be away from in-laws?) Nonetheless, likely due to the Depression, he was in San Antonio by 1930.

Mexican-American attorneys in Texas and the United States were few in the 1930s. In 1954 there were about two dozen Mexican-American lawyers in the state of Texas; most Mexican-American lawyers in 20th-century Texas appeared after 1970 due to financial aid, affirmative action and the Chicano movement.[24] There were eighty-five Mexican-American lawyers in San Antonio out of 700 from 1931 to 1967, most in the last decade.[25] According to the 1930 San Antonio census four Mexican Americans and four Mexican immigrants self-identified as lawyers. Tejanos included M.C. Gonzales, Ruben R. Lozano and Charles Ramírez. Gonzales became a LULAC co-founder while Lozano and Ramírez joined LULAC. Immigrants Emilio Leal, Mariano Viesca y Arizpe, Anacleto Martínez and Ricardo García Granados identified themselves as lawyers though there is no evidence they took or passed the Texas bar. James Tafolla Jr. was another by 1931 as well as N.A. Quintanilla.[26] Perales' friend Pablo González was yet another. There were enough Latino lawyers in San Antonio by 1936 to create a softball team which could play Latino doctors.[27] A list of San Antonio Latino attorneys in Perales' papers, likely targets for donations to the Henry B. González 1950 campaign, shows about fifteen male lawyers.[28]

The Great Depression of the 1930s made it a difficult decade for all, including lawyers. Perales worked at 509 Alamo National Building in August 1931.[29] He noted about his San Antonio business, "Business is very dull at present, doubtless due to the economic crisis."[30] In 1932 Canales advised M.C. Gonzales not to move to the Valley when he told him, "Other lawyers are struggling to make a living."[31] Around December 1932 Perales worked at 609 Houston Bldg. in San Antonio.[32] He became a notary public in 1933.[33] He toyed with the idea of moving to Rio Grande City in July 1933 since "business is very dull here and my expenses are high."[34] He made San Antonio his permanent home opening his law office in the firm of Still, Wright, Davis & Perales in the Gunter Building downtown near the Alamo in 1933.[35] In 1934 Perales was located at 104-5 Cassiano Building on 201 S. Laredo St.[36] In January1934 he was appointed Assistant Attorney to D.F. Davis, Bexar County attorney, likely the first Mexican American in the position.[37] National magazine *Commerce and Industry* called Perales "one of the leading Mexican American attorneys in the State of Texas as well as an outstanding legal authority on Latin American nations."[38] In January 1935 he was part of Stieler, Davis, Wright & Perales at 700-5 Gunter Building with partners Henry Stieler, D.F. Davis, and Arthur V. Wright.[39] So Perales had several law partners, some European Americans, in municipal and private practice. So by the mid-1930s the *Album de la Raza* magazine of San Antonio called Perales "without a doubt, the best known Mexican-American lawyer in the State of Texas, among officials in Washington and in several Central and South American countries where he has served on various commissions."[40]

Perales' law practice had some financial challenges during the Depression. One of Perales' 1939 bank statements from Alamo National Bank showed a balance of $320 in April; $87 in June; and $433 in July.[41] Perales spent significant funds to pay publisher Artes Gráficas for his book *En Defensa de mi Raza* in 1936.

One of the most important cases Perales was involved with was *Salvatierra vs. Del Rio ISD,* a Texas school desegregation case in 1931. Canales and Gonzales served as trial lawyers. According to attorney Michael Olivas, "After the 1930 Court of Appeals decision, it appears that the appellant's petition for writ of error was dismissed for want of jurisdiction on March 18, 1931 by the Texas Supreme Court. Then, on April 15, 1931, the motion for rehearing of the petition for writ of error was overruled. Next, the appellants, who by this time included Perales as co-counsel, filed their Statement as to Jurisdiction on Appeal to the US Supreme Court on July 27, 1931. The US Supreme Court dismissed the case for want of jurisdiction on October 26, 1931, noting that it was treating the papers whereon the appeal was allowed as a petition for writ of certiorari . . . certiorari denied." Olivas continued, "While J.T. Canales and Gonzales were the Salvatierra trial lawyers, along with John L. Dodson, of Del Rio, young Perales was listed on the brief for the 1931 Statement as to Jurisdiction on Appeal, which was eventually denied. This appears, at least by document review, to be the only time he joined these two Mexican-American colleagues in a formal case, joining together the first three Texas Mexican-American lawyers."[42] More information about Perales' role is not available. *LULAC News* also reported that George M. Mayer also represented Council 2 in the case.[43]

Perales and LULAC hoped the case would go to the Supreme Court. The front cover of *LULAC News*, LULAC's official organ, pictured the Washington capitol building with the words "On to Washington."[44] At the 1932 annual LULAC convention Perales suggested that if the US Supreme Court were to authorize the segregation of Mexican-descent children in the public schools he would relinquish his US citizenship.[45] But the case failed to reach the state level.

Perales also served as the key attorney in a case against the Hondo School district, southwest of San Antonio. There only eleven Latinos were allowed to attend the "main school" while other Latinos were "demoted from fifth to fourth grade in order to prevent them from being eligible to go to the 'main school.'"[46] Hondo was to build a "modern and well-equipped primary building" for Latinos.[47]

After more than ten years in the Depression, Perales gradually built a successful law practice in the 40s especially after World War II ended. US entrance into World War II in 1941 had improved the economy. According to Judge Lupe Salinas, "Perales did not have many impact litigation cases"[48] but had what Olivas noted appeared "to have been a successful general commercial trial and appellate practice."[49] This practice allowed Perales to live a middle-class lifestyle. In 1942 Perales felt good about his business telling friend Dr. Castañeda, "I have a very good business here . . ."[50] By 1943 Perales was looking for a new 1942 Buick Sedan.[51] In 1943 he also told friend J. Luz Sáenz, "I am making a good living in my profession and that is why I haven't accepted employment with Uncle Sam."[52] But the US government did not offer Perales employment either because he was of Mexican descent; lacked endorsements from Euro-American upper-level officials; Maury Maverick, ex-mayor of San Antonio, gave him a bad reference and/or he was being blacklisted.

Perales had a successful business but it would be a stretch to call it a "thriving" business."[53] Bank statements show that Perales had $2364 in November 1944 and $1680 in June 1946.[54] Perales had numerous clients but he performed much pro-bono work. Friend Castañeda told him in 1946, "You have a bad habit of not sending *in your* checks for collection until it is too late."[55] Perales did so on purpose.

According to Dr. Arnoldo Vento, son of Adela Sloss-Vento, "Activist Sloss-Vento, would often tell me how many of his cases were pro-bono. His generosity and economic sacrifice left him poor compared to other lawyers."[56] Sometimes, Perales took up the slack. For instance, in 1959 he paid $896 for "medical expenses for clients."[57]

In Feb. 1947 Perales worked at Davis, Wright & Perales law firm but by August 1948 he had his own law practice.[58] Around September 1947 he opened his office at the new International Building on Houston St., a block off of Commerce Street and next to the Mexican Consulate General and Mexican Chamber of Commerce, founded in 1929.[59] The building also housed the Alameda movie theatre which showed Spanish-language films. He was now situated in the "Mexican quarter," a six block area with numerous Mexican-owned businesses for Mexican-descent people.[60] His office was about a block from City Hall, about two blocks from the Bexar County courthouse, near two shaded parks, a block from the *mercado* (Market Square) and Mi Tierra restaurant founded in 1934. He would have seen activist and attorney M.C. Gonzales who worked for the Mexican Consulate and Mexican-descent businesspeople in this part of town. His office was also about a block from San Fernando Cathedral which he attended daily and he was also about a block from the West side. *La Prensa's* office was also not far on Santa Rosa Street across from Milam Square/Plaza del Zacate.[61] Previously he worked near the Alamo/tourist district which was more European American. Perales was now located in the heart of the Mexican-descent community's commercial center where businesspeople, newsmen, vendors, Mexican food and Mexican music were common. Close to all he loved, he must have appreciated this more supportive Mexican environment away from the Alamo and the central business district.

On occasion, Perales continued to ask friend and veteran attorney Canales for advice. In 1942 Canales wrote Perales about a will that Perales had prepared for Gertrudis Canales of Jim Wells County in South Texas and Canales responded asking him about specific clauses.[62] In 1947 Perales also asked Canales about "porciones," land allotments given under New Spain in the 1700s. He wrote Canales, "Porcion 74 is being partitioned in Starr County the early part of October. Martita and her folks have about 400 acres in it. You have had a lot of experience with partition suits in Rio Grande. Would you advise them to employ an attorney to represent them, or will it suffice for two or three members of the family to be present and ready to claim the acreage they consider themselves entitled to?"[63]

Puente Housing Desegregation Case, 1948

A key case that Perales tried in the 1940s was *Clifton v. Puente* related to racial real estate covenants. As early as 1923 Perales wrote an editorial criticizing racial real estate covenants in San Antonio.[64] These restrictive covenants were "agreements under which the owners of real estate agree to exclude the members of particular groups of people from residing in a specified area."[65] In the 1930s Perales criticized Congressional candidate Thurman Barret, a homebuilder from Harlendale neighborhood in San Antonio because he used restrictive covenants there.[66] In 1947 Perales complained to Congress about this issue when Mexican-descent veterans were denied housing; he wrote, "It is the real state (sic) developers who insist upon segregating our people generally and now have the effrontery to attempt to segregate the defenders of our country, the very men who made it possible for them to continue to exist." He added that the federal government should not "guarantee any loan or grant prioritiei for the acquisition of critical materials in any real estate addition in which Mexican-American veterans are denied the right to purchase a home simply because of their racial lineage."[67] Perales' protégée Gus Garcia also wrote about this practice: "Frankly, we came back from the war expecting an entirely different situation from that which we found. We came back to find that we could not buy homes because of restrictive covenants."[68]

This practice by the real estate industry reinforced the city's geographic racial segregation and prevented the Mexican ethnic middle class from realizing one benefit of its class privilege. Middle-class ethnics could not always offer their children a middle-class education due to these restrictions. One scholar noted, "restrictive racial covenants in property deeds helped preserve the racial homogeneity of vast segments of the urban areas. Mexican Americans and Anglos were separated as a consequence of de facto segregation housing patterns reinforced by de jure restrictive covenants in property deeds."[69] Alamo Heights, Olmos Park and Terrell Hills in San Antonio had these covenants.[70]

Abdon Salazar Puente bought a house in Mayfield Park in Southwest San Antonio. In 1946 ability-challenged veteran Mr. Humphreys bought the house and then sold it to Puente, a naturalized US citizen.[71] Humphreys said, "I believe that a G.I. of Latin-American descent has the same rights as any other American . . . and I believe that many of them are now being kept from owning their own homes because of restrictive clauses. I am convinced I am doing what is right in selling to Puente and I don't intend to back down."[72] After the neighbors and real-estate company obtained a temporary restraining order based on fear of property value decline, Puente approached the new city organization of Pan American Progressive Association (PAPA). It financed the case and provided legal counsel.[73]

Perales worked with co-counsel lawyer Cadena and J.M. Woods in *Clifton v. Puente,* 218 S.W.2d 272 (Tex. Civ. App.-San Antonio 1948, writ ref'd n.r.e.) According to Cadena, Henry B. González of PAPA asked Cadena if he would take the case "so we tried the case."[74] According to Lupe Salinas by then the US Supreme Court had already "ruled that state judicial approval of covenants that barred the sale of property to African American violated the Fourteenth Amendment's Equal Protection Clause.[75] The US Supreme Court decided *E. Shelly v. Kraemer.*

Perales wrote about Puente: "We won a victory in the Puente restrictive covenants case. Judge Tayloe patterned his decisions after that of the U.S. Supreme Court. The 'enemy' has appealed the case to the Fourth Court of Civil Appeals, but it will avail them nothing."[76] He added, ". . . we have them whipped for the reason that the U.S. Supreme Court has already spoken."[77] According to attorney García, both Perales and Cadena worked with PAPA and "obtained a favorable Court decision in a State Court which, from a strictly legal standpoint, went one step farther than the United States Supreme Court decision."[78] Thereafter LULAC sought to convince the Federal Housing Authority (FHA) to reject loans or approval to subdivisions with these restrictive covenants. National

LULAC responded quickly to a newspaper announcement in August 1949 titled, "South Side Not to Sell Land to Latin-Americans" with a protest letter to the US Attorney General.[79]

According to Olivas, Perales worked on two other key cases in the 1940s. These included: *Lozano v. De Martinez,* Court of Civil Appeals of Texas, San Antonio. July 22, 1942 164 S.W.2d 196; and *Alaniz v. State,* Court of Criminal Appeals of Texas. May 4, 1949 153 Tex. Crim. 374.

The 1950s was Perales' last decade. Perales had a secretary named Miss de la Torre in June 1952. She noted in one of Perales' letters: "dictated, but not read by Mr. Perales" so errors were to be excused and otherwise, Perales would catch them.[80] In 1958 niece Araceli Pérez lived with the Perales and since she was taking shorthand in school she helped Perales with filing and he dictated letters to her.[81] In the early 50s the Perales had a small real estate business[82] and on January 1, 1952 Perales obtained a real estate dealers license.[83]

Young lawyer José I. López joined Perales' firm by December 1957 likely due to Perales' declining health.[84] López attended Sidney Lanier High and Trinity University as well as the South Texas College of Law in Houston. He served in the Marines in Korea.[85] Letterhead read "Law Offices of Perales and López" located at 518 Houston St.[86] But apparently López left or did not work out because when Perales passed wife Marta hired lawyers to close pending legal matters. In June 1959 Perales had forty-one clients.[87] Perales' 1959 income taxes show his adjusted gross income was $3,551.[88] Attorney/scholar Olivas has outlined a number of Perales' cases in the 1950s.[89]

Around 1960 Perales had a law partner named Ronald Smallwood. After Perales purchased his dream home, a two-story house on the corner of Courtland St. with a lot next door. Perales planned to build his law office and library there before he passed in 1960.[90]

Raquel González' Murder Case, 1958

In 1958 Perales was so intrigued by what he called a "women's rights" case that he decided to volunteer his time despite his declining health. He collaborated with Colonel/attorney L.G. Mathews of

Brownsville in a case related to Raquel González of Georgetown near Austin. On August 14, 1958 Perales instructed friend and attorney Canales: "Please call up Mr. Mathews, attorney, Brownsville, and tell him that you know me; that I am the type of man that believes in justice; that I have been defending our race (out of Court most of the time) for about 40 years, etc. It so happens that I went to Brownsville recently and offered my services free of charge to a young lady named Raquel Gonzalez, who killed a man who had deceived her. The case appealed to me from the beginning. She gave me the name of her lawyer, and I told her that if her lawyer did not object to my participating in the case I would assist him: otherwise I would not. Accordingly, I wrote to Mr. Mathews the early part of this month, but so far I have not heard from him. So please give him a little background about myself. I want nothing out of the case. I just want to assist this poor, unfortunate girl if I can."[91] Perales felt that despite González' murder of her love interest, she had cause.

Cameron county (Brownsville, Texas area) deputy sheriff Bobby Solis reportedly wooed a reluctant González even though he was married and reportedly did not tell her so. He got her pregnant and later informed her that he was married and told her "don't bother me. The Hell with you. Don't call me here at the office." Perhaps out of the shame of an extra-marital affair, common in the 1950s, González left Brownsville and moved to Idaho. She wrote Solis a letter stating, "I will kill you" and actually did so.[92]

Perales volunteered to work on the case because he felt she was wronged and her honor stained. Indeed, she was allegedly lied to, she was allegedly seduced by a married man, and the man allegedly refused to take up fatherly and financial responsibilities. In short, Solis' immorality had permanently impacted a woman and their child leaving moral, social, work and financial implications for the rest of their lives. Perales sympathized with the hardship of a mother with a child or children. He clearly put aside the fact that she had violated one of the Ten Commandments: "Thou shall not kill."

Perales' Christian social take on the case is interesting. He saw González as an innocent victim of a man and perhaps as a woman without sexual desire. (But what if she had sexual desire? What if she seduced him?) This was not an era in which women openly claimed sexual desire. Perales believed in marriage especially for mothers and fathers. (What if she wanted a child and trapped Solis?) What if Solis told González that he was married and what if Gonzalez lied? Perales may have been bothered by the idea of a fatherless child, his own experience. And he also knew what it meant to miss a father's financial contribution. Perales assumed she told him the truth.

After the case ended Canales wrote Perales: "he [attorney Mathews] assured me that you rendered him valuable service, which resulted in a suspended sentence, almost a complete victory. I followed the trial in the newspapers, and when the State introduced in evidence the damaging letters which gave evidence of a premeditated act on the part of the defendant, we were a little apprehensive of the result and thought the jury would not recommend a suspended sentence, although I had thought the jury might do that. It is needless to say to you that the verdict rendered met with the approval of most of the people here. As I knew that you were assisting Judge Mathews voluntarily and without compensation, I thought that you, as well as Colonel Mathews, should be complimented for what I think is at least almost a victory."[93]

Once the case was won Perales explained to his co-counsel Mathews, "Rachel González wrote a new chapter in the history of progress of women in these United States of America" by establishing the following 'facts:' FIRST, that women have the right to defend their dignity and their honor. SECONDLY, that no man has a right to ruin the life of a young girl. THIRDLY, that when a man makes love to a girl and conceals the fact that he is already married, he will have to suffer the consequences. If he is single, he is expected to live up to his promise to marry the girl." He concluded, "She has set a good example for the women of America that they might know henceforth how to defend themselves. The women of America owe a debt of gratitude to Rachel González."[94] This was one of his Perales' last cases and one in which he claimed a victory for feminism.

While this secular reading of the case's outcome there is also a Christian reading here. In "Problemas del Hogar," (Problems at Home) one of Perales' newspaper articles, he warned of unaccompanied young women, men who promised matrimony, and men who might not be honorable gentlemen. Indeed, that is why Perales called for vigilance and "chaperoning," the idea that a woman's virginity needed protection and honor prized.[95] Perales believed that women needed protection. He believed marriage was sacred. And he believed it was the husband's duty to provide for a wife. Historian Mario García also noted that "What particularly disturbed Perales was the unfaithfulness of married men."[96] Perhaps Perales had also been embolded by the Catholic Apostolic Cursillo momentum of the 1950s.

Protégées
Gus Garcia

Perales served as a role model, mentor and colleague for several important emerging younger lawyers. He encouraged the pursuit of a legal career by Latinos as early as the 1920s.[97] Perales shaped and witnessed their rise in the profession; they became attorney Gus Garcia, attorney and professor of law Carlos Cadena and attorney and US ambassador of Argentina Vilma S. Martínez. All were impacted by LULAC. While his direct influence cannot be documented, he worked with them in civic organizations, advised them and served as a contemporary role model.

Garcia was born in Laredo in 1915 and moved to San Antonio in 1924. His father attended college in Missouri. According to widow Marta, Perales helped young Gus Garcia get into Main High School when he was sixteen. Garcia's mother asked Perales "to help her with the energetic young teenager. Gus would go to the law offices and help around keeping him off the streets and out of trouble."[98] García graduated high school at age 16 and was Thomas Jefferson High valedictorian. He attended the University of Texas at Austin (UTA) on scholarships and graduated with his BA in 1936 at age 20 and became a champion debater. He obtained his law degree from UTA in 1938. From 1939 to 1940 he served as LULAC legal advisor. He also filed a case for LULAC against the Cuero ISD for segregated schools in 1940. In 1941 he served as Vice-President of the Club Democrático Unión Fraternal.[99] He became first assistant city district attorney in San Antonio for three years before he was called upon by World War II.[100] He also served as assistant city attorney. (This is a position

Perales had served and likely a concession he got from Mayor Quin for Garcia.) Garcia later served as an infantry officer and judge advocate during World War II in Japan.[101] In the late 40s he joined the Mexican Consulate's office as a legal advisor.[102]

Perales supported Garcia's run for elected office. In April 1948 Perales supported Garcia in the San Antonio ISD race for school board, the position for which he ran and lost in 1946. According to one report in 1948 both Latinos and African Americans "built up an organization in every precinct, supporting the slogan "Latins for a Latin!" and the West side especially supported Garcia.[103] Perales greeted Garcia's victory with joy. He wrote friend Dr. Castañeda, "Well, at long last we have broken the ice and on Saturday we elected Gus C. Garcia to the School Board and the colored folks elected one of their own for the San Antonio Junior College Board. Needless to say, we are quite happy over it."[104] But shortly after Garcia's election it seems Castañeda and Perales were not sure about Garcia. By August 19, 1948 Castañeda wrote Perales, "I do not trust GG further than I can see him."[105] Perales did not write back to defend García. Garcia took up the cause of the School Improvement League which had been active since the mid-1930s and helped pass a school improvement bond.[106] In 1948 Garcia and other lawyers introduced *Delgado v. Bastrop* shortly after Dr. Castañeda sent Perales a copy of the *Mendez v. Westminster* case, the first major desegregation lawsuit in California with statewide impact and which ended separate schools for Latinos in 1946. Castañeda wrote Perales, "Now, then, why can't we get a similar case here? Lets [sic] think the matter over. Sánchez says he is doing something, but I doubt it."[107]

Though Perales did not take part in the *Delgado v Bastrop* case, the first major school desegregation lawsuit in Texas related to Latinos but he welcomed it as part of Gus Garcia's work.[108] Perales wrote, "Unquestionably, it is a good step in the right direction. It is indeed too bad the case did not go all the way up to the Supreme Court of the United States that the case might have been decided once for all times. The injunction against the Superintendent (L.A. Woods) is not valid, in my opinion. However, he has seen fit to try to scare the School Districts, and I hope his strategy will work. It may in some cases. On the other hand, we know here are a lot of stubborn School Boards who will probably fight to the last."[109] Perales' work to desegregate schools for La Raza became a legal reality. While critical of LULAC, Garcia was its member, lawyer and advocate. He helped to revise the 1949 LULAC constitution.[110] He also wrote to the *Wharton Spectator* newspaper who published that "Mexican peon labor is not my type." Garcia wrote "Since we feel confident that you believe in the development of our American way of life we are enclosing an application blank for membership in LULAC and trust that, after you become familiar with our aims and purposes, you will see fit to file a formal application for membership in our organization."[111]

In the early 1950s Garcia took a case which would propel his significance. By 1952 Perales wrote Castañeda, "Well, some people have made a big thing out of our young hero's trip to Washington, and they are having a big pow-pow to honor him to-morrow [sic] night. He came to me this morning and apologized for having sent me a 'stupid' letter (as he himself called it) over the George I. Sánchez matter. He acted very meek and humble. However, I do not intend to go, for several reasons, and one is that he thinks of me only when he needs me, when he wants to use me as in this instance."[112] (Garcia appeared before the Senate migratory labor committee headed by Hubert Humphrey on behalf of the American G.I. Forum (AGIF) or Garcia may have visited UNESCO (United Nations Educational, Scientific and Cultural Organization) in Washington, DC at this time.[113] Indeed, Garcia visited Perales to apologize for "that stupid letter which I never should have written to you."[114] Garcia had sided with Dr. Sánchez on the Wetback pamphlet issue and that is where Perales drew the line.

Perales refused to attend a testimonial dinner honoring Garcia.[115] That same day in 1952 Perales wrote, "I am not going to the banquet in his honor."[116] He also told activist J. Luz Sáenz, "I don't think they should invite Gustavo because he's on Sánchez' side and he will continue to defend him if given the opportunity. He and his close friend Idar think [they are] big because they spoke before a Congressional hearing and they keep talking about it."[117] Castañeda responded, "I agree on the attitude you have taken in regard to the Garcia dinner. He and a number of others are always trying to use everybody and to play both ends against the middle."[118]

Garcia would also serve as attorney in a Supreme Court case in 1954.[119] Right after his 1954 Supreme Court win, he traveled to Washington, DC to speak to politicians. Although Garcia was intelligent and reportedly shined like a "matador" at the Supreme Court, he had character flaws. As soon as he arrived in Washington, DC he got drunk, spending funds that civil rights supporters had raised. He may have had a mental illness and was an alcoholic. He felt a sense of entitlement, and was materialistic and unethical, passing around bad checks that finally got him disbarred. He enjoyed the limelight and accolades.

Tension between Garcia and Perales existed. It might also be attributed to Garcia's privileges over Perales. Garcia had a college-educated father and was raised middle class. Perales may have seen him as one who took his class privilege for granted and threw it away. Garcia was also younger and benefitted from openings that Perales helped create. They may have also competed in regards to intellect. Perales was also likely not happy when Garcia resigned from the school board. Garcia was also more liberal in relations to African Americans and worked with a coalition to win his school board election. Garcia was a liberal Democrat and Perales veered toward Republicanism and growing conservativism in the 1950s.

Political scientist Rodolfo Rosales considered Garcia more positively than Perales though perhaps due to his Chicano movement lens at the time. He noted, "On the one hand, Gus Garcia, although, driven by the same concerns that motivated Perales, challenged the system's neglect of the Chicano community through the legal process" and added, "Garcia's efforts reflected a more confrontational strategy for gaining inclusion. Besides setting the tenor for a civil rights agenda that has pervaded Chicano politics throughout the modern period, his efforts also initiated the conflict over strategies."[120] But Perales used the same legal process, used it first, and Garcia addressed the same issues as Perales. And at times both supported Republican candidates.

While the Salvatierra case was the most important school desegregation case for Mexican-origin people in the 1930s by the 1940s the key case would be *Delgado vs. Bastrop ISD* litigated by Garcia. Perales did not try Delgado which would officially desegregate schools for Mexican-descent people in Texas in 1948. It followed *Mendez v. Westminster* in California. That work was left to his protégées Carlos C. Cadena and Gus Garcia, both of San Antonio who Perales influenced or mentored. Perales wrote Garcia praising him for his work on Delgado.[121]

Carlos C. Cadena

Another of Perales' protégées was attorney Carlos Cadena. He was born in San Antonio in 1917 and was about 12 when Perales founded LULAC.[122] He attended San Antonio high school at St. Henry's Academy as possibly the only Mexican American there among many German Americans and graduated from the University of Texas at Austin law school in 1940.[123] He served as student editor of the *Texas Law Review*.[124] Young Cadena joined LULAC Council 16 in the 1930s.[125] Although third in his class and light-skinned, no law firm interviewed him for a job.[126] Around 1941 he worked as an attorney for the Back Tax Department in San Antonio.[127] From 1941 to 1943 he served as assistant city attorney in San Antonio, a position Perales had fought for Latinos to have. Drafted into World War II, he did not see combat action but served in Hawaii, Okinawa, Manila, South Dakota and Arizona. He then practiced law in Mexico City with Goodrich and Dalton for a year.[128] From 1947 to 1950 he was affiliated with the Archer, San Miguel & Cadena firm. During that time, he worked with Perales on the Puente case. (Cadena was on a list of approved Pan American Optimist Club members so they would have socialized there too.)[129]

Cadena also became a law professor. After two years at UTA as a student again from 1950 to 1952, he became a part-time professor and then full-time professor from 1947 to 1975 at St. Mary's University in San Antonio. He was the first Mexican-American law professor there and probably in the entire United States.[130] In 1953 he belonged to a committee on Latin American law in the Texas Bar Association, once speaking on "Our Heritage from Spain and Mexico as Reflected on our Texas Pleadings."[131] In 1961 he held the Burke Chair at the law school at St. Mary's.[132]

From 1954 to 1961 Cadena served as San Antonio city attorney. In 1960 Cadena ordered the police chief not to arrest students protesting segregated Woolworth lunch counters downtown, the first city in the South to do so.[133] In 1965 after Perales' death he was appointed by Governor John Connally to the Fourth Court of Appeals as associate justice "after considerable political pressure."[134] He was considered a "very highly regarded appellate judge." In 1977 Governor Dolph Briscoe appointed him Chief Justice of the Fourth Court of Appeals.[135] He and lawyers James DeAnda and Pete Tijerina of LULAC founded the Mexican American Legal Defense and Education Fund (MALDEF) in San Antonio in 1968 with financial assistance from the Ford Foundation due to the connections of Dr. George I. Sánchez, his professor and friend.[136] MALDEF became a permanent institution addressing major Latino legal issues in the United States. Cadena was MALDEF's first board president.[137]

Cadena became a highly successful attorney. According to historian Ignacio M. García, "Cadena . . . became the most successful Mexican American lawyer of his time and possibly of all time with four major victories, including three in the Supreme Court." He was involved in the *Clifton v. Puente* case on housing discrimination; *Delgado v. Bastrop* on Texas school segregation; and *Harvey v. the State of Texas* which allowed for various races to box one another. Garcia added, "No lawyer of his generation could claim such a judicial record, and only Reynaldo G. Garza, who became a federal judge in 1961, would rise as high in the profession."[138]

Cadena embraced emerging liberal ideas, including the inclusion of African Americans and allowing women's participation in juries. He "chastised Mexican American reformers for seeking to build a 'cultural wall' to keep away from other ethnic groups, particularly 'the ultra-progressive Negro-Americans."[139] Likewise, he saw his victory with the Hernández case as a potential argument against keeping women out of jury duty in Texas using the "class apart" theory. Indeed, Texas women would finally obtain jury duty in 1954.

Cadena was a humble man in contrast to the flamboyant Gus Garcia who called Cadena "the best brain of my generation."[140] According to historian Ignacio M. García, "his daughter remembers him as a shy man who seldom spoke about his accomplishments."[141] His law partners were surprised to learn he had argued before the Supreme Court three times. Garcia surmised, "Cadena seemed to have that quiet resolve that people of great character often do. He was quiet, humble, and methodical. He also knew how to meet his obligations well."[142] Cadena saw himself this way noting, "I usually kept quiet, stayed in the background, and when it looked like we could develop a good case—well, then I participated."[143]

Henry B. González

A third attorney who Perales influenced was Henry B. González, also of San Antonio. He was raised in a political family as his father was a mayor in the state of Durango, Mexico before immigrating to Texas. As mentioned in the early 40s no one would hire him and Perales made phone calls on his behalf; he became chief probation officer for Bexar County.[144] He later quit this position when he was not allowed to hire an African American.[145] He obtained his law degree from St. Mary's University in San Antonio in 1943.[146] He was thrown out of either a San Antonio or New Braunfels public park due to a "Whites Only" sign with Perales reportedly filing a "LULAC complaint."[147] González was repeatedly told, "A Mexican cannot win" in San Antonio[148] even though Gus Garcia had already won a school board position in 1948.

González worked with Perales in the Pan American Progressive Association (PAPA), founded in the late 1940s. In 1947 González was its executive assistant.[149] Among its new numerous board of directors were attorneys Perales, Cadena, M.C. Gonzalez, Gus C. Garcia, and Adolfo A. Garza; it was "directed by men."[150] According to political scientist Rosales PAPA was formed to address the lack of credit extended to Mexican-descent businesses by banks.[151] PAPA invited Perales as a guest speaker at its meeting at the Salón Pan Americano in the Casa Blanca Restaurant on May 26, 1948. The invitation stated, "We unquestionably consider you a great asset and leader in this our community."[152] González reportedly resigned due to disagreement in PAPA over how to address the issue of restrictive covenants.[153] This case was won by Perales and Cadena.

González ran for city council and was elected in 1953, the second Mexican American after Ruben R. Lozano, a LULAC member[154] and chapter 14 showed Perales' role in his campaign. In the same year, González pushed an ordinance desegregating all city-owned public facilities.[155] In 1956 he gained a seat in the Texas Senate and in 1958 ran for governor. A letter between Jack Danciger and Perales shows Perales may have been working on a dinner campaign fundraiser for González.[156] González and Maury Maverick also sought to fill a US Senate seat in 1961 but both lost to John Tower.[157] González was successful in becoming a Texas legislator in 1961 and then became the first Tejano in Congress from 1961 to 1999. He played a major role in ending the poll tax with the US Civil Rights Act of 1964.

Albert A. Peña Jr.

Albert A. Peña Jr. of San Antonio benefitted from the G.I. bill and graduated from law school in 1950 in Houston and would have also known Perales.[158] Peña Jr. claimed "I didn't have any role models"[159] though there were already a number of Latino lawyers in San Antonio, including his attorney father Albert Peña Sr. who attended John K. Weber School in San Antonio.[160] Peña served as LULAC Council 2 president and was a member of the AGIF.[161] In the 1940s he played a key role in organizing the Latin American Democrats, a local partisan group.[162] He would go on to file cases especially in Hondo, Texas in 1951 for the AGIF and in Lytle, Texas in 1952 for LULAC. He was elected Bexar County Commissioner, "the first person of Mexican ancestry to be elected, in 1956, to a major public office in urban Texas, that of Bexar County commission (San Antonio)."[163] He joined the Latin American Democrats in San Antonio in the 50s, ran for the state legislature in 1956 and became a member of the Bexar County Coalition in 1960 which sought to elect Mexican Americans, African Americans and labor leaders. The Coalition got Albert Peña Jr. elected to the Bexar County Commission in 1960.[164] Peña was a founder and state chair of the Political Association of Spanish Speaking Organization (PASO), a national organization founded in 1960 supporting the election of Latino candidates.[165] He was a transition figure between post World War II activism and the emerging Chicano movement. He was the first Tejano to advocate against the Vietnam War.[166]

Perales also served as a role model for aspiring Latino lawyers even decades later. Judge Lupe Salinas of Houston was impacted by Perales when he encountered *Are We Good Neighbors?* decades later. Salinas wrote, "I can honestly state that this is when my career in civil rights began to develop. The impact on me—as I read through his book in the UH [University of Houston] library during my pre-law years—was immediate. I saw the detailed affidavits that he obtained from victims of anti-Mexican racist practices."[167]

Vilma S. Martínez

While Perales influenced several key male attorneys, he seems to have impacted only two women who went on to become lawyers. In the 1950s he mentored young teenager Vilma S. Martínez. She was the daughter of personal friends, Salvador Martínez, a carpenter, and Marina, a homemaker. Martínez was raised only with the Spanish language but grew up on the East side in a racially mixed working-class neighborhood. She sought direction from her junior high school counselor but he/she "wouldn't cooperate"; the counselor directed her to a trade school. Perales likely directed her toward law school.

In 1977 San Antonio journalist Veronica Salazar of the *San Antonio Express News* began her story on Vilma Martínez, "Vilma S. Martinez is living proof that young women can have successful careers as long as they have determination and are willing to fight."[168] This was not Salazar's projection in 1977, it was Perales' projection in the 1950s. According to Salazar, Martínez "learned to help people through law at the age of 15 when she worked as an assistant to the well-known late civil rights attorney Alonso Perales." She worked for him the summer of 1958.

Perales not only allowed her in his office, he promoted her in one of his Architects column in *La Prensa*. He acknowledged her publically. The occasion of the article was Martínez' *quinceañera* (similar to a Sweet 16 celebration). He provided all the social information as to who presented her and who attended the event. He also applauded that she had attended Nuestra Señora de los Dolores where she received religious instruction. But Perales went on. He wrote, "Miss Martínez symbolizes to a perfection the kind of young woman that all young women should aspire to be."[169] He also wrote, "Es una señorita inteligente y brillante." (She is an intelligent and bright young woman.)

Martínez continued to encounter obstacles but like Perales persevered. Someone advised her against applying to UTA but she rejected this bad advice and finished in two and a half years with scholarships and part-time jobs. She went to Columbia University in New York and received her law degree in 1967. At Columbia she worked with the National Association for the Advancement of Colored People (NAACP) Legal Defense Fund. She became the first woman on the board of the Mexican American Legal Defense and Education Fund (MALDEF), founded in 1968. Attorneys in LULAC and the AGIF had in effect served as MALDEF for decades.[170] Martínez became its first woman president and general counsel from 1973 to 1982.[171] While there, MALDEF organized a Chicana Rights Project.[172] When asked about MALDEF's biggest accomplishment Martínez noted "that it has articulated for the country 'the fact that Mexican American citizens are being denied equal protection of the law." She later added, "Lawyers are particularly suited for that sort of effort since we are this country's articulators." She followed the lead of Perales, one our "country's articulators" and Mexican-American public intellectuals all his life.

Over the years, Martínez has remembered Perales' work and mentorship fondly. In the 1970s she said, "He helped a couple adopt a child; he helped a young widow whose husband was killed in a crop dusting accident."[173] In 2009 Martínez recalled Perales, "What I learned was that lawyers, through their education and training, are able to help people in times of need."[174] In 2018 she wrote, "Watching him work inspired me to consider becoming a lawyer. I was very much impressed with the help he was able to provide through his good ear and legal training . . . the time I had no idea what an important man and force he was for our Mexican American community."[175] Martínez emulated Perales in one other way. President Barack Obama named her US ambassador to Argentina in 2009, following Perales' lead as a US diplomat.[176]

Another woman who Perales inspired was Adelfa Botello who would go on to become the second Tejana lawyer in Texas.[177] Edna Cisneros of Falfurrias was the first in the 1950s.[178] After Botello graduated from high school in Cotulla, she wrote Perales. There is no evidence he responded. She followed her dream attending Southern Methodist University in Dallas in the late 60s and had a fruitful career.[179]

Conclusion

Alonso S. Perales' legal training at a prestigious university in the nation's capitol gave him confidence and intellectual capital to begin his civil rights campaign in Texas. Unique, he had already served as a US diplomat before he began lawyering. He worked with several partners, beginning with veteran Mexican-American attorney J.T. Canales and then with several European American partners. The Depression did not permit a profitable law business but Perales nonetheless played a role in *Del Rio ISD v. Salvatierra* which challenged segregated Mexican schools in Texas.

By the 1940s Perales had a successful private law firm and he took up pro-bono cases often. That was his wealth and success. Following a Supreme Court case, Perales and lawyer Carlos Cadena took up a case ending restrictive real estate covenants in San Antonio allowing people of color to live wherever they could afford.

In the 50s Perales took up a women's right case that showed him to be a man caring to women though his interest was based on traditional heterosexual Catholic sexual mores for women and men. Yet, the case showed he valued the idea of a woman's right to self-defense, even if it involved murder. This was unlikely for Perales since he was a devout Catholic.

While Perales' court record is not as significant as Cadena's and others, Judge Lupe Salinas, a Perales scholar, noted, ". . . his court record is very limited. His greatest contribution to the law, in my opinion, came from his indefatigable fight for Justice for his people, la Raza Mexicana." Also key is the fact that Perales inspired, mentored and/or impacted key attorneys Gus Garcia, Carlos Cadena, Henry B. González, Albert Peña Jr. and Vilma S. Martínez.[180] All were also impacted by LULAC's work. Perales worked with all of them. Garcia became an outstanding lawyer though Perales ultimately believed him opportunistic. He served as a legal advisor for LULAC. Cadena was a LULAC Council 16 activist in 1930s, became an attorney, a law professor and judge. He was the first Latino in San Antonio's city hall and argued three cases before the Supreme Court and also played a role in the founding of MALDEF. González became a city councilman, Texas state legislator in the 1950s and US Congressman in the 1960s. Perales helped him get a job, played a major role in his 1950 Texas legislature campaign and worked with him in PAPA. Peña Jr. was also a LULAC local president and would play a key role in the emerging Chicano movement.

Few women took up law before 1970 but Perales mentored Vilma S. Martínez. His mentorship would prove lasting not only because of her individual career but because of her role in MALDEF and its Chicana Rights Project which impacted women during the emerging Chicana movement of the 1970s. She also followed his lead and became a US diplomat as Ambassador to Argentina under Obama's US presidency.

Latino lawyers are still few today. Recall that Perales found Canales the only Latino lawyer in Texas in 1923. Some twenty had graduated from the University of Texas in Austin by 1950.[181] But by 2010 there were 51, 074 Latino lawyers and judges in the United States with 7,080 Mexican-American lawyers or judges in Calif.; 6, 569 in Texas; 979 in New Mexico; and 868 in Illinois.[182] Michael A. Olivas noted, "This is a world the early Latino and Latina lawyers would not recognize."[183] Likewise, Lupe Salinas wrote that in Houston in 1972 he knew the thirty Latino lawyers but in 2003 there were over 400.[184] Perales played a major role in creating this world. No twentieth-century Latino lawyer was more important.

CHAPTER 15
Politico

Alonso S. Perales was involved in numerous efforts at Mexican-American political empowerment at the city, county, state, national and international levels. Beyond his 1929-1960 activism already covered, he made even more contributions in politics. This chapter first reviews his political ideology inclusive of Mexican Americanism; pro-democracy; anti-political bossism, anti-communism and homosociality. Second, Perales' local, county, state and national participation in electoral politics is discussed. At the local and county levels, Perales helped initiate the Association of Independent Voters in San Antonio in the early 30s and the League of Loyal Americans (Loyals) and the Committee of One Hundred in the late 30s and 40s, all three Mexican-American efforts. The latter two associations contacted US presidents, Congressional members and political leaders in Mexico. Third, some of Perales' activism at the local, state and national level is delineated. At the national level, he testified before Congress in the 30s and 40s on Mexican immigration and employment discrimination. At the state level, Perales helped spearhead antiracist legislation in the Texas legislature in the 40s and 50s. Local efforts included supporting or opposing San Antonio mayors and his bid for the San Antonio ISD school board.

In 1930 the political status of the Mexican-descent people in San Antonio and in the state was grim. A questionnaire administered by Professor Oliver Douglas Weeks and filled out by a LULAC leader noted 75,000 members of La Raza in the city and 4,000 in the county. Of this 40,000 were US citizens and another 3,500 in the county.

Of this, 8,000 in the city paid the poll tax and 500 in the county. Of this approximately 5,000 voted in the last election and 250 in the county.[1] There was one elected Mexican-American man.

Perales' Political Ideology

Perales ideology consisted of several elements: democracy without political bossism, Mexican Americanism, anti-communism and homosociality.

Pro-democracy

Perales believed in democracy and democratic institutions. Historian Richard A. Garcia noted, "Perales was foremost an intellectual who worked to provide the vision of a new democracy for Mexican American citizens."[2] Perales claimed this "new" democracy for people of Latino descent. He believed that all machinations preventing Mexican Americans from participating in US democracy were undemocratic. This included the poll tax, the white man's primary, exclusion from political parties, lack of representation in government and taxation without representation. He also believed in the right to complain to government officials, the right to be heard, the right to advocate as to how taxes should be spent and the right to organize ethnic associations. Perales believed in "democratic ideals, ideals which he believes, are not to be understood as the right of white Americans only" as stated by literary scholar Donna Kabalen de Bichara.[3]

Anti-political bossism

Bossism had existed in San Antonio at least since 1885. Bosses still controlled elections there in the 1920s and 30s. The only temporary respite from bossism was the mayoral administration of Maury Maverick, a populist, from 1939 to 1941.[4] Mexican Americans had a minor role in the politics of San Antonio before the 1930s though Francisco Chapa played a key role in the 1910s.

Not only did Perales denounce Euro-Texan political bossism, he criticized Mexican Americans who aided bosses. He was critical of what historian Richard A. Garcia called "the lieutenants and the intermediaries between the political bosses and the Mexican community."[5] A LULAC member told scholar Paul S. Taylor, "We have three [kinds of] people to contend with: the American politicians, the Mexican [machine] politicians, who sacrifice their race for their own advantage, and the old Mexicans. The Mexican politician controls a few voters for what he can get out of them, and is afraid of our society . . . The Mexican politicians fight us and knock us and call us renegades, but after a while they join."[6] The "old Mexicans" criticized LULAC for its Mexican Americanism but some of their children would eventually become Mexican Americans who would also become LULAC supporters. Yet, while there were Mexican-American leaders who influenced others, San Antonio had no true Mexican-American boss in the 1930s unlike the role Charles Bellinger played for African Americans in the city.

San Antonio also witnessed a new kind of bossism by the Good Government League from 1955 to 1975 under Walter McAlister. It was the "political arm of the San Antonio economic and social elite," some twenty families, before 1972.[7] Over two decades it ran over eighty races and only lost three for city council seats. By the 1950s it ran a handful of acceptable Mexican-American candidates but not until then. In the 30s and 40s Mexican Americans were outsiders.[8]

Mexican Americanism

The most original and important ideology that Perales espoused was "Mexican Americanism," a term coined by historian Richard A. Garcia and in recent years promoted by scholar Aaron E. Sánchez.[9] Perales explained Mexican Americanism's goals in 1924 in *El Defensor* of Edinburg:

"We are not trying to deny our race. On the contrary, we are proud to have American blood running through are veins. And our purpose is not to ask, much less beg, Anglo Saxons to allow us to mingle socially with them. What we long for is the respect of our unalienable rights and privileges. We would like equality of opportunity in the various battlegrounds of life as well as the courts of justice. We would like for persons of Mexican descent in violation of the laws that govern our country to be tried before a competent Court of Justice and not be lynched . . . We would like to go to a theater, restaurant, dance hall, or any other establishment whose doors are wide open to the general public, whenever we feel like it. We do not want be arrested as is frequently done, with the mere excuse of our national origin. In one word, we ask for justice and opportunity to prosper. There you have our goal. There you have our objective."[10]

This was the essence of "Mexican Americanism"—recognition of the dignity of the Mexican-descent people; the right not to be lynched or discriminated; treatment as citizens of the United States with all its rights and privileges; fairness in the criminal justice system; and equal opportunity to compete in the labor market and advance in US society. Historian Ralph Morales has noted that Mexican Americans had been Texans since 1836 and Americans since 1845 and that "Americanism was not dependent on ethnicity."[11]

Throughout Perales' participation in politics he maintained a consistent message for the political evolution of Mexican Americans. As early as 1930 he advised: 1) pay the poll tax; 2) vote intelligently; 3) obtain civic instruction; 4) unite for Raza interests but stay away from political factions; 5) demand respect for the race; and 6) insist on adequate representation in government at the city, county and state levels.[12]

This was also a call for democracy to work for people of Mexican origin in the United States and a call for political participation especially through the vote. Perales believed that in a republic like the United States the act of voting was essential. From 1903 until the 1965 federal Voting Rights Act, Texas required a poll tax and Perales argued for its payment by voters themselves. Attorney Lupe Salinas has pointed out that Perales did not challenge the existence of the poll tax and simply advocated for its payment.[13] The poll tax was a burden on the working class.

Perales believed Mexican Americans had incentive to vote for and against specific individuals. For instance, they should vote against a sheriff "that tolerates and defends its deputies who unjustly arrest and often kill peaceful and law-abiding citizens or residents."[14] Or a mayor or commissioner who paved, cleaned and beautified Anglo neighborhoods but did not do the same for Mexican neighborhoods or school board members who built schools with bricks for whites but huts and *jacales* for "Mexicans" and did not permit "Mexicans" to attend high school. Perales believed voters should vote out racist whites.

Perales wrote extensively about the poll tax. For instance, in 1931 he published, "El Poll Tax y el Ciudadano" (The Poll Tax and the Citizen) in which he called upon "Americans of Latino origin" to pay the poll tax to stop racial abuses.[15] Five years later, he prepared a flyer or information sheet about the poll tax. He suggested the vote was the "most potent weapon" to get rid of bad politicians. He added, "Of course, without this the community elects them and can kick them out voting against them if they are incompetent, dishonest, unjust and good for nothing."[16] In 1942 Perales was active promoting the poll tax and explaining why the San Antonio mayoral race mattered[17] and three years later, in 1945, he wrote the newspaper article titled, "El 'Poll Tax' o Impuesto Electoral (The Poll Tax or Electoral Tax)."[18]

Anti-communism

While Perales believed in democratic ideology he was also anti-communist, domestic and foreign. He expressed anti-radical and anti-communist sentiment as early as 1928. He wrote LULAC co-founder J.T. Canales, "I believe that the best remedy that Uncle Sam could invent for radicals and bolshevists in the United States would be to ship them to Nicaragua, all expenses paid, and keep them there for about six months."[19] Most understood communism at the time as described by San Antonio mayor Maury Maverick, "As for Communism, all they knew was that it was Russian, unpatriotic, and sinful."[20] More evidence of Perales' anti-communism appeared in 1937 when at the national LULAC convention in Houston he wrote a resolution against communism and fascism and succeeded in getting it passed.[21] Also in 1937 he voiced opposition against domestic communists Donald Henderson and Emma Tenayuca, leaders of the Pecan Shellers' strike in San Antonio as shown in chapter 11.

Perales' also expressed anti-communist fervor in the 1950s when he wrote President Dwight Eisenhower about the Soviet Union and Cuba.[22]

He supported conservative Governor Allan Shivers, a fervent anti-Communist who tried to make Communist membership a capital offense. In 1954 Shivers called membership in the Communist Party "mass murder." Perales wrote Shivers "that is exactly what we Americans must insist that each and every candidate do in determining whether or now [sic] we are going to support him; and that any candidate who refuses to do that is not deserving of our consideration at the polls."[23] Perales said liberals Ralph Yarborough and State Representative Maury Maverick were "soft" on communism.

Besides supporting anti-communist Governor Shivers, Perales also supported Texas Congressman Martin Dies and US Senator Joseph McCarty. He wrote, "I have never supported Lyndon Johnson. On the contrary, I have fought him with all my might at times and on one occasion my support of Martin Dies caused Johnson to lose the election and enable 'Pappy' O' Daniel to win."[24] (Johnson began his political career as an avowed segregationist and Perales would not live past 1960 to see him as President pushing through national civil rights legislation. Perhaps Perales would have come to support President Johnson had he lived longer.) Perales supported US Senator Joe McCarthy, the most vocal anti-communist senator in the 1950s and the force behind the communist witch-hunt. Perales wrote friend Dr. Carlos Castañeda, "P.S. I am still a hundred percent for Senator McCarthy. It is too bad that for purely personal reasons the powers that be have gotten into an awful squabble and lost sight of the main objective which is to drive to communist rats out of the US Government."[25] But this anti-communist crusade also helped tear down the Congresso [sic] de Pueblos de Habla Española, a pro-Latino, pro-labor organization in California. The communist label often worked against progressive causes.

Perales' last statement on communism was to Canales. In 1959 he wrote, "Now if the Russians will only leave us alone and not try to impose their communism upon us and the rest of the Free World, I see no reason why we cannot continue to co-exist but it will have to be as President Eisenhower, has so well stated: 'Friendship in Peace and Freedom.' Nothing short of this will satisfy us."[26] Historian Richard A. Garcia was correct in stating that for Perales, communism was the anti-Christ.[27] We might also remember that Communists saw religion as the "opium of the people" and Perales was a strong Catholic. Ironically, Perales became a victim of McCarthyism in the 1950s. According to his daughter, "He was caught up in the McCarthy paranoia. He was placed on the watch list of the US government and was suspected of left-wing socialism and branded as radical in the eyes of many."[28] Future research efforts will likely discover this from a Freedom of Information search.

Homosociality

Perales inherited, reiterated and enacted the tradition of homosocial organizing in the Mexican-descent community, men with men and women with women. The 1910s saw mostly homosocial organizing among La Raza, but by the 1920s there was mixture of homosocial and heterosocial organizing. The 1920s also saw increased women's rights in the United States with women's suffrage being won in 1920 and even the rise of a woman governor in Texas. Nonetheless, Perales and others continued to exclude women from their own civic, political and philanthropic organizations. Moreover, while Perales supported Mexican-American women's vote he did not see the necessity of organizing women with men in LULAC in 1929.

Perales believed women maternal. In 1952 he wrote about women's participation in civic life, "Within the Mexican immigrant community this had already been instigated by the Mexican consulate and thus Mexico." Perales said, "It would be composed of Mexican women of no particular social status, so that, taking advantage of its kindness and giving spirit, along with the protection that the Commissions would grant and power that was semi-officially assigned, the Blue Cross would impart that other protection which can never be reached by the Government's effort nor, let us confess, the endeavors of men of goodwill. I am alluding to that protection which is not only bread, but love and comfort as well as enthusiasm. What I am referring to is the Christian and caring charity of our beautiful female colleagues."[29] Thus he assigned women the traits of benevolence, charity and moral reform consistent with the ideology of maternalism as noted by historian Gabriela González.[30]

Perales and LULAC supported the organization of Mexican-American women into women-only associations such as the League of Women Voters or the PTA. In his 1930 comments on Mexican-American political evolution he noted an active League of Women Voters. He wrote, "The Mexican American woman should join that League or form a Latin American women's voting league."[31] In February 1932 LULAC men installed and organized three Latin American PTAs for women.[32] (Here, the grandmother of Henry Cisneros, Carolina Munguia, would practice her maternal politics and civil rights work.) Likewise, Council 2 and 16 organized three boy-scout troops on the West side but none for girls.[33]

There were few examples of San Antonio Mexican-descent women crossing homosociality in political and civic life. In the late 1920s María L. Hernández organized a civic club along with her husband Pedro called the Orden Caballeros de América in San Antonio which allowed women and men. In 1932 Delphine Tafolla Swain ran for the San Antonio Board of Education but it is not known if Perales assisted her.[34] And in the late 1930s Mrs. Ruben R. Lozano was President of the Latin American Civic Club in San Antonio and Adela Jaime was active with the Democratic Party, especially assisting Maury Maverick.[35] Teacher Ester Pérez Carbajal's civic work with the Pan American Round Table paralleled Perales' and LULAC's work.[36]

The Order Sons of America's constitution included women's auxiliaries though none were organized throughout the 1920s. Women assisted nonetheless through women's clubs such as the Alpha Club in Corpus Christi. In spring 1933 women in Alice organized a LULAC entity. For some unknown reason Perales informed Canales that both men and women could become LULAC members. Canales wrote him in April 1933, "I am glad that I had this foresight when I wrote that article of the constitution in not limiting the membership to male persons. Now, with reference to whether it will be better to have our women organize separate from the men or whether to permit them to join the same council is a matter which I would like to let the supreme council decide. I will not undertake to decide such important question by myself."[37] However, Article 3, Section 1 on membership did not refer to the inclusion or exclusion of men or women and only addressed citizenship. A section on honorary membership mentioned "himself or herself." Canales also told Perales that he sent the Alice women a "charter No.1 as Ladies Auxiliary council." Another document suggests that J. Luz Sáenz may have organized the group which also included Adela Sloss-Vento. Perhaps Sloss-Vento was the organizer but there is no evidence that she joined. On May 7, 1933 Joe V. Alamia and J.M. Canales of Edinburg submitted a resolution "permitting Latin American women to organize on the same basis as men and to be known as Ladies LULAC Councils . . . [The women's chapters] are to have equal representation with men['s] councils at all conventions."[38]

Perales had little contact with women in LULAC. One of the only times Perales tried to reach women LULAC members, he signed a form letter initially signed by Council 16 President Charles Albidress. They sent a letter to Mrs. L.S. Perales, Alice Dickerson Montemayor, Mrs. Arnulfo Zamora, all of Laredo trying to influence them on who to vote for in the 1937 national presidency.[39] Other than that, Perales mostly ignored LULAC women. Montemayor, a prominent feminist in LULAC, was just beginning to make her mark in the League when Perales was exiting. She wrote him twice while he was national LULAC Inspector General but there is no evidence that he responded.[40]

Yet Perales did believe women should seek education, participate in civic life and vote.[41] He also advocated for women to attend night school in the 1930s.[42] In 1941 Perales listed women among people willing to work on a city election.[43] In "El Impuesto Electoral y el Porvenir de Nuestro Pueblo" (The Poll Tax and the Future of Our Community) in one of his Architects column he wrote, "Our women of Mexican origin should also pay their poll tax given they too have the right to vote and we need their help." [44] He included Adela Sloss-Vento and his sister-in-law Mrs. Santos Lozano (Francisca Pérez Lozano) in his *Are We Good Neighbors?* And, he supported women's right to fight back abusive men as shown in the Rachel González legal case in the 1950s. Moreover, he married a self-determined, intelligent woman and apparently it was her choice—not his—not to participate in Ladies LULAC.

Electoral Politics
The Association of Independent Voters, San Antonio, 1931-1933

Perales played a major role in founding the Association of Independent Voters (AIV) in San Antonio in the 1930s, one of the first groups to mobilize Mexican-American voters. Several local Mexican-American political organizations already existed in the 1930s, including a Westside Civic League led by attorney Ruben Lozano as president (1931)[45] and *Club Democrático* (1932).[46] In 1936 it sent a protest letter to the San Antonio mayor noting, "We members of the *Club Democrático* and American citizens of Mexican origin would like to indicate to you the conditions that prevail in our *colonia* so that you can immediately take action."[47] These groups sought to confront the political machine known as the People's Party in the city and tied to C.K. Quin who served as mayor from 1933 to 1943 with the exception of a term by liberal Maury Maverick.

Eleuterio Escobar, LULAC member and an Association of Independent Voters (AIV) past president, provided a first-hand account of AIV's origins. It was a non-partisan club seeking greater representation of Mexican Americans as elected officials as well as electing non-racist Euro-Texan officials.[48] Organized by Henry Guerra, the owner of a funeral home and later the first Mexican American to broadcast news in English on a major radio station in the city in 1939, the first preliminary meeting was attended by Escobar, Perales and John Solís. Solís' activism dated back to 1921 with the Order Sons of America and Escobar had joined the Order Knights of America in 1927. The AIV's first public meeting was held at Centro Mercantile on January 12, 1932 with thirteen in attendance.[49]

Perales and Solís outlined AIV's aims and purposes. The language of the "aims and purposes" suggests they were likely written by Perales. Among the aims were:

1. To participate in all local, state, and national political contests and support candidates who meet the following conditions:
   (a) Who have no prejudice against people of Latin descent.

(b) Who, if elected, will see, in so far as they may be able to do so, that people of Latin extraction get the same consideration as the Anglo-Saxons when their interests come before city, county, state, and national authorities for adjudication.

(c) Who, if elected, will see, in so far as they may be able to do so, that our race is given fair political representation in the city, county, state, and national governments.[50]

AIV was not yet ready to overtly state that it would support Latino candidates or did not believe it could garner enough votes for them. AIV's goals included equal representation on juries, payment of the poll tax, education, building needed schools and civic activism.[51]

However, Perales' notes included an agenda with some additional ideas. They were: "Every member must be politically independent until the Association decides which political party it is to endorse and support. Said party should be the one that offers our race the most advantage from the standpoint of justice and fair representation in the government. This can be ascertained by approaching spokesmen of each party. Once our Association makes its deadlines, every member will be in duty bound to vote for the same party."[52] But the idea of party loyalty was either not presented or rejected. And Perales himself would veer away from party loyalty.

A May 24, 1932 document lists officers as Eleuterio Escobar, President; Wenceslao Martínez, Vice-President, Pablo González, secretary; M.C. Trub, Assistant Secretary; and F. H. Flores, Treasurer. Perales probably chose not to serve as an elected officer but was on the twenty-one-member board of directors, all men.[53] (González and Trub would later join Perales in LULAC Council 16 in the 1930s.) Other members included Edmundo Mireles, a latter day LULAC member, educator, Spanish-language textbook writer, and husband to folklorist and educator Jovita Gonzalez.[54] Pablo Meza presided in 1934.[55]

At one event Perales called for adequate representation in city government, county and nation adding, "we are not content with our Raza working solely as street cleaners and trash collectors in the city of San Antonio and Bexar County."[56] The organization developed sample ballots and vetted candidates. One ballot shows no Mexican

198 CYNTHIA E. OROZCO

Americans running for any state or county positions except "committee men"; the ballot listed twenty-one Spanish-surnamed persons
under Precinct Committee member and it included one Latina, Adela
H. Jaime.[57] AIV also sent letters to all county candidates inviting them
for possible endorsement. The committee typically vetted thirty city
and county Democratic and Republican candidates. The screening
committee was composed of Henry Guerra, attorney N.A. Quintanilla, attorney Lozano, Perales and John Solís. Questions included: "If
we gave you our full support, how many Mexican Americans are you
going to place with good positions?" Candidates, most of who were
Euro-Texans, were often paternalistic. Among Escobar's papers is a
summary of candidate interviews dated June 11, 1932. Responses
included, "I was in school with Pable (sic) Meza, he was my best
friend"; "I always liked the Mexican people, we had a good maid
working for us for a long time, her name was Maria" or that "they had
Mexican blood in their veins." Candidate J.R. Burke said, "I don't
think anybody has a larger representation of Latin-Americans in [his]
office than I have. He said the Latin-Americans have always been his
friends. Anyone asking a favor from him was not turned down. He
said he felt entitled to a certain percentage of votes from our race in
payment of the favors he has given so far."[58] Likewise Maury Maverick, candidate for tax collector, said, "I will employ any person that is
capable and will discriminate against no race. Any candidate should
afford fair representation to the Latins and could do no more."[59]

Another document suggests Perales' influence in AIV and the
Mexican-descent community. In 1933 an AIV flyer titled "Attorney
Alonso S. Perales's Message to San Antonio's Mexican Colony" at the
top and went on to list AIV's name as well as its officials and board of
directors.[60] It noted, "If the federal government has confidence in Lic.
Perales we should too." It listed some state and county officials for
whom "Latino Americano citizens" should vote. It appealed to Latinos
in Spanish. Its endorsed ticket was W.O. Muray, Associate Justice court;
W.A. Williamson, state senator; Walter Tynam, district attorney; Hart
McCormick, district clerk; Frost Woodhull, county judge; J. Franklin
Spears, county attorney; George W. Huntress Jr., county clerk; J.S.
McNeel, sheriff; Maury Maverick, tax collector; Thomas G. Leighton,

County Treasurer; and Will W. Wood, Constable Precinct No. 1.[61] They also supported Latino allies such as J. Franklin Spears. Indeed, in the 1940s Spears worked with Perales and M.C. Gonzales to sponsor an antidiscrimination bill in the state legislature. (See chapter 12)

AIV also supported Mexican-American candidates. According to Escobar, Henry [Guerra] wanted to run for office and asked Escobar to run his campaign.[62] The group helped elect the first Mexican-American county judge secretary Col. Matias M. Trub; the first Mexican-American county clerk secretary; and a boxing commissioner.

The club used mass advertising and held mass meetings. It paid for 10,000 circulars, 100 posters and 9 radio talks.[63] Some 3,000 attended an event. The meetings sought to support attorney D.F. Davis, Bexar County district attorney and candidate for the position.[64] Speakers included Dr. Carlos E. Castañeda as well as María L. and Pedro Hernández of the Orden Caballeros de América. The club was having an impact.

Unfortunately, AIV was sabotaged by a *movida*, a political move. The club approved a resolution not to enter the gubernatorial race between Governor Ma Ferguson and Ross Sterling. But some sixty men arrived at an AIV meeting. In one night they amended the resolution not to get involved in gubernatorial elections, approved candidates, endorsed Sterling and had pre-printed thousands of circulars with AIV endorsing Sterling. Consequently, AIV "died that night of natural causes."[65] Later, Perales wrote Escobar that this was just the beginning. He wrote, "you and I will have to study this issue and see what we can do."[66] Perales was optimistic.

While San Antonio Mexican Americans did not achieve more significant electoral success until the late 1940s, they had begun to muster political muscle and could gain some political concessions such as appointments. By the early 40s when Mayor Maury Maverick ran again, Perales could claim on a radio address: "And before I forget it, Mr. Mayor, let me remind you that I have never said that I controlled 12,000 voters in the Western Section of the City. What I did say was that I had 12,000 voters backing me for the simple reason that these voters stand for the same principles that I advocate and because they know that Alonso Perales is not seeking any. . . ."[67] The Mexican-American electorate base of San Antonio had been activated.

League of Loyal Americans (Loyals), San Antonio, 1936-1946

Shortly before Perales left LULAC in 1937, he founded yet another civic organization—the League of Loyal Americans (Loyals). Once again Perales showed that he did not seek to be *the* leader or the one and only leader. He was happy with more activist groups and he would not let LULAC stand in his way. He wrote Canales in 1942: "As I have said to you before, it makes no differences what organizations each one of (sic) belongs to or what anyone says about us. . . . "[68] Perales did not care which organization he used; he just needed an organization because he valued his role in the context of collective action. The Loyals was the next association he used from the late 1930s and through the early 1950s.

This group in effect replaced Perales' LULAC Council 16. Perales explained to Dr. Carlos Castañeda, "I realize that being the Principal Founder of the League of United Latin American Citizens and having been so instrumental in making it what it is to-day (sic) it [is] most regrettable that I should have to take this course, but since we were 'kicked' out we see nothing else for us to do, if we are to continue to work for our people and our Nation. Our new name is The LEAGUE OF LOYAL LATIN AMERICANS."[69] This 1937 letter to Castañeda was written on the Loyals' stationary and there "Council Number Sixteen" appeared on the stationary though reference to the council disappeared over time. Its address was 2201 Saunders Ave. Officers were Pablo A. Meza, president; Gregorio R. Salinas, vice-president; E.F. Gabriel, secretary; and F.R. Flores, treasurer. Once again, Perales did not make himself the first president. He believed others capable and also wanted to prevent the charge that he simply desired leadership. In 1941 Perales was chair; Esteban Barrera, vice-chair; Charles Albidress Sr., secretary; and F.R. Flores, treasurer.[70]

The Loyals' aims and purposes were similar to LULAC's. They were: "To develop within the members of the Hispanic-American Race loyal and progressive citizens of the United States of America; to uphold and defend our American form of Government and our

American Institutions; to take an active interest in the civic, social and moral welfare of the community; to unite the members in the bonds of friendship, good fellowship and mutual understanding and to support benevolent, charitable, and educational undertakings; and for those purposes to establish subsidiary councils in different localities throughout the State of Texas; all as authorized by Section 2 of Article 1302 of the Revised Statutes of the State of Texas, 1925 Revision."[71] Its name revealed an awareness of Nazi, fascist and communist organizations prominent in the United States, Germany, Spain, Italy and Russia in the late 30s. It was overtly anti-communist.[72]

Perales acted as Director General along with fifteen men including Pablo A. Meza, Gregorio R. Salinas, E.F. Gabriel, Florencio R. Flores, Carlos Albidress, Pablo G. González, George L. Vann, Esteban Barrera, Matias C. Trub, Ernesto Vidales, Agustín A. González, Eleuterio Hernández, Alex G. Reyes, Lauro López, and Arcadio G. Reyes Sr.[73] No women were allowed. Perales was its "National Director General" in 1939 though there is no evidence it succeeded in crossing Texas borders.[74]

Loyals were active in numerous causes including racial classification by state and local governments. Perales represented the Loyals when racial classification became an issue in San Antonio.[75] In 1939 Perales worked as its attorney protesting the census racial classification issue when La Raza was labeled as "Mexican" instead of "white."[76] In August 1939 Mayor Quin agreed that statistical records would be changed as Perales suggested to "white, including Mexicans."[77]

Loyals also focused on housing. In 1937 it passed a resolution supporting the ten-million-dollar slum clearance which was advocated for by Father Carmelo Tranchese, the San Antonio Housing Authority and the San Antonio Junior Chamber of Commerce.[78] In 1939 it protested the actions by the Mexican Consulate and Mexican landlords who obstructed Tranchese's public housing initiative. They opposed those who rented houses/shacks to La Raza and asked the Mexican Consulate to consider the thousands of jobs that La Raza would have resulting from new construction.[79] In 1939 Loyals placed an ad in the newspaper *El Pueblo: El Periódico Hispano Americano de Tejas* asking readers to identify commercial firms that did not hire Mexicans.[80] In that same year they were involved in selecting the police chief.[81] The Loyals also addressed the red light district, an issue previously taken up by Council 16.[82] In 1939 Loyals also protested segregated facilities at Brackenridge Hospital in Austin, likely at the behest of Austin LULAC or Castañeda.[83]

In 1940 the association also began a Spanish-language newspaper/newsletter titled "Justicia Social" (Social Justice). It was "an annual publication for the civic engagement of the Hispanic American Conglomerate under the auspices of Council 16 of the League of Loyal Americans." While the publication was in Spanish the masthead had a flag in a circle with the words "Keep Old Glory Flying" suggesting US patriotism and another stating "United We Stand for Freedom, Equality, and Liberty for All."[84]

Initially the plan was to make Loyals a Texas group. Perales explained the plan to LULAC co-founder J.T. Canales: "First we intended to confine it to San Antonio, but we are being urged to organize chapters throughout the state. Therefore, we have completed a program that calls for the installation of 100 councils by January 1, 1938."[85] While it had three chapters in San Antonio by Feb. 1939 there is no evidence it became a state or national organization.[86] A 1939 document noted Perales as the National Director General with Gregorio R. Salinas as state president.[87] In 1940 Esteban Barrera served as state president. But resources, financial and human, were limited given the Depression and then World War II began. Moreover, it duplicated LULAC.

The Loyals existed through the 1940s. They organized a "Grandiosa Junta Política Anti-Maverick" (Grand Anti-Maverick Political Meeting) at Washington Irving School with music, Mexican singers and 1,000 seats for families.[88] In 1941, Castañeda said that Catholics had offered his name as possible ambassador to Mexico so he asked the Loyals to contact Cordell Hull in Washington, DC with its support.[89] During the war the Loyals placed pressure on city government to close the red light district near Fort Sam Houston, a campaign initiated by LULAC Council 16 in 1933.[90] In 1945 the Loyals also protested the ouster of the Mexican Consulate, a Mexican senator, and Mexican aviators from the park in New Braunfels. The Loyals wrote a letter to the editor of the *New Braunfels Herald* on August 1, 1945 complaining that the ouster occurred not because of "cleanliness or behavior" but "because they were Latins."[91]

Committee of One Hundred, San Antonio, 1941-1947

It seems that the Loyals or Perales realized they needed an overtly political arm so the veneer of one was created—the Committee of One Hundred. According to political scientist José Angel Gutiérrez his interview with Ruben Munguia of San Antonio suggested "The Committee of 100 was a group formed by Alonso Perales to circumvent the LULAC charter that prohibited partisan electoral activity." [92] Sociologist Sister Woods noted in 1948, "The Committee of the 100 is one of the few associations which is avowedly political in aim, being the political auxiliary of the League of Loyal Americans."[93] Before April 30, 1941 a "political club to be known as the Committee of One Hundred was formed." Its first chair was Perales; Vice-president Esteban Barrera; Secretary Charles Albidress; and Treasurer F. R. Flores. "Members accepted" were Ernesto Videles, Alex G. Reyes, Susano Díaz, Demetrio Ortega; José Solsona, Arcadio Reyes Jr., Reynolds Flores, Cristino D. Pérez and Rev. Tomás Garza.[94] Perales already had experience with *movidas* against AIV so he took leadership and the organization seems to be only by invitation since the first document mentioned "members accepted." This was truly Perales' political arm; in 1946 the Committee had stationary and its office location was Suite 714 Gunter Bldg., the same location as the Davis, Wright & Perales law firm.[95] The Committee held political rallies and openly supported its candidates.[96]

The Committee of 100 was likely a façade of at least 100 men speaking on behalf of La Raza.[97] No women were involved. Its charter was not filed with the Texas Secretary of State; it was likely just another name for the Loyals. No minutes of Committee meetings exist and nor has another list of Committee leadership been found. In 1943 Perales told Castañeda, "Our Committee of One Hundred is getting stronger every day."[98] A 1944 article by Perales published in *Fraternidad*, an anti-racism effort in Mexico, referred to two organizations but this may have a front.[99] A 1946 letterhead read, "Committee of

One Hundred, A Strictly Political Organization"[100] suggesting its work in electoral politics. Perhaps Perales took the name of the committee from Comité Contra Racismo (Committee against Racism) in Mexico with which he worked.

Perales represented the Committee of One Hundred and the Loyals in a testimony about FEPC before the US Congress in 1943. Perales said the Committee was "strictly a political organization" and that the League was civic and patriotic. He was chair of the Committee and director general of the Loyals. Yet he noted he represented a million Mexican Americans.[101]

The Committee also released a statement in March 1945 after Senator Eugenio Prado, head of Mexico's Congress, was discriminated. He wrote the president of the Pecos Chamber of Commerce about its treatment of Prado due to the racist exclusion at a local restaurant.[102] Perhaps it was this event that led Perales and LULAC to begin to work more closely with politicians in Mexico against the *bracero* program.

The Committee worked to pass the Texas antidiscrimination bill by Senator J. Franklin Spears. Perales wrote, "During my travels in Hispanic America, I have observed that the discrimination in Texas and other states of our Union against persons of Mexican or Hispanic descent is deeply resented by our neighbors to the South."[103] Perales cared about Latinos and Latin America.

In March 1944 Perales wrote President Franklin D. Roosevelt and asked for a federal law to prohibit humiliation "generally in any part of our country" to end segregationist practices. Noting that the "law is necessary in order to put an end to this painful situation immediately" since education was slow.[104] Later in December 1944 as Director General of the Committee he informed Senator Dennis Chávez they had sent him a list of 100 Texas cities and towns where discrimination "against Mexicans and Hispanic Americans generally" was practiced.[105]

In April 1944 Perales wrote of the Committee to Clare Booth Luce, US House of Representative for Connecticut, who had called for a resolution to investigate possible discrimination against minority groups in the military. In particular, he wanted to "make sure that racial prejudice is not carried to the battlefronts in such a manner that our soldiers of

Mexican extraction are sent to the firing line first and in great numbers and in preference to others of other racial lineages."[106] Moreover, in 1944 Perales wrote the Commanding General, Eighth Service Command, US Army providing him a list of more than a hundred Texas towns and cities which humiliated "American soldiers of Mexican descent." And he asked him to take steps to protect them immediately.[107]

Two year later, Perales wrote US President Harry Truman to congratulate him for his work "on behalf of the minority and forgotten groups in our country" which he said included three million Mexicans of American descent. He also hoped for approval of the Federal Employment Practices Commission bill."[108] In 1946 Perales wrote the Uvalde, Texas American Legion to report exclusion from public restaurants there including the Hangar VII Grill, the Dinette Cafe, Newport Cafe, Shadowland Cafe, Walgreen's Drug Store, Palace Drug Store, Uvalde Candy Shoppe, Manhattan Cafe, Casey Jones Cafe and Casal Cave. J.T. Canales's nephew had been denied service in the town.[109]

In 1947 Perales wrote to a Congressional committee about segregated real estate practices in San Antonio and criticized loan practices.[110] In that same year he sent the El Paso Commissioner of Immigration a letter about new contracts for migratory workers. He called for a living wage, "These workers, including the agricultural workers, should be paid a minimum of sixty cents per hours in order to subsist."[111]

The Loyals existed through 1947. In April 1947, Dr. Castañeda asked Perales if the Committee would donate to Houston LULAC council 60 member and attorney John J. Herrera who was running for the Texas senate campaign.[112] It supported the School Improvement League and Perales was listed as the Loyals' delegate to the group.[113] After 1947 the Perales papers make no mention of the Loyals. Perhaps Perales saw a new synergy after World War II and the Loyals morphed into the Pan American Progressive Association (PAPA). The Loyals was later followed by the Loyal American Democrats in the 1950s and the Bexar County Coalition by 1960 which included African Americans, liberal Mexican Americans and labor. The Coalition got Albert Peña Jr. elected to the Bexar County Commission in 1960.[114]

While it appears that the Committee had ended by 1947, another Mexican-American activist attacked Perales and his Committee in

1951. The *San Antonio Light* noted that American G.I. Forumer Ed Idar Jr. criticized Perales noting "His Committee of One Hundred is a dissident group organized by himself when he could not convince other Latin-American organizations to follow some outdated ideas on what is best for the group."[115] Were Perales' ideas outdated? It is true that he often believed he knew what was best for La Raza. But this was still a cheap shot from Idar Jr. Recall that Perales and Canales filed charges against his uncle Clemente Idar in the early 1930s and both Clemente and his father Eduardo Idar had left LULAC by 1932. Moreover, Idar attacked Perales because of his contrasting ideas and perhaps because Perales was becoming a Republican in the 1950s.

Committee of 100's Support for US Senator Dennis Chávez of New Mexico

The Committee also sought to impact national politics by supporting Senator Dennis Chávez of New Mexico. Perales was well aware of the significance of federal legislation and also noted that Senator Dennis Chávez was the only Latino in the US Congress. Recall by the late 1930s Perales was convinced that Latinos needed to get involved in federal policies. Chávez was a past LULAC member in New Mexico, a Perales ally and the Latino Congressman behind the FEPC. In the 1930s and early 40s he was the only Latino Congressperson but was joined by Antonio Fernández of New Mexico in the 1950s. Perales asked members to donate $10 to his Senate campaign since he was the only US senator of Mexican origin.[116] As Committee president Perales mailed out a form letter to "Estimados amigos" (Dear friends).[117] By May 1946 the Committee had raised $660. Perales added, "We expect to get $200.00 more within the next day or so, and we'll immediately remit it . . . I hope they are not disappointed at us poor Mexicans from Texas, altho [sic] if they are I do not blame them, as we really are behind the times in politics. Just think: folks who are worth a lot of money have pitched in $10.00 when they could just as well have contributed $100.00. Others who are well to do have contributed NOTHING. It is pitiful. Still, I hope they will not laugh at us but rather accept our small contribution as a token of friendship and good will, and above all, our admiration and respect for Senator Chávez."[118] By June 1946 Perales conceded, ". . . It is not so easy to raise money for political purposes among our people. We have not graduated yet. We still need a lot of education."[119]

Perales' Campaign for San Antonio School Board

Perales believed in honest and intelligent leadership and recognized that he was such a person. But he ran for office only once and it was for the school board. Perales had spent much of the 1930s fostering equal educational facilities in San Antonio. He realized that Latinos were needed on local school boards. A 1941 newspaper reported that in San Antonio 48,000 whites paid their poll tax compared to 10,500 Mexican Americans and 4,000 African Americans.[120] By 1944 Perales believed more Mexican Americans were voting and that a Mexican-American candidate could win. He wrote, "The unusually large number of voters who turned out for the recent school elections is most encouraging, indeed. When almost five thousand voters show up at the polls to say who shall rule the destinies of their school children, it means that from now on our schools will not be run by selfish business interests but by the citizens of the community."[121] So in April 1946 he ran for the San Antonio Independent School District school board.[122] At the time persons of Mexican descent were 1/3 of the city populace and 53% of the elementary school populace.[123] He wrote Dr. Castañeda, "Am running for the School Board. For the sake of our school children. I hope I'll win."[124]

Perales ran an up-hill battle since not only was he running against Euro-Texans, Mexican Americans who had paid their poll tax were few, Mexican-American poll tax payers did not always turn out to vote and he ran against incumbents. His campaign pledge began with a call for "adequate school facilities for EVERY CHILD," attention to juvenile delinquency and better pay for teachers. For Spanish-readers he asked, "Are you interested in progress?" and asked them to elect "one of our race that is worthy and protects the interests of our school children."[125] *La Prensa* also made it known that the position was unpaid.[126] Perales also tried to dissuade Euro-Texan fears by saying, "If you have a Latin on the board, he might be a valuable go-between for parents, children, and school attendance officers."[127] Little is known of his supporters though a two-page document noted, "We are one hundred percent for Alonso S. Perales for membership on the Board of Trustees of the San Antonio Independent School District because he is admirably qualified for the post."[128]

Perales ran against white incumbents, Paul Adams and J.E. Seibert, who pointed to Perales' race as a factor for voters to consider. They received support from Oliver Sawtell, past president of the San Antonio Builders' Exchange, who wrote to its members asking to "Let us keep our present School Board uncontaminated by destructive politics and politicians."[129]

After Perales lost the school board election he wrote friend Dr. Castañeda: "Well, I went down in glorious defeat. My adversaries managed to arouse the Anglos and they came out and beat me 2 to 1. I have one consolation, however, and that is that I defeated them in the western section 2 to 1, and at least in one box I beat them almost 3 to 1. What happened was that the Anglos turned out about 2800 strong and ours only came out to the strength of 1486 which is the total number of votes I received. Our people missed a wonderful opportunity. If they had only come out 3000 strong (and there are about 10,000 people qualified to vote in the school district, I venture to say), they would have sent the Anglos to an ignominious defeat. Well, they chose to remain at home and take it lying down, so that's that."[130] Apathy, voter education and voter mobilization were still obstacles.

Perales did not run for office again. According to his widow, "He felt that he would compromise himself if he held office" and "He always wanted to be free to defend his Raza without having to weigh political considerations."[131] Perales could have gotten on the school board, city council, county commission and state legislature had he decided to run again later. Attorney Gus Garcia, one of Perales protégées, however, won a seat on the school board two years later in 1948. Perhaps San Antonio's Mexican-American community learned its lesson with Perales and tasted the possibility of victory. Perales likely campaigned for Garcia.

Perales and San Antonio Mayors

Perales fought for and against specific San Antonio mayors. Maury Maverick was originally opposed to racial equality but evolved to support the causes of people of color and workers. In 1928 he wrote, "I do not believe in social equality of [sic] the races and act accordingly. . . ."[132] He joined Congress in 1935. By 1937 he advocated for equal pay for equal work but "he made no firm commitment to the concept of social equality between the races."[133] He also supported the white primary. African Americans delivered 5,000 votes through a political machine in the 1930s organized by African American political boss Charles Bellinger.[134] In 1937 Maverick was the only Southerner to vote against an anti-lynching bill.[135] In 1938 he claimed this vote cost his Congressional re-nomination[136] so he re-entered city politics and had to fight the Quin-Kilday-Bellinger ticket.[137] (African Americans received some patronage from white officials: they received 14% of the city's relief program though only 7 or 8% of the populace as their benevolent paternalism but not until the 1950s were African Americans a part of a liberal Texas coalition.[138])

Perales and San Antonio Maury Maverick had a long history. Perales supported him for mayor in 1939.[139] LULAC members were both pro-Maverick, a Democrat, as well as pro-C.K. Quin, a Republican.[140] Historian Richard A. Garcia noted, "The Mexican American for the first time had exhibited a knowledge of pressure politics, a consciousness of power, and an awareness of pragmatic (not nationalistic) politics. Education and knowledge were becoming political, and political knowledge was being translated into power."[141]

Mayor Maverick (1939-1941) made several promises to Perales. The city issued a major report in 1940 that concluded, "A growing consciousness of the people in power that discrimination against a strong segment of its population [the Mexicans] is not wise-in fact that it is not healthy politically, educationally, economically or socially to discriminate. Political recognition [must be extended to] its Latin American population."[142] While not written by liberals, it did mean that the business sector took note of Mexican Americans' role in politics. Maverick promised "a city ordinance to prohibit discrimination in public places; give the Mexicans adequate representation in appointive political positions; close the Red Light District or move it from the heart of the Mexican quarters; and instruct the police to treat Mexican prisoners the same as Anglos."[143]

Perales turned against Maverick when he failed to deliver.[144] Perales explained his disfavor toward Maverick in a letter to Dr. Castañeda, "Maverick and I fell out because he refused to pass an ordinance forbidding discriminations against persons of Hispanic descendent. Quin defeated Maverick, with my assistance, and passed the ordinance—an ordinance that will do more to get the peoples of the Americans together than anything Maverick has done. Yet, our Federal Government is listening to Maverick and penalizing me for having helped to defeat Maverick, the man who refused to pass the anti-Race-hatred ordinance."[145] Perales was correct. He was blackballed from federal employment during World War II in part because of Maverick's word against him.

Another fracture between the two was Maverick's OK to allow communist supporters of the Pecan Shellers' strike to use the city auditorium. In a prepared radio speech on KABC Perales called Maverick a "little dictator who has gained control of our City Government." He explained, "why we protested because they were renting the Municipal Auditorium to the Communists Homer Brooks and his wife Emma Tenayuca." And noted he had given "aid and comfort to such subversive elements. San Antonio's Americans of Mexican descent are not communists, fascists (sic) or nazists, and we strongly condemn anyone who is giving aid and comfort to these un-American elements."[146]

Perales was also upset at Maverick for his lack of substantial political appointments. A June 1940 *San Antonio Light* article read "Perales Sees Discrimination" and said Perales was critical of Maverick because of the "refusal to appoint for outstanding public office citizens whose surnames might be Pérez, García or Gonzales."[147] Perales believed political promises should be kept. He wrote, "To me a pledge is something to be carried out and not simply an empty utterance made during an electoral campaign to be forgotten after the election is won."[148] Perales was also mad because Maverick said prostitution was a "Spanish custom."[149]

Perales seems to have obtained some political concessions from Quin, Maverick's opponent. A San Antonio-political commentator, "Don Politico," wrote, "The don, when he observed the endorsement of Alonzo [sic] Perales of the Quin ticket, felt there was something concrete at its foundation." Quin "promises the Latin-Americans better representation in the higher branches of the city's services" and "will be returned to their police captaincies (sic) and probably will be given an assistant city attorney's post."[150] Either due to emerging business liberalism or pressure from the returning Mayor Quin the city passed "an ordinance saying that it is illegal for any business licensed by the City of San Antonio to discriminate. And if they did, they would lose their license."[151]

Perales did not make Maverick a permanent enemy. During World War II Maverick labeled Perales "an agitator by trade" and likely prevented him from any military intelligence post during the war. But by 1947 Perales was campaigning for Maverick again on KCOR Spanish-language radio.[152] And in 1951 Maverick set up a meeting for the School Improvement League with the San Antonio ISD board president with Perales attending. They continued to cooperate.

Perales and Texas Governors

Understanding their power, Perales began contacting Texas governors in the 1920s. He wrote Governors James Ferguson, Dan Moody and Miriam "Ma" Ferguson. He wrote Governor Jim Ferguson in the 1920s.[153] In 1927 he wrote Governor Dan Moody (1927-1931) about the assassination of some Mexican-descent men in Raymondville, Texas.[154] Moody did not respond. Perales then forwarded his concerns to US Senator Morris Shephard of Texas.[155] He also wrote Governor Miriam Ferguson on October 24, 1926 about racial violence.[156] Also, Perales and others placed newspaper ads in favor of candidates. He, Adela H. de Jaime, and Sra. María de Hernández, for example, supported a gubernatorial candidate in the 1930s.[157]

Perales had a rocky relationship with Governor Allan Shivers (1949-1957). He told Castañeda after the July 1952 elections, "It was a good protest vote against Shivers."[158] But then Perales supported Shivers in 1954. He believed that communism was the "decisive factor" in this gubernatorial campaign.[159] He even provided Shivers a list of men who campaigned against "Your Excellency": Gus Garcia, Dr. George I. Sánchez, Dr. Hector García, John J. Herrera, Ed Idar among others.[160] This is one of the few times Perales would turn against his Raza. This occurred after 1951 when Perales identified this group as his adversaries because of their pro-Wetback pamphlet stance. This was his lowest attack. In 1954 Perales was pro-Shivers. In August 1954 Perales and J.T. Canales wrote each other about their pro-Shiver stances. Canales noted that ". . . the labor unions like the CIO and its allies as well as the fanatical faction of the Democratic Party are arousing much opposition and exciting our Latin American community."[161] On September 13, 1954 Perales informed Castañeda that "In the counties where I campaigned for Governor Shivers such as Willacy, Hidalgo, and Cameron he won two to one. Before I arrived on the scene my recording had been broadcast widely throughout the Valley and so had yours." [162] He also wrote, "Por Qué Voté por el Gobernador Shivers" (Why I Voted for Governor Shivers) which appeared in *La Prensa* around before September 17, 1954 and in *La Verdad* of Corpus Christi.[163] As an elite, Perales could and did sway minds and votes, both for Democrats and Republicans. He sought to extract benefits for La Raza.

Perales and US Presidents

Perales wrote most US presidents from 1927 to 1960. He wrote Presidents Calvin Coolidge, Franklin Delano Roosevelt, Harry S. Truman and campaigned for Dwight D. Eisenhower. In February 1927 Perales wrote a US president for the first time when he protested the deaths of five men of Mexican descent in Willacy County in the Valley.[164] He sought federal government action to deal with this hate crime.[165] Coolidge did not respond.

As a representative of the Loyals, Perales contacted Roosevelt about racism at least three times in 1944.[166] He was mostly a Democrat until the 1950s when he became more conservative.[167] Joining Dr. George I. Sánchez and M.C. Gonzales, Perales met with US Vice President Henry Wallace and the Office of the Coordinator of Inter-American Affairs (OCIAA)'s director Nelson Rockefeller. They helped establish the Spanish-Speaking Minority Project within the Division of Inter-American Activities in the United States.[168]

Perales' lauded Truman and his creation of the President's Committee on Civil Rights. He also stated he feared the "Southern Block will filibuster to death every bill introduced pursuant to the Committee's recommendations."[169] Perales had faith in Truman but was eventually disappointed.

Perales supported Republican candidate Dwight D. Eisenhower for president. According to his daughter, he "worked arduously for the candidate. In all the small towns of South Texas, Perales held rallies for him. In small and large tents people would gather to hear."[170] Dr. Castañeda wrote, "On the political situation, I agree with you. I think we might just as well join the band wagon with Eisenhower. In the state I think we should work for Yarborough for Governor. Shivers is a D_ hypocrit[e]. Your Compadre Sáenz is right. I know how he has double crossed the Catholics also. I hope he gets defeated, but I doubt it. The Democratic Convention going on now is lot of Huey."[171] Perales supported Republican Shivers and not Democrat Yarborough.

Perales died before John F. Kennedy became president. Perhaps he would have returned to the Democratic Party especially since Kennedy was a Catholic.

Perales' Ties to the National Republican Party, 1950s

While Perales supported Republican Allan Shivers as governor, he believed Shivers had to deliver in the form of political appointments and payback for Mexican-American support. He expected him to appoint Mexican Americans to positions like judgeships. Moreover, he believed the local and national Republican Party should support this. He wrote both local and national Republicans to dissuade a run against Mexican-American Democrat candidate Fidencio M. Guerra who had been appointed by Shivers to the new 139th district court in Hidalgo County.[172] Democrat Guerra had to run for the office thereafter and Republican Van Culpepper ran against him.

At the local level Perales wrote John Q. Adams, an attorney, and District Committeeperson for the Republican Party about his support of Democrat Fidencio M. Guerra. He wrote, "As I said to you over the phone this afternoon, it would be a fatal blunder to permit Mr. Culpepper to make the race as a Republican nominee, if you really want to build the Republican Party in Texas. I for one feel very friendly toward the Republican Party right now and have ever since I campaigned in General Eisenhower's behalf two years ago, but I want to be encouraged instead of discouraged. I am certain thousands of Latin American citizens in Texas feel the same way." [173] He added, "PS: We have only one District Judge of Latin descent in Texas. Governor Shivers will appoint two more soon making only three in the entire State. Now you propose to take one away from us next November. Just think...."[174]

Perales also wrote National Republican Committeeman H.J. Porter to prevent Van Culpepper from running against Guerra. Perales wrote that because the "Latin American citizenry" would "interpret it as an unfriendly gesture on the part of the Republican Party toward our people in Texas."[175] However, Perales also wrote Canales, "I do not think there is much likelihood that the Republicans will withdraw their nominee."[176] Perales was right; Culpepper ran.

Perales' papers included election results. The November election favored Guerra with 7,484 votes versus 2,820 for Culpepper.[177] McAllen, Texas voted 464 for Guerra and 337 for Culpepper; Mexican-American voters outnumbered European Americans there and throughout the Valley and some Mexican-American Republicans may have crossed parties.[178] Perales' support for some Republican candidates may suggest his frustration with the Democratic Party or it could signal his anti-communism in the 1950s. Nonetheless, Texas was beginning to see the slow ascendancy of Republican rule in Texas. Mexican Americans, however, would play a miniscule role in this transition in the 1950s.

Conclusion

Alonso S. Perales' political ideology included Mexican Americanism, pro-democracy, anti-bossism, anti-communist and homosociality. His firm belief in homosociality in organizations prevented the empowerment of Mexican-origin women. He became a militant anti-communist supporting Martin Dies of Texas and US Senator Joseph McCarthy.

Perales worked all levels of government—city, state, national and international levels. He ran for the San Antonio school board only once and after he lost he did not run again. Even when it was clear that Perales could be elected years later, he chose not to run. His job was to support candidates he believed would uplift La Raza.

At the local level in San Antonio he promoted Mexican-American political empowerment. He used both the Association of Independent Voters, the Loyal American Citizens and the Committee of 100 in that endeavor. Some scholars have assumed the Loyals were the political arm of LULAC since LULAC did not officially permit involvement in electoral matters.[179] But it was officially independent but ideologically similar. Perales likely wrote the Loyals' aims and purposes and was the primary force behind the association; in essence it was his LULAC chapter. The Committee of 100 was a political arm of the Loyals operating at the local, state and national level with Perales again the force behind it. The Committee openly supported pro-Raza candidates and get out the vote efforts. It also entered national politics by supporting US Senator Dennis Chávez of New Mexico, the only Latino in Congress and an essential partner in pro-FEPC efforts. Perales testified before Congress and wrote Congressional members.

Perales regularly contacted those at the pinnacle of power—US presidents, Congressional members, Texas governors and San Antonio mayors. Perales contacted most of all the US presidents from Calvin Coolidge to Dwight D. Eisenhower; wrote Texas governors; and established relationships with San Antonio mayors, especially Mayor Maury Maverick. Perales expected concessions from those he supported and if they did not deliver for La Raza, he retracted support.

Perales was a Democrat until the 1950s when he became more conservative, shifting from Democrat to Republican likely because of his anti-communist stance and his greater religiosity that decade. Still, he sought concessions from Republicans to advance the interests of La Raza. So, at least in this instance he put race before political party assuming that is possible. Nonetheless, Perales was an effective gadfly and political activist for four decades. His work played a major role in the political uplift of Latinos in the United States.

CHAPTER 16
Public Intellectual

Alonso S. Perales was an elite college-educated lawyer who wrote for the general public who he might inform and motivate for social change and also for politicians he might influence. This chapter highlights Perales as a public intellectual and master of the media as he "employed all the discursive avenues available to him."[1] As Judge Lupe Salinas noted, he simply "assumed the duty of speaking for his people."[2] First, it examines the tradition of Mexican-American public intellectuals in the twentieth century. Second, it looks at reports of Perales' visual and oratorical appeal. Third, it reports on his speeches. Fourth, it focuses on his radio addresses and radio interviews. Fifth, it investigates the various modes of public writings he undertook: books, essays, newspaper articles and newspaper columns, news magazine articles, published letters and Congressional testimony. I also provide details behind the publication of his two books, *En Defensa de Mi Raza* (1936 & 1937) in two volumes and *Are We Good Neighbors?* (1948). Finally, the chapter discusses his speeches, radio addresses and radio interviews. Perales was not only one of the most prolific public intellectuals of the twentieth century; he was also the major intellectual behind "Mexican Americanism."

Mexican-American Public Intellectuals

According to historian Carlos Blanton, Dr. George I. Sánchez was the "single most important Mexican American intellectual between the Great Depression (1929) and the Great Society (1970)."[3] Historian Ignacio M. García also called Sánchez "the preeminent advocate of his generation."[4] Both are correct though Alonso S. Perales was the single most important Mexican-American public intellectual between the end of World War I (1919) and the Great Frontier (1960), preceding Sánchez, active for a longer span of time and writing more for the general public. Both were unusual due to an elite education rare for their generation and race. Both types of intellectuals were needed- Sánchez versed in social/political issues based on intellect and academic research addressing current issues and Perales versed in social/political issues based on intellect and legal training. Sánchez would also benefit from LULAC, the organization Perales created, and even serve as LULAC national president in the early 40s. Castañeda should also be added as another important intellectual though he did not write much for the public.

Perales provided everyday insight into current issues and attempted to reach the public every year and some years every week through newspapers. He wrote for a popular audience that was newspaper literate.[5] He had an affinity for newspapers—they gave him a voice and reached the largest reading audience possible at the time. In 1946 he wrote, "A newspaper is useful when it serves the interests of the collective."[6] Perales sought to influence and uplift the masses.

Law scholar Michael A. Olivas called Perales a public intellectual and historian Richard A. Garcia called him a "citizen intellectual." Perales simply "assumed the duty of speaking for his people."[7] No one gave him that "duty;" Perales felt it was his obligation to serve the community so as to educate, uplift and inspire. Mexican-origin academic intellectuals in the United States were few since there were no Historically Brown colleges established which could have fostered more academicians. There was no Mexican-American or Latino academic association for scholars to meet one another until the 1970s. Mexican-American academics were especially few and could only be found in Texas, New Mexico and California. In New Mexico before 1960 there was Spaniard Joaquín Ortega, Dr. Antonio Rebolledo (of Peruvian descent), Dr. Arturo Campa, Fray Angélico Chávez and Dr. George I. Sánchez, Anita Osuna Carr and Mela Sedillo. Community writers included women Fabiola Cabeza de Baca, Cleofas Jaramillo, Aurora Lucero White and Nina Otero Warren. In Texas before 1960 there was Sánchez who moved to Texas around 1940; Dr. Carlos E. Castañeda, a Mexican who grew up in Brownsville and naturalized in 1936; and historian/folklorist Jovita González. In the community there was Cleofas Calleros of El Paso; Jovita's husband Edmundo Mireles; and Emma Tenayuca in San Antonio. In California there was Ernesto Galarza who obtained a master's from Stanford in 1928 and a Ph.D. in History from Columbia University in 1944. Dr. Aurelio Espinosa of Colorado taught at Stanford and UNM. Luisa Moreno (of Guatemala descent) and Josefina Fierro de Bright were intelligent community activists. These were the most prominent intellectuals and among the most educated Mexican Americans. There were not more since few Mexican Americans reached college. As late as 1971 only 459 Spanish-surnamed persons graduated that year from the University of Texas at Austin.[8]

No national US Spanish-language newspaper existed during Perales' lifetime. Newspaper columnists and writers were other community writers and intellectuals but most of these were educated in Mexico and did not espouse Mexican-American themes. Indeed, Perales had to compete with them for the soul and future of Mexican-descent residents of Texas.

According to historian Richard A. Garcia, Perales was the "main architect" of a "new intellectual and cultural paradigm" of "Mexican Americanism."[9] And "Perales was foremost an intellectual who worked to provide the vision of a new democracy for Mexican American citizens."[10] He had "intellectual cosmopolitanism"[11] which was garnered in Alice, San Antonio, and most importantly in Washington, DC but grounded in and fostered by reading Spanish-language newspapers, especially *La Prensa*. Moreover, he was a Latin Americanist because of his diplomatic work. Racial pride was a cornerstone of this new paradigm; it was the self-worth and collective dignity of the Mexican people and Latinos in the United States that Perales cared about.

Perales engaged the public, both the Spanish-speaking world and European Americans, to educate and inform. He wrote Dr. Carlos Castañeda, historian and friend, about speaking to the San Antonio Business and Professional Women's Club (largely white) about Spanish missions or some other Texas history because ". . . the idea being to educate them on the merits of our Race so that they might feel more inclined to recognize us as worthy of consideration in all fields of human endeavor."[12] So Perales recognized the value of educating whites as well. Likewise, Perales wrote his second book *Are We Good Neighbors?* in English reaching both Mexican Americans and non-Raza.

Perales rarely addressed the intellectual condition of the Mexican-origin people though he constantly discussed their educational status. In the early 30s he wrote, "we must make it our business to raise our intellectual level."[13] However, most of his life was dedicated to the educational uplift of his people—the building of more and better schools, desegregating schools and supporting Latino college students.

Historian Emilio Zamora noted that Perales "wrote an astonishing number of works including newspaper articles, books, speeches, testimonies, resolutions and affidavits that recorded the feelings and views of hundreds of aggrieved Mexicans in Texas."[14] This, notwithstanding, as Olivas observed, "even though he was not an academic and did not have academic resources for this writing."[15] Literary scholar Donna M. Kabalen de Bichara noted, "his writing presents the voice of an intellectual who works toward constructing a public record intended to stand as a permanent fixture of discourse so as to formalize and verify what is true regarding the daily life experiences of his people."[16]

Perales' Visual Appeal

Historian Richard A. Garcia noted that Perales attracted people also for "his personality, his great enthusiasm and his stature as an articulate public speaker."[17] He was a dark man as his passport noted.[18] Perales referred to himself as "prieto"[19] (dark). When Mexican journalist Carlos Basañez Rocha attacked him in 1927 he wrote that some renegades (Perales and Sáenz) said with pride, "We are Mexicans by race, state (without seeing for a moment in the mirror their bronze color and their totally Indian aspect, the origin of their race, and not their nationality quite proudly 'I am an American.')"[20] Perales was proud of his racial origin and color. And he referred to color as a factor in discrimination; he wrote about "*piel morena*" (brown skin) in a publication in Mexico. Perhaps he was more cautious to mention this in English.[21] Nonetheless, there is no evidence that LULAC consciously sent out its "light-skinned representatives" as one historian suggested.[22]

Activist Adela Sloss-Vento described Perales' physical appearance. She recalled his "distinguished appearance"[23] as she described his looks to an academic. She described his physical delivery with his stance as erect and gestures animated. She said his speeches were mostly extemporaneous adding "his involvement and sense of mission gave his (sic) the needed inspiration, energy, and spirit."[24]

As a professional, Perales dressed for success. As a lawyer he wore suits with his 5'10 medium build, making him a tall man especially among La Raza.[25] Son Raimundo called him a "big man, tall in stature."[26] Photographs show a clean-shaven, well-groomed, well-dressed man and no photo shows him without a suit. Sometimes he wore a double-breasted suit and his pants ironed with pleats. But he was not self-conscious of his dress; only once did he and friend Dr. Carlos E. Castañeda speak of what they were wearing to an event.

Books

Perales wrote and published two volumes *En Defensa de Mi Raza* (1936; 1937) that served as the primary means that historians came to learn of him. Perhaps the idea of writing a book came from his friend J. Luz Sáenz who wrote a book on World War I in 1933. By 1936 Perales had already been active seventeen years since 1919. Likewise, 1937 marked the ten-year anniversary of the Harlingen Convention and LAC's founding. Perales explained to Castañeda as to why he wanted to write the book: "In other words, it is my hope that by putting these writings in book form others may be inspired to continue what I leave off."[27] He did not say he planned to make money or receive accolades.

En Defensa de Mi Raza

En Defensa de Mi Raza was the title of the two volumes. While typically translated as *In Defense of My People*, when Perales testified before Congress in 1943 he translated it to mean "In Defense of My Race."[28] Perales chose Artes Gráficas of San Antonio as his press likely because it was local and Mexican-American owned. Publisher

José C. Ramírez was also likely a LULAC member since he was named interim Director of Publicity under the J.T. Canales LULAC administration.[29] In 1936 and 37, Perales assisted with the publication of *En Defensa*, the first volume costing $360.00, the second $446.25, significant amounts during the Depression.[30] He sold each at 60 cents. Brother Luis Perales helped sell them in Laredo.[31]

The first volume included about twenty-five essays or news articles, mostly from *La Prensa*. It included his 1919 essay, about twenty-two essays from the 1920s and another twenty-three from the 1930s. Topics included education, voting, racial justice, health and LULAC's contributions. It did not refer to the Harlingen Convention or LULAC's founding.

The second volume included his photo, a foreword dedicated to Mexican children and youth in the United States, a one-page introduction, a prologue by Castañeda and a brief biography. It was followed by commentaries on the first volume written by Prof. Manuel A. Urbina, J. Luz Sáenz and Prof. J.A. Sauceda. Fifty-two editorials or letters written by Perales from 1928 to 1937, most originally appearing in newspapers followed as did, "El Verdadero Origen" (True Origins), an account of the founding of LULAC and a table of contents.

"True Origins" provides Perales' account and may have been written since Ben Garza, the first national president of LULAC, died that year.[32] Perales noted that he had the idea for LULAC in 1919 and that he spoke to Pablo González and Filiberto Galván of San Antonio about it. He then stated he went to Washington to study and prepare himself to help solve the community's problems in Texas. Through newspapers and these two friends he learned of the Order Sons of America and realized they did not meet his ideals. He then provided an account of the 1924 lecture tour, using excerpts from *El Fronterizo* newspaper of Rio Grande City in July 1927. He then mentions that the Latin American Citizens (LAC) was formed in Harlingen in 1927 but he does not mention the exclusion of Mexicans. Then he included some of his correspondence with Ben Garza and J.T. Canales. Garza's letter shows his reticence to become the first national president of the forthcoming LULAC. The documentation that Perales provides here does not show the work some San Antonio OSA members like M.C.

Gonzales, John Solís and Mauro Machado's made to foster this emerging civil rights movement. Nor does it focus on the limitations of the OSA or Tafolla Sr. except to say that Tafolla Sr. had been president from 1921 to 1929. Perales provided evidence here that he was the principal founder of LULAC. Those who purchased the book would have not heretofore known that Perales was the true founder. He also showed that Ben Garza played a minor role. Still, few bought the book and the myth of Garza's leadership had begun after he passed. Still, Perales included original sources for latter-day historians.

Volume two also included letters to the editor, protests against segregation in towns like San Angelo and New Braunfels, Texas and racial exclusion in Wharton, Texas. Most essays focused on immigration, the US census racial classification issue, housing and health. Several articles were about LULAC's work. Not a single title referred to "México Americanos;" they all referred to "Mexicanos."

Are We Good Neighbors? (1948)

One of the most important contributions by Perales in the 1940s was his documentation of racist acts in specific towns on specific dates in *Are We Good Neighbors?* Perales and the Committee of One Hundred had written President Franklin D. Roosevelt about 100 Texas towns with racist practices and received no response. Adela Sloss-Vento wrote a similar essay, "The Problem with Many Texas Towns" published before in 1943 which listed specific racist incidents in Corpus Christi, Kingsville and McAllen.[33] Moreover, M.C. Gonzales also gathered info on discriminatory acts in 100 Texas towns. In 1944 and 1945 Perales continued to ask readers for details about discriminatory acts at specific businesses or public accomodations in specific towns with specific dates.[34] Scholar George A. Martínez noted, "The affidavits supplied by Perales reveal white supremacism at work in the distribution of benefits, burdens, goods and services."[35]

Perales explained the impetus for the book. Citing a recent incident against Henrietta Castillo of the Bishop's Spanish-Speaking Committee in New Braunfels, Perales noted that "I believe the time has come to release all the evidence I have in the form of a book, and entitle it something like this: Discrimination—the Number One Problem in Texas; or, 'The Facts about Discrimination in Texas.' . . . I believe we have been patient enough . . . It will be all in English. Some Anglo-Americans in Texas claim they are not informed upon the subject. Well, here is their chance to learn all about the discrimination now going on in Texas."[36] Unlike *En Defensa*, this book was in English. Perales also wrote Sáenz, "I think the time has come to write a book titled: "Discrimination—the Number One Problem in Texas, or The Facts about Discrimination in Texas."[37] He noted he would use affidavits, "in other words, that is the evidence." Castañeda told him his book should not include discrimination in the title because whites would think the book was about African Americans[38] and proceeded to give him some ideas on book organization such as to place religious leaders first, maybe include a Euro-Texan and then a Mexican-American voice, and perhaps place persons of prominence first.[39] Later one afternoon, Castañeda helped him put the book together.[40]

The title *Are We Good Neighbors?* suggested it was a critique of the US Good Neighbor policy as well as a critique of racial segregation by white "neighbors." According to Gabriela González," "The title summoned a past marked by President Franklin Roosevelt's Good Neighbor foreign policy, with the goals of respecting Latin American nations' right to self-determination and unifying the western hemisphere" and was "an indictment of the United States for failing to be a good neighbor every time racial and cultural discrimination was practiced against people in Latin American or Americans of Latina American descent."[41] Pan-Americanism, the Good Neighbor policy and racism were major subjects in the book. It also contained an introduction by Castañeda and a short biographical listing of Perales' education, employment and civic work.

The book was organized into six parts: Part I, "The Problem as Seen by Others"; Part II, "The Problem on the National Level"; Part III, "Concrete Cases in Texas"; Part IV, "Articles and Comments"; Part V, "Correspondence and Comments"; and Part VI, "Mexican Americans in World War II." Part I included commentary by Archbishop Robert E. Lucey, Dr. Castañeda, oilman and liberal Jack Danciger and J. Luz Sáenz. It only addressed Texas, California and New Mexico which made it Southwestern. Part III included affidavits of discriminatory incidents, a list of racist towns in Texas and letters from those experiencing discrimination. Perales' list included towns across the state and contended that at least 150 Texas towns practiced discrimination.[42] "The Problem as Seen by Others" began with a statement by Archbishop Robert E. Lucey almost giving the book a christening over the optimistic racial project.[43] The book also included documents related to Perales' activism from 1928 to 1937 and his testimony in the 1930 Congressional hearing on Mexican immigration.

Affidavits of racial discrimination in Texas, some eighty pages, were the most important part of the book. It made individuals' private experiences into public, permanent record and legal documented systemic racism since Perales was a lawyer and notary public since 1933.[44] Michael A. Olivas noted, "the *testimonio* lead of *Are We Good Neighbors?*, the extraordinary work-extraordinary in the sense that there were very few such works in this genre, evidence of his lawyerly instincts."[45] Scholars Norma Adelfa Moulton and George A. Martínez also commented on Perales' methodology in *Are We* According to Mouton, "By collecting the cases of discriminatory practices directly from those who had experienced them and later bringing the worst cases to the attention of the public whether through his weekly column or through his political contacts in Washington, DC, Perales was instrumental in gaining recognition for the plight of the Mexican American in Texas and elsewhere and ameliorating the social condition of his community."[46] He gave numerous specific examples of anti-Mexican sentiment.

Martínez noted the book's anti-racist methodology and wrote, "The methodology of Alonso S. Perales in establishing the existence of widespread discrimination against Mexican Americans is consistent with recent critical race theory methodology and epistemology which had advocated 'Looking to the bottom' and seeking knowledge about issues race [raised] "in the particular of [people of color's] social reality and experience."[47] According to Martinez, this was "subjugatged knowledge" outside of the white/black civil rights paradigm.[48] Castañeda reminded Perales of this binary (white/black) when he told him to name his book differently. As scholar Richard Buitron noted, "In the manner of Progressive muckrakers like Upton Sinclair or Lincoln Steffens . . . Perales compiled the statements of Tejano activists, Anglo liberals and the affidavits of aggrieved Tejanos comprise the content of this compelling book."[49] Martínez also noted that the book used legal methodology, "Perales used the skills that he developed as a lawyer—i.e., taking sworn testimony—to advance his civil rights project. Perhaps only a lawyer would have thought to put people under oath in order to establish and prove the existence of discrimination."[50] And he added, "Perales insisted that it was necessary to impose legal constraints on the dominant group to bring an end to racial discrimination against Mexican Americans."[51]

Through this publication, Perales gave value to the experiences of everyday Latinos. According to scholar Lorena Gauthereau, his project "reveal [ed] the embodiment of racism in the United States. One after another, these accounts tell stories of everyday life: going out for dinner with family, spending time with friends, looking for employment, moving to a new house, riding the bus to school, or going to the barbershop for a haircut. Yet, for Mexican Americans in the 1940s, these activities are marked by disgust, hatred, shame, and even violence. This project highlights the personal history of racism, one that takes place in our neighborhoods to real people, rather than distanced through abstract statistics."[52]

Perales' *Are We* continued *En Defensa's* trajectory by documenting racial discrimination against people of Mexican-descent in Texas.[53] Perales offered his remedies to end discrimination there and in other states by: 1) promoting education in schools, churches, the press and radio; 2) ending segregated schools; and 3) passing state and federal legislation against discrimination.[54] Historian Zamora called the book "the single most important compilation of primary records that addressed the Mexican experience at midcentury."[55] No book on the Mexican-origin people compared to it in any other state.

Perales' *Are We* also referenced a few racist incidents from several other states. For instance, Mrs. Felix H. Morales of Houston reported on incidents experienced by two active duty Latino servicemen in Dodge City, Kansas who were asked to sit with African Americans at the movie theatre because they were not white.[56] While she likely harbored anti-African American sentiment, common among people of Mexican descent, she also pointed out white privilege and segregation. José Caballero of San Antonio wrote Perales about conditions in North Dakota where he went to work at a beet sugar company. He said the treatment there was "much worse than [the treatment] of Afro Americans in Texas" and that "they sell to them in the kitchen, but to us in this state of North Dakota not even in the kitchen [will they sell food to us]."[57] Senator Dennis Chávez of New Mexico also received these kinds of letters but they remained in his archive, unknown to the public. Perales made them public.

With this book, Perales sought to make it clear that anti-Latino sentiment was not restricted to Texas. He included statements by leaders from Los Angeles, Chicago and New Mexico. Eduardo Quevedo, president of the Coordinating Council for Latin-American Youth, said he represented seventy-two organizations with 15,000 members.[58] Frank Paz, President of the Spanish-Speaking People's Council of Chicago, said he represented 45,000 people from Chicago, part of Indiana and the southern part of Wisconsin including Milwaukee.[59] He discussed employment discrimination in the railroad, steel mills and packing industry.

Artes Gráficas also published this book. Mainstream presses were generally not interested in the Mexican-origin people before the 1970s. Witness rejection letters from major presses sent to Jovita González in the 1930s, J. Luz Sáenz in the 40s and Américo Paredes in 1958. Perales told Castañeda he was considering Artes Gráficas but was unsure if owner Ramírez would accept the project because of a possible lawsuit.[60] Perhaps Perales had some previous difficulty with his first book. Initially he had 100 books printed at the cost of $2.00 each since "The thing is to make it easy for people to buy it."[61] Perales advanced Artes Gráficas $500.[62] Overall, this book cost him $1,550 but he trusted with the help of God I may get every cent I put into it. I'll be happy if I come out even." [63] According to political scientist Benjamin Márquez, Perales said the printing cost was $2,475

($23,097 in 2010 dollars).[64] That was a lot of money but a wise, lasting investment in anti-racist work that cemented a legacy for Perales. Perales was disappointed that sales were limited and that "his people" did not support him.[65] But Perales was not a salesman—he was an activist attorney. Moreover, too many of "his people" could not read English, afford books or were under-educated. And too many European Americans disliked his people and did not want to be educated. Still, Perales sought to target Texas legislators, the Texas press, and the press in Mexico by asking white ally Jack Danciger if he would help support his effort by purchasing copies for them to which he agreed.[66]

Perales also relied on friends to promote the book. He asked activist friend Sáenz to get a resolution before the American G.I. Forum to get each council to buy five or six copies and give them to libraries and schools.[67] It is unlikely that he approached LULAC. Castañeda volunteered to give several to libraries and newspapers that would "bring it to the attention of millions."[68]

Are We had mixed reception. Thomas Bledsoe in *Southwest Review* said "he has called upon both legal training and his experience in research" and called the book a welcome addition joining other publications by Pauline Kibbe, Ruth Tuck and Malcom Ross of the ACLU. Noting that "he has called upon both legal training and his experience in research," he surmised, "Three points emerge from the book: the prevalence of discrimination through the Southwest and in other parts of the country; the immediate necessity that this discrimination be eliminated for the general well-being of the nation" and the call for "the enactment of anti-discrimination legislation, federal and state." [69]

Charles G. Kidder of the University of Texas at Austin's newspaper the *Daily Texan* gave a less positive review on Jan. 9, 1949. He wrote that it was "a weak effort to present the problem on a national and state level" and that Dr. Sánchez, "who has probably done more for this minority than any other man, receives only slight mention." But Kidder knew little of Perales' civil rights work and he did not know that Perales and Sánchez were no longer allies. Henry L. Roberts of *Foreign Affairs* also reviewed the book in July 1960.[70]

Perales' was vindicated when the San Antonio Pan American Progressive Association (PAPA) newsletter was released on December 1,
1948, reprinting Ted Deming's review, "San Antonio Lawyers Asks
Provocative Question" from a local newspaper. Deming called it "one
of those rare volumes of human thought which must be 'chewed and
digested' thoroughly." He noted that Perales "who is qualified to
speak from experience, indicts the people of Texas, and the Southwest
in general, for the rampant practice of prejudice and discrimination
against fellow Americans in a social order which is supposedly constructed OF and FOR free equal peoples."[71]

Pamphlets

In 1931 Perales published "El México Americano y la Política del
Sur de Texas" ("The Mexican American and the Politics of South
Texas"), a translation of an article by political scientist Oliver Douglas
Weeks and two one-page essays. Weeks sought to document the political significance of LULAC's founding as well as one by school
reformer J.O. Loftin.[72] Perales translated Weeks' article into Spanish
because he believed it would "stimulate interest in the 'poll-tax.'"[73]

Perales commented briefly on Weeks and added his own essays,
"El Poll Tax y el Ciudadano" (The Poll Tax and the Citizen) and
"Nuestra Evolución General" (Our General Evolution). Since Mexican Americans were emerging from decades of boss rule, payment of
the poll tax was key to their political empowerment. Perales asked
Latinos to pay the poll tax and stated, "If we American citizens of
Latino origin want to be respected, if we want to be prepared to vote
against all the candidates that have abused our brothers in race, mis-
treating them, humiliating them, assassinating them and denying them
justice when necessary, we need to pay our poll tax" and "we need to
do so before the first of February."[74] He printed over 500 copies perhaps with financial assistance from a one-page listing of supporters.
Activist Roberto E. Austin of Mission ordered 2,000 copies of one of
Perales' writings.[75] In 1939 Perales also wrote "Our Rights and Duties
as Citizens" which appeared in J. Montiel Olvera's, *First Year Book
of the Latin-American Population of Texas*.[76]

Newspapers

From no other source was Perales better known than through his newspaper articles, particularly in *La Prensa* of San Antonio. By June 1924 he had already written at least four newspaper essays as well as a letter to Governor James Ferguson which he published in 1921 in *El Latino-Americano* of Alice, Texas.[77] From the mid-20s to 1930 Perales utilized *Diógenes* of McAllen as his major voice piece.[78] And by 1930 *El Comercio* of Harlingen referred to Perales as a journalist.[79] Newspapers were his preferred weapon to wage war against racism and to advance civic and political empowerment. In 1946 he wrote, "The press is a necessity to solve said problems in a satisfactory manner and no one needs the invaluable help of free press as much as minorities do."[80]

Historian Emilio Zamora noted Perales' work in the press, ". . . no one else matched Perales' ceaseless protests and persistent calls for unity, frequently through Spanish-language newspapers . . ."[81] Perales' activism in print inspired Adela Sloss-Vento to do the same though as a wife and mother, she wrote much less.[82] Nevertheless, considering gender she too left a most impressive record in Spanish and English in South Texas newspapers.

Perales wrote opinion-editorials and letters to the editor for several English-language newspapers including the *Washington Post*, *San Antonio Express* and the *San Antonio Light*. San Antonio had at least three English dailies[83] while Texas had no statewide English-language newspaper before 1960. Except for one *Washington Post* essay, he did not write for non-Texas newspapers or for a national audience.

Those Spanish-language newspapers Perales wrote for in Texas included: *El Latino-Americano* (Alice); *La Prensa* (San Antonio), *El Pueblo* (San Antonio), *El Monitor* (Falfurrias), *El Fronterizo* (Rio Grande City), *Diógenes* (McAllen), *Las Novedades* (Kingsville),[84] *Evolución* (Laredo), *La República* (El Paso); and *La Verdad* (Corpus Christi).[85]

Of all the newspapers listed, *La Prensa* was Perales' preferred forum. He largely depended on the newspaper owned by Ignacio Lozano, a Mexican immigrant.[86] La Raza would have been in worst shape without it. Sloss-Vento called it "that great daily newspaper that was like a blessing from God in those difficult days, because it lent all its assistance to our cause and carried the message to the Mexican-American public."[87] Its public also included Mexican immigrants and Latinos. *La Prensa* had a political bent that was oriented toward Mexico, *México de afuera*, and Latin America. It also had a conservative bent and condemned socialism.[88] It is unknown whether Perales agreed with Castañeda that *La Prensa* was anti-American and typically against the Mexican government, at least up until 1930.[89]

While *La Prensa* covered Mexico, Latin America and international news, it gave Mexican Americans like Perales a Tejano voice. Lozano, himself, had served as managing editor of San Antonio's *El Imparcial de Texas*, an activist newspaper under F.A. Chapa's direction, so he understood Tejanos.[90] "Lozano understood the importance of a Mexican consciousness of collectivity in a world rapidly becoming Americanized," historian Richard A. Garcia noted.[91] In the same manner, historian Brandon H. Mila noted that *La Prensa* "accepted and validated the Mexican Americans' political strategies without criticism."[92] Perales was given carte blanche, as is seen in a letter Perales wrote Sáenz, "Sometimes I also get desperate but then I think about our access to the press. We should maintain contact with our community. *La Prensa* is a good means of communication because it circulates a lot through the state."[93] Indeed, my mother Aurora E. Orozco wrote a poem about a boy selling *La Prensa* in the streets of a Mercedes, Texas barrio.[94]

Perales considered this newspaper his right hand. In 1926 he wrote "Viva *La Prensa*-La Tribuna de la Raza," (Long live *La Prensa*-La Raza's Tribune) calling it the tribune of "Nuestra Raza" (Our Race).[95] In fact, most of the articles published in the second volume of *En Defensa* were first published in *La Prensa*. Around 1936 Perales had a section appearing regularly in the newspaper.[96] *La Prensa* closed after Perales' death; it closure would have been a tremendous blow to him.

Perales served as columnist for both *La Prensa* and *La Voz Católica* (*The Catholic Voice*). From 1945 to 1959 Perales' *La Prensa* column was titled "Arquitectos de Nuestros Propios Destinos"[97]

(Architects of Our Own Destiny). The column promoted upward mobility and economic health for individuals and the collective of La Raza.[98]

As noted, Perales began writing in 1919 and continued in earnest throughout the 1920s. In 1924 Perales protested lynching; he wrote, "We would like for persons of Mexican descent in violation of the laws that govern the country to be tried before a competent Court of Justice and to not be lynched, as was the unfortunate young man Elias Villarreal Zarate in Weslaco, Texas on November 1921."[99] In October 1924 he also wrote, "El Ideal de los México-Americanos," (Mexican American Goals) calling for the rights and privileges of citizenship and progress without whites' interference.[100] Also in 1924 he wrote, "La Evolución de los México-Americanos"[101] (The Evolution of the Mexican Americans). This essay foresaw the major themes of his life: "What is the goal of Mexican Americans? Are they trying to Americanize themselves? Do they want to deny their race? Do they beg Anglo Saxons to allow them to mingle socially with them?"[102]

In October 1926 he protested to Governor Miriam Ferguson[103] and in August 24, 1926 the *Washington Post* published an article called "Restriction for Peon?" in which Perales defended Mexican peons as honorable and efficient and responsible for the wealth that cotton produced in Texas.[104] On September 25, 1926 *Diógenes* of McAllen announced his response to "rude and unwarranted" attacks on Mexican peons. These examples show how Perales worked to publicize his acts.

On February 2, 1927 *La Prensa* reported that federal authorities were investigating the deaths of several murders in Willacy County in the Valley.[105] In February 1927 Perales wrote US President Calvin Coolidge about the deaths of the five men.[106] That same month Perales sent a letter of protest to Texas Congressman Morris Sheppard and Texas Governor Dan Moody.[107] And in 1928 he wrote "Problemas de Nuestra Raza en Estados Unidos" (Problems of Our Race in the United States) for *Diógenes*.[108] These are some of his most noteworthy articles published before 1929.

Perales began his column *Arquitectos de Nuestro Destino* (Architects of Our Own Destiny) in August 1945. The column ran without any subtitles throughout 1945 but by 1946 Perales offered titles defining his topics, such as "Vigorosa campaña en pro del pago del impuesto electoral" (Strong campaign for the Poll Tax); "El Comité Coordinador de San Antonio entra en acción" (The San Antonio Coordinating Committee in Action); "México honra y favorece al Estado de Texas una vez más" (Mexico honors the State of Texas Once More); "Nuestra Democracia a prueba una vez más"(Our Democracy is put to the test once more); "Nuestros hermanos de San Angelo laboran por el bien de nuestro pueblo" (Our San Angelo brothers work for the community's well-being); "El conocimiento de las dos culturas mantendrá la amistad de los dos pueblos" (Familiarity with the two cultures will keep the friendship between the two communities); "Cómo solucionar el problema de los sheriffs, condestables y policías" (How to solve the sheriffs, constables, and police problem); "Democracia recibe un tremendo revés" (Democracy Hits Reverse); "¿Nos conviene segregarnos dentro de la Legión Americana?" (Does segregation within the American Legion benefit us?); "Promoviendo la Doctrina del Buen Vecino" (Promoting the Good Neighbor Policy); "Nuestros Veteranos México-Americanos deben aprovechar las oportunidades Educativas" (Our Mexican-American Veterans should take advantage of Educational Opportunities); and "Vamos a limpiar y a embellecer nuestros solares" (Let's clean and beautify our yards.).[109]

Perales' column in his last years, 1954 to 1959, included the following titles: "Justo Reconocimiento a Nuestro Pueblo" (The Just Recognition of Our Community); "Hagámonos Fuertes Pagando el Impuesto Electoral: ¡Salve, Oh (yes oh) Raza Latina!" (We Are Strengthened by Paying Our Poll Tax, Save Our Latin Race); "Representación Para Los Nuestros en el Gobierno del Estado de Texas" (Our Representation in Texas State Government); "Triunfo de un Candidato México-Americano" (Victory by a Mexican-American Candidate) (about Fidencio M. Guerra); "El Pueblo Hispano de Texas Estamos de Placemes" (The Hispanic Community in Texas); "Continúa el Entusiasmo con Motivo de la Reaparición de *La Prensa*" (Support Continues for the Reappearance of *La Prensa*); "Cartas de Nuestros Lectores" (from Saginaw, Michigan) (Letters from our Readers); "Gran Manifestación Pública de Nuestra Fe" (Great Public

Manifestation of Our Faith); and "Honor Eterno a Las Madres" (Eternal Honor to Our Mothers).[110]

News Magazines

Perales also wrote a few essays for *LULAC News*, the League's monthly news magazine, since the early 1930s. He believed in informing LULAC members by sharing lectures, etc. once a week or at least twice a month."[111] He was aware that his writings inspired his readers. This news magazine reached New Mexico and Washington, DC by the 1930s and California, Arizona and Colorado before World War II. By the 1950s it reached the Midwest and parts of the East Coast, but Perales was no longer writing for it.

Perales wrote five essays specifically for *LULAC News* in the 1930s.[112] All essays reflect his self-recognition as a leader and explain how leadership was a trait from which all could benefit. In "Training for Leadership" he called for all Raza town and city leaders to organize night schools for the masses.[113]

Perales also wrote for several other news magazines, including *Pan American*, a San Antonio news magazine, which began in 1944 under the auspices of LULAC council 2 member Jacob Rodríguez.[114] He also wrote for *Revista Latino Americana* published in Mission in the Valley and edited by Gilberto Díaz.[115] *Fraternidades*, a bilingual news magazine of Mexico's Comité Contra Racism (Committee Against Racism), an anti-fascist effort, also included some of Perales' essays.[116]

Published Letters

Letters are typically private and not part of public intellectual work. On some occasions Perales informed newspapers of letters he had sent so the public would understand key issues. Scholar Donna Kabalen de Bichara, in her reading of the letters indicates that they "express[ed] counter-hegemonic cultural politics that are situated within a Third-space that can be understood as a site of struggle or alternative space of enunciation that emphasizes a sense of identity as well as the transmission of specific cultural politics and values."[117] For instance, in 1921 Perales informed *El Imparcial de Texas* that he had written a letter of protest to Governor James Ferguson about his demeaning comments about Mexicans in the *Ferguson Forum*.[118] Likewise, when Perales published *En Defensa* he included a letter he wrote the mayor of San Angelo, Texas condemning segregation in the town's municipal auditorium.[119]

Congressional Testimony

Perales testified at several US Congressional hearings. In 1930 he argued that a quota against Mexicans should not be established if the rationale was due to racist thinking of Mexicans as a racially inferior people. He presented his case, answered questions, submitted his resume and accompanying evidence. He said he had reason to believe Mexicans were being excluded because they were not of "Teutonic" or "Nordic extraction."[120] Perales was well aware of intellectual and social scientific justifications of racism and submitted a listing of his diplomatic work to show his worthiness. He also included social science documentation on the history, culture and racial makeup of people from Mexico. He included statistics that demonstrated the racial distribution of the Mexican people as "mestizo (white and Indian)"; "pure Indian" as 59% and 29%, respectively. He also included excerpts from books such as *Social Psychology* by Floyd Henry Allport; Caspar Whitney in "What's the Matter with Mexico?"; Frank Tannenbaum, *The Mexican Agrarian Revolution*; George McCutcheon McBride, *The Land System of Mexico*; *The Republic of Mexico, Its Agriculture, Commerce, and Industries*; Carlton Beal's work on Mexico; L. Spence *Mexico of the Mexicans*; Robert N. McLean *That Mexican*; and Oliver Douglas Week's essay on LULAC.[121] This bibliographical essay shows Perales' sought to appeal to their intellect showing he was aware of current academic research about Mexico written in English.

Perales also testified for Senate Bill 101 for the FEPC on behalf of the Loyals in 1943 and 1944. He again submitted his resume; notarized incidents of race discrimination; a statement by Archbishop Lucey from *Are We Good Neighbors?*; an editorial from *Novedades* of Mexico City; and the testimony of a man who stormed Normandy Beach in World War II and the names of members of the Loyals.[122]

Orator

There are a few studies of Chicano oratory such as Dr. Héctor P. García; United Farm Workers' leader César Chavez; land grant activist Reies López Tijerina; and United Farm Workers' leader Dolores Huerta.[123] One study focused on Chicano protest rhetoric after 1960[124] and Hammerback and Jensen noted, "rhetoric functions to construct reality for listeners or readers and thereby influences their behavior. . . ."[125] Rhetorical discourse is used to "induce attitudes and influence activism—formed and furthered the protest."[126]

Perales began his career as an orator in college in Washington, DC. where he spoke about Mexican President Álvaro Obregón before the *Círculo Español* (Spanish-speaking Circle) of George Washington University in 1920.[127] A newspaper reported, "The speaker briefly sketched Mexico's history, described its government and constitution, and drew attention to the land question."[128] Another newspaper article titled "Urges Deep Study of Spanish Laws" reported Perales' speech to the Spanish-American Atheneum meeting in 1922.[129] He also spoke to the Secular League, an open forum in Washington addressing the topic "The Truth about Mexico"[130] and by 1924 Perales considered himself an orator; a 1924-*San Antonio Light* article on "Border Aliens" included the subtitle "Orator of Mexican Descent."[131]

According to historian Richard A. Garcia, Perales had a "booming voice"[132] and several who actually heard and saw Perales also wrote of his oratorical skills. Adela Sloss-Vento said Perales "spoke with great enthusiasm of our problems"[133] and added, "I can still hear their [Perales', Canales', Sáenz'] voices in the meetings and courtrooms, speaking to the people with all their heart and with the sincerity that characterize them. I seem to hear them urging the people to unite and protest the hate and injustice. Their sonorous voices were like those of a magic bell, reaching out to the heart of the Latin American people"[134] Tristán Longoria, a LAC member in La Grulla in the

Valley, said, "I remember attorney Alonso S. Perales as a young distinguished man, full of enthusiasm, with much humanity toward his
brothers. With this optimism and humanity, he magically united
everyone."[135] Son Raimundo also recalled his "loud, strong, authori-
tative voice." [136] Two photos show Perales' hand gestures, one above
his head and another with a clenched fist.[137]

There are a few reports of Perales' oratorical skills. A 1942 *calavera* (Spanish-language playful, mocking poem) noted his "*palabras
sonoras*" (loud words).[138] Professor Gilbert R. Cruz, a historian from
Texas, heard Perales speak in the late 1940s and wrote me the following note:

> Perales represented a new generation of articulate professio-
> nals, emerging middle class business men and battle scarred
> veterans proud of their bicultural heritage. He possessed an
> impressive speaking voice that thundered with conviction.
> His capacity to use both languages with enormous facility and
> skill captivated his audience. I swelled with pride upon hea-
> ring his voice. So did everyone else. . . . He projected immen-
> se loyalty to the institutions that were paramount in the lives
> of his people, notably the extended family, role of the Ancient
> Church, and the grandeur of his culture. There was no ques-
> tion about his moral courage. He spoke with an almost a deep
> religious feeling of purpose. Perales was tough, driven and
> endowed with an optimism to combat an adversary basking in
> triumphal boasting."[139]

San Antonio news reporter Paul Thompson called him "Mr. Peri-
cles," a reference to the Greek orator who argued for democracy.[140]
Son Raimundo recalled seeing his dad in the courtroom, "My daddy
began talking in a very loud and deep voice, very different from what
I was used to hearing. He clutched his fist and the room was quiet
except for my daddy's strong and forceful voice."[141]

There are many reports of Perales' numerous speaking engagements. In March 1932 friend and attorney J.T. Canales wrote M.C.

Gonzales, "Perales has been delivering lectures on political subjects. His hobby is 'true democracy' and 'Government of the people, for the people, and by the people.'"[142] Also in March 1932 Gonzales wrote Canales, "Perales told one of my friends that he had gone to Edinburg at the special request of Bravo and that he and Bravo had sought to make a political speech . . . ."[143]

In June 1940 Perales gave a talk titled, "What Kind of Education do Latin-Americans Want for their Children?" He answered we "want the same kind." He quoted Merrill M. Colins' essay "Let Us Teach Democracy" from the *Texas Outlook*. He added, "Ours must be a war against prejudice, ignorance, injustice, and poverty . . . We must teach and practice the doctrine of Jesus Christ having as its theme love and tolerance." He believed that the teachers in public schools wielded great influence over youth. He noted, "We hope the day will soon come when adequate school facilities will be available in every community in Texas for the children of Mexican descent. By adequate school facilities we mean good school buildings and equipment, adequate playgrounds and equipment, and well-paid teachers who not only possess the necessary educational qualifications, but who also have a sympathetic attitude toward and understanding of Texas' inhabitants of Mexican extraction."[144] He also spoke before educators, likely University of Texas professors.

Around April 1952 he was invited to speak about "Power at the Polls" and wrote various friends about the number of Latino elected officials in their counties to prepare.[145] He wrote Canales of Brownsville and attorney John J. Herrera of Houston LULAC Council 60. These are only a few examples of the hundreds if not thousands of speeches Perales gave in his lifetime.

Radio Addresses and Radio Interviews

Perales accessed the radio to reach a broad audience in Spanish and English. San Antonio opened its first radio station, WOAI, in 1922.[146] According to political scientist Benjamín Márquez as early as 1924 "in his radio programs, he reminded community members that they were a dignified and proud people and challenged Anglos to recognize the merits and virtues of a 'dignified and noble race.'"[147]

Spanish-language radio was available in San Antonio by the 1930s.[148] That decade there were no Spanish-language radio stations and only Spanish-language hour program slots. In the 1930s Spanish-language music was played on KONO, WOAI (Chucho Martínez' program), KMAC (Mexican Commercial Hour), WOAL (Latin Melodies) and KABC (La Hora Latina).[149] Rene Capistrán González had a half-hour program called "La Voz de la Raza" on KACB and KONO had La Estrella from 1933 to 1935.[150] Perales was on the Spanish-language radio stations KABC and KCOR as well on the English-language KIWW, KMAC and KONO.[151] In Spanish he addressed his listeners as "Mis distinguished conciudadanos" (My distinguished co-citizens).[152] In 1936 he addressed radio station KMAC about an art contest sponsored by Club Copelia, a Mexican women's club. He went on to discuss leadership for the progress of his race.[153]

Perales spoke on a wide range of topics. In 1932 on "La Voz de la Raza" he talked about the importance of graduating from high school. It would "mean that in over time we would have more professionals, business and industry owners and fewer chaffeurs, servers and workers with a pick and shovel."[154] He observed that in San Antonio those Latinos who worked in the day could opt to attend three law schools and one college at night. He said each graduate would be "One more leader for our Raza in this country." And more men and women who could solve educational, economic, social and political problems. Recall that in the 1930s San Antonio colleges had 350 students but only nine had Spanish surnames. On March 3, 1941 he spoke on KONO radio on the topic "What Does It Take to get the Peoples of the Americas Together."[155] In a 1943-radio address Perales said, "We are going to show the world that we have just and legitimate aspirations, that we have self pride, dignity and racial pride; that we have a very high concept of our American citizenship; that we have great love of our country."[156] Perales also had a weekly radio address on KIWW around August 1950.[157]

Spanish-language TV was not available until 1955 when it was developed in San Antonio by businessman and past LULAC National President Raoul Cortez.[158] As late as 1979 sound recordings of Perales were available in his archive but when the archive was made available to researchers in 2009 none had survived.[159] Perhaps radio archives have some.

Conclusion

Alonso S. Perales was the most prolific public intellectual of Mexican descent in the twentieth century. As one of the few Mexican-American college graduates and lawyers in his time, he understood the power of the written and spoken word. He used many written formats available to him: books, newspapers, news magazines, Congressional testimonies, affidavits, essays and published letters.

Perales' books serve as lasting testaments to his work despite less than successful sales. *En Defensa de Mi Raza* documented his work from 1919 to 1937 and offers critical information about his involvement in the founding of LULAC. Using affidavits that Perales solicited from everyday Mexicans and Mexican Americans, *Are We Good Neighbors?* criticized the lack of good neighborliness by white Texans and pointed to an ineffective US Good Neighbor policy in Texas and the nation.

No other public intellectual of Mexican descent did more in the 20th century. Collectively, not only was Perales a master of the media, he was adept at using various media as tools to reach a broad audience. He was an articulate and powerful writer, and reports suggest that Perales was an effective orator. He accessed radio with prepared addresses; was interviewed on the radio; and used radio to lobby for political candidates. Perales' primary message was Mexican Americanism, anti-racism against Latinos, political empowerment, economic uplift, cultural validation, Christian aims and family strength. And he brought racism against Mexican-descent people to the attention of all.[160]

CHAPTER 17
US Diplomat in Latin America

Alonso S. Perales spent most of his life battling racism against Mexican Americans and other Latinos in the United States. However, he was also involved in the foreign affairs of the US government and the affairs of Nicaragua Americans in the United States. The US was extensively involved in Mexico, Central America, South America and the Caribbean in the 1920s and 1930s through its interventions, military and diplomatic. Between 1925 and 1933 Perales served on thirteen diplomatic missions.[1] As an employee of the US government, Perales participated in US-sponsored plebiscites, inter-American dispute settlements and complex trade agreements.[2] Thus Perales had numerous ties to different Latin American nations. And as an employee of the Nicaraguan government, he conducted activities as Nicaragua's consulate from 1934 to 1960 with direct ties to Nicaraguan Americans in the United States.

This chapter addresses Perales' Pan-Americanism in three locations: at home in the United States, in Latin America and on the world stage. It begins with Perales' early thoughts on Latin America and his preparation for diplomatic work. Second, it reveals his work in North America (Mexico); Central America (Nicaragua); South America (Bolivia, Paraguay, Chile, Peru); and the Caribbean (Cuba, Dominican Republic). Third, it points to his Pan-Americanism at the Texas state level. Fourth, it addresses his work in inter-American conferences where he sought a Latin American stage for the problems of La Raza. Fifth, it shows his diplomacy on behalf of Nicaragua when Perales worked as a Consulate for Nicaragua in the United States.

Sixth, it explores Perales' role at the founding of the United Nations, a world stage, where he officially represented Nicaragua in 1948 but also served as an ambassador for La Raza. Finally, it describes how Perales benefitted personally and professionally from his diplomatic work while also promoting possible diplomatic work by Latinos.

Perales' Latin American work occurred during a time when the United States began to shift relations with Latin America. According to Thomas M. Leonard and Thomas L. Karnes, Pan-Americanism is "Broadly defined . . . cooperation between the Western Hemisphere nations in a variety of activities including economic, social, and cultural programs; declarations; alliances; and treaties—though some authorities narrow the definition to include political action only. However, the specific definition must always be partly in error, and the broad one borders on the meaningless."[3]

Perales' Early Thoughts on Latin America

Perales' made few public statements about Latin America throughout his life though further investigation into Perales' newspaper work might reveal otherwise. In 1928 he described conditions found in nations with slow capitalist development though he did not call it that. He wrote that conditions there were the same as when Christopher Columbus found them: "Ignorance, poverty, dusty towns and city, unhygienic and backwardness predominates in Latin America."[4] Here he presented a stereotype of the wide-ranging civilizations and tribal life found by Europeans. Perales likely already knew Columbus found subsistent tribes in the Caribbean; that Hernán Cortés encountered the impressive, rich city of Tenochtitlán in the Aztec empire; that the Mayas had numerous city-states; and that Francisco Pizarro was amazed by the Incas in Peru. Perales had seen some places in Latin America (though which ones is not known) but created this broad stereotype. Later in his lifetime, he would write against these stereotypes.

Perales wrote J.T. Canales and Ben Garza, two Tejanos, his impressions of Nicaragua in the 1920s. In 1928 he wrote Canales, ". . . the Nicaraguans have made very little progress since Columbus discovered America [. . .] I believe that the best remedy that Uncle Sam could invent for radicals and bolshevists in the United States would be to ship them to Nicaragua, all expenses paid, and keep them here for about six months."[5] Perales likely visited too many slowly developing nations and/or poor regions within those nations in this decade.

He also wrote Ben Garza comparing Nicaragua with Mexican quarters in the United States. "Confidentially, friend Garza, I will tell you that I find Managua very hot, dusty, filthy and backward. However, I will not criticize these people, for I feel that I have no right to. Although I am an American citizen and the United States is the leading country in the world, I belong to the Mexican-American component element of our nation, and as a racial entity we Mexican-Americans have accomplished nothing that we can point to with pride. If I were to criticize Nicaraguans for their filthy and backward towns and cities they would in all probability retort: 'How about your Mexican villages (otherwise known as Mejiquitos in San Antonio, Houston, Dallas and other Texas cities and towns?' I believe I would have to agree with them that our Mexican districts in the United States are just as filthy and backward as Managua."[6]

But Perales did not believe Latin America inferior to the United States. He criticized Harry L. Foster's book *A Gringo in Manana-Land* (1924) who wrote, "We know that not all gringos are superior to all Latin Americans but we are sure that man per man, lawyer per lawyer, doctor per doctor, soldier per soldier and farmer per farmer, the Anglo-Saxon is superior to [the] Latin American in physical fitness, intelligence, education, aptitude and character, if not refinement."[7]

Perales came to look upon Mexico favorably. First, in later years he wrote proudly about the Aztecs and Mayas, indigenous tribes of Mexico, holding both an empire and city-states respectively. Secondly, he wrote positive views about his visits to the cities of Monterrey and Saltillo in the 1920s, and Mexico City in the 1930s and 40s.[8] In "Impresiones de un Viaje a Mexico" (Impressions of a trip to Mexico) in 1934 in *En Defensa de Mi Raza*, he stated that after his visit to Mexico City he came to the "conclusion that Mexico is not only a rich and beautiful country but it should also call itself a nation of art because of its natural beauty and also because all of its sons are artists."[9] Visiting Monterrey, he noted the wonder of Mexico's industrial progress, its highways and its engineers who were just as capable as others in the world. He was also impressed with Monterrey's factories. He hoped that Mexican-descent people in Texas might visit Mexico to see its wonders and arts "so they can see the beauty and grandeur that is Mexico and moreover so they can get rid of the racial inferiority complex which has been imposed on us in Texas."[10]

Preparation for Diplomatic Work

Given the limitations of being born working class, an orphan and a Mexican American in Texas, Perales had excellent preparation for diplomatic work. First, his early years had prepared him in Spanish. He left Texas with at least a seventh-grade education and business skills obtained at Draughon's of San Antonio. He gained more stenographic experience in World War I. As soon as he was released from active service he completed the equivalent of his high school degree in Washington, DC. Then he attended George Washington University (GWU) and its law professors gave him lessons in diplomatic Spanish.[11] Several found Perales to be versed in "Hispanic protocol." Perhaps this amounted to insider knowledge about salutations, appropriate touching and timing. The 1978 program dedicating a school named after him in San Antonio noted, "His knowledge of Hispanic protocol along with his skills in translating and interpreting also proved invaluable in these sensitive missions."[12] Perhaps "Hispanic protocol" referred to his ability to speak Spanish and/or perhaps it was assumed his being Latino made diplomacy easier for the United States.

Perales' positions toward US intervention in Latin America are not fully known. Interestingly enough while Perales was at GWU he participated in a debate with Rutgers University and for which the topic was the "US should care to protect, by armed force, capital invested in foreign lands except after formal declaration of war."[13] Perhaps the broadest question to ask about Perales' work in diplomacy is whether he supported US intervention in Latin America. Did he prop up "support for American imperialists' intervention in Latin America and, in particular, Central America . . . (?)"[14] as historian Mario T. García has surmised? As an employee of the United States, to what extent did he have flexibility in assisting any country in Latin America? In 1936 in an address before the local Pan American Round Table he stated, "No state has the right to intervene in the internal or external affairs of another" and said the United States needed to "Pan-Americanize the Monroe Doctrine," a re-statement that the European nations should not intervene in Latin America.[15]

Dominican Republic, 1922

Perales began his diplomatic work in the Dominican Republic in the Caribbean. Freed from Spain in 1844, its government was filled with autocrats and did not see peaceful transfer of power from one freely elected president to another until 1978. The US government occupied the Dominican Republic with troops from 1916 to 1924 so as to recover $300 million owed to US private businesses. The US evacuated troops in 1924.

Perales joined the Diplomatic Corps as secretary to Sumner Welles in July 1922.[16] Another source reported he joined the Latin American division of the Department of State in October 1922.[17] He served as an assistant to Welles in the Dominican Republic and Special Assistant to the President in Santo Domingo, its capitol.[18] He was a Spanish-English stenographer and translator. One article noted "He showed unusual qualifications for secretarial work. As a result, immediately following Mr. Welles' appointment, he was named as secretary and interpreter to Minister Welles."[19] He earned $250 a month.[20] Perales may have also assisted with the US withdrawal of US troops in the Dominican Republic.[21] Perales' letter to *El Siglo*, likely a San Antonio newspaper, noted "my brief stay in this country has been extremely pleasant."[22] In July 1926 Perales was offered work as a lawyer in the Dominican Republic.[23]

While his stay was pleasant, the Dominican Republic would experience short-lived peace and prosperity with Horacio Vásquez as leader but followed by dictator and strong man Rafael Leonidas Trujillo (1930–1961).

Central America, 1922-24

Perales' next assignment was in Central America though exactly where is unknown. He served as secretary to US Senator Burt Wheeler and the US delegation to the Conference on Central American

Affairs from December 1922 to January 1923 for which he received $250 a month.[24] He worked as Spanish-English stenographer and translator to the delegation. In 1923 he was also Assistant to the Inter-American High Commission in Washington, DC.[25] Later, between Fall 1927 and December 30, 1928 he wrote Adela Sloss-Vento that he had been to Central America, South America and Cuba.[26]

Peru, Chile and Bolivia, 1925

The US sent past World War I military commander John Pershing and chief attorney Perales to Peru, Chile and Bolivia to settle a dispute over land and access to nitrates.[27] Perales served as attorney and interpreter for the US Delegation, Plebiscitary Commission of the Tacna-Arica Arbitration from 1925-1926.[28] In late 1929 the United States mediated between Chile, Peru and Bolivia in the Tacna/Arica dispute over access to nitrates. An 1866 treaty between Bolivia and Chile allowed both countries to share revenue of a nitrate rich desert area. An 1874 treaty redefined benefits and extended control over Tacna and Arica for ten years and planned a plebiscite. In the 1880s conflict erupted. Bolivia allowed Chilean companies to mine nitrate deposits. The plebiscite was never held and finally in the 1920s the United States offered to mediate. Chile reportedly controlled the town of Arica including its police and transportation system; a plebiscite was to include a vote by Chileans and Peruvians.[29]

Joining in June 1925 Perales' role was assistant on the plebiscite board and election investigator and examiner taking testimonies for the Plebiscitary Commision Tacna-Arica Arbitration.[30] At this point if not earlier he was affiliated with the Division of Latin American Affairs, Department of State.[31] He earned $250 per month plus actual expenses during the period of service.[32] One source suggests he began "as clerk, then by promotion as law Clerk and interpreter then by promotion as attorney and interpreter."[33] Peru got Tacna and Chile got Arica while Bolivia left discussions without any land or money.[34] The work took Perales to Arica and Perales hoped he might visit some capitol cities in the continent.[35] One of Perales' superiors wrote of his service, "The high class of assistance you were able to render the investigating committee of the commission by virtue of your legal training, your unusual familiarity with both English and Spanish and your intimate understanding of the disposition of the people of Latin America, were particularly valuable."[36]

Cuba (1927-1928); Mexico (1928); Bolivia & Paraguay (1929); and Cuba & Panama (1930)

In January 1927 Perales was in Cuba.[37] In 1928 he was Special Assistant to the US delegation to the Sixth International Conference of American States held there. From 1928 to 1929 he served as Special Assistant to the US Delegation to the International Conference of American States on Conciliation and Arbitration.[38] This 1928 conference was a major Pan American conference that saw the United States shifting away from overt intervention toward more capitalist cooperation with Latin America.

Perales also conducted official diplomatic work in or with Mexico. In 1926 he worked with the Mexican American Claims Commission.[39] In 1928 he worked as attorney for the Agency of the United States, General and Special Claims Commission, United States and Mexico.[40] He was offered $3,250 as his annual salary.[41] Perales tried to become a consulate of Mexico but activist M.C. Gonzales held that coveted position. Perales took it upon himself in the 1940s to organize relations between himself as a representative of La Raza and the Mexican government as noted in chapter 12.

In April 1929 Perales used stationary from the Commission of Inquiry and Conciliation, Bolivia and Paraguay.[42] Delegates to this commission included Mexico, Columbia, Bolivia, Paraguay, Uruguay, Cuba and the United States. Mrs. Perales joined him on this mission.[43] He served as Special Legal Assistant of the Secretariat General of the Commission.[44] Some of this work was also in Washington, DC.[45] Perales was in Cuba in 1929 around the time Charles Lindberg's flew across the Atlantic Ocean.[46] Perales acted as Assistant to the US Delegation, Congress of Rectors, Deans and Educators in Havana.[47] By 1930 Perales had also served or visited Panama.[48]

Nicaragua, 1928 and beyond

Perales' most lengthy diplomatic work was in Nicaragua. In 1913 the United States sought the right to construct a canal through Nicaragua. In 1914 the United States also signed the Bryan-Chamorro Treaty. Perales served as legal advisor to three US electoral missions in Nicaragua in 1928, 1930, and 1932.[49] In 1928 he served as Attorney, US Electoral Mission in Nicaragua.[50] In 1927 Francis White and General Frank R. McCoy of the US Department of [State?] invited Perales to serve on a mission in Nicaragua by the order of President Calvin Coolidge. According to friend Santos de la Paz, "Perales was called to Washington, D.C. by Franklin Delano Roosevelt's recommendation that Perales was the proper person that could diplomatically represent the interests of the United States in halting an uprising in Nicaragua."[51] (But he meant President Coolidge.) By May 1928 he and Marta settled in Managua.

Perales addressed Nicaraguan electoral fraud. There he served as legal advisor to Lieutenant Inteli and Lieutenant Salguera working on the issue of political party conventions.[52] With US oversight, the 1928 election was considered successful with an 88% turnout and a victory for liberals. Reportedly electoral results were seen as a success by conservatives, liberals and the United States.[53] Perales wrote friend Fortino Treviño his thoughts about his work: "The presidential elections were verified on the 4th of this month with the Liberal Party winning. It was an orderly, peaceful, and honest election. Never had such a thing been seen in the history of Nicaragua. Both the winners and losers were satisfied with the results."[54]

McCoy commended Perales: "I wish to express my sincere appreciation of the splendid service you have rendered . . . your professional knowledge and ability, tact, mastery of the Spanish language and thorough understanding of Latin-American character and customs, have been of great help to me in the solution of the many and perplexing problems which it was foreseen would arise in connection with the work of a Mission of this kind."[55]

In 1930 Perales was Legal Adviser to the US Electoral Mission in Nicaragua.[56] He wrote his father-in-law that he was "Representante de Presidente de los Estados Unidos overseeing the election of senators and representatives."[57] He stayed from June 1930 to December 2, 1932 and returned to San Antonio on December 20, 1932.[58] According to Perales, Captain [unidentified] Johnson said, "I have kicked myself a hundred times for not having brought Perales with me when I first came here."[59] After the mission Admiral Woodward praised Perales' "thorough knowledge of Nicaraguan code law and electoral precedent in this and other Latin American governments, your acquaintance with the points of view of the Nicaraguan citizenry, its political leaders, and its public officials . . . your efforts on behalf of the Electoral Mission and the people of Nicaragua have reflected great credit upon yourself and the United States Government . . . Your official presence in Nicaragua has been of substantial benefit to that Republic in the administration of its political affairs."[60] Several attempts to kidnap Perales occurred in Nicaragua but US Marines were assigned to protect his residence thereafter.[61]

In February 1932 Perales contacted Lieutenant General Charles F.B. Price of the State Department to let him know he wanted to serve on another electoral mission in Nicaragua. Immediately after his national LULAC presidency in May 1932, Perales began his last diplomatic mission there. Perales left the United States on May 21, 1932 and finished his work in Nicaragua by December 1932.[62]

These missions in Nicaragua made Perales an ideal candidate for a Consulate position in the United States. No Latino besides Nicaraguan Americans in the United States knew more about Nicaragua. Few Latinos were lawyers and few as well educated. In April 1934 he received a certificate as Consul, ad honorem from the president. In 1935 Perales was a Nicaraguan delegate to the foreign trade conference held in Houston. In April 1936 he received a certificate from President Anastacio Somoza naming him Consulate.[63] He was officially appointed in May 1937.[64]

Perales as General Nicaragua Consulate, 1937-1960

Nicaragua employed Perales as Consul General for Nicaragua from 1937 to 1960.[65] Historian Arturo Rosales noted that this appointment became "a position he parlayed into being able to participate in

Pan American level activity."[66] A 1942 letter by Perales states it was an honorary position that paid no compensation and that he was "not required to swear allegiance to Nicaragua, and I am free to resign at any time."[67] It is not clear what he meant by "allegiance."

Perales' ties to Nicaragua did not authorize him to speak on discrimination against Latinos in the United States but he did so nonetheless. Few Nicaraguan Americans lived in Texas or the United States. Historian Emilio Zamora wrote, "Nicaraguan officials, for example, rarely expressed Mexico's level of concern over racial discrimination or over the United States' history of intervention."[68] In 1940 or 1950, there were few Nicaraguan Americans in the United States. One of a few known and active Nicaraguans in Texas was labor activist Humberto Silex of El Paso.[69]

Perales was silent on domestic issues within Nicaragua from the 1930s to 1960 and especially its undemocratic politics under generations of the Somoza family. There was considerable resistance by Nicaraguans against President Anastacio Somoza. In 1945 5,000 students organized major protests; in 1947 the Communist Party was declared illegal there; and the 1950 constitution declared only two legal parties.[70] Perales probably disagreed with protests and hated communists but probably disagreed with controlling party access. His direct correspondence with President Anastacio Somoza is sparse. Perales did send him a note congratulating him on Nicaragua's anniversary on United Nations Conference on International Organization stationary.[71] He also wrote Somoza about his suggestions to get the US government to designate him as a delegate or advisor to the delegation to a Caracas, Venezuela conference because he was "interested in our American countries establishing a pact to combat communism in these territories."[72] He also mentioned to him that he had worked on the Eisenhower presidential campaign. He wrote later noting that his attempts to attend the conference failed. He stated that in his opinion neither the Treaty of Bogotá or the InterAmerican Treaty of Reciprocal Assistance of Rio de Janeiro (Tratado Interamericano de Asistencia Recíproca de Río de Janeiro) "are sufficiently ample to cope with the situation created in Guatemala, for instance."[73] Guatemala had democratically elected a communist as president in 1954.

On one occasion Perales sought to introduce US millionaire Frank J. Gravis to President Anastacio Somoza in hopes that he might develop the oil industry there. Perales wrote "Sin duda que el impulso y desarrollo de la industria petrolera en Nicaragua sería la gran cosa para el país" (Undoubtedly, the development of the oil industry in Nicaragua would be a big thing for the country.) And he mentioned a *Time* magazine article dated December 19, 1955. He noted that Gravis was aware that "Nicaragua's subsoil promises much."[74] If Gravis entered Nicaragua, this would have likely meant jobs for Nicaraguans though low paid, some profit for Nicaraguan elites, and hefty profits for Gravis.

Nicaraguans in the United States had little visibility until the 1980s and Perales did not live to see their surge. In 1970 there were only 28,620 Nicaraguans in the United States but by 1990 there were 202,658. In the late 1970s the anti-Somoza Sandinistas including Daniel Ortega launched a revolution leading middle-class and wealthy Nicaraguans to flee to the United States in the 1980s and 90s. The son of Anastacio Somoza, Luis, had replaced his father and the revolution was against him, and his son "Tachito." Conservative Tachito moved to the United States and lives in Miami today.[75]

Pan American Conferences, 1927-1933

In January 8, 1927 Perales attended the US delegation to the Pan American Congress in Havana, Cuba and had J.T. Canales serve as General Pro Tem of the Latin American Citizens League (LAC).[76] Perales received an invitation from Francis White of the US State Department to serve as a US delegate to the Sixth Pan American Conference also in Havana in January 1928.[77] This was one of the conferences that began a major shift in US Latin American policy.

In 1933 Perales sought to serve as a delegate to the Seventh International Conference of American States.[78] In August 1933 Perales asked Dr. Carlos E. Castañeda to write Senators Morris Sheppard, Tom Conally and Congressman Richard Kleberg of Texas to endorse him as a US delegate to a conference to be held December 1934 in Uruguay.[79] Sheppard apparently did not respond.

After 1933 the United States consented to a non-intervention pact into Latin America. This led to the rise of President Franklin Delano Roosevelt's Good Neighbor Policy. The United States would continue to intervene nonetheless as evidenced in Guatemala and Cuba in the 1950s and in El Salvador in the 1980s. The United States also continued to prop up dictators like Rafael Trujillo in the Dominican Republic and Anastacio Somoza in Nicaragua.

The US government did not call upon Perales after 1933. Around 1933 the United States entered a new era of US/Latin American relations. At the local level there were organizations like the Pan American Round Table in which local residents sought to theoretically do their part. As early as 1920 Perales spoke favorable about the Pan American Union, the Pan American Federation of Labor, the Pan American Round Table and various Chambers of Commerce that were promoting international understanding.[80] In 1936 Perales apparently gave a speech encouraging but also condemning the Pan American Round Table, Rotary Club, Lions Club, Kiwanas and Chamber of Commerce for ignoring blatant racial murders. He chastised the "abnormal" attitude toward Mexicans and noted that "Public opinion does not favor the Mexican." He asked them to be "True Americans, and Genuine—Not Hipocrites [sic]-Pan Americans."[81] By 1941 Perales stated that "Pan American organizations and service clubs with Pan American leanings have failed to do anything about it."[82] He broke publicly with the Pan American Round Table of Texas because they ignored "the growing injustices and humiliations that are daily being directed against the Mexican residents in Texas."[83] Later, however, by 1948 he would still come to preside over the Pan American Optimists which used the Pan American name and was mostly a charitable club but with a solely Latino membership.

To have greater success in world affairs particularly World War II, the United States was forced to address a few of its Jim Crow practices. The United States wanted Mexico as an ally since it was concerned about Axis entry into the United States. The United States created the Office of the Coordinator of Inter-American Affairs (OCIAA) with Nelson Rockefeller as its head.[84] While Rockefeller created an adviso-

ry committee no Latinos were members. Rockefeller sent field representatives to Texas and California including Tom Sutherland of Texas.
As early as 1937, Perales began addressing improving Mexico-US
relations but eventually focused on the US' official new Good Neighbor Policy. He specifically discussed the Good Neighbor Policy for the
first time in his book of collected essays in April 1937, mentioning
President Franklin D. Roosevelt and "Pan-Americanismo" by name.[85]
When the United States entered the war in 1941 the nation increased its
Pan American rhetoric. He even saw how Mexican polo players could
play a role.[86] They could do so as "*elementos cultos y dignos*" (cultured
and dignified elements), people of the arts, sciences and sports.

Perales' regular and persistent calls for non-discrimination inter-
faced with the US' Good Neighbor Policy one day at lunch in West
Texas. The President of Mexico's Congress Eugenio Prado entered a
Pecos, Texas restaurant called the Lone Star Cafe in March 1945. This
incident was captured not only in *La Prensa* but in Mexico's newspapers "reminding everyone that some Texans insisted on treating Mexicans differently regardless of how this contradicted the United States'
alliance with Mexico and its declared wartime aim of promoting and
protecting the democratic rights of Mexican in the United States."[87] As
historian Zamora noted, "the war against fascism opened a Mexican
fight on the home front against discrimination that matched the Double
V campaign associated with the African American cause."[88]

Perales belonged to several legal bar organizations attempting to
use his membership as political leverage for Pan Americanism. In
1948 he was a member of five associations: San Antonio Bar Association, the Texas State Bar Association, the American Bar Association,
the Inter-American Bar Association and the American Society of
International Law.[89] Perales also belonged to the committee on Latin
American law under the Texas Bar Association.[90] Perales did not join
an organization for socializing or status. For instance, as a delegate of
the Texas Bar Association he introduced a resolution at the Congress
of the Inter-American Bar Federation in 1944 calling for federal legislation with penalties and sanctions for violations of civil rights
against citizens and "aliens."[91] After it passed unanimously there he
got state representative Gabe Garrett of Corpus Christi to introduce it

as a bill though few other Texas legislators showed any interest.[92] In 1944 Texas was not interested.

By the 1940s Perales was joining international associations. In 1944, for instance, he was a member of La Asociación Nacional de Abogados (of Mexico) and he attended the Third Inter-American Bar Association conference in Mexico City.[93] He got the Inter-American Bar Federation conference to denounce US racism in 1944. Joined by M.C. Gonzales and J.T. Canales, he "managed to convince the General Assembly to adopt a revised version of a resolution he had authored which called on the delegates to seek the adoption of civil rights legislation in their respective countries."[94] He referred to a 1928 international treaty that the United States signed in Cuba "to extend to aliens residing and or in transit through their territory, all individual guarantees extended to their own national, and the enjoyment to essential civil rights."[95]

As historian Zamora has shown Perales sought to "advance the cause for civil rights legislation at four international assemblies."[96] These "hemispheric venues"[97] included the Inter-American event in 1944; the Inter-American "Chapultepec" Conference on Problems of War and Peace, also in Mexico City in 1945; and the founding meeting of the United Nations in San Francisco in 1948. For Perales true Pan Americanism was not about "banquets or superficial acts of good will," he called for "a genuine Americanism and a enduring, true international friendship" enacted in a Christian way."[98]

Texas Good Neighbor Commission

As the United States at least tokenly shifted toward a US Good Neighbor Policy, Perales sought to get Texas to enact its own Good Neighbor Policy. Again, the 1930s saw the United States change its more overt interventionist policy toward Latin America to a more benign Good Neighbor Policy under President Franklin D. Roosevelt due to fear of pro-German sentiment on the eve of World War II. In 1940 when the federal government established the office of Inter-American Affairs, Governor Coke Stevenson created the Texas Good Neighbor Commission (GNC) in 1943.[99] He did so to appease Perales, Gonzales, and LULAC's efforts to get state anti-discrimination laws. The GNC had little funding and no legal teeth.

But Perales, M.C. Gonzales and others sought a way to leverage the GNC. They gathered complaints of racial discrimination and presented them to the GNC to leverage Mexico against the United States. Historian Thomas Guglielmo noted that in the last four months of 1943 the GNC received 117 formal complaints from LULAC, Mexican consuls and individuals.[100] Perales and Gonzales "forwarded complaints by Mexican Americans to the Good Neighbor Commission to the State Department."[101] They sent them to the US state department to make Texas racism against Mexican immigrants an international offense to Mexico since the US needed workers during the war. William Blocker, US Consul in Reynosa, Mexico was especially critical of these interventions by Gonzales and Perales. He wrote, "More and more I am convinced that Mr. M.C. Gonzalez (sic) and Mr. Alonso S. Perales, and probably Dr. George Isidore Sánchez, of the University of Texas, are responsible for the majority of the cases that have been filed by the Mexican Embassy with the Department."[102]

Perales also criticized the GNC when liberal Pauline Kibbe was fired.[103] Kibbe was also manager of the "Oficina Anglo-Espanola" and a member of the Business and Professional Women of San Antonio.[104] She authored an important and timely book *Latin Americans in Texas* documenting race discrimination in 1947. Yet, historian Carlos Blanton has since documented she was a mole.

Perales at the Founding of the United Nations, 1948

Perales inserted himself in Pan Americanism and even world affairs when he participated in the founding of the United Nations considered the "most important international forum on human rights."[105] According to historian Zamora, he "announced publicly that he would be representing Mexican nationals and US born-Mexicans, giving voice to their fight against discrimination and inequality in the United States."[106] No Mexican-descent organization was invited or gave him authority to represent them. Perales simply felt he was their ambassador; he even announced publicly that he would be representing their interests.[107]

The conference organizing the United Nations took place in San Francisco in June 1945. Perales attended as part of the delegation from

Nicaragua. Zamora noted that "Nicaraguan officials had dispensed with tradition and assigned one of the coveted positions in their delegation to a person who had been born and raised in the United States. . . . His selection and assignment may have seemed odd to a casual observer. . . . By the time the first UN meeting took place, Perales had served as Nicaraguan Consul General in San Antonio, Texas for eleven years; he also had participated in at least thirteen U.S. diplomatic missions in Latin American since the 1920s."[108] Perales wrote co-activist J. Luz Sáenz about his UN experience on the Organization's letterhead. Perales wrote "We are completing the Magna Carta."[109] He added, "I did all I could to include provisions in the Carta that would end discrimination and give our people equal rights to progress and happiness."[110] According to historian Zamora, "Perales managed to convince the General Assembly to adopt a revised version of a resolution he had authored which called on the delegates to seek the adoption of civil rights legislation in their respective countries."[111] Attorney and LULAC leader Gus Garcia also attended.[112]

Personal and Professional Benefits of Diplomatic Work

Perales benefitted tremendously from his diplomatic work. International travel provided amazing legal, linguistic and cultural experiences and opportunities in Latin America. Perales traveled to Mexico, Nicaragua, Paraguay, Uruguay, Chile, Bolivia, Cuba, Dominican Republic, Panama and the West Indies. Perales' Latin American consciousness/*Latinidad* was strengthened. Previous chapters showed his hemispheric consciousness did not begin with the US government's Pan Americanism of the 1930s, World War II or his work with the United Nations in the 1940s as historian Zamora surmised. His Latin American consciousness began in the 1910s in Alice, Texas and not outside of the United States and not only after 1941. His knowledge of the Spanish language and newspapers like *La Prensa* had already crafted a Latin Americanist. His travels to numerous Latin American countries saw his hemispheric consciousness expanded, affirmed and solidified.

Perales saw little difference between Latin Americans and Mexican-descent people. He saw *Mexiquitos* (Little Mexicos i.e. Mexican barrios in Texas towns and cities) in Nicaragua. Historian Brandon H. Mila concluded with great insight: "Perales did not simply participate in three different electoral missions; he spent the equivalent of two years of his life living in Nicaragua. His time spent in Nicaragua changed Perales, he was not an entirely new man, but he viewed the world differently which is expressed in his future work. By 1932, Perales had gained a hemispheric approach to the world and began participating in Pan American level politics, conventions, and conferences."[113] While Perales seems to have been much aware of Latin American issues, he focused most of his efforts on Mexican Americans and then Nicaraguan Americans in the United States. He did not write about Latin America much, not even about Mexico.

Perales grew to love the people of Nicaragua. In 1931 when an earthquake hit there, he appealed to the Mexican people in San Antonio for help. In April he wrote "Un Llamamiento Para que los Mexicanos Ayuden a las Víctimas de Nicaragua" (A Call to Mexicans to Help Nicaragua Victims) for *La Prensa*. He stated, "Nicaraguans are our blood brothers because they, like us Mexicans, are descendants from either pure Spanish blood or pure indigenous blood and through their veins flow both bloods. Additionally, their language is Spanish and their customs and ideologies are identical to ours."[114] Here, Perales, laid out his rationale for including Latin Americans as members of La Raza based on blood, language, customs and ideology. Here, he acknowledged Spanish, indigenous and mestizo roots though silent on African/ Arab heritage. In 1933 Perales told *LULAC News* he had "nothing but praise and words of kindness for the heroic people of Nicaragua."[115]

In a different and less racist era Perales' experience may have qualified him to be Secretary of State or President of the United States. Professionally, Perales' diplomacy qualified him to serve as consulate for Nicaragua most of his adult life and that apparently provided steady income for Perales. Had Perales been a European American, he may have been appointed to higher positions. Perales believed that all his appointments before 1933 had been non-political, probably meaning he was not selected at the behest of any politician.[116] Perales understood that his race and activism worked against him; he was disappointed in the failure by upper-level statesmen to acknowledge him.

According to historian Arturo Rosales, "He attempted to obtain various positions on diplomatic missions but was constantly rejected in the 1930s even though he knew State Department officers in high places."[117] Where was Sumner Welles? Pershing? Rosales added, "I suspect that his zealous dedication to civil rights might have sabotaged his chances in the Foreign Service . . ."[118] Recall that in fall 1942 Perales attempted to obtain a position with the Civil Service Commission. Perales wrote Sumner Welles and US Representativde Kilday about possible appointments. He noted that "about ten San Antonio attorneys of Mexican descent have tried to get commissions in the Army, but have been unsuccessful . . . It seems that we just simply are not wanted in high positions."[119]

Perales' work with the Federal Employment Practices Commission (FEPC) in the 1940s and other anti-racism work further prevented other federal and diplomatic appointments especially during WWII. According to Rosales, US Consulate in Reynosa, Mexico William Blocker "quickly identified him as a mettlesome troublemaker in more than one piece of correspondence in the files of his confidential report. This probably led to Perales not receiving a commission in the military [during World War II] which he strenuously sought."[120] Overseas activities in Latin America by Perales also lead to FBI surveillance of LULAC.[121]

In the political/civic arena, Perales' diplomatic work gave him yet another venue from which to speak—an international platform. Rosales continued, ". . . he found these diplomatic skills useful building an international and diplomatic platform for exposing violations of the rights of Mexican Americans."[122] According to historian Zamora, "Through his role in hemispheric diplomacy, Perales brought international attention to the discriminatory treatment of Mexicans in the American Southwest."[123] Perales continued to hope. Reporting on the UN conference he wrote in *La Prensa*, "despite all the efforts in favor of incorporating a list of human rights, everything suggests that we will not achieve this now, but that in the end the basic principles that will guarantee those rights will have been pesented."[124]

Perales was at the UN meeting not only out of secular concerns, he also had a religious mission. In an essay titled "The Antonians" he asked whether "is it not high time we Catholic men wake up and do something about it?" "It" referred to "When we go to a United States Conference to write a charter designed to preserve the peace of the world and we outlaw God from our deliberations, when we some people question the right of our Government to have a diplomatic representative at the Vatican that our Nations might commune with God through His Supreme Representative on this earth. . . ."[125] Perales mixed religion and politics.

Hiring and Appointing Latino Diplomats to Latin America

Though Perales had numerous personal benefits from working in Latin America, he sought this opportunity for other Latinos too. In 1933 he wrote US Senator Morris Sheppard of Texas about this idea. He wrote: "I take the liberty of addressing you to suggest that in the future our Government give us American citizens of Latin extraction the opportunity of representing our country in Latin American Republics [. . .]. ". . . we could serve as a link between the two great peoples. Doubtless, our Government could secure the services of several qualified Latin Americans in Texas, New Mexico, Arizona, California, and Puerto Rico. In Texas, for instance, our Government could engage Judge J.T. Canales, of Brownsville, the writer and others."[126] Not only was he suggesting Mexican Americans but also Puerto Ricans.

Perales asserted his qualifications to serve in more advanced diplomatic posts. He added, "Personally, I consider myself qualified for service as a lawyer and adviser on international affairs in the Department of State in Washington, or as a Counsel or of Embassy, or even as a Minister of some small Latin American Republic." He told him he had twelve different assignments since 1922. "Most of these, however, have been minor assignments, the highest having been that of Adviser."[127] Sheppard responded with a generic letter suggesting he follow channels for employment and simply ignored his call for Latino diplomats since he himself as a typical Euro Texan did not like "Mexicans."[128]

San Antonio tax collector Maury Maverick was the only non-Latino who took Perales' diplomatic experience seriously. In 1933 he wrote, "I make this statement outright: That Perales is eminently fitted for any diplomatic position in a Spanish-speaking country, and

this by culture, temperament, education, and racial background."[129]
He was qualified for non-Spanish-speaking nations as well. Still, the
United States was hardly ready for Latino diplomats much less a Lati-
na diplomat.

Conclusion

While Perales served his country, the United States, as a diplomat,
it is difficult to assess whether he equally served his "hermanos de
raza," (racial brethren) Latin Americans in Latin America, since he
served at the behest of the United States and its national and class
interests. As an interpreter, he may have been in the middle and to
what extent he may have helped or hurt specific nations in Latin
America we will never know. Moreover, the Latin American heads of
state that he met in the pre-1940 era were elites who did not typically
work for the interests of working-class and indigenous people, peas-
ants and women. Future historians will have to dig into diplomatic
sources to answer these questions.

Perales' Pan-Americanism in Latin America was aligned with US
state interests. As an interpreter, he likely did what he was told. However, as a Latino he hoped that the status of Latin American nations
would improve. As a Latino he also hoped that non-discrimination of
Latin American-descent people would become the norm in the United States. He frowned upon prejudice toward Latin Americans. But
Perales' optimism was unfounded. Perales' own Pan-Americanism
did not involve condemning the elected or dictatorial leaders of Latin
American nations and their lack of democracy. Nor did it call for re-
structuring of Latin American nations. He was silent on dictator
Anastacio Somoza in Nicaragua. In this sense, Perales worked with
dictators and did not publicly criticize Nicaraguan autocrats—they are
still in place in 2021.

Nicaragua did not see democracy or economic stability with the
Somoza dictators from 1937 to 1979. Anastacio Somoza entered the
presidency in 1937 and ruled until 1956; he was followed by son Luis
from 1956 to 1963; and then by grandson son Anastacio "Tachito"
from 1967 to 1972 and 1974 to 1979. The Sandinista National Libera-
tion Front, revolutionaries, finally brought the Somoza administration

down. In 1979 Sloss-Vento wrote Perales' wife Marta, "I have seen such sad things on TV. The desolation and killings of innocent civilians. I am so glad Somoza is out. God wants a return to peace."[130] Daniel Ortega was one of the anti-Somoza revolutionaries and became president. However, in 2021 he is still president and revolutionaries are now fighting him. Consequently, impoverished migrants and those fleeing violence are currently migrating to the United States.

While Perales' international work did not advance the lives of ordinary Latin Americans, he acted as a Pan American ambassador domestically inside the United States. Perales used any Pan American opportunity to advance Latino interests. He sought to use the Texas Good Neighbor Commission to push for better neighborliness by whites in Texas. And he used the GNC to argue for better treatment of Mexicans and *braceros* in Texas. He used US relations with Mexico as leverage to do so.

On the world stage, Perales appointed himself to serve as a Latino ambassador at the United Nations. While officially representing Nicaragua he acted as unofficial ambassador for all Latinos in the United States where he sought to advance civil rights.

Perales benefitted personally and professionally from his diplomatic work though he was still treated as a "Mexican" and as an "agitator." He did not receive an ambassadorship to any Latin American country. His call for Latinos as US ambassadors fell on deaf ears. President John F. Kennedy appointed the first Mexican-American ambassador Raymond Telles who had been elected as mayor of El Paso with the assistance of LULAC and Ladies LULAC in the early 1960s. Julian Nava would serve as an ambassador to Mexico in 1980 under President Jimmy Carter. However, it is no coincidence that the one young woman Perales mentored in his law office, Vilma S. Martínez, would become Ambassador to Argentina from 2009-2013 under President Barack Obama. Perales' ambition and hemispheric consciousness is seen in her.

Perales' international Pan-American work seems to have been contradictory to his domestic Pan-American work in the United States. Unfortunately, Perales was not in a position of power to do more for Latin America.

PART III
Private Life

CHAPTER 18
Religion

Alonso S. Perales wrote, "Without God, we are nothing and nobody."[1] This chapter examines Perales' religiosity as a Christian. Perales was fundamentally a Catholic and lived a moral life though historian Mario T. García called him a secular priest, confessor and missionary.[2] Four themes are examined in this chapter: Perales' private practices as a Catholic including his memberships in voluntary associations; his socio-political gospel; the Catholic Church's institutionalized racism; and Perales' thoughts on Mexican-descent Catholic masculinity and womanhood.

Private Practices

Perales was likely introduced to Catholicism by his parents and then by the Treviño family in Alice. The archives provide no information about his religious practices until the 1940s. Beyond ordinary church attendance Perales apparently took some religion classes. He was schooled in Moral Theology. In September 1947 he took "A Course in Moral Theology for Catechists" from Reverend Raymond F. O'Brien, C.M., S.T D.[3] As a Christian, Perales probably attended Catholic mass every day or at least did so in his adult, married years. In 1951 he told friend Dr. Carlos E. Castañeda, "Then too we had very strenuous week working and attending the Novena at San Fernando (I attended every day both morning and evening). . . ."[4] San Fernando was a historic cathedral dating to the 1720s in downtown San Antonio which promoted Spanish/Mexican Catholicism and was walking distance from Perales' law firm. When Castañeda's brother died

Perales noted, "Every morning when I go to Mass I remember him and pray for him."[5] Activist Adela Sloss-Vento noted, "I ought to point out that on May 8th (Mother's Day) our defender attended two masses and received the sacrament as usual. His religiosity was exemplified by his taking communion every day before going to the office. For him, God was like the air we breathe. Perhaps that is why in the Angelus Funeral Home at San Antonio, Texas several priests attended, said the responses for the dead, and spoke in his favor. Not only was he the tireless and loyal defender of the Mexican-American people, but he was also a good Christian man, always close to God."[6]

Perales was active with San Fernando church in San Antonio. In January 1954 Perales wrote friend J.T. Canales, "Mrs. Perales and I are having a Mass said at San Fernando Cathedral 'en acción de gracias' (in Thanksgiving)." "We are very grateful to God because he is restoring your health."[7] On occasion Perales also attended retreats such as one by St. Anthony's Seminary in 1951[8] and some Catholic conferences such as the 1947 National Catholic Women's Conference in El Paso.[9]

The Perales family practiced ordinary daily Catholic activities. Daughter Marta Carmen remembered, "The quintessential element of our family was our Catholicism, our faith. From the time we were little toddlers and could talk we learned all our prayers. Nightly we knelt and prayed the Rosary, which Daddy led whenever he was home."[10] She added, "During the month of May, he took us to the Cathedral to carry flowers to the Blessed Mother, Queen of Heaven. My brothers played dress up like priests. Daddy had bought them a plastic set with Chasuble and altar linen, which they placed on our children's folding card table. Then pretended to give Mass and for communion they used fish food wafers as communion hosts."[11]

While Perales was religious, most of his letters were secular. He wrote his best friend, fellow Catholic, and fellow Knights of Columbus member Dr. Carlos E. Castañeda often but their letters were not about religion. Still, their Catholicism cemented a tighter bond. Perales wrote few religious salutations to Castañeda. One read, "the best of everything and may GOD continue to bless you and all your dear ones."[12] By August 1956 he responded to Castañeda much like the one Castañeda had sent him: "Yes, the Lord certainly has been good to me and to you. I likewise never cease thanking Him. I remember you in my prayers every morning. May God bless you and keep you and your dear family safe, in good health, and happy always."[13] A 1956 letter from Perales to Zapata County judge and past LAC member Manuel Bravo noted, "We are well, thank the Lord."[14]

Most of Perales' charitable contributions went to the church. His 1959 income tax return shows he made contributions to Our Lady of Sorrows, San Fernando Cathedral, Daughters of Mary Immaculate, St. Joseph's Retreat House and Guadalupe Community Center.[15]

Membership in Catholic Organizations

Perales was active with Catholic groups, most connected to San Fernando. A 1947 biographical article noted he was president of the Holy Name Society and a charter member of San Fernando Post, Catholic War Veterans of America.[16] He was also a member of the Knights of Columbus Council 787.[17] A 1948 biographical note showed he was an advisory board member of the National Catholic Community Service of San Antonio and executive board member of the Archdiocesan Union of Holy Name Societies in the city.[18] A 1952 resume reports that he was president of the Holy Name Society, a member of the National Catholic Community Service of San Antonio and a member of the Catholic War Veterans.[19] So Perales was also a leader at his church and perhaps among San Antonio Catholics and/or Mexican-descent Catholics. This religious leadership may have provided him more believability and status in his ethnic community as well.

Moreover, Perales worked with religious leaders including Father Carmelo Tranchese and Archbishop Robert E. Lucey for better housing and non-discrimination.

Socio-Political Gospel

Perales believed religion central to humanity but he may not have believed examining world religions. He wrote, "To know which is the true religion it is not necessary to know and study all religions. This would be impossible."[20] He only cared about Christianity and specifically Catholicism.

According to historian Mario T. García, Perales "employed Catholic social doctrine as a way of influencing Anglos, especially policy-makers about the civil rights concerns of Mexican Americans . . ."[21] Thus, he engaged in "unofficial preaching or his political unconsciousness linked to faith to citizenship . . ."[22] In this sense, his Catholicism was part of his cultural citizenship[23] and he wanted to "show the outside world that Mexican Americans represented a strong and observant religious American people."[24] In a 1940 speech he said, "We must teach fair play, brotherhood of man, love of One's neighbors, and unselfishness. We must teach and practice the doctrine of Jesus Christ having as its theme love and tolerance."[25]

García also argued, "For Perales, embracing God was the only way not only to be saved in Heaven, but for happiness and goodness in this world. But, as noted, Perales' advice did not just have, in my opinion, a personal objective but a political or quasi-political one. That is, Mexican Americans by being good Catholics were also asserting that they were good American citizens. As such, Perales' columns represented a form of Mexican-American jeremiad or "'political sermon.'"[26] García argued that he typically made "almost authoritarian pronouncements."[27] He correctly noted, "his thinking always carried a clear normative message."[28]

Perales believed in religious instruction in public schools and felt like its lack was "causing much damage to our country."[29] So he did not believe in separation of church and state. He also charged that the United Nations, the international organization fostering peace after 1948, did not reflect the Christian faith.[30] Perales did not promote Christianity but rather Catholicism as the only true religion.[31] He denounced the YMCA for suggesting that all religions were acceptable.[32] Here, he was particularly narrow. Perales told Castañeda in February 1948, "These fellows form a part of a conspiracy, with headquarters perhaps in Mexico City, to ridicule and bring our Church into disrepute."[33] These fellows included Protestants and Masons.

Perales believed Christianity could save the world. With the separation of church and state in the United States, Perales felt that Christians had to seek out more indoctrination outside of churches. He noted, "The truth is that we sense the destruction of the world and we know that God is the only one who can save us."[34] Perales also believed an individual powerful with God's help. He wrote, "We have to understand how to help ourselves. That is, with the help of God, our progress depends in large part on ourselves."[35]

Perales' religious beliefs also influenced his thinking on living wages for workers.[36] He quoted a Father Birch in 1947, "One of the sins that cries out for God's vengeance is the denial to the worker of a just wage and our pontiffs have stressed that a just wage is one that makes it possible for a man to live a [sic] reasonable comfort and frugality with his family."[37] In a Por Mi Religión (For My Religion) column titled "Más Sobre el Problema de los Braceros y Los Trabajadores Migratorios" (More on the Problem of Braceros and Migratory Workers) while quoting Archbishop Lucey who called communists the enemies of the working community, he also stated that paying workers fifty cents an hour was a shame for Christianity.[38]

To what extent Perales may have "preached" to others is unknown. According to one account San Antonio newspaperman Frank Trejo said that "late in his life, Perales embraced religion and would accost people on the street to preach the Word."[39] Perales intertwined his Catholicism with his work as an attorney in advocating for social justice; he was even a member of the Catholic Lawyers Guild.[40]

Perales on the Catholic Church's Institutional Racism

Perales realized that the Catholic Church itself employed institutional racism but he rarely openly criticized it. The church created churches for the Mexican descent separate from Euro-Texans throughout Texas.[41] As noted in chapter 12, Perales called for equality: "Equal in the trenches, but also equal in the factories, in the stores, in the schools, in the churches, in the restaurants, in the barbershops, in the theatres, and everywhere else."[42] In Midland, Texas in 1944 two Mexican boys were asked to leave a church designated for white Catholics only.[43] Perales likely worked with the Bishops' Committee for the Spanish Speaking established in 1945 to address the Church's institutional racism.[44]

Perales attacked the Church more privately. He wrote friend Castañeda, "We go to conferences and lambast everybody else for discriminating and segregating our people, but our Catholic Friends (some of them) reserve the right to do it themselves and do not wish to be reminded that it is a sin to do so, that is unchristian, undemocratic, etc." He added, "Isn't that a hell of a state of affairs?"[45] He noted that "prejudiced" lay Catholics had "petty foolish tactics" to "ostracize" 'our people.'"

Perales' Column in *La Voz Católica*

Perales expressed his religiosity in his column "Por mi religión" (For My Religion) from 1951 to 1960 for the San Antonio Catholic newspaper, *La Voz*.[46] Perhaps it is no coincidence that the decade that he wrote about religion was also his most conservative era—his era of anti-Communism and the time he supported Republicans. But it was also the decade when he had a family and more health problems. His topics included marital infidelity, juvenile delinquency, dating, and rape.

The column appeared right around the time when Perales' illness became more serious. Titles in 1951 included "Retiro Espiritual Que Mucho Nos Beneficiara" (Spiritual Return that Benefits Us); ¡Salve, O, Cristo Rey! (Salvation, Oh Christ the King); "Debemos Formar Hogares Indestructibles"(We should Make Indestructable Homes); "A Proposito de Hogares Indestructibles" (How to Make an Indestructable Home); "Asistir a la Iglesia con Regularidad es Rendir Homenaje de Gratitud a Dios" (Helping the Church with its Regular Homage to God); "Problemas Hogarenos Que Exigen Solución" (Domestic Problems that Need Solutions); "Cuando se Pierde la Fe se Pierde Todo" (When Faith is Lost, all is Lost); "La Instrucción Religiosa es Una Imperiosa Necesidad" (Religious Instruction is a Necessity); and Cartas de Nuestros Lectores" (Letters from Our Readers).[47] Luis Alvarado, J. Luz Sáenz' son-in-law and LULAC leader, complimented Perales noting, "I consider his column very spiritually stimulating and indispensable."[48] These writings were also shared on KCOR radio because daughter Martha Carmen remembered "Every Sunday I heard him [-] this eloquent man speak on the KCOR program, "Por Mi Religión."[49]

Perales' Thoughts on Masculinity, Womanhood and Marriage

Perales addressed masculinity. He wrote, "I want to stress that we men are even more obligated than women to demonstrate our *religiosity* [Perales' emphasis] given that the deplorable state of the world has been created by us *men* [Perales' emphasis] and not by women.[50] Men needed to participate in religious retreats which he saw as "a place where we can recharge our spiritual batteries" . . . and from which "we will return to our homes as better men."[51] They could participate in the Knights of Columbus, bible study groups, conferences, or read Catholic magazines.

Mexican American parents should not permit daughters to date boys with cars since this might invite sexual opportunity suggesting that parents should expect their sons to be heterosexual and sexually active. Yet, according to García, he also "lectured young women to also fight back."[52] He believed women had rights. This is especially seen in his volunteer work in the Rachel González legal case in chapter 14.

Perales also wrote about women's obligations as good women and good wives. He expected women to get men to attend church; he wrote, "We lovingly ask wives to induce their husband and young children to attend the missions." He asked wives to "motivate them to attend the missions and you will see how things change in your House. What happens is that most men are under the mistaken impression that only women are obligated to be religious and that is not the case."[53]

Perales also wrote about the sacrament of marriage. He believed that "marriage next to the priesthood was the highest and most important vocation."[54] He explained, "What is matrimony? Is it just a civil contract as some say? Yes, it is a civil contract made by men, but under God it is much more than that. It is a sacrament especially when it is contracted by the representatives of God on earth. What is marriage? Is it just a ceremony that permits one to get married one day and then abandon it the next? What rights and obligations does marriage entail? Does marriage allow a man to treat his wife like a slave and that she has the obligation to accept this treatment, injustices, and shame (*sin vergüenza*) [sic]. Does it mean that a husband can spend all his earnings at the cantina? Does it mean that a man can come home drunk and abuse his wife and children without them protesting? Does it mean that a husband can have extramarital affairs? Does it mean that a husband can hit his wife and suffer no consequences? Does it mean that a husband can be an absolute tyrant at home and that his wife has to accept this?"[55] Here it is clear that Perales saw men as the bread earners; did not believe in spousal abuse; and did not believe in adultery. He believed in an amicable partnership though Perales himself was mostly an absent husband and absent father. According to García, Perales had a "patriarch [al] view of marriage."[56] Perales was the breadwinner but Marta readily socialized outside the home as an independent woman.

Conclusion

Perales' faith directed his social, civic, and political activities. His religiosity allowed him to pursue his civic and political goals. He was active in numerous Catholic organizations. His Mexican Americanist themes were intertwined with his moral beliefs in the equality of "man." He criticized the practice of segregated Catholic churches though it was not his loudest cry.

Perales was a traditional Catholic with traditional views on heterosexual marriage, masculinity, and womanhood. He expected men to be faithful husbands and expected women to lead men to church. He was respectful and caring toward women as permitted through Christianity though still excluding them from LULAC.

Perales' written will was his last religious statement. It read, "I desire and direct that my body be buried in a decent and Christian-like manner."[57] He firmly believed as he told activist and friend Adela Sloss-Vento, "While God gives us life and health there is hope."[58]

CHAPTER 19
Character

Alonso S. Perales' character was one of his finest attributes. As early as 1922, when Perales was only 24, *Las Noticias* of Laredo which was an Idar family newspaper noted, "Perales is a known defender of our causes and had done so with a clean conscience."[1] This chapter discusses Perales' character—the good and the bad. His positive qualities were numerous—he was personable, charitable, brave, dedicated, tenacious, persistent, pragmatic and optimistic. Likewise, his firm belief in collective empowerment and enlightened leadership should be noted. He sought collective empowerment for Mexican immigrants, the working class, youth and college students. Moreover, he was not an opportunist. His less-than-stellar qualities included being uncompromising, being a know-it-all (one who claims full knowledge), making political *movidas* (moves) and occasionally having petty jealousies.

Before addressing his character, let us not forget that Perales was born poor and became an orphan at an early age. Yet he accessed every opportunity at hand—especially educational opportunities—to advance himself. He could speak both to self-improvement as well as the collective improvement of the race.

Poets wrote about Perales' qualities during his lifetime. Perhaps the poets recognized him more than any other group. Luckily the literary *calavera* tradition of *Día de los Muertos* (Day of the Dead), which playfully mocks prominent individuals, captured Perales' essence. Co-activist Adela Sloss-Vento honored him more than any other person. She organized her last tribute to him in a small red book, her manifesto and monument—it was a remarkable feat.[2] Her son Dr. Arnoldo Carlos Vento believed his mother's character to be like that of Perales, J. Luz Sáenz, and J.T. Canales; he wrote: "While the judicious four [Perales, Sloss-Vento, Canales, and Saenz] shared a spirit of collaboration, they also had in common bilingualism, integrity, veracity, sincerity, candidness, magnanimity, unselfishness, and moral rectitude."[3]

The Good Qualities of Alonso Perales
A Personable Man

Perales was already a preeminent figure before he immersed himself in civil rights activism. He received glowing letters of recommendation from his business college, his first major employer (Frank Saddlery), his army superior and from several attorneys, all Euro-Americans. Draughon's president wrote that Perales was "a very loyal American citizen." He added that he was a "splendid young man, strictly honest, sober, upright in every respect and we feel sure that he would make good in any position . . ."[4] G.W. Parish, President of Draughon's Practical Business College, also wrote of Perales in 1925, "I have always considered you as one of my best friends."[5] J.B. Andrews, department manager at Frank Saddlery Company noted, "He is my most valuable assistant in my work here." Edwin Keller, who was with the same company noted, "I have formed a strong personal attachment for the lad, because of his clean habits and superior individuality."[6] His army officer reported that he "was well liked by his associates and by the officers with whom he worked."[7] In 1924, attorney Bat Corrigan wrote, "He is a young man of splendid character, a hard worker, conscientious, and his honesty and integrity is unquestioned."[8] Attorney G. Woodson Morris wrote, he was of "very high moral character" and "extremely studious and very desirous of making his mark in the world."[9] Perales' persona allowed him to foster friendships or solid acquaintances with middle-class and elite whites, transgressing racial boundaries. In 1928, Texas Congressman John N. Garner said he was a "man of high character and superior ability." Perales had solid support from numerous white professional acquaintances and past employers.

By the 1940s, Perales' references included national and international figures. By the 1940s, his reference list included Anastacio Somoza, Nicaragua's president and Mexico's president Manuel Ávila Camacho; Sumner Welles, Under Secretary of State, US Department of State; Congressman Paul Kilday of San Antonio; Mayor C.K. Quin of San Antonio; and numerous military leaders from the US army, navy and marines.[10] (Noticeably absent from his own list were M.C. Gonzales, Mayor Maury Maverick and Dr. George I. Sánchez.)

A Charitable Man

Perales was generous with his time, money and skills. A 1931-document noted, "He personally and at his own expense organized the Brownsville, Laredo, McAllen and La Grulla councils of said League."[11] When he wrote the wife of Ben Garza, the first national LULAC president, after Garza died in 1937, Perales noted his own eighteen years of service to La Raza, which he had provided free of charge. In an interview with the *Chicano Times,* his widow Marta recalled one incident when Perales helped a "poor Mexican lady" get her coat back after it had been confiscated by a merchant. According to the woman, she had been making payments on her coat for several years; it can be inferred that this went on too long and she paid more than she owed. The merchant asked Perales, "Why are you helping that poor Mexican woman?" The *Times* reported, "Perales became even more infuriated and answered back, "What do you think I am?"[12] Perales understood what it meant to be poor. He must have also noted that the woman was making payments, but that the merchant was taking advantage of her lack of financial savvy.

Sloss-Vento and Perales' family members also recalled his generosity.[13] Much of his legal work was pro-bono and cannot be documented. His daughter Marta Carmen recalled his generosity toward his clients. She wrote, "A Hispanic wife or a Hispanic parent would call him or go by his office asking for him to help them. He would have to take us with him to bail the client out of jail. He would sit us on the bench in front of the officers while he attended to the paperwork. Needless to say, more often than not he [would] cover the cost . . . Upon release of the client the wife or parent would gratefully thank him and embrace him with tears."[14] Wife Marta wrote, "He did not care about money nor about getting rich, charity is what he cared about."[15]

Rarely did Perales write about his own giving to La Raza. However, in 1956 he revealed his thoughts about his life of giving to Nicaraguan President Anastacio Somoza: ". . . I am poor because, since I returned from Nicaragua in 1932, I have dedicated a lot of my time to defending the interests of our Hispanic race free of charge. I am not sorry for doing so because I have great satisfaction sacrificing for what I believe in. At the same time, everything has its limits, and, now, after forty years of service to my race, I plan to dedicate more time to my business and advocating more for my wellbeing and that of my family."[16] Perales was not poor, but he could have had a lot more money.

A Brave Man

Perales and all the early civil rights activists operated in a dangerous time, especially in the 1920s. That decade the Ku Klux Klan was active in South Texas and several lynchings of people of Mexican-descent occurred, which Perales protested. Sloss-Vento noted, ". . . these early leaders fought alone to open the way and that is why today, it is not as difficult for the present generation as it was for our leaders in the twenties, thirties and forties. It was a time when it was dangerous to even speak of justice.[17] While they were not alone, these activists did risk their lives.

Attorney Carlos Cadena also praised Perales for his work during these decades of racial violence against Mexicans. Cadena stated, "They had a bad atmosphere at that time". He added that Alonso and Manuel Gonzales had been shot at in West Texas.[18] Cadena noted that more modern-day "rabble-rousers" [a likely reference to Chicano Movement activists] "can get up and make all the speeches they want to and nobody shoots at them. But Alonso and Manuel Gonzales, they to some extent risked their lives."[19] He concluded, "And now a lot of these young 'rabble-rousers' think of them as "Uncle Toms."[20]

A Dedicated, Tenacious, Persistent Man

Perales was stubbornly dedicated to La Raza. LULAC co-founder Sáenz called him "tenacious."[21] His wife Marta wrote, "Every obstacle that he encountered gave him a firmer determination to accomplish his objectives."[22] Sloss-Vento wrote that he had "an invincible [sic] spirit."[23] Santos de la Paz, editor of *La Verdad* of Corpus Christi noted, "He fought for equality for the Mexican-Americans like no one else has or ever will. He did it diplomatically and with vigor, not with scandals, riots or marches."[24] While this is a critique of the methods traditionally associated with the Chicano Movement, it is true that few nationally recognized activist leaders were as persistent as Perales, with perhaps the exception of Dolores Huerta of the United Farm Workers or Dr. Rudy Acuña, professor of history. Perales and Dr. Carlos E. Castañeda encouraged one another to continue the struggle. Castañeda reminded him, "Remember the slogan of Time: 'The fight goes on in a thousand fronts.'"[25]

Judge and scholar Lupe Salinas found Perales to be an assertive militant. He wrote, "Perales honestly came across as somewhat assertive" and "appeared to be somewhat of a militant, almost demanding equality."[26]

A Pragmatic and Optimistic Man

Perales was both a pragmatist and an optimist. One political scientist wrote, "it is surprising how pessimistic he was about the prospects for social change."[27] He said that Perales "doubted Anglo Americans could be trusted."[28] It was not trust Perales lacked, but rather he recognized that centuries of racist socialization were part of the foundation of Texas history, culture and identity. Still, Perales cooperated with a few white allies and was optimistic about prospects for social change. Perales encountered few white liberals, and they failed to appear in any of the organized groups to which he belonged. He said that the federal and state governments "could . . . send us a corps of Anglo-American lecturers and writers to wage a vigorous campaign among our Anglo-American friends and fellow-citizens designed to form in the minds of their listeners a sympathetic attitude toward the Mexican people."[29] But he knew this would never happen. Perales was a realist. LULAC fought racial hegemony and the consensus that supported it "but they have the approval of a majority of the Anglo-American people in Texas, and the proof is that they [the majority] have never done anything to prevent the minority from continuing to humiliate the people of Mexican origin. . . ."[30] He told Castañeda in a letter that the problem "is really among ninety-five percent, if not ninety-nine, of the people in the Southwest. It may be that only 20% actually come out and openly express their feelings, but they have the backing of the rest, who, on the QT, say 'Amen.'"[31] Perales understood white privilege and he especially understood the press' role in maintaining it.

Perales would not have endured decades of work without believing La Raza could alter their condition. Perales urged La Raza to step out of "lethargy."[32] And though he was thinking positively, he also shared his despair with friend Castañeda. He noted, "Well, it showed that we cannot afford to quit lest they sink us deeper into the depths of misery and humiliation. Gosh! And to think that we have to fight the battle almost single-handed, as our people will just simply not back us up. They seem so indifferent toward it all. The only time they show interest is when they are hurt. On the spur of the moment they holler 'murder,' but they then go to sleep and forget about it."[33]

Collective Empowerment

Perales did not blame La Raza's oppression on La Raza. In 1927, Perales wrote, ". . . the conqueror can't assimilate conquered people. Reason: Snobbishness on the part of our fellow citizens of Nordic extraction."[34] And, in 1940, he wrote, "Ours must be a war against prejudice, ignorance, injustice, and poverty."[35] Thus, La Raza had to organize itself to fight its own collective oppression.

Perales believed foremost in the collective empowerment of La Raza—the community of Mexican Americans, Mexicans in the United States and Latinos regardless of citizenship. Like all LULAC members, he realized participation in electoral politics was an essential part of Raza empowerment. US citizens could vote, support candidates, serve on juries, run for office and serve as office holders. The 1929 LULAC Constitution Aim and Principle 13 read: "With our vote and influence we shall endeavor to place in public office men who show by their deeds, respect and consideration for our people."[36] Unfortunately, he did not foresee or advocate for women serving as elected officials.

Perales sought to empower the community of Mexican descent, including the poor and under-educated. In 1926, he defended the Mexican "peon" [37] as honorable and worthy people.[38] As LULAC national president, Perales also dealt with the issue of health, especially tuberculosis, since it impacted the poorest in the community.

Perales questioned almost all authority, including the authority of the presidents of the United States. In 1927, he wrote President Calvin Coolidge but received no response. A second letter to Coolidge noted, "much to my regret, [I] have to inform my fellow-citizens of Mexican extraction that I failed in my efforts to induce our Government to take action in the case I have alluded to, since neither Your Excellency nor the governor of Texas . . . even acknowledged receipt of the communications[,] in which I asked you to be good enough to use your good offices to bring the slayers of defenseless citizens[,] above mention[ed][, before the bars of justice."[39] Perales' criticism fell on deaf ears likely because he was of Mexican descent. But he tried to reach the highest authority in the United States.

Perales valued collectivism over individualism. He would "choose to situate himself as part of the Mexican-American collectivity."[40] As literary scholar Donna Kabalen de Bichara noted, "Interestingly, Alonso S. Perales chose not to focus on the personal 'I' but rather to document the 'threads' of his life project through the conservation of letters, articles and other types of writing that point to the narrative and argumentative discourse related to a community of people of Mexican descent; this is, his endeavors focus on 'mi raza'/my people/ and he clearly situates himself as a member of this cultural group."[41] He did not choose the "I" but a "community of people of Mexican descent."[42] Note that he did not write an autobiography, though he published some autobiographical notes about LULAC's founding in his 1937 book *En Defensa de Mi Raza*. He mostly took pride in the accomplishments of others. For instance, in 1952 he lauded the "noble and grandiose labor social charity of numerous organizations in San Antonio like the Clínica Mexicana, Cruz Azul and the Bexar County Public Health Association.[43]

Early on, Perales stated that the Mexican-American civil rights movement was not about one person. In the 1920s, he wrote, "No man is big enough to impede our progress or prevent our unification. A fraction is not larger than the whole. I will not stand in the way; on the contrary, I will do everything in my power to achieve those ends. Now, if everyone [sic] of our leaders would assume this same attitude, I am certain that our labors would be crowned with success."[44] And, in the 1950s, Perales and other LULAC founders were not attempting to establish "control."[45]

Perales' collectivism is particularly important because, too often, LULAC members have been described as self-interested or self-serving. Indeed, a 1996 study of LULAC asked how to "understand LULAC's evolution as an organization because it analyzes the individual's reasons for participation in an organization. . . ."[46]

Perales believed in civic organizations' ability to help realize Raza progress. Speaking on the need to participate in San Antonio Latino groups, he noted, "I urge that we take notice of our individual obligations with respect to the collective."[47] Members were to be composed of "conscious individuals who understand perfectly their responsibility to the community."[48]

Deflecting attention from himself, Perales ran for elected office only once. He ran for the San Antonio Independent School District: he lost and never ran for office again.[49] Even though Perales lost, he was only momentarily disillusioned. Perales campaigned for those who he believed had La Raza's interest at heart. For example, he wrote about his political preferences for mayoral candidates such as Maury Maverick, a liberal and CIO supporter. But he also broke ties with Mayor Maverick, when he failed to keep political promises he had made to La Raza.[50] In 1990, attorney Carlos Cadena said the following about Perales: "Oh yes, he—a very sincere—he would NOT take a political job. He was active in campaigns. And he would support actively those people he thought would be fair. And lots of them after they got elected offered him a job, and he said, "NO." Cadena added, "He would say, "I'm going to keep an eye on you. If you don't half-way keep your promise—I'm going to oppose you."[51]

Perales campaigned for individuals but did not show a preference for a particular political party, in part because both Democrats and Republicans were racist. In the 1930s, Perales and other Mexican Americans created the Association of Independent Voters, a sign that Mexican Americans were dissatisfied with both parties.[52] Perales supported candidates who considered the interests of La Raza, which can be seen in this 1930 list of conditions for support:

1) When the candidate or the whole ticket did not, in any way, denigrate or insult the Mexican community;
2) If the candidate or ticket advocated placing Mexican Americans on jury duty; and
3) If they advocated placing Mexican Americans in city or county government positions.[53]

He also warned,

"Our support of a political party or faction in Bexar County should be conditioned upon two things:

1. That no insults be cast upon our race at any time by members of said political party or faction.
2. Fair political representation for our race in the city and county government. We should have at least the following offices:
   • County Commissioner
   • Justice of the Peace
   • Assistant District Attorney
   • Assistant County Attorney
   At least 35% of all District and county minor offices.
   • City commissioner
   • Assistant City Attorney
   At least 25% of all city minor offices.
   one seat in the state legislature."[54]

He believed that "in election time they [Latinos] must support men who were unquestionably friends of our race." Perales was not interested in tokenism. In 1940, he resigned as board member of the San Antonio Board of Public Health because he did not want to be a mere figurehead, objecting to the lack of Spanish-surnamed employees in city government.[55] And, as I noted in Chapter 13, he expected Republicans to advance the interests of La Raza.

Perales did not privilege politicians who were of higher class or had more education. He believed that any person without formal education could be intelligent. In the 1920s, he wrote "as far as our cause is concerned, we do not need educated politicians but sincere and honest men [who] really and truly endeavor to improve the condition of our people in Texas."[56]

Uplifting the Working Class

Perales sought to uplift the working class through education, organization and advocating for fair wages. He fought to desegregate, provide access to schools and increase and improve school facilities. A better educated populace could fight for its rights.

One example of his concerns for the working class was his advocacy for adult education. In 1934, in *El Porvenir* of San Antonio he wrote "Lo que Significan Para Nosotros Las Escuelas Para Adultos," (What Schools for Adults Mean for Us). He wrote, "Education for adults is undeniably the key to a rapid solution of our social-civic problems, since our adult fellow citizens will be better prepared to participate, actively and intelligently, in societies that have as an objective the promotion of phases of social activity."[57] He wanted raise the educational level of the working through adult education and night school for Latinos. He argued that "all Mexicans regardless of citizenship" should take these classes.[58] He helped to establish a night school open to women and people of all ages regardless of their citizenship.[59] In 1934, LULAC Council 16 supported a night school attended by 1,400 at Sidney Lanier School, which was on the West side of San Antonio. He also sent a petition protesting the school's proposed closure in September 1934.[60] At another time, he joined Henry B. González in teaching a night class. Perhaps, Perales proved his caring nature when he himself taught at this night school. He was qualified to teach at a law school or a college, but he did not seek out those opportunities. He also told Sloss-Vento that San Juan, Texas needed a night school.[61]

While Perales believed organizations could act as a foundation for social justice, he did not attempt to organize the working class into LULAC. Perhaps he believed this would require them to become educated first. Surely, he supported their involvement in mutual aid societies and any other civic groups. Perales did not argue for unionization; he had limited contact with unions or union officials.

Perales advocated for better wages for workers (including farmworkers). The liberal American Civil Liberties Union leader Malcom Ross noted that Perales and others celebrated a pay raise for Mexican-American skilled workers in 1948. Ross reported, "The prosperous San Antonio Mexican-Americans who staged this dinner for the four upgraded workers, themselves made speeches celebrating the triumph . . . Their tidy bank balances, their pleasant homes, their confidence in their own abilities could not make them fully citizens of the United States so long as the great mass of their people were set apart and kept in squalor."[62] This was apparently a compliment, and not an underhanded one, of their morality and the actions they took to uplift La Raza.

Uplifting Mexican immigrants

Despite the official exclusion of Mexicans in LULAC, Perales concerned himself with Mexican immigrants too. But he did not make the lives of Mexicans in Mexico his business. He wrote, "We Texas Mexican origin residents, irrespective of citizenship, have civic and social problems that need solving."[63] He realized racism trumped citizenship. In a 1928 letter to attorney and LULAC co-founder Canales, he noted, "the murderers did not stop to think whether or not this [sic] would-be victims were American citizens or not."[64] [In other words, they were all treated as "Mexicans."] Even after the Harlingen Convention, Perales noted, "The object of the organization is to promote the general welfare of Mexican-Americans and Spanish-speaking peoples generally throughout Texas."[65] He cared about Mexican nationals and Latinos in the United States.

Perales also sought to inform the undocumented about the law. His 1937 book *En Defensa de Mi Raza* included "Notes toward Immigration Laws of the United States of America" because he wanted to inform immigrants about changes to citizenship laws after 1924. It was determined that after July 1, 1924 immigrants would not become citizens if they entered the country without documents.[66] He also let immigrants know of a free citizenship manual.[67] No doubt, Perales filed many pro-bono cases for the poor, including unauthorized immigrants.

Uplifting Students and Youth

Empowering La Raza included the empowerment of youth and college students. In 1931, Perales addressed the student body and teachers at Sidney Lanier Junior High School in San Antonio.[68] He argued for Boys Scouts as a standing LULAC committee though he left out the girls. He himself was a Boy Scout leader. Perales helped to advance working-class youth who sought out opportunities. His most significant mentorship was that of Vilma S. Martínez, the daughter of a carpenter and homemaker, who went on to become an attorney in the 1960s and diplomat in Argentina in the 2010s. But his most important work in uplifting youth was helping to initiate the School Improvement League in San Antonio in the 1930s.

Perales also supported college students. The idea of offering LULAC scholarships may have been either his or Canales. He visited the college club, the Latin American Club of the University of Texas at Austin, during his 1930-31 LULAC presidency and attempted to create a council there.[69] (Perhaps he planted the seed for LULAC for students Edmundo Mireles and Jovita González who were there at the time; George I. Sánchez also heard him speak there.) In 1942, Perales helped a Nicaraguan at the University of Texas at Austin and wrote, "I see a good opportunity here to start a number of Nicaraguan students on the way to the University of Texas."[70] Perales saw college students as future leaders who might in turn aid La Raza.

Enlightened Leadership

Leadership qualities mattered to Perales. He argued for character and believed there were character traits to be avoided: slothfulness, timidity, egotism and *envidia*.[71] He emphasized intelligence, honesty and selflessness. He wrote:

1. Our leaders must be intelligent in order that they may best guide the destiny of our race in this country.
2. They must be honest. They must really believe in and practice what they preach. They must not deceive our race by organizing it under false pretenses.
3. They must be unselfish. They must place the general welfare of all above their own. For instance, in election times they must support men who are unquestionably friends of our race.[72]

Perales listed the "moral assets," qualities needed in leaders:

1) They must be honorable beyond reproach, so that they shall neither deceive nor exploit our unfortunate Race in Texas.
2) They should be highly active, in order that our general progress may be attained more rapidly, and also be brave and not fear to demand justice whenever their rights as citizens of the United States are violated;
3) They must be intelligent so as to better direct our destinies both as citizens, as well as members of our Race."[73]

Perales' concept of leadership allowed many to lead; he noted, "Everyone has a talent. It doesn't matter how small. And this talent should be developed if society is to elevate itself."[74] He believed the role of the leader was to dedicate their time to guiding others.[75] Unfortunately, Perales did not advance women's leadership. But he complimented existing women leaders, such as Adela Sloss-Vento and María L. Hernández in San Antonio.

Perales was not elitist. In 1928, he either suggested or agreed to the idea that Ben Garza should be the League's first president. He wrote, "Ben is a very active young man, has money and, although he says he did not receive a very good education, I believe he would make a good President."[76] Perales did not assert his own college education or law degree over Garza. He did not argue that only lawyers, the college-educated or professionals were qualified to preside over LULAC. Perales believed in educating ordinary people about politics. He wrote a simple question and answer essay or flyer "El "Poll-Tax o Impuesto Electoral" (The Poll Tax or Electoral Tax), so that the working class and undereducated people could understand the political process.[77]

Moreover, Perales believed that formal education and white-collar skills mattered. Perales commented about the skills LULAC National President Canales should look for in a proposed secretary. In a letter he wrote to JT Canales, he stated: "Now, for Secretary General you should have someone who can write English well and is ACTIVE; a man who will answer all correspondence promptly and who will take a real interest in the affairs of our League." But he added a caveat, "Of course, it goes without saying that he must be LOYAL to YOU, my friend; otherwise, the other qualifications will be superfluous."[78]

As a community leader, Perales was exceptional because he cared about La Raza, LULAC and its leadership. "The only reason I am working so hard is because I firmly believe that this League of ours is destined to become the greatest thing of its kind that we Mexican-Americans have ever had in our entire history," he wrote.[79] And it was in the active committee that he saw the results of what LULAC could accomplish.[80] Likewise, he believed leaders needed to dedicate each day "POR EL PROGRESO DE MI RAZA"[81] (FOR THE PROGRESS OF MY PEOPLE).

Perales cared deeply about who led LULAC. In 1927, he wrote about future LULAC leadership, "Our organization is destined to be the greatest thing of its kind we Mexican-Americans ever had, but we must keep the reigns in good hands."[82] On advocating for Pablo G. González over Ermilio Lozano as potential LULAC national president, he noted "I am trying to safeguard the interests of our League. That's all."[83] He did not want LULAC to fall apart. Likewise, in April

1934 he noted, "delegates, with few exceptions, do not take trouble to think." And he added that LULAC members needed to "elect a man who is qualified in every respect.[84] He wanted qualified male leaders and as a result liked to choose or influence who would be LULAC's national presidents.[85]

Perales also wanted men who had a track record in LULAC to serve as national presidents. In 1937, he signed a document showing dissatisfaction with the 1937-38 president-elect. He signed (or may have written) a form letter signed by Council 16 president, Charles Albidress, which complained that "anyone can become President General even if they have not worked on behalf of our Raza or League and even if they have been a member for only a few days."[86]

Likewise, Perales believed in multiple organizations, not just LULAC or his own, having the power to move the civil rights agenda forward. Again, as Perales noted in a letter to Canales, "it makes no difference what organizations each one of [sic] belongs to or what anyone says about us . . ."[87] Perales believed in strong leaders and in effective organization beyond the capacities of individual leaders or, even of himself. Also, in 1948, Perales talked about spreading leadership around; he told Castañeda: "What is worrying me is that we have entirely too many civic organizations, and in a number of them the leaders are the same. We are wearing ourselves out attending so many meetings."[88] He did not see the civic clubs as competitive but as complementary.

A Non-Opportunistic Man

Perales was not an opportunist, taking advantage of others, seeking status or power for his own sake. He did not seek to be the first LULAC national president, nor did not seek the presidency of a LULAC local council. He sought public office only once. He wrote, "I harbor no ill-feeling toward any man or group of men who seek to achieve personal fame and glory by holding themselves out as guardians and defenders of our race." He also stated that he felt "impelled to say vehemently that [he] must decline, [. . .] to identify [him]self with any man or group of men who would use our downtrodden race as an instrument whereby to further selfish, individual ends."[89] Additionally, Perales did not make himself the official head of the Loyals. In fact, he saw himself as part of a larger movement — not as "the" movement. In 1929, he wrote Canales "everyone who assisted ought to be given just credit therefor (sic)."[90]

Literary scholar Dr. Arnoldo Carlos Vento also noted that Perales did not seek power for himself when he cited him: "It matters little who among Mexican-Americans ascends to power . . . as long as they are capable and sincere... that they be men that are more interested in the well-being of the collective mass rather than their own personal self."[91] Perales stated this repeatedly. When Perales was elected Pan American Optimist Club president in 1948, he wrote, "I was not a candidate and had not even dreamed of being so honored, so I am still stunned."[92] This humility is from a man who became president of small local service club but who, had he not been Latino, could have easily been a President of the United States.

In terms of status, Perales could have cast himself as one of the most outstanding Mexican-American leaders in the United States in the 1930s, but he did not. Only a handful of men or women — such as Senator Dennis Chávez or New Mexican state legislator Concha Ortiz y Pino — could have cast themselves in this manner. Despite the fact that Perales was the most active public Mexican-American intellectual from the 1920s to 1960s, he did not seek attention or self-aggrandizement. Instead, he wanted publicity only to further the cause.

The Bad
An Uncompromising Man

At times Perales had an uncompromising attitude as is evident in the assessment of two of his close friends. In letters that Canales wrote to Dr. Carlos E. Castañeda, he spoke frankly about the threat that Perales might resign from LULAC in 1930 over the Gonzales/Idar incident. In a letter dated March 21, 1920 Canales told Castañeda that, "Perales should not be so uncompromising."[93] The latter agreed and replied a couple days later, "I cannot agree with Mr. Perales. Harshness in such cases has a limit and I believe in this case mercy, such as you have exercised in the trial was the most judicious course to follow."[94] (LULAC's trial allowed M.C. Gonzales to stay in

LULAC and Perales did not resign.) Michael A. Olivas also noted in his research that Perales "was so intolerant of groups and ideas he disliked."[95]

Mexican critic Carlos Basañez Rocha, of *Mexico en el Valle,* suggested in the 1920s that Perales "perceived himself as the judge and protector of the Mexican people."[96] This was an accurate assessment. Recall, that at the Harlingen Convention of 1927, he orchestrated the foundation of an organization that could offer a Mexican-American perspective on the fate of the Mexican-origin people, which included the Mexican immigrant community. He assumed he and Mexican Americans knew best what kind of leadership and organization Mexican immigrants needed. Likewise, he tried to coordinate the 1952 Latin American Convention in Mission from afar as an organized response to the publication of the racist Wetback pamphlet. He also attempted to stifle the democratic process of meetings to prevent them from not going his way. For example, he told Sáenz not to allow opponents or critics to speak at the anti-Wetback Pamphlet conference.[97]

Perales also believed that he knew which politicians would best serve the interests of the people of Mexican descent. Perales did not attempt to control LULAC but he did try to direct it.[98] He did what he could do to determine who the next national president would be. According to one political scientist, "During election years, Perales believed he knew which candidates were best qualified for office and thought less of those who disagreed with him."[99] Sometimes those who read newspapers, listen to the news, keep up with politics and/or who talk to a wide range of persons might be better informed. But it is easy to misjudge candidates. Opportunists, criminals and perverts have been elected. Democrats might argue that Perales made a mistake by supporting any Republican or vice-versa. And Perales was stridently anti-Communist in the 1950s, though some US Communists had the interests of the working-class in mind.

Perales could be paternalistic. He wrote, "Frankly speaking, I am somewhat disappointed to learn that the Corpus Christi Council of the Order of the Sons of America and the Order of the Knights of American have not yet joined the League of Latin-American Citizens."[100] Even the exclusion of Mexican immigrants from LULAC membership had a ring of paternalism. Except Perales was right. A Mexican immigrant-led organization might have fallen apart due to the deportations of the 1930s. I would argue, however, that LULAC might have inspired parallel Mexican organizations composed of men and women. Indeed, the original discussion was about creating two major organizations based on citizenship. But the Mexican community in Texas could speak for itself and did not act to establish such an organization. It was fractured by class, competing ideologies and loyalties. And poverty prevented many from participating.

Perales was also politically vindictive. This is seen in three major incidents. The first is the threat of deportation of Mexican critics. (See Chapter 7 on the Harlingen Convention.) The second is his attack on M.C. Gonzales and Clemente Idar. (See Chapter 22 on Friends and Frenemies.) And the last is his threat of filing a lawsuit or of firing of Dr. George I. Sánchez. (See Chapter 14 on the 1950s.) He did not tolerate serious criticism of his ideas or political actions, especially if these critiques were public. According to Perales, in 1953 *Joe v. Alamia* "actually went out of his way to libel and defame me recently when I went to the Valley to campaign for Governor Shivers." Perales wrote than Alamia contributed to the publication of a poster defaming him, and that he had flunkies calling him both "Vendido" and "Republicano" at an event.[101] Perales helped defeat Alamia in his bid for re-election as Criminal District Attorney for Hidalgo County. Perales later told Castañeda, "He had everything I did against him coming to him."[102]

Perales, like others, had his share of *envidia* or petty jealousies. He wrote Sáenz, "Jealousy is common among our leaders and pseudo-leaders."[103] It is true that on occasion Perales was a political target. Sloss-Vento noted, "Often, our leaders were persecuted by politicians, Anglos, and in some cases by our own people."[104] Likewise, Perales was critical of those he felt were lacking, incompetent or egotistical. Perales also expressed the occasional jealousy, as with attorney Gus Garcia, who received more accolades than Perales. Although Perales was just as deserving if not more.

Conclusion

Perales was an outstanding figure with few flaws. Ironically, the first persons to recognize his strong character were all whites, his first major supporters in his employment, in the army and in his early legal work. Perales was giving, brave, optimistic and community-minded. He sought to empower La Raza, immigrants and youth. However, Perales did not advance women's empowerment by not including them in non-segregated LULAC chapters and this impacted generations of women in Texas. Even though he orchestrated attacks on several political enemies who disagreed with him, threatened several of his critics with deportation and expressed occasional petty jealousies, Perales was by far a stellar figure.

Perales was a caring man and this is evident in his care for his Raza family. Perales was more than "generous"—he gave his life for La Raza. He used his intellect, education, bilingualism and middle-class status as well as his writing, oratorical and leadership skills to further the lives of Latinos and redeem La Raza in the United States. As an educated, middle-class man he could have sat on his laurels and basked in middle-class comfort but that was not his choice. Moved by his humanity and his Christian beliefs, he chose a life of dedication instead. Perales was a good man and his weaknesses should be attributed to his humanity. Only his affront to women, in segregating them into Ladies LULAC, proved to be a lasting affliction.

CHAPTER 20
Family

Alonso S. Perales was a family man. Losing his brother, father, mother and two sisters while he was still young must have played a key role in his desire to have his own family. This chapter investigates his wife Marta Engracia Pérez's background, especially her class status and her thoughts on civil rights activism, particularly for women. First, the question related to Perales and his wife's relationship to LULAC will be discussed, and whether she advocated for women's inclusion in LULAC. In previous chapters it was indicated that Perales believed women should be segregated into Ladies LULAC councils. Second, this chapter looks at their courtship, their marital relations and their relations with the children they adopted in 1950. Third, it analyzes Perales' relations with his nephew, Alonso M. Perales who went on to become a professional with a PhD in Latino and Latin American Studies. Finally, the chapter describes the family's life after his death.

Marta Engracia Pérez, Wife

In his early 20s, Perales sought a romantic partner and married Marta Engracia Pérez of Rio Grande City on November 26, 1922.[1] Marta was his perfect match. Her father's background made her a good fit for Alonso. She was born on April 16, 1901 in the Rio Grande City area to Sylvestria Peña and Casimiro Pérez-Álvarez.[2] Pérez-Álvarez was a descendant of the 1787 Spanish land grant recipient Pedro José Pérez, and by the 1900s, the family had managed to retain some of this land. Pérez-Álvarez was a rancher, a US marshal and a publisher of two Spanish-language newspapers, *El Voluntario* and *El Bien Público*. *El Voluntario*, called itself an "organ of the México-

Texano element."[3] He had received at least a junior high school education in Texas, and had then attended private school in Mier, Tamulipas and Ateneo Fuentes College in Saltillo, Coahuila in Mexico. This allowed him to be versed in world geography and to operate a private Mexican school in South Texas in the early 1890s. He was a member of Club Washington Hidalgo in Rio Grande City. In 1900, he was a census enumerator; a US Marshall from 1902 to 1914; a county food administrator during World War I; a US government scout during the Mexican border raids; and a postmaster in 1924. Marta's mother was likely a homemaker and taught her the social graces fitting of her gender and class. Since the Pérez Alvarez family was a patrician family, who had inherited land dating back to the 1700s, Marta grew up in a family with significant intellectual, educational, political and civic capital.[4] She was solidly middle class.

Marta grew up in a large family. Her siblings included Hilda (1899); Fulgencio Manuel (1904); Francisca (1905); Librada (1906); Estela (1910); María Celia (1910); Toraldo (1913) and two infants who died.[5] Francisca, Estela and Celia expressed their political intellect throughout the twentieth century. Francisca wrote letters to the editor on civic and political matters and she was not a member of Ladies LULAC. Celia published an essay on political campaigns in Starr, County, at age 17, in an Edinburg, Texas newspaper.[6]

Marta finished high school and attended college in the 1920s, at Our Lady of the Lake University in San Antonio, making her exceptional among Mexican-American women of that time. She began college in 1917 and finished two years of college before marrying Alonso. She completed her degree in the late 20s after socializing with parents of Nicaraguan Violeta Chamorro.[7] Marta also received a certificate from Universidad Nacional de México Cursos de Extensión Universitaria (UNAM Extension) of San Antonio in Texas in 1944, where she studied Spanish and Inter-American Relations.[8] Marta and Alonso also opened a bookstore in San Antonio, likely during the post-World War II years, suggesting her intellectual and business acumen and ambition.

Courtship and Love

Marta and Alonso met at a dance at the Casino Mexicano in San Antonio. They corresponded through letters until they married in 1922.

Once married, they socialized at the Casino where they danced and mixed with the local Mexican middle class and the emerging Mexican-American middle class. One leader referred to the Casino as a "beautiful center of aristocracy, beauty, and culture," this was perhaps an exaggeration, though potential members needed a sponsor, letters of recommendation and had to be voted in.[9] Members reportedly included bankers, businessmen, industrialists, farmers, newspapermen and professionals where some 300 couples attended socials in the 1930s.[10] In 1937, Perales served as master of ceremonies for an annual spring dance sponsored by the club for women of Mexican-descent, Club Swastika.[11]

After Perales met Marta, they corresponded because he was still living in Washington, DC. Perales wrote her love letters but only one remains; it reads,

My Unforgettable Martita:

Today 15 days ago I wrote you a letter telling you that I had resolved to continue studying some more time, but that I want to marry you as soon as possible. I also asked you if you thought your father would consent for you to come to this city to marry me. To this date I have not received your response. Why do you punish me this way? Why are you taking so long to respond to a letter as important as that one? Why do you not write at least some lines telling me something in respect to our situation? Why are you so ungrateful with me, Love of Mine? Huh? Huh? Does it not occur to you that I will be anxious to know what you think about our situation? Imagine how I am here imagining thousands of things. I say: Did she misinterpret my letter and feels offended by me? Did her father feel offended? Did the letter not arrive? I don't know what to think. Tomorrow is Saturday and if I do not receive a letter from you, you can imagine the splendid Sunday that I will have. What I tell you in my letter does not mean that we will not get married given the case that your father will not want for you to come here and contract marriage with me.

No, no . . . life of mine. We will get married as soon as possible. That is, as soon as I can make the trip and arrange everything properly.

Many kisses.
Your Alonso
Yours Always

Perhaps Marta and her parents expected a more personal or formal proposal? Perhaps she/they expected a wedding in Rio Grande City? Shortly after this letter was written, Perales returned to Texas to marry Marta and then they returned to Washington, DC. The family likely approved of Alonso, who was an ambitious, accomplished and an educated man of character.

Marta in the Marriage

According to historian Richard A. Garcia, "Perales supported an idealized situation where the husband was the breadwinner and the wife and mother did not work outside the home, but instead stayed at home and took care of the children."[12] This is partly true. The family likely had only one car throughout their lifetime, so Alonso drove to work and she stayed home. But one document showed that Marta did some secretarial work for him, so, at times, she may have accompanied him to his office. She attended social events both with Alonso and on her own. Moreover, there were no children in their marriage for three decades, and they had a nanny for the earliest years with the children, at least.

Moreover, Marta did not "stay at home" when Perales traveled to Latin America. Most of Perales' work obligations gave his wife travel opportunities. She traveled to many of the countries where Perales worked. Historian J. Gilberto Quezada interviewed her, and he wrote "She traveled extensively with her husband on thirteen diplomatic missions."[13] A 1932 *La Prensa* article was titled, "Los Esposos Perales Van a Managua, Nicaragua."[14] This likely made her one of the most well-traveled Latinas in the United States. To what extent she remained inside her living quarters during their travel is unknown. There were some occasions when she did not travel with her husband. For instance, Perales traveled to Chile in 1925 without her. Perales told his father-in-law, "pues la verdad es que no estamos contentos separados" (The truth is that we are not happy separated.)[15] She stayed in Rio Grande City while he was in South America.

Marta likely attended to all the domestic chores in their household before the children arrived but there is evidence they had a maid in the early 1950s, when the couple had adopted children. Perales wrote, "well, we had a young woman helping us in the house and she slept there and she was there all the time."[16] But, by December 1954, there was no maid or assistant.[17] Later, however, they did have a housekeeper named Dalilia Fernández.

Despite her "wifedom," Marta had her own identity though it was not related to a career or to civil rights like Alonso's. She was a singer, pianist, inventor and bookstore owner, so she partly stepped out of gender boundaries. She had a long history as a singer and musician. In 1924, a Rio Grande City newspaper reported she played the piano during her visit to her family home.[18] While living in Washington, in 1926, she rented a piano.[19] In June 1931, Perales wrote, "We are enjoying life in San Antonio. Mrs. Perales is beginning to sing again and to go out with me."[20] Perhaps she had fallen into depression after her sister's Celia's death. Marta also participated in a recital at the San Pedro Playhouse in San Antonio in 1941. *La Prensa* reported, "The third part of the presentation was a Mrs. Marta P. de Perales, soprano the aria of 'Il Trovatore, 'D'amo sull'all rosee,' accompanied by the tenor Antonio Gutierrez."[21] In 1947, she sang the aria "Aida" for the Cosmopolitan Club of Opera at the Municipal Auditorium, at an event to benefit the San Antonio Social Welfare and Legal Aid Bureau."[22] And, in 1948, she participated in a benefit for a new Sacred Heart Convent in McAllen.[23] She shared her talent to benefit others, at least on these occasions. She also composed music.[24]

Besides being a singer and pianist, Marta was also an inventor. She invented a rotary filing cabinet for which she obtained a patent. The *San Antonio Light* reported, ". . . she first got the idea for her unique design while doing secretarial work for her husband and watching him struggle in opening and closing his filing cabinets."[25] She conceptualized at least three inventions and successfully obtained a patent for one of them. Besides the revolving filing cabinet, she developed a thread holder to hold the thread when the spool was not in use[26] and she also invented some type of "bank trap."[27]

The Perales also had a bookstore, likely opened after World War II and through the early 1950s. A bookstore would have gotten Marta out of the house, allowing her to pursue intellectual and cultural interests and fostering social contact. When the Perales adopted children, they closed it because they had no one to manage it.[28]

Marta also took opportunities to pursue her outside social and educational interests by joining club life, and attending social events where she mixed with the middle class and the elites of San Antonio. Her husband's occupation and activism gave her numerous occasions to socialize. She joined the Pan American Round Table (PART), an inter-racial women's (but overwhelmingly white) organization promoting better US/Latin American relations, Pan Americanism and Good Neighborliness.[29] While her class position allowed her some access to socializing with white women, race relations were still strictly codified and segregation was still the norm.

In the 1940s, she was "instrumental in the founding of the Pan American League" which apparently organized free childcare for barrio mothers.[30] The Pan American Optimist Club, of which Perales was a member and later became the president, offered a Ladies Day meeting regularly in which she also participated.[31] In 1957, she was a member of the Council of International Relations.[32] She was also a member of the Women's Auxiliary of the San Antonio Bar Association.[33] In 1966, she was given a certificate from the María R. Magnon Memorial Black and White Ball.[34] So, while Marta was Perales' wife, she was not simply a domestic helpmate.

While Perales' wife was not involved in civil rights efforts, Marta's sister Mrs. Francisca Pérez de Lozano (Mrs. Santos V. Lozano) was much more vocal. She wrote four letters to the *Valley Morning Star* in Harlingen in 1947, protesting discrimination, praising Mexican workers, the greatness of Mexico and Latin American men's patriotism.[35] Her sister Estela was contacted by politician Lloyd Bentsen in 1948, and she ran for county commissioner in 1978.[36] In this sense, her sisters were more political than Marta.

There is no evidence Marta joined Ladies LULAC in San Antonio, which was founded there in the 1930s.[37] Marta's activities matter, especially in understanding that since she was not interested in being a civil rights activist herself, she did not influence or change Perales' position on women in LULAC. It seems to be that she was comfortable with homosocial practices in civic organizations, of men congregating with men and women with women as was expected of both during that time.

Husband & Wife

Assessing marital relations is a difficult endeavor for a third party. Neither Marta nor Alonso are alive to testify or correct my findings. Their marriage stayed intact for thirty-eight years. They also decided to adopt children late in their marriage, which could either be a sign of a successful or distressed marriage.

Only three written sources offer any evidence of their relationship. According to Perales' nephew, Alonso M. Perales, who had a similar name to his uncle, Alonso S. had a temper with his wife. His nephew Alonso M. said, "He had a temper, too. And she (Marta) would trigger that temper right away. There were things that he did that she don't [didn't] care for."[38] These are his observations or his feelings, and they come from personal contact he had with the couple.

A second source showed that Perales had some conflicts with his wife, though it is not possible to assess how common this was. He wrote his friend Dr. Carlos E. Castañeda: "I lost my temper, but I was driven to it. I have felt miserable ever since." (Today, those familiar with anger management might say that each person is in charge of his or her own emotions and reactions.) Perales continued, "To think that one cannot have peace and happiness, or at least peace, just because the other party insists on making both of us unhappy by the constant nagging and by constantly embarrassing and humiliating me even in the presence of our friends." Perales asked to meet with the Castañedas again ". . . but this time with the understanding that all conversation regarding other women (alleged rivals) and all accusations from our wives toward us will be taboo."[39]

Perales also took some responsibility, in their marriage and for his parenting, when he apologized for being an "egotist."[40] Once, when Marta and the children were visiting in Rio Grande City, he wrote, "I understand that I should not be so selfish and I should grant you your wishes, even though I may suffer in the absence of all of you."[41] Did he admit to being an "egotist" because he did not give her enough attention or as much as she wanted? Was he an egotist because he did not spend enough time with the children? We have no further insight into this conflict in their relationship from his perspective or from hers; the archive contains no letters from Marta to Alonso.

There was love in their relationship, as the 1922 love letter Perales wrote Marta confirms as does a letter from 1953. The latter opens with, "Dear and unforgettable Martita"[42] and goes on to say: "Tú, mi viejita linda, y mis hijitos reciban el cariño inmenso y los besitos de este su esposo y padre."[43] He called her "Martita," signifying affection and she reciprocated with him "Chito,"[44] an affectionate term. Friend Castañeda wrote in January 1955, "Martita grande looks well also and so much more contented than in the old days,"[45] perhaps referring to the fact that the Perales family now included children.

Children

Because they had no children, the couple adopted in the 1950s. It is possible that the childless couple drew attention to themselves, since it was uncommon for couples, especially of Mexican descent, not to have children. Several families asked them to adopt theirs.[46] "The whole world knew they had no children," noted their daughter.[47] Marta would have especially been the focus of gossip. Alonso had already shown his love for children, not only through his civic work in the 1930s, but also as a Boy Scouts troop advocate and troop leader in 1946.[48] In 1950, when Marta was 49 and Alonso was 52, they adopted Alonso Saul Perales Jr., Marta Carmen and Raimundo Alfonso.[49] Marta Carmen was adopted first at the age of four months; then Alonso Saul, who was four years old; and then Raimundo Alfonso at two weeks old.[50] Their friend Adela Sloss-Vento noted that by then Alonso was "ill and tired."[51] In an interview with Marta Carmen, she shared that her father taught her to introduce herself as follows: "Soy Marta Carmen Perales y Pérez, hija adoptiva del Licenciado Perales y la Señora Marta Perales y Pérez, a sus órdenes."[52]

In a letter found in the archive, it is evident that Alonso loved and cared for his children. In this letter he wrote to Marta who, along with the children, were visiting relatives in Rio Grande City he asks Marta, "How are my lovely children who I care for so much? How is my lovely Mami [Marta Carmen], my most beautiful and precious Popi [Raimundo] and my funny, loving and beautiful Junior [Alonso Jr.]."[53] A year later, Perales wrote Castañeda that "the children are growing all am just crazy about him [them] . . ."[54] and Castañeda told Perales his was a "happy family" in 1955.[55] Moreover in the correspondence with his friend J.T. Canales, Perales shared intimate details about the family's traditions before bedtime: "The story of Moses and Joseph I will hand to Martita when I go home tonight, so that she may tell same as bedtime stories to our three children."[56] As a stay-at-home mother, she played a more active role in the lives of their children given that Perales spent little time at home. It is believed that Perales typically attended mass before going to work probably from 8 to 5, worked on Saturdays and often attended meetings at night.

But as a loving dad on occasion, Perales also took the children and his niece Araceli to his workplace, where they would play in his office and go the ice cream parlor nearby. [57] His son Raimundo recalled that they would first "stop at the small café across the street from the red courthouse building. [And] We would then go to his office in the Alameda building and I would run to be the first to sit on his big brown chair that would go back like a rocking chair. He would just laugh and say, 'A que mijito'."[58]

Blanca E. Perales, Alonso Jr.' wife, shared that her husband told her Alonso Sr. would "go out of his way to give them the best Christmas. One year he said that he bought him a whole cowboy outfit with hat and boots. Also a horse—the one that was made out of [a] stick."[59] Alonso's second son, Raimundo, remembered that one time his mother asked Perales to spank Raimundo, and instead of doing that, his father, "put his finger to his lips and whispered that [I] was to begin crying as he hit the bed with the belt. I was very good at pretending that I was indeed crying. My daddy never did give me a spanking. He was very good to me and my sister and brother. My sister says he did the same ritual with my brother Jr."[60] This memory of a loving and caring father would be supported by Marta Carmen through our conversations: "My Daddy showered us with love, hugs & kisses. We were pampered."[61]

The Perales children had a father for less than a decade. He was not able to imbue them with his passion for civil rights.

In 1958, Perales' niece Araceli moved in with Perales' family. She finished high school at Jefferson High and Perales helped to prepare her for college. According to Araceli Pérez Davis, "The first thing that I remember was that he and I walked to the San Antonio College administrative office (behind his residence) and he introduced me to the president. Tío Alonso was planning on my attending SAC as soon as I graduated. I remember he would help me with my school assignments at night after he worked all day at his law office. After I graduated I enrolled in college and he paid for the semester."[62]

Alonso Jr. only lived to age 52.[63] He attended Our Lady of Sorrows Catholic School, and then finished high school at Thomas Jefferson. He immediately joined the Army and was wounded by an explosive mine in Viet Nam. Later, he worked in the US Attorney's office assisting with legal work. He was 52 when he passed in 2001.[64]

Perales' Nephew

While Perales' children were too young to inherit his activist spirit, it was passed on to his nephew Alonso M. Perales. His nephew would drive his uncle "to gatherings held in huge revival tents on the outskirts of towns."[65] He received a scholarship funded by Canales in 1952, for which Perales had served on the committee.[66] Alonso M. obtained a Ph.D. from the University of Texas at Austin with the dissertation, "The Effects of Teacher-oriented and Student-oriented Strategies on Self-concept, English Language Development, and Social Studies Achievement of fifth grade Mexican American Students." In 1974, he served as bilingual director of San Antonio ISD and worked with the district for thirty-five years. He was also a Fulbright Scholar in Applied Linguistics in Ecuador and El Salvador.[67] Dr. Alonso M. Perales wrote four books, including *Brujas, Lechuzas y Espantos*, a children's book.[68] It is evident that like his uncle, he also had a Latin Americanist and literary bent.

Marta after Alonso S. Perales' Death

His wife Marta spoke publicly about Alonso several times after his death. She did so in 1962, at his reinternment to a second cemetery location; at a LULAC chapter founders' banquet in 1962; and at the national annual LULAC convention in Albuquerque in 1990.[69] In 1960, she told the funeral audience, "He was born a leader and nothing could stop his march because men who are born for that come to this world once in a century."[70]

After Perales died in 1960, Marta had to hold the family together. She and the children had a long life without a husband and father. There is no evidence of there being any love interests in Marta's life afterwards nor did she work outside of the home for wages. She was about 60 years old when Alonso died, in an era when that age was considered elderly.

Marta also had to close her husband's law practice. Lawyer Ronald Smallwood, Perales' law partner, agreed to help her do so, but when he did not follow through she resorted to contacting him through letters and she eventually had to hire another lawyer to help.[71] Lawyer Charlie Albidress Jr., the son of Charles Albidress and LULAC Council 16 and Loyals member, also helped tie up Perales' legal matters.[72]

Marta faced some financial challenges as a woman without a career and with young children. She received death benefits from Sociedad de la Unión, which Alonso had joined in 1935.[73] She also received $233 a month from Social Security for herself and her children in 1960. She seemed to keep up with her husband's charities until she was unable to continue as is evidenced in a letter she wrote in 1965 to the George Washington University Alumni Annual Fund, "Due to the responsibility that I have in supporting and educating our three adopted children, I regret not to be able to contribute to the

Alumni Annual Fund."[74] Luckily, she had oil and gas royalties in Starr County and rental property to supplement her income.

The Perales' had entered the real estate business in 1951 and two years later, in 1953, they had created a small realty company called Perales Realty Company. It may have been established after they closed the bookstore. In 1955, the Perales' bought two lots from Salvador and Marina P. Martínez, parents to Vilma S. Martínez that they proceeded to rent to tenants.[75] In this way, the family obtained rent from several properties. Marta would sell her house on Courtland St. and buy one on North Drive after her husband's death.[76] Overall, however, their family paid the price of Alonso's decades of activism, pro-bono work and generosity; they were left with limited wealth upon his death and no pension.[77]

Although Marta did not seem to engage in civil rights activism— her name is not listed among the women who attended the founding LULAC convention in February 1929, she did participate in a handful of civil rights actions. In 1957, she wrote to the editor to complain about Mexican boys in Colorado not being permitted to carry an American flag. She believed any person exhibiting US patriotism should not be discriminated against.[78] She also must have written Senator Edward Kennedy because he responded noting, "I share your feelings of concern with regard to the plight of the migrant workers . . ."[79] On a visit to Rio Grande City, Marta joined a farmworkers' march with César Chávez and she walked to the Alamo and then presumably to Austin.[80] However, she was apparently not happy with the rise of the term "Chicano" because in 1977, she wrote, "There is one thing that disturbs me. I do not approve of a generation that has given our race a new name or pseudonym to distinguish or classify us."[81] In 1980, she wrote Governor William Clements about the location of a proposed state prison in Starr County.[82] She also wrote a letter in support of José Ricardo García, candidate for the Edgewood School District Board in 1988.[83]

This is the extent of the activism that Marta Perales was engaged in that can be supported through archival research. Her daughter Marta shared that her mother often "preferred playing the piano and singing for her husband at the end of a day" instead of participating in marches, her upper middle class upbringing often defined the activities that she, a mother and wife, could be involved in and even though her mother loved the work her father did, "she didn't like the (poor) people he helped."[84] Perales' nephew Alonso M. referred to Marta as "snobbish," perhaps alluding to her middle-class ways[85] that are best understood within the concept of *"gente decente,"* the high society of reason, manners and culture.[86]

After Perales died, Marta carried on a lengthy friendship with Adela Sloss-Vento through correspondence. While they talked about various topics, including their health, they mostly discussed preserving Alonso S. Perales' legacy. Marta spent the rest of her life caring for her children and grandchildren. She raised intelligent, successful and articulate children.[87]

Conclusion

Perales found his soul mate in Marta Pérez Peña, daughter of the prominent Casimiro Pérez-Álvarez. Casimiro was symbolic of all Perales strived for: middle-class status, political activism, civic engagement, educational achievement, ethnic pride and intellectual activism. In Marta, Alonso found class status, an educated woman and an intellectually curious woman. She was also proud of her ethnicity and smart, even owning a book store. She was more than the stereotypical idea of a "wife."

Like some, Perales struggled with his temper. He admitted to Marta that he was an "egotist," perhaps because she and the children needed more attention than he provided. (In no other way was Perales an egotist.) The addition of children seems to have elevated the family's happiness though it added financial pressures. This may have led the Perales into a small real estate business in the 50s.

Perales must have had a stable relationship with his wife Marta, since they adopted children late in their lives, after almost thirty years of marriage. While Marta was a homemaker, she continued her interests as singer and pianist, consistent with her middle class background. She also took up nontraditional activities as an inventor and did some clerical work for Alonso, but just how much is not clear. She may have helped organize some of his archives and most likely opened the Perales' bookstore, which required both intellectual and business acumen.

Raised with class privilege as the daughter of Casimiro Pérez-Álvarez, Marta easily accessed middle-class social life. She spent a significant amount of time without Perales at home all of her life. Perhaps Marta's middle-class upbringing, which likely emphasized the importance that girls have ladylike manners, molded her without an activist vein although her father was civically involved. She was not a member of Ladies LULAC, and there is no evidence that she was critical of the idea of homosocial chapters for men and women.

All the evidence suggests that Perales was a most excellent father. Though his time at home was limited, he took his children to the office on Saturdays and even, to the courthouse. He showered the children with love and gave them extra treats. Perales was unable to pass on his activist torch to his young children because he passed away early. He also extended care to his niece and nephew as well, helping to educate them and instilling the value of education and activism in nephew Dr. Alonso M. Perales. His nephew not only earned a Ph.D., he also became an administrator in bilingual education, an author of books for Latino children and a Latin American folklorist. Dr. Alonso M. Perales made activism and education a family tradition.

With Perales' death, his family bore the brunt of the sacrifices Perales had made for his activism. They endured decades without a father and without his earnings. (He had forsaken wealth decades before.) Nonetheless, today the family understands that Perales gave up his family time for the cause of Mexican Americanism.

CHAPTER 21
Friends and Frenemies

Although Alonso S. Perales was a busy man, he made time for friends. From the early 1920s to the early 1950s, he was a busy, married man. In the 1950s, he was a man with three children. He wrote friends and visited them, though they were mostly activists like himself. Perales used letter writing to maintain his friendships, all of which were civic in nature. Several of Perales' close relationships can be understood through his correspondence. He did not write anyone for casual chit-chat nor did he use letters to stay connected to his relatives, with perhaps the exception of his father in law Casimiro Pérez-Álvarez. He did not gossip about others unless the gossip related to political differences. While the telephone was commonly available since the 1920s, his use of the phone is unknown. Perhaps given long-distance fees, letter-writing proved to be an affordable means of communication for him.

This chapter discusses Perales' relationship with friends and frenemies, all of whom had a role in the Mexican-American civil rights movement, including friendships with his inner circle of activists: J. Luz Sáenz, J.T. Canales, Dr. Carlos E. Castañeda and Adela Sloss-Vento. In an era of homosociality, when heterosexual men socialized with men and heterosexual women socialized with women, Sloss-Vento, was his only woman friend. The chapter also mentions his close friends in San Antonio and South Texas. While most of his friends were Mexican Americans, he maintained a friendship with Jack Danciger, an oilman and rancher of Fort Worth, Texas who was originally from Taos, New Mexico, with whom he corresponded between 1944 and 1959.[1]

Finally, this chapter also examines Perales' adversaries, men with whom Perales had a conflict. These men were also major civil rights activists, with whom Perales had working relationships, but with whom he also had ideological and/or personality differences. These included attorney M.C. Gonzales and educator Dr. George I. Sánchez.

Civic friendships
J. Luz Sáenz

Alonso S. Perales and J. Luz Sáenz were friends. The Perales papers at the University of Houston and the Sáenz papers at the University of Texas at Austin show they only had sporadic correspondence over the decades—less than twenty letters have survived. They likely had regular contact in the 1920s when they both were in the Valley and in the 1930s when they both were active with LULAC. They organized a Valley lecture tour together in 1924. Later, Sáenz frequently moved from one teaching job to the next in South, Central and West Texas because he was considered a pro-Raza agitator. And, since he was married and had nine children, he did not have much leisure time or money.

Perales and Sáenz had much in common: both were from Alice; both were veterans; both were highly educated; both were impacted by Eulalio Velásquez (or Pablo Pérez); and both were infused with an activist spirit. Sáenz was Perales' senior and had ten years of experience as an activist in the Agrupación Protectiva Mexicana in the 1910s which had South Texas chapters before he met Perales. Likewise, Sáenz had contacts across South Texas that were useful to Perales. They had cordial relations and there is no evidence of conflict between them. In 1942, Perales noted, "It has been a long, long time since you and [I] have conversed together. Next time you visit San Antonio please let me know in order that we may have lunch together. I want to see you and to have a good chat with you as we used to in days gone by."[2]

When Sáenz died Perales wrote an article memorializing him, "An Interesting Letter about a Great Mexican Leader," which

appeared in *La Verdad* of Corpus Christi on September 14, 1952.[3]
Perales wrote J.T. Canales about Sáenz's character and stated that he
is "a man of sincerity and honor. He is one of the few men in whom I
have implicit confidence. He harbors no illegitimate or selfish ambitions and I'll guarantee you that he will never turn a traitor to our
cause."[4] Sáenz died in 1952 before Perales.

J.T. Canales

The second major friendship Perales had was with J.T. Canales.[5]
Perales met Canales through his father-in-law, Casimiro Pérez
Alvarez.[6] Perales contacted Canales in the 1920s; both were from
South Texas, had become attorneys and had attended elite law schools
outside of Texas. Factors possibly working against a closer relationship between the two were their age, social and religious differences,
geography and Canales' limited socializing outside of his home due to
his condition as a germaphobe. Canales was nineteen years older,
lived most of his adult life in Brownsville, Texas[7] and may have practiced both Judaism and Catholicism. Perales asked him for advice
related to his career, legal issues and finances. What drew them
together was their civil rights activism, their attorney status, their
South Texas culture, the Spanish language, their anti-Communist
beliefs, and in the 1950s, their support for the Republican Party.[8]
Their correspondence spanned the 20s, 30s and 50s even though there
were some years when they did not exchange letters. There is no evidence they visited one another on a regular basis because when
Perales visited South Texas, he often went to Rio Grande City—100
miles from Brownsville.

When Perales wrote that there seemed to be a wrong impression
of all the work he did as National President of LULAC from 1930 to
1931 from some of his colleagues who may have believed that he had
done "nothing for the League" and proceeded to write a memo documenting his activism in this period, it is likely that Canales wrote
"Some of the things Alonso S. Perales has done for the League of
United Latin American Citizens,"[9] a document that described Perales'
contributions to LULAC. Perales likely returned the favor when he
praised Canales with a pamphlet he published in the 1930s.[10] He also

printed a flyer to campaign for Canales as LULAC national president in 1933.[11]

Perales and Canales did not agree on everything. For instance, they disagreed on whether LULAC members should have supported the national presidency of Mauro Machado (1933-1934). Perales opposed him, and Canales initially favored him. In 1935, Canales wrote Dr. Carlos E. Castañeda that "our mutual friend, Lic. Perales has undertaken lately to oppose anything I do" and, thus, Canales had decided to become a little less passive in LULAC.[12]

Perales and Canales were ethical men who did not seek power or control, though both could have commanded it. They equally believed in civil rights organizations and principled leadership. In the 1940s, Perales wrote Canales about their activism outside of LULAC, since both had quit the organization in the late 1930s. Perales wrote "As I have said to you before, it makes no difference what organizations each of [us] belongs to or what anyone says about us. . . ."[13]

Perales also came to Canales' defense on a serious issue in 1956. Canales made some comments about Judge Ezequiel D. Salinas of Laredo, one of the few Mexican-American judges in the pre-1960 era, and Salinas filed charges against Canales for libel. Perales asked Salinas to drop the charges. There is no evidence in the Canales or Perales papers that Canales asked Perales to intervene but the following letter, from May 1956, documents Perales's request to Judge Salinas, ". . . it would make me very happy to see you drop the suit for damages which you have against Honorable J.T. Canales . . . I have not read the articles, but I know that Judge Canales did not intend to libel you. He is the dean of the Latin American lawyers in Texas, and it is my feeling that we owe him every consideration."[14] Salinas did not look upon Perales' intervention favorably, retorting, "Your (sic) and your kind wife's intervention is one of many indirect and round-about ways which your dean has employed and is employing to get out of confronting on the witness stand, and under oath, the lied which he publicized about me—not one time—but during a course of six months, and continued them from time to time until recently."[15] Again, there is no evidence in the Perales or Canales correspondence that Canales sought this intervention on his behalf, and I doubt that a phone call might have been made. The last exchange between Canales and Perales was in 1960 when Perales wrote: "in me you have a sincere, loyal and true friend who has been with you always and will be at all times."[16]

The two were close enough that, on two occasions, Perales asked Canales for money. On behalf of Perales' compadre, Jesús María (?), Perales asked Canales for an $800 loan so that Jesús María could buy a boiler and tumbler for his business.[17] In July 1953, he asked Canales for a $30,000 loan to buy a house which he planned to put in Canales' name until he could buy it from him. Perales noted that his own house was worth at least $15,000 and he had a lot on Dwyer Street two blocks from the courthouse worth $10,000.[18] Canales did not respond (thus turning down the request). They remained friends and Perales later joked to Canales, "As the saying goes, 'Folks visit a cactus only when it has fruit.'"[19] Perales readily dropped the idea.

The last letter was from Perales to Canales was written in 1960 and that is where Perales wrote, "in me you have a sincere, loyal and true friend who has been with you always and will be at all times."[20] Perales died a few months later. The elder J.T. Canales died in 1978.

Dr. Carlos E. Castañeda

Perales' and Dr. Carlos E. Castañeda's relationship constituted the third major friendship of Perales' life. Perales was Castañeda's contemporary. He was a professor and his intellectual equal.[21] Castañeda was born in Camargo, Tamaulipas, Mexico, but grew up in Brownsville, and had a much more privileged life than Perales as the son of a teacher.[22] He attended the University of Texas at Austin (UTA), where he completed an MA in history in 1923 and a Ph.D. in 1932. Castañeda lived in Austin and worked as a librarian and professor of Latin American history at UTA. He and Perales were both immersed in activism and intellectual activity; engaged in work in Latin America; enjoyed travel in Latin America; and were both married Catholic men. Castañeda wrote twelve books and eighty articles but was also an activist.[23] In his own words, Castañeda considered himself "militant".[24] According to historian Virginia Raymond, their shared Catholicism was their "deepest bond."[25] Both were members of the

Knights of Columbus, an organization honoring religious fraternalism and charity. At times Castañeda was a LULAC member and at others he was its ally. It is not clear when Perales and Castañeda met. One of Castañeda's papers was read at the 1929 LULAC constitutional convention although neither he or Perales attended. In 1935, Castañeda taught at Our Lady of the Lake in San Antonio, this perhaps gave the two an opportunity to solidify their friendship outside of short exchanges when they ran into each other at events.[26]

Their most important activist role was their work with the Federal Employment Practices Commission (FEPC) where Castañeda worked as a senior examiner, regional director and then as special assistant to the FEPC chairman for Latin American Problems.[27] Perales was not employed by FEPC but worked on its behalf with Castañeda. The latter worked with African Americans more than Perales especially in his FEPC work. The Texas Negro Chamber of Commerce, the Dallas NAACP, and the Dallas Council of Negro Organizations wrote letters in his behalf.[28]

Due to their geographical proximity, the Perales and Castañeda families socialized. In a letter that Perales wrote, he references their close friendship: "Dear Friend: Yes, it is too bad we have not had the opportunity of a chat in a long time. We just have not been able to make the connection. Well, here is hoping it will not be long now. Bring Mrs. Castañeda and the children and let's have a good get-together here. We'll have a few drinks and then we'll find a good place to eat. And all the time we'll be conversing and going over matters of mutual interest. We really have a lot to talk about."[29]

Their epistolary relationship lasted across the peak of both of their professional lives. Between 1927 and 1958, they wrote hundreds and hundreds of letters, typically every week or every two weeks if one of them was busy. Historian Raymond commented on their ties: "The men corresponded with each other about local, state, national, and church politics; activities of the Knights of Columbus, Holy Name Society, and other Catholic organizations; the comings and goings of priests; their research; public addresses, and their families. In their extensive letters, Castañeda and Perales asked for each other's assistance in locating employment for young people—mostly men—they had mentored; they gossiped about rivals and overrated (in their view) ostensible allies such as Paula [Pauline] Kibbe and George Sanchez; they asked for and dispensed advice; and they dined together with their families."[30]

They shared their disappointments in civil rights and politics. In May 1942, Castañeda wrote, "It was good to have a frank talk with you. It did me a lot of good because I could see in all you said an exact replica of my own experiences. Well, my friend, the Lord gives everyone his cross to bear[,] and I guess we have ours where least suspectec (sic), I mean in my case. . . . the Lord never gives a cross heavier than the miserable sinner can bear, so maybe we will make out."[31]

Perales wrote, "Only through the development of a group of well-trained, sincere, and earnest leaders can the beautiful ideals of the League of United Latin American Citizens be realized."[32] Both Perales and Castañeda saw limitations in some LULAC councils. For instance, Castañeda joined the local LULAC council in Del Rio, where he served as superintendent of the San Felipe School District after taking a leave from UTA in the 30s, and he felt that the council was "not doing much of anything. I have quit going to their meetings, but I am keeping in touch with what they are doing."[33] Likewise, Castañeda was likely a member of Austin LULAC, founded in the late 30s. He also urged that endowed scholarships to be created in memory of Spanish and Mexican patriots of Texas and of World War I. He hoped scholarship recipientswould become trained leaders serving the Latino community.

Perales and Castañeda both typically signed off with their complete names and avoided expressing their emotions; still, their relationship could be called a "bromance" under 21st-century parameters. Perales also provided a shoulder for Castañeda to lean on. Once, when Perales felt the press had slighted Castañeda, he said he would write his own essay titled "Ecos, de la Gran Ceremonia" (Echoes of the Grand Ceremony). Perales signed his letter, "Your sincere friend and ss (?) that appreciates you" on October 21, 1941.[34] After Castañeda was slighted by the press, Perales continued to sometimes sign his letters "Your friend." Castañeda would write, "Sincerely your friend" or "Sincerely yours." Given the cultural norms before 1960, it is not surprising that neither said more. Perhaps Perales said it all when he sent Castañeda an essay titled "Solid People" which discussed the traits of friends.[35] Castañeda revealed his professional woes to Perales in 1951. These problems were especially hard to resolve since he was the only person of color in the UTA history department. When Professor Charles Hackett died, his history class on Mexico was assigned to another instructor instead of Professor Castañeda. Castañeda told Perales, "None of my suggestions have been taken into account, in other words I have been completely ignored, in spite of my rank, term of service, and my publications, recognition in the United States in my field, and my recognition abroad." He added, "The thing that is worst is that there is little or nothing that I can do about it. There is no explanation for this conduct on the part of the chairman other than prejudice both because of religion and racial origin. [. . .] Fortunately, I have tenure, so they cannot discharge me."[36] In 1948, only a few years earlier, he had written an essay referring to people of Mexican descent in American society as the "second-class citizen."[37] Castañeda's experience still has resonance for professors of color today—discrimination at all levels, despite a Ph.D., tenure, publications or experience. Castañeda was still a "Mexican" in the ivory tower just like Perales was a "Mexican" in the world of diplomacy and other upper levels of US federal employment.

They also shared failures and successes, gave each other advice and promoted one another. Castañeda lamented his failure to get an appointment to the Texas State Historical Survey Committee and the Board of Texas Historical Foundation.[38] In 1951, when Castañeda considered taking a job in Washington, DC, Perales suggested he would "shine more at Texas U than in Washington and thus bring us more prestige as an ethnic group." He added, "In Washington you would be one of many brilliant starts. Not so in Texas, where you are one of FEW brilliant stars."[39] Castañeda also worked to get Perales the Spanish Merit award and the University of Texas Alba Club's Latin American of the year award.[40] In 1952, Perales was delighted to receive a photograph of Castañeda,[41] "a great American, a real Christian and a true friend." Castañeda passed on April 3, 1958. This hurt Perales deeply. Perales died two years later.

Adela Sloss-Vento

Perales' fourth major friendship was with Adela Sloss-Vento, a woman who was only three years younger than him. She initiated their relationship when she wrote him a letter in 1927 to introduce herself to him. While many of his letters to her were lost by Sloss-Vento over the years or were mailed to others in her effort to share them, her collection contains twelve envelopes from Perales' law office in the 30s, 40s and 50s[42] and six letters that Perales sent her in the 1950s.[43] The Perales collection has a significant body of their correspondence, likely more than a hundred letters. While Perales lived in San Antonio, he sometimes visited the Valley and the Vento family after she married in 1935.

It is interesting that Perales and Sloss-Vento developed a strong relationship because there is no evidence that Perales invited her to join LULAC or Ladies LULAC. He seemed to have traditional ideas of a woman's place in society. Historian Mario T. García noted that Perales cannot be fully understood "without understanding the centrality of his Catholic faith". This Catholicism included traditional gender roles.[44] While he was a "new Mexican-American man," this new man was not new in terms of his gender relations, except for his becoming friends with Sloss-Vento. For instance, Perales was largely responsible for the exclusion of women in LULAC—he was a Mexican-American man of his time. He was clearly aware of gender when he wrote Eduardo Idar in 1928 to "Please make another effort to keep the Boys together."[45] And he believed Mexican American women should, instead, involve themselves in the Spanish-Speaking PTA.[46] Clemente Idar, who sought to include women in the Order of the Sons of America, was more modern in his understanding of gender relations. He was one of three co-authors of the Order Sons of America constitution and it allowed for ladies auxiliaries.[47]

Sloss-Vento strengthened her relationship with Perales when she started to honor him in newspapers in the early 1930s, in *La Prensa* and *LULAC News*. Years later, in March 1952, Sloss-Vento wrote about Perales in *La Prensa* and *La Voz*, the Spanish-language newspaper of the Catholic Action and Social Justice Center published by the San Antonio archdiocese, on the occasion of Spain awarding Perales a Medal of Civil Merit. Sloss-Vento's letter to *La Prensa* about the honor was titled "To Attorney Alonso S. Perales, Defender of Justice and Racial Dignity"[48] and in it, she noted, "The noble struggle of Alonso Perales will always be great and everlasting. His name will always sound to us as magic music that speaks of hope, faith, honor, justice and liberty."[49]

Perales saw Sloss-Vento as his near equal. Literary scholar Donna Kabalen de Bichara suggested that Perales was Sloss-Vento's mentor, that he functioned as an "elder" guiding a "novice," instructing her on how to open an adult night school in San Juan.[50] That was not the case. Perales was only three years older than her and she was no novice. But, sometimes Perales' strategy as an activist was to tell others what to do and how.[51] The scholar also interpreted Perales' note to Sloss-Vento, which advised her to ignore a murder case and get busy with the adult classes as a gendered response. Kabalen de Bichara said that Sloss-Vento was "speaking outside the limits that were culturally imposed upon women during this time period."[52] That is who Sloss-Vento was and that is exactly what she did. Moreover, Perales himself taught adult classes, so teaching was not a strictly gendered activity.

Perales appreciated and admired his friend and co-activist Sloss-Vento. She initiated the relationship, in November 1927, as a recent high school graduate (though she was then 26) when she thanked him for his work in founding the Latin American Citizens League (LAC). His next letter to her, in December 1928, told her that three organizations were planning to unite in what would become LULAC. By the late 30s, his letters would address her as "Distinguished and Most Esteemed Mrs. Vento;" she was married.[53] Moreover, Perales thanked and praised Sloss-Vento for her articles. In a letter, he wrote:

> While I am extremely busy I did not want this day to pass without offering you my most sincere congratulations for that splendid article that appeared in *La Prensa* today regarding the Anti-Discrimination Law No. 909 that is pending in the

Texas Legislature. I am well aware of your thoughts and feelings on this matter and I know that you [] always fought and
collaborated with the objective of linking the friendship of
those two great races within the Western Hemisphere.

I can do no less than applaud you and it gives me great
pleasure when I see you succeed as you have today.

My most affectionate regards to you and your husband,

Your Sincere Friend and Assured Servant,
Alonso S. Perales"[54]

Perales was quick to congratulate her for her intellect in her articles and letters. He readily acknowledged their male to female relationship as friends and activists.

Perales also privately thanked her throughout her life. In 1947, he
wrote her, "I have always admired your work and I thank God for giving us people like you who are sincere and not self-interested and who
focus on the progress and advancement of our people."[55] He added
that her article was "magnificent." In 1948, his P.S. in a letter read: "I
sincerely congratulate you for your beautiful work on behalf of our
people. I always read your letters and articles with great interest. Forward. I thank God we have leaders like you."[56] In another 1948 letter
he wrote, "I'm happy, thank God, we have leaders like you."[57] And,
in 1954, he wrote her several letters as "Sra. Doña Adela S. de Vento,"
Doña signifying a title of respect in Mexican culture. In that letter he
noted, "Too bad there aren't more people like you who seek to solve
our problem."[58] And he addressed her as "my distinguished and fine
friend."[59]

At no time did Sloss-Vento prove her loyalty to her friend Perales
more than when he was under public attack for his stance on the "Wetback pamphlet." Dr. George I. Sánchez and Ed Idar Jr. did not agree
with him. Idar Jr. publicly attacked him. Sloss-Vento wrote Perales on
December 12, 1951 stating: "I have just received your two letters and
am aware of the gross response by Dr. Sanchez (sic) . . . Don't worry
Licenciado . . . You will always live in the heart of all patriotic citizens . . ."[60]

Perales' publicly recognized Sloss-Vento though she lauded him much more. He spoke of her pen and called her an "articulista" (essayist). His book *Are We Good Neighbors?* included her essay "Cheap Labor Does Not Pay in the Long Run"[61] along with other well-respected contributors. Perales also attended an event in San Antonio to honor Sloss-Vento, but she did not attend. He was planning to acknowledge her—perhaps as a writer, activist or leader—in an article for *La Prensa* in the early 60s but he died before he could do so. She noted, "He had even asked for a photograph of myself (sic) for an article he was writing noting my zeal in collaborating in favor of our cause."[62] She was, in her words, "by his side."[63]

Perhaps in a different era Perales would have done more to promote Sloss-Vento, who was a major civil rights activist and public intellectual in Texas. Also, he could have offered to edit the manuscript she sent him or helped to see it published. However, Perales did attempt to honor her right before his own death and the Perales papers include a four-page biography of her. However, it is unclear if he or she wrote it.[64] In the correspondence between Perales and Castañeda, "Mrs. Vento" is only mentioned once in a letter to Castañeda, "Yes, I have read the article written by Mrs. Vento entitled 'Nos perjudican y nos subajan' (They discriminate against us and subjugate us) and I have written to her expressing my deep appreciation."[65]

Sloss-Vento documented the life and character of Perales better than anyone. According to historian Richard A. Garcia, "Adela Sloss-Vento captures a few of his notable qualities: his intellectuality, his dedication to humanity, his devotion to all Americans of Mexican descent and Mexican workers, and in spite of all his responsibilities, his ability to be and live free," adding that Perales had all the "qualities of a patriot, a humanitarian, and one who loves justice and seeks to protect the rights of others."[66]

Perales transgressed traditional gender norms in corresponding with Sloss-Vento and had she been a traditional woman, she would have corresponded with Marta Perales, not Alonso, while he was alive. Lastly, although Adela, Alonso and their spouses and children visited with one another socially there is only one letter between Adela and Marta before Alonso Perales died in 1960. Only after

Perales' death did Sloss-Vento begin a significant relationship and correspondence with Marta. The two women grew close through letters and phone calls; they had a shared mission—to memorialize Perales' life and save his archives.

Friends in San Antonio and South Texas

Other men that Perales considered to be his friends included Pablo González, son of Dr. González, and Filiberto Galván, whom he met in the 1910s. Later, key friends in San Antonio included Eleuterio Escobar, Leonides González, Dr. Hesiquio N. González and Laureano Flores.[67] Eleuterio Escobar was a member of LULAC Council 16; Leonides González was a Mexican political exile and business manager of *La Prensa* and, like Perales, González promoted education and the preservation of Mexican culture. He was also father to Henry B. González—Texas legislator and later US Congressman.[68] Dr. Hesiquio N. González was the son-in-law of J.T. Canales.

Laureano Flores was a political ally and worked with the San Antonio Post Office of Censorship during World War II,[69] a job that Perales also performed during World War I. Flores contributed regularly to *La Prensa* and filed a complaint with the FEPC.[70] Flores wrote an essay titled, "La Candidatura del Lic. Perales," (Lic. Perales' Candidacy) noting Perales' legacy "as a defender of Mexican rights is typical. He is an open book with plenty of facts and bitter struggles, already in the press, already in the Tribune, already in the field of the politics, etc. Continually struggling at the expense of sacrifices, at the expense of his own time and money."[71] Flores also served as a director of the Committee of One Hundred[72] and Perales included one of his essays in *Are We Good Neighbors?*[73]

Perales and Eleuterio Escobar met in San Antonio while he was a member of the Order of the Knights of America, later of Council 2 of LULAC and then of Council 16 of LULAC.[74] Escobar was a patron and supporter of Perales' pamphlet publication "El México Americano y la Política de Sur in 1931."[75] He took over the work that Perales began after Council 16's Committee on Public Schools investigated inferior schools on the West and South side of San Antonio. This eventually became the Liga Pro-Defensa Escolar/School Improvement League.

Lifelong friends from South Texas included Roberto Austin and Felipe García of Mission; Fortino Treviño of Alice; Santos de la Paz, originally from Alice, but who moved to Corpus Christi; and Judge Manuel Bravo of Zapata County. Roberto Austin not only supported Perales' in his work towards better education for the underserved communities, he also bought numerous copies of Perales' South Texas politics pamphlet. In the 30s, Austin wrote to Perales about improving school facilities in Mission.[76] Felipe García and Perales met at Camp Travis during World War I and helped organize a LAC council in Mission around 1928.[77] Both Austin and García joined the legal complaint against the Mission School District in a desegregation case.[78] Manuel Bravo was one of the original men who attended the May 1929 LULAC constitutional convention.

Fortino Treviño was more like family than a friend. Treviño "knew Mr. Perales as a small boy in the town of Mr. Perales' birth, Alice, Texas. Mr. Treviño also personally knew Nicolas and Susana Perales, proud parents of Alonso S. Perales, as well as their entire family."[79] He volunteered in WWI.[80] Treviño and his wife were very involved in LULAC activities: his wife was elected president of Ladies LULAC 1 in Alice[81] and he was elected as the first LULAC president in Alice in May 1932. He re-gifted a diary someone gave him and gave it to Sáenz. In 1939, in his role as notary public, Treviño signed an affidavit related to Perales' birth certificate.[82] Perales referred to Treviño as "compadre" or "muy estimado compadre"[83] and he and his wife sought to raise funds for the Perales monument.[84] Treviño and Perales corresponded intermittently between 1928 and 1958.[85] When Perales published his book, *En defensa de mi raza,* Treviño toured the Valley selling the book. Records in the archive show that he sold ten to Eleuterio De la Garza in Brownsville.[86]

When Perales and his children visited Treviño in Alice, they sometimes stayed at his home. His son Raimundo recalled, "Mr. Treviño would call me 'Papi Boy.' I thought Mr. Trevino was the best barber in Alice as he would always cut my hair and my brother's hair as well as daddy['s] when we were in Alice. Mr. Trevino also owned a Kiddie Park with rides and cotton candy. Daddy was sure to take us to the Kiddie Park. I could tell he was also enjoying the Kiddie Park because he was laughing with Mr. Trevino while watching us and eating an ice cream cone. I think vanilla was his favorite."[87]

Santos de la Paz, originally from Alice, was another friend during the 1940s. He was the editor of *La Verdad* (Corpus Christi)[88] and during Perales' funeral noted, ". . . it is important that you know that the inspiration of helping the cause of the Mexican-American was instilled in me by Perales. I, too, am from Alice, Texas, and am very proud to have known Perales the way I did."[89] De la Paz was one of Perales' confidantes at the Latin American Convention in Mission in 1952. He also fought injustice and as a result of his criticism of a racist sheriff in Live Oak County near Corpus Christi, he was jailed. His newspaper business was also set on fire and sustained $4,000 in damages.[90] His newspaper existed at least until March 27, 1953.

Perhaps Perales' best Anglo-Texan friend was Jack Danciger, a Fort Worth oilman and rancher originally from Taos, New Mexico. Danciger grew up speaking Spanish. He began his correspondence with Perales in June 1944, after reading Perales's essay, "Mexicans Shall Defend Themselves against Discrimination in Texas" in *La Prensa*. He wrote him "It is a sad commentary on the decency and respectability of Texans when a brilliant Mexican Attorney such as you are finds it necessary to write such an article pointing your finger of 'I accuse' at so many unthinking Morons in Texas who parade as Americans."[91] This seems to have been the start of their friendship.

Adversaries

Like all people, Perales had political disagreements and some people he disliked. There were individuals with whom he had conflict but with whom he also had a working relationship because their shared cause was more important than their personal feelings. His most outstanding adversaries were M.C. Gonzales and Dr. George I. Sánchez.

Perhaps Perales' earliest nemesis was Manuel C. Gonzales, OSA member, OKA president, Harlingen convention attendant and co-founder of LULAC. They had much in common, including that they were both from South Texas, were veterans with clerical experience, worked as lawyers and for consulates and both were civil right leaders and political elites. Gonzales ran for the state legislature in 1930,[92] worked for the Mexican consul and served as assistant counsel to the minister of foreign relations.[93]

Their strongest disagreement occurred at LULAC's Harlingen convention. There was controversy with regards to Gonzales representing the Mexican consulate there. Perales later wrote Canales, "although Gonzales betrayed us in Harlingen and stabbed you and me a little later, if the San Antonio boys want him as their leader it should make no difference to us, as we shall have little or nothing to do with him. However, we must insist on one hundred percent loyalty and devotion to our League and the principles for which it stands from every leader and member thereof."[94]

In early 1930s, another conflict arose over Perales' role at a 1930 Congressional hearing testimony. According to Canales, "by orders of our President General, Hon. Ben Garza, and Mr. J.T. Canales, a member of said organization" appeared before Congress. Also, according to Canales, LULAC Vice-President M.C. Gonzales and LULAC member Clemente Idar wired the president of the American Federation of Labor, William Green, to indicate that neither Perales nor Canales had a right to speak on behalf of LULAC.[95] According to Canales, Gonzales and Clemente Idar knew he was "not only the Honorary President General of the League but the duly accredited representative of the league at Washington." Thereafter, the Canales resolution suggested they apologize to Perales personally and publicly in the press and submit to a trial jury before two selected League delegates. The trial occurred and Gonzales was found to be compliant. Later charges were dropped.[96]

Perales also wrote both Clemente N. Idar and M.C. Gonzales a letter, which ended with the following statement: "The next time you decide to send telegrams to committees in Washington, be sure you know what you are talking about. Do not make asses of yourselves as you did on this occasion. Men of your age, who profess to be leaders of our race, must know how to better behave. You have made a fool of our League with your telegram."[97]

This is the only letter or piece of writing I came across in which Perales used near-profanity. Canales prepared the "Wolves in Sheep Clothing" essay and a resolution about the "Idar-Gonzalez incident" which required that both men apologize. Gonzales did but when Idar refused, LULAC expelled him. This incident ended all contact between Perales and both Clemente Idar and his brother, Eduardo Idar, and it is likely that Idar brothers ceased their contact with LULAC.[98]

Perales and Gonzales had conflict once again over the issue of the existence of two LULAC councils (Council 2 and Council 16) in San Antonio. Their disagreements likely led to the formation of Council 16. One of Perales' memos discussed this issue: "M.C. G. called on me today and said that he had some difficulty with his friends . . . Escobar called the meeting." . . . "That they had heard my radio talk of last Wednesday night (January 6th) and had interpreted it as the forerunner of this meeting, as tho (sic) I was preparing the ground for it, and they had not like[d] that." . . . "That they felt that Mr. Escobar and the others would endeavor to push me to the front and hold him down. That they would expect the whole group to push both him and me to the front on an equal footing; for instance, if I ran for the legislature, to run him also." . . . "That he wanted my assurance that I would not accept either the temporary or permanent chairmanship of the organization." . . . ". . . the idea being not to make it appear that I or he were leaders in this movement." . . . "That if his group were not treated fairly, they would form another organization."[99]

There was also some pettiness on the part of Perales. In another incident, in the 1930s, Gonzales interrupted Perales' talk on segregation. Gonzales yelled out, "no, no, haga bien or haga mal mi país, mi país hace bien."[100] ("No. No. Right or wrong. My country first.) Likewise, there is a scribbled note in the Perales papers noting that Gonzales was in a car outside of a political event. The note on the back of a page insert about the Pecan Shellers reads, "Manuel C. Gonzales is in the outside crowd in a car."[101] Perales' papers also include a photo of Gonzales in a publication marked with an X, though who drew it is unknown. Perhaps Perales' animosity towards Gonzales became especially well known in 1975, when the widow Perales called Gonzales an "enemy" in a newspaper interview. According to Sra. Perales, M.C.

Gonzales and Tafolla (Sr.? or Jr.?) campaigned against him. Perhaps in the LULAC presidential bid or the school board position(?). I don't believe Gonzales campaigned against his LULAC presidential bid or his bid for the San Antonio school board but I doubt he went out of his way to support him.

Despite their disagreements both men continued to work with one another for the greater good. In the 1930s, they worked together on the *Del Rio vs. Salvatierra* case in the 1930s and served on the board of directors for the Association of Independent Voters in San Antonio. Perales presided over the Del Rio LULAC regional convention during M.C. Gonzales' administration (1931-1932).[102] They cooperated on fighting for state legislation, for proposed anti-discrimination bills in the state legislature in 1941 and on FEPC issues in the 40s. Likewise, in 1948, both were members of the Pan-American Optimist Club, with Perales as president and Gonzales as secretary.[103] They did not always agree or get along, but they acknowledged one another's significance. When I interviewed M.C. Gonzales in 1979, he did not malign Perales.

Moreover, both Gonzales and Perales worked for consulates. Gonzales was legal counsel for the Mexican Consulate while Perales was counsel for Nicaragua. The job with the Mexican Consulate was a job that Perales was well qualified for and had applied for, but Perales did not settle in Texas permanently until 1932. By then Gonzales had been given the job. In 1934, Gonzales was named assistant counsel to the minister of foreign relations in the Claims Commission between Mexico and the United States.[104] In 1943, he became Consul for Guatemala.[105]

A statement made by Gonzales at an event in 1944, in which he called Ben Garza "the father of LULAC," may have infuriated Perales with just cause.[106] Yet, when Perales was honored by Spain, Gonzales wrote him a letter of congratulations. Gonzales began his letter by asking Perales if he might congratulate him: "May I be permitted to express my sincere congratulations? Also, may I be permitted to state that I consider it a distinct privilege to be counted among your many friends?"[107]

Historian Richard A. Garcia interviewed Gonzales for his book on San Antonio's Mexican-American middle-class community and surmised, "It seems to me that the differences between Gonzales and Perales were accentuated by life-style, personal idiosyncrasies, and Perales' emphasis on his Mexicanness as opposed to Gonzales' emphasis on his Americanness."[108] Both men emphasized Mexicanness and Americanness, but Perales was most likely influenced by Mexican culture and institutions since he attended a private Mexican school. And Perales also had more experience in Latin America.

Dr. George I. Sánchez

Sánchez quickly befriended Perales after he moved to Texas from New Mexico. Sánchez was a UT Austin graduate student when LULAC was taking shape in the early 1930s, though it did not reach Austin until the late 30s. The two met when Perales addressed the Latin American Club at UTA in 1931. Sánchez wrote Perales shortly after and shared his thoughts on the *Salvatierra* case, suggesting expert advice on pedagogy as a rationale for school exclusion.[109] Sánchez made Texas his permanent home in 1940 when he joined the University of Texas at Austin faculty. He became National President of LULAC in 1940.

But there is evidence they were not close as early as 1941. By then, Perales was working outside of LULAC.[110] In a letter to FEPC authorities, Sánchez did not recommend Perales as a possible candidate for FEPC work even though he recommended M.C. Gonzales, who did similar work to that of Perales.[111] Sánchez' and Perales' correspondence is almost nil which is surprising given their cause.[112] Perales also joined Sánchez, then-national LULAC president, to meet with Nelson Rockefeller about a Latin American Research and Policies Commission.[113] According to historian Natalie Mendoza, as LULAC national president, Sánchez began efforts to access the US/Good Neighbor policy. Sánchez traveled with Perales and M.C. Gonzales to plan a Spanish Speaking Minority Project in the Division of Inter-American Activities in the United States.[114] Sánchez did inform Perales of the $17,000 grant that the University of Texas at Austin received from the Office of the Coordinator of Inter-American Affairs in 1941 and sought to keep him informed.[115]

In 1948, when Perales compiled his book, *Are We Good Neighbors?*, he did not include an essay by Sánchez, even though he included works by many of his peers. This could be because of their conflict, or Perales could have simply felt Sánchez already had significant access to publishing. Perhaps Sánchez felt slighted. Besides their conflict over the "Wetback Pamphlet" in the 1950s, (discussed in more detail in chapter 13), the two also had conflict over religion. Attorney Gus Garcia wrote Perales, "I know you do not like George Sanchez because you classify him as an atheist. You might as well put me in the category of a non-Christian since I am not eligible to partake of the Sacraments. I believe, however, that George Sanchez and I are far better Christians and Catholics—at least according to the definition given by Pope Leo XII—than hypocrits (sic) . . . ."[116] Sánchez' wife divorced him in 1946, which Perales would have likely frowned upon.[117]

Even though Perales and Sánchez did not get along, they cooperated on some issues. They worked together on the Texas Committee on Pan-American Group Work Fellowships.[118] In 1948, Perales wrote Castañeda to support and praise Sánchez, "Our friends Sanchez, Gus Garcia et al won a victory in the School Segregation case. It is a partial victory to be sure, but half a loaf is better than none."[119] There was also general support of one another until the "Wetback" controversy which initiated a permanent break. At that moment, both used acerbic words. In a curt note that Sánchez sent Perales, he states, "It is with a certain degree of both amusement and amazement that I read your letter of December 5. I am amazed that a lawyer of your experience should presume to act as judge, jury, and executioner on a matter that is not within your competence. I am amused that, after much presumption, you should think that you are thereby entitled to demand anything of me."[120]

Sánchez also wrote Dr. Hector P. García, "I'm quite hurt and grieved that Perales and *La Verdad* should attack me in such an unwarranted manner. After all, I'm guilty of nothing—unless sticking my neck out for them and for my people generally constitutes guilt. The fact that both of them are notorious fools is no excuse. I'm tempted to sue *La Verdad* [for libel] and destroy the sheet."[121] Sánchez also wrote a friend that Perales was "a pathetic figure, a psycho-neurotic with delusions of grandeur."[122] But Perales did not have delusions of grandeur. Both Sánchez and Perales were grand.

In October 1954, Perales told Castañeda when he discussed, "Those guys (George Sanchez and company) certainly have their nerve. Now they are claiming the credit for the appointment of the special judges when as a matter of fact they tried their best to prevent their appointment by trying to defeat Shivers at the polls! The nerve."[123] Yet, both Perales and Sánchez would have supported Mexican-American Democratic judges Reynaldo Garza/Fidencio Guerra, despite the fact that Perales had become a Republican in the 1950s and that Sánchez was a lifelong Democrat.

Perales had little contact with Dr. Hector P. García, but any possibility of friendship with him ended due to his political alignment with Sánchez on the Wetback pamphlet. According to historian Ignacio M. García, "As a young man, he had witnessed old-time reformers such Alonso Perales, Manuel Gonzalez, J.T. Canales, and others rally the Mercedes Mexicans to be concerned about their rights and their treatment."[124] Perales wrote Dr. García only two letters, one to congratulate him for the Three Rivers case in 1948, in which national attention was brought to the refusal of a Three Rivers, Texas, cemetery to bury a Mexican-American veteran. The other letter Perales wrote to Dr. García was related to the Wetback pamphlet controversy in 1951. The two were in opposite camps.[125] Sánchez believed the report documented social and economic conditions while Perales felt it exacerbated racist attitudes.

Conclusion

Perales had many friends and several adversaries, most related to Mexican-American activism. Most of Perales' closest friends were of Mexican descent except for Jack Danciger, a few white reformers and church men. Most, if not all, of his friends were civic leaders and all, but one, were men. Perales' friendship with Adela Sloss-Vento was an anomaly. There is no evidence he was close to any Nicaraguan-Americans despite serving as Consulate General for Nicaragua for about thirty years. There were few Nicaraguan Americans in San Antonio or Texas.

Perales' friendships shifted over the decades. In the late 1910s, he was close to Draughon's Business college students Filiberto Galván and Pablo González. In the 1920s, perhaps J. Luz Sáenz was his closest friend since both of them moved constantly throughout the decade. During the early 1930s, J.T. Canales was his closest friend. Dr. Castañeda and Perales began corresponding in 1927, but their letters became more frequent in the 1940s. Castañeda then became his best friend. Adding to the analysis by historian Marianna Bueno, this chapter contributed to our knowledge of Castañeda as an activist, not just a historian. Activism and intellect tied the two together. He befriended Sloss-Vento in 1927, and they remained close friends, especially corresponding in the 40s and 50s.

While he was active in LULAC in the 1930s, few LULAC members were close to Perales except for Sáenz, Canales, Castañeda and Fortino Treviño, who was both a family member and friend.

Like all politicos, Perales had adversaries. These included his nemesis M.C. Gonzales and Dr. George I. Sánchez. Still, Perales was a man who moved beyond petty jealousies to forward the cause of Mexican Americans, as was the case with his ties to Gonzales. Like any human, he made social comparisons. However, he did not forgive Dr. George I. Sánchez (and Dr. Hector P. García) for what he considered an unforgiveable insult to the people of Mexican descent, their support of the Wetback pamphlet.

At times, Perales may have felt he had few friends. When he was awarded the Spanish Merit award, in 1952, in San Antonio he noticed those in attendance: only six Pan American Optimist members, none from the Mexican Chamber of Commerce and none from LULAC. Were M.C. Gonzales, Gus Garcia, Carlos Cadena or Henry B. González there? Perales lamented, "It is a good thing I have friends in other circles and do not have to depend upon them."[126] Exactly who he meant by "them" is not clear. Perales' wife and children were likely in attendance as was Castañeda and those were the people who mattered most to him. While Perales may have had few close friends, he continued to extend his hand to La Raza.

CHAPTER 22
Health and Death

Alonso S. Perales was not yet sixty when he died. He had suffered two strokes and two heart attacks earlier in his life.[1] It's true people of his generation had a shorter life span than we do today, but perhaps he may have lived longer had he not dedicated his life to serving the public. Perales' lifestyle reflected the work ethic of his generation and the life of activists who too often place themselves second to their activism. His wife Marta contemplated, "It was natural that all the suffering eventually affected his heart and his health in general."[2] This chapter first addresses Perales' health and death by focusing on his medical issues, especially his high blood pressure. Second, reports of his death are discussed as well as tributes honoring him after he died. Much of this chapter is based on correspondence between Perales and his dear friend Dr. Carlos E. Castañeda.

Health Issues

Alonso S. Perales lived a typical middle-class lifestyle of a Mexican-American man before the 1960s. His health reflected the diet, exercise and medical ailments common in his time. While he was an optimist, was religious and likely had a satisfying career, family life and friends, he had "middle age" health challenges in his forties and fifties. In his late 20s, before traveling to Latin America, he weighed 130 lbs. but gained 32 lbs. while there.[3] Today, with healthier eating options available, knowledge about exercise, better medicine or better alternatives to prescriptive medicine, his life might have been extended. Perales believed God was all powerful giving life; he expressed, "Without God, we are nothing and nobody."[4] Yet, without less work, less stress, better eating, relaxation and more exercise we cannot live to old age.

Perales rarely took vacations. In 1928, he traveled to San Francisco.[5] In October 1948, Perales attended a Bishops Committee for the Spanish-Speaking of the Southwest in El Paso, it was a work trip with a vacation attached.[6] None of his letters referred to any vacations, though he did tell Canales once that he rested when he traveled to Rio Grande City, his wife's hometown. His wife Marta may have benefitted from travel to Latin America in the 1920s, but there is no evidence that Perales traveled there for fun. He did travel to New Orleans, Mexico City, Monterrey and Saltillo. Apparently, he and Marta traveled through New Orleans regularly to catch ships in the days before air travel.[7] His papers also include magazines from Barcelona, Montserrat in the Caribbean and the Canary Islands.[8]

In 1942, at age 44 Perales developed high blood pressure. In October 1942, he interviewed with the US Navy about employment during World War II, but his blood pressure was 175 and he was rejected.[9] That month Perales knew he had health problems and he went on a diet.[10] By November 17, 1942 his blood pressure was down to 142, still high by today's standards.[11]

Perales first mentioned his health issues to his friend Castañeda in 1944. He wrote, "Frankly, I was all worn out that day because, the day before the Conference began at Austin we were "*padrinos*" at a wedding at 5:30 A.M. Then Sunday night we went to a dance and were up until midnight . . . run-down condition. . . ."[12] Then in 1948, he wrote Castañeda twice about expanding the leadership base or having fewer organizations because "we are wearing ourselves out attending multiple meetings."[13] In 1949, Perales told Castañeda he was worried about Castañeda's hectic lifestyle but not his own; in a PS at the end of letter he noted, "Please slow down as much as possible. Remember: good health is essential. I am afraid you are working too hard, and are always on the go. Cut your speed down to half and you will live longer."[14]

The 1950s would see Perales and his inner circle beginning to experience serious health issues or death. In 1950, Perales had a "slight stroke" due to his high blood pressure.[15] In January 1951, his brother-in-law Hernan Contreras wrote, "...we are sorry to hear your blood pressure is again giving you trouble."[16] In March 1951 Perales wrote Castañeda telling him, "The Doctor told me I could go to work, but to take it easy. I am devoting a few hours daily at first, until I recover fully. I will take good care of myself this time, believe me."[17] His friend J.T. Canales also expressed concern in 1951: "I was very sorry to hear that you suffered a stroke last October," and "I am afraid that this is due to your over-work. You must remember that you are no longer a young man and that as we age we have our limitations. I want you to take good care of yourself for we still need your counsel and leadership."[18] In November 1951, Perales wrote friend J. Luz Sáenz, "That afternoon you came I felt real bad because of my blood pressure, fatigue, tiredness and that's why I didn't offer to take you where you wanted to go. . . . ." But Perales continued to be active. By 1952, his friend Adela Sloss-Vento was aware of his bad health.

Perales was also worried about Castañeda's health. In 1952, Perales told Castañeda, "Now, don't you turn around and die because then I will be in a hell of a fix."[19] A few months later, another friend died and Perales told Castañeda, "Please take good care of yourself, slow down and take it easy, as I don't want to lose any more of my real friends. I have lost enough already."[20] But on November 14, 1953 Castañeda suffered a heart attack.[21] In 1954, Perales wrote about Bishop Fitzsimon who had been admitted to the Santa Rosa Hospital in San Antonio. "Too bad, but there again we have the consequences of keeping a fast pace. It seems that it just simply cannot be done indefinitely. In this respect, I admire Secretary of State [John Foster] Dulles and Prime Minister Churchill. More power to them. I know I could not do it."[22] Castañeda noted in October 1954, "I believe that you and I should start an association of "elder statesman a la Baruch" to sort of work for the general good, quietly and unostentiously, [sic] scientifically and systematically."[23] (Bernard Baruch was an advisor to Presidents Woodrow Wilson and Franklin Delano Roosevelt.)

In 1955, Castañeda wrote Perales, "What you told me about your marching and its effect has worried me a bit. You need to take care of yourself. I notice you have gained wait (sic). . . . exercise not violently but regularly a little each day, such as walking ten or fifteen minutes a day." "And to eat few starches, sweets, and fats."[24] In May 1956, Castañeda had another heart attack.[25] By July 1956, Perales had been diagnosed with angina pectoris. Perales wrote Castañeda, "I think so too because when I get excited, lift up something heavy or walk fast I feel a pain in the chest."[26] In September 1956, Perales told Castañeda, "I don't drive the automobile either on Doctor's orders. When we went to the Rio Grande Valley recently my poor wife had to do all the driving. All together she drove about 500 miles."[27] In October 1956, Perales told Castañeda that "I am feeling a case of nerves right now. I don't know whether the medicine I have been taking have affected my nervous system or what it is. I sleep well though, thank God."[28] By December 1956, Perales was back in his office.[29]

In February 1957, Perales mentioned that ". . . life has been miserable with these depression spells."[30] In February, Perales said he was taking neorosine but did not tell his doctor; his blood pressure was 140 over 60 and 145 over 65.[31] (Neorosine can result in dizziness, insomnia, nervousness, light-headedness, nausea, diarrhea, headaches and fatigue.) Castañeda told him he was taking Meritren quarter-grain tablets and suggested Perales take them too.[32] It may have been around this time that his wife Marta, according to daughter Marta Carmen, "Had thrown away all his medications during a period when he showed signs of a pending nervous breakdown."[33]

Perales wrote Castañeda in March 1957, "Your letter has encouraged and cheered me up a great deal. One does get discouraged at times. The thing is that I do not feel exactly the same as before. I feel the nervous tension. I tell my Doctor and he said to me 'aguantanse.' [Just deal with it.] I attribute my nervous condition to the pills I am taking coupled with my diet. I take the equanil (the same as the Miltowns) tablets and a pink pill daily and I must say that I feel better as a result."[34]

An April 1958 letter to Canales from Perales noted that he was taking Meritren tablets. He wrote, "they have helped me a great deal."[35] Finally, on April 4, 1958 Castañeda died after three heart attacks in the 1950s.[36] This must have been a terrible blow to Perales.

His best friend, confidant and co-activist was gone. Perhaps he grew depressed, ate worse or exercised less. Perales' health declined.

By October 1958, Perales was writing his insurance company noting that he had lost six months of work due to illness.[37] In May 1959, Perales injured his right hand. Perales' income taxes reveal he spent significant amounts on prescriptions and doctors' bills in 1959 and 1960. In 1959 he spent $640 on medical expenses and $450 at the pharmacy.[38] Sloss-Vento got on a bus to visit him in San Antonio in March 1959, suggesting he was quite ill.[39]

On February 16, 1960 Perales wrote Canales noting there was an upcoming LULAC anniversary on Feb. 17, 1960. He said, "I was invited, following your suggestion, to be principal speaker, but my doctor told me to avoid all excitement and I believe such an event would cause me to become somewhat excited." Judge Fidencio M. Guerra of the Valley, who Perales had supported, spoke in his place with Perales in attendance.[40]

Luckily, before Perales passed in May 1960, he was celebrated, interviewed and photographed by *La Prensa* for its February 14, 1960 issue, forty-one years after LULAC's founding anniversary on Feb. 17, 1929. The front-page headlines in red noted "Será Conmemorada Brillantemente La Fundación del 'LULAC'" (LULAC's Founding will be Commemorated with Great Fanfare) with the subtitle "Evoca el Lic. Perales Esfuerzos del Pasado." (Lic. Perales Discusses Past Efforts). Perales acknowledged some memorable victories; he said, "For sure they were times of struggle. Now I have in my soul the satisfaction of results." He added, ". . . we have Henry Gonzales as Senator; Albert Peña as county commissioner; José Olivares and Jose San Martín as city councilmen, and Fidencio Guerra and Osvaldo García as district judges. And these are many, but many examples that we can have. And I don't want to forget to mention the case of Lic. Carlos C. Cadena, the first lawyer in city hall."[41]

Perales must have also felt proud of LULAC Council 2's activities. Political scientist Benjamín Márquez surmised: "By the end of the 1950s, the league [LULAC] as a whole had begun to focus more and more on local, non-controversial 'civic' issues, activities which would benefit not only Mexican Americans but the entire community or nation."[42] But consider the following account by Frank Jasso of LULAC Council 2 who reported on its recent actions in the same newspaper issue that lauded Perales. Jasso reported the following LULAC activities: the 1960 Testimonial Dinner to founders, the Feria de las Flores for LULAC scholarships and the forthcoming national convention in San Antonio. He also listed the following civic actions: "the intensive program to arouse interest for parents to enroll their pre-school children in local Schools of 400 words, that will enable the youngsters to compete with their first days in elementary school. . ."; "recent civil action of the local LULAC group has been opposing the sewer tax; in favor of having Robt. B. Green as the site for the University of Texas Medical School. We oppose the present poll tax, against the new automobile insurance law; in favor of five new Bexar County Courts. We inaugurated "Operation Spotlight" in an attempt to open new and more profitable employment opportunities for members of our ethnic group. Other issues that were acted upon by our San Antonio Council includes establishment of a Fair Employment Code in San Antonio, favored Federal Public Housing; appointed committee to study juvenile gang problems; made study on legislation on Texas migratory labor; oppose wholesale wetback labor importation; fought for retention of Bolivar Library as depository of Spanish, historical, and folkloric literature. We flayed the sales tax and urged stronger wage and hour laws in Texas. We have pointed out the lack of Spanish-name representation on state boards."[43]

Contrary to scholar Márquez' supposition, local and civic issues mattered, were numerous, and were often controversial.

Another kudos, received right before Perales' death, was the receipt of a letter from the *Encyclopedia of American Biography* in March 1960 announcing possible inclusion in a forthcoming edition.[44] Another civil rights success was achieved before his death—San Antonio became the first major city in the South to integrate its lunch counters, especially for African Americans and in which attorney Carlos Cadena played a role.[45] After his death, privately-owned but publicly used facilities voluntarily desegregated in 1963; some 655 hotels, motels and restaurants did so with only two motels and one restaurant refusing.[46]

Other activists experienced similar bouts of bad health. Attorney Gus Garcia died in 1962. By the mid-60s, Dr. George I. Sánchez, who was eight years younger than Perales, had "tuberculosis, high blood pressure, a bad back and creaky ankles and hips."[47] However, he lived until 1972, and would participate in the rise of the Political Association of Spanish Speaking Organization, witness the Raza Unida Party, Mexican-American high student walkouts, the Chicano movement and co-found Mexican American Studies at the University of Texas at Austin. Canales passed in 1976. Sloss-Vento died in 1998. And Cadena died in 2001.

Reports of his Death

Both English and Spanish-language local, regional, state, national and international newspapers wrote obituaries. The *San Antonio Light* and *San Antonio Express* noted he was survived by his wife, his children, his brother Louis Perales and his nephew Alonso M. Perales.[48] The *New York Times* noted that he served as Nicaraguan Consul General, a United Nations counselor, a LULAC founder and author.[49]

The Spanish-language press also reported his death in *La Prensa*, and *La Voz*, a Catholic newspaper.[50] Perales was first buried in San Antonio but was reburied in Alice, Texas on October 15, 1960.[51]

Tributes

Sloss-Vento dedicated the rest of her life to fostering his legacy. She had lauded his contributions as early as the 1930s. Now, with health issues as an elderly woman, she continued this work nonetheless. She wrote a poem to the Perales family, "A un árbol de orquídeas" (To an orchid tree).[52] In 1960, she wrote the tribute "Memorias del Fallecimiento del Gran Defensor, Lic. Alonso S. Perales, el Día (9 de mayo 1960) por la Sra. Adela Sloss de Vento, Edinburg, Texas."[53] (Memories of the Death of the Great Defender, Lic. Alonso S. Perales) She was his most vocal public supporter. Her greatest contribution to his legacy was her small book, *Alonso S.*

Perales, His Struggle for the Rights of Mexican Americans, published in 1977. She wrote, "They [Perales, Canales, Saenz] have sacrificed their health, time and even their money and they have had bad times and have battled the enemies of our cause. But their patriotism, optimism and their great love for the Latin American community and its well-being has conquered all."[54]

Conclusion

The official cause of Perales' death was high blood pressure but perhaps stress, caused by overexposure to racism and his herculean efforts to battle racism, contributed to his premature death. His conscience made him an activist but perhaps he undertook too much activism. Perales typically attended church early in the morning, worked all day and attended meetings at night. His friend Dr. Carlos E. Castañeda remarked that Perales' exercise was limited. Perales' health began to decline in his forties and affected him throughout his fifties.

The international, national, state, regional and local press reported on Perales' death because he was an important man. The *New York Times* covered it. But it was his friend and fellow activist Adela Sloss-Vento who played the most important role in honoring his legacy with her biography, *Alonso S. Perales, His Struggle for the Rights of Mexican Americans.*

La Prensa of San Antonio captured a photo of Perales and this is the best final visual commentary on Perales: a proud and happy attorney surrounded by his books and newspapers, true to his morals, his spiritual and political beliefs and with a smile on his face, knowing that he had spent over four decades of his life defending the dignity of Mexican Americans, Mexicans and Latinos in the United States. When Perales died, he left Latinos and especially Mexican Americans in a more advanced state of affairs. A reportedly happy family man, with a wife and children, and a faithful Catholic, he believed his maker would finally let him rest in peace.

PART IV
Perales on Trial

CHAPTER 23
In Defense of Perales in Latino History

Heretofore Alonso S. Perales had not been the subject of a biography by a professional historian. His papers have only been available to the public since 2009. Nonetheless, over the years, historians and political scientists have commented on him in articles and books on LULAC. This chapter dialogues with Latino history scholars' assessment of Perales and LULAC on the following critical issues: 1) Mexican Americanism; 2) citizenship, including attitudes toward Mexican immigrants; 3) Latino consciousness; 4) Latin American consciousness; 5) whiteness, including racism against African Americans; 6) class, including attitudes toward the working class, unions and elitism; 7) political ideology (conservativism, liberalism, including attitudes toward communism); and 8) gender.

This chapter also elaborates on contributions that Perales and LULAC made to the advancement of the civil rights and interests of people of Mexican descent. These include: 1) being pro-democracy; 2) fighting racism against Latinos; 3) advocating for Latino self-determination and self-help; and 4) fostering pride in the Spanish language, Latino culture and Latino history.

Mexican Americanism

Historian Aaron E. Sánchez noted that Perales articulated an "emerging imaginary" called "Mexican Americanism."[1] Historian Richard A. Garcia originally referred to this development as well, calling it the 'Mexican-American mind'. Historian Mario T. García referred to it as the 'Mexican-American generation.' Sánchez wrote,

"The intellectual project of re-conceptualizing US-Mexican belonging as American citizens was a departure from previous modes of imagining in US-Mexican thought. This change required a reformulation of the position of US-Mexicans in the region, the nation and the world. Calling themselves Mexican American invoked a direct intent and entailed an ideological shift. They were responding to the international implications of changes in citizenship and the evolving homeland politics in the Southwest in the years after the Mexican Revolution. Many US-Mexicans found themselves outside of the mainstream American social imaginary, and they also found themselves excluded from the imagined community of *México de afuera*. This meant many people were on a search for belonging. For a group of US-Mexicans, they were Americans-including the exclusive racial, class and linguistic connotations the word carried with it . . . Perales . . . and . . . LULAC cooperated in ideas that while not necessarily hegemonic were definitely homogenizing."[2] Historian Francisco Rosales also referred to "Mexican Americanism" and I find this terminology to be appropriate and insightful.

Scholar Sánchez' Mexican-American "imaginary" was also a legal fact and a cultural reality. Mexican Americans were born in the United States of America. To call oneself "Mexican American" was an assertion of having been born in the United States, of being a US citizens, and of having been partly Americanized and likely being able to speak English. Some had been here for generations and were not necessarily the sons or daughters of recent Mexican immigrants. Houstonian and LULAC national president John J. Herrera, for example, was a seventh generation Texan.[3]

In Texas, Mexican-American identity also co-existed with Mexican (or *Mexicano* in Spanish) identity. In the 1920s, "Mexican American" appeared challenging "México-Texano," a term specifying regional identity for Mexican Americans in Texas. Claiming Mexican Americanism involved using the term "Mexican American" in English, claiming United States citizenship, and calling the United States home. Historian Ignacio M. García noted, "Being Mexican American was contingent on their believing in American society, and their yearning for full acceptance."[4] Perales and LULAC staked a claim for citizenship, identity and rights. Literary scholar Donna M. Kabalen de Bichara wrote, "Perales' life project that involved deconstructing systems of thought that attempt to radically limit the rights of Mexican Americans as citizens of the United States."[5] To claim Mexican Americanism was to claim a birthright.

White Anglo-Texans resisted the claim by Americans of Mexican descent of being "Mexican American." Whites mostly referred to persons of Mexican descent as 'Mexican' despite their US citizenship. In the 1920s, when whites named the "Mexican problem," they included Mexican Americans in this "problem". Ignacio M. García noted that, even in the 1950s, the United States "did not really have a place for Mexican Americans," and " too often Mexican Americans had been the subject of an occasional story in *Look* or *Life* magazine, or periodically showed up in a government report commenting on their poverty" or "simply discounted them."[6] The black/white binary of race relations was prominent.

Mexican Americans were invisible in the US public's consciousness. Scholar and LULAC president Dr. George I. Sánchez called Mexican Americans "orphans" and "forgotten people."[7] Perales explained the task at hand: "how to teach the average Anglo Americans to recognize the American Mexican as an 'American' and at the same time, how to teach the American Mexican to realize and recognize the fact that he [is] an American, without arousing the national resentment, hatred, and animosity created in him by his daily treatment by other Americans."[8]

Mexican Americanism had both temporal and regional significance. Historian Sánchez noted, "By the end of the 1950s and the beginning of the 1960s, Mexican-Americanism was ideologically developed and mature. Mexican-Americanism had spread across the nation; it was no longer limited to Texas."[9] However, during the 1940s, in Texas and elsewhere, it should be noted that "Latin American" resurfaced to promote Pan-Americanism and the new Good Neighbor Policy because of World War II. Likewise, there was regional variation by state. For instance, in New Mexico "Mexican American" never took hold.[10] However, Mexican Americanism as an ideology asserting US citizenship did take hold in New Mexico in the

1930s with LULAC. To wit, New Mexico was the second state to embrace LULAC and at least five national presidents came from New Mexico in the 1930s and 40s, including Dr. George I. Sánchez. Likewise, historian Rosales noted that in California Mexican Americanism arose with the Mexican American Movement developed by college students and their newspaper *Mexican Voice* in the 1930s. The same ideology developed in Arizona is the Latin American Clubs which had 5,000 members from the 1930s to the 50s and could be seen in its bilingual newsletter *El Latino Americano*.[11]

Central to Mexican Americanism was the redemption of La Raza. Historian Gabriela González argues, "Redeeming la raza was as much about saving them from traditional modes of thought and practices that were perceived as hindrances to progress as it was about saving them from race and class-based forms of discrimination that were part and parcel of modernity."[12] It did not include a remedy for gender discrimination, though women enacted maternalism as an alternative strategy.

Citizenship, Including Attitudes toward Mexican Immigrants

Claiming Mexican Americanism meant claiming US citizenship and rejecting Mexican citizenship. Mexican Americans could not claim Mexican citizenship because they were not legal citizens of Mexico—dual citizenship did not yet exist at that time. Perales understood that Anglo-Americans typically made little distinction between Mexican Americans and Mexicans in the United States.

Perales and LULAC both excluded Mexican nationals in the United States from their organizations' while simultaneously representing them. The 1927 Harlingen convention privileged US citizens as members of the emerging LAC organization. Mexican nationals were overwhelmingly not allowed in LULAC, though the League permitted a few select Mexican individuals to join. Dr. Carlos E. Castañeda joined while he was still a citizen of Mexico until he was naturalized in 1936. Yet, in 1946, John J. Herrera of Houston LULAC council 60 read the constitution to mean "that Mexican nationals were eligible for membership if they promised to seek U.S. citizenship."[13] And Félix Tijerina, national LULAC president in the 1950s, was a Mexican national.[14] But mostly LULAC excluded Mexicans from its ranks. LULAC did not officially change its constitution excluding non-US citizens (Mexican immigrants) until the 1980s. As decades passed, the English language was more commonly used in LULAC meetings in some towns and cities, which would have alienated Mexicans. Also, over time LULAC published fewer *LULAC News* and LULAC documents in Spanish. LULAC went the same way most Mexican Americans and Mexicans were going—assimilating into the dominant culture though not all were doing so at the same pace, depending on family tradition, proximity to the border and the availability of Spanish radio, TV and Spanish cultural practices. Cultural critic Tomas Ybarra Frausto reminds us that "All Mexicans [in the US] are potential Chicanos [Mexican Americans]."[15] Some were naturalized into US citizenship over time. Some had children born in the United States who were Mexican Americans and US citizens. Some have acculturated to become Mexican Americans over time. Some have become Mexican Americans linguistically over time. At the same time, LULAC has also re-Mexicanized and become Latinized, thanks to the waves of Mexican immigrants in the 1970s and 2000s migrating to the United States. For example, there are Spanish-dominant LULAC councils today and some of the LULAC website is bilingual. Puerto Ricans in the United States and Puerto Rico also joined the League in the 1990s, adding more Spanish language use to LULAC events.

Despite their official exclusion, the work of Perales and LULAC still benefitted Mexican citizens.[16] Fraternal clubs like the Order of the Sons of America and the Order of the Knights of America serviced all of La Raza. LULAC's work to desegregate schools and build new ones benefitted all of La Raza. Not once did LULAC argue that public schooling should only benefit US citizens (Mexican Americans). In 1944, LULAC co-founder M.C. Gonzales noted that "the work of Lulac, which has indirectly benefitted Mexican citizens as well. . . ."[17] Communist Emma Tenayuca also acknowledged LULAC worked for all Mexicans in the United States.

While LULAC excluded Mexicans, it simultaneously called for an end to discrimination against all Mexicans. One historian suggested, "They simply could not continue to exclude non-US citizens at the same time as they were calling for an end to discrimination in the Americas."[18] Yet, it did. Perales and LULAC sought to include all Latinos regardless of citizenship as beneficiaries of anti-discrimination legislation in the 40s and 50s. Historian Thomas Guglielmo noted, ". . . their battle for Caucasian rights legislation sought to protect all people of Mexican or Latin American descent, not simply those who were citizens of the United States."[19] Not once did LULAC condone economic discrimination against Mexican immigrants or Latino immigrants. Indeed, historian Zamora referred to LULAC's work during WWII and with the FEPC as "Pan-Mexican."[20]

Despite Perales' call for LULAC councils to be composed of US citizens, he did not exempt Mexican immigrants from civic responsibility. In 1934, one of his essays noted, "I will take this opportunity to say with emphasis that the responsibility of the future of our race in this country belongs to Mexican leaders without attention to citizenship."[21]

Perales considered Mexicans his "hermanos de raza" (brethren by race). His first essay in the second volume of *En Defensa de Mi Raza* noted "mis hermanos de raza, tanto a los ciudadanos Americanos como a los ciudadanos mexicanos residentes en Estados Unidos"[22] (my brothers by race, the American citizens as well as the Mexican citizens who reside in the United States). Historian Zamora noted, "Perales consistently maintained that all Mexicans, regardless of citizenship or length of residence in the United States, faced the same discriminatory fate."[23]

Perales' attitude and treatment of Mexican nationals did not change over time. He did not change his position in the 1920s, and he voiced it especially clearly at the Harlingen convention, or in the 1930s during Mexican deportation, or in the 1940s when the ideology of Pan Americanism was becoming pronounced, or in the 1950s during the height of the Bracero Program.

Zamora also revealed that Perales and LULAC cooperated with the Mexican government and organizations in Mexico on its strategy to end the discrimination against and exploitation of *braceros*. It cooperated with Mexican presidents, Mexican Congressmen, the

Comité pro México de Afuera (Committee for the Protection of Mexicans Abroad) and Comité Mexicano Contra el Racismo (Mexican
Committee against Racism). Moreover, scholar Jose Angel Gutiérrez
has noted that LULAC "has consistently been defined as an agent of
Mexico."[24]

LULAC's position on the Bracero Program has been misunderstood as anti-Mexican. One historian wrote, "LULAC had no clear
interest in the condition of bracero workers" and "LULAC leaders
had few good things to say about poor Mexicans."[25] LULAC and
Perales did not favor the Bracero Program, because it was based on
labor exploitation and the condition of people of Mexican-descent
people in Texas was already bad, without adding more poverty and
racism to the community with the arrival of new Mexican immigrant
workers. Perales consistently said good things about poor Mexicans.
His friend Melisio Pérez of Alice called Perales "un buen amigo de
sus paisanos"[26] (a good friend to his countrymen).

Some have asked to what degree Perales and LULAC were anti-
Mexican. One scholar claimed LULAC "disapproved of increasing
[the] number of Mexican immigrants."[27] He wrote, "In the short term,
the league concluded that one way to protect second and third-gener-
ation Mexican Americans was to draw a line between itself and Mexican nationals."[28] But LULAC merely acknowledged the different
legal status' (one privileged in the US with US citizenship and the
other not). LULAC was silent on the US deportation raids and campaigns, in the 1930s, and might have taken up this cause had they been
primarily based in California.

Latino Consciousness

An early criticism of Perales and LULAC, particularly voiced in
the 1970s, was that LULAC used 'Latin American' as a euphemism
for 'Mexican.' According to one historian, "Since 'Latin,' like 'Spanish,' called to mind the members' European rather than Indian ancestry, that term was thought less offensive than 'Mexican.'"[29] This criticism did not take into account Perales' and LULAC's pride in being
Latino. Perales publicly expressed this pride as early as during his
George Washington University college days, when he took Spanish

classes and participated in a Spanish club. As scholar Felix Padilla has suggested, Latino consciousness is created when Latinos from different nations or peoples encounter one another in sizeable group settings.[30] Perales "became" a Latino (in his case, a person of Mexican descent interacting with other Hispanics from other Hispanic countries) in Washington, DC the place where he would have encountered more people who were not of Mexican descent than he typically did in Alice or San Antonio. This would be the first time besides his World War I stint in San Antonio that he would be a part of a highly multicultural community. Perales addressed Latino peoples as early as the 1920s, a time when the term "Latino" was rarely used.[31]

Perales' 1928 essay, "Problemas de Nuestra Raza en Los Estados Unidos" (Problems of Our People in the United States) mentioned not just Mexican Americans and Mexicans but also Latinos.[32] So his Raza was broader than just the people of Mexican descent. In the 1930s, he applauded a recreation center for Mexicans and Latinos.[33] He wrote about the benefits of the Parent Teacher Association (PTA) for Latinos.[34] He discussed scholarships for Latinos, not just for people of Mexican descent.[35]

My book, *No Mexicans,* documents how the word "Latin American" in the LULAC name came from Alonso Perales. "Latin American" was used as a means of expressing solidarity with any Spanish-speaking person in the United States. The LULAC constitution referenced "Spanish-speaking persons." In the 1920s, almost all Latinos spoke Spanish. The LULAC's membership application did not ask if one was of Mexican descent; it only asked about citizenship, occupation and gender. Male Latinos were welcome in LULAC.

Perales pointed to discrimination against Latinos. Anti-Mexican sentiment meant anti-Latino sentiment; Euro-Texans did not distinguish between Latinos. One draft of a non-discrimination bill Perales and LULAC tried to pass stated, "The term 'Mexican or Latin-American origin' as used in this Act shall mean any person who is a citizen of Mexico or any of Countries of Central or South American, or who is related in the third degree by affinity or consanguinity to any person who is or was a citizen of any of these countries or places."[36] In 1941, during the US government's brief support of Pan-Americanism, he wrote ex-boss and Undersecretary of State Sumner Welles about discrimination against Venezuelans in New Braunfels, Texas. Venezuelan air force pilots training in San Antonio were asked to move to the Latin American tables in a public park.[37] In 1944, Perales stated before the Inter-American Bar Federation, ". . . I wish to make clear that in that section of the United States when the word 'Mexican' is used it is intended to include all citizens of the Latin-American Republics."[38] In March 1944, in a letter to President Franklin Delano Roosevelt Perales noted that not only persons of Mexican descent were discriminated but also "Venezuelans, Hondurans and Argentinians, some of them members of the Armies of said countries, have also been discriminated against."[39] In March 1945, in a letter to the press he referred to "his travels in Hispanic America, I have observed that the discrimination in Texas and other states of our Union against persons of Mexican descent or Hispanic descent is deeply resented by our neighbors to the South."[40] Perales' *Are We Good Neighbors?* referred to practices against "the Mexican and Spanish speaking people in the United States, as well as throughout the Western Hemisphere."[41]

Perales did not speak of Latinidad or Latino unity, whether imagined or not.[42] He did not attempt to construct an artificial unity but included Latin Americans in his activism when their well-being required it. In Texas, the Mexican-origin people's presence was dominant and there were few Latinos in San Antonio. Still, in the early twentieth century, the Spanish language united them.

Part of Perales' Latino consciousness was his embrace of the multiple identities in the Latino past and present. He referred to his people as Mexicans, Americans, Mexican Americans, Spanish, Latin American and as La Raza. He did so because they had a hybrid, multicultural, multi-national past and present. They saw themselves as both "Americans" and "Mexicans." When they referred to themselves as "Americans," they acknowledged their place in United States society and their national origin. When they called themselves "Americans," they resisted European American racialization. When they referred to themselves as "Mexicans," they acknowledged their racial, ethnic and national origin and identities. When Latin American was used, they recognized their parallel history to others of Latin American national origin. Again, Perales did not give the indigenous, Arab and African origin of Latin American much attention.

Latin American Consciousness

Not only was Perales inclusive of Latinos, he also had a hemispheric consciousness that included Latin America. By 1933, *Lulac News* reported he "has nothing but praise and words of kindness for the heroic people of Nicaragua."[43] Perales referred to Latin Americans as "hermanos de raza"[44] (racial brethren). "Latin American" in the name of LULAC was designed to be an inclusive term. Historian Neil Foley erroneously surmised, "LULAC members constructed new identities as Latin Americans in order to arrogate to themselves the privileges of whiteness routinely denied to immigrant Mexicans, blacks, Chinese, and Indians."[45] Foley not only assumed "Latin American" meant white (despite the multi-racial and multi-cultural heritage of people from Latin America), he assumed Mexican Americans/LULAC members were treated differently than Mexican immigrants. Perales referred to his Latin American ethnic heritage as part Spanish and Indian. Neil Foley added, "When many middle-class Mexican Americans identified themselves as 'Latin Americans' rather than 'Mexicans,' they did so less in solidarity with other Latin Americans than to avoid the label 'Mexican,' which in the Southwest was a moniker for racial inferiority. For these Mexican Americans, the identity markers 'Latin American' and 'Anglo American' suggested a harmonious symmetry between whites of 'Latin extraction' and whites of European or Anglo-Saxon ancestry, in contradistinction to Negroes, Chinese, Japanese, Indians, and other nonwhite citizens who had yet to achieve the status of hyphenated Americans, much less their constitutional rights as U.S. citizens."[46] But Mexican Americans were not Mexicans and Perales and LULAC never accepted that 'Mexican' was an undesirable term or that people of Mexican descent were inferior; indeed, they waged war against this racialization.

Perales saw little difference between Latinos or Latin Americans from different nations. He wrote, "the Nicaraguans are our blood brothers because they, like us Mexicans, are descendants from either pure Spanish blood or pure indigenous blood or through their veins flow both. Additionally, their language is Spanish and their customs and ideologies are identical to ours."[47] While he wrote disparaging comments about Latin American living conditions in the 1920s, he did not disparage the Latin American people. Moreover, he said that Mexican American living conditions were similar.

Perales' Latin American consciousness developed over time. It developed from his 1) earliest learning likely from Velásquez or his library or his students; 2) *La Prensa's* Mexicanness and its Latin American content; 3) his likely socializing with Latinos in Washington, DC and/or in college; and 4) his diplomatic work in Latin America.[48] An offense against Mexicans was an offense against all Latin Americans. For instance, in 1923 he considered the racist western film *The Bad Man* "an insult to the official representatives of the Mexican government and all the other Hispano American diplomatic staff members living in Washington who, although they are not Mexicans, resent as much as we do the outrages inferred to our race by virtue of the ties of blood and language that connect us."[49]

Perales had a hemispheric consciousness as historian Zamora has argued. Along with Drs. Carlos E. Castañeda and George I. Sánchez, they were among the elite Mexican Americans with ties to multiple Latin American nations. Speaking before a Congressional committee in 1945, Perales said, "The discriminatory situation in Texas is truly a disgrace to our Nation. Mexicans—regardless of citizenship—and, for that matter, citizens of Honduras, Venezuela, Colombia, Argentina and the other republics, have been humiliated merely because they happened to be of Spanish and Mexican descent, time and again."[50]

Whiteness Including Attitudes toward African Americans

One of the recent myths about Perales and LULAC was his/its position on whiteness. The 1929 LULAC constitution made no reference to whiteness or to color. But it specifically referred to pride in racial origin. US society was color-conscious with laws referencing color and whiteness since its colonial days under England and under Spain. From 1878 to 1952, there were fifty-two cases in which US judges identified those who were and were not white.[51] The 1925 Texas Civil Code called for separate schools for 'Whites' and 'Colored' people. 'Colored' was defined as "all persons of mixed blood descended from negro ancestry."[52] Texas often used a racial binary of white and colored.

Historian Ignacio M. García has noted that "Mexican Americans were seen as anything but white in the way they were treated in the labor markets, in the political arena, in the schools and in the social arena."[53] Garcia added, "It served no purpose, before Brown and Board of Education [1954] to be colored in the United States. It offered very few protections and added many additional burdens. If Mexican Americans wanted 'color,' whites were more than willing to give them the burdens that came with it."[54] Historian Francisco Rosales also noted, "if they [Mexican Americans] were to be classified as colored, it could subject them to de jure segregation."[55] Indeed, according to Texas law, "colored" meant African American. Texas courts recognized only black and white "races", a binary that made color a complex issue for people of Mexican descent. Scholar María Portillo Saldaña noted people of Mexican descent in the United States had a "fabricated racial dichotomy" based in US law that after 1930 offered them the choice between "white" or "colored," a binary option. Perales "chose" the identity that offered privilege instead of oppression.

In 1920, the US census deemed persons of Mexican descent "white." But they were deemed "Mexican" in 1930, a unique racial category distinct from "white" and "colored". This change did not represent the United States' approval of people of Mexican descent people and their ethnicity; the US believed this was not an ethnicity to be proud of. Perales and LULAC protested. For them, being labeled 'Mexican' in 1930 was close to being labeled "colored" with its additional racist burdens. According to historian Foley, when Perales and LULAC fought for the white classification, "By embracing whiteness, Mexican Americans have reinforced the color line that has denied people of African descent full participation in American democracy" and "In pursuing White rights, Mexican Americans combined Latin American racialism with Anglo racism, and in the process separated themselves and their political agenda from the Black civil rights struggles of the forties and fifties."[56] But these were not "white rights"—these were US rights the constitution extended to citizens which Perales demanded.[57] Likewise, Zamora believed LULAC and the GI Forum attacked segregation "not on the ground that this racial practice was morally wrong, but because Mexicans were ostensibly white."[58] According to historian Benjamin Johnson, "Interpretations by whiteness scholars end up marginalizing the more racially progressive aspects of LULAC and help perpetuate the mistaken notion that the organization and its members had cut themselves off from Mexican culture and politics, including discourses of race that did not revolve around whiteness."[59] He continued, "whiteness scholars 'put words in their subjects' mouths to compensate for the absence of first-hand perspectives by the historical actors themselves." For instance, they have implied that 'Latin American' meant 'white.' And even though Perales and LULAC often referred to 'our race' which meant 'a notion of peoplehood distinct from Anglo-Americans,' they still argue that LULAC claimed sole membership in the white race. When in fact, some LULAC members referred to the 'Mexican race.'"[60]

LULAC was founded because racism was immoral, Perales wrote that Mexican Americans should "energetically and constantly combat the acts that denigrate" them as non-white.[61] This was a claim to legal rights based on citizenship. Legal scholar George Martínez correctly observed that Perales "sought to establish the rights of Mexican Americans as a distinctive group as opposed to founding such rights on a claim that Mexican Americans were members of the white race."[62]

Perales did not seek a possessive investment in whiteness. Perales was a person of color raised in the barrio, attending the public schools with both its racist and exclusionary curriculum under the racial hegemony of Texas. On rare occasions, he expressed opinions that showed he had internalized colonialism, a force which all persons of Mexican descent in the United States are subject. In one essay, he called upon La Raza to be clean and to save money. There was a racial script under the 'Mexican problem' that Mexicans were dirty. He believed saving was one virtue Anglo-Saxons had.[63] But Perales also pointed out that whites earned higher wages due to white privilege, and that the working class needed higher wages. In the thousands of documents written by Perales, I found only one example of Perales showing deference to a white person. He did so with Governor Allan Shivers in 1954, when he praised Shivers for his anti-communism calling him "Your Excellency."[64] But Perales stated whites did La Raza no favors by permitting social mingling with them.

Perales' thoughts on racial origin were expounded upon in a 1930 US Congressional document. He wrote about race in the written testimony he submitted to Congress. He noted the "Mexicans descend from the two great races, the Indian and Spanish. That, of course, does not make them Nordic or Teutonic." He added, "The greater part of Mexican people are either Indian or Mestizo." He used tables like a scholar in his testimony, noting that a mestizo was white and Indian, and they represented 60% of the population, while purely Indian Mexicans represented 30% of the population. So, in his national testimony addressing white Congressmen, Perales stated that he was of mestizo origin.[65] He described the Spanish as white despite centuries of mixture from Africa, the Middle East and other parts of Europe. And he asserted Mexico's Indianness as well. Perales had no problem revealing his indigenous racial origin.

Perales did not like the "white or colored" binary. In a 1939 "Memorandum on Conditions in San Antonio," Perales advised "Say: 'Anglo-American Women' instead of 'White Women.'" The less we use the word "white" in contradistinction to the word "Mexican', the better it will be." Still, Perales referred to La Raza as members of the Caucasian race. Perales stated, "Mexicans belong to the Caucasian Race . . ."[66] He accepted the label of "white" as part of the political strategy for the empowerment of La Raza, or at least he accepted that people of Mexican descent be categorized as "other white."[67]

Complicating Perales' claim of whiteness even more is how he qualified this whiteness. On several occasions he said he was "white **but** Mexican" or "white **and** Mexican." In fact, while he claimed to be a member of Caucasian race, he also added that he had "Mexican blood."[68]

Thus, he acknowledged La Raza was "off-white" or as we would say today, "of color", or an identifiable ethnic group, or a class apart. Because of these qualifications, it cannot be emphatically stated that Perales said he was white.

And while Perales referred to people of Mexican descent as Caucasian, he simultaneously referred to "La Raza," suggesting a differentiation from whiteness or from a white race. While 'La Raza' suggested "the people," it still had racial connotations signifying difference from the dominant society. Attorney and scholar Lupe Salinas noted that use of 'La Raza' suggested Latinos regarded themselves as "an identifiable group, distinctive from other whites."[69] Perales was aware that the idea of calling La Raza 'white' may have insinuated a lack of pride in Mexican identity. He explained to the state health officer of Austin, "the only reason we had not done so was because we are very proud of our racial extraction and we did not wish to convey the impression that we are ashamed to be called Mexicans."[70]

So, Perales and LULAC not only had to articulate their relationship to the US racial imaginary of white and colored (black) with a dash of brown after 1920, they also had to address the Latin American racial imaginary of mestizaje. Perales embraced racial hybridity [at least Spanish and Native American], Latin Americanness and Mexicanness. Perales referred to La Raza as "Mexican or Latin-American origin" and "of the Caucasian or Indian race."[71] Perales said Mexican Americans were Caucasians "who have Indian blood."[72] So, his idea of his race was not just belonging to one race and even included an understanding of his indigenous origin/blood/race.

In summation, Perales claimed multiple racial origins. He claimed to be white, Caucasian, Spanish, Indian and Mexican. As scholar María Portillo Saldaña has noted, persons of Mexican descent in the United States have a "fabricated racial mestizaje." Perales readily pointed to his Mexican, Indian and Spanish past. It did not include a specific tribal identity though he referenced the Aztecs and Mayas and not any nomadic or small tribe. It included no African or Middle Eastern past or any other Europeans in Mexico; no Asian heritage was mentioned.

Perales and LULAC constantly shifted identities to suit their political needs because race was socially constructed and fluid. Historian Laura Cannon added, "Men and women of various ethnic groups constantly negotiated the social definitions of "white" and "nonwhite."[73] Historian Ignacio M. García noted, "It would, however, be more accurate to say that middle-class Mexican Americans were unsure where they fit in the mosaic of American society."[74]

African Americans

Perales had racist attitudes toward African Americans. Perales grew up in Alice, Texas with its racist ideology and practices against African Americans. He would have witnessed racist treatment of African Americans from both whites and members of La Raza. In San Antonio, Perales lived among La Raza, again separate from African Americans who mostly lived on the East side. He likely had limited contact with them during World War I. Perales may have had more contact with African Americans in Washington, DC, but his attitudes were not changed there. His contact with Latin American nations had some populations of African-descent but this did not impact him either.

Only a few of Perales' racist statements against African Americans are documented. He said people of Mexican descent should not "jumble them in as Negroes, which they are not."[75] He mostly believed taking up the African American civil rights cause would mean the failure of La Raza's cause. He wrote, ". . . the negro is entitled to JUSTICE, but if we champion his cause, we are doomed."[76] In 1941, Perales argued for a Texas campaign "to end all racial prejudices in so far as members of the Caucasian race are concerned."[77] However, during efforts to extend the existence of the Federal Employment Practices Commission in the 1940s, Perales contacted African American leader A. Phillip Randolph about making a permanent FEPC.[78] However, Perales made little effort to foster more cooperation with African Americans and African Americans exerted little effort on this front either. Each group dealt with its own battle separately.[79] Yet, Perales did congratulate President Dwight Eisenhower for sending troops to Little Rock, Arkansas to enforce the integration of African American students in public schools in the early 1950s.[80]

Historians have used three specific incidents as evidence of LULAC's racism. First, in 1936 El Paso's Frank Galvan, national LULAC president, sent a letter "To all LULAC councils" that the Census Bureau "has insulted our race in classifying us as colored in their statistics reports." He asked that councils "protest" to respective

"Congressmen."[81] Second, LULAC Council 16 Secretary Gregory R. Salinas cited racial [and possible sexual] interaction between African American men and a Mexican-American woman. He wrote, "let us tell these negroes that we are not going to permit our manhood and womanhood to mingle with them on an equal social basis."[82] Third, in the 1950s LULAC national president Félix Tijerina banned African Americans from his Houston restaurant.[83]

A few LULAC leaders' positions on potential Brown/Black civil rights organizations' cooperation evolved over time especially in the 1940s. First Castañeda stated, "Mexican employees should use the same facilities as other white employees; under Texas law they are white, and have a legal right to insist on not being classified as colored."[84] Castañeda originally held the idea that "We have no objection to segregation . . . of Negroes in one . . . [facility], and Anglos and Latin-Americans in another."[84] But later he supported Texas legislation which would have banned discrimination against Mexican Americans, African Americans and Afro-Latinos from Latin America.[85] And, by 1947, he believed Mexican Americans should address discrimination against African Americans and Mexican Americans.[86] Castañeda had significant contact with African Americans as he worked in the Federal Employment Practices Commission in the 1940s. In 1947, he told Perales, "As I have told you repeatedly we must began [sic] to establish a basis for cooperation in political action with the Negro Group. Politically they are much better organized then (sic) our own people. Their problems and ours are similar and as Mr. Weslery said they feel that every gain made by Latin Americans is an indirect gain for them and they have greater confidence in a Latin American in office than in an Anglo American."[87] Dr. George I. Sánchez collaborated with African American civil rights leaders Thurgood Marshall and sociologist Charles Johnson.[88] Historian and attorney Virginia Raymond found that Castañeda and John J. Herrera of Houston, 1952-53 national LULAC president, believed Mexican Americans should join forces with African Americans.[89] Overall, Castañeda, Sánchez and Herrera were more open to working with African Americans than was Perales.

Class

Perales and LULAC have been criticized for having a class bias. Perales and LULAC were middle class. Perales' contemporary Emma Tenayuca chided Perales and LULAC on the issue of class bias in the late 1930s. She first joined a LULAC ladies' auxiliary in San Antonio as a teenager but was later exposed to Marxist theory and became active in labor unions and the Communist Party. She and husband Homer Brooks wrote, "In the past, its [LULAC's] viewpoint was colored by the outlook of petty-bourgeoisie native-born, who seek escape from the general oppression that has been the lot of Mexican people as a whole. It meant an attempt to achieve Americanization, while barring the still unnaturalized foreign-born from membership." They called LULAC's work a "sterile path." Yet in the same essay they added, "In Texas they have led successful strategies against segregation in public schools, parks, etc., not only in behalf of American citizens, but of all Mexicans . . . [T]his important organization of the Mexican middle class will play an increasing role in the general movement for Mexican rights."[90]

In 1945, Tenayuca again criticized LULAC, though this time in her diary. She was critical of LULAC's attempts or strategies to seek an anti-discrimination law in the Texas legislature. After LULAC sent 1000 letters to the Women's Federation Clubs of Texas and American Legions, she wrote, "But my opinion is that only a strong mass movement supported from all sections of the population can bring about provable action by the state legislature. There is an opportunity now to enlist the support of all sections of the population, Catholics, Jews, Chambers of Commerce, labor, etc. . . . . The usual procedure of the LULAC may get the work done for the sake of the Mexican people, but there is no room for the small politicking of the LULAC."[91] A campaign to send a thousand letters was a mass effort. LULAC could have been more strategic in its coalition work, yet it is also true that these sectors, which were controlled by whites, were barely starting to stand up for Latinos. Interestingly enough, in the mid-40s she worked with LULACer Jacob Rodriguez's *Pan American* newsletter in San Antonio. By the time Tenayuca wrote this diary entry she was already outside of mass politics due to government surveillance. While she became a role model of resistance during the Chicano movement and thereafter, Perales' liberal path proved more lasting than Tenayuca's.[92] LULAC's so-called "small politicking" proved large over time. And while Tenayuca is better known than Perales, his impact was greater. Perales was highly cognizant of "economic discrimination." His 1944 resolution at the Congress of the Inter-American Bar Federation in Mexico City poignantly noted, "Traditionally the Mexican has been assigned the heaviest, dirtiest and most poorly remunerated work both in the industrial and agricultural fields." He explained: "1) He is refused employment. 2) He is denied an opportunity to acquire higher knowledge, and secure better positions. 3) He is refused promotions on the basis of seniority and qualifications. 4) He is paid smaller wages than the Anglo-Saxon for the same kind of work."[93] All of Perales' FEPC work benefitted Latino and Latina skilled workers.

Perales believed in fair wages and fair treatment for workers, not wage disparities. In a 1936 letter LULAC sent to local businessmen, he wrote "In order for the Mexican to educate himself and his children and to live in good and sanitary housing it is absolutely indispensable that he receive for his labor a wage that will permit him to live a normal human life. I firmly believe that if employers who hire Mexican workers would raise their wages [,] they would be performing not only a humanistic act but that it would benefit the whole community economically."[94] The letter was sent to "Los Industriales y Hombres de Negocio" (Industrialists and Businessmen) with Perales listed as the first signature and his title as "Presidente de la Comisión Pro-Aumento de Jornales," (President of the Workers' Raise Increase Commission), a LULAC Council 16 committee. Business leaders who received this letter probably threw it away. A kind letter to employers was not enough. Perales also criticized the dual wage system that paid Mexicans one wage and whites another.[95] And he attacked child labor.[96]

Cultural studies scholar George Martínez explained LULAC and Perales' position on unions. "Perales' ideological rigidity made him suspicious of labor unions, even as poorly paid agricultural workers struggle[d] to organize in Texas and other parts of the Southwest . . . he offered no alternate to unionization and did not say how civil rights activism was different from labor organizing, or how it might help society's most vulnerable workers."[97] Perales did not promote unions and labor organizing enough. LULAC was all about uplifting the poor through ethnic consciousness, Mexican Americanism and anti-racism but not through class consciousness and unionization. Thus his/their approach to ethnic/national oppression was limited by a middle-class perspective.

Perales' position on the Pecan Shellers' strike of the late 1930s, a major conflict in San Antonio over wages, is not clear-cut. In 1938, Perales and LULAC supported the Pecan Shellers' strike on the condition that communist Tenayuca be kicked out.[98] Perales was "President de la Comisión Pro-Aumento de Jornales de la Liga de Ciudadanos Unidos Latinoamericanos." He said, "To remedy our people's problems they need to be paid what their work is worth". He suggested La Raza speak to representatives of the pecan factories, noting that workers could only afford $5.00 rent per month.[99] But Perales withdrew his support of the strike because of Tenayuca's communism. Considering the 1937 pact between Russia and Germany, Perales' anti-Communism can be understood. One historian said LULAC supported the "police suppression of the pecan shellers' strike" but offered no evidence.[100] Historian Laura Cannon has showed that LULAC Council 2 and the Loyals ultimately took up the pecan shellers cause. Moreover, analysis of several other strikes in the 1930s, such as an onion workers' strike in Laredo, suggests LULAC was supportive of striking workers.[101]

Perales and LULAC's focus on the desegregation of public accommodations was not elitist or class based. Segregation affected all persons of Mexican descent including the fair-skinned, the educated, the political elites and the wealthy. He complained about the denial of service to people of Mexican descent in public establishments, which extended to people from all social classes, including service men, Mexican diplomats and migratory workers.[102] The insult was the same regardless of class status. Historian Zamora has noted that diplomats and migrant workers were equally affected. Historian Thomas Guglielmeo has noted that Pauline Kibbe, Good Neighbor Commission secretary, said that segregation was most common in the "fourth and fifth-class" establishments that poor and working-class Mexicans and Mexican Americans could afford.[103] Perales also concerned himself with the political education of the working class of Mexican descent and its economic welfare. One historian stated that LULAC was "inclined to ignore the plight of the poor Mexican workers."[104] Political scientist Benjamin Márquez noted, "One major charge hurled at LULAC by Chicano activists was that it focused on discrimination only as it would affect its middle-class constituency but showed little concern about political education and the economic welfare of such people as migrant farmworkers."[105] Perales and LULAC addressed some worker issues, including those of farm workers and migrant workers. Perales' worked to have *braceros* banned from Texas in the early 40s and argued against their exploitation. LULAC was not a union but most of its activities were about the political and economic empowerment of workers; LULAC spent significant attention on access to schools empowering the working class and gave minor attention to college access for the few who were fortunate to graduate from high school. Perales and LULAC supported the Federal Employment Practices Commission (FEPC), suggesting that labor rights were civil rights. Historian Emilio Zamora concluded "LULAC has not always confined itself to civil rights."[106]

Even LULAC's work for education has been misinterpreted as elitist. One historian acknowledged protests against segregated schools by the Mexican-American middle class but suggested these were "essentially class-specific protests" that "pressed for the rights of the respectable educated Mexicans", and that they simply presented their campaigns "in the name of the Mexican community."[107] Their protests were indeed on behalf of the entire community for members of all classes. Historian Gabriela González has argued that the significant work undertaken by the Mexican-American middle class in civil rights work must be respected. They were motivated by middle-class notions of respectability but also by social justice.[108] In fact, Perales referred to "social justice" when denouncing horrendous housing in San Antonio in the 1930s.

LULAC's educational goals were focused on working-class uplift. A 1935 unsigned LULAC essay stated, "The first step that must

be taken in this great human endeavor is the improvement of the educational attainments of our people. The principles of democracy are
so simple that the strongest appeal (sic) of them is to the educated
man . . . our first duty is to enlarge the education of our people and
this is the reason The League of United Latin American Citizens is
more interested in the schools and educational institutions of our state
than in any other of our government institutions."[109] Perales supported night schools, which sought to reach the working-class people
whose days may have ended at 5pm. In fact, in 1934 he saw the creation of adult night schools as "a new era in the evolution of Latin
Americans in this city and state" noting that 1400 Spanish-speaking
adults were attending Sidney Lanier High School in the evenings.[110]

Perales also supported scholarships for Latino students, because
too few were educated and middle class. It was through education—
high school graduation and college graduation that grew the middle
class. Perales did not want a middle class for its own sake—that is
individual class mobility—he expected new middle-class members to
lead La Raza and act on its behalf for empowerment. Perales stated,
". . . education will enable us to enjoy life better; it will make us more
useful citizens; it will increase our earning power and thus raise our
standard of living and our social position. We must encourage the education of our people by all means at our command."[111] He understood
the relationship between language, education and class. He explained,
"Due to this segregation Latin American children never learn the English language well and they are thus prevented from pursuing higher
studies which (sic) might enable them to reach a higher economic
level when they attain their majority; as a further consequence great
masses of underpaid laborers are formed for the future."[112] Historian
Rosales was unable to finish his biography of Perales, but one of his
theses was "as shall be seen the civil rights issues tackled by organizations like LULAC would benefit the working classes more than any
other group if the efforts were successful."[113]

Among Perales' papers, I found only one example of class bias or
condescension. He gave Dr. Carlos E. Castañeda the opportunity to
speak at a Fiesta de la Raza celebration sponsored by the Pan American

Optimists in San Antonio. Perales wrote, "In a crowd like that [of] course, there is always the riff-raff who cannot appreciate it because of their ignorance. All they want is entertainment, and of the most ordinary type at that. Bring them a clown and they are perfectly satisfied."[114] This was a classist statement. Perhaps he had grown accustomed to listening to his wife's piano, classical music and operetta singing.

Liberalism, Conservativism, Anti-communism

A political scientist called LULAC's political history "solidly conservative." [115] But Perales rarely waivered from LULAC's political ideological foundation, liberalism.[116] Indeed, LULAC was "liberal and pragmatic" as historian Richard A. Garcia has noted.[117] Free-market enterprise unencumbered by racism was its economic ideology.

Another historian called LULAC "sheepish" and "complacent."[118] But, contrary to the statement that LULAC only addressed non-controversial issues and local issues, it addressed controversial issues like the Pecan Shellers Strike, state, national and international issues as well. LULAC did not address the deportation of Mexicans and Mexican Americans in the 1930s, but it addressed hundreds of other issues head on. The 1960 *La Prensa* report of San Antonio council 2's activities alone conflict with characterizations of LULAC as only involved in non-controversial issues.

Historians should not present a binary understanding of pre-World War II (associated with LULAC) and post-World War II civil rights activism (associated with the American G.I. Forum) as simply "conservative" versus "progressive." One historian noted, "The new ideas emerging from progressive Mexican-American leaders following World War II emphasized results in economic anti-discrimination struggles over the desire that Anglo leaders in the State accept them as social equals."[119] Pre-World War II leaders and LULAC members were not deferential to whites, and they did address economic discrimination. One historian has suggested that Perales "did not necessarily embrace the tactic of publicly embarrassing racists."[120] In fact, Perales called out racists all his life through his writing and deeds.

Anti-communism

Perales was conservative in his anti-communism. Historian Richard A. Garcia noted, "Perales did not propose a radical or ideological approach to solving the problems of Mexican Americans. Instead, his philosophy pragmatically fused ethnicity and citizenship."[121] Perales was a liberal, not a radical. He did not believe in radical ideologies like communism or socialism.

While the ideology of communism was developed in the nineteenth century, during Perales' adult life, between 1920 and 1960, he witnessed numerous international Communist threats. Communism arose in Russia in 1919 as did the US Communist Party. Perales grew up in the era that saw the banning of radical ideologies in the United States due to World War I. Moreover, communism as practiced by Russia, North Vietnam, China and Cuba was not progressive. Communist Russia saw the genocide of twenty million under dictator Joseph Stalin. China's communism after 1948 made the ideology a global threat. North Vietnam and North Korea also became communist. Cuba fell to communist dictatorship in 1958. Communism was an international threat and Perales saw the rise of these repressive regimes.

Perales made anti-Communist statements at least by 1939. A newspaper reported, "Perales bitterly opposes the present policy of the CIO and A.F.O.L of admitting Communists, Nazis or Fascists in their ranks. 'We are ready to fight all 'isms,' he said as he thumped his desk, "Nazism, Fascism, Communism—we will fight anyone who advocates them.'"[122] In the late 1930s, Perales wrote, "We neither need nor desire the advice, assistance or support of the Communists or any other un-American group."[123] Communists, Nazis and fascists did not all share the same beliefs, but Perales believed them all to be totalitarian. US Communists had the interests of the working class in mind, but Perales did not acknowledge this.

Political scientist Benjamín Márquez correctly described Perales as a "fervent anti-communist."[124] This would especially be true in the 50s. "At the same time, his unyielding anti-communist stance conflicted with his stand on the need to respect the Constitution of the United States, even when it disallowed an American citizen the opportunity to engage in free speech," wrote scholar and attorney Lupe Salinas.[125] Márquez also noted that Perales "condemned the American Civil Liberties Union for protecting the first amendment rights of groups espousing revolutionary politics."[126] And Perales criticized attorney Gus Garcia for defending a company that he believed to be "communistic."[127] Perales also supported the fanatical Martin Dies of Texas in the 1950s. Perales was naïve in not understanding that the label of "communist" could also work against Latinos and progressive causes. For instance, anti-FEPC Congressmen cried "communism" as a rationale to end this federal agency that fought racism.

Gender

While historians and political scientists have criticized Perales and LULAC for class bias, they have been silent on the issue of gender. Perales and LULAC operated under patriarchal heterosexual norms before 1970. Perales argued for the initial inclusion of men (and the tacit exclusion of women). Perales believed women and men in LULAC should work separately and he supported the idea of segregated councils for women called Ladies LULAC, which were authorized in 1933. He validated the dominant tendency in Texas Mexican-descent society to organize and segregate by gender—this homosociality would afflict Mexican-origin women in Texas until the 1970s.

Much of US and Texas society before the 1970s was organized according to the principle of homosociality, so Perales was in tune with the times. Ladies LULAC existed until the 1970s, when the rise of Chicana feminism led to gender-mixed councils. The era of what sociologist Sister Woods called "patriarchal citizenship" died slowly in Texas.[128] In effect, Perales' support of Ladies LULAC marginalized women's roles as civic activists from the 1930s to 1970.

LULAC's Contributions

Besides Perales and LULAC's civic and political actions across the decades, they promoted the dignity of the people of Mexican descent and Latinos as well. They promoted anti-racism toward Latinos, self-determination and self-help and pride in the Spanish language, culture and heritage.

Anti-Racism Toward Latinos

Perales and LULAC opposed racism. Perales noted, "Racial discrimination is practiced in Texas against the people of Mexican origin by a minority of Anglo-Americans it is true, but they have the approval of a majority of the Anglo-American people in Texas, and the proof is that they never done anything to prevent the minority from continuing to humiliate the people of Mexican origin for the simple fact of being of said origin."[129] Most whites were complicit with this racism.

Few anti-racist organizations existed in Texas, though there was the Southern Association for the Prevention of Lynching by white women and NAACP composed of white people and African Americans. Perhaps the most "radical" white ally was the benign Pan American Round Table! Liberal whites in Texas, including Jews, were extremely rare before 1950. Dr. Carlos Castañeda noted "liberal groups in our area are rare as hen's teeth."[130] However, the Bunn family of the Midwest assisted with a contribution in the 1940s, and then other white liberals contributed to the formation of the American Council of Spanish Speaking Persons in the 1950s, which with Perales had no connection. It was Sánchez, not Perales, who successfully accessed liberal funding. A more liberal Texas political coalition would begin to appear in the 1950s.

While Perales noted the tenacity, persistence, culture and foundation of racism he did acknowledge a few white allies. During his Congressional testimony in 1930, before the Box Bill, he noted the following as friends of the people of Mexican descent: Gaspar Whitney, Frank Tanenbaum, George McCutcheon, Hermann Scheizner, Carlton Beal, L. Spence, Robert W. McLean, O. Douglas Weeks and L.W. Maus.[131] Indeed, it was Weeks who documented 1920s Mexican-American civil rights organizing. Perales also cooperated with white allies such as San Antonio politician Maury Maverick and state legislator J. Franklin Spears. Perales also included white allies Archbishop Robert Lucey and Jack Danciger in his book *Are We Good Neighbors?*

La Raza could not depend on help from the government—Texas state government and the federal government were part of the problem as they were controlled by racist whites. Political scientist Matthew Gritter noted that the federal government provided no assistance to the Mexican-American civil rights movement until 1942, when the Federal Employment Practices Commission (FEPC) was extended to include Latinos suffering employment discrimination. Congressman Dennis Chávez of New Mexico intervened on Latinos' behalf. But FEPC was short lived as Southern conservatives, Western Republicans and other racists got their way, defunding the World War II era agency.

Congress did little to improve the lives of Latinos. The federal government was silent on lynching and Congress failed to pass an anti-lynching bill despite the persistence of African Americans. This is to say, since the 1911 anti-lynching campaign in Laredo by La Raza, over thirty years had gone by without US government assistance to stop lynching against people of Mexican descent.[132] Congress did not approve a minimum wage until the 1930s and then, it excluded farmworkers and domestics, two occupations which were typically those of people of color and specifically, those of women of color. Congress did not outlaw the South's poll tax practice until 1964, and it did not ban racial segregation of public accommodations until 1965.

As part of Perales' anti-racism, he was especially bothered by stereotypes in his fight against white supremacy.[133] He wrote, "so long as there are people among the Anglo Saxons who unjustly classify ALL the Latin Americans as indigent, ignorant riff-raff, so long shall there be Latin Americans who will refuse to cooperate with you in civil affairs."[134] He fought stereotypes of Mexicans as peons in the *Washington Post* in May 1923.[135] In the 1930s, he was upset about an article about the San Antonio Westside portraying chile queens and other food vendors and asked the author to visit with him about her essay on "Cosmopolitan San Antonio."[136] He also fought the idea that prostitution was a Spanish custom in San Antonio.[137] Much of his battle against the "Wetback pamphlet" in the 1950s was due to the stereotypes it perpetuated of Mexicans as lazy, dirty and full of lice.

Self-determination & Self-help

Perales and LULAC were patterned on self-determination and self-help. Perales' foundational principle was "Our community can help itself."[138] He believed in the tradition of mutual aid societies dating back to the 1850s with self-help as an ethic in the community of Mexican descent in the United States. Again, there were around 100 mutualistas in Texas in 1900. In San Antonio, there were thirty mutual aid societies around 1920 and the Mexican government established the Comisiones Honoríficas and Cruz Azul in the 1920s. Historian Julie Leininger Pycior found that this self-help ethic transitioned and took other forms after the Depression, and that it continues today in an evolved form.[139]

Perales did not believe that mutual aid societies were the best vehicle for Raza uplift. Instead, he created the new civic group LULAC. Perales argued that, "We Latin-Americans must organize. We must get out of the rut and forge ahead. Let us catch up with and keep abreast of our hard driving fellow-citizens of Anglo-Saxon extraction. To accomplish this, no man should be allowed to stand in our way. No man is big enough to block our progress. A fraction is not larger than the whole. For the sake of posterity and the good name of our race, let us get together, my Friends, and begin to solve our great problems. We can only do it thru a well-disciplined, solid, powerful organization."[140]

This solid, powerful organization was typically based at the local level and in rural communities. It was typically led by English-speaking, educated, middle-class leaders who could take on the dominant society with greater success. Local councils were supported by regional meetings, conferences and an annual statewide/national conference. Leadership changed annually, without control from any one locality or council. Before the 1970s, all expenses were paid for by La Raza, especially its middle class. If or when a council failed, LULAC leaders would return to re-group and re-organize old and new members. This cycle continues to repeat itself and has worked for over ninety years.

Perales believed education was the best tool for racial uplift so he fought against segregated inferior schools, lack of schools, condemned tracking and promoted scholarships. Tracking was the practice used by schools to pre-determine an educational/career path deemed appropriate for students based on their race and gender. Nonwhite students were not encouraged to pursue educational or professional goals. He wrote Dr. Castañeda, "We want our children to have ample opportunity to become educators, doctors, engineers, lawyers, merchants, industrial leaders, pharmacists, or bakers, mechanics, carpenters, bricklayers, etc. If they feel like it. But we do not want them to become any of these things against their will and inclinations, and most certainly we do not want our school system to mold their setups that our children cannot become anything but artisans."[141] Perales respected artisans as both his father, and the father of his adopted home, Cresencio Treviño, were artisans. But he also believed in access to education and to middle-class jobs for Raza. He recognized that upward mobility through education was painfully slow but still believed it to be the best path. Beyond the slow path of education to reach the middle class, Perales called for interventions in civic policy and in practices that were perpetuated by the dominant white society. Perales could not even conceive of becoming upper class.

Pride in Latino Culture, Heritage and the Spanish Language

While LULAC and Perales espoused loyalty to the United States, as Latinos, they also expressed pride in being Latino. The Order of the Sons of America and LULAC co-founder John Solis stated, "We were always proud of our ancestry and heritage, and we were always proud of being American. We were not trying to be Gringo."[142] As early as 1929, Perales wrote, "ought to be our proof that our efforts to be rightfully recognized as citizens of this country do not imply that we wish to become scattered nor mush less abominate our Latin heritage, but rather on the contrary, we will always feel for it the most tender love and the most respectful veneration."[143] In "Our Attitude toward History" in *El Paladin*, a Corpus Christi LULAC newspaper, Perales wrote, "we solemnly declare once and for all to maintain a sincere and respectful reverence for our social origin of which we are proud. This ought to be our proof that our efforts to be rightfully recognized as citizens do not imply that we wish to become scattered or much less abominate our Latin heritage."[144] He said, ". . . we are not fundamentally inferior."[145]

Perales recognized the unique history of people of Mexican descent in the United States. He was proud of his Mexican/Mexican American identity, history and culture. He noted, "The Mexican people do not pertain to a fundamental inferior race. The history of our people proves this." He added, "Mexicans are descendants of two great peoples: the indigenous and the Spanish."[146] He wrote about the "sophisticated civilization the Indians created."[147] He referred to Cuauhtémoc and Father Miguel Hidalgo with pride.[148] He noted, "Americans should not despise and slander, but rather welcome, even salute and respect the founders [La Raza] of this continent."[149]

Perales also acknowledged Tejano leaders in history. Shortly after 1936, the 100th anniversary of the Texas Revolution, Perales brought attention to the Tejanos Antonio Navarro and Francisco Ruiz who had signed the Texas Declaration of Independence. He also lauded those who were connected to the fight at the Alamo such as Juan Seguin and Antonio Menchaca. He called Tejano Juan Cortina, who used violence against white Texans in the 1850s, "a true citizen and true champion of justice and a defender of Mexicans in Texas."[150] He did not recognize any women.

Perales was fully bilingual, bicultural and bi-literate and was proud of his Latino heritage, the Spanish language, Latino culture and Latino history. Most of his published work was in Spanish. Some of his letters to other Mexican Americans were in Spanish or were bilingual. He advocated for bilingualism. During his LULAC presidency he himself translated the constitution of LULAC into Spanish.[151] His first book, *En Defensa de Mi Raza* was in Spanish and targeted Latino readers but his second book *Are We Good Neighbors?* was in English and sought a Euro-American and bilingual Latino audience. As more Latinos were accessing public schools in the United States, it was necessary to write in English to reach them. Perales had fought for that inclusion and advancement in public schools.

A few scholars have suggested that LULAC supported English-only policy. Early Chicano studies scholar Américo Paredes wrote, "The LULACS were trying to teach their children not to speak Spanish."[152] Living in Brownsville he visited with J.T. Canales, a bilingual LULAC leader, who espoused pro-English themes. But Canales lived next to the Mexican border, spoke Spanish and wrote in Spanish and he wanted Mexican Americans to learn English. According to another historian, "LULAC abandoned Spanish."[153] Both Perales and Canales ensured that English became the official language of LULAC. "English as a second language was considered imperative, because often more than 90% of the Mexican children in Texas could not speak English" in the 1930s, noted historian Richard A. Garcia.[154] English was also a tool of defense against oppression and a way to successfully live in the United States. As late as 2005, another author in a Latino-American history series book wrote, "LULAC encouraged their members to take up U.S. ways and give up Latino culture." Perales and LULAC typically promoted speaking English but also biculturalism and bilingualism; they were proud of Latino culture and organized in the League as ethnic Latinos. LULAC has always been synonymous with ethnic pride.

Conclusion

From the 1970s to the 1990s, most scholars were prejudiced against Perales and LULAC because of their Chicano movement bias against the middle class and assimilation. (Ironically, many of us accessed higher education and middle-class status due to the educational victories won by LULAC, which our generation inherited.) They also used few sources to make broad claims, since there was not yet a Perales archive or LULAC archive. The LULAC archives were available after 1980.

In the 1990s, several scholars began to look at Perales and LULAC's progressive work in the civil rights arena. Among them, I analyzed Perales' and LULAC's gender politics and pointed to women's oppression within LULAC. Scholars can now use the thousands of primary sources in numerous LULAC archives in places like Austin, Houston, El Paso, Albuquerque and Iowa City.

But the 2000s saw the rise of whiteness studies which blemished LULAC's reputation again. These works utilized few sources but made broad generalizations. The 2010s has seen a greater understanding of Perales and of LULAC. Scholars published in the Michael A. Olivas anthology on Perales used the Perales archive, providing historical context. But the bias against Perales and LULAC persists. A book review of the Olivas' anthology in 2014 even rehashed common myths.[155] And in 2017, the Chicano movement activist and political scientist José Angel Gutiérrez stated that LULAC did not "even encourage the payment of the poll tax."[156]

Historian Richard A. Garcia has captured Perales' essence best. By placing him within the context of Mexican San Antonio, his class and his times, he explained Perales' thinking and actions as such: "Struggle, but democratically; demand the rights of a U.S. citizen, but remain proud of the Mexican heritage, in other words, equality not privilege, cultural pluralism not assimilation, justice not discrimination, pride not inferiority, literacy not illiteracy and economic self-responsibility not welfare."[157] In short, his motto was struggle.

Perales had a militant attitude against white privilege. Perhaps his most radical statement came in the mid-1920s when he said Latinos were not seeking to mingle with whites as if it was an honor. It is ironic that Perales, one of the people who struggled the most, has not only been forgotten and misunderstood but maligned as an apologist.

CHAPTER 24
Conclusion

Alonso S. Perales was this nation's greatest Latino ambassador inside of the United States though he was silent on the oppression of Latin Americans south of the Rio Grande River. As an employee of the US government and the Nicaraguan government he was unable to criticize US policies in Latin America or criticize the lack of democracy in the Dominican Republic and Nicaragua. His "full professional written and oral proficiency in both English and Spanish" as well as his advanced education and legal training made him an unusual figure.[1] He was even more unusual as a self-made man.

For decades activist Adela Sloss-Vento's writing and research promoted leader Perales as a friend to La Raza. She dedicated her life to documenting his contributions and civil rights endeavors. She tried to get LULAC to more earnestly recognize Perales; around 1977 she wrote, "Letters have been sent to the State Director of LULAC, to the President Generals in the past by myself, by the widow, Mrs. Marta Perales and others regarding the above information, but no answer had been received."[2] In 1974, she wrote, "And I ask, what more can one ask of an outstanding citizen as Mr. Perales?"[3] Indeed, he advocated and organized against the notion of the ideology of the "Mexican problem" which emerged in the 1920s.

On the occasion of Perales' award from Spain in 1951, LULAC co-founder M.C. Gonzales also recognized Perales' legacy. He congratulated him because he "blazed a trail" noting, "Our racial brothers are now serving on juries, are now voting, are now owning real estate, and our children as now being taught to love the flag and the principles of democracy in non-segregated schools."[4] Gonzales, also a World War I veteran, witnessed Perales' battles.

About twenty years after Gonzales' letter was written, Henry Cisneros, Ph.D., San Antonio mayor in the 1970s, wrote Perales' wife stating, "Many of us who were not even born at the time he [Alonso S. Perales] was working are now reaping the benefits of his pioneering work." He wrote, "We take very lightly the benefits that we are now receiving in the form of educational opportunities, governmental fairness, job accessibility, and business opportunities that would never have existed had not men like your husband literally given their lives to the cause."[5]

Attorney and scholar Michael A. Olivas explained how exceptional he was. He noted, "He was without equal either in his community or that of the larger community, finding extensive public involvement in his law practice, organizational involvement and leadership, the Catholic Church, efforts to gain elected office, diplomatic and international participation, lobbying and advocacy before governmental entities, private correspondence, writing op-eds and media venues, publishing books and recording public and private instances of discrimination engagement in a number of other discourses that allowed him to seek equality. . . ."[6] In his introduction to the book, *In Defense of My People, Alonso S. Perales and the Development of Mexican-American Public Intellectuals,* Olivas went on to defend Perales,"One of the many canards applied to Mexican-Americans by those who do not know better is that we have passively accepted our fate and did not work to resist the many depredations visited upon the community. If there is any single figure whose entire life did not conform to this stereotype, it was Alonso S. Perales, who worked tirelessly and effectively in defense of his Raza."[7] Years later Olivas lamented, "We need more leaders like Alonso S. Perales to assist in the battle for Latino equality." He asked fellow lawyers and academics to ask themselves if they too were indeed "good neighbors" empowering others.[8]

In the early 2000s, Judge Albert Peña Jr., past President of LULAC Council 2 of San Antonio, said that he was "perplexed why such a historic leader is forgotten to a generation."[9]

San Antonio and Alice, Texas would do well to claim Perales as a lauded native son. As recently as 2018, a survey of the history of Latino rights organizations in San Antonio began in the 1960s.[10] San Antonians celebrated their 300th year anniversary without mentioning Perales or LULAC. The efforts of the Order of the Sons of America as early as 1921 and LULAC need to be acknowledged.

Before there was US House of Representative Joaquin Castro and US Secretary of Housing and candidate for US president Julián Castro of San Antonio in the 2010s, there was Mayor Henry Cisneros; before Henry Cisneros there was Judge Albert Peña Jr; before Peña there was Congressman Henry B. González and attorneys Gus Garcia and Carlos Cadena. Attorney Vilma Martinez should also be acknowledged. Willie Velásquez, founder of the Southwest Voter Registration Project in San Antonio in the 1970s, also followed Alonso S. Perales' work promoting the importance of voting.[11] There were still others before Perales but none as important in the fight for Latino civil rights.

President Theodore Roosevelt captured the essence of activist warriors like Perales in the following quote:

"The credit belongs to the man who is actually in the arena; whose face is marred by dust and sweat and blood . . . who spends himself in a worthy cause; who at best knows in the end the triumph of high achievement, and who at the worst, if he fails, at least fails while daring greatly—so that his place shall never be with those cold and timid souls who neither know[12] victory nor defeat."[13]

Gladiator Alonso S. Perales was the man in the arena. No person did more to fight for Latinos. The broadsheet *La Calavera* said it all: "He was a mover and man of ideas. A powerful man . . . in a fight."[13] A master of the medium, he exerted power through civic engagement, political empowerment, educational uplift, and intellectual vigor. "Respect the Mexican" was his battle cry for his pueblo and his gente (community and people). Not only was Perales a civil rights gladiator at the local, state, national, and international arenas, he was a builder. Not only did he construct LULAC, he was a principal architect of Latino and Latina destiny.

Selected Bibliography

Archival and Primary Sources

The most important collection on Alonso S. Perales is the Alonso S. Perales Collection at the M.D. Anderson Library, University of Houston. I took several hundred pages of hand-written notes of 1920s documents in 1979; they includes notes on some items no longer in the Perales collection and are referred to as Cynthia Orozco Notes on Perales (ON), 1979. The Dr. Carlos E. Castaneda collection at the Benson Latin American Collection at the University of Texas at Austin contains the most letters written by Perales. Many of Perales' newspaper writings can be found in *La Prensa* and *La Voz Católica,* both of San Antonio. Most LULAC archives are located at the Benson including *LULAC News*. Some are digitized at repositories.lib. utexas.edu.

Manuscript Collections

Bancroft Library, University of California at Berkeley (BL)
Gamio, Manuel, Papers (MG)
Taylor, Paul S., Papers (PST)

Benson Latin American Collection, University of Texas at Austin (BLAC)
Alderete, Chris (CA)
Castañeda, Carlos E., Papers (CC)
de Luna, Andrés Sr., Collection (ADL)
Escobar, Eleuterio Jr., Papers (EE)
Garcia, Gustavo (Gus), Papers (GG)

Garza, Ben. Collection (BG)
Gonzales, Manuel C. Collection (MCG)
Idar, Clemente N. Papers (CI)
League of United Latin American Citizens Archive
Montemayor, Alice Dickerson (ADM)
Munguia, Romulo (RM)
Order Sons of America (OSA), Council 5, Records
Sáenz, José de la Luz, Collection (JLS)
Weeks, Oliver Douglas, Papers (ODW)

*Dolph Briscoe Center for American History, University of Texas at
Austin (DB)*
Castañeda, Carlos Eduardo (CC2)
Pérez Álvarez, Casimiro, Papers (CPA)

Center for Southwest History, University of New Mexico
Chávez, Dennis, Papers (DC)

Cushing Library, Texas A&M University at College Station
Contreras, Hernan (HC)

Houston Metropolitan Research Center
Hernandez, Alfred, Papers. (AH)

Institute of Texan Cultures, University of Texas at San Antonio
Photography collection

Library of Congress, Washington, DC
Federal Employment Practices Commission

M.D. Anderson Library, University of Houston
Perales, Alonso S. Collection (AP)

South Texas Archives, James C. Jernigan Library, Texas A&M University at Kingsville

Canales, J.T., Estate Collection (JTC)
Perales, Alonso S. Collection (AP2)

Private Collections
Orozco, Dr. Cynthia E., Ruidoso, New Mexico (CO)
Sloss-Vento, Adela, Papers, Austin, Texas (ASV)

Newspapers

El Paladín, (Corpus Christi) UCLA Chicano Studies Research Center
La Prensa (San Antonio)
La Voz Católica (San Antonio)

Correspondence, Email, Telephone Conversations
Carrizales, Martha Perales, 2017-2019
Martínez, Vilma, 2018
Mireles, Celia, 2018-2019
Perales, Raimond, 2018-2019
Pérez Davis, Araceli, 2018-2019
Sloss-Vento, Adela, 1978-1980
Tenayuca, Emma, 1980-1984

LULAC News

Benson Latin American Collection, University of Texas at Austin; Dolph Briscoe Center for American History (DB), University of Texas at Austin; Houston Metropolitan Research Collection; Center for Southwest Research, University of New Mexico; Paul S. Taylor Collection (PST), University of California at Berkeley; Library of Congress, Washington DC.

Oral Histories

Judge Carlos C. Cadena with Juan Gilberto Quezada, January 31, 1991, Bexar County Historical Commission, San Antonio Public Library
Author with MC Gonzales, 1979
Author with John C. Solis, 1980

Dissertations and Theses

Cannon, Laura E. "Situational Solidarity: LULAC's Civil Rights Strategy and the Challenge of the Mexican American Worker, 1934-1946," Ph.D. diss., Texas Tech Univerity, 2016.

Cannon Dixon, Laura. "Police Brutality Makes Headlines: Retelling the Story of the 1938 Pecan Shellers' Strike," master's thesis, Indiana State University, 2010.

Chandler, Charles Ray. "The Mexican American Protest Movement," Ph.D. diss., Tulane University, 1968.

Knox, William John. "The Economic Status of the Mexican Immigrant in San Antonio, Texas,"master's thesis, University of Texas, 1927.

Lynch III, Michael John. "South Texas Renaissance Man: The Humanitarian, Political, and Philanthropic Activities of Judge J.T. Canales," master's thesis, Texas A&M University at Kingsville, 1996.

Mendoza, Natalie. "The Good Neighbor Comes Home: The State, Mexicans and Mexican Americans, and Regional Consciousness in the US Southwest during World War II." Ph.D. diss., University of California at Berkeley, 2016.

Mila, Brandon H. "Hermanos de Raza: Alonso S. Perales and the Creation of the LULAC Spirit," master's thesis, University of North Texas, 2013.

Morales III, Ralph Edward. "Hijos de la Gran Guerra: The Creation of the Mexican American Identity in Texas, 1836-1929," Ph.D. diss., Texas A&M University, College Station, 2015.

Pycior, Julie Lenninger. "La Raza Organizes: Mexican American Life in San Antonio 1915-1930, As Reflected in Mutualista Activities," Ph.D. diss., University of Notre Dame, 1979.

Rosales, Rodolfo. "The Rise of Middle Class Politics in San Antonio, 1951 to 1985," Ph.D. diss., University of Michigan, 1991.

Woods, Sister Frances Jerome. "Mexican Ethnic Leadership in San Antonio, Texas." Catholic University of America, Washington DC, 1947.

Wilson, Leigh Ann. "Fighting Two Devils: Eleuterio Escobar and the School Improvement League's Battle for Mexican and Mexican American Students," Education in the San Antonio, Texas Public Schools from 1934 to 1958," Ph.D. diss., University of Memphis, 2011.

Government Documents

Articles of Incorporation, Texas Secretary of State
   Club Protector Mexico-Texano, 3 November 1921
   Loyal Latin American League, December 1937
   Order of the Knights of America, 22 October 1927
   Order of the Sons of America, 4 January 1922
   Order of the Sons of Texas, 15 June 1923
US Congress. House. Commission on Immigration and Naturaization. Hearings on the U.S. Congress. House. Committee on Immigration. Hearings on Western Hemisphere. 71st Cong., 2nd Sess. 1930.

Articles

Christian, Carole E. "Joining the American Mainstream: Texas's Mexican Americans During World War I." *Southwestern Historical Quarterly* 92:4 (April 1989): 559-598.

Foley, Neil. "Becoming Hispanic: Mexican Americans and the Faustian Pact with Whiteness," *New Directions in Mexican American Studies*, ed. Neil Foley. Austin: Center for Mexican American Studies, University of Texas at Austin, 1997: 53-70.

García, Mario T. "Mexican Americans and the Politics of Citizenship: The Case of El Paso, 1936." *New Mexico Historical Review* 59 (April 1984): 187-204.

Garcia, Richard A. "Alonso S. Perales: The Voice and Visions of a Citizen Intellectual," in *Leaders of the Mexican American Generation, Biographical Essays*, ed. Anthony Quiroz. Boulder: University Press of Colorado, 2015: 85-118.

Garcia, Richard A. "The Mexican-American Mind: A Product of the 1930s." In *History, Culture, and Society: Chicano Studies in the*

1980s, ed. Mario T. García, et al. Ypsilanti, Michigan: Bilingual Press/Editorial Bilingue, 1983: 67-94.

Gritter, Matthew. "Elite Leadership, People of Mexican Origin, and Civil Rights: Dennis Chávez and the Politics of Fair Employment," *Congress & the Presidency* 44 (2017): 143-156.

Guglielmo, Thomas A. "Fighting for Caucasian Rights: Mexicans, Mexican Americans, and the Transnational Struggle for Civil Rights in World War II Texas," *Journal of American History* 92:4 (March 2006): 1212-1237.

Gutiérrez, José Angel. "Chicanos and Mexicans Under Surveillance, 1940-1980," *Renato Rosaldo Lecture Series Monograph* 2, Series 1984-5. Tucson: Mexican American Studies and Research Center, University of Arizona, 1986: 29-58.

Johnson, Benjamin H. "The Cosmic Race in Texas: Racial Fusion, White Supremacy, and Civil Rights Politics," *Journal of American History* 98:2 (September 2011): 404-419.

Kauffman, Al. "The Birth of Latino Rights Organizations" *300 Years of San Antonio and Bexar County*, ed. Claudia R. Guerra and Char Miller. San Antonio: Hamilton Books, Trinity University, 2018.

Limón, José E. "El Primer Congreso Mexicanista de 1911: A Precursor to Contemporary Chicanismo." *Aztlán* 5:1-2 (1974): 85-115.

Lipman-Blumen, Jean. "Toward a Homosocial Theory of Sex Roles: An Explanation of the Sex Segregation of Social Institutions," *Signs* 1:3, Part 2 (Spring 1976): 15-31.

Locke, Joseph L. "The Heathen at Our Door: Missionaries, Moral Reformers and the Making of the 'Mexican Problem.'" *Western Historical Quarterly* 49:2 (Summer 2018):127-153.

Morales, Cynthia A. "A Survey of Leadership, Activism and Community Involvement of Mexican American Women in San Antonio, 1920-1940," *Journal of South Texas* 13:2 (Fall 2000):193-206.

O'Connor, Karen and Lee Epstein. "A Legal Voice for the Chicano Community: The Activities of the Mexican American Legal Defense and Educational Fund, 1968-82." In *The Mexican American Experience: An Interdiscplinary Anthology*, ed. Rudolfo O. De la Garza, et. al. Austin: University of Texas Press, 1985.

Orozco, Aurora. "Mexican Blood Runs Through My Veins," *Speaking Chicana, Voice, Power, and Identity*, ed. Leticia Galindo and María Dolores González. Tucson: University of Arizona, 1999: 106-122.

Orozco, Cynthia E. "Alice Dickerson Montemayor: Feminism and Mexican American Politics in the 1930s," in *Writing the Range: Race, Class, and Culture in the Women's West* (Norman: University of Oklahoma Press, 1997): 434-456.

Orozco, Cynthia E. "Beyond Machismo, La Familia, and Ladies Auxiliaries: A Historiography of Mexican-Origin Women's Participation in Voluntary Associations and Politics in the U.S., 1870-1990." *Perspectives in Mexican American Studies* 5 (Tucson: Mexican American Studies & Research Center, University of Arizona, 1995): 1-34.

Orozco, Cynthia E. "Ladies LULAC," *Readers' Companion to U.S. Women's History*, ed. Wilma Mankiller, Gwendolyn Mink, Marysa Navarro, Barbara Smith, Gloria Steinhem. (Boston: Houghton Mifflin Co., 1998): 378.

Orozco, Cynthia E. "Regionalism, Politics, and Gender in Southwestern History: The League of United Latin American Citizens' (LULAC) Expansion into New Mexico from Texas 1929-1945," *Western Historical Quarterly* XXIX: 4 (November 1998): 459-483.

Perales, Alonso S. "El México Americano y La Política del Sur de Texas: Commentarios." (San Antonio: Artes Gráficas, 1931) Trans. and commentary. Oliver Douglas Weeks. "The Texas—Mexican and the Politics of South Texas." *American Political Science Review* 24 (August 1930): 606-627.

Pérez Davis, Araceli, "Marta Pérez de Perales," *El Mesteño* 4:37 (October 2000): 16-17.

Portillo Saldaña, María Josefina. "How many Mexicans [is] a horse worth?" The League of United Latin American Citizens, Desegregation Cases and Chicano Historiography." *South Atlantic Quarterly* 107:4 (Fall 2008): 809-831.

"Reisler, Mark. "Always the Laborer, Never the Citizen: Anglo Perceptions of the Mexican Immigrant during the 1920s," *Pacific Historical Review* 45:2 (May 1976): 231-254.

Salinas, Alicia. "Alice, Texas," *New Handbook of Texas*. ed. Ronnie C. Tyler, Douglas Barnett, and Roy Barkley. 1: Austin: Texas State Historical Association, 1996: 105-106.

Tenayuca, Emma and Homer Brooks, "The Mexican Question in the Southwest," *The Communist*, March 1939: 257-268.

Weeks, O. Douglas. "The League of United Latin American Citizens: A Texas-Mexican Civic Organization," *Southwestern Political and Social Science Quarterly* 10:3 (December 1929): 257-278.

Books

Almaráz, Félix D. *Knight without Honor: Carlos Eduardo Castañeda*. College Station: Texas A&M University, 2000.

Behnken, Brian D. *Fighting Their Own Battles: Mexican Americans, African Americans, and the Struggle for Civil Rights in Texas*. Chapel Hill: University of North Carolina Press, 2014.

Blanton, Carlos Kevin. *George I. Sánchez, The Long Struggle for Integration*. New Haven: Yale University Press, 2015.

Carrigan, Walter D. and Clive Webb. *Forgotten Dead: Mob Violence against Mexicans in the United States, 1848-1928*. Oxford: Oxford University, 2013.

Chacon, Justin Akers. *Radicals in the Barrio: Magonistas, Socialists, Wobblies, and Communists in the Mexican American Working Class*. Chicago: Haymarket Books, 2018.

Foley, Neil. *Quest for Equality, the Failed Promise of Black-Brown Solidarity*. Boston: Harvard University Press, 2010.

García, Ignacio M. *Hector P. García: In Relentless Pursuit of Justice*. Houston: Arte Público Press, 2002.

García, Mario T. *Católicos: Resistance and Affirmation in Chicano History*. Austin: Universityof Texas Press, 2008.

García, Mario T. *Mexican Americans, Leadership, Ideology & Identity*. New Haven: Yale University Press, 1989.

Garcia, Richard A. *Rise of the Mexican American Middle Class, San Antonio 1929-1941*. College Station: Texas A&M Press, 1991.

González, Gabriela. *Redeeming La Raza, Transborder Modernity, Respectability, and Rights*. Oxford: Oxford University Press, 2018.

Gritter, Matthew. *Mexican Inclusion: The Origins of Anti-Discrimination Policy in Texas and the Southwest.* College Station: Texas A&M University, 2012.

Handbook of Texas. 3 vols. Austin: Texas State Historical Association, 1952, 1976.

In Defense of My People, Alonso S. Perales and the Development of Mexican-American Public Intellectuals. Ed. Michael A. Olivas. Houston: Arte Publico Press, 2012.

Kaplowitz, Craig. *LULAC, Mexican Ameericans, Civil Rights, and National Policy.* College Station: Texas A&M University, 2006.

Leaders of the Mexican American Generation, Biographical Essays. Ed. Anthony Quiroz. Boulder: University of Colorado, 2015.

Lynch, Michael and Carlos Larralde. *Judge J.T. Canales, Latino Civil Rights Leader, an Intimate Portrait.* London: Lambert Academic Publishing, 2015.

Márquez, Benjamín. *LULAC: The Evolution of a Mexican American Political Organization.* Austin: University of Texas Press, 1993.

Muñoz Martínez, Monica. *The Injustice Never Leaves You, Anti-Mexican Violence in Texas.* Boston: Harvard, 2018.

New Handbook of Texas. Ed. Ronnie C. Tyler, Douglas E. Barnett, and Roy R. Barkley. 6 vols. Austin: Texas State Historical Association, 1996.

Olivas, Michael, A. *Colored Men and Hombres Aquí: Hernández v. Texas and the Rise of Mexican American Lawyering.* Houston: Arte Público Press, 2006.

Orozco, Cynthia E. *Agent of Change, Adela Sloss-Vento, Mexican American Civil Rights Activist and Texas Feminist.* Austin: University of Texas, 2020.

Orozco, Cynthia E. *No Mexicans, Women or Dogs Allowed: The Rise of the Mexican American Civil Rights Movement.* Austin: University of Texas Press, 2009.

Perales, Alonso S. *Are We Good Neighbors?* San Antonio: Artes Gráficas, 1948; reprint New York: Arno Press, 1974.

Perales, Alonso S. *En Defensa de Mi Raza.* 2 vols. San Antonio: Artes Gráficas, 1936, 1937.

Pycior, Julie Leninger. *LBJ and Mexican Americans, The Paradox of Power*. Austin: University of Texas Press, 1997.

Ramirez, José A. *To the Line of Fire!: Mexican Texans and World War I*. College Station: Texas A&M University, 2009.

Rosales, F. Arturo. *Chicano!: The Mexican American Civil Rights Movement*. Houston: Arte Público Press, 1997.

Rosales, Rodolfo. *The Illusion of Inclusion: The Untold Political Story of San Antonio*. Austin: Center for Mexican American Studies, University of Texas Press, 2000.

Sáenz, J. Luz. *Los México Americanos en la Gran Guerra y su Contingente en pro de la Democracia, la Humanidad y La Justicia*. San Antonio: Artes Gráficas, 1934.

Saunders, Lyle and Olen E. Leonard. *The Wetback in the Lower Rio Grande Valley of Texas*. Inter-America Education Occasional Papers, no. 7. Austin: University of Texas, 1951.

Sloss-Vento, Adela. *Alonso S. Perales, His Struggle for the Rights of Mexican-Americans*. San Antonio: Artes Gráficas, 1977.

Testimonio: A Documentary History of the Mexican American Struggle for Civil Rights. Ed. F. Arturo Rosales. Houston: Arte Público Press, 2000.

The Politics of San Antonio, Community, Progress, and Power. Ed. David R. Johnson, John A. Booth, and Richard J. Harris. Lincoln: University of Nebraska, 1983.

The World War I Diary of Jose de la Luz Saenz. Ed. Emilio Zamora with Ben Maya. College Station: Texas A&M University, 2014.

Vargas, Zaragosa. *Labor Rights are Civil Rights: Mexican Workers in Twentieth-Century America*. Princeton: Princeton University Press, 2005.

Vento, Arnoldo Carlos. *Adela Sloss-Vento, Writer, Political Activist, and Civil Rights Pioneer*. Lanham: Hamilton Books, 2017.

Villanueva Jr., Nicolas. *The Lynching of Mexicans in the Texas Borderlands*. Albuquerque: University of New Mexico, 2017.

Zamora, Emilio. *Claiming Rights and Righting Wrongs in Texas, Mexican Workers and Job Politics during World War II*. College Station: Texas A&M University Press, 2009.

Digital Sources

"Alonso Perales: El Paladín de la Raza, A Champion for Civil Rights," https://www.ebsco.com/blog-archives/article/alonso-perales-el-paladin-de-la-raza-a-champion-for-civil-rights Accessed Oct. 8, 2019.

Alonso S. Perales Conference & Exhibit: Marta Perales Carrizales speaks about her father. https://www.youtube.com/watch?v=Dw_iLAVDwNY Accessed on September 2, 2019.

Alonso S. Perales Conference & Exhibit: Raymond [Raimundo] Alfonso speaks about his father. https://www.youtube.com/watch?v=OcT8q4nObi A Accessed on September 2, 2019.

Gauthereau, Lorena. "Are We Good Neighbors?: Mapping Discrimination Against Mexican Americans in 1940s Texas." https://www.arcgis.com/apps/MapJournal/index.html?appid=80b15409a9d742318cd80b18e6157e76 Accessed on July 19, 2019.

Quezada, J. Gilberto. "Alonso S. Perales Pioneer Leader of the Mexican American Civil Right Movement," Somos Primos, September 2015. http://www.somosprimos.com/sp2015/spsep15/spsep15.htm Accessed on July 1, 2018.

Timeline: Life of Alonso S. Perales

1898—born in Alice, Texas

1904—father died, age 6; picked cotton; laid railroad ties

1910—mother died, age 12; joined brothers selling tamales door to door

1915—attended Draughon's Business College, San Antonio

1915—worked as stenographer and translator at Frank Saddlery Company, San Antonio, Texas

1918—army field clerk in World War I, San Antonio, Texas

1918—first newspaper report of Perales' activities

1919—wrote first newspaper essay for *La Evolucion,* Laredo, Texas

1920—received honorable discharge from army

1920—worked at US Department of Commerce, Washington, DC

1921—wrote letter protesting Texas Governor James Ferguson's racist commentary

1922—attended George Washington University, Washington, DC

1922—married Marta Engracia Perez Alvarez of Rio Grande City, Texas

1922—joined US Diplomatic Corps as secretary to Sumner Welles; began work as diplomat

1923—worked for San Antonio Chamber of Commerce

1925—admitted to bar in Texas

1925—served as chief attorney, Tacna/Arica Arbitration under John J. Pershing & President Calvin Coolidge

1926 — earned law degree from George Washington University

1926 — wrote protest letter to *Washington Post* about Mexican workers

1927 — wrote first newspaper article for *La Prensa,* San Antonio, Texas

1927 — wrote letter of protest to President Calvin Coolidge about racial violence in Raymondville, Texas

1927 — joined law firm Canales and McKay, McAllen and Rio Grande City, Texas

1927 — co-organized Harlingen, Texas convention which excluded Mexicans; co-founded Latin American Citizens League (LAC) in the Lower Rio Grande Valley, Texas

1929 — principle founder, League of United Latin American (LULAC) at Corpus Christi, Texas

1930 — testified in Congressional hearing on Mexican immigration along with J.T. Canales on behalf of LULAC

1930 — re-published essay by Oliver Douglas Weeks about LULAC's founding adding his own commentary

1930 — made San Antonio, Texas, his permanent home

1930-1931 — presided over national LULAC as second president

1930s — addressed radio audiences in Spanish and English

1931 — counseled *Del Rio ISD v. Salvatierra* lawsuit, first class-action desegregation case on behalf of children of Mexican descent in Texas

1933 — joined Still, Wright, Davis, and Perales law firm, San Antonio, Texas

1933 — founded LULAC Council 16, San Antonio, Texas

1934 — co-founded Association of Independent Voters, San Antonio, Texas

1934 — worked for Bexar County Attorney's office, San Antonio, Texas

1936-37 — authored *En Defensa de Mi Raza* (*In Defense of My People*) (2 volumes)

1937 — seceded from LULAC; founded League of Loyal Americans, San Antonio, Texas

Late 1930s—founded Committee of 100, San Antonio, Texas

1938-1960 appointed Consul General of Nicaragua

1938—denounced Emma Tenayuca, communist leader of the San Antonio Pecan Shellers' strike

1939—testified before US Congressional hearing on Mexican immigration

1940—100 LULAC men's councils and 20 Ladies LULAC councils existed

1940—resigned from San Antonio Board of Public Health

1941—initiated Racial Equality Bill #909 in Texas legislature along with attorney M.C. Gonzales

1942—diagnosed with high blood pressure

1943-1945—worked with Federal Practices Employment Commission (FEPC), the first federal civil rights agency addressing racial discrimination against people of color in employment

1944—testified before US Congressional hearing in favor of the FEPC

1945—fought for Spears bill in Texas legislature to ban racial discrimination

1945-1959—served as columnist for *La Prensa* newspaper, San Antonio, Texas

1945—represented Nicaragua and Latinos at founding of the United Nations, San Francisco, Califonia

1946—ran unsuccessfully for San Antonio Independent School District board

1946—raised funds for US Senator Dennis Chávez of New Mexico, the only Latino in Congress

1948—opened Perales law firm

1948—wrote book *Are We Good Neighbors?* documenting racism in Texas and criticizing token Pan Americanism

1948—supported *Delgado vs. Bastrop* case ending school segregation of Mexican-descent children in Texas

1948—acted as lawyer in Puente case banning restrictive covenants in real estate, San Antonio, Texas

1948—president of the Pan American Optimist Club, San Antonio, Texas

Late 40s—opened small book store with wife Marta

1950—suffered slight stroke

1950—campaigned for Henry B. Gonzalez for Texas legislature

1951—denounced publication of the "Wetback pamphlet" overseen by Dr. George I. Sánchez

1951-60—served as columnist of "Por Mi Religión," *La Voz*, a Catholic newspaper, San Antonio

1951—adopted three children

1952—awarded Spain's Medal of Civil Merit

1952—received titular membership from Spain

1952—worked on another anti-discrimination bill in Texas legislature

1952—friend J. Luz Sáenz died

1952—campaigned for Republicans Dwight Eisenhower for US president and Allen Shivers for Texas governor

1954—played minor role in *Hernandez vs. Texas* case at US Supreme Court

1958—best friend Dr. Carlos E. Castañeda died

1958—mentored 15-year-old Vilma S. Martínez, future lawyer, MALDEF leader and US Ambassador to Argentina

1958—pro-bono work on Rachel Gonzalez case, a women's rights case

1958—joined board of directors, Pan American Progressive Association (PAPA), San Antonio, Texas

1960—died; buried in San Antonio, Texas

1960—body moved to Collins Cemetery, Alice, Texas

1960s—efforts to create a park, monument or school honoring Perales

1972—first Chicano Studies academician inquired about Perales' papers

1974—Perales Elementary School dedicated in San Antonio, Texas

1975—*Chicano Times* of San Antonio wrote "Who Was Alonso S. Perales?"

1977—Adela Sloss-Vento published *Alonso S. Perales, His Struggle for the Rights of Mexican-Americans*

1979—Orozco, University of Texas at Austin undergraduate, used Perales' papers

1980—Orozco wrote senior honors thesis on origins of LULAC

1980—LULAC archive created at University of Texas by Ruben Bonilla, National LULAC president

1989—Richard Garcia's book on San Antonio's Mexican-American middle-class is published

1996—Orozco's brief biography of Perales is published in *New Handbook of Texas*

2003—Hector Saldaña's "Unsung Hero" about Perales published in *San Antonio Express*

2007—Perales recognized at annual National LULAC convention, Albuquerque, New Mexico

2009—Orozco's book, *No Mexicans, Women or Dogs Allowed* on origins of LULAC is published

2009—Perales archive obtained by US Hispanic Literary Recovery Project and deposited at the University of Houston

2012—Perales conference sponsored by the US Hispanic Literary Recovery Program, Houston, Texas

2012—Michael A. Olivas' edited book on Perales, *In Defense of My People: Alonso S. Perales and The Development of Mexican-America Public Intellectuals* published by Arte Público Press

2014—Brandon H. Mila wrote master's thesis on Perales

2021—This book is published more than sixty years after Perales' death and more than ninety years after LULAC was founded

Notes

ACKNOWLEDGEMENTS

[1]F. Arturo Rosales' book manuscript on Perales (2016) included chapters titled: 1) Alice, Context for ASP Life; 2) The Perales Family; 3) The Rise of Mexican Americanism; 4) The Great War and Mexican Americanism; 5) The Rise of Mexican Americanism and Tejanismo in Texas; and 6) Historical Causality of Tejano Identity. He had not completed chapters beyond 1920.

INTRODUCTION

[1]Prof. M.A. Urbina, "El Defensor de la Raza" in Adela Sloss-Vento, *Alonso S. Perales, His Struggle for the Rights of Mexican Americans* (San Antonio: Artes Gráficas, 1977), 99. Urbina was member of the Loyals organization in the 1940s. Original text: El Defensor de la Raza/Cinco lustros ha que una voz vibrante/En tribunales de Texas se escucha,/Y ante congresos resuena constante/La airada voz que sin descanso lucha/Doquiera defiende libertades [en gente]/Contra el injusto descriminador/Que impugnando derecho de gentes/Rompe a la unión su armonía y valor/La voz proclama la fraternidad/A todos los hombres de América/Que pueden labrarse la felicidad/De la soñada justicia Homérica/En la voz de Americanos leales/Que reclama derecho y justicia/En los labios de Alonso S. Perales/Contra el pérfido que anida malicia/En la voz que llama enciende/De equidad en alma Mexicana/Que con hábil presteza defiende/A la raza Indo-Hispano-Americana.

[2]Hector Saldaña, "Unsung Hero of Civil Rights 'Father of LULAC' a Fading Memory," *San Antonio Express,* September 14, 2003.

[3]Marta Pérez de Perales, "Al Pueblo de Alice," October 15, 1960, Alonso S. Perales (hereafter AP), M.D. Anderson Library, University of Houston, Box 10, Folder 6.

[4]Prof. Benjamín Cuellar Sr., "El Paladín de la Raza Lic. Alonso S. Perales fue Condecorado," *Revista Latino-Americana* 4:10 (April 1952), AP, Box 11, Folder 16.

[5]Saldaña; Emilio Zamora, "Connecting Causes, Alonso S. Perales, Hemispheric Unity, and Mexican Rights in the United States," *In Defense of My People, Alonso S. Perales and the Development of Mexican-American Public Intellectuals,* ed. Michael A. Olivas (Houston: Arte Público Press, 2012), 294.

[6]Joseph Orbock Medina, "The Trials of Unity: Rethinking the Mexican-American Generation in Texas, 1948-1960," *In Defense,* 72.

[7]Lupe S. Salinas, "Legally White, Socially Brown: Alonso S. Perales and His Crusade for Justice for La Raza," *In Defense,* 93.

[8]Richard A. Garcia, *The Rise of the Mexican American Middle Class, San Antonio 1929-1941* (College Station: Texas A&M University, 1991), 275. Garcia referred to both Perales and Gonzales as LULAC's principal fathers but Gonzales played no role writing the LULAC constitution.

[9]Brian Gratton and Emily Klancher Merchant, "La Raza: Mexicans in the US Census," *Journal of Policy History,* 28:4 (October 2016): 537-567. https://www.cambridge.org/core/journals/journal-of-policy-history/article/la-raza-mexicans-in-the-united-states-census/2D20 DBCD1360E3648D AB50A9ACBC525D Accessed August 15, 2019.

[10]*Alma Latina,* April 1932, 1, 12, Paul S. Taylor Collection, no box, no folder, Bancroft Library, University of California at Berkeley.

[11]The Alpha Club of Corpus Christi also honored him in the 1930s. While the article is now missing, it was listed on p. 23 of the J.T. Canales Estate Papers inventory and was located in Box 436, Folder 20. J.T. Canales Estate Collection (hereafter JTC), South Texas Archives, James Jernigan Library, Texas A&M University, Kingsville.

[12]Adela Sloss, "The League of United Latin Americans by It's (sic) Founder, Atty. Alonso S. Perales," AP, Box 3, Folder 37; Adela Sloss, "Importancia de la Liga de Ciudadanos Latino Americanos," *LULAC News,* December 1932: 15, Dolph Briscoe Center for American History (hereafter DB), University of Texas at Austin.

[13]Cynthia E. Orozco, "Adela Sloss-Vento," *Latinas in the United States: An Historical Encyclopedia,* ed. Vicki L. Ruiz and Virginia Sánchez-Korrol (Bloomington: Indiana University Press, 2006), 686-687.

[14]"Address delivered by M.C. Gonzales at the Latin Quarter on the occasion of a banquet given by LULAC Council #2 in his honor, San Antonio, Texas," November 9, 1944, AP, Box 3, Folder 47.

[15]Adela Sloss-Vento, *Alonso S. Perales, His Struggle for the Rights of Mexican-Americans* (San Antonio: Artes Gráficas, 1977). 10.

[16]Sloss-Vento, 10.

[17]*La Calavera,* November 2, 1942, AP, Box 10, Folder 30. Translated by Irma Orozco.

[18]Ibid, November 1949, AP, Box 10, Folder 30. Also see the November 1945 *calavera* about Perales in the same location.

[19]J. Luz Sáenz, "España Tributa Honores a un Texano," *Revista Latino-Americana,* April 1952, 23, AP, Box 11, Folder 16.

[20]Sloss-Vento, 30-31.

[21]Letter to Alonso S. Perales from the Alba Club, Elmo López, President, April 5, 1952, José de la Luz Sáenz Papers (hereafter JLS), Benson Latin American Collection (hereafter BLAC), University of Texas at Austin, Box 2, Folder 1.

[22]"Alonso S. Perales, Honored by the Institute of Hispanic Culture," October 1952, AP, Box 1, Folder 1.

[23]"Letter from Danciger Reports on Perales," *San Antonio Express News*, May 18, 1960, Alonso S. Perales Papers (hereafter AP2), Texas A&M, Kingsville, Box 1, Folder 5. This small Perales collection in Kingsville consists of a few folders in one box.

[24]Letter to Mrs. Alonso S. Perales from Zoe Esteele, May 25, 1960, AP, Box 1, Folder 1.

[25]Tony Cruz, President, Downtown LULAC Council No. 363, "In Memory of Alonzo (sic) S. Perales, LULAC Founder and Texas

Civic Leader," 2nd Annual Founders-Awards Banquet, San Antonio Public Library (hereafter SAPL), Texana Room, San Antonio Archival File, Organizations, LULAC.

[26]Sloss-Vento, 74.

[27]Ibid, 74.

[28]Letter to Muy estimada Comadre from Mr. and Mrs. Fortino Treviño, June 25, 1965, AP, Box 10, Folder 5.

[29]"Alice's New High School to be Named After City," *Corpus Christi Caller,* September 10, 1969, AP, Box 14 oversize.

[30]"Petition Recommends High School Be Named for Alonso S. Perales," *Alice Echo,* September 9, 1969, AP, Box 10, Folder 5.

[31]Resolution by Luis Alvarado, Feb. 12, 1960, LULAC Hall of Fame, AP, Box 3, Folder 40.

[32]Gilberto M. Hinojosa, "Alonso S. Perales," Opinion: IMAGE Documentary, Chan (Channel?) 12-11-30 am, AP, Box 10, Folder 10.

[33]Letter to Joe Benitez, National LULAC President from Adela Sloss-Vento, 1974, AP, Box 4, Folder 34.

[34]Letter to Joe Benítez, National LULAC President, from Marta Perales, June 14, 1974, AP, Box 4, Folder 8.

[35]Golden Years Appreciation Banquet Program, a Banquet Honoring Distinguished Mexican-Americans, September 16, 1974, San Antonio, Dr. Cynthia E. Orozco Papers (hereafter CO), Ruidoso, New Mexico.

[36]"An Interview with Mrs. Perales," *Chicano Times,* Feb. 14 thru Feb. 28, 1975, AP, Box 14.

[37]Ibid.

[38]Alonso M. Perales, "Alonso S. Perales," Alonso S. Perales Elementary School, 1977 program, AP2, Box 1, Folder 5.

[39]Sloss-Vento, 96.

[40]https://www.worldcat.org/title/alonso-s-perales-his-struggle-for-the-rights-of-mexican-americans/oclc/436461757&referer=brief_results Accessed September 2, 2019.

[41]Sloss-Vento, 22.

[42]Cynthia Orozco, "Mexican and Mexican American Conflict at the Harlingen Convention of 1927: The Genesis of LULAC," Senior honors thesis, University of Texas at Austin, 1980, CO.

[43]Cynthia E. Orozco, *No Mexicans, Women or Dogs Allowed: The Rise of the Mexican American Civil Rights Movement* (Austin: University of Texas, 2009), chapter 6.

[44]Cynthia E. Orozco, "Alonso S. Perales," *New Handbook of Texas* (hereafter *NHOT*) eds. Ronnie C. Tyler, Douglas E. Barnett, and Roy R. Barkley 5 (Austin: Texas State Historical Association, 1996): 148-149.

[45]"Name of Scholarship Leads to Controversy," *San Antonio Express News,* September 17, 1994, SAPL, Texana Room, Vertical Files, Organizations.

[46]Guy H. Lawrence, "LULAC co-founder Alonso Perales honored," *Corpus Christi Caller,* February 16, 1999, CO.

[47]Araceli Pérez Davis, "Marta Pérez de Perales," *El Mesteño* 4: 37 (October 2000): 16.

[48]Josh Gottheimer, *Ripples of Hope: Great American Civil Right Speeches* (New York: Basic Civitas Books, 2003); George A. Martinez, "Alonso S. Perales and the Effort to Establish the Civil Rights of Mexican Americans as Seen through the Lens of Contemporary Critical Legal Theory: Post-racialism, Reality Construction, Interest Convergence, and Other Critical Themes," *In Defense,* 119-150.

[49]Martinez.

[50]See https://www.txhistoricalmarker.com/text?page=15&text=newspapers

[51]Mario T. García, *Católicos: Resistance and Affirmation in Chicano Catholic History* (Austin: University of Texas Press, 2014).

[52]Cynthia E. Orozco, "Alonso S. Perales and His Struggle for the Civil Rights of La Raza through the League of United Latin American Citizens (LULAC) in Texas in the 1930s: Incansable Soldado del Civismo Pro-Raza," *In Defense,* 3-28.

[53]Letter from Mario T. García to Marta Pérez Perales, May 5, 1982, AP, Box 10, Folder 2.

[54]Letter to Mrs. Alonso S. Perales from José E. Limón, August 29, 1972, AP, Box 10, Folder 3.

[55]Letter to Mr. Manuel Bernal from Lester L. Klein, no month, 23, 1970, AP, Box 10, Folder 3.

[56]Letter to Dear Mrs. Perales from Donna R. Tobias, May 1, 1979, AP, Box 10, Folder 3.

[57]Letter to Marta Pérez Perales from Elvira Chavaria, May 26, 1981, AP, Box 10, Folder 1.

[58]Letter to Sra. Marta Pérez de Perales from Margo Gutiérrez, October 25, 1988, AP, Box 10, Folder 5.

[59]Email to Cynthia E. Orozco from Margo Gutiérrez, May 14, 2001 and June 11, 2001, CO. She sent this email to numerous scholars.

[60]García, *Rise,* 169. Shortly after, the Church appropriated the paper, made it anti-communist, and published in English.

[61]*In Defense of My People.*

[62]Martinez, *In Defense,* 135.

[63]Cynthia E. Orozco, "Gustavo C. García," 3 *NHOT:* 84.

[64]Brandon H. Mila, "Hermanos de Raza: Alonso S. Perales and the Creation of the LULAC Spirit," master's thesis, University of North Texas, 2013.

[65]Richard A. Garcia, "Alonso S. Perales, the Voice and Visions of a Citizen Intellectual," *Leaders of the Mexican American Generation, Biographical Essays,* ed. Anthony Quiroz (Boulder: University of Colorado, 2015), 85.

[66]Emilio Zamora, "Connecting Causes, Alonso S. Perales, Hemispheric Unity, and Mexican Rights in the United States," *In Defense,* 293.

[67]Three major publications did not mention him. See Char Miller, *San Antonio, a Tricentennial History* (Austin: Texas State Historical Association, 2018); *300 Years of San Antonio and Bexar County,* ed. Claudia R. Guerra and Char Miller, (San Antonio: Hamilton Books, Trinity University Press, 2018); and *San Antonio: Our Story of 150 Years in the Alamo City* (San Antonio: Staff of the San Antonio Express-News, 2015). I presented on Perales at the 50th anniversary conference of the 1968 US Civil Rights Commission hearings on Mexican Americans in San Antonio in November 2018.

[68]No author, "The Laredo Trio," *Lulac News,* August 1931, n.p., Dolph Briscoe Center for American History, University of Texas at Austin.

[69]Carlos Basañez Rocha, "Falsos Apostóles y Malos Políticos," *México en el Valle,* September 19, 1927, Cynthia E. Orozco Notes of Alonso S. Perales Papers (hereafter ON), 1979, CO, 95.

[70]Carlos Kevin Blanton, *George I. Sánchez, The Long Struggle for Integration* (New Haven: Yale University Press, 2015), 154.

[71]No author, Poster, "For Sale, A Goat of the Sharyland Breed" signed The Association of Goat Raisers, ca. 1954, Carlos E. Castañeda Papers, BLAC, Box 34, Folder 3.

[72]"Ya Llego el Circo Perales," AP, Box 14 oversized. See also "Catecismo del Condado de Hidalgo," another pro-RalphYarborough and anti-Allen Shivers flyer.

[73]Flyer, "The Circus Perales of San Antonio, Texas has already arrived," August 24, 1954, AP, Box 1, Folder 10.

[74]"A Letter from Mrs. Marta Pérez Perales," 1977 (letter written for Adela Sloss-Vento book), AP, Box 10, Folder 6.

[75]Letter to Lawrence W. Cramer from Maury Maverick, June 10, 1942, Federal Employment Practices Commission (FEPC), Library of Congress, Washington, DC, Box 339, Legal Division, Southwest-Mexicans, Folder: Southwest Hearing-Background Material.

[76]José Angel Gutiérrez, "Chicanos and Mexicans under Surveillance: 1940-1980," *Renato Rosaldo Lecture Series Monograph* 2 (Tucson: Mexican American Studies & Research Center, Spring 1986) Series 1984-85, 29-58.

[77]Email to Cynthia E. Orozco from Marta Carmen Perales Carrizales, November 20, 2018.

[78]José E. Limón, "Transnational Triangulation: Mexico, the United States, and the Emergence of a Mexican American Middle Class," in *Mexico and Mexicans in the Making of the United States,* ed. John Tutino (Austin: University of Texas, 2012). Limón incorrectly dated this Texas middle class as a post-World War II phenomena.

[79]Cynthia E. Orozco, "Alice Dickerson Montemayor: Feminism and Mexican American Politics in Texas in the 1930s," *Writing the Range: Race, Class, and Culture the in the American Women's West,* ed. Elizabeth Jameson and Susan Armitage (Norman: University of Oklahoma Press, 1997): 435-456. On Ladies LULAC see Cynthia E. Orozco, "Ladies LULAC," 3 *NHOT:* 1-2 and "League of

United Latin American Citizens" *Latinas in the United States,* 378-380.

[80]Michael Omi and Howard Winant, *Racial Formation in the United States: From the 1960s to the 1980s* (New York: Routledge and Kegan Paul, 1987).

[81]Ibid, 64.

[82]See Juan Gómez-Quiñones, *Chicano Politics, Promise, and Reality, 1940-1980* (Albuquerque: University of New Mexico Press, 1990).

[83]Historian J. Gilberto Quezada from Laredo commented that the term "Mexican American" was rarely used in Laredo in the 1940s or 50s; he encountered the term for the first time at a university in San Antonio in 1967. Email from J. Gilberto Quezada to Cynthia E. Orozco, January 5, 2018.

[84]Félix Padilla, *Latino Ethnic Consciousness, The Case of Mexican Americans and Puerto Ricans in Chicago* (Notre Dame: University of Notre Dame Press, 1985), 4-5.

[85]*Testimonio: A Documentary History of the Mexican American Struggle for Civil Rights,* ed. F. Arturo Rosales (Houston: Arte Público Press, 2000), 106.

[86]"Relaciones entre Mexicanos, México-Texanos y Americanos," ca. 1930, Manuel Gamio Papers (hereafter MG), Bancroft Library, University of California at Berkeley. Original text: "El méxico-texano, que tiene sangre mexicana y sentimientos americanos, es en mi concepto un producto híbrido; ama a los Estados Unidos, pero más especialmente a Texas, porque nació aquí, rinde culto a la bandera americana porque se lo enseñaron en la escuela, se siente parte integrante de este gran pueblo y por lo tanto, se cree superior a hombres de su misma raza que vienen de México."

[87]Sánchez, 97.

[88]Ibid. See Paul S. Taylor, *An American-Mexican Frontier: Nueces County, Texas* (Chapel Hill: University of North Carolina Press, 1934), 241.

[89]Limón. 90. Original text: "Con profunda peña hemos visto a maestros mexicanos enseñando inglés a niños de su raza, sin tomar para nada en cuenta el idioma materno que cada día se va olvidando más y cada día van sufriendo adulteraciones y cambios que hieren mate-

rialmente al oído de cualquier mexicano por poco versado que esté en el idioma de Cervantes. Si en la escuela americana a la que concurren nuestros niños se les enseña la Biografía de Washington y no la de Hidalgo y en vez de hechos gloriosos de Juárez se le refieren las hazañas de Lincoln, por más que éstas sean nobles y justas, no conocerá ese niño las glorias de su Patria, no la amará y hasta verá con indiferencia a los coterráneos de sus padres."

[90]William John Knox, "The Economic Status of Mexican Immigrants in San Antonio, Texas," master's thesis, University of Texas at Austin, 1927, 23-24.

[91]Sister Frances Jerome Woods, "Mexican Ethnic Leadership in San Antonio, Texas," Ph.D. diss., Washington, DC: Catholic University, 1949, reprint (New York: Arno Press, 1976) 4-5, 117.

[92]Ibid, 4-5.

[93]Woods, 66.

[94]See Marco Portales, *Crowding Out Latinos, Mexican Americans in Public Consciousness* (Philadelphia: Temple University Press, 2000). Despite Perales' public writings, he is not mentioned in this book.

CHAPTER 1

[1]This chapter is based on Chapter 1, "The Mexican Colony of South Texas" in Cynthia E. Orozco, *No Mexicans, Women or Dogs, The Rise of the Mexican American Civil Rights Movement* (Austin: University of Texas, 2009); Gabriela González, *Redeeming La Raza, Transborder Modernity, Race, Respectability, and Rights* (Oxford: Oxford University, 2018), 6.

[2]See Daniel D. Arreola, *Tejano South Texas: A Mexican American Cultural Province* (Austin: University of Texas, 2001).

[3]David G. Gutiérrez, "Migration, Emergent Ethnicity and the 'Third Space': The Shifting Politics of Nationalism in Greater Mexico," *Journal of American History* 91:3 (September 1999), 906-931.

[4]Richard A. Garcia, *Rise of the Mexican American Middle Class, San Antonio 1929-1941* (College Station: Texas A&M University, 1991), 15.

[5]John A. Booth and David R. Johnson, "Power and Progress in San Antonio Politics, 1836- 1970," *The Politics of San Antonio, Community, Progress, & Power,* ed. David R. Johnson, John A. Booth, and Richard J. Harris (Lincoln: University of Nebraska Press, 1983), 17.

[6]Tucker Gibson, "Mayoralty Politics in San Antonio, 1955-1979," *The Politics of San Antonio,* 121.

[7]Garcia, *Rise,* 318.

[8]F. Arturo Rosales' book manuscript on Perales (2017), chapters 1 and 7.

[9]Rosales book manuscript, (2017) chapters 2, 20. Dr. Raymond Johnson, the first African American to get a Ph.D. from Rice University in Houston, attended this school.

[10]Nicholas Villanueva Jr., *The Lynching of Mexicans in the Texas Borderlands* (Albuquerque: University of New Mexico, 2017), 169.

[11]Juanita Luna-Lawhn, "The Mexican Revolution and the Women of El México de Afuera, the Pan American Round Table, and the Cruz Azul Mexicana," *War Along the Border, the Mexican Revolution and Tejano Communities,* ed. Arnoldo De León (College Station: Texas A&M University, 2012), 156-175.

[12]See Nancy A. Aguirre and Elise Urrutia, "A Place in Exile," *300 Years of San Antonio & Bexar County,* ed. Claudia R. Guerra and Char Miller (San Antonio: Maverick Books, Trinity University Press, 2018).

[13]Ralph Edward Morales III, "Hijos de la Gran Guerra: The Creation of the Mexican American Identity in Texas, 1836-1929," Ph.D. diss., Texas A&M University, College Station, 2015, 163.

[14]Garcia, *Rise,* 245.

[15]Alonso S. Perales, "'Nuestra Evolución General," in Alonso S. Perales, "El México Americano y la Política del Sur de Texas," 13, Benson Latin American Collection (hereafter BLAC), University of Texas at Austin.

[16]"Carta al Sra. Alberta Besch," in Alonso S. Perales, *En Defensa de Mi Raza* 2 (San Antonio: Artes Gráficas, 1937), 97. Original text: "La actual colonia Mexicana de San Antonio es más progresista que la colonia Mexicana hace veinte años."

[17]Villanueva, 167.

[18]Robin Doak, *Struggling to Become American, 1899-1940* (New York: Infobase Publishing, 2007), 94.

[19]Mark Reisler, *By the Sweat of Their Brow, Mexican Labor 1900-1940* (Westport, Conn.: Greenwood Press, 1976):143; Arnoldo De León, *They Call Them Greasers: Anglo Attitudes toward Mexicans in Texas, 1821-1900.* (Austin: University of Texas, 1983): 105.

[20]Richard A. Garcia, "Alonso S. Perales: The Voice and Visions of a Citizen Intellectual," *Leaders of the Mexican American Generation, Biographical Essays,* ed. Anthony Quiroz (Denver: University of Colorado, 2015), 91.

[21]Michael A. Olivas, "The Legal Career of Alonso S. Perales," *In Defense,* 317; William D. Carrigan and Clive Webb, *Forgotten Dead: Mob Violence Against Mexicans in the United States, 1848-1928* (Oxford: Oxford University Press, 2013), 35-62.

[22]Perales, *En Defensa* 1 (San Antonio: Artes Gráficas, 1936), 6-7.

[23]Interview with Mr. Gonzáles, September 1967, Transcription Notes, Vertical file, "Mexican, Associations," Institute of Texan Cultures, University of Texas at San Antonio.

[24]In Re: Sgt. Macario García by John J. Herrera, ca. Sept. 1945, Alonso S. Perales Papers (hereafter AP), M.D. Anderson Library, University of Houston, Box 5, Folder 49.

[25]Malcolm Ross, "Our Personal Relations with Mexicans," Alonso S. Perales, *Are We Good Neighbors?* (New York: Arno Press, 1974, reprint), 70.

[26]"Protesta Contra La Segregación de Nuestra Raza en New Braunfels," in Perales, *En Defensa de Mi Raza* 2 (San Antonio: Artes Gráficas, 1937), 97.

[27]Notes on *The Argus,* Mid-April, No. 1927, Transcript of John Box immigration files, 91, Oliver Douglas Weeks Papers (hereafter ODW), BLAC.

[28]H.T. Manuel, *The Education of Mexican and Spanish-Speaking Children in Texas* (Austin: Fund for Research in the Social Sciences, 1930), 61-2.

[29]"Varios Clubs Discuten el Asunto de las Chozas y Tejabanes en San Antonio," in Perales, *En Defensa* 2: 50-51. Original text: "la tendencia general de nuestros conciudadanos angloamericanos es edu-

car a la niñez Mexicana en chozas y jacales mientras que para los
niños angloamericanos construyen magníficos edificios de ladrillo;
hay varias poblaciones en Texas donde nuestra niñez Mexicana no
puede asistir a la escuela superior porque las autoridades escolares
no se los permite."

[30]Leigh Ann Wilson, "Fighting two 'devils': Eleuterio Escobar and
the School Improvement League's Battle for Mexican and Mexican
American Students' Educational Equality in the San Antonio, Texas
Public Schools from 1934 to 1958," Ph.D. diss., University of Memphis, 2011, 7.

[31]Neil Foley, *Quest for Equality: The Failed Promise of Black-Brown
Solidarity* (Boston: Harvard University Press, 2010), 117.

[32]Ruth L. Martínez, "The Unusual Mexican: A Study in Acculturation," master's thesis, Claremont College, 1942.

[33]Philis Barragan Goetz, *Reading, Writing, and Revolution, Escuelitas and the Emergence of a Mexican American Identity in Texas*
(Austin: University of Texas, 2020).

[34]Response of LULAC Councils to questionnaire, Oliver Douglas
Weeks Papers, Box 1, Folder 8, BLAC.

[35]Perales, "El México Americano y La Política del Sur de Texas," 6.

[36]Jovita González, "Social Life in Cameron, Starr, and Zapata Counties," master's thesis, University of Texas at Austin, 1930, 93-4.

[37]"Letter to White Man's Union Association of Wharton County,"
July 5, 1937, in Perales, *En Defensa de Mi Raza* 2, 94; Laura Cannon Dixon, "Police Brutality Makes Headlines: Retelling the Story
of the 1938 Pecan Shellers' Strike," master's thesis, Indiana State
University, 2010, 16.

[38]"Ejemplo de la Boleta Apoyada Por la Asociación de Votantes Independientes," Eleuterio Escobar Papers, BLAC, Box 2, Folder 1;
Cynthia A. Morales, "A Survey of Leadership, Activism and Community Involvement of Mexican American Women in San Antonio,"
Journal of South Texas, 13:2 (Fall 2000) 199; Email from Martha
Lopez to Cynthia E. Orozco, February 4, 2018. Lopez is her granddaughter.

[39]"Presidents of Local Councils," ca. mid-1930s, AP, Box 3, Folder
37.

[40]*1929 Texas Agricultural and State Industrial Guide,* 262-89; *Members of the Texas Legislature, 1846-1962* (Austin: Texas Legislature, 1962), Dolph Briscoe Center for American History, University of Texas at Austin.

[41]José Angel Gutiérrez, *Albert A. Peña Jr., Dean of Chicano Politics* (East Lansing: Michigan State University, 2017), 48-49.

[42]García, 315.

[43]Gutiérrez, 254. See Gutiérrez's "Note on County Government" for details of San Antonio Latino electoral empowerment over the decades.

CHAPTER 2

[1]Birth certificate, Alonso S. Perales Papers (hereafter AP), M.D. Anderson Library, University of Houston, Box 1, Folder 1.

[2]F. Arturo Rosales book manuscript on Perales (2017), chapter 2, 4-5.

[3]Letter to Mrs. Ben Garza from Alonso S. Perales, July 30, 1937, AP, Box 4, Folder 18.

[4]Email to Cynthia E. Orozco from Marta Carmen Perales Carrizales, November 19, 2018.

[5]Ibid.

[6]Rosales book manuscript, chapters 2 and 11. The information about tamale sales came from Rosales' interview with Marta Perales Carrizales, January 14, 2012.

[7]"An Interview with Mrs. Perales," *Chicano Times*, Feb. 14 thru Feb. 28, 1975, 9, AP, Box 14 oversized.

[8]*The World War I Diary of José de la Luz Sáenz,* edited and with an Introduction by Emilio Zamora, Translated by Emilio Zamora with Ben Maya (College Station: Texas A&M University Press, 2014), 298.

[9]Jesse Nazario, "Fortino Treviño," https://tshaonline.org/handbook/online/articles/ftr43Accessed July 15, 2019.

[10]*The World War I Diary,* 298.

[11]Ibid.

[12]Gilberto M. Hinojosa, "Alonso S. Perales," May 5, 1970, Opinion: IMAGE Documentary, Chan (channel?) 12, 11:30 am, AP, Box 10, Folder 10.

[13]Email to Cynthia E. Orozco from Marta Carmen Perales Carrizales, November 19, 2018.

[14]Rosales book manuscript, (2017) chapter 2, 12-13.

[15]Ibid.

[16]Rosales book manuscript, (2017) chapter 1, 18. Nicolasa Perales' 1919 death certificate named the Salazar mortuary. Rosales located and identified this item.

[17]Emilio Zamora, "José de la Luz Sáenz: Experiences and Autobiographical Consciousness," *Leaders of the Mexican American Generation, Biographical Essays*" ed. Anthony Quiroz (Boulder: University Press of Colorado, 2015): 31-33.

[18]Zamora, 31-33.

[19]Quoted in Adela Sloss-Vento, *Alonso S. Perales, His Struggle for the Rights of Mexican Americans* (San Antonio: Artes Gráficas, 1977), 9; Lupe S. Salinas, "Legally White, Socially Brown: Alonso S. Perales and His Crusade for Justice for La Raza," *In Defense of My People, Alonso S. Perales and the Development of Mexican-American Public Intellectuals,* ed. Michael A. Olivas (Houston: Arte Público Press, 2012), 78. My *Handbook* article noted he graduated in 1918 from high school but was incorrect. Orozco, "Alonso S. Perales," *New Handbook of Texas* (hereafter NHOT), ed. Ronnie C. Tyler, Douglas E. Barnett, and Roy R. Barkley 5 (Austin: Texas State Historical Association, 1996):148-149.

[20]"An Interview with Mrs. Perales."

[21]*The World War I Diary*, 2.

[22]Zamora, "José de la Luz Sáenz: Experiences," 31.

[23]Rosales, Perales book manuscript, (2017) chapters 2 and 6, 13.

[24]Ibid, 32.

[25]Ibid.

[26]Alicia Salinas, "Alice, Texas," https://tshaonline.org/handbook/online/articles/hea01 Accessed May 22, 2018.

[27]Agnes G. Grimm, "Eulalio Velásquez," https://tshaonline.org/handbook/online/articles/fve04Accessed May 22, 2018.

[28]*The World War I*, ftnt. 7, 478.

[29]Ibid, 13.

[30]Ibid, 19.

[31]Ibid, 70-71.

[32]Ignacio M. García, *White But Not Equal, Mexican Americans, Jury Discrimination, and the Supreme Court* (Tucson: University of Arizona, 2009), 90.

[33]Grimm.

[34]Rosales book manuscript, (2017) chapter 6, 15-16.

[35]Letter to Sr. Lic. Alonso S. Perales from Eulalio Velásquez, October 9, 1937, AP, Box 3, Folder 6.

[36]Agnes G. Grimm, "Pablo Pérez," https://tshaonline.org/handbook/online/ articles/fpe33Accessed on September 22, 2018.

[37]Letter to J. Luz Sáenz from Miss Elena (Zamora?), José de la Luz Sáenz Papers (hereafter JLS), Benson Latin American Collection (hereafter BLAC), University of Texas at Austin, Box 2, Folder 1. She wrote him, "Many years have passed since you've graduated at the Alice Hi [sic] when I taught there."

[38]Cynthia E. Orozco, "María Elena Zamora O'Shea," 4 NHOT: 1176-1177.

[39]Orozco, "O'Shea."

[40]Stationary, Letter from Franco Pérez to Sr. Carlos E. Castañeda, April 30, 1929, Carlos E. Castañeda Papers, BLAC, Box 34, Folder 6.

[41]Letter to Honorable Judge Winchester Kelso from JBA (J.B. Andrews), February 19, 1924, AP, Box 1, Folder 4.

[42]Letter to Eduardo Idar from Alonso S. Perales, November 4, 1927, AP, Box 4, Folder 10; see also Letter to J.T. Canales from Alonso S. Perales, November 2, 1927, AP, Box 4, Folder 10.

[43]National University School of Economics and Government report card, Fall 1929-30, AP, Box 1, Folder 13. He made an 85 with 75 a passing grade.

[44]Rosales book manuscript, (2017) chapter 2, 5. Rosales interviewed nephew Alonso M. Perales, April 28, 2009, and daughter Martha Pérez Carrizales, January 14, 2012.

[45]Daniel D. Arreola, *Tejano South Texas, a Mexican American Cultural Province* (Austin: University of Texas, 2002), 131.

[46]Richard A. Garcia, *Rise of the Mexican American Middle Class, San Antonio, 1929-1941* (College Station: Texas A&M University, 1991), 38.

[47]Ibid, 53.

[48]Ibid, 84.

[49]"Draughon's School of Business," *The Encyclopedia of Arkansas History and Culture* http://www.encyclopediaofarkansas.net/encyclopedia/entry-detail.aspx?entryID=5308 Accessed September 14, 2018.

[50]Letter "To Whom It May Concern" from G.W. Parish, president, Draughon's Practical Business College, April 17, 1918, info on stationary, AP, Box 1, Folder 4.

[51]Brandon H. Mila, "Hermanos de Raza, Alonso S. Perales and the Creation of the LULAC Spirit," master's thesis, University of North Texas, 2013, 11; "School Record of Alonso S. Perales," ca. 1924, AP, Box 1, Folder 26. Filed as "correspondence," this is the best source on Perales' early education.

[52]Letter to Honorable Judge Winchester Kelso from J.B. Andrews, AP, Box 1, Folder 4.

[53]Application for appointment as army field clerk, 1918, AP, Box 1, Folder 8.

[54]Marta Pérez Perales, "Biography of Alonso S. Perales," n.d. (1972?) AP, Box 10, Folder 10. This brief unpublished biography consisting of about four pages was written by Perales' daughter.

[55]Zamora, "José de la Luz Sáenz," 52, ftnt. 19.

[56]"Conferencias Culturales Pro-Raza," Flyer, August 3, 1927, Cynthia E. Orozco Notes of Perales Papers (hereafter ON), 1979, 34. Galvan was one of four men on "El Comité."

[57]Marta Pérez Perales, "Biography."

[58]Letter to "To Whom It May Concern" from G.W. Parish, April 17, 1918, AP, Box 1, Folder 4.

[59]Mila, 11; Letter to Whom It May Concern from A. Wallach, L. Frank Saddlery Co., April 4, 1918, AP, Box 1, Folder 4. The company became the Straus-Frank company in 1920 and after 2004 became a subsidiary of General Parts, Inc. located at 1964 South Alamo Street.

[60]Letter to US Civil Service Letter to US Civil Service Commission from AP, Jan 3, 1923, AP, Box 1, Folder 8.

[61]Letter to Friend Perales from J.B. Andrews, February 19, 1924, AP, Box 1, Folder 4.

[62]Rosales book manuscript, (2017) chapter 2, 25.

[63]Marta Pérez Perales, "Biography," 8.

[64]Rosales book manuscript, (2017) chapter 6, 19.

[65]"El Sr. Alonso S. Perales," *El Latino Americano,* 1918, ON, 1979, 285.

[66]Aaron E. Sánchez, *"Mendigos de nacionalidad:* Mexican-Americanism and Ideologies of Belonging in a New Era of Citizenship, Texas, 1910-1967," *In Defense of My People, Alonso S. Perales and the Development of Mexican-American Public Intellectuals,* ed. Michael A. Olivas (Houston: Arte Público Press, 2012), 97-118.

[67]Alonso S. Perales, "Principios Contraproducentes Para La Americanización en Estados Unidos," *En Defensa de Mi Raza* 1 (San Antonio: Artes Gráficas, 1936), 1-2. See also *La República,* November 16, 1919; *La Época,* November 16, 1919. Original text: "Todas estas injusticias han sido cometidas en personas de carácter irreprochable, tanto de un punto de vista social como intelectual. Cierto es que la distinciones desfavorables a veces suelen ser indispensables debido a las costumbres y conducta de algunas personas, en cuyo caso deberían aplicarse INDIVIDUAL y NO COLECTIVAMENTE, como ha sucedido en muchas ocasiones, basadas en los méritos de una persona e impuestas de acuerdo y no sobre todos los miembros de una raza."

[68]Rosales book manuscript, (2017) chapter 4, 19.

[69]Emory S. Bogardus, *The Essentials of Americanization* (Los Angeles: University of Southern California Press, 1919), 12; *The Ordeal of Assimilation: A Documentary History of the White Working Class,* ed. Stanley Feldstein and Lawrence Costello (Garden City, N.Y.: Anchor Press, 1974), 357-358.

[70]Allen F. Davis, *Spearheads of Reform: The Social Settlements and the Progressive Movement, 1890-1914* (New York: Oxford University Press, 1967); "Mexican Christian Institute," 1, Vertical Files, "Mexican Americans," Dolph Briscoe Center for American History

(hereafter DB), University of Texas at Austin; Colby D. Hall, *Texas Disciples; A Study of the Rise and Progress of that Protestant Movement Known as Disciples of Christ or Christians* (Fort Worth: Texas Christian University Press, 1953), 221; María Cristina García, "Agents of Americanization: Rusk Settlement and the Houston Mexicano Community, 1907-1950," in *Mexican Americans in Texas History* ed. Emilio Zamora, Cynthia E. Orozco, and Rodolfo Rocha (Austin: Texas State Historical Association, 2000), 121-138.

[71]Bogardus, 12, 21; White, 2.

[72]Supplement to the Senate Journal, Regular Session of the 36th Legislature, 1919, 177, (Testimony of Captain Hansen), DB.

[73]William E. Leuchtenberg, *The Perils of Prosperity, 1914-1932* (Chicago: University of Chicago Press, 1958), 45; Simmons, 68. Emphasizing patriotism, the movement also led to the suppression of radicalism. See Emilio Zamora, "Mexican Labor Activity in South Texas, 1900-1920," Ph.D. diss., University of Texas at Austin, 1983, 180; Emilio Zamora Jr. "Chicano Socialist Labor Activity in Texas, 1900-1920," *Aztlán* 6:2 (Summer 1975): 221-36, and Neil Foley, *The White Scourge: Mexicans, Blacks, and Poor Whites in the Texas Cotton Culture* (Berkeley: University of California Press, 1997).

[74]Joe B. Franz, *Texas A Bicentennial History* (New York: W.W. Norton & Company, Inc., 1976), 171; Thomas F. Gosset, *Race, the History of an Idea in America* (Dallas: Southern Methodist University Press, 1963), 371; John J. Mahoney, "Training Teachers for Americanization," *Bulletin* 12 (Washington, DC: Government Printing Office, 1920), 42.

[75]Guadalupe SanMiguel Jr., *'Let Them All Take Heed' Mexican Americans and the Campaign for Educational Equality in Texas, 1910-1981* (Austin: University of Texas at Austin, 1987), 65.

[76]Letter to Hon. Alonso S. Perales from M.C. Gonzales, March 21, 1952, AP, Box 12, Folder 1.

CHAPTER 3

[1]This chapter is based on chapter 2 "Ideological Origins of the Movement" in *No Mexicans, Women or Dogs Allowed: The Rise of the Mexican American Civil Rights Movement* (Austin: University of Texas at Austin, 2009), 50-57. See F. Arturo Rosales, book manuscript on Perales (2017), chapter 4. His chapter was titled "The Great War and Mexican Americanism." The World War I experience of Latinos continues to be overshadowed by World War II and more often than not civil rights development is attributed to the second war though significant developments occurred after World War I. In 2015, for example, scholar Maggie Rivas-Rodríguez stated, "But Mexican civil rights gained momentum after World War II, when returning Mexican-American veterans were determined to challenge the disparities their people faced." Maggie Rivas-Rodríguez, *Texas Mexican Americans & Postwar Civil Rights* (Austin: University of Texas, 2015), 5.

[2]José A. Ramírez, *To the Line of Fire!: Mexican Texans and World War I* (College Station: Texas A&M University, 2009), 22.

[3]Ibid.

[4]Ben Wright, "War Time, A Century Later, the Shadow of World War I Still Looms on Campus," *Alcalde* (March-April 2017), 46-47.

[5]*The World War I Diary of José de la Luz Sáenz,* edited and with an introduction by Emilio Zamora; translated by Emilio Zamora and Ben Maya (College Station: Texas A&M University, 2014), 114.

[6]Laurie E. Jasinski, "San Antonio," https://tshaonline.org/handbook/online/ articles/hds02Accessed May 27, 2018.

[7]Laura Cannon Dixon, "Police Brutality Makes Headlines Retelling the Story of the 1938 Pecan Shellers' Strike," master's thesis, Indiana State University, 2010, 6; Katherine Nelson Hall, "San Antonio, Military City," *300 Years of San Antonio & Bexar County,* ed. Claudia R. Guerra and Char Miller (San Antonio: Hamilton Books, Trinity University Press, 2018), 231-239.

[8]See Ralph Edward Morales III, "Hijos de la Gran Guerra: The Creation of the Mexican American Identity in Texas, 1836-1929," Ph.D. diss., Texas A&M University, 2015.

[9]Rosales book manuscript, (2017) chapter 5, 10.

[10]Ramírez, 22.

[11]Ibid, 45.

[12]Letter to US Civil Service commission from Alonso S. Perales, Jan 3, 1923, Alonso S. Perales, (hereafter AP), M.D. Anderson Library, University of Houston, Box 1, Folder 8.

[13]Morales, x.

[14]Ramírez, 33.

[15]Ramírez, 20.

[16]Adela Sloss-Vento, *Alonso S. Perales, His Struggle for the Rights of Mexican Americans* (San Antonio: Artes Gráficas, 1977), 92.

[17]Ramírez, 35.

[18]Ibid, 36.

[19]Ibid, 23.

[20]Ibid, 44.

[21]Ibid, 58.

[22]Ibid, 107.

[23]*The World War I Diary,* 10.

[24]2018 University of Texas at El Paso calendar for month of August 2018, published by the C.L. Sonnichsen Special Collections Department.

[25]Rosales book manuscript, (2017) chapter 4, 11.

[26]Letter to US Civil Service commission from Alonso S. Perales, Jan 3, 1923, AP, Box 1, Folder 8.

[27]Memorandum from Dept. Adjutant to Mr. Alonso Perales, October 17, 1918, AP, Box 1, Folder 7.

[28]Application to Field Clerk, September 19, 1918, AP, Box 6, Folder 4.

[29]Special Orders Note, War Dept. from Secretary of War Peyton C. March, General Chief of Staff, November 29, 1918, AP, Box 1, Folder 8.

[30]Rosales book manuscript, (2017) chapter 1, 10-11; Ancestry.com. U.S., World War I Draft Registration Cards, 1917-1918 [online database]. Provo, Utah: Ancestry.com Operations Inc., 2005. This item was located by F. Arturo Rosales.

[31]Brandon H. Mila, "Hermanos de Raza: Alonso S. Perales and the Spirit of LULAC," University of North Texas, master's thesis, 2013, 11.

[32]Certificate, Honorable discharge, Jan 6, 1920, Headquarters Cavalry Officers' Training School, Camp Stanley, Texas. Perales received a Victory Medal per G.O. 48, W.D. 1919, AP, Box 1, Folder 7.

[33]Bureau of Standards, HND to Alonso Perales, January 2, 1920; Albert Fensch from Ft. Houston Depot to Mr. Brimmer, Jan 6, 1920, AP, Box 1, Folder 4.

[34]Nicholas Villanueva Jr., *The Lynching of Mexicans in the Texas Borderlands* (Albuquerque: University of New Mexico, 2017), 168.

[35]Alonso S. Perales, "Principios Contraproducentes Para la Americanización en Estados Unidos," *En Defensa de Mi Raza* 1 (San Antonio: Artes Gráficas, 1936), 1-2. Original text: "pero el propietario de dicho hotel se rehusó a aceptarlo exponiendo como razón que en su hotel no se admitían mexicanos, fueran or no ciudadanos americanos. Unos cuantos meses después que regresaron de Francia varios méxico-americanos después de haber participado en todos los combates librados por la famosa División 90."

[36]*The World War I Diary,* 113, 404. Other veterans from Alice included Lupe García, Manuel Flores, Florencio Heras, Sixto Flores and Jesús López.

[37]Ramírez, 28.

[38]Cynthia E. Orozco, "Manuel C. Gonzales," *New Handbook of Texas* ed. Ronnie C. Tyler, Douglas E. Barnett, and Roy R. Barkley 3 (Austin: Texas State Historical Association, 1996): 227.

[39]Ramírez, 52.

[40]Perales did not "go East" during World War I as reported by Michael A. Olivas. See *In Defense of La Raza: Alonso S. Perales and the Development of Mexican American Public Intellectuals,* ed. Michael A. Olivas (Houston: Arte Público Press, 2012), xi, 41; Villanueva Jr., 167.

CHAPTER 4

[1]"Para Washington," ___?___ Americano (Alice), 1920, Alonso S. Perales (hereafter AP), M.D. Anderson Library, University of Houston, Box 12, Folder 2.

[2]"$3,000 a Year in Picturesque Santo Domingo," *Getting Ahead*, III: 3, ca. 1923, Cynthia E. Orozco Notes of Alonso Perales Papers, 1979 (hereafter ON), 8.

[3]Enrique S. Puma, "District of Columbia," *Latino America, A State-by-State Encyclopedia*, ed. Mark Overmyer-Velázquez (Westport, Conn.: Greenwood Press, 2008) 2, 157-158. Puma's chronology of Latinos in DC begins in 1800, continues with the first Latino in Congress in 1822 and abruptly skip to the 1960s. More research on this topic is needed.

[4]Letter to US Civil Service Commission from Alonso S. Perales, January 13, 1923, AP, Box 1, Folder 8.

[5]Memorandum to Mr. Alonso Perales from Department Adjutant, October 17, 1918, AP Box 1, Folder 7.

[6]Letter to US Civil Service Commission from Alonso S. Perales, January 13, 1923, AP, Box 1, Folder 8.

[7]Letter to Mr. Alonzo (sic) Perales from John T. Doyle, Sec. US Civil Service Commission, March 3, 1923, AP, Box 1, Folder 8.

[8]"$3,000 a Year in Picturesque Santo Domingo," *Getting Ahead*, 3:3, ON, 160.

[9]See marriage announcement of Alonso S. Perales and Marta Pérez, Hernán Contreras Papers (hereafter HC), Cushing Library, Texas A&M University, College Station, Box 2, Folder 7.

[10]Letter to Hilda and Lola Pérez from Marta Pérez de Perales, August 27, 1926, AP, Box 10, Folder 9. Original text: "Estoy pasando mejor tiempo porque tengo más amigas y Chito tiene más tiempo de llevarme a visitarlas y si él no me lleva, voy yo sola, y así siquiera tengo con quién platicar también una señora joven que está en el teléfono nos ha simpatisado mucho, también me gusta ir abajo a platicar con ella, ella es muy buena nomás ve en el cajón de nosotros que hay cartas para mí y me las manda con los sirvientes . . ."

[11]https://digital.lib.uh.edu/collection/perales/item/4 Notes on the photo cite Washington, DC as the location.

[12]"School Record of Alonso S. Perales," AP, Box 1, Folder 26.

[13] Washington Preparatory School, 1921-1922 catalog, 20, AP, Box 1, Folder 13; Letter to Hugh J. Fegan, Assistant Dean, Georgetown Law School, October 9, 1926, AP, Box 1, Folder 13. The document includes a photo of the 1921 graduating class. See also "School Record of Alonso S. Perales," AP, Box 1, Folder 26.

[14]"S.A. Lawyer is Named to Tacna-Arica Board," *San Antonio Light*, June 28, 1925, AP, Box 12, Folder 2.

[15]"Who's Who in the American Electoral Mission of Nicaragua," 1930, AP, Box 8, Folder 12.

[16]Letter to Honorable Dean, George Washington University Law School from Alonso S. Perales, October 8, 1926, AP, Box 1, Folder 13.

[17]"School Record of Alonso S. Perales," AP, Box 1, Folder 26.

[18]Ibid.

[19]Letter to Alonso S. Perales from H.L. Clamp, September 2, 1925, AP, Box 1, Folder 26.

[20]Photo, Senior Prom, National University Law School, December 4, 1926, AP, Box 14 oversized.

[21]https://en.wikipedia.org/wiki/National_University_School_of_Law Accessed August 26, 2018.

[22]Report Card, Fall 1929-30, National University School of Economics and Government, AP, Box 1, Folder 12.

[23]Certificate, Universidad Nacional de México Cursos de Extensión Universitaria, 1944, AP, Box 14 oversized.

[24]"Spanish Club Observes Makes New Plans and Rules," n.d. (ca. 1920), unidentified newspaper; "Spanish Club Observes Cervantes Day Program," n.d. (ca. 1920), and "Gives Spanish Play," n.d. (ca. 1920), AP, Box 12, Folder 2.

[25]Letter to J.T. Canales from Alonso S. Perales, October 12, 1927, AP, Box 4, Folder 35.

[26]Letter to J.T. Canales from Alonso S. Perales, n.d. (ca. 1929), AP, Box 4, Folder 10.

[27]Alonso S. Perales, "Las Sociedades Como Medio de Progreso," *En Defensa de Mi Raza 2* (San Antonio: Artes Gráficas, 1937), 17. Original text: "Los pueblos que no cuentan con sociedades culturales, comerciales, cívicas, sociales, etc., sino que dependen enteramente del gobierno para su desenvolvimiento, son por lo general los pueblos más retrógrados del mundo."

[28]Marta Pérez Perales, "Biography of Alonso S. Perales," n.d. (ca. 1972), AP, Box 10, Folder 10.

[29]Letter to US Civil Service Commission from Alonso S. Perales, January 3, 1923, with two-page listing of Perales' jobs written by Perales, AP, Box 1, Folder 8.

[30]"Lic. Alonso S. Perales," *Las Noticias*, no date, AP, Box 12, Folder 2.

[31]"De Paseo," *El Fronterizo*, June 23, 1923, AP, Box 12, Folder 2.

[32]"El Señor A.S. Perales También Presentará Su Examen De Leyes," *El Nacional*, June 8, 1924, AP, Box 12, Folder 2.

[33]"Personales," *El Centro del Valle* (Mercedes), April 29, 1924, AP, Box 12, Folder 2.

[34]"Alonso Perales Locating Here," *McAllen Daily Press*, July 8, 1927, AP, Box 12, Folder 2.

[35]"Mis Proyectos Para el Futuro Inmediato," *Diógenes*, July 2, 1927, AP, Box 12, Folder 2.

[36]"Un México-Texano Que Honra a Su Raza," *Diógenes*, October 2, 1926, AP, Box 12, Folder 2. The full subtitle was "Brillante Carrera del Lic. Alonso S. Perales."

[37]Letter to Eduardo Idar from Alonso S. Perales, November 7, 1927, AP, Box 4, Folder 24.

[38]See Joseph L. Locke, "The Heathen at Our Door: Missionaries, Moral Reformers and the Making of the 'Mexican Problem,'" *Western Historical Quarterly 49:2* (Summer 2018): 127-153.

[39]"Americanism and the Americanized Mexican," February 17, 1920, HC, Box 2, Folder 7.

[40]Donna M. Kabalen de Bichara, "Self-Writing and Collective Representation: The Literary Enunciation of Historical Reality and Cultural Values," *In Defense of My People, Alonso S. Perales and the Development of Mexican-American Public Intellectuals*, ed. Michael A. Olivas (Houston: Arte Público Press, 2012), 247.

[41]"Un Americano Sale a la Defensa de los Mexicanos," *El Imparcial de Texas*, 1921, ON, 6. Original text: "hace que los mexicanos y todos los que amamos a México, le estemos agradecidos."

[42]Lupe S. Salinas, "Legally White, Socially Brown: Alonso S. Perales and His Crusade for Justice for La Raza," *In Defense*, 87.

[43]Benjamín Marquez, "In Defense of My People: Alonso S. Perales and the Moral Construction of Citizenship," *In Defense*, 36.

[44]Emilio Zamora, "Connecting Causes: Alonso S. Perales, Hemispheric Unity, and Mexican Rights in the United States," *In Defense*, 309.

[45]Letter to Col. L.M. Maus from Alonso S. Perales, April 22, 1921, HC, Box 1, Folder 17; Letter to Misses Hilda and Lola Pérez from Marta Pérez de Perales, August 27, 1926, AP, Box 10, Folder 9.

CHAPTER 5

[1]This chapter is based on information from chapter 3 "Rise of a Movement" in Cynthia E. Orozco, *No Mexicans, Women or Dogs Allowed: The Rise of the Mexican American Civil Rights Movement* (Austin: University of Texas Press, 2009), 65-91.

[2]Carlos Morales, KWBU News, "The Long and Forgotten History of Texas' Mutualistas," December 30, 2016, *https://www.houstonpublicmedia.org/ articles/news/2016/12/30/182220/the-long-and-forgotten-history-of-texas-mutualistas/* Accessed July 5, 2019.

[3]"La Sociedad 'Hijos de América,'" *La Prensa*, November 7, 1921, 1; "Constitution and By-Laws of Order Sons of America Council No.1, San Antonio, Texas," (San Antonio: OSA, June 15, 1922), 45, José Limón Papers, Long Beach, California.

[4]Cynthia E. Orozco, "Clemente Idar," *New Handbook of Texas* ed. Ronnie C. Tyler, Douglas E. Barnett, and Roy R. Barkley 2 (Austin: Texas State Historical Association, 1996): 813-814.

[5]"Constitución y Leyes de la 'Orden Hijos de América,'" San Antonio, Texas, 1927, Oliver Douglas Weeks Papers (hereafter ODW), Benson Latin American Collection (hereafter BLAC), Box 1, Folder 3.

[6]Araceli Pérez Davis, "Marta Pérez de Perales," *El Mesteño* (Mar. 1999) 4:37, 16.

[7]Arnoldo Vento (?) Translation of Alonso S. Perales, "El Verdadero Origen de La Liga de Ciudadanos Latino Americanos" in Alonso S. Perales, *En Defensa de Mi Raza* 2 (San Antonio: Artes Gráficas, 1937), 101-116, Alonso S. Perales Papers, M.D. Anderson Library, University of Houston (hereafter AP), Box 3, Folder 36.

[8]"Abogarán Por Sus Derechos los México Texanos," unidentified newspaper, 1923, Cynthia E. Orozco Notes of Alonso Perales Papers (hereafter ON), 1979, 9.

[9]"Hoy Hace Un Año," *El Nacional,* July 11, 1924, ON, 14. Ibid. Original text: "Que esos hombres de raza mexicana se marcharon un día a los campos de batalla y expusieron sus vidas en defensa de la bandera de las barras y estrellas y que aquellos hermanos que tuvieron la suerte de regresar con vida se entristecen ahora que ven que la antipatía que les tenían los americanos desde hace casi un siglo continúa y aumenta de día en día pero que ya estaban dispuestos a 'Ser a Ser'."

[10]Letter to Alonso S. Perales from J.T. Canales, November 4, 1925, AP, Box 4, Folder 10.

[11]Petition, December 1, 1925, OSA, Corpus Christi, Paul S. Taylor Papers (hereafter PST), Bancroft Library, University of California, Berkeley, Carton 12, Folder 30.

[12]Articles of Incorporation, Order Knights of America, October 22, 1927, Texas Secretary of State Office. The OKA constitution has not been located. "Objects and Principles," *OKA-NEWS* 1:2 (December 1927), n.p., ODW, Box 1, Folder 2.

[13]Letter to H.M. Johnston (Sec. San Angelo LULAC #27), May 31, 1932, José Tomás Canales Estate Papers, James Jernigan Library, Texas A&M University, Kingsville, Box 436B, Folder: LULAC, May 1932.

[14]Form Letter to Sr. Don ____ from Alonso S. Perales, no month, 1924, AP, Box 3, Folder 38.

[15]"Éxito de una conferencia en Kingsville," July 22, 1924, ON, 22.

[16]Donna M. Kabalen de Bichara, "Self-Writing and Collective Representation: The Literary Enunciation of Historical Reality and Cultural Values," *In Defense of My People, Alonso S. Perales and the Development of Mexican American Public Intellectuals,* ed. Michael A. Olivas (Houston: Arte Público Press, 2012): 252; Adela

Sloss-Vento, *Alonso S. Perales, His Struggle for the Rights of Mexican-Americans* (San Antonio: Artes Gráficas, 1977): 7.
[17]Arnoldo Vento (?) Translation of Alonso S. Perales, "El Veradero."
[18]"La Labor que va a Desarrollar el Lic. Perales," *El Fronterizo,* July 2, 1927, ON, 32.

CHAPTER 6

[1]This chapter is based on chapter 5 "The Harlingen Convention of 1927: No Mexicans Allowed," in Cynthia E. Orozco, *No Mexicans, Women or Dogs Allowed: The Rise of the Mexican American Civil Rights Movement* (Austin: University of Texas Press, 2009), 120-150.
[2]"La labor que Va a Desarrollar el Lic. Perales," *El Fronterizo,* July 2, 1927, Cynthia E. Orozco Notes of Alonso S. Perales Papers (hereafter ON), 1979, 32.
[3]Aaron E. Sánchez, *"Mendigos de nacionalidad:* Mexican-Americanism and Ideologies of Belonging in a New Era of Citizenship, Texas 1910-1967," *In Defense of My People, Alonso S. Perales and the Development of Mexican American Public Intellectuals,* ed. Michael A. Olivas (Houston: Arte Público Press, 2012), 101.
[4]"Perales Chairman of Committee," *McAllen Daily Press,* August 19, 1927, ON, 73.
[5]Letter to J.T. Canales from Alonso S. Perales, September 1, 1927, Alonso S. Perales Papers (hereafter AP), M.D. Anderson Library, University of Houston, Box 4, Folder 10.
[6]Brandon H. Mila, "Hermanos de Raza: Alonso S. Perales and the Creation of the LULAC Spirit," master's thesis, University of North Texas, 2013, 26.
[7]F. Arturo Rosales book manuscript on Perales (2017), chap. 3, 14.
[8]Richard A. Garcia, *The Rise of the Mexican American Middle Class in San Antonio 1929-1941* (College Station: Texas A&M University, 1991), 259.
[9]Copies of letters to Mauro Machado, Rubén Lozano and Clemente Idar from Alonso S. Perales, September 10, 1927, ON, 89, 91, 92.
[10]Mila, 32. Perales' essay was "Insidiosos Ataques," *Las Noticias,* October 10, 1927.

CHAPTER 7

[1]This chapter is based on chapter 6 "LULAC's Founding" in Cynthia E. Orozco, *No Mexicans, Women or Dogs Allowed: The Rise of the Mexican American Civil Rights Movement* (Austin: University of Texas Press, 2009), 153-157.

[2]Letter to James T. Tafolla Sr. from Alonso S. Perales, August 26, 1927, Alonso S. Perales (hereafter AP), M.D. Anderson Library, University of Houston, Box 4, Folder 35.

[3]Letter to J.T. Canales from Alonso S. Perales, October 31, 1927, AP, Box 4, Folder 10.

[4]Letter to Adela Sloss-Vento from Alonso S. Perales, November 7, 1927, Adela Sloss-Vento Papers (hereafter ASV), Austin, Texas.

[5]Program, League of Latin American Citizens of the Valley, October 19, 1927, AP, Box 3, Folder 36.

[6]Letter to J.T. Canales from Alonso S. Perales, October 31, 1927, AP, Box 4, Folder 10; Brandon H. Mila, "Hermanos de Raza: Alonso S. Perales and the Creation of the LULAC Spirit," master's thesis, University of North Texas, 2013, 46-49.

[7]"Suggestions made by Alonso S. Perales," Andres De Luna, Sr. Papers (hereafter ADL), Benson Latin American Collection (hereafter BLAC), University of Texas at Austin, Box 1, Folder 3.

[8]"Suggestions made by Alonso S. Perales."

[9]Letter to Alonso S. Perales from Ben Garza, September 24, 1927, AP, Box 4, Folder 18.

[10]Letter to J.T. Canales from Alonso S. Perales, October 31, 1927, AP, Box 4, Folder 10.

[11]Letter to Eduardo Idar from Alonso S. Perales, November 2, 1927, AP, Box 4, Folder 24 and 35.

[12]Letter to Eduardo Idar from Alonso S. Perales, November 4, 1927, AP, Box 4, Folder 24.

[13]Letter to Alonso S. Perales from J.T. Canales, November 9, 1927, AP, Box 4, Folder 10 and 35.

[14]Mila, 50-51.

[15]"Constitución y Leyes de la 'Liga de Ciudadanos Americanos de Origen Latino,'" AP, Box 3, Folder 35.

[16]Letter to J.T. Canales from Alonso S. Perales, November 2, 1927, AP, Box 4, Folder 10.

[17]Letter to J.T. Canales, Alonso S. Perales, Santiago Tafolla, and Bernardo de la Garza from Eduardo Idar, November 19, 1927, AP, Box 4, Folder 24.

[18]"Constitución y Leyes," AP, Box 3, Folder 5.

[19]1. Desarrollar dentro de los miembros de nuestra raza, el mejor, más puro y perfecto tipo de un verdadero y leal ciudadano de los Estados Unidos de América.

2. Destruir de raíz de nuestro cuerpo político todos los intentos y tendencias a establecer distinciones entre nuestros ciudadanos y compañeros a causa de raza, religión o posición social, como contrario al verdadero espíritu de la Democracia y que repugnan con nuestra Constitución y Leyes.

3. Usar todos los medios legales a nuestra mano, para lograr que todos los ciudadanos en nuestro país disfruten de iguales derechos; que les sea extendida la igual protección de las leyes de este país y se les concedan iguales oportunidades y privilegios.

4. La adquisición del idioma inglés, que es el idioma oficial en nuestro país, es necesario para disfrutar de todos nuestros derechos y privilegios, por lo que declararamos que sea el idioma oficial de esta organización y protestamos, por lo mismo, aprenderlo, hablarlo y enseñarlo a nuestros hijos.

5. Declararnos solemnemente de una vez para siempre, mantener un culto respetuoso y sincero por nuestro origen racial, y nos enorgullecemos de ello.

6. Cada uno de nosotros se considera con responsabilidad igual en nuestra Institución, a la que voluntariamente juramos subordinación y obediencia.

7. La Liga de Ciudadanos Americanos de Origen Latino no es un club político; pero, como ciudadanos conscientes, participaremos en las contiendas de política local, del Estado y de la Nación, bajo un punto de vista de interés colectivo, desatendiéndonos y abjurando de una vez para todas, cualquier compromiso de carácter personal que no esté en armonía con estos principios.

8. Ayudaremos con nuestros votos e influencia al encumbramiento político de individuos que con hechos demuestren respeto y consideración para los nuestros.

9. Encumbraremos como líderes nuestros a aquellos que entre nosotros por su integridad y cultura muestran ser capaces de orientarnos y dirigirnos rectamente.

10. Mantendremos medios de publicidad para difundir estos principios, extender las ramificaciones de nuestra organización y consolidarla.

11. Nos opondremos a toda manifestación radical, violenta que tienda a crear conflictos y violar la paz y tranquilidad del país.

12. Estimularemos la creación de instituciones educativas para ciudadanos Americanos de origen latino, y prestaremos nuestro apoyo a las ya existentes.

[20]Letter to Alonso S. Perales from J.T. Canales, February 15, 1928, AP, Box 4, Folder 10.

[21]Questionnaire, League of Latin American Citizens, ca. 1928, AP, Box 3, Folder 35.

[22]"Constitución y leyes," AP, Box 3, Folder 35.

[23]Letter to Alonso S. Perales from J.T. Canales, February 15, 1928, AP, Box 4, Folder 10.

[24]Manual for Use by The League of United Latin American Citizens, ca. 1928, Oliver Douglas Weeks Papers (hereafter ODW), BLAC, Box 1, Folder 3.

[25]Alonso S. Perales, *En Defensa de Mi Raza* 2 (San Antonio: Artes Gráficas, 1937), 101.

[26]No title, *Valley Review*, April 2, 1931, AP, Box 9, Folder 37.

[27]Mila, 46.

[28]Ibid, 43.

[29]"Minutes of the First Meeting of the League of Latin-American Citizens," August 29, 1927, AP, Box 3, Folder 42; see also Box 3, Folder 36; Liga de Ciudadanos Americanos de Origen Latino agenda, n.d. (ca. 1927), AP, Box 3, Folder 35.

[30]"Program for Meeting of League of Latin-American Citizens to be held October 23, 1927," AP, Box 3, Folder 37.

[31]Mila, 44.

[32]Letter to J.T. Canales from Alonso S. Perales, December 21, 1927, AP, Box 4, Folder 10.

[33]Letter to Alonso S. Perales from Ben Garza, October 27, 1927, AP, Box 4, Folder 18.

[34]Letter to J.T. Canales from Alonso S. Perales, January 2, 1928, AP, Box 4, Folder 10.

[35]Letter to Mr. Ben Garza from Alonso S. Perales, June 22, 1928, ADL, Box 1, Folder 3.

[36]Letter to Eduardo Idar from Alonso S. Perales, November 4, 1927, AP, Box 4, Folder 24.

[37]Perales, *En Defensa* 2: 101-116.

[38]Letter to Alonso S. Perales from Eduardo Idar, March 20, 1928, ASV.

[39] Perales, *En Defensa* 2: 104.

[40]Letter to J.T. Canales from Alonso S. Perales, October 31, 1927, AP, Box 4, Folder 10.

[41]Perales, *En Defensa* 2: 113; Mila, 81; Edward D. Garza, "League of United Latin-American Citizens," master's thesis, Southwest Texas State Teachers College, 1951, 6. He used the February 17, 1929, minutes.

[42]Arnoldo Vento (?) Translation of Alonso S. Perales, "El Verdadero Origen de la Liga de Ciudadano Latino Americanos," in Alonso S. Perales, *En Defensa de Mi Raza* 2 (San Antonio Arte Gráficas, 1932), 101-116, AP, Box 3, Folder 36," 17.

[43]Perales, *En Defensa* 2: 115.

CHAPTER 8

[1]This chapter is based on Chapter 6 "LULAC's Founding" in Cynthia E. Orozco's *No Mexicans, Women or Dogs Allowed: The Rise of the Mexican American Civil Rights Movement* (Austin: University of Texas, 2009). Historian Brandon H. Mila suggested that my overall interpretation presented Perales as having had a minor role in LULAC's founding. My goal in *No Mexicans, Women or Dogs Allowed, the Rise of the Mexican American Civil Rights Movement* was to show that LULAC evolved from a social movement, not the product of an individual, and credited all founders. It pointed to the

Order Sons of America of San Antonio founded in 1921 before Perales returned to Texas. Yet, Mila emphasized Perales was the true founder of LULAC. See Brandon H. Mila, "Hermanos de Raza: Alonso S. Perales and the Spirit of LULAC," master's thesis, University of North Texas, 2013, 6, 105.

[2]"Program for To-day's (sic) Meeting," n.d., Alonso S. Perales Papers (hereafter AP), M.D. Anderson Library, University of Houston, Box 3, Folder 35.

[3]"Program."

[4]Translation notes of *El Paladín,* February 22, 1929, 4-5, Oliver Douglas Weeks Papers, Benson Latin American Collection (hereafter BLAC), Box 1, Folder 11, University of Texas at Austin.

[5]Oliver Douglas Weeks, "The League of United Latin American Citizens: A Texas-Mexican Civic Organization." *Southwestern Political and Social Science Quarterly* 10:3 (December 1929): 263.

[6]Principles adopted unanimously by the Committee on Feb. 17, 1929, AP, Box 3, Folder 35.

[7]Ibid.

[8]Letter from Alonso S. Perales to Mr. E. Escobar, April 14, 1929, Eleuterio Escobar Jr. Papers, BLAC, Box 1, Folder 13.

CHAPTER 9

[1]This chapter is based on Chapter 6 "LULAC's Founding" in Cynthia E. Orozco, *No Mexicans, Women or Dogs Allowed: The Rise of the Mexican American Civil Rights Movement* (Austin: University of Texas Press, 2019); Letter to J.T. Canales from Carlos E. Castañeda, February 15, 1929, Carlos E. Castañeda Papers (hereafter CC), Box 2, Folder 6, Benson Latin American Collection (hereafter BLAC), University of Texas at Austin.

[2]Local Rules of Order and By-Laws, 1929, Alonso S. Perales Papers (hereafter AP), M.D. Anderson Library, University of Houston, Box 3, Folder 35. This is consistent with "LULAC Milestones," *LULAC News,* February 1940, 16, Alice Dickerson Montemayor Collection (hereafter ADM), BLAC.

[3]J. Gilberto Quezada, "Alonso S. Perales Pioneer Leader of the Mexican American Civil Rights Leader," *Somos Primos,* September 2015, http://www.somosprimos.com/sp2015/spsep15/spsep15.htm Accessed July 1, 2018.

[4]"To the Honorable Supreme Council of the League of United Latin American Citizens," March 5, 1930. (Articles of Impeachment) Paul S. Taylor Collection (hereafter PST), Bancroft Library, University of California at Berkeley, Carton 12, Folder 37.

[5]Letter to Luis Alvarado from J.T. Canales, Sept. 6, 1960, Jose T. Canales Estate Collection (hereafter JTC), Texas A&M University, James Jernigan Library, South Texas Archives, Box 436, Folder 23.

[6]Letter to Luciano Santoscoy from J.T. Canales, September 29, 1953, JTC, Box 436, Folder 23.

[7]Three-page short history of LULAC by J.T. Canales, September 29, 1953, attached to Letter to Luciano Santoscoy, JTC.

[8]"In Our Mailbox," *LULAC News* (April 1954): 2 (Letter from J.T. Canales to Mr. Armendariz), William Flores Papers, BLAC; Draft, United Latin American Citizens constitution, ca. March 1929, Adela Sloss-Vento Papers, (hereafter ASV) Austin, Texas; Letter to Honorable Felix Tijerina from J.T. Canales, October 26, 1957, AP, Box 4, Folder 10; and Letter to Luis Alvarado from J.T. Canales, September 7, 1960, JTC, Box 436, Folder 23.

[9]United Latin American Citizens constitution, ca. February 1929, ASV.

[10]Lupe S. Salinas, "Legally White, Socially Brown: Alonso S. Perales and His Crusade for Justice for La Raza," *In Defense of My People, Alonso S. Perales and the Development of Mexican-American Public Intellectuals,* ed. Michael A. Olivas (Houston: Arte Público Press, 2012), 81.

[11]Constitution, League of United Latin American Citizens (LULAC), 1929, Oliver Douglas Weeks (hereafter ODW), BLAC, Box 1, Folder 4.

[12]Suggestions made by Alonso S. Perales, Andrés De Luna Papers (hereafter ADL), BLAC, Box 1, Folder 3.

[13]Constitution, LULAC, 1929, 7-8.

[14]Ibid, 5.

[15]Oliver Douglas Weeks, "The League of United Latin American Citizens: A Texas-Mexican Civic Organization," *Southwestern Political and Social Science Quarterly* 10:3 (December 1929), 264.

[16]Minutes of founding convention by Andrés De Luna, February 17, 1929, ADL, Box 1, Folder 3; Draft, "Aims and Purposes of This Organization," and Draft, United Latin American Citizens constitution, ca. March 1929, ASV.

[17]Constitution, LULAC, 1929, 8.

[18]Alonso S. Perales, "La Unificación de los México Americanos," September 9, 1929, *La Prensa,* Dolph Briscoe Center for American History, University of Texas at Austin.

[19]See Letter to Alonso S. Perales from J.T. Canales, April 17, 1933. See https://digital.lib.uh.edu/collection/perales/item/57, Accessed June 1, 2019.

[20]Letter to Mr. Luciano Santoscoy from J.T. Canales, September 29, 1953, JTC, Box 436B, Folder: LULAC, 1953-1954.

[21]Manual for use by The League of Latin American Citizens, ODW, Box 1, Folder 3; "LULAC Milestones," *LULAC News,* February 1940, 16, JTC, Box 436, Folder 23; Richard A. Garcia, *Rise of the Mexican American Middle Class in San Antonio, 1929-1941* (College Station: Texas A&M University, 1991), 273.

[22]Gabriela González, *Redeeming La Raza, Transborder Modernity, Race, Respectability, and Rights* (Oxford: Oxford University Press, 2018), 171.

CHAPTER 10

[1]"The Convention of the L. of U.L.A.C. Which Met in McAllen Sunday was Great Success," *El Paladín,* June 28, 1929, Translation, Oliver Douglas Weeks Paper (hereafter ODW), Benson Latin American Collection (hereafter BLAC), University of Texas at Austin, Box 1, Folder 10; Oliver Douglas Weeks, "The League of United Latin American Citizens: A Texas-Mexican Civic Organization." *Southwestern Political and Social Science Quarterly* 10:3 (December 1929), 267.

[2]*El Paladín,* November 1, 1929; November 22, 1929; November 29, 1929; December 13, 1929; January 3, 1930, ODW, Box 1, Folder 10.

³Weeks, 270.

⁴Paul S. Taylor, *An American-Mexican Frontier: Nueces County, Texas* (Chapel Hill: University of North Carolina Press, 1934), 315.

⁵Cástulo Gutiérrez, "Para los que no conocen nuestra institución," (LULAC Council 16 section), *El Popular,* (Del Rio) ca. 1930, Ben Garza Papers, Box 1, Folder 2, BLAC. Original text: "No son los fines de esta Liga americanizar a los mexicanos, ni mucho menos para relegar al olvido el idioma español, como maliciosamente se propia. Porque los méxico-americanos, mientras no nos elevemos al nivel de ciudadanos, no seremos más que conquistados." He added, "Pero cuando que estos mismos, una vez teniendo hijos aquí les eviten tomar parte en la maquinaria política de esta tierra, creyendo que pueden incorporarlos en cuerpo y alma la patria mexicana."

⁶Ibid, Original text: "Podrán y es muy precioso incorporar su alma y espíritu en las cosas mexicanas, pero su cuerpo no, es imposible prácticamente, sin vivir en México, o mejor dicho, sin dejar de vivir en Estados Unidos."

⁷Ibid, Original text: "Sino toda la familia mexicana, aún hasta la de México."

⁸Ibid, Original text: "Traerán también beneficios para los ciudadanos mexicanos, quienes son nuestros padres, abuelos y amigos."

⁹Taylor, 271.

¹⁰Alonso S. Perales, "La Unificación de los México-Americanos," *La Prensa,* September 6, 1929, 9, Dolph Briscoe Center for American History (hereafter DB), University of Texas at Austin.

¹¹Letter from Andrés De Luna to Carlos Castañeda, April 13, 1929, Carlos Eduardo Castañeda Papers (hereafter CC), BLAC.

¹²Weeks, 264.

¹³Letterhead, Letter to "To Whom It May Concern" from J.T. Canales, December 30, 1932, Alonso S. Perales Papers (hereafter AP), M.D. Anderson Library, University of Houston, Box 3, Folder 36.

¹⁴"Carta Dirigida Por Los Concilios de San Antonio Numeros 16, 12 y 2 de La Liga De Ciudadanos Unidos Latinoamericanos a los Industriales y Hombres de Negocios y Otras Personas de San Antonio, Texas, Solicitando un Jornal Más Alto par los Trabajadores

Mexicanos," Alonso S. Perales, *En Defensa de Mi Raza* 1 (San Antonio: Artes Gráficas, 1936): 66-67.

[15]Cynthia E. Orozco, "Regionalism, Politics, and Gender in Southwestern History: The League of United Latin American Citizens' (LULAC) Expansion into New Mexico from Texas, 1920-1945, *Western Historical Quarterly* 29:4 (1998), 459-483.

[16]Ibid.

[17]Cynthia E. Orozco, "Texas Association of Mexican American Chamber of Commerce," *New Handbook of Texas* (hereafter *NHOT*), ed. Ronnie C. Tyler, Douglas E. Barnett, and Roy R. Barkley 5 (Austin: Texas State Historical Association, 1996), 1975.

[18]Justin Akers Chacón, *Radicals in the Barrio: Magonistas, Socialists, Wobblies, and Communists in the Mexican-American Working Class* (Chicago: Haymarket Books, 2018), 432.

[19]J.T. Canales, Untitled, Resume of proceedings, LULAC, San Diego, Texas, February 16, 1930 conference, Paul S. Taylor Col- lection (hereafter PST), Carton 12, Folder 38, Bancroft Library University of California at Berkeley.

[20]*El Paladín,* May 7, 1931, UCLA Chicano Studies Research Center (hereafter CSRC); *LULAC News,* May 1933, DB.

[21]Letter to J.T. Canales from Alonso S. Perales, May 13, 1932; J. T. Canales, "To Whom This May Concern," May 24, 1932; J.T. Canales, "To Whom This May Concern," December 30, 1932, AP, Box 3, Folder 36.

[22]Benjamín Márquez, *LULAC: The Evolution of a Mexican American Political Organization* (Austin: University of Texas, 1993), 27.

[23]"Presidents of Local Councils," n.d., AP, Box 3, Folder 37.

[24]Richard A. Garcia, *Rise of the Mexican American Middle Class in San Antonio, 1929-1941* (College Station: Texas A&M Press, 1991), 315.

[25]Letter to Alonso S. Perales from J.T. Canales, May 17, 1932, AP, Box 4, Folder 10.

[26]Letter to J.H. Contreras from AP, April 2, 1934, AP, Box 4, Folder 14; see also March 20, 1934 letter, AP, Box 4, Folder 15.

[27]Letter to Mauro Machado from AP, June 2, 1932, AP, Box 4, Folder 29.

[28]*LULAC News,* November 1934, AP, Box 4, Folder 6.

[29]Letter to H.H. Contreras from AP, April 2, 1934, AP, Box 4, Folder 14.

[30]Letter to Alonso S. Perales from J. Luz Sáenz, April 29, 1934, AP, Box 4, Folder 28.

[31]Moisés Sandoval, *Our Legacy: The First Fifty Years* (Washington, DC: LULAC, 1979); "Editorial," *LULAC News,* August 1931, 3, DB.

[32]Letter to AP from J.T. Canales, Aug. 7, 1931, AP, Box 4, Folder 10; "To the Various Councils of the League of United Latin-American Citizens," June 1, 1932, AP, Box 3, Folder 38.

[33]Tomás A. Garza, "The Kingsville Convention," *LULAC News,* August 1931, 4, DB.

[34]Letter to Fernando Ximenez from J.T. Canales, April 3, 1933, AP, Box 4, Folder 11.

[35]Letter to Candelario V. Barrientos from AP, May 31, 1933, AP, Box4, Folder 9. Original text: "En cuanto a la depresión, pues parece que todos estamos siendo víctimas de ella."; "No hemos pagado nuestras cuotas porque no tenemos dinero, pero el pabellón de la LULAC continúa flameando."

[36]Letter to Candelario V. Barrientos from AP, May 31, 1933, AP, Box4, Folder 9.

[37]Letter to M.C. Gonzales from J. Reynolds Flores, President LULAC Council 2, July 11, 1931, José T. Canales Estate Collection(hereafter JTC), James Jernigan Library, Texas A&M University, Kingsville, Correspondence Anglo-Latin Good Relations Committee, Box 436.

[38]Alonso S. Perales, *En Defensa* 2 (San Antonio: Artes Gráficas, 1937), 81.

[39]Letter to Hon. J.T. Canales from M.C. Gonzales, October 26, 1931, JTC, Box 436B, Folder: Correspondence, June-Dec. 1932. This 1931 document is located in the 1932 folder.

[40]Resolution presented by Mr. J.T. Canales to the Supreme Council of the United Latin American Citizens, February 16, 1930, CC, Box 9, Folder 6.

[41]Testimony of J.T. Canales, House, Committee on Immigration, Hearings on Western Hemisphere Immigration, 71st Congress, 173.

[42]Ibid, 180.

[43]Ibid.

[44]Ibid, 180-181.

[45]*Testimonio, A Documentary History of the Mexican American Struggle for Civil Rights,* ed. F. Arturo Rosales (Houston: Arte Público Press, 2000), 91-92. One recent encyclopedic article incorrectly suggested Perales was LULAC president at the time of the 1930 Congressional hearing. See "Alonso S. Perales," *Latinos, Great Lives from History,* ed. Carmen Tafolla and Martha P. Cotera 3 (Ipswich, MA: Salem, 2012), 701-702.

[46]Alonso S. Perales, "Nuestra Próxima Convención y el Porvenir de Nuestra Niñez Escolar," *En Defensa* 1: 84.

[47]"Elogios al Lic. A. Perales por la labor desarrollada en pro de la Raza Mexicana," *La Prensa,* ca. June 1929, Ben Garza Collection (hereafter BG), Box 1, Folder 2, BLAC.

[48]"Ben Garza Goes to Washington to Aid in Fight on Immigration Bills," unidentified newspaper, n.d. (circa June 1930), BG, Box 1, Folder 2.

[49]Garcia, *Rise,* 106.

[50]Letter to Carlos E. Castañeda from JTC, March 21, 1930, CC, Box 9, Folder 6.

[51]See the photo appearing in "Golden Years Appreciation Banquet, A Banquet Honoring Distinguished Mexican-Americans," IMAGE banquet, September 16, 1974, Cynthia E. Orozco Papers, Ruidoso, New Mexico.

[52]Letter to "Mr. President" from Alonso S. Perales, May 4, 1931, AP, Box 3, Folder 40.

[53]Unsigned [J.T. Canales ?], List of "Some of the things Alonso S. Perales has done for the League of United Latin American Citizens," ca. 1931, AP, Box 3, Folder 40.

[54]Letter to "Mr. President."

[55]"Alonso S. Perales, Past National President," https://lulac.org/about/history/past_presidents/alonso_perales/ Accessed August 17, 2019.

[56]Letter to "Mr. President."

[57]Letter to J.T. Canales from AP, ca. 1930, AP, Box 4, Folder 10.

[58]Circular #2, *El Paladín*, April 4, 1930, CSRC.

[59]"Plática sostenida por el Lic. Alonso S. Perales en la transmisión de La Voz de la Raza la noche del 23 de Marzo de 1932," AP, Box 8, Folder 15; see also Box 8, Folder 16.

[60]*LULAC News*, November 1934, Alfred Hernández Papers, Houston Metropolitan Research Library.

[61]Letter to Hon. J.T. Canales from Alonso S. Perales, May 19, 1932, JTC, Box 436B, Folder Correspondence, LULAC, May 1932.

[62]Unsigned [J.T. Canales?], List of "Some of the Things that Alonso S. Perales," ca 1931, AP, Box 3, Folder 40.

[63]"To the Members of the League of United Latin American Citizens," *LULAC News*, December 1932, 6, DB.

[64]Brandon H. Mila, "Hermanos de Raza Alonso S. Perales and the Spirit of LULAC," master's thesis, University of North Texas,2015, 96.

[65]"Documents related to segregation of Mission, Texas Mexican Students," December 30, 1930, AP, Box 3, Folder 40.

[66]F. Arturo Rosales, "Writing a Biography of Alonso Sandoval Perales," *In Defense of My People, Alonso S. Perales and the Development of Mexican-American Public Intellectuals,* ed. Michael A. Olivas (Houston: Arte Público Press, 2012), 279.

[67]Rosales, 278.

[68]Edward D. Garza, "LULAC: League of United Latin-American Citizens," master's thesis, Southwest Texas State Teachers College, 1951, 14-15.

[69]"Arrangements for San Antonio Convention," *LULAC News,* November 1931, 10, DB.

[70]Letter to Fernando Ximenes from Alonso S. Perales, March 10, 1932, AP, Box 4, Folder 36.

[71]Letter to Sir and Brother from Alonso S. Perales, April 27, 1932, JTC, Box 436B, Folder: Correspondence, LULAC, Jan-April 1932.

[72]Ibid.

[73]Letter to Hon. M.C. Gonzales from J.T. Canales, March 2, 1932, JTC, Box 436B, Folder: Correspondence, LULAC, Jan-April 1932.

[74]Letter to J.T. Canales from AP, March 18, 1933, AP, Box 4, Folder 11.

[75]Minutes, Robstown Special Convention, June 1, 1932, AP, Box 3. See Letter to Hon. A. S. Perales from J.T. Canales, June 1, 1932, JTC, Box 436, Folder: Correspondence, LULAC, June-Dec. 1932.

[76]"To the Various Councils of the League of United Latin-American Citizens," June 1, 1932, AP, Box 3, Folder 38.

[77]Letter from A. Perales to J.T. Canales, May 17, 1932, AP, Box 4, Folder 10.

[78]Ibid.

[79]"The Parade of Past Presidents General," *LULAC News,* June 1947: 23, 29, AP, Box 4, Folder 7.

[80]Photo, 1934 Special LULAC convention, San Antonio, AP, Box 14 oversized.

[81]Thomas Kreneck, *Mexican American Odyssey, Félix Tijerina, Entrepreneur and Civic Leader, 1905-1965* (College Station: Texas A&M University, 2001): 67-68.

[82]Letter to John W. Brown, State Health Officer from Alonso S. Perales, November 28, 1936, AP, Box 4, Folder 9.

[83]*LULAC News,* July 1937, n.p., Bonilla-Wilmot Papers, BLAC.

[84]"Program for Activities Recommended by the retiring Pres. General to Local Councils," AP, Box 3, Folder 35.

[85]Resolution introduced by AP, May 16, 1934, AP, Box 3, Folder 42.

[86]"Dr. Berchelmann Report Approved," *San Antonio Express,* February 23, 1939, AP, Box 9, Folder 38.

[87]Ibid.

[88]"The Parade of Past Presidents General," *LULAC News,* June 1947, 23, 29, AP, Box 4, Folder 7.

[89]See Letter to Mauro Machado from Alonso S. Perales, February 28, 1934, CC, Box 33, Folder 11.

[90]Letter to Dr. Carlos E. Castañeda from Alonso S. Perales, April 2, 1934, CC, Box 33, Folder 11.

[91]Kreneck, 67-68.

[92]Letter to John W. Brown, State Health Officer from AP, November 28, 1936, AP, Box 4, Folder 9.

[93]*LULAC News,* July 1937, n. p., LULAC Archive, BLAC.

[94]"Resumen de Resoluciones presentados por el Lic. Alonso S. Perales, Delegado del Concilio Num. 16, de San Antonio, Texas, de la Liga de Ciudadanos Unidos Latinoamericanos, en la Novena Convención Anual de la Liga, verificado en Houston, Texas, los días 5 y 6 de Junio de 1937," Perales, *En Defensa* 2 (1937), 74-75.

[95]Ibid.

[96]Letter to L.A. Woods from Alonso S. Perales, February 18, 1938, AP, Box 4, Folder 36.

[97]Letter to Manuel C. Gonzales from AP, January 30, 1931, Perales, *En Defensa* 2 (1937): 88-89.

[98]Garcia, *Rise,* 287.

[99]Letter to "Dear LULAC Brother" from M.C. Gonzales and Tomás F. Garza, April 14, 1932, AP, Box 4, Folder 20.

[100]Letter to J.T. Canales from Alonso S. Perales, n. d., ca. 1930, AP, Box 4, Folder 10.

[101]Letter to M.C. Gonzales from Juan Solis, May 18, 1931, JTC, Box 436, Folder 20.

[102]Letter to J.T. Canales from Alonso S. Perales, May 17, 1932, JTC, Box 4, Folder 10.

[103]Garcia, *Rise,* 287.

[104]"A Letter to 'San Antonio Council No. 2 of the LULAC' from President General J.T. Canales," n. d., AP, Box 4, Folder 3.

[105]Letter to J.T. Canales from Alonso S. Perales, May 27, 1932, AP, Box 4, Folder 10.

[106]Letter to Alonso S. Perales from J.T. Canales, February 21, 1933, AP, Box 10, Folder 4; Letter to J.T. Canales from AP, May 27, 1932, AP, Box 4, Folder 10.

[107]Transcript, Memorandum: Conditions in San Antonio, Texas, Proposed revisions/corrections by Perales, February 23, 1939, AP, Box 3, Folder 42.

[108]Garcia, *Rise,* 294.

[109]Letter to Antonia Gomez from Alonso S. Perales, January 11, 1933, AP, Box 4, Folder 20. She is one of a few women who wrotePerales.

[110]Letter to Dr. Carlos E. Castañeda from Alonso S. Perales, November 14, 1933, CC, Box 33, Folder 11.

[111]Laura E. Cannon, "Situational Solidarity: LULAC's Civil Rights

Strategy and the Challenge of the Mexican American Worker, 1934-1946," Ph.D. diss., Texas Tech, 2016, Chapter 5, n.p.

[112]Letter to Don Eleuterio Escobar from Alonso S. Perales, November 22, 1932, Eleuterio Escobar Papers (hereafter EE), BLAC. Original text: "El mayor obstáculo parece ser satisfacer las ambiciones de popularidad y notoriedad de algunos individuos y aunque para ello tengamos que suprimir or cuando menos controlar las de otros."

[113]Unsigned letter (AP?) to J.T. Canales, May 13, 1932, AP, Box 4, Folder 10.

[114]"By Their Fruit Ye Shall Know Them," *LULAC News,* April 1933, 4, DB.

[115]Transcript, Memorandum: Conditions in San Antonio.

[116]Transcript on founding of LULAC Council 16, March 18, 1933, AP, Box 3, Folder 37; "Lic. P.G. Gonzales, Pres. del Nuevo Concilio," *LULAC News,* April 1933, 17, DB; Letter to R.S. Menefee, Pres. San Antonio Board of Education from Greg Salinas, April 9, 1934, Eleuterio Escobar Papers (hereafter EE), BLAC, Box 1, Folder 12; Letter from Louis Wilmot to Gregory R. Salinas, August 13, 1936,Andrés De Luna Sr. Papers (hereafter ADL), BLAC, Folder 14; "List of members of LULAC Council #16," EE, Box 2, Folder 2.

[117]Eleuterio Escobar, First Autobiography Draft, 1c, 19, EE.

[118]"Memorandum," Jan. 12, no year, ca. 1934,AP, Box 3, Folder 42.

[119]"Resolved by Council 16 of the LULAC, at its meeting of May 16, 1934," Resolution introduced by Alonso S. Perales, AP, Box 3, Folder 42.

[120]The Latin American cadets referred to the fact that LULAC got Maury Maverick's help to appoint Zeferino Martínez to West Point; no title, *LULAC News,* Feb. 1937.

[121]Letter to Antonia Gómez from Alonso S. Perales, January 11, 1933, AP, Box 4, Folder 20: Gálvan-González; Memo of LULACCouncil 16, Accomplishments, no date, AP, Box 1, Folder 12; "Resume of the Work Done by San Antonio Council No.16 of LULAC during the year 1936-1937," AP, Box 3, Folder 42.

[122]"Resolved by Council No. 16."

[123]"LULAC Council No. 2 Membership Roster," (ca. 1930s); "List of Members of LULAC Council #16," EE, Box 2, Folder 2 and printed form letter, AP, Box 3, Folder 42.

[124]"List of Approved Prospective Members," ca. mid-1930s, AP, Box 3, Folder 36.

[125]Sister Frances Jerome Woods, "Mexican Ethnic Leadership in San Antonio," Ph.D. diss., Catholic University of America, Washington, DC, 1947, 87; reprint (New York: Arno Press 1976).

[126]"La Liga de Ciudadanos Unidos Latino Americanos," ca. mid-1930s, AP, Box 14, Folder: Newspapers articles saved: Perales' life & work.

[127]"Resume of the Work."

[128]Perales, *En Defensa* 1:24.

[129]"La Petición Formal Para Que se Construya Una Plaza de Estilo Netamente Mexicano," Perales, *En Defensa* 1: 24.

[130]Flyer, "Se Abren Las Escuelas Gratis Para Adultos," ca. 1934, CC, Box 33, Folder 11.

[131]"Survey made by the Committee on Public School Buildings and Recreational Facilities of the LULAC," September 27, 1934, AP, Box 3, Folder 35.

[132]Stationary, AP, Box 3, Folder 42.

[133]Letter to Ignacio E. Lozano from Dr. Orlando F. Gerodetti, Jan 15, 1935, AP, Box 4, Folder 20.

[134]"Solicitando Facilidades Escolares Para Nuestra Niñez," Perales, *En Defensa* 2: 72.

[135]Letter to Eleuterio Escobar from L.A. Woods, State Superintendent, 1934, EE, Box 3, Folder 17.

[136]Letter to the Honorable Board of Trustees, San Antonio Independent School District from President of Council 16 and chairman of Committee of Public School Buildings and Playgrounds, 193?, AP, Box 3, Folder 42.

[137]Resolution by Carlos Albidress, pres. of SA Council 16 and Charles A. Ramírez, SA Council 2 (likely written by Perales), ca. 1937, AP, Box 3, Folder 35.

[138]Letter to John W. Brown, M.D., State Health Office from AP, Nov. 28, 1936, AP, Box 4, Folder 9.

[139]Ibid.

[140]"Letter from Frank J. Galvan Jr., LULAC National President, to "All LULAC Councils," Oct. 8, 1936, AP, Box 4, Folder 20.

[141]Thomas A. Guglielmo, "Fighting for Caucasian Rights: Mexicans, Mexican Americans, and the Transnational Struggle for Civil Rights in World War II Texas," *Journal of American History* (March 2006), 1215.

[142]"El Que no Llora no Mama," *LULAC News,* February 1937, 4, LULAC Archive, BLAC; Letter to W. B. Carssow, Texas House of Representatives, January 14, 1937, AP, Box 4, Folder 15.

[143]Mario T. García, *Católicos: Resistance and Affirmation in Chicano Catholic History* (Austin: University of Texas, 2004), 66.

[144]Ibid, 66-67.

[145]"Resumen de Resoluciones presentadas por el Lic. Alonso S. Perales," Perales, *En Defensa* 2: 74-75.

[146]Craig A. Kaplowitz, *LULAC, Mexican Americans and National Policy* (College Station: Texas A&M University, 2004), 26.

[147]Letter to J.T. Canales from Alonso S. Perales, March 7, 1938, AP, Box 4, Folder 11.

[148]Speech presented by Mr. Charles Albidress Sr., Mach 13, 1977, dedication of the Alonso S. Perales Elementary, San Antonio in Adela Sloss-Vento, *Alonso S. Perales: His Struggle for the Rights of Mexican Americans* (San Antonio: Artes Graficas, 1977), 96-97.

[149]"Resume of the Work Done by San Antonio Council No. 16 of the League during the year 1936-1937," AP, Box 3, Folder 42.

[150]"Varios Clubs Discuten el Asunto de las Chozas y Tejabanes en San Antonio," *En Defensa* 2, 48-52

[151]"Resume of the Work Done."

[152]"Protestan los 'LULACS' por un Suceso," Perales, 2, 27.

[153]"Resume of the Work Done."

[154]"Protestan los 'LULACS' por un Suceso," *La Prensa,* January 25, 1936, AP, Box 9, Folder 42.

[155]Letter to J.T. Canales from Alonso S. Perales, January 14, 1934, AP, Box 4, Folder 11.

[156]Letter to Carlos Castañeda from Alonso S. Perales, April 2, 1934, AP, Box 4, Folder 43.

157Letter from Alonso S. Perales to J.T. Canales, April 3, 1933, AP, Box 4, Folder 11.

158Ibid.

159Letter from Frank J. Galván Jr.

160Form letter from President Charles Albidress, President Council 16, May 22, 1937, AP, Box 3, Folder 37. Original text: "cualquiera puede llega a ser Presidente General, aunque no haya trabajado para nuestra Raza o nuestra Liga y aunque tenga unos cuantos días de ser socio."

161Letter to Dr. Carlos E. Castañeda from Alonso S. Perales, September 14, 1937, CC, Folder Perales.

162Jacob I. Rodríguez, "Truth Will Out," *LULAC News,* August 1937, 21, Alice Dickerson Montemayor Papers, BLAC.

163Rodríguez, "Truth Will Out."

164J.T. Canales, "The Right of LULAC Councils to Secede and Form a Rival Organization," *LULAC News,* Oct. 1937, LULAC Archive, BLAC.

165Resolutions at National LULAC Convention, listed in *LULAC News,* July 1937, LULAC Archive, BLAC; *LULAC News,* March 1938: 19-20, LULAC Archive, BLAC.

166Transcript, Memorandum: Conditions in San Antonio.

167Letter to Perales from unknown, ca. 1937, AP, Box 4, Folder 9.

168"Machine Politics and Methods in LULAC," *LULAC News,* August 1939: 21-22, LULAC Archive.

169Letter to H.H. Contreras from Alonso S. Perales, April 2, 1934, AP, Box 4, Folder 14.

170Letter to Alonso S. Perales from Adolfo de la Garza, June 18, 1937, AP, Box 4, Folder 20: Galván-González.

171Letter to AP from Adolfo de la Garza, June 18, 1937, AP, Box 4, Folder 20.

172No title, 11th Annual LULAC Convention Program, June 3-4, 1939, LULAC Archive, BLAC.

173Letter to Mr. Luis Alvarado from J.T. Canales, JTC, Sept. 6, 1960, Box 436B, Folder, Correspondence-LULAC, 1953-1954.

174Transcript, Memorandum: Conditions in San Antonio.

[175]Alonso S. Perales, *Are We Good Neighbors?* reprint (New York: Arno Press, 1974), 6.

[176]Neil Foley, *Quest for Equality, the Failed Promise of Black-Brown Solidarity* (Boston: Harvard University Press, 2010), 90.

[177]Ibid, 109.

[178]Ibid, 126.

[179]Letter to Dr. Carlos E. Castañeda from Alonso S. Perales, May 14, 1954, CC, Box 34, Folder 3. Original text: "'Los envidiososos' se oponían a cuanta resolución presentaba Perales nada más porque era Perales."

[180]"LULAC Job Praised," *San Antonio Light,* February 21, 1957, AP, Box 9, Folder 43.

[181]Letter to Alonso S. Perales from J.T. Canales, April 29, 1958, JTC, Box 431B, Folder 15.

[182]Letter to Honorable J.T. Canales from Alonso S. Perales, May 2, 1958, JTC, Box 431B.

[183]Letter to Honorable J.T. Canales from Alonso S. Perales, January 20, 1960, JTC, Box 436B.

[184]No author (Andrés De Luna?), "History of LULAC," *LULACNews,* February 1940, 5-8, ADM.

[185]George I. Garza, "Founding and History of LULAC," *LULAC News,* May 1955, 5, 8, LULAC Archive, BLAC.

[186]"Latin Group is Headed by Valley Man," *Brownsville Herald,* October 3, 1937.

[187]Woods, "Mexican Ethnic Leadership," 197.

[188]Margie Aguirre, "California LULAC, a History of Patriots with Civil Rights," 2009, http://www.californialulac.com/?page_id=70 Accessed September 23, 2018. List of presidents of LULAC local councils, ca. mid-30s, AP, Box 3, Folder 37. Jake Rodríguez established Council 58 there.

[189]Woods, 107.

[190]Ibid, 108.

[191]Ibid.

[192]Cynthia E. Orozco, List, LULAC General Officers, 1929 to 1965, Cynthia E. Orozco Papers, Ruidoso, New Mexico.

[193]George I. Garza, "Founding and History of LULAC," *LULAC News,* May 1955, LULAC Archive, BLAC.

[194]"Foreword," *LULAC Handbook,* Published by the 1960-1961 Administration, M.C. Gonzales Collection, BLAC.

[195]Márquez, *LULAC: The Evolution of a Mexican American Organization* (Austin: University of Texas, 1993), 63.

[196]"LULAC: 50 Years of Accomplishment," *San Antonio Express News,* February 14, 1979, San Antonio Public Library, Texana Room, Vertical Files, "Organizations."

[197]Letter to Clifford Forster, Staff Counsel, American Civil Liberties Union from George I. Sánchez, January 4, 1949, George I. Sánchez Papers, BLAC, Box 37, Folder 10.

[198]Foley, 126.

[199]Lorena Oropeza, *¡Raza Sí! ¡Guerra No!: Chicano Protest and Patriotism during the Vietnam War Era* (Los Angeles: University of California Press, 2005), 52. No evidence was provided.

[200]José Angel Gutiérrez, "Chicanos and Mexicanos under Surveillance: 1940-1980," *Renato Rosaldo Lecture Series Monograph 2,* Series 1984-5 (Tucson: Mexican American Studies and Research Center University of Arizona, Spring 1986): 29-58.

[201]Rodolfo Acuña, *Occupied America: A History of Chicanos* (New York: Harper & Row, 1981), 310.

[202]Carlos Kevin Blanton, *George I. Sánchez, The Long Struggle for Integra-tion* (New Haven: Yale University Press, 2015), 79.

[203]*Testimonio, A Documentary History of the Mexican American Struggle for Civil Rights,* ed. F. Arturo Rosales (Houston: Arte Público Press, 2000), xviii.

[204]Rosales, 105.

[205]Garcia, *Rise,* 122.

[206]Gutiérrez, 36.

CHAPTER 11

[1]Melita M. Garza, *They Came to Toil, Newspaper Representation of Mexicans and Immigrants in the Great Depression* (Austin: Uni- versity of Texas, 2018).

[2]Laura E. Cannon, "Situational Solidarity: LULAC's Civil Rights Strategy and the Challenge of the Mexican American Worker, 1934-1946," Ph.D. diss., Texas Tech University, 2016, Chapter 5, n.p. This chapter relies on Cannon's work on the Pecan Shellers strike.

[3]Julie Leininger Pycior, *LBJ & Mexican Americans, The Paradox of Power* (Austin: University of Texas, 1997), 41.

[4]Richard A. Garcia, *Rise of the Mexican American Middle Class, San Antonio, 1929-1941* (College Station: Texas A&M University, 1991), 37.

[5]Ibid, 179.

[6]Alonso S. Perales, *En Defensa de Mi Raza* 1 (San Antonio: Artes Gráficas, 1936), 16.

[7]García, 39.

[8]"The Seggregation [sic] of Mexican School children at Del Rio," *LULAC News* (August 1931), n.p, Dolph Briscoe Center for American History, University of Texas at Austin.

[9]Rodolfo A. de la Garza, "Our School Children," *LULAC News* (November 1932), 9, LULAC Archive, Benson Latin American Collection (hereafter BLAC).

[10]Mario T. García, *Mexican Americans, Leadership, Ideology, and Identity, 1930-1960* (New Haven: Yale University Press, 1989), 66. See his chapter "Education and the Mexican American: Eleuterio Escobar and the School Improvement League of San Antonio."

[11]Leigh Ann Wilson, "Fighting Two Devils: Eleuterio Escobar and the School Improvement League's Battle for Mexican and Mexican American Students, Education in the San Antonio, Texas Public Schools from 1934 to 1958," Ph.D. diss., University of Memphis, 2011, 71, 15.

[12]Wilson, 73, 84.

[13]Cynthia E. Orozco, "School Improvement League," *New Handbook of Texas* (hereafter *NHOT*), ed. Ronnie C. Tyler, Douglas E. Bar-

PIONEER OF MEXICAN-AMERICAN CIVIL RIGHTS: ALONSO S. PERALES

nett, and Roy R. Barkley 5 (Austin: Texas State Historical Association, 1996): 925-926.

[14]Richard A. Gambitta, Robert A. Milne, and Carol R. Davis, "The Politics of Unequal Educational Opportunity," *The Politics of San Antonio, Community, Progress, and Power,* ed. David R. Johnson, John A. Booth, and Richard J. Harris (Lincoln: University of Nebraska, 1983), 143.

[15]Wilson, 73, 84.

[16]Orozco, "School Improvement League," 925-926.

[17]Gambitta, et. al, 143.

[18]Lupe S. Salinas, "Legally White, Socially Brown: Alonso S. Perales and His Crusade for Justice for La Raza," *In Defense of My People, Alonso S. Perales and the Development of Mexican-American Public Intellectuals,* ed. Michael A. Olivas (Houston: Arte Público Press, 2012), 88.

[19]Gilberto Juan Quezada interview of Carlos Cadena, January 31, 1991, Bexar County Historical Commission, San Antonio Public Library.

[20]Wilson, 99.

[21]Ibid, 101.

[22]Félix D. Almaráz Jr., *Knight without Armor: Carlos E. Castañeda* (College Station: Texas A&M University, 2000), 302-303.

[23]Wilson, 116.

[24]Laura Cannon Dixon, "Police Brutality Makes Headlines: Retelling the Story of the 1938 Pecan Shellers' Strike," master's thesis, Indiana State University, 2014, 14.

[25]Garcia, *Rise,* 38; Cannon Dixon, "Police Brutality," 7.

[26]Garcia, *Rise,* 72.

[27]Ibid, 39.

[28]Ibid, 55.

[29]Letter to Dr. Thomas Dorbandt from unsigned, likely ASP, November 27, 1933, AP, Box 5, Folder 33.

[30]"Resume of the Work Done by San Antonio Council 16," AP, Box3, Folder 42.

[31]Cannon, "Situational," Chap. 5, n.p.; Donald Zelman, "Alazan-Apache Courts," *Southwestern Historical Quarterly,* 87 (July 1983-April 1984) 87:2, 123-150. See also *War on Slums in the Southwest:*

Public Housing and Slum Clearance in Texas, Arizona, and New Mexico, 1935-1965 (Temple University Press, 2014).

[32]According to Matt Meier and Margo Gutiérrez, "In the 1930s he was selected by President Franklin D. Roosevelt as an advisor on Mexican American concerns" but no evidence has been found. See "Alonso S. Perales," *Encyclopedia of the Mexican American Civil Rights Movement,* ed. Matt Meier and Margo Gutiérrez (Westport, Conn.: Greenwood Press, 2000), 180-181.

[33]Araceli Pérez Davis, "Marta Pérez de Perales," *El Mesteño,* 4:37 (March 1999), 16.

[34]"Resumen de Resoluciones presentadas por el Lic. Alonso S. Perales, Delegado del Concilio Num. 16, de San Antonio" Perales, *En Defensa* 2: 74.

[35]Laurie E. Jasinski, "San Antonio, Texas," https://tshaonline.org/handbook/online/articles/hds02 Accessed May 27, 2018.

[36]Letter to Hon. Morris Sheppard from Alonso S. Perales, January 4, 1939, AP, Box 5, Folder 6.

[37]"Committee on Housing for Bexar County," AP, Box 5, Folder 25.

[38]Benjamín Márquez, "In Defense of My People: Alonso S. Perales and the Moral Construction of Citizenship," *In Defense* 32.

[39]Letter to Alonso S. Perales from Carlos E. Castañeda, August 22, 1935, Carlos E. Castañeda Papers (hereafter CC), Benson Latin American Collection (hereafter BLAC), University of Texas at Austin, Box 33, Folder 11.

[40]Letter to Dr. Carlos E. Castañeda from Alonso S. Perales, September 2, 1935, CC, Box 33, Folder 11.

[41]Cannon, "Situational," 17-18.

[42]Ibid, 2.

[43]Ibid, 5.

[44]Ibid, 8.

[45]Garcia, *Rise,* 60-61.

[46]See *America's Lowest Paid Workers* (San Antonio: Pecan Shellers Union, 1939).

[47]Garcia, *Rise,* 55.

[48]Ibid, 63.

[49]Cannon, "Situational," 2.

[50]Ibid, 34.

[51]As a young woman she joined a San Antonio LULAC Ladies auxiliary in the early 1930s but had been radicalized.

[52]Garcia, *Rise,* 271.

[53]Cannon, "Situational," 39-40.

[54]Ibid," 57.

[55]Ibid, 61.

[56]Garcia, *Rise,* 60.

[57]Ibid, 98.

[58]Transcript, Memorandum: Conditions in San Antonio.

[59]Zaragosa Vargas, *Labor Rights are Civil Rights, Mexican American Workers in Twentieth-Century America* (Princeton: Princeton University Press, 2005), 81.

[60]Ibid, 137.

[61]"Toma Impetu el Movimiento de los Lulacs en Pro de Aumento de Jornaleros Para los Mexicanos," n.d., ca. late 1930s, AP, Box 1, Folder 39. Original text: "la situacion de nuestra gente es indispensable que a les pague lo que valúe su trabajo."

[62]Garcia, *Rise,* 40.

[63]Emma Tenayuca and Homer Brooks, "The Mexican Question in the Southwest," *The Communist,* March 1939: 265-266, Dolph Briscoe Center for American History, University of Texas at Austin.

[64]Justin Akers Chacón, *Radicals in the Barrio: Magonistas, Socialistys, Wobblies, and Communists in the Mexican American Working Class* (Chicago: Haymarket Books, 2018), 480.

[65]Sister Frances Jerome Woods, "Mexican Ethnic Leadership in San Antonio, Texas," Ph.D. diss, Washington, DC, Catholic University, 1947; reprint (New York: Arno Press, 1976), 55.

[66]Garcia, *Rise,* 39.

[67]Woods, 28.

[68]Garcia, *Rise,* 129.

[69]Cynthia A. Morales, "A Survey of Leadership, Activism and Community Involvement of Mexican American Women in San Antonio, 1920-1940," *Journal of South Texas* 13:2 (Fall 2000): 199; Cynthia E. Orozco, "Clínica de la Beneficencia Mexicana," *NHOT* 2: 162-163.

[70]F. Arturo Rosales book manuscript on Perales, (2017), chapter 2, 26.

[71]Letter to the Business and Professional Men of San Antonio from B.B. Buck, November 27, 1933, AP, Box 5, Folder 33.

[72]Letter to Miss Panay Nichols from Alonso S. Perales, November 3, 1933, AP, Box 5, Folder 33.

[73]Program, First Latin-American Health Week, April 1 to 7, 1934, AP, Box 5, Folder 33.

[74]Ibid.

[75]"A propósito de la convención de la asociación anti-tuberculosis del Estado de Texas," Perales, *En Defensa* 1: 77.

[76]See AP, Box 5, Folders 31-34.

[77]Draft, "To the Honorable Commissioner's court of Bexar County, Texas," ca. 1941, AP, Box 1, Folder 10. This item is on the back of "Lista de personas que están dispuestos a cooperar en la campaña electoral municipal de 1941."

[78]"Resignation Action Demanded by Perales," *San Antonio Express,* June 20, 1940, AP, Box 9, Folder 36.

[79]Demetrio Rodríguez attended the dedication of the Alonso S. Perales Elementary School. See "Alonso S. Perales Elementary School Dedication Program," 1974, AP, Box 1, Folder 1. He filed Rodríguez vs. San Antonio I.S.D. in 1971. See Cynthia E. Orozco, "Rodríguez v. San Antonio I.S.D," *NHOT* 5: 658-659.

CHAPTER 12

[1]Historian Joseph Orbock Medina claimed, "More conservative Mexican-American leaders, especially those from the Valley could enjoy a significant degree of parity with Anglos of their same class." See Joseph Orbock Medina, "The Trails of Unity: Rethink- ing the Mexican-American Generation in Texas, 1948-1960," *In Defense of My People, Alonso S. Perales and the Development of Mexican-American Public Intellectuals,* ed. Michael A. Olivas (Houston: Arte Público Press, 2012), 58. It is not clear who is he speaking about.

[2]Félix D. Almaráz Jr., *Knight Without Armor, Carlos Eduardo Castañeda, 1898-1958* (College Station: Texas A&M University, 1999), 265.

[3]Letter to Captain C.F. Detweiler, US Air Corps from Alonso S. Perales, May 29, 1942, Alonso S. Perales Papers (hereafter AP), M.D. Anderson Library, University of Houston, Box 1, Folder 7.

[4]Lt to Major General Arthur W. Brown from Alonso S. Perales, April 10, 1942, AP, Box 1, Folder 7.

[5]Letter to Colonel M.B. Ridgway, War Dept. from Alonso S. Perales, May 8, 1942, AP, Box 1, Folder 7.

[6]Letter to Cpt. C.F. Detweiler, US Air Corps from Alonso S. Perales, May 29, 1942, AP, Box 1, Folder 7.

[7]Letter to Lic. Alonso S. Perales from C.E. Castañeda, July 9, 1942, Carlos E. Castañeda Papers (hereafter CC), Benson Latin American Collection (hereafter BLAC), University of Texas at Austin, Box 34, Folder 1.

[8]Letter to Major Gen. Arthur W. Brown from Alonso S. Perales, July 27, 1942, AP, Box 1, Folder 7; Letter to John W. Bailey Jr. Esquire, Acting Chief, Division of Foreign Service Personnel, Dept. of State from Alonso S. Perales, July 5, 1942, AP, Box 1, Folder 7.

[9]Letter to Dr. Carlos E. Castañeda from Alonso S. Perales, July 10, 1942, CC, Box 34, Folder 1.

[10]Letter to Major General Arthur W. Brown from Alonso S. Perales, July 27, 1942, AP, Box 1, Folder 7.

[11]Letter to Mr. John W. Bailey Jr., Division of Foreign Services Personnel, August 3, 1942 from A.W. Brown, AP, Box 1, Folder 7. Brown was a retired Major General.

[12]Letter to Alonso S. Perales from Major General Arthur W. Brown, August 3, 1942, AP, Box 1, Folder 7.

[13]Letter to Major General Arthur W. Brown, Aug. 27, 1942 from Alonso S. Perales, AP, Box 1, Folder 7.

[14]Letter to Major Gen. Arthur W. Brown from Alonso S. Perales, September 11, 1942, AP, Box 1, Folder 7.

[15]Letter to Alonso S. Perales from Major General Brown, Sept. 14, 1942, AP, Box 1, Folder 7.

[16]Letter to Major General Arthur W. Brown from Alonso S. Perales, August 27, 1942, AP, Box 1, Folder 7.

[17]Letter to Major General Arthur W. Brown from Alonso S. Perales, September 11, 1942, AP, Box 1, Folder 7.

[18]Letter to Dr. Carlos E. Castañeda from Alonso S. Perales, September 16, 1942, CC, Box 34, Folder 1.

[19]Ibid.

[20]Carlos Kevin Blanton, *George I. Sánchez, The Long Fight for Mexican American Integration* (New Haven: Yale University Press, 2015), 69.

[21]Letter to Director of Naval Officer Procurement, New Orleans from AP, Oct. 18, 1942, AP, Box 1, Folder 6.

[22]Letter to Dr. Carlos E. Castañeda from Alonso S. Perales, October 15, 1942, CC, Box 34, Folder 1.

[23]F. Arturo Rosales, "Writing a Biography of Alonso Sandoval Perales," In Defense *In Defense of My People, Alonso S. Perales and the Development of Mexican-American Public Intellectuals,* ed. Michael A. Olivas (Houston: Arte Público Press, 2012), 281.

[24]Mario T. García, *Católicos, Resistance and Affirmation in Chicano History* (Austin: University of Texas, 2008), 73.

[25]Transcript, KONO Broadcasting Station, March 3, 1941, "What Does It Take to Get the Peoples of the Americas Together?," AP, Box 8, Folder 19.

[26]Alonso S. Perales, "Como Se Trabaja en Tejas Contra La Discriminación Racial," *Fraternidad,* December 1944 (Mexico City), 6-7, AP, Box 14, Folder 8. Original text: "Porque cualquier manifestación discriminatoria por razón de diferencia racial, significa, hoy día, una valiosa ayuda para el enemigo común contra el que lucha todo el mundo civilizado: el nazifascismo."

[27]"Citations to the Congressional Medal of Honor for Six LatinAmericans of the State of Texas," in Alonso S. Perales, *Are We Good Neighbors?* reprint (New York: Arno Press, 1974), 289-293.

[28]Letter to Honorable Paul J. Kilday, Member of the US House of Representatives from Committee of One Hundred League of Loyal Americans, by Alonso S. Perales, Director General, in "Record of Mexican-Americans in World War II," Perales, *Are We,* 283. This counters Aaron E. Sánchez's statement "Although Perales recognized that Mexican Americans were dying in disproportionate numbers, he did not complain." See Aaron E. Sánchez, *"Mendigos de*

nacionalidad: Mexican-Americanism and Ideologies of Belonging in a New Era of Citizenship, Texas 1910-1967," *In Defense,* 110.

[29]Márquez, "In Defense of My People: Alonso S. Perales and the Moral Construction of Citizenship," *In Defense,* 44.

[30]Craig A. Kaplowitz, *LULAC, Mexican Americans and National Policy* (College Station: Texas A&M University Press, 2005), 42.

[31]Ibid, 43.

[32]Emilio Zamora, *Claiming Rights and Righting Wrongs in Texas, Mexican Workers and Job Politics during World War II* (College Station: Texas A&M University Press, 2009), 72.

[33]Matthew Gritter, "Elite Leadership, People of Mexican Origin, and Civil Rights: Dennis Chávez and the Politics of Fair Employment," *Congress & the Presidency* 44 (2017), 144-145.

[34]Gritter, "Elite," 146.

[35]Matthew Gritter, *Mexican Inclusion: The Origins of Anti-Discrimination Policy in Texas and the Southwest* (College Station: Texas A&M University, 2012), 88.

[36]Unidentified author, "The Facts About Job Discrimination," Perales, *Are We,* 262.

[37]"Report from the Congress of the Inter-American Bar Federation Held in Mexico City" *Fraternidades,* 1944, 7, AP, Box 14, Folder 8.

[38]Gritter, *Mexican Inclusion,* 128.

[39]Letter from Julián A. Hernández to Dear Sir (Senator Dennis Chávez), June 12, 1948, Dennis Chávez Papers (hereafter DC), Center for Southwest Research, University of New Mexico, Box 10, Folder 21.

[40]Memo to Will Maslow, Director of Field Operations from Dr. Carlos E. Castañeda, March 3, 1944, DC, Box 93, Folder 1.

[41]Neil Foley, *Quest for Equality, the Failed Promise of Black-Brown Solidarity* (Boston: Harvard University Press, 2010), 62.

[42]"Statement of Dr. Carlos E. Castañeda, Special Assistant on Latin-American Problems to the Chairman of the President's Committee on Fair Employment Practice (sic), before the Senate Committee on Labor and Education in the Hearings Held September 8, 1944, on S bill 2048, to prohibit discrimination because of race, creed, color, national origin or ancestry," 4, Carlos Eduardo Castañeda Collection

(hereafter CC2), Dolph Briscoe Center for American History, University of Texas at Austin. This is a second Castañeda collec- tion.
[43]Almaráz Jr., 221.
[44]Ibid, 229.
[45]Ibid.
[46]"Cases of Discrimination (Employment)," Federal Employment Practices Commission (hereafter FEPC), National Archives, Washington, DC, Box 339, Folder: Southwest Hearing-Background Material.
[47]Juan Gómez-Quiñones, *Chicano Politics, Promise and Reality, 1940-1990* (Albuquerque: University of New Mexico, 1990), 89.
[48]Almáraz Jr., 217. According to Almaráz, Castañeda promoted himself, M.C. Gonzales, Arturo Vásquez employed at a censorship office in El Paso, all of Texas, and Dr. Arturo Campa and Antonio Fernández of New Mexico as well as several white liberals like Dr. Herschel T. Manuel of Texas.
[49]Foley, *Quest,* 59-62.
[50]No author, "The Facts About Job Discrimination," *Are We,* 261-262.
[51]F. Arturo Rosales, "Writing a Biography of Alonso Sandoval Perales," *In Defense,* 276.
[52]Gritter, *Mexican Inclusion,* 93.
[53]Ibid, 71.
[54]Ibid, 89
[55]FEPC March 12, 1945 hearing notes, DC, Box 9, Folder 38.
[56]George A. Martínez, "Alonso S. Perales and the Effort to Establish the Civil Rights of Mexican Americans as Seen through the Lens of Contemporary Critical Legal Theory: Post-racialism, Reality Construction, Interest Convergence, and Other Critical Themes," *In Defense,* 123.
[57]Alonso S. Perales, "El Comité Presidencial de Prácticas Justas de Empleo y la Compañía Shell," *La Prensa,* February 11, 1945, AP, Box 9, Folder 42.
[58]Letter to Dennis Chávez from Alonso S. Perales, August 15, 1938; Letter to Dennis Chávez from Committee of One Hundred, August 29, 1944, AP, Box 10, Folder 48.
[59]Telegram from Dennis Chávez, Senate Committee on Education and Labor, September 2, 1944, AP, Box 10, Folder 48.

[60]Gritter, "Elite," 145.

[61]Ibid, 147.

[62]Foley, 88.

[63]"Backers of FEPC Bill throw in the Sponge; Cloture Vote to End Filibuster in Senate," *San Antonio Express,* February 8, 1946, AP, Box 9, Folder 40.

[64]Alonso S. Perales, "Nuestra Democracia Recibe un Tremendo Revés," *The Pan-American,* 1:12 (December 1946): 12, AP, Box 11, Folder 6.

[65]Letter to Lawrence W. Cramer from Maury Maverick, June 10, 1942, FEPC, Box 339, Legal Division, Southwest-Mexicans, Folder: Southwest Hearing-Background Material.

[66]Gritter, *Mexican Inclusion,* 66-67.

[67]Richard A. Garcia, *Rise of the Mexican American Middle Class, San Antonio, 1929-1941.* (College Station: Texas A&M University, 1991), 302.

[68]Dr. Carlos E. Castañeda, "Statement on Discrimination Against Mexican-Americans in Employment," Perales, *Are We,* 59.

[69]"Group told San Antonio Minorities Must Again Expect Low Wages," unidentified newspaper, October 2, 1945, AP, Box 9, Folder 43.

[70]Foley, 84.

[71]Thomas A. Guglielmo, "Fighting for Caucasian Rights: Mexicans, Mexican Americans, and the Transnational Struggle for Civil Rights in World War II Texas," *Journal of American History* 92:4 (March 2006), 1215.

[72]Transcript, Alonso S. Perales, "What Does it Take."

[73]Zamora, 112.

[74]Virginia Marie Raymond, "Faithful dissident: Alonso S. Perales, Discrimination, and the Catholic Church," *In Defense,* ftnt. 3, 215.

[75]Guglielmo, 1220.

[76]Ibid, 1220.

[77]Ibid, 1220.

[78]Letter to Dr. Carlos E. Castañeda from Alonso S. Perales, January 25, 1941, CC, Box 33, Folder 12.

[79]Benjamín Márquez, "In Defense of My People: Alonso S. Perales and the Moral Construction of Citizenship," *In Defense,* 40.

[80]Guglielmo, 1221.

[81]Letter to Dr. Carlos E. Castañeda from Alonso S. Perales, March 19, 1943, CC, Box 34, Folder 1.

[82]Guglielmo, 1222.

[83]Ibid, 1223.

[84]Ibid.

[85]Ibid, 1225.

[86]Ibid, 1227.

[87]Ibid, 1228.

[88]Ibid, 1229.

[89]Alonso S. Perales, "The J. Franklin Spears Anti-Discrimination Bill," *Free Press for Texas,* February 9, 1945, AP, Box 14, Folder 7 or 9.

[90]Ibid.

[91]Letter to His Excellency Franklin Delano Roosevelt from Alonso S. Perales, Committee of One Hundred Mexican American Citizens, League of Loyal Americans, March 31, 1944, Perales, *Are We,* 279.

[92]Gabriela González, *Redeeming La Raza, Transborder Modernity, Race, Respectability, and Rights* (Oxford: Oxford University, 2018), 167.

[93]"Caucasian' Bill Refused," *San Antonio* n.d. (1945), AP, Box 9, Folder 32.

[94]Zamora, 219.

[95]Guglielmo, 1230.

[96]"Está en peligro de fracasar el Proyecto de Ley Antidiscriminato- rio," *Revista Latino-Americana,* Mayo de 1951, AP, Box 11, Fold er 16.

[97]Sister Frances Jerome Woods, "Mexican Ethnic Leadership in San Antonio," Ph.D. dissertation, Catholic University of America, Washington, DC, 1947; reprint (New York: Arno Press, 1976), 85.

[98]Woods, 105.

[99]Ibid, 114.

100Constitution of the Pan-American Optimist Club of San Antonio, Texas, ca. 1949, AP, Box 5, Folder 21.

101Woods, 113.

102Letter to Dr. Héctor Urrutia from Alonso S. Perales, February 24, 1949, AP, Box 5, Folder 21.

103Letter to Dr. Carlos E. Castañeda from Alonso S. Perales," April 8, 1948, CC, Box 34, Folder 2

104Woods, 112.

105Ibid, 113.

106Lic. Alonso S. Perales, "Un Club Cívico que Labora Por El Progreso y el Bienestar de Nuestra Niñez y Nuestra Juventud Mexicana," La Prensa, March 14, 1947, AP, Box 9, Folder 10.

107Woods, 109.

108Letter to Sr. Roberto Garces from Alfredo Flores, October 4, 1949, AP, Box 5, Folder 21.

109Letter to Dr. Carlos E. Castañeda from Alonso S. Perales," CC, Box 34, Folder 2.

110Letter to Sr. Don Jesús María Canales from Alonso S. Perales, November 26, 1948, AP, Box 5, Folder 21; Pan American Optimist Club, Statement of Assets and Liabilities, September 30, 1949, AP, Box 5, Folder 21. Henry Ramos Rodríguez received $300 to attend Trinity University in San Antonio; ? (unidentified name) Guerrero received funds to attend St. Mary's University in the city; and (unidentified) Lopez received funds to attend Trinity.

111Financial Statement, Pan-American Optimist Club, December 31, 1949, AP, Box 5, Folder 21.

112No title, Document begins "Durante esta semana el programa de radio," n.d. (ca. 1949), AP, Box 5, Folder 21.

113John Hart Lane, "Voluntary Associations Among Mexican American in San Antonio, Texas: Organizational and Leadership Characteristics," Ph.D. diss., University of Texas at Austin, 1968 reprint (New York: Arno Press, 1976), 87.

CHAPTER 13

[1] Letter to Dr. Carlos E. Castañeda from Alonso S. Perales, February 27, 1951, Carlos E. Castañeda Papers (hereafter CC), Benson Latin American Collection (hereafter BLAC), University of Texas at Austin, Box 34, Folder 3.

[2] Letter to Alonso S. Perales from Filiberto R. Rodríguez, December 13, 1951, José de La Luz Sáenz Papers (hereafter JLS), BLAC, Box 5, Folder 17.

[3] Roberto R. Calderón, "Tejano Politics" *New Handbook of Texas* (hereafter *NHOT*) ed. Ronnie C. Tyler, Douglas E. Barnett and Roy R. Barkley 5 (Austin: Texas State Historical Association, 1996): 239-242.

[4] Ibid.

[5] Anne W. Hooker, "Carlos Bee" https://tshaonline.org/handbook/online/articles/fbe23 accessed on May 28, 2018.

[6] Oral History Interview with Albert Peña Jr, 1996, http://library.uta.edu/tejanovoices/xml/CMAS_015.xml, accessed on June 21, 2018. He was interviewed by Dr. José Angel Gutiérrez. Info about Guerra running for state representative came from Letter to Dr. Carlos E. Castañeda from Alonso S. Perales, July 29, 1952, CC, Box 34, Folder 3.

[7] "An Interview with Mrs. Perales," *Chicano Times,* February 14 to February 28, 1975, 12, Alonso S. Perales (hereafter AP), MD Anderson Library, University of Houston AP, Box 14 oversize.

[8] "An Interview."

[9] Postcard form, August 1, 1950 from Muy estimado amigo from Alonso S. Perales, AP, Box 1, Folder 10.

[10] Letter to Compadre from Alonso S. Perales, August 8, 1950, AP, Box 1, Folder 23.

[11] "Meeting of Business Men's Club for Henry Gonzales," n.d., AP, Box 1, Folder 10.

[12] "Plática sustentada por el Lic. Alonso S. Perales a Través de la Estacion KIWW a las 7 de la tarde, el Jueves, 24 de Agosto de 1950," AP, Box 8, Folder 20. Original text: "Ni un solo votante México-

Americano debe quedarse sin votar por Henry B. González para la Legislatura de Texas "

[13]"Plática, English Translation: "Being that it is just and necessary to have legislators of Mexican heritage in the aforementioned legislature because by being from our racial heritage, they will try harder and be more interested in making laws that benefit ALL inhabitants of the state."

[14]See documents in AP, Box 1, Folder 10.

[15]Rodolfo Rosales, "The Rise of Middle Class Politics in San Antonio," Ph.D. diss., University of Michigan, 1991, 58-62.

[16]Ibid, 80.

[17]Letter to Dr. Carlos E. Castañeda from Alonso S. Perales, Aug. 10, 1956, CC, Box 34, Folder 3.

[18]Letter to J.T. Canales from Carlos E. Castañeda, May 13, 1957, CC, Box 9, Folder 7.

[19]See Julie Leininger Pycior, "Henry B. González," *Profiles in Power: Twentieth-Century Texans in Washington,* ed. Kenneth Hendrickson and Michael Collins, (Austin: Texas State Historical Association, 1993; revised edition, 2004), 294-308.

[20]David Montejano, *Quixote's Soldiers: A Local History of the Chicano Movement, 1966-1981* (Austin: University of Texas Press, 2010).

[21]"A Bill to be Entitled," ca. 1951, AP, Box 4, Folder 2.

[22]Letter to Dr. Carlos E. Castañeda from Alonso S. Perales, Feb. 23, 1951, CC, Box 34, Folder 3.

[23]Alonso S. Perales, "Está en Peligro de Fracasar el Proyecto de Ley Antidiscriminatoria," *Revista Latino-Americana,* May 1951, 5, AP, Box 11, Folder 16.

[24]Braceros were Mexican immigrants who were officially authorized to enter the US based on an international labor agreement by both the US and Mexico. The Bracero Program began so as to serve labor needs during World War II but business found this exploitative labor arrangement so profitable they lobbied to continue the program successfullyuntil 1964 when US labor organizations stopped the program.

[25]Letter to Dr. George I. Sánchez from Alonso S. Perales, Dec. de 1951 (unspecified day), George I. Sánchez Papers (hereafter GIS), BLAC, Box 62, Folder 8.

[26]Letter to Alonso S. Perales from J.T. Canales, November 28, 1951, AP, Box 4, Folder 10.

[27]Ibid.

[28]Joseph Orbock Medina, "The Trials of Unity: Rethinking the Mexican-American Generation in Texas," *In Defense of My People, Alonso S. Perales and the Development of Mexican-American Public Intellectuals,* ed. Michael A. Olivas (Houston: Arte Público Press, 2012), 63.

[29]Letter to Dr. Héctor P. García from Alonso S. Perales, December 8, 1951, JLS, Box 5, Folder 17.

[30]Letter to Prof. J. Luz Sáenz from Alonso S. Perales, December 11, 1951, JLS, Box 2, Folder 1. Original text: "Si 6 or 12 hombres de nuestra raza del Valle se amarran los pantalones, pueden entablar una demanda por medio millión de dólares por daños y perjuicios en contra de la Universidad de Texas."

[31]"Editor Attacks Censoriousness of Wetback Pamphlet's distinction in Texas," *La Verdad,* December 28, 1951, AP, Box 14, Folder 11. The word "censoriousness" was used.

[32]Ibid.

[33]Letter to Dr. George I. Sánchez from George J. Garza, National President, LULAC, January 14, 1952, GIS, Box 37, Folder: loose.

[34]Benjamín Márquez, "In Defense of My People: Alonso S. Perales and the Moral Construction of Citizenship," *In Defense,* 36.

[35]Orbock Medina, 65.

[36]"Sobre los Inauditors Insultos Lanzadas en Contra de los Mexicanos en un Librero Que Públicamente se ha Dicho, Fue Costeada su Impresión con Fondos de la Universidad de Texas," *La Verdad,* February 22, 1952, Cynthia E. Orozco notes of Alonso S. Perales Papers, 289.

[37]Orbock Medina, 63. He wrote, "Some conservative Mexican Americans, including Alonso S. Perales and J. Luz Sáenz met at Mission on March 9, 1952 and passed a harsh resolution " But Perales did not attend.

[38]Letter to Professor J. Luz Sáenz from Santos de la Paz, Jan. 21, 1952, JLS, Box 2, Folder 1.

[39]Letter to Adela Sloss-Vento from Alonso Perales, March 5, 1952, JLS, March 5, 1952, Box 5, Folder 17. Original text: "No voy aten-

der . . . opinión que la junta deber ser de gente del Valle nada más, con excepción del Sr. De la Paz quien debe asistir bajo toda circunstancia . . . para que no se diga que nosotros los de afuera fuimos los agitadores, mi deseo es que usted, el Professor Sáenz y el Sr. De La Paz trabajen en perfecta armonía antes, durante y después de la junta."

[40]Letter to Mi estimado amigo Luz from Alonso S. Perales, March 6, 1952, AP, Box 2, Folder 1. Original text: "No permitan debates y no dejen a los de San Antonio y Corpus (es decir, del campo enemigo) que cojan la batuta. Ni los dejen hablar. No me sorprendería si llevaran a Gustavo y o otros para tratar de echarles a perder su junta . . . No permitan debates sobre el folleto."

[41]"En Mission Será la Conferencia Para Debatir el Folleto Respeto a Mexicanos," La Prensa?, n.d., GIS, Box 20, Folder: Newsletter No. 5.

[42]Emilio Zamora, "José de la Luz Sáenz, Experiences and Autobiographical Consciousness," Leaders of the Mexican American Generation, Biographical Essays, ed. Anthony Quiroz (Boulder: University Press of Colorado, 2015), 54, ftnt. 35. He cited Alonso Perales, "Quienes son los mexicanos que residen en Texas?," La Verdad, March 1952.

[43]Committee Report to the Convention, March 1951, GIS, Box 62, Folder 8.

[44]Letter to Professor J. Luz Sáenz from Alonso S. Perales, February 2, 1952, JLS, Box 2, Folder 1; "Draft of Resolutions Adopted by Leaders of the Latin American Citizens of the Lower Rio Grande Valley," no author, JLS, Box 2, Folder 1. Original text: "Las autores de las resoluciones son tú y De La Paz. No se les olvides. Vale."

[45]"Draft of Resolution Adopted by Leaders of the Latin American Citizenry of the Lower Rio Grande Valley," AP, Box 3, Folder 40.

[46]Letter to M.C. Gonzales from Maury Maverick Jr., February 26, 1953, with note from Maury to Dr. George I. Sánchez, GIS, Box 37, Folder: M. Miscellaneous.

[47]Ignacio M. García, Viva Kennedy, Mexican Americans in Search of Camelot (College Station: Texas A &M University, 2000), 15.

[48]Quoted in Matthew Gritter, "Elite Leadership, People of Mexican Origin, and Civil Rights: Dennis Chávez and the Politics of Fair Employment," *Congress & the Presidency* 44 (2017): 145.

[49]Letter to Mr. M.C. Gonzales from George I. Sánchez, February 23, 1943; Letter to Dr. George I. Sánchez from M.C. Gonzales, March 1, 1943, GIS, Box 38, no folder, loose.

[50]Letter to J.O. Loftin from Roger Baldwin, November 6, 1945, GIS, Box 37, no folder, loose. Sánchez and Gonzales were the two key Latino contacts.

[51]Cynthia E. Orozco, "American Council of Spanish-Speaking Persons," *NHOT* 1: 146-147.

[52]Ibid.

[53]Letter to Dr. Carlos E. Castañeda from Alonso S. Perales, August 8, 1951, CC, Box 34, Folder 3.

[54]Alonso S. Perales, "Un Decidido Defensor de Nuestra Raza en Texas in 1859," (Arquitectos de Nuestros Propios Destinos) *La Prensa,* no date, JLS, Box 5, Folder 17.

[55]Orbock Medina, 56.

[56]Letter to Dr. Carlos E. Castañeda from Alonso S. Perales, April 28, 1952, CC, Box 33, Folder 10.

[57]Letter to Alonso S. Perales from Carlos E. Castañeda, July 23, 1951, CC, Box 33, Folder 12.

[58]Resolution of merger, Texas Pro-Human Relations Fund Committee and Latin American convention of South Texas, May 4, 1952, AP, Box 5, Folder 27.

[59]Draft, Anglo-Latin Good Relations Committee constitution, n.d. (1952), Jose Tomás Canales Estate Collection (hereafter JTC), James C. Jernigan Library, South Texas Archive, Texas A & M University, Kingsville, Box 436B, Folder: LULAC, 1952.

[60]Letter to H.N. González from J.T. Canales, April 24, 1952, JTC, Box 436B, Folder: LULAC, 1952. He also suggested *La Verdad* of Corpus Christi serve as the new official organ.

[61]Orbock Medina, 57.

[62]Ibid.

[63]Aims and Purposes, Anglo-Latin Good Relations, AP, Box 5, Folder 27.

[64]Orbock Medina.

[65]Ibid, 65; 70-72. He argued LULAC of the 1950s was "weighted toward the elite" and that pro-labor, popular interests "challenged LULAC in the 1950s." Finally, he concluded, "Ed Idar Jr, George Sánchez, and Hector García successfully refocused ethnic activism from middle class assimilation to social justice for Mexican-American workers . . . " This binary of pre-World War II and post-World War II activism requires more nuance.

[66]Ibid, 64.

[67]Historian Richard A. Garcia suggested Perales accompanied attorney Carlos Cadena and Gus Garcia at the Supreme Court but he did not. Richard A. Garcia, "Alonso S. Perales: The Voice and Visions of a Citizen Intellectual," *Leaders,* 91.

[68]Ignacio M. García, *White But Not Equal, Mexican Americans, Jury Discrimination, and the Supreme Court* (Tucson: University of Arizona, 2009), 97, 144-45.

[69]Gilberto Juan Quezada interview of Carlos Cadena, January 31, 1991, Bexar County Historical Commission, San Antonio Public Library.

[70]Mario T. García, *Mexican Americans: Leadership, Ideology, and Identity* (New Haven: Yale University Press, 1989), 50.

[71]Letter to J.T. Canales from Carlos Cadena, October 28, 1953, Box 431 B, JTC; Letter to Hon. J.T. Canales from Alonso S. Perales, October 28, 1953, Box 431B, JTC.

[72]Quezada interview with Carlos Cadena.

[73]José Angel Gutiérrez, *Albert A. Peña Jr., Dean of Chicano Politics* (East Lansing: Michigan State University Press, 2017), 36.

[74]Teresa Palomo Acosta, "Alba Club," *NHOT* 1: 92-93.

[75]Letter to Professor J. Luz Sáenz from Alonso S. Perales, February 26, 1952, JLS, Box 2, Folder 1. Original text: "Gracias a Dios que alguien (aunque sea allá, lejos, en España) tiene una palabra de aliento para los que como tú y yo hemos gastado nuestras vidas combatiendo las injusticias que se han cometido, y se siguen cometiendo, con nuestra raza "

[76]*Revista Latino-Americana,* April 1952, AP, Box 11, Folder 16.

[77]Letter to Alonso S. Perales from Elisa G. de Longoria, March 20, 1952, AP, Box 12, Folder 1 1. Original text: "como siempre siendo el paladín y libertador de nosotros, los Latinos."

[78]Letter to Alonso S. Perales from J.T. Canales, March 19, 1952, AP, Box 4, Folder 10.

[79]Letter to Carlos E. Castañeda from J.T. Canales, April 1, 1952, CC, Box 2, Folder 7.

[80]"Otra Honrosa Distinción Concedida al Lic. don Alonso S. Perales," *Revista Latino-Americana,* December 1952, AP, Box 11, Folder 16.

[81]Conversation with Carlos Cansino, ca. 1997; Jennifer Binder, "A Biography of Carlos Cansino," University of New Mexico, History 283 Research Paper, ca. 1999, Dr. Cynthia E. Orozco Papers, Ruidoso, New Mexico. He was an acquaintance when I taught at the University of New Mexico at Albuquerque from 1997-2000. See Carlos Espinosa Cansino Papers, Center for Southwest Research, University of New Mexico.

[82]Binder, 6-8.

[83]Cansino appeared in the PBS film *¡Chicano, The Mexican American Civil Rights Movement! History of the Mexican American Civil Rights Movement.*

[84]Stan Steiner, *La Raza, the Mexican Americans* (New York: Harper & Row, 1970), 291.

[85]Richard A. Garcia, *Rise of the Mexican American Middle Class, San Antonio,* 1929-1941 (College Station: Texas A&M University, 1991), 305.

CHAPTER 14

[1]Letter to Hugh J. Fegan, Assistant Dean, Georgetown Law School from Alonso S. Perales, October 9, 1926, Alonso S. Perales Papers (hereafter AP), M.D. Anderson Library, University of Houston, Box 1, Folder 13.

[2]Alonso S. Perales, *En Defensa de Mi Raza* 1 (San Antonio: Artes Gráficas, 1936), 10-11. This chapter benefitted from essays by Michael A. Olivas and Lupe S. Salinas in *In Defense of My People, Alonso S. Perales and the Development of Mexican-American Pub-*

lic Intellectuals, ed. Michael A. Olivas (Houston: Arte Público Press, 2012).

[3]"90 Take Legal Exams," unidentified newspaper, ca. June 8, 1924, AP, Box 13, Folder 2.

[4]Letter to H.C. Clamp from Alonso S. Perales, September 6, 1924, Cynthia Orozco Notes of Perales Papers (hereafter ON), 288.

[5]Letter to Honorable Dean, George Washington University from Alonso S. Perales, October 8, 1926, AP, Box 1, Folder 13.

[6]"Jóvenes Mexicanos Que Serán Pronto Abogados," *El Nacional,* June 8, 1924, ON, 13.

[7]Letter to State Board of Legal Examiners from Bat Corrigan, April 17, 1924, AP, Box 1, Folder 4.

[8]Letter to Alonso S. Perales from Mann, Neel & Mann, April 9, 1925, Hernan Contreras Collection (hereafter HC), CushingLibrary, Texas A&M University, College Station, Box 1, Folder 17; Letter to Sr. Casimiro Pérez Alvarez from Alonso S. Perales, April12, 1925, Box 1, Folder 17, HC.

[9]Letter to Honorable Judge Winchester Kelso from JBA (J.B. Andrews), February 19, 1924, AP, Box 1, Folder 4.

[10]Letter to Gentlemen, The Board of Legal Examiners from Carl C. Wurzbach, April 8, 1924, AP, Box 1, Folder 4.

[11]"Officers of the U.S. Naval Services on duty with the United States Electoral Mission to Nicaragua," pamphlet, AP, Box 2, Folder 32; Letter to Sr. Casimiro Pérez Alvarez from Alonso S. Perales, June 14, 1925, HC, Box 1, Folder 17.

[12]ON, 4. (Note by me based on conversation with Marta Pérez Perales.)

[13]Letter to Alonso Perales from J.T. Canales, October 9, 1926, AP, Box 4, Folder 10.

[14]Letter to J.T. Canales from Alonso S. Perales, October 9, 1926, AP, Box 4, Folder 10.

[15]Letter to Alonso Perales from J.T. Canales, October 9, 1926, AP, Box 4, Folder 10.

[16]Letter to J.T. Canales from Alonso S. Perales, November 4, 1926, AP, Box 4, Folder 10.

[17]Letter to J.T. Canales from Alonso S. Perales, April 11, 1927 and April 26, 1927, AP, Box 4, Folder 10.

[18]Letter to J.T. Canales from Alonso S. Perales, May 1, 1927, AP, Box 4, Folder 10.

[19]Adela Sloss-Vento, *Alonso S. Perales, His Struggle for the Rights of Mexican Americans* (San Antonio: Artes Gráficas, 1977), 7. See also *In Defense of My People,* xiv.

[20]"Will Organize 'American of Mexican Descent' Society," *McAllen Daily Press,* August 11, 1927, ON, 41.

[21]Letter to Inolvidada Martita from Alonso, January 11, 1928, AP, Box 10, Folder 3.

[22]Letter to Dr. Carlos E. Castañeda from Alonso S. Perales, June 28, 1951, Carlos E. Castañeda Papers (hereafter CC), Benson Latin American Collection (hereafter BLAC), University of Texas at Austin, Box 33, Folder 9.

[23]Letter from Alonso S. Perales to Eleuterio Escobar, April 14, 1929, Eleuterio Escobar Papers (hereafter EE), Box 1, Folder 13, BLAC.

[24]Michael A. Olivas, "The Legal Career of Alonso S. Perales," *In Defense,* 315.

[25]"1923—First start in business," (1923-1967 Mexican American lawyers in San Antonio info), EE, Box 1, Folder 28.

[26]"1923—First start in business"; Lic. Alonso S. Perales, "El Mexico Americano y la Política del Sur de Texas," (San Antonio: Artes Gráficas, 1931), 2, BLAC.

[27]"Official score card of 3rd annual softball contest Lawyers vs. Doctors, July 9, 1939, AP, Box 1, Folder 11.

[28]List of Latino attorneys, ca. 1950, AP, Box 1, Folder 10. This list included Frank Alvarado, Efraín Arredondo, Carlos Cadena, Henry Castillo, E.G. García, Gus C. Garcia, A.A. García, Ruben R. Lozano, Rafael M.M (unidentified name), Albert A. Peña Sr., N.A. Quintanilla, Charles A. Ramírez, Alberto U. Treviño and Matias Zertuche.

[29]Ad, *LULAC News,* August 1931, n.p, Dolph Briscoe Center for American History, University of Texas at Austin.

[30]Letter to Miss Nina Romeyn from Alonso S. Perales, June 25, 1931, AP, Box 12, Folder 4.

[31] Letter to M.C. Gonzales from J.T. Canales, March 26, 1932, J.T. Canales Estate Collection (hereafter JTC), Box 436, Folder 20, South Texas Archives, James Jernigan Library, Texas A&M University, Kingsville.

[32] Letterhead, Letter to Whom It May Concern from J.T. Canales, AP, Box 3, Folder 36.

[33] Notification of appointment as notary public in Bexar County, June 1, 1953, AP, Box 1, Folder 6.

[34] Letter to Emilio S. Perales from Alonso S. Perales, June 12, 1932, AP, Box 2, Folder 11.

[35] "Interview with Mrs. Perales," *Chicano Times,* Feb. 14 thru Feb. 28, 1975, AP, Box 14 oversized.

[36] Letterhead, Letter to Dr. Carlos E. Castañeda from Alonso S. Perales, January 30, 1934, CC, Box 33, Folder 11.

[37] Letterhead, Letter to Dr. Carlos E. Castañeda from Alonso S. Perales, April 2, 1934, CC, Box 33, Folder 11.

[38] "Prominent Texas Attorney Secures Further Honors," *Commerce & Industry,* November 1934, CC, Box 34, Folder 1; Typed reprint of article from *Album de la Raza* (San Antonio), January 15, 1934, CC, Box 34, Folder 1.

[39] Letterhead, Letter to Dr. Carlos E. Castañeda from Alonso S. Perales, January 29, 1935, CC, Box 33, Folder 11; Letter to Sr. don Casimiro Pérez Alvarez from Alonso S. Perales, January 2, 1935, HC, Box 2, Folder 18.

[40] Translation of part of article, *Album de la Raza,* January 15, 1934.

[41] Alonso S. Perales, Alamo National bank statement, April to July 1939, AP, Box 6, Folder 40.

[42] Olivas, "The Legal Career, S. Perales," *In Defense,* 335.

[43] Tomás A. Garza, "Forward to Washington!," *LULAC News,* October 1931, AP, Box 4, Folder 4.

[44] *LULAC News,* October 1931, AP, Box 4, Folder 4.

[45] Mario T. García, *Católicos: Resistance and Affirmation in Chicano Catholic History* (Austin: University of Texas at Austin, 2010), 74.

[46] Lupe S. Salinas, "Legally White, Socially Brown: Alonso S. Perales and His Crusade for Justice for La Raza," *In Defense,* 88.

[47] Salinas, 88.

[48]Ibid, 93.

[49]Olivas, 336.

[50]Letter to Dr. Carlos E. Castañeda from Alonso S. Perales, October 15, 1942, CC, Box 34, Folder 1.

[51]Letter to Dr. Carlos E. Castañeda from Alonso S. Perales, May 20, 1943, CC, Box 34, Folder 1.

[52]Letter to Prof. J. Luz Sáenz from Alonso S. Perales, February 4, 1942, José de La Luz Sáenz Papers (JLS), BLAC, Box 2, Folder 1. Original text: "Yo estoy ganándome la vida muy bien en mi profesión, y por eso no he aceptado empleo con el Tío Samuel."

[53]Richard A. Buitron Jr., *The Quest for Tejano Identity in San Antonio, 1913-2000* (New York: Routledge, 2004), 30.

[54]Alonso S. Perales, statement of account, National Bank of Commerce, November 1944 and June 1946, AP, Box 6, Folder 39.

[55]Letter to Mr. A.S. Perales from Carlos E. Castañeda, April 8, 1946, CC, Box 34, Folder 2.

[56]Arnoldo Carlos Vento, *Adela Sloss-Vento, Writer, Political Activist, and Civil Rights Pioneer* (Lanham: Hamilton Books, 2017), 54.

[57]"Expenses during the year of 1959 made by Mr. Perales,"AP, Box 1, Folder 5.

[58]Letterhead, letter to J. Luz Sáenz from Alonso S. Perales, February 24, 1947 and August 3, 1948, JLS, Box 2, Folder 1, BLAC.

[59]Letter to Dr. Carlos E. Castañeda from Alonso S. Perales, Aug. 23, 1947, CC, Box 34 Folder 2.

[60]Daniel D. Arreola, *Tejano South Texas, a Mexican American Cultural Province* (Austin: University of Texas, 2002), 136-137, 141.

[61]Arreola, 139.

[62]Letter to Mr. Alonso S. Perales from J. T. Canales, March 2, 1942, JTC, Box 431B.

[63]Letter to Hon. J.T. Canales from Alonso S. Perales, Sept. 15, 1947, JTC, Box 431B.

[64]Salinas, 87.

[65]Legal document, no title, begins "This Court has before it a case involving the validity of racial restrictive covenants on real property," ca. 1947, AP, Box 6, Folder 5.

[66]Salinas, 87.

[67]Letter to Honorable Joint Committee on Housing of the Congress of the United States from Alonso S. Perales, Committee of One Hundred, League of Loyal Americans, October 29, 1947, Alonso S. Perales, *Are We Good Neighbors?* reprint (New York: Arno Press, 1976), 229-230.

[68]Lupe S. Salinas, "Gus Garcia and Thurgood Marshall: Two Legal Giants Fighting for Justice, *Thurgood Marshall Law Review* (Spring 2003) 28: 145-175.

[69]Richard A. Gambitta, Robert A. Milne, and Carol R. Davis, "The Politics of Unequal Educational Opportunity," *The Politics of San Antonio, Community, Progress, and Power,* ed. David R. Johnson, John A. Booth, and Richard J. Harris (Lincoln: University of Nebraska Press, 1983), 142.

[70]Ibid, 142.

[71]Sister Jerome Frances Woods, "Mexican Ethnic Leadership in San Antonio," Ph.D. dissertation, Catholic University, Washington, DC, 1947; reprint (New York: Arno Press, 1976), 101.

[72]Woods, 102.

[73]Ibid.

[74]Gilberto Juan Quezada interview with Carlos Cadena, January 31, 1991, Bexar County Historical Commission, San Antonio Public Library.

[75]Salinas, 83.

[76]Letter to Dr. Carlos E. Castañeda from Alonso S. Perales, June 30, 1948, CC, Box 34, Folder 2.

[77]Ibid.

[78]Letter from Gus C. García to Mr. Raoul A. Cortez, June 6, 1950, George I. Sánchez Papers (hereafter GIS), BLAC, Box 37, Folder: Gus Garcia.

[79]"South Side Not to Sell Land to Latin-Americans," *San Antonio Evening News,* August 17, 1949.

[80]Letter to Dr. Carlos E. Castañeda from Alonso S. Perales, June 13, 1952, CC, Box 34, Folder 3.

[81]Email to Dr. Cynthia E. Orozco from Araceli Pérez Davis, November 20, 2018.

[82]Law Firm Ledger, 1952, AP, Box 7, Folder 14. A notation states "Received from Perales Realty Company, the sum of $40.00 Oct. 13-1953" and a list of twenty-four people with notation "want homes."

[83]Real Estate Dealers License from Texas Real Estate Commission, January 1, 1952, AP, Box 6, Folder 38.

[84]Letterhead, Letter to J.T. Canales from Alonso S. Perales, December 24, 1957, JTC, Box 436, Folder 13.

[85]"Se Recibe de Abogado," ca. 1957, newspaper unidentified, Francisco Arturo Rosales notes.

[86]Letter to Honorable J.T. Canales from Alonso S. Perales, October 16, 1958, JTC, Box 431B.

[87]Law Firm Ledger, 1959, AP, Box 7, Folder 15.

[88]Alonso S. Perales, 1959 income tax return, AP, Box 1, Folder 5.

[89]Olivas, 319. *Mendoza v. Mendoza,* Court of Civil Appeals of Texas, San Antonio, February 4, 1953 255 S.W.2d 251; *Powe v. Powe,* Court of Civil Appeals of Texas, San Antonio, April 28, 1954 268 S.W.2d 558; and *Barrera v. Barrera,* Court of Civil Appeals of Texas, San Antonio (October 24, 1956) 294 S.W.2d 865; *Ydrogo v. Haltom,* Court of Civil Appeals of Texas, Eastland, May 10, 1957, 302 S.W.2d 670; *Villarreal v. U.S.,* 254 F. 2d 595 (5th Cir. 1958); and *Valdez v. Amaya,* Court of Civil Appeals of Texas, San Antonio, September 9, 1959 327 S.W. 2d 708.

[90]Email to Cynthia Orozco from Marta Carmen Perales Carrizales, November 18, 2018.

[91]Letter to Honorable J.T. Canales from Alonso S. Perales, August 14, 1958, JTC, Box 431B, Folder 15.

[92]"Rachel Gonzalez Testimony Heard," unknown newspaper, n.d., 1958, AP, Box 9, Folder 42.

[93]Letter to Hon. Alonso S. Perales from J.T. Canales, November 13, 1958, JTC, Box 431B.

[94]Letter to Honorable L.G. Mathews from Alonso S. Perales, November 3, 1958, JTC, Box 436, Folder 13.

[95]Alonso S. Perales, "Problemas del Hogar," manuscript, May 8, 1952, AP, Box 7, Folder 18.

[96]Mario T. García, "Alonso S. Perales and the Catholic Imaginary: Religion and the Mexican-American Mind," *In Defense,* 161.

[97]Benjamín Márquez, "In Defense of My People: Alonso S. Perales and the Moral Construction of Citizenship," *In Defense*, 37. See Alonso S. Perales, "¡Jóvenes México-Americanos, estudiad derecho!" Alonso S. Perales, *En Defensa* 1: 11.

[98]Email to Cynthia E. Orozco from Marta Carmen Perales Carrizales, November 20, 2018.

[99]Stationary, Letter to Alonso S. Perales from C. Campa, April 29, 1941, AP, Box 6, Folder 16.

[100]Márquez, "In Defense of My People: Alonso S. Perales," *In Defense*, 39.

[101]Ignacio M. García, *White But Not Equal, Mexican Americans, Jury Discrimination, and the Supreme Court* (Tucson: University of Arizona, 2009), 55.

[102]Ibid, 55.

[103]Woods, 98.

[104]Letter to Dr. Carlos E. Castañeda from Alonso S. Perales, April 5, 1948, CC, Box 34, Folder 2.

[105]Letter to Alonso S. Perales from Carlos E. Castañeda, August 19, 1948, CC, Box 34, Folder 2.

[106]Anthony Quiroz, "'I Can see No Alternative Except to Battle it out in Court:'" "Gus García and the Spirit of the Mexican American Generation," *Leaders of the Mexican American Generation, Biographical Essays,* ed. Anthony Quiroz (Boulder: University Press of Colorado, 2015), 212.

[107]Virginia Marie Raymond, "Faithful Dissident: Alonso S. Perales, Discrimination, and the Catholic Church," *In Defense*, ftnt. 23, 217.

[108]Woods, 103.

[109]Letter to Dr. Carlos E. Castañeda from AP, June 30, 1948, CC, Box 34, Folder 2.

[110]Cynthia E. Orozco, "Gustavo C. Garcia," *New Handbook of Texas* (hereafter NHOT) ed. Ronnie C. Tyler, Douglas E. Barnett, and Roy R. Barkley 3 (Austin: Texas State Historical Association, 1996), 84.

[111]Quiroz, 215.

[112]Letter to Dr. Carlos E. Castañeda, February 12, 1952, CC, Box 34, Folder 3.

[113]Note from Judge Lupe Salinas to Dr. Cynthia E. Orozco, November 5, 2018; "Address Delivered by Gus C. Garcia at his Testimo-

nial Dinner, February 13, 1952, San Antonio," Cristóbal Alderete Papers (hereafter CA), BLAC, Box 2, Folder 8.

[114]Letter to Dr. Carlos E. Castañeda from Alonso S. Perales, February 19, 1952, CC, Box 33, Folder 10. A major motion film is in the works about Gus Garcia. See Raul A. Reyes, "Remembering Gus Garcia, Mexican-American Civil Rights Pioneer," https:www.nbc-news. com/news/latino/remembering-gus-garcia-mexican-ameri-can-civil-rights-pioneer-n786391. Acessed August 24, 2017.

[115]See "Address Delivered by Gus C. Garcia at his Testimonial Dinner, February 13 1952, San Antonio, Casa Blanca Restaurant," CA, Box 2, Folder 8.

[116]Letter to Professor J. Luz Sáenz from Alonso S. Perales, February 12, 1952, JLS, February 12, 1952, Box 2, Folder 1. Original text: "No voy al banquete en su honor."

[117]Ibid. Original text: "No creo que deben invitar a Gustavo porque él está a favor de Sánchez y lo defenderá allí mismo si le dan la oportunidad. Él y su íntimo Idar creen que hicieron mucho porque dijeron ante el Comité del Congresso que ya tantas veces se habiá dicho . . ."

[118]Letter to Alonso S. Perales from Carlos E. Castañeda, February 15, 1952, CC, Box 33, Folder 10.

[119]Lupe S. Salinas, "Gus Garcia and Thurgood Marshall: Two legal giants fighting for justice," *Thurgood Marshall Law Review* (2003) 28: 145-175.

[120]Rodolfo Rosales, "The Rise of Chicano Middle Class Politics in San Antonio 1951 to 1985," Ph.D. diss., University of Michigan, 1991, ftnt. 26, 47.

[121]Raymond, *In Defense,* 200.

[122]Martin Donell Kohout, "Cadena, Carlos Christian," http://www.tshaonline.org/handbook/online/articles/fcaas. Accessed August 24, 2017.

[123]Gilberto Juan Quezada interview with Carlos Cadena, January 31, 1991, Bexar County Historical Commission, San Antonio Public Library.

[124]Ricardo Romo, "Carlos Cadena: World War II Veteran and Civil Rights Advocate," *La Prensa,* August 16, 2018. https://laprensa-

texas.com/carlos-cadena-world-war-ii-veteran-and-civil-rights-advocate/Accessed September 17, 2019.
[125]"List of Approved Prospective Members," Council 16?, n.d., AP, Box 1, Folder 37.
[126]Quezada with Cadena.
[127]Márquez, 39.
[128]"Carlos Cadena," St. Mary's Law School Exhibit, http://tarlton. law.utexas.edu/first-year-societies/carlos-cadena, Accessed April 16, 2018.
[129]"List of Approved Prospective Members," ca. 1949, AP, Box 5, Folder 21.
[130]Olivas, "The Legal Career,"335.
[131]Typed copy, San Antonio Light, January 18, 1953, AP, Box 9, Folder 38.
[132]Quezada with Cadena.
[133] Romo, "Carlos Cadena."
[134] Ignacio M. García, 147.
[135] Ibid, 196.
[136]Olivas, 335-336.
[137]Quezada with Cadena.
[138] Ignacio M. García, 196.
[139] Ibid, 150.
[140]Ibid, 56.
[141]Ibid, 125.
[142]Ibid, 141.
[143]Quezada with Cadena. A calavera was written about Cadena. See "Judge Carlos Cadena," "Las Tremendas Calaveras, Suplemento Anual de la Revista Cultural 'Cosmos,'" Nov. 1976, AP, Box 11, Folder 16.
[144]Banquet.
[145]https://en.wikipedia.org/wiki/Henry_B._González. Accessed September 18, 2018.
[146]Martin Donell Kohout, "Henry Barbosa Gonzalez," http://www. tshaonline.org/handbook/online/articles/fgo76. Accessed July 27, 2018.
[147]Salinas, 84.

[148]Clarke Newton, *Famous Mexican-Americans* (New York: Dodd Mead, 1972), 77.

[149]Kohout.

[150]"P.A.P.A. on the March," PAPA pamphlet, CC, Box 34, Folder 2.

[151]Rosales, 43.

[152]Letter to Mr. Alonso S. Perales from Felix J. Cerda, May 15, 1948, AP, Box 5, Folder 14.

[153]Rosales, 44.

[154]Kohout; José Angel Gutiérrez, *Albert A. Peña Jr., Dean of Chicano Politics* (East Lansing: Michigan State University Press, 2017), 52.

[155]Rosales, 78.

[156]Letter to Lic. Alonso S. Perales from Jack Danciger, May 26, 1958, AP, Box 4, Folder 51.

[157]Rosales, 79.

[158]*Testimonio, A Documentary History of the Mexican American Struggle for Civil Rights,* ed. F. Arturo Rosales (Houston: Arte Público Press, 2000), 205.

[159]Oral History Interview with Albert Peña Jr., 15, Center for Mexican American Studies, Special Collections, University of Texas at Arlington Libraries. Dr. José Angel Gutiérrez conducted this interview in 1996.

[160]Gutiérrez, 12.

[161]Rosales, "The Rise," 62.

[162] Gutiérrez, 48-49.

[163]Ibid, 33-41.

[164]Oral History Interview with Albert Peña Jr., np.

[165]"Albert A. Peña Jr.," Golden Years Appreciation Banquet, A Banquet Honoring Distinguished Mexican Americans, September 16, 1974, Dr. Cynthia E. Orozco Papers, Ruidoso, New Mexico.

[166]Rosales, "The Rise of Chicano," 81.

[167]Email from Judge Lupe Salinas to Cynthia Orozco, November 7, 2018.

[168]Veronica Salazar, "Determination should mean victory," *San Antonio Express News,* August 21, 1977.

[169]Alonso S. Perales, "Fiesta Quinceañera de una Damita Ejemplar," (Arquitectos de Nuestros Propios Destinos) *La Prensa*, November 23, 1958, AP, Box 9, Folder 42. Original text: "la señorita Martínez simboliza a perfección el tipo de damita que toda señorita debería de ser."

[170]Maggie Rivas-Rodríguez, *Texas Mexican Americans & Postwar Civil Rights* (Austin: University of Texas Press, 2015), 116.

[171]"Vilma Socorro Martínez," *Encyclopedia of the Mexican American Civil Rights Movement,* ed. Matt S. Meier and Margo Gutierrez (Westport, Conn.: Greenwood Press, 2000): 141-142.

[172]Rivas-Rodríguez, 116; Cynthia E. Orozco, "Chicana Rights Project," *NHOT* 1:69; Lori A. Flores, "A Community of Limits and the Limits of Community: MALDEF's Chicana Rights Project, Empowering the 'Typical Chicana,' and the Question of Civil Rights, 1974-1983," *Journal of American Ethnic History,* (Spring 2008) 27: 3, 81–110.

[173]Janet Morey and Wendy Dunn, *Famous Mexican Americans* (New York: Cobblehill Books, 1989), 66.

[174]Letter from Vilma S. Martínez to the Alonso S. Perales Conference Organizers, December 21, 2011, *In Defense,* iii.

[175]Email from Vilma S. Martínez to Cynthia Orozco, May 29, 2018. Perhaps Jorge Rangel of Alice, Texas also knew of Perales. Not only did he become an attorney, in 1972 he co-authored an article on segregated Mexican schools for the *Harvard Civil Rights-Civil Liberties Law Review.* See Jorge C. Rangel and Carlos M. Alcala, *Harvard Civil Rights-Civil Liberties Law Review* 7:2 (March 1972).

[176]http://www.en.wikipedia.org/wiki/Vilma_Socorro_Mart%ADnez Accessed August 31, 2012.

[177]Info provided by Judge Lupe Salinas. Email from Judge Lupe Salinas to Cynthia Orozco, November 7, 2018.

[178]Teresa Palomo Acosta, "Edna Cisneros Carroll," *Handbook of Texas,* http://www.tshaonline.org/handbook/online/articles/fcarr. Accessed July 27, 2019.

[179]See "Longtime Dallas lawyer, civil rights activist Adelfa Callejo dies at 90," January 2014 accessed at https://www.dallasnews. com/obit-

uaries/obituaries/2014/01/25/longtime-dallas-lawyer-civil-rights-activist-adelfa-callejo-dies-at-90 Accessed November 13, 2018.
[180]Attorney Joseph F. Ceniceros to Mrs. Alonso S. Perales, January 12, 1971, AP, Box 10, Folder 1.
[181]Olivas, xi.
[182]Ibid, "The Legal Career," 315.
[183]Ibid, 316.
[184]Salinas, "Gus Garcia and Thurgood Marshall," 17.

CHAPTER 15

[1]"Responses of LULAC Councils to Questions from Weeks, 1930," Oliver Douglas Weeks Collection, Box 1, Folder 8, Benson Latin American Collection (hereafter BLAC), University of Texas at Austin.
[2]Richard A. Garcia, "Alonso S. Perales: The Voice and Visions of a Citizen Intellectual," *Leaders of the Mexican American Generation,* ed. Anthoy Quiroz (Boulder: University Press of Colorado, 2015), 91.
[3]Donna Kabalen de Bichara, "Self-Writing and Collective Representation: The Literary Enunciation of Historical Reality and Cultural Values," *In Defense of My People, Alonso S. Perales and the Development of Mexican-American Public Intellectuals,* ed. Michael A. Olivas (Houston: Arte Público Press, 2012), 244.
[4]Garcia, 206.
[5]Ibid, 286.
[6]Ibid, 267.
[7]Thomas A. Baylis, "Leadership Changes in Contemporary San Antonio," *The Politics of San Antonio, Community, Progress, and Power,* ed. David R. Johnson, John A. Booth, and Richard J. Harris (Lincoln: University of Nebraska, 1983), 99; David Montejano, *Quixote's Soldiers, A Local History of the Chicano Movement, 1966-1981* (Austin: University of Texas, 2010), 14-15.
[8]Tucker Gibson, "Mayoralty Politics in San Antonio, 1955-1979," *The Politics,* 122.
[9]Richard A. Garcia, *Rise of the Mexican American Middle Class in San Antonio, Texas, 1929-1941* (College Station: Texas A&M Uni-

versity, 1991), 252; Aaron E. Sánchez, "Mendigos de nacionalidad: Mexican-Americanism and Ideologies of Belonging in a New Era of Citizenship, Texas 1910–1967," *In Defense,* 97–118.

[10] *Testimonio: A Documentary History of the Mexican American Struggle for Civil Rights,* ed. F. Arturo Rosales, (Houston: Arte Público Press, 2000), 167.

[11] Ralph Edward Morales III, "Hijos de la Gran Guerra: The Creation of the Mexican American Identity in Texas, 1836-1929," Ph.D. diss., Texas A&M University, College Station, 2015, 165.

[12] Alonso S. Perales, "El México Americano y la Política del Sur de Texas," (San Antonio: Artes Gráficas, 1931), 11, BLAC.

[13] Lupe S. Salinas, "Legally White, Socially Brown: Alonso S. Perales and His Crusade for Justice for La Raza," *In Defense,* 92.

[14] Perales, "El Mexico Americano." Original text: "que tolera y defiende a sus diputados que injustamente arrestan, y a veces privan de la vida, a ciudadanos o residents pacíficos y honrados "

[15] Lic. Alonso S. Perales, "El Poll Tax y el Ciudadano," in Perales, "El México Americano," 12.

[16] Alonso S. Perales, "El 'Poll-Tax' o Impuesto Electoral," *En Defen- sa de Mi Raza* 2 (San Antonio: Artes Gráficas, 1937), 62. Original text: "Claro que sí, pues sin eso el pueblo es el que los elige, el pueblo es el que debe echarlos fuera, votando en contra de ellos, si son funcionarios incompetentes, deshonestos, injustos y buenos para nada."

[17] "Plática Sustentada por Alonso S. Perales a través de los micrófonos de la 'Hora Nacional' el día 29 del actual," no date, Alonso S. Perales Papers (hereafter AP), M.D. Anderson Library, University of Houston, Box 8, Folder 19.

[18] Alonso S. Perales, "El 'Poll Tax' o Impuesto Electoral."

[19] Letter to J.T. Canales from Alonso S. Perales, June 9, 1928, AP, Box 4, Folder 10.

[20] Rodolfo Rosales, "The Rise of Chicano Middle Class Politics in San Antonio, 1951 to 1985," Ph.D. diss., University of Michigan, 1991, ftnt. 16, 46.

[21] "Resumen de Resoluciones presentadas por el Lic. Alonso S. Perales, Delegado de Concilio Num. 16 de San Antonio " *En Defensa de la Raza* 2 (San Antonio: Artes Gráficas, 1937), 75.

[22]Benjamín Márquez, "In Defense of My People: Alonso S. Perales and the Moral Construction of Citizenship," *In Defense,* 42.

[23]Virginia Marie Raymond, "Faithful Dissident: Alonso S. Perales, Discrimination, and the Catholic Church," *In Defense,* 201; Letter from Alonso S. Perales letter to Allan Shivers, August 19, 1954, AP, Box 2, Folder 20.

[24]Letter to Dr. Carlos E. Castañeda from Alonso S. Perales, May 14, 1954, Carlos E. Castañeda Papers (hereafter CC), BLAC, Box 34, Folder 3.

[25]Letter to Dr. Carlos E. Castañeda from Alonso S. Perales, May 14, 1954, CC, Box 34, Folder 3.

[26]Letter to Honorable Judge J.T. Canales from Alonso S. Perales, December 28, 1959, José T. Canales Estate Collection (hereafter JTC), James Jernigan Library, South Texas Archives, Texas A&M University at Kingsville, Box 431B.

[27]Garcia, *Rise,* 317.

[28]Email to Cynthia E. Orozco from Marta Carmen Perales Carrizales, November 20, 2018.

[29]*Testimonio,* 147-148. See "Preparación Para un Hogar Feliz," *La Voz,* May 23, 1952, AP, Box 28, Folder 23.

[30]Gabriela González, "Jovita Idar: The Ideological Origins of a Transnational Advocate for La Raza," *Texas Women: Their Histories, Their Lives,* ed. Elizabeth Hayes Tuner, Stephanie Cole, and Rebecca Sharpless (Athens: University of Georgia Press, 2015), 114; Gabriela González, *Redeeming La Raza, Transborder Modernity, Race, Respectability, and Rights* (Oxford: Oxford University Press, 2018).

[31]Perales, "El México Americano, Comentarios,"11.

[32]"La Liga de Ciudadanos Latino-Americanos Logra Instalar Una Asociación Más de Padres y Maestros," *Alma Latina:* 10, M.C. Gonzales Papers, BLAC, Box 1, Folder 2.

[33]M.C. Trub, "Boy Scouts and Scouters in L.U.L.A.C," *LULACNews,* Nov. 1934, Alfred Hernández Papers, Houston Metropolitan Research Center.

[34]No title, *San Antonio Express,* March 18, 1932, AP, Box 1, Folder 12.

[35]"Presidents of Local Councils," no date, AP, Box 1, Folder 37. This item is dated by the fact that New Mexican LULAC councils are included and they appeared in the mid 1930s.

[36]Letter to Mrs. Ester Pérez de Carvajal from Alonso S. Perales, June 11, 1940, AP, Box 1, Folder 23; "Presidents of Local Councils," n.d., AP, Box 3, Folder 36. This civic club was not a LULAC chapter.

[37]Letter to My dear Friend Perales from J.T. Canales, April 17, 1933, AP, https://digital.lib.uh.edu/collection/perales/item/57 Accessed September 9, 2019.

[38]"Brief Resume of the Work Accomplished at the Del Rio Annual Convention," *LULAC News,* May 1933, 13, Dolph Briscoe Center for American History, University of Texas at Austin.

[39]Form letter, "Liga de Ciudadanos Latino-Americanos," May 22, 1937, AP, Box 1, Folder 37.

[40]Letter to Alonso S. Perales from Mrs. F.I. Montemayor, Nov. 15, 1936, AP, Box 4, Folder 1.

[41]Perales, "El Poll-Tax o Impuesto Electoral," *En Defensa,* 2: 64.

[42]Perales, "Lo Que Significa Para Nosotros Las Escuelas Para Adultos," *En Defensa,* 2: 22.

[43]"Lista de personas que están dispuestas a cooperar en la campaña electoral municipal de 1941," (note), AP, Box 1, Folder 8.

[44]Lic. Alonso S. Perales, "El Impuesto Electoral y el Porvenir de Nuestro Pueblo," *La Prensa,* January 11, 1948, AP, Box 9, Folder 10. Original text: "Nuestras damas de origen mexicano también deben pagar el impuesto electoral, sin falta, puesto que tienen el derecho de votar, necesitamos su ayuda. El voto de la mujer México-Americana nos es indispensable para el triunfo."

[45]Perales, "El México Americano y La Política," 2.

[46]Letter to Alonso S. Perales from C. Campa, April 28, 1941, AP Box 6, Folder 16. The stationary notes the group was founded December 1,1932.

[47]Garcia, 271.

[48]"Association of Independent Voters," Eleuterio Escobar, First Autobiography draft, 1c, Eleuterio Escobar Papers (hereafter EE), BLAC.

[49]Handwritten notes by Perales of April 20, 1932 meeting, Association of Independent Voters, AP, Box 1, Folder 12. Perales dates the organization's founding date here.

[50]"Aims & Purposes of the Association of Independent Voters, 1932," EE, Box 2, Folder 1.

[51]"Aims & Purposes of the Association of Independent Voters," n.d, ca. 1932, AP, Box 5, Folder 18.

[52]"Tentative Agenda for Tuesday's Meeting," January 18, 1932, AP, Box 3, Folder 42.

[53]Stationary, Association of Independent Voters, May 25, 1932, EE, Box 2, Folder 1.

[54]Letter to Hon. Henry A. Guerra, Chairman of Membership Committee from Alonso S. Perales, May 14, 1932, AP, Box 1, Folder 12.

[55]"Un Concurrido Mitin Hubo El Jueves," *La Prensa,* July 14, 1934, AP, Box 9, Folder 40.

[56]Summary of special meeting, Asociación de Votantes Independientes at Casino Mexicano hall, n.d. (ca. 1932), AP, Box 1, Folder 10. Original text: "que no estamos contentos conque los de nuestra raza ocupen únicamente puestos de barrenderos y recogedores de basura en el gobierno de la ciudad de SA y el del condado de Bejar." . . . "uniéndose para presenter un frente solido."

[57]"Ejemplo de la Boleta Apoyada por la Asociación de Votantes Independientes," EE, no box, no folder.

[58]Unsigned letter to Hon. E. Escobar, President, Association of Independent Voters, June 11, 1932, EE, Box 2, Folder 1.

[59]Ibid.

[60]"Mensaje del Lic. Alonso S. Perales a la Colonia Mexicana de San Antonio, Texas," 1933, EE, Box 2, Folder 1. Original text: "Mensaje del Lic. Alonso S. Perales a la Colonia Mexicana de San Antonio, Texas. Si el gobierno federal ha demostrado confianza al Lic. Perales; nosotros también debemos tenerla."

[61]"Mensaje." This is also located in AP, Box 1, Folder 8.

[62]Letter from Eleuterio Escobar to Alonso S. Perales, October 5, 1932, EE, Box 2, Folder 1.

[63]Minutes, Association of Independent Voters, January 27, 1932, AP, Box 1, Folder 12.

[64]"Un Concurrido Mitin Hubo El Jueves," *La Prensa,* July 14, 1934. The subtitle was "Tres Mil Personas Asistieron al efectuado en la Escuela Navarro."

[65]Letter to J.T. Canales from Alonso S. Perales, AP, Box 4, Folder 10.

[66]Mario T. García, *Mexican Americans, Leadership, Ideology, and Identity, 1930-1960* (New Haven: Yale University Press, 1989), 65.

[67]"Radio Talk to be Made by Alonso S. Perales, Local Attorney, Over Station KABC, Friday May 2nd,? (no year identified) at 6:46 P.M," AP, Box 8, Folder 20.

[68]Letter to J.T. Canales from AP, March 13, 1942, JT, Box 431, Folder 15.

[69]Letter to Dr. Carlos E. Castañeda from Alonso S. Perales, September 14, 1937, CC, Folder: Perales.

[70]"At a meeting to be held Wednesday April 30, 1941," AP, Box 8, Folder 20.

[71]"Memorandum, Subject: Conditions in San Antonio, Texas," February 23, 1939, AP, Box 3, Folder 42.

[72]"Arrangements Completed for Huge Americanism Meeting," n.d. (ca. late 1930s?), AP, Box 1, Folder 37.

[73]Charter, The League of Loyal Americans, No. 72540, Filed in office of the Secretary of State, December 21, 1937.

[74]"Arrangements Completed for Huge Americanism Meeting," *San Antonio Express* (?), n.d. (ca. late 1930s), AP, Box 3, Folder 37.

[75]"White Classification in Vital Statistics to Include Mexicans," *San Antonio News,* August 19, 1939, AP, Box 14, Folder 7.

[76]Ibid. [77] Ibid.

[78]Resolution by the League of Loyal Americans, AP, Box 3, Folder 42.

[79]García, 271.

[80]Ibid.

[81]"League of Loyal Americans OK's Importing of Police Chief," *San Antonio Evening News,* July 26, 1939, AP, Box 9, Folder 32.

[82]"Dr. Berchelmann Report Approved," *San Antonio Express,* February 23, 1939, AP, Box 9, Folder 38.

[83]Mario T. García, *Católicos, Resistance and Affirmation in Chicano History* (Austin: University of Texas, 2008), 75.

[84]"Justicia Social," 1:2 (Diciembre 1940), CC, Box 22, Folder 10. Original text: "órgano anual editado en Pro de Fomento Cívico entre el Conglomerado Americano de origen Hispano, bajo el patrocinio del Concilio Núm. 16 de 'The League of Loyal Ameri- cans.'" It is also located in AP, microfilm reel 2.

[85]Letter to JT Canales from Alonso S. Perales, 1937, JTC, Box 436, Folder 13.

[86]"Memorandum, Subject: Conditions in San Antonio, Texas," February 23, 1939, AP, Box 3, Folder 42.

[87]"Salinas Elected head of League," unknown newspaper, July 16, 1939, AP, Box 9, Folder 41.

[88]Poster, "Grandiosa Junta Política Anti-Maverick Patrocinada por El Comité de los 100," AP, Box 14.

[89]Letter to Hon. Alonso S. Perales from C.E. Castañeda, November 4, 1941, CC, Box 33, Folder 12; "Statement of Dr. Carlos E. Castañeda, Special Assistant on Latin-American Problems to the Chairman of the President's Committee on Fair Employment Practice (sic), before the Senate Committee on Labor and Education in the Hearings Held September 8, 1944, on S bill 2048, to prohibit discrimination because of race, creed, color, national origin or ancestry," 1, Carlos Eduardo Castañeda Papers (hereafter CC2), Dolph Briscoe Center for American History, University of Texas at Austin. This isa second minor Castañeda collection.

[90]Laura E. Cannon, "Situational Solidarity: LULAC's Civil Rights Strategy and the Challenge of the Mexican American Worker, 1934-1946," Ph.D. diss., Texas Tech, 2016, chapter 5, n.p.; "Dr. Berchelmann Report Approved," *San Antonio Express,* February 23, 1939, AP, Box 9, Folder 38.

[91]Sister Frances Jerome Woods, "Mexican Ethnic Leadership in San Antonio," Ph.D. diss, Catholic University of America, 1947, reprint (New York: Arno Press, 1976), 35-36.

[92]José Angel Gutiérrez, "Chicanos and Mexicans Under Surveillance: 1940-1980," *Renato Rosaldo Lecture Series Monograph* (Tucson: Mexican American Studies & Research Center, Spring 1986), 55, ftnt 20.

[93]Woods, 104.

[94]"At a meeting to be held Wednesday April 30, 1941," AP, Box 8, Folder 20. Members are listed in a 1943 Congressional testimony. More familiar names included Charles Albidress Sr., Florencio R. Flores, Charles Albidress Jr., Laureano Flores, Manuel A. Urbina, and Dr. Carlos E. Castañeda. See Perales, *Are We Good Neighbors?* reprint (New York: Arno Press, 1974), 133.

[95]Letter on stationary, Letter to Estimados amigos from Alonso S. Perales, May 9, 1946, JLS, Box 2, Folder 1.

[96]Woods, 104.

[97]I found no evidence of Anglo members.

[98]Letter to Dr. Carlos E. Castañeda from Alonso S. Perales, March 9, 1943, CC, Box 34, Folder 1. His address here in 1943 was Suite 714, Gunter Building.

[99]"Como Se Trabaja en Tejas Contra la Discriminación Racial," *Fraternidad,* December 1, 1944, AP, Box 11, Folder 6.

[100]Letter to Estimados Amigos from Alonso S. Perales, President, Committee of One Hundred, May 9, 1946, José de la Luz Sáenz Papers (hereafter JLS), BLAC, Box 2, Folder 1.

[101]Testimony of Alonso S. Perales before US Congress, 1943, *Are We* 114-115.

[102]Letter to Guy Walker, President, Pecos Chamber of Commerce, March 29, 1945 from Alonso S. Perales, Committee of One Hundred, League of Loyal Americans, Perales, *Are We,* 265.

[103]"Press Statement of Alonso S. Perales, Director General of the Committee of One Hundred and the League of Loyal Americans," Perales, *Are We,* 266.

[104]Letter to His Excellency Franklin Delano Roosevelt from Alonso S. Perales, March 31, 1944, Perales, *Are We,* 278-280. See 258 ftnt 15 for more correspondence between Perales and FDR in 1944 in Julie Leininger Pycior, *LBJ & Mexican Americans, the Paradox of Power* (Austin: University of Texas, 1997).

[105]Letter to Dennis Chávez from Director General, Committee of One Hundred, League of Loyal Americans, December 14, 1944, AP, Box 10, Folder 48.

[106]Letter to Honorable Clare Boothe Luce, Member of the US House of Representatives from Alonso S. Perales, Committee of One

Hundred, League of Loyal Americans, April 15, 1944, Perales, *Are We,* 277.

[107]Letter to Commanding General, Eighth Service Command, United States Office from Alonso S. Perales, Committee of One Hundred American Citizens of Mexican Descent, League of Loyal Americans, November 16, 1944, Perales, *Are We,* 275-276.

[108]Letter to His Excellency Harry S. Truman from Alonso S. Perales, Committee of One Hundred, February 8, 1946, Perales, *Are We,* 273.

[109]Letter to Hon. Martin Kessler from Alonso S. Perales, League of Loyal Americans, December 12, 1946, Perales, *Are We,* 258.

[110]Letter to Honorable Joint Committee on Housing of the Congress of the United States from Alonso S. Perales, Committee of One Hundred, The League of Loyal Americans, October 29, 1947, Perales, *Are We,* 229-230.

[111]Letter from Alonso S. Perales, Committee of One Hundred, League of Loyal Americans to Watson Miller, Commissioner of Immigration, November 24, 1947, Perales, *Are We,* 228-229.

[112]Letter to Mr. Alonso S. Perales from Carlos E. Castañeda, April 11, 1947, CC, Box 34, Folder 2.

[113]Affiliation card of League of Loyal Americans with the Liga Pro Defensa Escolar, EE, Box 2, Folder 1.

[114]Oral History Interview with Albert Peña Jr., CMAS 15, Special Collections, University of Texas at Arlington Libraries. This interview was by Dr. José Angel Gutiérrez in 1996.

[115]"Study Attack Draws Retorts," *San Antonio Light,* December 9, 1951, Adela Sloss-Vento Papers (hereafter ASV), Austin, Texas.

[116]Ibid.

[117]Fundraising form letter for Dennis Chávez from Alonso. S. Perales, May 9, 1946, JLS, Box 2, Folder 1.

[118]Letter to Dr. Carlos E. Castañeda from Alonso S. Perales, April 19, 1946 and May 23, 1946, CC, Box 34, Folder 2.

[119]Letter to Dr. Carlos E. Castañeda from Alonso S. Perales, June 13, 1946, CC, Box 34, Folder 2.

[120]Don Politico, "Poll Tax Still Curtails Negroes," *San Antonio Express-News,* January 30, 1941, AP, Box 1, Folder 10.

[121]"Statement of Alonso S. Perales on the Recent School Board Election," *The Pan-American,* 1: 12 (1946), AP, Box 11, Folder 6.

[122]Vote for Alonso S. Perales card, April 6, 1946, CC, Box 34, Folder 2.

[123]No title, document begins "We are one hundred percent," ca. 1946, AP, Box 1, Folder 1.

[125]"Statement of Alonso S. Perales, Candidate for Trustee of the San Antonio Independent School District," 1946, AP, Box 5, Folder 20. Original text: "Es Ud. interesado en el progresso" "a uno de nuestra raza que vale por y proteje los intereses de nuestra niñez escolar."

[126]"El Lic. Perales lanza su candidatura para miembro del consejo escolar," *La Prensa,* March 10, 1946, AP, Box 9, Folder 38.

[127]"Perales Seeks Board Post," San Antonio unidentified newspaper, March 26, 1946, AP, Box 9, Folder 41.

[128]No title, begins "We are one hundred percent."

[129]"Letter from Oliver Sawtelle, past president, San Antonio Builders' Exchange to Fellow Members, April 3, 1946," *The Pan-American* 1:12 (1946), 5, AP, Box 11, Folder 6.

[130]Letter to Dr. Carlos I. Castañeda from Alonso S. Perales, April 9, 1946, CC, Box 34, Folder 2.

[131]"An Interview with Mrs. Perales," *Chicano Times,* AP, Box 14 oversize.

[132]Judith Kaaz Doyle, "Maury Maverick and Racial Politics in San Antonio, Texas, 1938-1941," *African Americans in South Texas,* ed. Bruce A. Glasrud (College Station: Texas A&M University 2011), 208.

[133]Ibid, 210.

[134]Ibid.

[135]Ibid, 213.

[136]Ibid, 214.

[137]Ibid, 216.

[138]Ibid, 206, 213.

[139]Richard A. Garcia, *The Rise,* 213.

[140]Ibid, 213.

[141]Ibid, 214.

[142]Ibid, 216.

[143] Woods, 104. Woods is referring to Perales and Maverick but does not cite their names.

[144] Garcia, 216.

[145] Letter to Dr. Carlos E. Castañeda from Alonso S. Perales, March 9, 1943, CC, Box 34, Folder 1; Letter to Alonso S. Perales, October 21, 1942, CC, Box 34, Folder 1.

[146] "Radio Talk to be made by Alonso S. Perales, Local Attorney, Over Station KABC, Friday, May 2nd," unidentified source, no date, AP, Box 8, Folder 20.

[147] "Perales sees Discrimination," *San Antonio Light,* June 29, 1940, AP, Box 14, Folder 4.

[148] "Resignation Action Demanded by Perales," *San Antonio Express,* June 20, 1940, AP Box 9, Folder 36.

[149] "Indigna Humillación Para el Pueblo Mexicano," newspaper insert, no date (ca. 1940), AP, Box 9, Folder 36.

[150] "Candidates Know Efforts would be wasted," *San Antonio Light,* April 20, 1941, AP Box 14, Folder 9.

[151] Gilberto Juan Quezada interview with Carlos Cadena, January 31, 1991, Bexar County Historical Commission, San Antonio Public Library.

[152] "Plática por el Lic. Alonso S. Perales en favor de la planilla Maverick, el 20 de Mayo de 1947, a Través de la Estación KCOR," AP, Box 8, Folder 19.

[153] Donna M. Kabalen de Bichara, "Self-Writing and Collective Representation: The Literary Enunciation of Historical Reality and Cultural Values," *In Defense,* 247.

[154] "Por Donde Principiar," *Las Noticias,* May 14, 1927, Cynthia Orozco Notes of Alonso S. Perales Papers, 1979, 31.

[155] Letter to the Honorable Morris Sheppard from Alonso S. Perales, January 13, 1927, AP, Box 5, Folder 6.

[156] "Protest to Miriam Ferguson," October 24, 1926, newspaper clipping, AP, Box 9, Folder 32.

[157] "Nuestro Voto Razonado por su Excelencia, Candidato a Reelección para Gobernador de Texas," (newspaper insert), CC, Box 33, Folder 11.

[158]Letter to Dr. Carlos E. Castañeda from Alonso S. Perales, July 29, 1952, CC, Box 34, Folder 3.

[159]Note on back of envelope to Consul of Nicaragua, no date, AP, Box 1, Folder 12.

[160]Virginia Marie Raymond, "Faithful Dissident. Alonso S. Perales, Discrimination, and the Catholic Church," *In Defense,* 201.

[161]Letter to Hon. Alonso S. Perales from J.T. Canales, August 20, 1954, CC, Box 431B. Original text: ". . . los grupos laboristas, como C.I.O. y sus aliados, lo mismo que un grupo fanático del partido demócrata le están dando mucha contra y exitando a nuestro pueblo Latino-Americano . . ."

[162]Letter to Dr. Carlos E. Castañeda from Alonso S. Perales, September 13, 1954, CC, Box 34 Folder 3.

[163]"Por Qué Voté por el Gov. Shivers," *La Verdad,* September 17, 1954, AP, Box 9, Folder 42.

[164]Salinas, "Legally White," *In Defense,* 81; Letter to the President from Alonso S. Perales, February 14, 1927, AP, Box 2, Folder 13.

[165]Letter to President Calvin Coolidge from Alonso S. Perales, February 14, 1927, AP, Box 2, Folder 13.

[166]Perales, *Are We,* 278-281.

[167]Benjamín Márquez, "In Defense of My People: Alonso S. Perales and the Moral Construction of Citizenship," *In Defense,* 29. Márquez notes that he was a member of the Democratic Party.

[168]Natalie Mendoza, "The Good Neighbor Comes Home: The State, Mexicans and Mexican Americans, and Regional Consciousness in the US Southwest during World War II," Ph.D. diss., University of California at Berkeley, 2016, 34.

[169]Perales, *Are We,* 63. This is a letter from Perales to Mr. Robert K. Carr, US President's Committee on Civil Rights.

[170]Email to Cynthia Orozco from Marta Carmen Perales Carrizales, November 20, 2018; "Rally speaker," No title, *Brownsville Herald,* n.d. (ca. 1952), AP, Box 9, Folder 32.

[171]Letter to My dear friend Perales from Carlos E. Castañeda, July 4, 1952, CC, Box 34, Folder 3.

[172]"Local Lawyer Appointed to Judge's Post," *McAllen Monitor,* September (no date specified) 1947, AP, Box 9, Folder 41.

[173]Letter to Honorable John Q. Adams from Alonso S. Perales, Sept. 17, 1954, CC, Box 431B.

[174]Ibid.

[175]Letter to Dr. Carlos E. Castañeda from Alonso S. Perales, September 17, 1954, CC, Box 34, Folder 3.

[176]Letter to Honorable J.T. Canales from Alonso S. Perales, October 9, 1954, CC, Box 431B.

[177]"General Elections Nov. 2nd 1954, Judge 139th, District Court," AP, Box 4, Folder 3.

[178]Ibid.

[179]Richard A. Garcia, "Alonso S. Perales: The Voice and Visions of a Citizen Intellectual," *Leaders of the Mexican American Generation, Biographical Essays,* ed. Anthony Quiroz (Boulder: University of Colorado, 2015), 108. Garcia incorrectly believed it was a "sanctioned representative of LULAC" and he incorrectly added that it died only after 1974 when LULAC could lobby directly. See 112-113 ftnt. 3.

CHAPTER 16

[1]Michael A. Olivas, "Introduction, Alonso S. Perales, The Rule of Law and the Development of Mexican-American Public Intellectuals," *In Defense of My People, Alonso S. Perales and the Development of Mexican-American Public Intellectuals,* ed. Michael A. Olivas (Houston: Arte Público Press, 2012), ix.

[2]Lupe S. Salinas, "Legally White, Socially Brown: Alonso S. Perales and His Crusade for Justice for La Raza, *In Defense,* 93.

[3]Carlos Kevin Blanton, *George I. Sánchez, The Long Fight for Mexican American Integration* (New Haven: Yale University Press, 2015).

[4]Ignacio M. García, *White But Not Equal, Mexican Americans, Jury Discrimination, and the Supreme Court* (Tucson: University of Arizona, 2009), 10. García mentioned M.C. Gonzales but not Perales.

[5]Benjamín Márquez, "In Defense of My People: Alonso S. Perales and the Moral Construction," *In Defense,* 31.

[6]Alonso Perales, "Un periódico es útil cuando sirve los intereses de la colectividad," *La Prensa,* Feb. 13, 1946, Alonso S. Perales (here-after AP), M.D. Anderson Library, University of Houston, Box 8, Folder 5. Original text: "Un periódico es útil cuando sirve los intereses de la colectividad."

[7]Salinas, *In Defense,* 93.

[8]*Spanish-Surnamed American College Graduates, 1971-72, Compiled by Cabinet Committee on Opportunities for the Spanish-Speaking* (Washington DC, 1971-72), 51.

[9]Richard A. Garcia, "Alonso S. Perales: The Voice and Visions of a Citizen Intellectual," *Leaders of the Mexican American Generation, Biographical Essays,* ed. Anthony Quiroz (Boulder: University of Colorado, 2015), 86.

[10]Ibid, 91.

[11]Ibid, 108.

[12]Letter to Dr. Carlos E. Castañeda from Alonso S. Perales, November 7, 1941, Carlos E. Castañeda Papers (hereafter CC), Benson Latin American Collection (hereafter BLAC), University of Texas at Austin, Box 33, Folder 12.

[13]Alonso S. Perales, "My Message to United Latin American Citizens," n.d., AP, Box 1, Folder 41. This is dated by the mention of the J. Luz Sáenz WWI memorial which was in the works before 1932.

[14]Emilio Zamora, "Connecting Causes: Alonso S. Perales, Hemispheric Unity, and Mexican Rights in the United States," *In Defense,* 305.

[15]Michael A. Olivas, "The Legal Career of Alonso S. Perales," *In Defense,* 336.

[16]Donna M. Kabalen de Bichara, "Self-Writing and Collective Representation: The Literary Enunciation of Historical Reality and Cultural Values," *In Defense,* 244.

[17]Richard A. Garcia, *Rise of the Mexican American Middle Class in San Antonio, 1929-1941* (College Station: Texas A&M University, 1991), 283.

[18]Salinas, 91.

[19]Márquez, 34-35.

[20]Letter fragment, September 10, 1927, Cynthia E. Orozco notes of Alonso S. Perales Papers (hereafter ON), 1979, 102.

[21]"Cómo Se Trabaja en Tejas Contra La Discriminación Racial," *Fraternidad,* December 1, 1944, AP, Box11, Folder 6.

[22]Historian Laura E. Cannon makes this assumption but provided no evidence. See Cannon, "Situational Solidarity: LULAC's Civil Rights Strategy and the Challenge of the Mexican American Worker, 1934-1946," Ph.D. diss., Texas Tech, 2016, chapter 5.

[23]Adela Sloss-Vento, *Alonso S. Perales, His Struggle for the Rights of Mexican-Americans* (San Antonio: Artes Gráficas, 1977), 7.

[24]Letter to Mrs. Donna Tobias from Mrs. Adela Sloss-Vento, May 4, 1979, Adela Sloss-Vento Papers, Austin.

[25]Special passport to Dominican Republic as Spanish-English translator and stenographer, no. 8136, October 30, 1922, AP, Box 1, Folder 6. The passport reported his height.

[26]Alonso S. Perales Conference & Exhibit: Raymond [Raimundo] Alfonso Perales speaks about his father. https://www.youtube.com/watch?v=OcT 8q4nObiA Accessed October 23, 2019.

[27]Letter to Dr. Carlos E. Castañeda from Alonso S. Perales, September 6, 1936, CC, Box 33, Folder 12.

[28]"Statement of Alonso S. Perales, Chairman, Committee of One Hundred, Director General, League of Loyal Americans, San Antonio, Texas," Alonso S. Perales, *Are We Good Neighbors?* reprint (New York: Arno Press, 1974), 115.

[29]J.T. Canales?, "A Quien Corresponde," May 23, 1932, AP, Box 1, Folder 36.

[30]Letter to Mrs. Ben Garza, July 30, 1937 from Alonso S. Perales, AP, Box 4, Folder 18.

[31]Letter to Luis S. Perales from Alonso S. Perales, November 5, 1936, AP, Box 2, Folder 11.

[32]See Alonso S. Perales, "El Verdadero Origen de la Liga de Ciudadanos Unidos Latinoamericanos," *En Defensa de Mi Raza* 2 (San Antonio: Artes Gráficas, 1937), 101-116; Cynthia E. Orozco, "Bernardo F. Garza," *New Handbook of Texas,* ed. Ronnie C. Tyler, Douglas E. Barnett, and Roy R. Barkley 2 (Austin: Texas State Historical Asso-

ciation, 1996), 105; Cynthia E. Orozco, "Ben and Adelaida Garza Fought for Equality," *Corpus Christi Times,* July 2, 1999; and Cynthia E. Orozco, "Ben Garza, LULAC's First President," *Corpus Christi Caller,* August 22, 2017.

[33] Adela Sloss-Vento, "The Problem of Many Texas Towns," *El Heraldo,* September 16, 1943, Adela Sloss-Vento Papers, Austin.

[34] Norma Adelfa Mouton, "Changing Voices: Approaching Modernity from Mexican to Mexican American to Chicano in the Epistolary Archives of Alonso S. Perales," *In Defense,* 223.

[35] George A. Martínez, "Alonso S. Perales and the Effort to Establish the Civil Rights of Mexican Americans as Seen through the Lens of Contemporary Critical Legal Theory: Post-racialism, Reality Construction, Interest Convergence, and Other Critical Themes," *In Defense,* 124.

[36] "Letter to Dr. Carlos E. Castañeda from Alonso S. Perales, February 24, 1947, CC, Box 34, Folder 2.

[37] Letter to Professor J. Luz Sáenz from Alonso S. Perales, February 24, 1947, José Luz Sáenz Papers (hereafter JLS), BLAC, Box 2, Folder 1.

[38] Letter to Alonso S. Perales from Carlos E. Castañeda, Feb. 26, 1947, CC, Box 34, Folder 2.

[39] Letter to Mr. Alonso S. Perales from Carlos E. Castañeda, April 2, 1947, CC, Box 4, Folder 2.

[40] Letter to Dr. Carlos E. Castañeda from Alonso S. Perales, Sept. 25, 1947, CC, Box 34, Folder 2.

[41] Gabriela González, *Redeeming La Raza, Transborder Modernity, Race, Respectability, and Rights* (Oxford: Oxford University Press, 2018), 183-184.

[42] Letter to Editor, *New Braunfels Herald,* August 1, 1945 from Alonso S. Perales, Committee of One Hundred, League of Loyal Americans, Perales, *Are We,* 264.

[43] Archbishop Robert Emmet Lucey, "Democracy and Church-Related Schools," Perales, *Are We,* 46-52.

[44] Notification of appointment as Notary Public in Bexar County, June 1, 1933, AP, Box 1, Folder 5.

[45] Olivas, "The Legal Career of Alonso S. Perales," *In Defense,* 317.

[46]Norma Adelfa Mouton, "Changing Voices: Approaching Modernity from Mexican to Mexican American to Chicano in the Epistolary Archives of Alonso S. Perales," *In Defense,* 223, 236.

[47]George A. Martínez, "Alonso S. Perales and the Effort to Establish the Civil Rights of Mexican Americans as Seen through the Lens of Contemporary Critical Legal Theory: Post-racialism, Reality Construction, Interest Convergence, and Other Critical Themes," *In Defense,* 125.

[48]Ibid, 126-127.

[49]Richard Buitron Jr., *The Quest for Tejano Identity in San Antonio, 1913-2000* (New York: Routledge, 2004), 32. On newspapermen see "Cuatro periodistas Mexicanos en Texas en el Siglo XIX," *La Prensa,* Feb. 13, 1938, second section; this was cited in Emilio Zamora's dissertation.

[50]Martínez, 125.

[51]Ibid, 133.

[52]See the digital project, Lorena Gauthereau, "Are We Good Neighbors?: Mapping Discrimination Against Mexican Americans in 1940s Texas." https://www.arcgis.com/apps/MapJournal/index. htm l?appid=80b15409a9d742318cd80b18e6157e76 Accessed on July 19, 2019.

[53]Ibid.

[54]Perales, *Are We,* 8-9.

[55]Zamora, 7.

[56]Mouton, 232; See Letter to Alonso S. Perales from Mrs. Félix H. Morales, April 17, 1944, AP, Box 2, Folder 7.

[57]Mouton, 233.

[58]"Statement of Eduardo Quevedo, President, Coordinating Council for Latin-American Youth, Los Angeles, California," Perales, *Are We,* 110.

[59]"Statement of Frank Paz, President of the Spanish-Speaking People's Council of Chicago," Perales, *Are We,* 111-114.

[60]Letter to Dr. Carlos E. Castañeda from Alonso S. Perales, April 8, 1947, CC, Box 34, Folder 2.

[61]Letter to Dr. Carlos E. Castañeda from Alonso S. Perales, March 29, 1948, CC, Box 34, Folder 2.

[62]Ibid.

[63]Letter to Dr. Carlos E. Castañeda from Alonso S. Perales, Jan. 21, 1949, CC, Box 34, Folder 2.

[64]Márquez, ftnt. 9, 48.

[65]Ibid, 45.

[66]Letter to Honorable Jack Danciger from Alonso S. Perales, January 19, 1951 and Letter to Alonso S. Perales from Jack Danciger, January 21, 1951, AP, Box 4, Folder 51.

[67]Letter to J. Luz Sáenz from Alonso S. Perales, March 20, 1950, JLS, Box 2, Folder 1.

[68]Letter to Mr. A.S. Perales from C.E. Castañeda, October 20, 1948, CC, Box 34, Folder 2.

[69]Book review by Thomas Bledsoe, *Southwest Review,* Spring 1949, 196-197, AP, Box 11, Folder 36.

[70]Book review by Henry L. Roberts, *Foreign Affairs,* July 1960.

[71]Untitled document beginning "The recently published 'Are We Good Neighbors?'," ca. December 1948, AP, Box 10, Folder 17.

[72]Oliver Douglas Weeks, "The League of United Latin-American Citizens: A Texas-Mexican Civic Organization," *Southwestern Political and Social Science Quarterly* 10:3 (1929), 257-278.

[73]Letter to Roberto Austin from AP, Jan. 8, 1932, AP, Box 4, Folder 9.

[74]Alonso S. Perales, "El Poll Tax y el Ciudadano," in *El México Americano y la Política del Sur de Texas,* (San Antonio: Artes Gráficas, 1931), 10, BLAC. Original text: "Por lo que respecta a nosotros los ciudadanos Americanos de origen latino, si queremos estar preparados para votar todo candidato que haya abusado de nuestros hermanos de raza, maltrátandolos, humillándolos, asesinándolos o negándoles la justicia cuando la merecen, debemos pagar el 'Poll Tax,'" and "hay que hacerlo antes del día primero del próximo mes de Febrero."

[75]Perales also wrote a pamphlet about Canales. Lic. Alonso S. Perales, "El Lic. José T. Canales Como Presidente General," (San Antonio: professionally printed by Perales?, April 30, 1932), AP, Box 4, Folder 8.

[76]Garcia, *Rise,* 113, ftnt7.

[77]*El Nacional,* June 8, 1924, AP, Box 12, Folder 2; "Réplica a Mr. James E. Ferguson, Carta Abierta," *El Latino-Americano* (Alice), ca. January 3, 1921, Casimiro Pérez Alvarez Papers, Box: Newpapers, Dolph Briscoe Center for American History, University of Texas at Austin.

[78]Alonso S. Perales, *En Defensa de Mi Raza* 2 (San Antonio: Artes Graficas, 1937), 1-15. All the essays Perales included in *En Defensa* before 1930 *Diógenes* published.

[79]"El Periodista Perales en Masatepe," *El Comercio,* October 5, 1930, AP, Box 9, Folder 41. Masatepe is in Nicaragua.

[80]Alonso S. Perales, "Un periódico es útil cuando sirve los intereses de la colectividad," *La Prensa,* February 13, 1946, AP, Box 8, Folder 5. Original text: "La prensa es indispensable para la solución satisfactoria de dichos problemas, y nadie necesita tanto de la valiosa ayuda de la prensa libre come los grupos minoritarios."

[81]Zamora, 294.

[82]Arnoldo Carlos Vento, *Adela Sloss-Vento, Writer, Political Activist, and Civil Rights Pioneer* (Lanham: Hamilton Books, 2017); Cynthia E. Orozco, *Agent of Change: Adela Sloss-Vento, Mexican American Civil Rights Activist and Texas Feminist* (Austin: University of Texas, 2020).

[83]Laura Cannon Dixon, "Police Brutality Makes Headlines: Retelling the Story of the 1938 Pecan Shellers' Strike," master's thesis, Indiana State University, 2010, 22.

[84]Kabalen de Bichara, 250.

[85]Ibid, 250.

[86]Maggie Rivas-Rodríguez, "Ignacio Lozano, The Exile Publisher who Conquered San Antonio and Los Angeles," *American Journalism* 21:1 (Winter 2004), 75-87.

[87]Sloss-Vento, 67.

[88]Garcia, *Rise,* 105.

[89]Letter to J.T. Canales from Carlos E. Castañeda, February 26, 1930, CC, Box 9, Folder 6.

[90]F. Arturo Rosales book manuscript, (2017), chapter 3, 10.

[91]Garcia, *Rise,* 200.

[92]Brandon H. Mila, "Hermanos de Raza: Alonso S. Perales and the Spirit of LULAC," master's thesis, University of North Texas, 2013, 25.

[93]Letter to Professor J. Luz Sáenz from Alonso S. Perales, May 28, 1952, JLS, Box 2, Folder 1. Original text: "Yo también a veces me desespero, pero luego pienso que tenemos necesidad de la tribuna. Debemos mantener el contacto con nuestros pueblos. *La Prensa* es un buen medio de comunicación porque circula mucho por el Estado."

[94]Aurora E. Orozco, *"La Prensa," El Tercer Piso* (newsletter of the Center for Mexican American Studies, University of Texas at Austin), 1979. As a work-study student, I co-founded and co-edited this newsletter.

[95]Alonso S. Perales, "Viva *La Prensa*-La Tribuna de la Raza!," *La Prensa,* October 24, 1926, AP, Box 9.

[96]"Conferencias del Lic. Alonso S. Perales," *La Prensa,* 1936, AP, Box 9, Folder 33.

[97]Sloss-Vento, 83.

[98]Alonso S. Perales, "Nuestros hermanos de Drafton, North Dakota se quejan de la discriminación." *La Prensa,* June 22, 1947, AP, Box 9, Folder 43 and "Cómo Solucionar el Problema de los Agentes de la Policía," *La Prensa,* April 28, 1946, Box 9, Folder 43. Perales wrote about racism in any town such as Drafton, North Dakota.

[99]Richard A. Garcia, "Alonso S. Perales, The Voice and Visions of a Citizen Intellectual," *Leaders of the Mexican American Generation,* ed. Anthony Quiroz (Boulder: University of Colorado, 2015), 91.

[100]Márquez, "In Defense," 34.

[101]Ibid, 34, 36.

[102]Alonso S. Perales, *En Defensa de Mi Raza* 1 (San Antonio: Artes Gráficas, 1936), 28-29.

[103]"Protesta to Miriam Ferguson, October 24, 1926," AP, Box 9, Folder 32.

[104]"El Lic. Alonso Perales Triunfó en Su Defensa De Peón Mexicano," *Diógenes,* September 25, 1926, Cynthia Orozco Notes of Perales Papers, 1979 (hereafter ON), 29.

[105]"Están Investigando las Autoridades Federales la Muerte de Mexicanos en El Condado de Willacy, Texas," *La Prensa,* February 2, 1927, ON, 30.

[106]Salinas, 81; Letter from Alonso S. Perales to the President, February 14, 1927, AP, Box 2, Folder 13.

107"Tribuna del Pueblo," *La Prensa,* February 21, 1927, AP, Box 9, Folder 42; "Por Dónde Principiar," *Las Noticias,* May 14, 1927, ON, 31.

108Kabalen de Bichara, 248; Salinas, 81.

109AP, Box 9.

110AP, Box 9, Folder 25. This folder is dated 1954 to 1959.

111Letter to J.T. Canales from Alonso S. Perales, ca. 1930, AP, Box 4, Folder 10.

112Alonso S. Perales, "Training for Leadership," *LULAC News* (hereafter *LN*), Feb. 1933, 5, Dolph Briscoe Center for American History, University of Texas at Austin; "Our Obligations and Community Progress," LN, Mar. 1933, 6-7, DB; "Training for Leadership," LN, Apr. 1933, 8, DB; "Our League and the Education of Our People," LN, Mar. 1937, no page, LULAC Archive, BLAC; "The Test of a Good LULAC Council," LN, July 1937, no page, LULAC Archive. Two essays were titled "Training for Leadership."

113Alonso S. Perales, "Our Obligations and Community Progress, *LN,* March 1933, 6-7, DB. This and other *LULAC News* can be accessed at repositories.lib.utexas.edu.

114Emma Tenayuca also worked for this magazine.

115*Latino-Americana Revista,* (1952), AP, Box 11, Folder 16.

116"Fraternidades," AP, Box 11, Folder 6.

117Kabalen de Bichara, 242.

118"Un Americano sale a la defensa de los Mexicanos," *El Imparcial de Texas,* nd, 1921, ON, 163.

119"Protesta Contra la Segregación de Nuestra Raza en San Angelo," *En Defensa* 2: 73-74.

120Testimony of Alonso S. Perales, House, Committee on Immigration, Hearings on Western Hemisphere Immigration, 71st Congress, 2nd Session, 1930, 182.

121Testimony, 182-189.

122Statement of Alonso S. Perales, Chairman, Committee of One Hundred, Director General, League of Loyal Americans, San Antonio, Texas," in Alonso S. Perales, *Are We,* 114-133.

123Michelle Kells, *Dr. Hector García, Everyday Rhetoric and Mexican American Civil Rights* (Carbondale, Ill.: Southern Illinois University Press, 2006) and John C. Hammerback and Richard J.

Jensen, *The Rhetorical Career of César Chávez* (College Station: Texas A&M University, 2003).

[124]John Hammerback, Richard J. Jensen, and José Angel Gutiérrez, *A War of Words: Chicano Protest in the 1960s and 1970s* (Westport, Conn.: Greenwood Press, 1985).

[125]Ibid, 6.

[126]Ibid, 5-6.

[127]"Addresses on Mexico," 1920, AP, Box 12, Folder 2.

[128]"Lauds Obregón's Rule in Mexico," n.d. (ca. April 1922), AP, Box 12, Folder 2.

[129]"Urges Deep Study of Spanish Laws," April 13, 1922, unidentified newspaper, AP, Box 12, Folder 2.

[130]"Miscellaneous," n.d., (ca. 1922), no newspaper name, (likely *Washington Star*), AP, Box 12, Folder 2.

[131]"Border Aliens to be Taught US Ways," *San Antonio Light,* August 1, 1924, AP, Box 9, Folder 36.

[132]Garcia, "Alonso S. Perales," *Leaders,* 109.

[133]Sloss-Vento, 7.

[134]Ibid, 62-63.

[135]Ventos, *Adela Sloss-Vento,* 68.

[136]Alonso S. Perales Conference & Exhibit. Raymond [Raimundo] "Alfonso Perales Speaks about his Father" youtube.com/watch?v= Oct8q4nOb:iA Accessed November 1, 2018.

[137]See the photo "Rally Speaker," *Brownsville Herald,* ca. 1952, ASP, Box 9, Folder 36.

[138]"Perales," *La Calavera,* November 2, 1942, ON, 139.

[139]Letter to author from Prof. Gilbert R. Cruz, August 9, 1999, Dr. Cynthia E. Orozco Papers, Ruidoso, New Mexico.

[140]"An Interview with Mrs. Perales," *Chicano Times,* February 14 to February 28, 1975, AP, Box 14 oversized.

[141]Email to Cynthia E. Orozco from Raimundo Alfonso Perales, November 19, 2018.

[142]Letter to M.C. Gonzales from J.T. Canales, March 2, 1932, J.T. Canales Estate Collection (hereafter JTC), James Jernigan Library, Texas A&M University, Kingsville, Box 436B, Folder: Correspondence-LULAC-Jan.-April 1932.

143Letter to Hon. J.T. Canales from M.C. Gonzales, March 28, 1932, JTC, Box 436B, Folder: Correspondence, LULAC, 1953-1954.

144Speech, "What Kind of Education do Latin-American Citizens Want for their Children," June 13, 1940, CC, Box 33, Folder 12. June 13, 1940.

145Letter to Dr. Carlos E. Castañeda from Alonso S. Perales, April 18, 1952, CC, Box 34, Folder 3.

146Laurie E. Jasinski, "San Antonio, Tx," https://tshaonline.org/ handbook/online/articles/hds02 Accessed May 27, 2018.

147Márquez, 32.

148Tony R. De Mars, "Buying Time to Start Spanish-Language Radio in San Antonio: Manuel Davila and the Beginning of Tejano Programming," *Journal of Radio Studies* (2014) 12:1, 74-84.

149Garcia, *Rise,* 83.

150Ibid, 106.

151Márquez, 36-38.

152Ibid, ftnt. 1, 47.

153"Palabras de Lic. Alonso S. Perales a Traves de la Estación KMAC con Motivo de un Concurso Artistico," *En Defensa* 2: 60-61.

154Alonso S. Perales, "Plática Sustentada por el Lic. Alonso S. Perales en la Transmisión de 'La Voz de la Raza' la Noche del 8 deJunio de 1932," *En Defensa* 2: 15. Original text: ". . . significará que en lo sucesivo tendremos más profesionistas, comerciantes e industriales y menos choferes, meseros y trabajadores de pico y pala."; "un líder más para nuestra raza en este país."

155Emilio Zamora, "Connecting Causes," *In Defense,* 298.

156Héctor Saldaña, "Unsung hero of civil rights 'Father of LULAC' a fading memory," *San Antonio Express-News,* September 14, 2003.

157Márquez, 37.

158Jasinski.

159Letter to Dear Mrs. Perales from Donna R. Tobias, May 1, 1979, AP, Box 10, Folder 5.

160Joseph Orbock Medina suggested Perales "did not necessarily embrace the tactic of publicly embarrassing racists." Perales pointed more so to systemic racism rather than individual racists. See Joseph Orbock Medina, "The Trials of Unity: Rethinking the Mexican-American Generation in Texas," *In Defense,* 55.

CHAPTER 17

[1]"An Interview with Mrs. Marta Perales," *Chicano Times,* February14 to February 28, 1975, Alonso S. Perales Papers (hereafter AP), M.D. Anderson Library, University of Houston, Box 14.

[2]Emilio Zamora, "Connecting Causes: Alonso S. Perales, Hemispheric Unity, and Mexican Rights in the United States," *In Defenseof My People, Alonso S. Perales and the Development of Mexican-American Public Intellectuals,* ed. Michael A. Olivas (Houston: Arte Público Press, 2012), 300. This chapter especially benefitted from Zamora's essay and Brandon H. Mila, "Hermanos de Raza: Alonso S. Perales and the Creation of the LULAC Spirit," master's thesis, University of North Texas, 2015.

[3]Thomas M. Leonard and Thomas L. Karnes, "Pan-Americanism," Encyclopedia.com https://www.encyclopedia.com/social-sciences-and-law/political-science-and-government/international-organizations/pan-americanism2. Accessed on July 5, 2019.

[4]Alonso S. Perales, "Problemas de Nuestra Raza en Estados Unidos," 2, *En Defensa de Mi Raza* 2 (San Antonio: Artes Gráficas, 1937), 6. Original text: "Ignorancia, pobreza, y poblaciones y ciudades polvosas, antihigiencias, insalubres y retrogradas predominan en la América latina."

[5]Letter to J.T. Canales from Alonso S. Perales, June 9, 1928, AP, Box4, Folder 10.

[6]Letter to Mr. Ben Garza from Alonso S. Perales, June 22, 1928, Andres de Luna Papers, Benson Latin American Collection (hereafter BLAC), University of Texas at Austin (hereafter UTA).

[7]Alonso S. Perales, "Problemas de Nuestra Raza en Estados Unidos," III, *En Defensa* 2, 9. Original text: "Sabemos que todos los gringos no son superiores a todos los latinoamericanos, pero estamos seguros de que hombre por hombre, abogado por abogado, doctor por doctor, soldado por soldado, y agricultor por agricultor, el anglo-sajón supera al latino-americano en físico, inteligencia, educación, aptitud, y carácter, si no en refinamiento."

[8]Alonso S. Perales, "Impresiones de un Viaje a México," *En Defensa* 2: 22; "Regreso de México el Lic. Perales," *La Prensa,* August 20, 1924, AP, Box 12, Folder 7.

[9]Ibid, 23. Original text: "conclusión de que México no es solamente un país rico y hermoso, sino que debería llamarse el país del arte, tanto por su belleza natural, como el hecho de que cada uno de sus hijos es un artista."

[10]Ibid, 23. Original: " . . . para que vieran lo bello y lo grande que es México y, sobre todo, para que se les borre de la mente ese complejo de inferioridad racial que el anglosajón ha querido imponernos en Texas."

[11]Araceli Pérez Davis, "Marta Pérez de Perales," *El Mesteño* (Mar. 1999) 4:37, 16.

[12]Alonso S. Perales Elementary School Dedication Program, AP, Box 1, Folder 1.

[13]"Intercollegiate debate, Rutgers University vs. George Washington University," n.d. ca. 1923, AP, Box 1, Folder 13.

[14]Mario T. García, "Alonso S. Perales and the Catholic Imaginary: Religion and the Mexican American Mind," *In Defense,* 155.

[15]"Resume of Address Made by Alonso S. Perales before the Pan American Round Table," November 16, 1936, AP, Box 8, Folder 9.

[16]Lupe S. Salinas, "Legally White, Socially Brown: Alonso S. Perales and His Crusade for Justice for La Raza," *In Defense,* 77.

[17]No title, October 31, 1922, AP, Box 12, Folder 2.

[18]No title, *El Siglo,* October 31, 1922, Cynthia E. Orozco Notes onPerales Papers (hereafter ON), 1979, 7.

[19]"$3,000 a Year in Picturesque Santo Domingo," *Getting Ahead,* III: 3, 1, ON, 8.

[20]Draughon Testimonies, July 1922, AP, Box 12, Folder 2.

[21]"Importantes Declaraciones de Mr. Welles a un Redactor de 'El Mundo' de Puerto Rico," July 27, 1922, unidentified newspaper, AP, Box 12, Folder 2.

[22]"El Sr. Perales Asistente del Comisionado Welles se despide de Sto. Domingo," *El Siglo,* ca. 1923, AP, Box 12, Folder 2. Original text: "mi breve estancia en este país ha sido sumamente agradable."

[23]Letter to Marta Perales from Alonso S. Perales, July 10, 1926, Hernán Contreras Papers (hereafter HC), Cushing Library, Texas A&M University, College Station, Box 1, Folder 17.

[24]"San Antonio Man Names Assistant to Plebiscite Board," unidentified newspaper, ca. 1924, AP, Box 12, Folder 2; Marta Perales, "Biography of Alonso S. Perales," n.d., ca. 1972?, AP, Box 10, Folder 10; Letter to Mr. Alonso S. Perales from Charles E. Hughes, Department of State, December 2, 1922, AP, Box 1, Fold-er 8. The ending date come from Marta.

[25]Mila, 18.

[26]Arnoldo Carlos Vento, *Adela Sloss-Vento, Writer, Political Activist, and Civil Rights Pioneer* (Lanham: Hamilton Books, 2017), 178.

[27]Salinas, 77.

[28]Mila, 18

[29]"Pershing to Sail for Tacna-Arica Meeting July 20," *Washington Post,* July 4, 1925, AP, Box 12, Folder 2.

[30]"San Antonio Man Named Assistant on Plebiscite Board," *San Antonio Express,* June 30, 1925; "San Antonian Named Tacna-Arica Examiner," unidentified newspaper, April 28, 1926, AP, Box 12, Folder 2; Letter to Don Casimiro Pérez Alvarez from Alonso S. Perales, November 3, 1925, Hernan Contreras Papers (hereafter HC), Cushing Library, Texas A&M University, College Station, Box 1, Folder 17.

[31]Letter to Sr. Don Casimiro Pérez Alvarez from Alonso S. Perales, June 25, 1925, HC, Box 1, Folder 17.

[32]Letter to Sr. Casimiro Pérez Alvarez from Alonso S. Perales, June 14, 1925, HC, Box 1, Folder 17.

[33]"Alonso Perales Locating Here," *McAllen Daily Press,* July 8,1927, AP, Box 12, Folder 2.

[34]Almaráz Jr.

[35]"Correspondencia," *El Buen Público,* Nov. 7, 1925, AP, Box 12, Folder 2.

[36]"Plebiscite Commission Member Given Praise," unidentified newspaper, 31, 1926, AP, Box 12, Folder 2.

[37]Letter to J.T. Canales from Alonso S. Perales, November 30, 1927, AP, Box 4, Folder 10.

[38]Mila, 18

[39]Letter to Sr. Don Casimiro Pérez Alvarez to Alonso S. Perales, September 23, 1926, HC, Box 1, Folder 17.

[40]Mila, 57.

[41]Ibid; Arnoldo Vento (?) Translation of Alonso S. Perales, "El Verdadero Origen de La Liga de Ciudadanos Latino Americanos" in Alonso S. Perales, *En Defensa de Mi Raza* 2 (San Antonio Artes Gráficas, 1937), AP, Box 3, Folder 36.

[42]Letter from Alonso S. Perales to Mr. E. Escobar, April 14, 1929, Eleuterio Escobar Papers (hereafter EE), Benson Latin American Collection (hereafter BLAC), University of Texas at Austin.

[43]Commission of Inquiry and Conciliation Bolivia and Paraguay, (Washington: US Government Printing Office, 1929), AP, Box 11, Folder 36.

[44]Card of identification, Special Legal Assistant of the Secretariat General of the Commission, March 13, 1929, AP, Box 1, Folder 6.

[45]Mila, 19.

[46]Pérez Davis, 16.

[47]"United Nations Principles Applied to Texas' Discrimination Problem," *San Antonio News,* March 15, 1951, AP, Box 9, Folder 32.

[48]Letter to Miss Lola Pérez from Marta Pérez Perales, November 1, 1930, HC, Box 1, Folder 17.

[49]"Alonso Perales," *LULAC News,* June 1937, LULAC Archive, BLAC; "Perales named Consul General," May 19, 1937, AP, Box 12, Folder 2.

[50]Mila, 18.

[51]Adela Sloss-Vento, *Alonso S. Perales: His Struggle for the Rights of Mexican Americans* (San Antonio: Artes Gráficas, 1977), 84.

[52]Mila, 59-61.

[53]Ibid, 63.

[54]Letter to Fortino Treviño from Alonso S. Perales, November 8, 1928, AP, Box 2, Folder 22. Original text: "Aquí se verificaron las elecciones presidenciales el 4 del actual, habiendo triunfado el Partido Liberal. Fue una elección ordenada, tranquila y honesta. Jamás se había visto cosa semejante en la historia de Nicaragua. Tanto los victoriosos como los vencidos quedaron contentos con los resultados."

[55]Mila, 63.

[56]Ibid, 96; F. Arturo Rosales, "Writing a Biography of Alonso Sandoval Perales," *In Defense,* 280.

[57]Letter to Don Sr. Casimiro Pérez Alvarez from Alonso S. Perales, June 4, 1930, HC, Box 1, Folder 17.

[58]"To the Members of the League of United Latin American Citizens," *LULAC News,* June 1932, 6, Dolph Briscoe Center for American History (hereafter DB), UTA.

[59]Letter to Sr. Don Casimiro Pérez Alvarez from Alonso S. Perales, November 2, 1930, HC, Box 1, Folder 17.

[60]Mila, 102.

[61]Pérez Davis, 16.

[62]Mila, 100; "To the Members of the League of United Latin American Citizens," *LULAC News,* December 1932: 6, DB.

[63]Certificate, Consul ad honorem from Presidente de la República de Nicaragua, April 5, 1934; Certificate, Consul from Presidente de la República de Nicaragua, April 16, 1936, AP, Box 14, oversized.

[64]"Perales Named Consul General," May 19, 1937, *San Antonio Express News*, AP, Box 12, Folder 2.

[65]Zamora, 290.

[66]Rosales, "Writing," *In Defense,* 280.

[67]Letter to Honorable Board of Economic Warfare from Alonso S. Perales, September 30, 1942, AP, Box 1, Folder 24.

[68]Zamora, 290.

[69]*The Mexican American and the Law* (New York: Arno Press, 1974), 14. Born in Nicaragua in 1902 Silex arrived in 1920 and had seven children in the United States. He filed for naturalization in 1942 and had naturalization hearings in 1947, defended by the American Council for Protection of the Foreign Born.

[70]Harvey K. Meyer, *Historical Dictionary of Nicaragua* (Lanham, Md.: Rowman & Littlefield, 1972), 110, 175, 428-429.

[71]Letter to Presidente Somoza y Señora from Alonso Perales y Señora, May 27, 1945, AP, Box 2, Folder 38.

[72]Letter to Su Excelencia, Don Anastacio Somoza, Presidente de la República de Nicaragua, February 3, 1954, AP, Box 2, Folder 38.

Original text: "interesado en que nuestros Países Americanos concierten un pacto para combatir el comunismo en estas tierras."
[73]Letter to Su Excelencia. Original text: "son suficientemente amplios para hacer frente la situación creada en Guatemala, por ejemplo."
[74]Letter to Su Excelencia, Don Anastacio Somoza from Alonso S. Perales, January 6, 1956, AP, Box 2, Folder 38. Original text: "el sub- suelo de Nicaragua promete mucho."
[75]Prominent Nicaraguan Americans today include Congresswoman and Democrat Hilda Solís of California, political commentator, TV personality and Republican Ana Navarro, Professor James Quesada of San Francisco, Professor Enrique Ochoa of Los Angeles and Bianca Jagger, ex-wife of Mick Jagger of the Rolling Stones and human rights activist.
[76]Perales, "True Origins," 7.
[77]Mila, 56.
[78]Letter to Senator Tom Connally from C.E. Castañeda, August 18, 1933, AP, Box 4, Folder 43.
[79]Letter to Dr. Carlos E. Castañeda from Alonso S. Perales, August 16, 1933, Carlos E. Castañeda Papers (hereafter CC), BLAC, Box 33, Folder 11.
[80]A. Perales, "Réplica a Mr. James E. Ferguson," *El Latino-Americano,* January 14, 1920, Casimiro Pérez Alvarez Papers, Box Newspaper collection, DB.
[81]"A Las Mesas Redondas PanAmericanas, Clubes de Rotarios, Leones y Kiwanis, Cámaras de Comercio y Demás Organizaciones Interesadas en Formar Buena Voluntuad y Cooperación Entre Los Pueblos de México y Los Estados Unidos de América," Alonso S. Perales, *En Defensa* 1: 78-82.
[82]Transcript, Alonso S. Perales, "What does It Take to Get the People of the Americas Together?", KONO Radio Station, March 3, 1941, AP, Box 8, Folder 19.
[83]Zamora, *In Defense,* 297.
[84]Neil Foley, *Quest for Equality, the Failed Promise of Black-Brown Solidarity* (Boston: Harvard University Press, 2010), 32.
[85]"Protesta Contra la Segregación de Nuestra Raza en San Angelo," *En Defensa* 2: 73-74.

[86]Alonso S. Perales, "Visitantes Mexicanos Que Mucho Nos Benefician," *En Defensa* 2: 668-69.

[87]Emilio Zamora, *Claiming Rights and Righting Wrongs in Texas: Mexican Workers and Job Politics during World War II,* (College Station: Texas A&M University, 2008), 105.

[88]Ibid, 97-98.

[89]Alonso S. Perales, *Are We Good Neighbors?* reprint (New York: Arno Press, 1974), 6.

[90]Typed copy, *San Antonio Light,* January 1, 18, 1953, AP, Box 9, Folder 38.

[91]"Report from the Congress of the Inter-American Bar Federation Held in Mexico City," AP, Box 14, Folder 8.

[92]"United Nations Principles Applied to Texas' Discrimination Problem" 1944, AP, Box 9, Folder 36.

[93]Certificate, La Asociación Nacional de Abogados, August 1944, AP, Box 1, Folder 2.

[94]Zamora, 301

[95]"Report from the Congress of the Inter-American Bar Federation Held in Mexico City," *Fraternidad,* 1944, AP, Box 14, Folder 8.

[96]Zamora, *Claiming Rights,* 112.

[97]Lecture Announcement, "The Charles L. Wood Lecture Series Featuring Dr. Emilio Zamora," TechAnnounce, Texas Tech University, October 18, 2013. https://techannounce.ttu.edu/Client/ViewMessage.aspx?MsgId=157530. Accessed on July 15, 2019.

[98]"Varios Clubs Discuten el Asunto de las Chozas y Tejabanes en San Antonio," in Perales, *En Defensa* 2: 52. Original text: "no conbanquetes ni manifestaciones superficiales de buena voluntad." And "un Americanismo genuino y una amistad internacional perdurable y verdadera."

[99]George N. Green, "Good Neighbor Commission," https://tshaonline.org/handbook/online/articles/mdg02. Accessed May 28, 2018.

[100]Thomas Guglielmo, "Fighting for Caucasian Rights: Mexicans, Mexican Americans, and the Transnational Struggle for Civil Rights in World War II Texas," *Journal of American History* 92:4 (March 2006), 1218.

[101]Carlos Kevin Blanton, *George I. Sánchez, The Long Struggle for Integration* (New Haven: Yale University Press, 2015), 78.

[102]Blanton, 78.

[103]Sloss-Vento, 26.

[104]Letter to Dr. Carlos E. Castañeda from Nerva S. Buzzo, June 25, 1941, CC, Box 8, Folder 16.

[105]Zamora, "Connecting Causes," 289

[106]Ibid, 288.

[107]Ibid.

[108]Ibid.

[109]Letterhead, Letter to J. Luz Sáenz from Alonso S. Perales, June 21, 1945, José de la Luz Sáenz Papers (hereafter JLS), BLAC, Box 2, Folder 1. Original text: "Ya estamos terminando la Magna Carta."

[110]Letter to Sr. Prof. J. Luz Sáenz from Alonso S. Perales, June 21, 1945, JLS, Box 2, Folder 1. Original text: "Hice todo lo que pude por incluir en la Carta disposiciones destinadas a acabar con la discriminación y a dar a los nuestros iguales oportunidades para progresar y ser felices."

[111]Zamora, "Connecting Causes," 301.

[112]Ignacio M. García, *White But Not Equal, Mexican Americans, Jury Discrimination, and the Supreme Court* (Tucson: University of Arizona, 2009), 55.

[113]Mila, 102.

[114]Mila, 98. Original text: "los Nicaragüenses son hermanos de raza nuestros porque ellos, al igual que nosotros los mexicanos, o son de sangre española pura o de sangre india pura o por sus venas circulan ambas. Además, su idioma es el español y sus costumbres e ideología son idénticas a las nuestras."; "Un Llamamiento Para que los Mexicanos Ayuden a las Víctimas de Nicaragua," *La Prensa*, April 13, 1931, AP, Box 1, Folder 12.

[115]"Brother Alonso S. Perales Home Again," *LULAC News*, January 1933, 9, AP, Box 4, Folder 4.

[116]Letter to Dr. Carlos E. Castañeda from Alonso S. Perales, August 16, 1933, CC, Box 33, Folder 11.

[117]Rosales, 280.

[118]Ibid.

[119]Letter to Dr Carlos E. Castañeda from Alonso S. Perales, October 6, 1942, CC, Box 34, Folder 1.

[120]Rosales, 281.

[121]Hector Saldaña, "Unsung hero of civil rights 'Father of LULAC' a fading memory," *San Antonio Express-News,* September 14, 2003; José Angel Gutiérrez, "Chicanos and Mexicans Under Surveillance: 1940-1980," Renato Rosaldo Lecture Series Mongraph, 2 (Tucson: Mexican American Studies and Research Center), 29-58.

[122]Rosales, 280.

[123]Zamora, "Connecting Causes," 289.

[124]Ibid, 303.

[125]Alonso S. Perales, "The Antonians," manuscript, ca. 1945, AP, Box 7, Folder 18.

[126]Letter to Honorable Morris Sheppard from Alonso S. Perales, February 6, 1933, AP, Box 5, Folder 6.

[127]Ibid.

[128]Letter to Alonso S. Perales from Morris Sheppard, March 21, 1935, AP, Box 5, Folder 6.

[129]Letter to Senator Tom Connally from Maury Maverick, May 31, 1933, AP, Box 1, Folder 26.

[129]Letter to Mrs. Martia (sic) Perales from Adela Sloss-Vento, July 19, 1979, AP, Box 10, Folder 5. Original text: "He visto cosas tan tristes por la televisión de la desolación y matanzas con los inocentes civiles. Que bueno que ya Somoza se salió y Dios quiere que vuelva a ver paz."

CHAPTER 18

[1]Hector Saldaña, "Unsung hero of civil rights 'Father of LULAC' a fading memory," *San Antonio Express News,* September 14, 2003.

[2]Mario T. García, "Alonso S. Perales and the Catholic Imaginary: Religion and the Mexican American Mind," *In Defense of My People: Alonso S. Perales and the Development of Public Intellectuals,* ed. Michael A. Olivas (Houston: Arte Público Press, 2012), 153, 169.

[3]"A course in Moral Theology for Catechists" materials, September 1947, Alonso S. Perales Papers (hereafter AP), M.D. Anderson Library, University of Houston, Box 7, Folder 22.

[4]Letter to Dr. Carlos E. Castañeda from Alonso S. Perales, September 24, 1951, Carlos E. Castañeda Papers (hereafter CC), Benson Latin American Collection (hereafter BLAC), University of Texas at Austin, Box 34, Folder 3.

[5]Letter to Dr. Carlos E. Castañeda from Alonso S. Perales, June 30, 1948, CC, Folder 34, Folder 2.

[6]Adela Sloss-Vento, *Alonso S. Perales, His Struggle for the Rights of Mexican-Americans* (San Antonio: Artes Gráficas, 1977), 66-67.

[7]Letter to Honorable José T. Canales from Alonso S. Perales, January 27, 1954, CC, Box 431B.

[8]Letter to Dr. Carlos E. Castañeda from Alonso S. Perales, June 28, 1951, CC, Box 33, Folder 10.

[9]Mario T. García. *Católicos: Resistance and Affirmation in Chicano Catholic History* (Austin: University of Texas Press, 2010), 61.

[10]Email to Cynthia Orozco from Marta Carmen Perales Carrizales, November 20, 2018.

[11]Ibid.

[12]Letter to Dr. Carlos E. Castañeda from Alonso S. Perales, June 16, 1954, CC, Box 34, Folder 3.

[13]Letter to Dr. Carlos E. Castañeda from Alonso S. Perales, Aug. 10, 1956, CC, Box 34, Folder 3.

[14]Letter to Honorable Manuel J. Bravo from Alonso S. Perales, August 27, 1948. Historian J. Gilberto Quezada of San Antonio mailed me this source.

[15]Alonso S. Perales, 1959 Income tax return, AP, Box 1, Folder 5.

[16]"Alonso S. Perales," The Parade of Past Presidents General, *LULAC News,* June 1947, 25, 29, AP, Box 4, Folder 6.

[17]Letter to Dr. Carlos E. Castañeda from Alonso S. Perales, June 28 1951, CC, Box 33, Folder 10.

[18]Alonso S. Perales, *Alonso S. Perales, Are We Good Neighbors?;* reprint (New York: Arno Press, 1974), 6.

[19]García, *Católicos,* 60-61.

[20]Untitled manuscript, beginning "Religión, decíamos el otro día, es el conjunto," May 4, 1959, AP, Box 7, Folder 18. Original text: "Para conocer cual es la religión verdadera no es necesario conocer y examinar todas las religiones pues esto fuera imposible."

²¹García, "Alonso S. Perales," 152.

²²Ibid, 154.

²³Ibid, 69.

²⁴Ibid, 153.

²⁵García, *Católicos,* 72.

²⁶García, "Alonso S. Perales,"153.

²⁷Ibid, 153.

²⁸Benjamín Márquez, "In Defense of My People: Alonso S. Perales and the Moral Construction of Citizenship," *In Defense of My People,* 31.

²⁹García, "Alonso S. Perales,"167.

³⁰Ibid, 155-156.

³¹Ibid, 154.

³²Ibid, 168.

³³Letter to Dr. Carlos E. Castañeda from Alonso S. Perales, Feb. 28, 1948, CC, Box 34, Folder 2.

³⁴Alonso S. Perales, "El Mundo Necesita Mucho de Instrucción Religiosa," manuscript, n.d. (ca. 1945), AP, Box 7, Folder 18. Original text: "La verdad es que presentimos la destrucción del mundo y sabemos que Dios es el único que nos puede salvar."

³⁵García, *Católicos,* 62.

³⁶Ibid, 64.

³⁷Ibid.

³⁸"Más Sobre El Problema de los Braceros y Los Trabajadores Migratorios," Por Mi Religión, *La Voz Católica,* May 16, 1958, AP, Box9, Folder 32.

³⁹Juan Montoya, "A Nugget Found in Orive Palmito Hill Homestead Reveals Chicano Historical Treasure, https://rrunrrun. blogspot.com/ 2011/10/nugget-found-in-uribe-homestead-reveals. html. Accessed on July 3, 2019. This is a blog titled "El RRun RRun."

⁴⁰Obituary, unidentified newspaper, May 1960, AP, Box 1, Folder 1.

⁴¹Roberto R. Treviño, "Facing Jim Crow: Catholic Sisters and the 'Mexican Problem in Texas,'" *Western Historical Quarterly,* 32:2 (Summer 2003), 139-164.

⁴²García, *Católicos* 73.

[43]Virginia Marie Raymond, "Faithful Dissident: Alonso S. Perales, Discrimination, and the Catholic Church," *In Defense,* 174.

[44]Sister Frances Jerome Woods, "Mexican Ethnic Leadership in San Antonio," Ph.D. diss., Catholic University, Washington, DC, 1947; reprint (New York: Arno Press, 1976), 94.

[45]Letter to Dr. Carlos E. Castañeda from Alonso S. Perales, April 26, 1951, CC, Box 33, Folder 10.

[46]AP, Box 8, Folders 21-35.

[47]AP, Box 8, Folder 21.

[48]Letter to Reverend Carlos Quintana from Luis Alvarado, Editor, *La Voz,* May 9, 1958, AP, Box 1, Folder 23.

[49]Email to Cynthia Orozco from Marta Carmen Perales Carrizales, November 20, 2018.

[50]García, "Alonso S. Perales," 163.

[51]Ibid, 163.

[52]Ibid, 164.

[53]Alonso S. Perales, "Las Santas Misiones y Nuestro Bienestar," manuscript, AP, Box 7, Folder 18. Original text: "Solicitamos muyencarecidamente la ayuda de las señoras esposas para inducir a sus esposo e hijos jóvenes a que asistan a las Misiones"; "Anímelos a que asistan a las Misiones y verá como cambiarán las cosas en su hogar. Lo que ocurre es que la mayor parte de los hombres están en la impresión errónea de que nada más las mujeres están obligada a ser religiosos y no es así."

[54]García, "Alonso S. Perales," 160.

[55]Ibid, 161-162.

[56]Ibid, 158.

[57]Last Will and Testament, Alonso S. Perales, March 20, 1961, filed May 23, 1960, AP, Box 1, Folder 1.

[58]Letter to Señora Adela S. Vento from Alonso S. Perales, August 11, 1947, AP, Box 5, Folder 8. Original text: "Mientras Dios nos da vida y salud habrá esperanza." (While God gives us life and health there is hope.)

CHAPTER 19

[1]"Lic. Alonso S. Perales," *Las Noticias*, 1922, Alonso S. Perales Papers (hereafter AP), M.D. Anderson Library, University of Houston, Box 12, Folder 2. Original text: "El lic. Perales es un conocido defensor de nuestros causas y ha actuado con limpia conciencia."

[2]Adela Sloss-Vento, *Alonso S. Perales and His Struggle for the Rights of Mexican-Americans* (San Antonio: Artes Gráficas, 1977).

[3]Arnoldo Carlos Vento, *Adela Sloss-Vento, Writer, Political Activist, and Civil Rights Pioneer* (Lanham: Hamilton Books, 2017), 74.

[4]Letter to "To Whom It May Concern" from G.W. Parish, President, Draughon's Practical Business College, April 17, 1918, AP, Box 1, Folder 4.

[5]Letter to Alonzo (sic) Perales from G.W. Parish, June 3, 1925, AP, Box 1, Folder 4.

[6]Letter to My Der See (sic) from Edwin Keller, October 16, 1918, AP, Box 1, Folder 2.

[7]Letter to My dear Mr. Brimer from Albert Fensch, Asst. CC, So. Dept., Jan. 6, 1924, AP, Box 1, Folder 4.

[8]Letter to State Board of Legal Examiners from Bat Corrigan, Attorney at law, April 17, 1924, AP, Box 1, Folder 4.

[9]Letter to "To Whom It May Concern" from G. Woodson Morris, April 8, 1924, AP, Box 1, Folder 4.

[10]"List of persons who might be written to regarding the character and qualifications of Mr. Alonso S. Perales, of San Antonio, Texas," n.d. (ca. 1942), AP, Box 1, Folder 7.

[11]"Some of the things Alonso S. Perales has done for the League of United Latin American Citizens," ca. May 1931, AP, Box 3, Folder 40.

[12]"An Interview with Mrs. Perales," *Chicano Times*, Feb. 14 thru Feb. 28, 1975, AP, Box 14: Oversize.

[13]Vento, *Adela Sloss-Vento*, 54.

[14]Email to Cynthia E. Orozco from Marta Carmen Perales Carrizales, November 20, 2018.

[15]Marta Pérez Pérales, "Al Pueblo de Alice," 1960, AP, Box 10, Folder 1. Original text: "El dinero para él no era importante. Jamás ambicionó hacerse rico, la caridad era lo que le importaba."
[16]Letter to Señor General don Anastacio Somoza from Alonso S. Perales, January 11, 1956, AP, Box 2, Folder 38. Original text: ". . . estoy pobre porque desde que regresé de Nicaragua en 1932, gran parte de mi tiempo lo he dedicado a la defensa y los intereses de nuestra raza hispana gratuitamente. No me pesa haberlo hecho, pues es grande la satisfacción que se siente cuando uno se sacrificapor sus semejantes. Al mismo tiempo, todas las cosas tienen su límite, y yo, hoy día, después de más de cuarto de siglo al servicio de mi raza, procuraré dedicar más tiempo a mi negocio y a propugnar más por el bienestar mío y de mi familia."
[17]Sloss-Vento, 12.
[18]Gilberto Juan Quezada interview with Carlos Cadena, January, 31, 1991, Bexar County Historical Commission, San Antonio Public Library.
[19]Ibid.
[20]Ibid.
[21]J. Luz Sáenz, "Lulacs are civic patriotic organization," *El Paso Herald Post*, February 23, 1953.
[22]"A Letter from Mrs. Marta Pérez Perales," (letter written for Adela Sloss-Vento book), ca. 1977, AP, Box 10, Folder 6.
[23]Sloss-Vento, 18.
[24]Santos de la Paz, "How I Remember Alonso S. Perales," Sloss-Vento, *Alonso. S. Perales*, 83.
[25]Letter to Lic. Alonso S. Perales from C.E. Castañeda, January 24, 1941, Carlos E. Castañeda Papers (hereafter CC), Benson Latin American Collection (hereafter BLAC), University of Texas at Austin, Box 33, Folder 12; Letter to Dr. Carlos E. Castañeda from Alonso S. Perales, October 16, 1942, CC, Box 34, Folder 1.
[26]Lupe S. Salinas, "Legally White, Socially Brown: Alonso S. Perales and His Crusade for Justice for La Raza," *In Defense of My People, Alonso S. Perales and the Development of Mexican-American Public Intellectuals* ed. Michael A. Olivas (Houston: Arte Público Press, 2012), 92-93.

[27]Benjamín Márquez, "In Defense of My People: Alonso S. Perales and the Moral Construction of Citizenship," *In Defense*, 30.

[28]Ibid.

[29]Transcript, Alonso S. Perales, "What Does It Take to get the Peoples of the Americas Together?," KONO Radio Station, March 3, 1941, 4-5, AP, Box 8, Folder 19.

[30]Richard A. Garcia, *The Rise of the Mexican American Middle Class, San Antonio, 1929-1941* (San Antonio: Texas A&M Univer- sity Press, 1991), 284.

[31]Márquez, 40.

[32]Alonso S. Perales, "Problemas de Nuestra Raza en Estados Unidos" III, *En Defensa de mi Raza 2* (San Antonio: Artes Gráficas, 1937), 7.

[33]Letter to Carlos Castañeda from Alonso S. Perales, April 9, 1946, CC, Box 34, Folder 2.

[34]Letter to J.T. Canales from Alonso S. Perales, October 31, 1927, AP, Box 4, Folder 10.

[35]AP speech, "What Kind of Education Do Latin-American Citizens Want for Their Children," June 13, 1940, AP, Box 8, Folder 11.

[36]Cynthia E. Orozco, *No Mexicans, Women or Dogs Allowed: The Rise of the Mexican American Civil Rights Movement* (Austin: University of Texas, 2009), 238.

[37]"El Lic. Alonso Perales Triunfó en su Defensa del Peón Mexicano," *Diógenes*, September 25, 1926, Cynthia E. Orozco Notes on Perales Papers (hereafter ON), 1979, 29.

[38]Márquez, "In Defense," *In Defense*, 37.

[39]Salinas, "Legally White," *In Defense*, 82; See Alonso S. Perales to the President, April 30, 1927, AP, Box 2, Folder 13.

[40]Donna M. Kabalen de Bichara, "Self-Writing and Collective Representation: The Literary Enunciation of Historical Reality and Cultural Values," *In Defense*, 245.

[41]Ibid, 243.

[42]Ibid.

[43]Alonso S. Perales, "Nueva Evolución General," *Revista Latino-Americana* (May 1953), 9, AP, Box 11, Folder 16.

[44]Perales, *En Defensa 2*, 113.

[45]Joseph Orbock Medina, "The Trials of Unity: Rethinking the Mexican-American Generation in Texas, 1948-1960," *In Defense*, 56.

[46]Benjamín Márquez, *LULAC: The Evolution of a Mexican American Political Organization* (Austin: University of Texas, 1993), 4.

[47]Alonso S. Perales, "Las Sociedades Como Medio de Progreso," *En Defensa* 2: 17. It originally appeared in *Álbum de la Raza*, Jan, 15, 1934. Original text: "Urge que nos demos cuenta de nuestras obligaciones individuales respecto de la colectividad."

[48]Ibid. Original text: ". . . personas conscientes que comprendenperfectamente sus obligaciones para con la comunidad."

[49]Interview with Mrs. Perales, *Chicano Times*, February 14 to February 28, 1975, 12, AP, Box 14.

[50]"Mensaje del Lic. Alonso S. Perales a la Colonia Mexicana de San Antonio, Texas," ca. 1930s, AP, Box 1, Folder 9; Rodolfo Acuña, *Occupied America, A History of Chicanos,* 7th ed. (New York: Pearson, 2011), 152; Alonso S. Perales?, "La Verdadera Causa y Razón de la Ruptura de Relaciones Entre Maverick and Perales," ca. 1940, AP, Box 8, Folder 11.

[51]Quezada interview.

[52]Letter to Alonso S. Perales from J. Luz Sáenz, March 22, 1934, AP, Box 4, Folder 28.

[53]Garcia, *Rise*, 287.

[54]Alonso S. Perales?, no title, ca. 1938 AP, Box 4, Folder 3.

[55]"Perales sees Discrimination," *San Antonio Light*, June 29, 1940; "Peticiones en Favor de los Mexicanos de San Antonio, Texas," *La Prensa*, June 24, 1940, AP, Box 14, Folder 7.

[56]Brandon Mila, "Hermanos de Raza: Alonso S. Perales and the Spirit of LULAC," master's thesis, University of North Texas, 2013, 68.

[57]Kabalen de Bichara, 250.

[58]Perales, *En Defensa* 1, 21. Original text: "todos los mexicanos, sin considera- ción de ciudadanía."

[59]"Se Establece en San Antonio una Escuela," *La Prensa*?, ca.1933, AP, Box 8, Folder 10.

[60]Letter to San Antonio Chamber of Commerce from Educational Committee, Council 16, AP, Box 3, Folder 41; Letter to J. Luz Sáenz from AP, March 17, 1934, AP, Box 4, Folder 28.

[61]See Cynthia E. Orozco, *Agent of Change: Adela Sloss-Vento, Mexican American Civil Rights Activist and Texas Feminist* (Austin: University of Texas, 2020), 119.

[62]Malcolm Ross, "Our Personal Relations with Mexicans," Alonso S. Perales, *Are We Good Neighbors?* (San Antonio: Artes Gráficas, 1948; reprint New York: Arno Press), 73.

[63]Lic. Alonso S. Perales, "Visitantes Mexicanos que Mucho Nos Benefician," *En Defensa* 1: 69. Original text: "Nosotros los habi- tantes de origen mexicano de Texas, sin consideración a ciudadanía, tenemos problemas cívicos-sociales importantísimos que solucio- nar."

[64]Letter to J.T. Canales from Alonso S. Perales, January 2, 1928, AP, Box 4, Folder 10.

[65]Typescript in English, news report of the Harlingen Convention, 1927, AP, Box 3, Folder 38.

[66]"Apuntes Sobre Las Leyes de Inmigración de Los Estados Unidos de América," *En Defensa* 2: 76-77.

[67]Alonso S. Perales, "Catecismo Cívico de los Derechos y Deberes de los Ciudadanos Americanos," *En Defensa* 2:75.

[68]Flyer delivered at the Convention Hall, Edinburg, (LULAC annual conference), "Mr. President," (form letter) May 4, 1931, AP, Box 3, Folder 40.

[69]Ibid.

[70]Letter to Carlos E. Castañeda from Alonso S. Perales, 1942, CC, Box 34, Folder 1.

[71]Alonso S. Perales, "Problemas de Nuestra Raza en Estados Unidos," *En Defensa* 2: 4.

[72]Transcript by AP?, AP, Box 3, Folder 39.

[73]Arnoldo Vento (?) Translation of Alonso S. Perales, "El Verdadero Origen de La Liga de Ciudadanos Latino Americanos" in Alonso S. Perales *En Defensa de Mi Raza* 2 (San Antonio: Artes Gráficas, 1937), 101-116; 5, AP, Box 3, Folder 36.

[74]Perales, *En Defensa* 1:20. Original text: "Cada hombre tiene un talento, no importa cuan pequeño sea este, y este talento debe ser desarrollado si la sociedad se ha de elevar más"

[75]"Palabras del Lic. Alonso S. Perales a Través de La Estación KMAC con Motivo de un Concurso Artístico," *En Defensa* 2:61.

[76]Ms., AP, LULAC related, 2, AP, Box 3, Folder 39.

[77]Lic. Alonso S. Perales, "El 'Poll-Tax' o Impuesto Electoral," *En Defensa* 2: 62-65.

[78]Letter to J.T. Canales from Alonso S. Perales, May 27, 1932, AP, Box 4, Folder 10.

[79]Letter from AP to J.T. Canales, November 2, 1927, AP, Box 4, Folder 10.

[80]Letter to Antonia Gómez from AP, January 11, 1933, AP, Box 4, Folder 9.

[81]"Palabras del Lic. Alonso S. Perales a Través de la Estación KMAC con Motivo de un Concurso Artístico," *En Defensa* 2, 61.

[82]Letter to J.T. Canales from AP, Oct. 31, 1927, AP, Box 4, Folder 10.

[83]Letter to Alonso S. Perales from J.T. Canales, April 3, 1933, AP, Box 4, Folder 11.

[84]Letter to H.H. Contreras from Alonso S. Perales, April 2, 1934, AP, Box 4, Folder 14.

[85]Letter to J.T. Canales from AP, March 18, 1933, AP, Box 4, Folder 11; Letter to J.T. Canales from AP, January 14, 1934; Letter to J.T. Canales from AP, April 2, 1934, AP, Box 4, Folder 11.

[86]"Liga de Ciudadanos Latino-Americanos," May 22, 1937, AP, Box 3, Folder 37.

[87]Letter to J.T. Canales from Alonso S. Perales, March 13, 1942, José Tomás Canales Estate Collection (hereafter JTC), Jernigan Library, South Texas Archives, Texas A&M University, Kingsville, Box 431, Folder 15.

[88]Letter to Dr. Carlos E. Castañeda from Alonso S. Perales, Aug. 28, 1948, CC, Box 34, Folder 2.

[89]Ms., AP, LULAC related, 2, AP, Box 3, Folder 39.

[90]Note to J.T. Canales from unsigned, ca. 1929, AP, Box 4, Folder 10.

[91]Vento, 11.

[92]Letter to Dr. Carlos E. Castañeda from Alonso S. Perales, April 8, 1948, CC, Box 34, Folder 2.

[93]Letter to Carlos E. Castañeda from J.T. Canales, March 21, 1930, CC, Box 9, Folder 6.

[94]Letter to J.T. Canales from Carlos E. Castañeda, March 22, 1930, CC, Box 9, Folder 6.

[95]Olivas, *In Defense*, xvii.

[96]Brandon H. Mila, "Hermanos de Raza: Alonso S. Perales and the Creation of the LULAC Spirit," University of North Texas, 2013, 27.

[97]Letter to J. Luz Sáenz from Alonso S. Perales, March 6, 1952, J. Luz Sáenz Papers (hereafter JLS), BLAC, Box 2, Folder 1.

[98]Joseph Orbock Medina stated, "When LULAC initially formed, the founders imagined they had achieved a substantial measure of control over the direction of Mexican-American civil rights activ- ity, but post-war developments showed that the LULAC monopolyhad been broken." But monopoly was not a goal of LULAC or LULAC founders and there were many local organizations. See Joseph Orbock Medina, "The Trials of Unity: Rethinking the Mexican-American Generation in Texas," *In Defense*, 56.

[99]Márquez, "In Defense," 45. See Letter to Carlos E. Castañeda from Alonso S. Perales, September 13, 1954, CC, Box 34, Folder 3.

[100]Arnoldo Vento (?) Translation of Perales, "El Verdadero."

[101]Letter to Dr. Carlos E. Castañeda from Alonso S. Perales, September 13, 1954, CC, Box 34, Folder 3; "For Sale, A Goat of the Sharyland Breed," attachment to Sept. 13, 1954 letter, CC, Box 34,Folder 3.

[102]Letter to Dr. Carlos E. Castañeda from Alonso S. Perales, September 13, 1954, CC, Box 34, Folder 3.

[103]Letter to Prof. José Luz Sáenz from Alonso S. Perales, November 21, 1951, JLS, Box 2, Folder 1. Original text: "La envidia es mucha entre nuestros líderes y pseudo-líderes "

[104]Sloss-Vento, *Alonso S. Perales*, 7.

CHAPTER 20

[1]Wedding announcement, Alonso S. Perales Papers (hereafter AP), M.D. Anderson Library, University of Houston, Box 1, Folder 1.

[2]Items 1-4, AP, Box 10, Folder 9.

[3]Cynthia E. Orozco, "Casimiro Pérez Álvarez," *New Handbook of Texas*, (hereafter *NHOT*) ed. Ronnie C. Tyler, Douglas E. Barnett, and Roy R. Barkley 5 (Austin: Texas State Historical Association,

1996):151. The family corrected the date to 1787. The San José de la Mulada ranch received a Texas Historical Commission Marker in 2017; see "Starr County Ranch Recognized with Historical Marker," http://www.krgv.com/story/35180852/starr-county-ranch-recognized-with-historical-marker Accessed on May 28, 2018. See also "Sunday Speaker Series presents Araceli Pérez-Davis: Casimiro Pérez Alvarez, Lawman of the Rio Grande," https://most history.org/sunday-speaker-series-presents-araceli-perez-davis-casimiro-perez-alvarez-lawman-of-the-rio-grande/Accessed on August 11, 2018.

[4] Obituary, *Laredo Times*, January 20, 1936, AP, Box 10, Folder 9.

[5] Casimiro Pérez-Álvarez Collection Finding Aid, compiled by Phyllis Kinnison, 2015, 4, Museum of South Texas History, Edinburg.

[6] Celia Pérez-Álvarez, "___ng Political Campaigns in Starr County, Texas," *The Review* (Edinburg) December 8, 1928, Hernan Contreras Papers (hereafter HC), Texas A&M University, College Station, Box 2, Folder 5.

[7] Araceli Pérez Davis, "Marta Pérez de Perales," *El Mesteño* (Oct. 2000) 4:37, 16.

[8] Certificate, Universidad Nacional de México Cursos de Extensión Universitaria, 1944, AP, Box 14.

[9] Richard A. Garcia, *Rise of the Mexican American Middle Class, San Antonio, 1929-1941* (College Station: Texas A&M University, 1991), 99, 103.

[10] Garcia, 99, 102.

[11] Garcia, 61.

[12] Garcia, 158.

[13] J. Gilberto Quezada, "Alonso S. Perales Pioneer Leader of the Mexican American Civil Rights Movement," *Somos Primos*, Sep- tember 2015. https://www.somosprimos.com/sp2015/spsep15/spsep15. htm Accessed July 1, 2018.

[14] "Los Esposos Perales Van a Managua, Nicaragua," *La Prensa*, n.d., 1932. This was included in the F. Arturo Rosales materials sent to me by Arte Público Press but had no specific date.

[15] Letter to Don Casimiro Pérez-Álvarez from Alonso S. Perales, November 3 1925, HC, Box 1, Folder 17.

[16]Letter to Prof. J. Luz Sáenz from Alonso S. Perales, November 21, 1951, José de la Luz Sáenz Papers, Benson Latin American Collection (hereafter BLAC), University of Texas at Austin, Box 2, Folder 1. Original text: "pues teníamos a una muchacha ayudándonos en casa y allí dormía y estaba todo el tiempo."

[17]Letter to Dr. Carlos E. Castañeda from Alonso S. Perales, December 14, 1954, Carlos E. Castañeda Papers (hereafter CC), BLAC, Box 2, Folder 3.

[18]"Tertulia," unidentified newspaper, July 26, 1924, AP, Box 12, Folder 2.

[19]Letter to Sr. Don Casimiro Pérez-Álvarez from Alonso S. Perales, September 9, 1926, HC, Box 1, Folder 17.

[20]Letter to Miss Nina Romeyn from Alonso S. Perales, June 25, 1931, AP, Box 12, Folder 4.

[21]"Ecos del Recital Ofrecido por la Prof. Luisa Bonancini Lauro," *La Prensa*, June 8, 1941, AP, Box 12, Folder 7. Original text: "La tercera parte fue presentación de otra cantante de relieve, la señora Marta P. de Perales, soprano el aria de 'Il Trovatore,' 'D'amo sull'all rosee,' acompañado por el tenor Antonio Gutierrez."

[22]"Sra. Marta Pérez de Perales," *La Prensa*, May 18, 1947, AP, Box 9, Folder 41.

[23]"The Operatic con be Given Here May 17," *Valley Evening Monitor*, May 2, 1948, AP, Box 9, Folder 42.

[24]"Bel Canto," June 4, 1955, AP, Box 10, Folder 6. This item is 70 pages.

[25]"Rotary Filing Cabinet Invented by S.A. Woman," *San Antonio Light*, February 27, 1953, AP, Box 4, Folder 8.

[26]Letter to Mrs. Marta Perales from J.A. Heard, Patent Developers, April 12, 1966, AP, Box 10, Folder 3.

[27]"Statement of Mrs. Marta Perez de Perales Regarding her Bank Trap Invention," April 13, 1954, AP, Box 10, Folder 3.

[28]Letter to J.T. Canales from Alonso S. Perales, March 20, 1957, AP, Box 4, Folder 10.

[29]Adriana Ayala, "Negotiating Race Relations through Activism: Women Activists and Women's Organizing in San Antonio, Texas during the 1920s," Ph.D. diss., University of Texas at Austin, 2005.

[30]Pérez Davis, 17.

[31]Letter to Dear Madam from Edmund Galvan, January 24, 1949, AP, Box 10, Folder 2.

[32]Membership card, Mrs. Alonso S. Perales, January 1, 1967 to December 31, 1957, Council of International Relations, AP, Box 1, Folder 6.

[33]The Women's Auxiliary of the San Antonio Bar Association, Year Book, 1946-47 and 1954-1955, AP, Box 7, Folder 2.

[34]Certificate, Mrs. Alonso S. Perales, Maria R. Magnon Memorial Black and White Ball, December 10, 1966, AP, Box 1, Folder 2.

[35]Alonso S. Perales, *Are We Good Neighbors?* reprint (New York: Arno Press, 1974), 238-244. See also Mrs. Santos V. Lozano, "All Kinds of People," *Valley Morning Star,* no specific date, 1947, AP, Box 10, Folder 10 and Mrs. Santos V. Lozano, "La Sociedad LULAC," no source, no date, AP, Box 10, Folder 17.

[36]Letter to Estela Contreras from Lloyd Bentsen, September 1, 1948 and "Excerpt from a newspaper announcing Estela Contreras' campaign for County Commissioner of Precinct 4," HC, Box 1, Folder 19 and Box 2, Folder 5.

[37]Cynthia E. Orozco, "Ladies LULAC," *New Handbook of Texas* ed. Ronnie C. Tyler, Douglas E. Barnett, and Roy Barkley (Austin: Texas State Historical Association, 1996) 4: 130-131.

[38]Hector Saldaña, "Unsung Hero of Civil Rights, 'Father of Lulac' a Fading Memory," *San Antonio Express News*, Sept. 14, 2003.

[39]Letter to Dr. Carlos E. Castañeda from Alonso S. Perales, Aug. 29, 1946, CC, BLAC, Box 34, Folder 2.

[40]Letter to "Mi muy querida e inolvidable Martita" from "Tu esposo," August 16, 1953, AP, Box 10, Folder 3. Original text: "Comprendo que no debe ser tan egoísta y que debo concederte tus deseos, y aunque yo sufra aquí por la ausencia de ustedes."

[41]Ibid.

[42] Ibid.

[43] Ibid.

[44]Letter to Misses Hilda and Lola Pérez from Marta Pérez de Perales, August 27, 1926, AP, Box 10, Folder 9; English translation: "To you, my lovely wife and children, I—your husband and father—send all my love and kisses."

⁴⁵Letter to Mr. Alonso S. Perales from Carlos E. Castañeda, Jan. 11, 1955, CC, Box 34, Folder 3.

⁴⁶Email to Cynthia Orozco from Marta Perales Carrizales, November 20, 2018.

⁴⁷Ibid.

⁴⁸Membership Card, Chairman, Troop 91, San Antonio Boy Scouts, March 31, 1946, AP, Box 1, Folder 6.

⁴⁹Pérez Davis, 17; Email to Cynthia Orozco from Marta Perales Carrizales, November 20, 2018.

⁵⁰Email to Cynthia Orozco from Marta Carmen Perales Carrizales, November 19, 2018.

⁵¹Adela Sloss-Vento, *Alonso S. Perales, His Struggle for the Rights of Mexican-Americans* (San Antonio: Artes Gráficas, 1977), 67.

⁵²Email to Cynthia Orozco from Marta Carmen Perales Carrizales, November 20, 2018. "I am Marta Carmen Perales y Pérez, adopted daughter to Attorney Perales and Mrs. Marta Perales y Pérez, at your service."

⁵³Letter to Sra. Doña Martita Pérez de Perales from "Tu Esposo," August 16, 1953, AP, Box 10, Folder 9. Original text: "[¿Cómo] están mis hijitos lindos a quienes tanto quiero? [¿Cómo está] mi Mami encantadora, mi Papi relindo [lindo?] y precioso, y mi Junior gracioso, cariñoso y lindo?"

⁵⁴Letter to Dr. Carlos E. Castañeda from Alonso S. Perales, June 16, 1954, CC, Box 34, Folder 3.

⁵⁵Letter to Mr. Perales from Carlos E. Castañeda, March 16, 1955, CC, Box 34, Folder 3.

⁵⁶Letter to Honorable J.T. Canales from Alonso S. Perales, April 23, 1958, José Tomás Canales Estate Collection (hereafter JTC), Jernigan Library, South Texas Archives, Texas A&M University, Kingsville, Box 436, Folder 13.

⁵⁷Email to Cynthia Orozco from Blanca E. Perales, November 20, 2018.

⁵⁸Email to Cynthia Orozco from Raimundo Alfonso Perales, Nov. 19, 2018.

⁵⁹Email to Cynthia E. Orozco from Blanca E. Perales, November 20, 2018.

⁶⁰Email from Raimundo Perales.

[61]Email to Cynthia Orozco from Marta Carmen Perales Carrizales, November 20, 2018.
[62]Email to Cynthia Orozco from Araceli Pérez-Davis, November 20, 2018.
[63]https://www.findagrave.com/memorial/5184125/alonso-s_-perales, Accessed July 29, 2019.
[64]Email to Cynthia Orozco from Blanca E. Perales, November 20, 2018.
[65]Saldaña, "Unsung Hero of Civil Rights."
[66]Letter to J.T. Canales from Carlos E. Castañeda, Alonso S. Perales, and Fortino Treviño, July 31, 1952, CC, Box 9, Folder 6.
[67]F. Arturo Rosales book manuscript, 2017, Chap. 2, 30.
[68]"Alonso M. Perales," https://artepublicopress.com/browse-and-order-books/?swoof=1&woof_text=alonso%20m.%20perales Accessed May 6. 2018.
[69]Speech before Downtown LULAC Council No. 363, Nov. 12, 1962, AP, Box 10, Folder 2.
[70]Marta Pérez de Perales, "Al Pueblo de Alice," October 15, 1960, AP, Box 10, Folder 6. Original text: "Lider nació, y nada pudo con- tener su marcha, por que (sic) los hombres que nacen para eso, vie- nen al mundo uno cada siglo."
[71]Letter to Mr. William L. Ellis from Mrs. Alonso S. Perales, January 3, 1963, Box 10, Folder 2.
[72]Law Firm ledger, 1959, 80, AP, Box 7, Folder 15.
[73]Membership letter from Sociedad de la Unión, January 7, 1935, AP, Box 1, Folder 1.
[74]Letter to Mr. J. Harry La Brum from Mrs. Alonso S. Perales, May 21, 1965, AP, Box 10, Folder 3.
[75]Warranty Deed, March 10, 1959, AP, Box 6, Folder 38.
[76]Contract, Marta P. Perales, seller, to José L. Rangel, buyer, 325 E. Courtland, San Antonio, August 30, 1969 and Contract Lt. Col. Gerald Masey et ux Dorothy, seller, to Marta Perales, September 8, 1969, AP, Box 6, Folder 38.
[77]See AP, Box 6, Folder 38 Law Firm-Real Estate Business. This includes an earnest money contract on 410 North Drive and Warranty Deed from Salvador and Marina P. Martínez, March 10, 1959.
[78]"Letter to the editor" from Mrs. Marta Pérez de Perales, February 24, 1957, unidentified newspaper, AP, Box 12, Folder 7.

[79]Letter to Mrs. Marta Pérez Perales from Senator Edward M. Kennedy, July 18, 1967, AP, Box 10, Folder 3.

[80]Pérez Davis, 17.

[81]"A Letter from Mrs. Marta Perez Perales, 1977, (Letter for Adela Sloss-Vento book), AP, Box 10, Folder 48.

[82]Letter to William P. Clements, Governor from Mrs. Perales, June 10, 1980, AP, Box 10, Folder 1.

[83]"Carta Abierta," April 29, 1988, signed by Marta Pérez Perales and Luis Alvarado Sr., Ex-Director National Legislation, LULAC, AP, Box 10, Folder 3.

[84]Saldaña.

[85]Ibid.

[86]See Gabriela González, *Redeeming La Raza, Transborder Modernity, Race, Respectability, and Rights* (Oxford: Oxford University, 2018), 128.

[87]See children Marta Carmen Perales Carrizales and Raimundo Perales speak articulately and affectionately about their father on You Tube. Alonso S. Perales Conference & Exhibit: Marta Perales Carrizales speaks about her father—https://youtu.be/Dw_iLAVDwNY, YouTube and Alonso S. Perales Conference & Exhibit: Raymond [Raimundo] Alfonso Perales speaks about his father— https://youtu.be/OcT8q4nObiA, YouTube.

CHAPTER 21

[1]Jack Danciger photo, back of photo, writing by Marta Perales noted he was "muy amigo de Alonso." Alonso S. Perales (hereafter AP), M.D. Anderson Library, University of Houston, Box 12, Folder 2. See Box 4, Folders 49, 50, and 51 for correspondence with Danciger. See also "Mr. Jack Danciger, A Friend of the Americas," *South Pacific Mail*, December 11, 1947, AP, Box 9, Folder 32. Danciger grew up in Taos, New Mexico, speaking only Spanish. He made his lawyer available to Fort Worth Mexican Americans and later became an ambassador to Chile. See also Malcom Ross, "Our Personal Relations with Mexicans," Alonso S. Perales, *Are We Good Neighbors?* reprint (New York: Arno Press, 1974), 69.

[2]Letter to Honorable J.T. Canales from Alonso S. Perales, March 13, 1942, José T. Canales Estate Collection (hereafter JTC), Texas A&M University, South Texas Archives, Jernigan Library, Box 431B.

[3]Emilio Zamora, "Jose de la Luz Sáenz: Experiences and Autobiographical Consciousness," *Leaders of the Mexican American Gener- ation, Biographical Essays*, ed. Anthony Quiroz (Boulder: Univer- sity of Colorado, 2015), 49. Original text: "Interesante Carta de un Gran Líder Mexicano."

[4]Letter to J.T. Canales from Alonso S. Perales, Jan. 2, 1928, AP, Box 4, Folder 10.

[5]See the photo of the J.T. Canales Texas Historical Commission marker established in 2009. See http://www.waymarking.com/way-marks/WMK8FA_JT_Canales Accessed on August 24, 2017.

[6]Cynthia E. Orozco notes of Perales Papers (hereafter ON), 1979, 2-3.

[7]Michael Lynch and Carlos Larralde, *Judge J.T. Canales, Latino Civil Rights Leader, An Intimate Portrait* (Saarbrucken: Lap Lambert Academic Publishing, 2015), 76-77.

[8]Lynch and Larralde, 9.

[9]Unsigned (J.T. Canales?), List of "Some of the things Alonso S. Perales has done for the League of United Latin American Citizens," ca. May 1931, AP, Box3, Folder 40.

[10]Letter to Dr. Carlos E. Castañeda from Alonso S. Perales," September 14, 1937, Carlos E. Castañeda Papers (hereafter CC), Benson Latin American Collection (hereafter BLAC), University of Texas at Austin, Box 34, Folder 2.

[11]"EL Lic. Jose T. Canales Como Presidente General," flyer by Lic. Alonso S. Perales, 1933, AP, Box 4, Folder 2.

[12]Letter to Dr. Carlos E. Castañeda from J.T. Canales, October 26, 1935, CC, Box 2, Folder 6.

[13]Letter Lic. Alonso S. Perales, "El Lic. José T. Canales Como Presidente General," (San Antonio: professionally printed by Perales?, April 30, 1932), AP, Box 4, Folder 8; Letter to J.T. Canales from Alonso S. Perales, March 13, 1942, JTC, Box 431, Folder 15, Jerni-

gan Library, South Texas Archives, Texas A&M University, Kingsville.

[14]Letter to Hon. Ezequiel D. Salinas from Alonso S. Perales, May 29, 1956, JTC, Box 431.

[15]Letter to Alonso S. Perales from Ezequiel D. Salinas, ca. May 30, 1956, JTC, Box 431. See June 2, 1956 response by Perales where she states Canales did not solicit or pay him to do so.

[16]Letter to J.T. Canales from Alonso S. Perales, March 17, 1960, JTC, Box 431, Folder 15.

[17]Letter to Hon. J.T. Canales from Alonso S. Perales, May 1, 1944, JTC, Box 431B.

[18]Letter to Honorable J.T. Canales from Alonso S. Perales, July 7, 1953, JTC, Box 431B.

[19]Letter to J.T. Canales from Alonso S. Perales, March 24, 1944, JTC, Box 431B. Original text: "Dice el dicho que 'al nopal lo viene a ver nomás cuando tiene tunas.'"

[20]Letter to J.T. Canales from Alonso S. Perales, March 17, 1960, JTC, Box 431, Folder 15.

[21]Félix D. Almaráz, *Knight without Armor: Carlos Eduardo Castañeda, 1896-1958* (College Station: Texas A&M University, 1998). Another biography of Castañeda is needed to capture his activism; historian Marianne Bueno alluded to this in her essay; see Marianne M. Bueno, "Intellectually He Was Courageous; in Public Action He Was Cautious and Prudent": A Reassessment of Carlos E. Castañeda's Wartime Service, *Latina/os and World War II: Mobility, Agency, and Ideology*, ed., Maggie Rivas-Rodriguez and Benjamin Olguín (Austin: University of Texas, 2014), 95-112.

[22]Mario T. García, *Mexican Americans, Leadership, Ideology & Iden- tity* (New Haven: Yale, 1989), 232.

[23]Letter to JT Canales from Carlos E. Castañeda, October 14, 1941, CC, Box 2, Folder 6.

[24]Virginia Marie Raymond, "Faithful Dissident: Alonso S. Perales, Discrimination, and the Catholic Church," *In Defense of My People, Alonso S. Perales and the Development of Mexican-American Public Intellectuals*, ed. Michael A. Olivas (Houston: Arte Público Press, 2012), 206.

516 CYNTHIA E. OROZCO

[25]Almaraz, 146.

[26]Bueno, 95.

[27]Ibid, 111.

[28]Perales, *Are We Good Neighbors?* (New York: Arno Press, 1970, reprint), 133; Letter to Dr. Carlos E. Castañeda from Alonso S. Perales, August 13, 1948, CC, Box 34, Folder 2.

[29]Raymond, 206.

[30]Letter to Sr. Lic. Alonso S. Perales from Carlos E. Castañeda, May 20, 1942, CC, Box 34, Folder 1. I found that they assisted young men and women alike though young men were brought to their attention more often.

[31]Richard A. Garcia, *Rise of the Mexican American Middle Class, San Antonio, 1929-1941* (College Station: Texas A&M University, 1991), 253.

[32]Letter to Alonso S. Perales from Carlos E. Castañeda, March 5, 1934, CC, Box 33, Folder 11.

[33]Postcard to Muy Estimado Amigo from Alonso S. Perales, October 14, 1941, CC, Box 33, Folder 12. Original text: "Su amigo sincere y s.s. que mucho lo aprecia."

[34]George Matthew Adams, "Solid People" enclosed in Letter to Dr. Carlos E. Castañeda from Alonso S. Perales, July 5, 1945, CC, Box 34, Folder 1.

[35]Letter to A.S. Perales from Carlos E. Castañeda, March 3, 1951, CC, Box 34, Folder 3.

[36]Carlos Castañeda, "The Second-Rate Citizen and Democracy" in Perales, *Are We*, 17-20; Richard A. Garcia, *Rise*, 302-303.

[37]Letter to Mr. Alonso S. Perales from Carlos E. Castañeda, Dec. 9, 1954, CC, Box 34, Folder 3.

[38]Letter to Dr. Carlos E. Castañeda from Alonso S. Perales, June 28, 1951, CC, Box 33, Folder 9.

[39]Letter to Mr. Alonso S. Perales from Carlos E. Castañeda, March 26, 1952, CC, Box 34, Folder 3.

[40]Letter to Dr. Carlos E. Castañeda from Alonso S. Perales, August 9, 1952, CC, Box 34, Folder 3.

[41]See José de la Luz Sáenz Papers (hereafter JLS), BLAC, Box 2, Folder 1.

[42]Arnoldo Carlos Vento, *Adela Sloss-Vento, Writer, Political Activist, and Civil Rights Pioneer* (Lanham: Hamilton Books, 2017), 53. See also Cynthia E. Orozco, *Agent of Charge: Adela Sloss-Vento, Mexican Amerian Civil Rights Activist and Texas Feminist* (Austin: University of Texas Press, 2020).

[43]Mario T. Garcia, "Alonso S. Perales and the Catholic Imaginary: Religion and the Mexican-American Mind," *In Defense*, 162, 168.

[44]Brandon H. Mila, "Hermanos de Raza: Alonso S. Perales and the Creation of the LULAC Spirit," master's thesis, University of North Texas, 2013, 65.

[45]Cynthia E. Orozco, "Spanish-Speaking PTA," *New Handbook of Texas*, ed. Ronnie C. Tyler, Douglas E. Barnett, and Roy R. Barkley 5 (Austin: Texas State Historical Association, 1996), 13-14.

[46]Orozco, *No Mexicans*, pp. 196-219.

[47]Mrs. Adela S. Vento, "Lic. Alonso S. Perales, Defensor Campeón de la Dignidad Racial," *La Voz*, March 28, 1952, Adela Sloss-Vento Papers (hereafter ASV), Austin, Texas; Sloss-Vento, 30. For a 1950s homage to Canales see Gilberto Diaz, "J.T. Canales: Un Insigne Jurista y un Osado Defensor de Nuestra Raza," *Revista Latino-Americana* (Mission, Texas) V: 11: 3, 5, Adela Sloss-Vento Papers (hereafter ASV), Austin, Texas. Canales appeared on the magazine's cover.

[48]Adela Sloss-Vento, *Alonso S. Perales, His Struggle for the Rights of Mexican Americans* (San Antonio: Artes Gráficas, 1977), 30-31. The article is titled, "To Attorney Alonso S. Perales, Defender of Justice and Racial Dignity," *La Prensa*, March ?, 1952. See also J. Luz Sáenz, "España Tributa Honores a un Texano," *La Prensa*, March 31, 1952, 6, ASV.

[49]Donna M. Kabalen de Bichara, "Self-Writing and Collective Representation: The Literary Enunciation of Historical Reality and Cultural Values," *In Defense*, 254. She also mistakenly called Perales Sloss-Vento's mentor in "Expressions of Dissent in the Writings," 201.

[50]See Orozco, *No Mexicans* and Cynthia E. Orozco, "Alonso S. Perales and His Struggle for the Civil Rights of La Raza through the

League of United Latin American Citizens (LULAC) in Texas in the 1930s" *In Defense*, 3-28.

⁵¹Kabalen de Bichara, "Self-Writing," 254-255.

⁵²Vento, 179-180.

⁵³Ibid.

⁵⁴Letter to Señora Adela S. Vento from Alonso S. Perales, August 11, 1947, ASV. Original text: "Yo siempre he admirado su obra, y he dado gracias al Ser Supremo por habernos dado personas como usted que sincera y desinteresadamente se preocupan por el progreso y bienestar de nuestro pueblo."

⁵⁵Letter to Sra. Adela S. Vento from Alonso S. Perales, October 22, 1948, ASV. Original text: "La felicito sinceramente por su bella labor en pro de nuestro pueblo. Siempre leo sus cartas y sus artículos con el mayor interés. ¡Adelante! Me alegra mucho que a Dios gracias, tengamos líderes come usted."

⁵⁶Letter to Sra. Adela S. Vento from Alonso S. Perales, October 22, 1948, ASV.

⁵⁷Letter to Sra. Doña Adela S. de Vento from Alonso S. Perales, October 5, 1954, ASV. Original text: "Qué lástima que por no haber más personas como usted que se interesan de veras en solucionar el problema"

⁵⁸Ibid.

⁵⁹Letter to Licenciado Alonso S. Perales from Adela S. de Vento, December 12, 1951, ASV.

⁶⁰Lic. Alonso S. Perales, "Arquitectos de Nuestros Propios Destinos," "El Precio de la Desunión," June 21, 1953, ASV. Original text: "Es muy inteligente, activa, entusiasta y sincera y su labor noble y constructiva la ha hecho acreedora al título de excelente líder cívica de nuestro pueblo en este país." See Perales, *Are We*, 247-249. Sloss-Vento's essay appeared in Part IV, Articles and Comments. It originally appeared in the *Harlingen Valley Morning Star*.

⁶¹Sloss-Vento, *Perales*, 66.

⁶²Sloss-Vento, *Perales* (Austin: Eagle Feather Institute, First E Book Edition, 2008), viii. Son Dr. Arnoldo Vento reprinted this edition of his mother's book.

[63]Unsigned, Alonso S. Perales?, "La Señora Adela S. de Vento," ca. 1960, AP, Box 8, Folder 14. She noted, "He had even asked for a photograph of myself (sic) for an article he was writing noting my zeal in collaborating in favor of our cause." See Sloss-Vento, *Perales*, 66.

[64]Letter to Dr. Carlos E. Castañeda from Alonso S. Perales, Sept. 17, 1954, CC, Box 34, Folder 3.

[65]Richard A. Garcia, "Alonso S. Perales, The Voice and Visions of a Citizen Intellectual," *Leaders*, 107.

[66]Letter to Honorable José T. Canales from Alonso S. Perales, January 27, 1954, JTC, Box 431B; Letter to Honorable J.T. Canales from Alonso S. Perales, October 16, 1958, JTC, Box 431B. He mentioned "our good friend Roberto E. Austin."

[67]Nora E. Rios McMillan. "Leonides Gonzalez," https://tshaonline.org/handbook/online/articles/fgo72, Accessed May 22, 2018.

[68]Emilio Zamora, *Claiming Rights and Righting Wrongs in Texas, Mexican Workers and Job Politics during World War II* (Austin: University of Texas, 2009), 238. See Flores' "Ordenanza Contra los Prejucios Raciales Dictada Por El Mayor Lic. C.K. Quin," *La Prensa*, Nov. 9, 1941, AP, Box 14, Folder 7.

[69]Ibid, 127.

[70]Laureano Flores, "La Candidatura del Lic. Perales" *La Prensa*, March 17, 1946, AP, Box 9, Folder 43.

[71]Perales, *Are We*, 133.

[72]Laureno Flores, "Discrimination in Texas," Perales, *Are We*, 40-44. Original text: "Su historia como Defensor de los derechos del Mexicano es tradicional. Es un libro abierto pletórico de hechos y de luchas amargas, ya en la Prensa, ya en la tribuna, ya en el campo de la política, etc. Continuamente en lucha a costa de sacrificios, a costa de su propio tiempo y dinero."

[73]Mario T. García, *Mexican Americans, Leadership, Ideology & Identity* (New Haven: Yale University Press, 1989), chapter 3, 62-83 and Cynthia E. Orozco, "Eleuterio Escobar," *New Handbook of Texas* 2: 889-890.

[74]Alonso S. Perales, "El México-Americano y la Política del Sur" (San Antonio: Artes Gráficas, 1931), 2.

[75]Letter to Alonso S. Perales from Roberto Austin, January 13, 1932, Alonso S. Papers (hereafter AP2), South Texas Archives, James Jernigan Library, Texas A & M Kingsville. This is a second Perales collection consisting of a few folders.

[76]Sloss-Vento, 92-93.

[77]Lawsuit, 79th District Court of Hidalgo County, AP, Box 5, Folder 49.

[78]Statement of Fortino Treviño, April 8, 1977 in Sloss-Vento, 87.

[79]Jesse Nazario, "Fortino Trevino," https://tshaonline.org/handbook/online/articles/ftr43 Accessed July 15, 2019.

[80]"The League of United Latin American Citizens, Presidents of Local Councils," ca. early 1930s, AP, Box 3, Folder 37.

[81]Birth certificate, Alonso S. Perales, December 21, 1939 signed by Emilio S. Perales and notarized by Andres de Luna and Fortino Treviño, AP, Box 1, Folder 1.

[82]Letter to Fortino Treviño from Alonso S. Perales, September 16, 1938, AP, Box 2, Folder 22.

[83]Letter to Sr. Fortino Treviño from Alonso S. Perales, October 7, 1940, AP, Box 10, Folder 5.

[84]AP, Box 2, Folder 22.

[85]Postcard, Fortino Treviño to Alonso S. Perales, September 8, 1937, AP, Box 2, Folder 22.

[86]Email to Cynthia E. Orozco from Raimundo Alfonso Perales, November 19, 2018.

[87]See De La Paz v. State lawsuit in 1955. See https://law.justia.com/cases/texas/court-of-criminal-appeals/1955/27552-3.html Accessed July 27, 2018.

[88]Sloss-Vento, 85.

[89]Arnoldo Carlos Vento, *Adela Sloss-Vento, Writer, Political Activist, and Civil Rights Pioneer* (Lanham: Hamilton Books, 2017), 193-195.

[90]Letter to Lic. Alonso S. Perales from Jack Danciger, June 6, 1944, AP, Box 4, Folder 49.

[91]"MC Gonzalez endorsed for state office," June 6, 1930, M.C. Gonzales Papers (hereafter MCG), BLAC, Folder 1.

[92]"San Antonio Lawyer Given Mexican Post," June 21, 1934, unidentified newspaper, MCG, Folder 1.

[93]Mila, 72-73.

[94]"Resolution Presented by Mr. J.T. Canales to the Supreme Council and the Delegates of the various councils of the United Latin American Citizens' League in convention assemble at San Diego, Texas on February 16, 1930, for the purpose of celebrating their first anniversary"; Untitled, Resume of proceedings, LULAC, Feb. 16, 1930, Paul S. Taylor Collection (hereafter PST), Bancroft Library, University of California at Berkeley, Carton 12, Folder 38.

[95]"In the Matter of the Charges Filed by Alonso S. Perales Against M.C. Gonzales," PST.

[96]Mila, 90-94

[97]Letter to J.T. Canales from Carlos E. Castañeda, February 5, 1930 and March 11, 1930 and "Wolves in Sheep Clothing," CC, Box 9, Folder 6.

[98]Memorandum (written on the back of Perales 1931 "A mis hermanos to Nicaragua"), AP, Box 3, Folder 42.

[99]"Fue Un Acontecimiento La Convención de la Liga de Ciudadanos en Edinburg," La Prensa, May 5, 1931, ASV; Vento, 14.

[100]"Humillación," AP, Box 9, Folder 40.

[101]"To the Various Councils of the League of United Latin-American Citizens," June 1, 1932, AP, Box 1, Folder 38.

[102]"Nueva Mesa Directiva del Club Optimista Pan-Americano de San Antonio, Texas," Mosaicos (San Antonio, 1948): 6, Rómulo Munguía Papers, Box 12, BLAC.

[103]"San Antonio Lawyer Given Mexican Post," June 21, 1934, newspaper unknown, MCG, Box 1, Folder 1.

[104]"M.C. Gonzales made Consul in Guatemala," newspaper unknown, August 20, 1943, MCG, Box 1, Folder 1.

[105]Address delivered by M.C. Gonzales at the Latin Quarter on the occasion of a banquet given by Council 2 of LULAC in his honor," November 9th, 1944, AP, Box 3, Folder 36.

[106]Letter to Alonso S. Perales from M.C. Gonzales, March 21, 1952, AP, Box 12 Folder 1.

[107]Garcia, Rise, ftnt. 98, 355.

[108]Letter to A.S. Perales from George I. Sánchez, April 30, 1931, AP, Box 2, Folder 19.

[109]On Sánchez see Ruben Flores, *Backroad Pragmatists, Mexico's Melting Pot and Civil Rights in the United States* (Philadelphia: University of Pennsylvania, 2014).

[110]Almaráz, 217.

[111]Letter to Alonso S. Perales from George I. Sánchez, April 7, 1943, AP, Box 2, Folder 19.

[112]Carlos Kevin Blanton, *George I. Sánchez, The Long Fight for Mexican American Integration* (New Haven: Yale, 2015), 76.

[113]Natalia Mendoza, "The Good Neighbor Comes Home: The State, Mexicans and Mexican Americans, and Regional Consciousness in the US Southwest during World War II," Ph.D. diss., University of California at Berkeley, 2016, chapter 2, "Reluctant Neighbors: The Limitations of Federal Support for Mexicans and Mexican Americans in World War II Texas," 34-54.

[114]Letter to Alonso S. Perales from George I. Sánchez, February 17, 1943, AP, Box 2, Folder 19.

[115]Letter to Alonso S. Perales from Gus Garcia, December 5, 1951, Dr. George I. Sánchez Papers (hereafter GS), BLAC, Box 37, Folder: Gus Garcia.

[116]Blanton, 112.

[117]Texas Committee on Pan-American Group Work Fellowships, GIS, Box 13, "George Sanchez biographical material."

[118]Letter to Dr. Carlos E. Castañeda from Alonso S. Perales, June 30, 1948, CC, Box 34, Folder 2.

[119]Letter to Alonso S. Perales from George I. Sánchez, December 5, 1951, AP, Box 2, Folder 19.

[120]Blanton, 154

[121]Ibid.

[122]Letter to Dr. Carlos E. Castañeda from Alonso S. Perales, October 29, 1954, CC, Box 34 Folder 3.

[123]Ignacio M. García, *Hector P. García: In Relentless Pursuit of Justice* (Houston, Texas: Arte Público Press, 2002), 35-36.

[124]Letter to Hector P. García from Alonso S. Perales, March 15, 1949; Letter to Hector P. García from Alonso S. Perales, February 15,

1951, AP, Box 4, Folder 20. See also García, *Hector P. Garcia*, 136-137, 360.

[125]Letter to Dr. Carlos E. Castañeda from Alonso S. Perales, March 22, 1952, CC, Box 34, Folder 3.

CHAPTER 22

[1]Email to Cynthia E. Orozco from Marta Carmen Perales Carrizales, November 20, 2018.

[2]"A Letter from Mrs. Marta Perez Perales," (Letter from Marta Perales for Adela Sloss-Vento book), ca. 1977, Alonso S. Perales (hereafter AP), M.D. Anderson Library, University of Houston, Box 10, Folder 6.

[3]Letter to Sr. Don Casimiro Pérez Alvarez from Alonso S. Perales, January 5, 1927, Hernan Contreras Collection (hereafter HC), Box 1, Folder 17, Cushing Library, Texas A&M University, College Sta- tion.

[4]Hector Saldaña, "Unsung Hero of Civil Rights 'Father of LULAC' a Fading Memory," *San Antonio Express News*, September 14, 2003.

[5]Letter to Fortino Treviño from Alonso S. Perales, November 8, 1928, AP, Box 2, Folder 22.

[6]Letter to Dr. Carlos E. Castañeda from Alonso S. Perales, Oct. 1, 1948, Carlos E. Castañeda Papers (hereafter CC), Benson Latin American Collection (hereafter BLAC), University of Texas at Austin, Box 34, Folder 2.

[7]Letter to Daddy and Mother (Casimiro Pérez-Álvarez and mother) from Marta Pérez Perales, November 29, 1930, HC, Box 1, Folder 17.

[8]Travel magazines, AP, Box 1, Folder 11.

[9]Letter to Dr. Carlos E. Castañeda from Alonso S. Perales, October 15, 1942, CC, Box 34, Folder 1.

[10]Ibid.

[11]Letter to Dr. Carlos E. Castañeda from Alonso S. Perales, November 17, 1942, CC, Box 34, Folder 1; 10; Letter to Director of Naval Officer Procurement from Alonso S. Perales, Nov. 21, 1942, AP, Box 1, Folder 7.

[12]Letter to Dr. Carlos E. Castañeda from Alonso S. Perales, May 3, 1943, CC, Box 34, Folder 1.

[13]Letter to Dr. Carlos E. Castañeda from Alonso S. Perales, Aug. 26, 1948, CC, Box 34, Folder 2.

[14]Letter to Dr. Carlos E. Castañeda from Alonso S. Perales, Oct. 20, 1949, CC, Box 34, Folder 2.

[15]Letter to Dr. Carlos E. Castañeda from Alonso S. Perales, October 12, 1950, CC, Box 34, Folder 3.

[16]Letter to Alonso S. Perales from Hernan Contreras, January 26, 1951, AP, Box 1, Folder 26.

[17]Postcard to Dr. Carlos E. Castañeda from Alonso S. Perales, Nov. 25, 1950, CC, Box 34, Folder 3.

[18]Letter to ASP from J.T. Canales, March 19, 1951, AP, Box 4, Folder 10.

[19]Letter to Dr. Carlos E. Castañeda from Alonso S. Perales, June 19, 1952, CC, Box 34, Folder 3.

[20]Letter to Dr. Carlos E. Castañeda from ASP, July 12, 1952, CC, Box 34, Folder 3.

[21]Letter to Alonso S. Perales from Carlos E. Castañeda, November 27, 1953, CC, BLAC, Box 34, Folder 3.

[22]Letter to Dr. Carlos E. Castañeda from Alonso S. Perales, June 16, 1954, CC, Box 34, Folder 3.

[23]Letter to Dr. Carlos E. Castañeda from Mr. Alonso S. Perales, October 14, 1954, CC, Box 34, Folder 3.

[24]Letter to Mr. Alonso S. Perales from Carlos E. Castañeda, Jan. 11, 1955, CC, Box 34, Folder 3.

[25]Félix D. Almaráz, *Knight without Armor, Carlos E. Castañeda* (College Station: Texas A&M University, 1999), 328.

[26]Letter to Doctor Dr. Carlos E. Castañeda from Alonso S. Perales, July 12, 1956, CC, Box 34, Folder 3.

[27]Letter to Dr. Carlos E. Castañeda from Alonso S. Perales, September 19, 1956, CC, Box 34, Folder 3.

[28]Letter to Dr. Carlos E. Castañeda from Perales, October 26, 1956, CC, Box 34, Folder 3.

[29]Letter to Mr. Alonso S. Perales from Castañeda, December 3, 1956, CC, Box 34, Folder 3.

[30]Letter to Dr. Carlos E. Castañeda from Alonso S. Perales, Feb. 12, 1957, CC, Box 34, Folder 3.

[31]Ibid.

[32]Letter to Mr. Alonso S. Perales from Carlos E. Castañeda, Feb. 20, 1957, CC, Box 34, Folder 3.

[33]Email to Cynthia Orozco from Marta Carmen Perales Carrizales, November 20, 2018.

[34]Letter to Dr. Carlos E. Castañeda from AP, March 18, 1957, AP, Box 34, Folder 3.

[35]Letter to Honorable J.T. Canales from Alonso S. Perales, April 23, 1958, CC, Box 431B.

[36]Carlos E. Castañeda Papers Finding Aid, BLAC.

[37]Letter To Whom It May Concern (insurance company) from Alonso S. Perales, May 2, 1958, AP., unknown box, unknown folder.

[38]Alonso S. Perales income tax returns, 1959 & 1960, AP, Box 1, Folder 5.

[39]Letter to Adela Sloss-Vento from Alonso S. Perales, March 16, 1959, AP, Box 5, Folder 9.

[40]Letter to Honorable J.T. Canales from Alonso S. Perales, February 16, 1960, Jose T. Canales Estate Papers (hereafter JTC), South Texas Archives, James C. Jernigan Library, Texas A&M University, Kingsville, Box 431B.

[41]"Ser Conmemorada Brillantemente La Fundación del 'LULAC,'" *La Prensa*, February 14, 1960, JTC, Box 431B. Original text: "Fueron tiempos de lucha-agrega. Ahora me queda en el alma la satisfacción del deber cumplido. Y la prueba mayor que se puede esgrimir para demostrar mis aseveraciones es ver como tenemos un Henry González, como Senador; un Alberto Peña, como Comisionado del Condado; un José Olivares y un José San Martín como miembros del Concilio de la Ciudad; un Fidencio Guerra y un Osvaldo García, como Jueces de Distrito. Y así, son muchos, pero muchos, los ejemplos que podemos poner. Pero no quiero dejar de señalar el caso del Lic. Carlos C. Cárdenas, que ese el primer abogado del City Hall."

[42]Benjamín Márquez, *LULAC: The Evolution of a Political Organization* (Austin: University of Texas, 1993), 59.

[43]"LULAC Celebrates 31 Years of Progress," (Letter from Frank Jasso, President, Council 2), Ad in *La Prensa*, Feb. 14, 1960, JTC, Box 431B.

[44]Letter to Mrs. Alonso S. Perales from Zoe Esteele, March 25, 1960, AP, Box 1, Folder 1.

[45]Laurie E. Jasinski, "San Antonio, Texas, https://tshaonline.org/handbook/online/articles/hds02 Accessed May 27, 2018.

[46]David Montejano, *Quixote's Soldiers, A Local History of the Chicano Movement, 1966-1981* (Austin: University of Texas, 2010), 15.

[47]Carlos Kevin Blanton, *George I. Sánchez, the Long Fight for Mexican American Integration* (New Haven: Yale, 2015), 253.

[48]"Alonso S. Perales," (obituary), *San Antonio Light*, May 10, 1960, AP, Box 1, Folder 5. "Nicaraguan Consul Dies," *San Antonio Express*, May 10, 1960, Cynthia E. Orozco notes of Perales Papers (hereafter ON), 1979, 290.

[49]"Alonso S. Perales," (obituary) *New York Times*, May 10, 1960, 37, AP, Box 1, Folder 5.

[50]*La Prensa*, May 11, 1960; "Lic. Perales Fallecido," *La Voz*, May 13, 1960, ON.

[51]Adela Sloss-Vento, *Alonso S. Perales, His Struggle for the Rights of Mexican-Americans* (San Antonio, 1977), 68.

[52]Arnoldo Carlos Vento, *Adela Sloss-Vento, Writer, Political Activist, and Civil Rights Pioneer* (Lanham: Hamilton Books, 2017), 16.

[53]Sra. Adela Sloss de Vento, "Memorias del Fallecimiento del Gran Defensor," May 9, 1960, Adela Sloss-Vento Papers, Austin, Texas.

[54]Unsigned, "La Señora Adela S. de Vento" biography, ca. 1960?, AP, Box 8, Folder 14. Original text: "Ellos han sacrificado su salud, su tiempo, aun puesto su dinero y han pasado malos ratos y bochornos con los enemigos de nuestra causa, pero su gran patriotismo, su optimismo, fue su gran cariño hacia el pueblo Latino Americano deverlo feliz lo ha vencido todo."

CHAPTER 23

[1]Aaron E. Sánchez, "Mendigos de nacionalidad: Mexican-Americanism and Ideologies of Belonging in a New Era of Citizenship, Texas,

1910-1967," *In Defense of My People, Alonso S. Perales and the Development of Mexican-American Public Intellectuals*, ed. Michael A. Olivas (Houston: Arte Público Press, 2012), 104.

[2]Ibid, 114.

[3]Thomas H. Kreneck, "Mr. LULAC, the Fabulous Life of John J. Herrera," *Leaders of the Mexican American Generation, Biographical Essays*, ed. Anthony Quiroz (Denver: University of Colorado, 2015), 231.

[4]Ignacio M. García, *White But Not Equal, Mexican Americans, Jury Discrimination, and the Supreme Court* (Tucson: University of Arizona, 2009), 126.

[5]Donna M. Kabalen de Bichara, "Self-Writing and Collective Representation: The Literary Enunciation of Historic Reality and Cultural Values," *In Defense*, 241.

[6]García, 141. Ignacio M. García's quote addressed Mexican-American legal status in the 1950s but captures some key ideas relevant to the 1920s.

[7]Neil Foley, *Quest for Equality, The Failed Promise of Black-Brown Solidarity* (Boston: Harvard University Press, 2010), 35.

[8]David Gutiérrez, *Walls and Mirrors, Mexican Americans, Mexican Immigrants, and the Politics of Ethnicity* (Berkeley: University of California 2005), 84.

[9]Sánchez, 112.

[10]See Laura Gómez, *Manifest Destinies: The Making of the Mexican American Race* (New York: New York University, 2007). The absence of a "Mexican American" identity in New Mexico is based on my observations after over twenty years in the state.

[11]F. Arturo Rosales book manuscript on Perales (2017), Chapter 3, 29.

[12]Gabriela González, *Redeeming La Raza, Transborder Modernity, Race, Respectability, and Rights* (Oxford: Oxford University, 2018), 5.

[13]Emilio Zamora, "Connecting Causes: Alonso S Perales, Hemispheric Unity, and Mexican Rights in the United States," *In Defense*, 296.

[14]Thomas Kreneck, *Mexican American Odyssey, Félix Tijerina, Entrepreneur and Civic Leader, 1905-1965* (College Station: Texas A&M University, 2001), 108, 310.

[15]Tomás Ybarra-Frausto, "Frameworks of Identity in the 1980s," *The Decade Show* (Museum of Colorado?, 1990), 95.

[16]Sánchez, 104. He wrote, "The new groups of the 1920s were not creating fraternity . . ."

[17]Address by M.C. Gonzales, November 9, 1944, Banquet by LULAC Council 2 in his honor, Alonso S. Perales Papers (hereafterAP), M.D. Anderson Library, University of Houston, Box 3, Folder 36.

[18]Zamora, 296. He noted, "Perales and other fellow founders of LULAC seemed willing to alienate Mexican nationals for the sake of establishing an ethnic organization in 1927. This changed by the 1930s . . ."

[19]Thomas A. Guglielmo, "Fighting for Caucasian Rights: Mexicans, Mexican Americans, and the Transnational Struggle for Civil Rights in World War II Texas," *Journal of American History* 92:4 (March 2006), 1232.

[20]Emilio Zamora, *Claiming Rights and Writing Wrongs in Texas, Mexican Workers and Job Politics during World War II* (College Station: Texas A&M University, 2009),16.

[21]Alonso S. Perales, "Las Sociedades Como Medio de Progreso," *En Defensa de Mi Raza* 2 (San Antonio: Artes Gráficas, 1937):18. Original text: "Y aquí juzgo oportuno decir con énfasis que la responsabilidad del porvenir de nuestra raza en este país es de los líderes mexicanos sin consideración a ciudadanía."

[22]Alonso S. Perales, "Problemas de Nuestra Raza en Estados Unidos," *En Defensa*, 2: 4.

[23]Zamora, "Connecting Causes," *In Defense*, 295.

[24]José Angel Gutiérrez, "Chicanos and Mexicans Under Surveillance: 1940-1980," Renato Rosaldo Lecture Series Monograph, 2 (Tucson: Mexican American Studies & Research Center, Spring 1986), 51.

[25]Craig A. Kaplowitz, *LULAC, Mexican Americans and National Policy* (College Station: Texas A&M University, 2005), 42.

[26]Untitled manuscript by Melisio Pérez, April 1952, AP, Box 10, Folder 17.

[27]Benjamín Márquez, *LULAC: The Evolution of a Mexican American Political Organization* (Austin: University of Texas Press, 1993), 29.

[28]Ibid, 30.

[29]John R. Chávez, *The Lost Land: The Chicano Image of the Southwest* (Albuquerque: University of New Mexico, 1984), 113.

[30]Félix M. Padilla, *Latino Ethnic Consciousness: The Case of Mexican Americans and Puerto Ricans in Chicago* (Notre Dame: University of Notre Dame, 1985), 4-5.

[31]Alice, Texas had a newspaper called *Latino Americano* and San Angelo, Texas had one called *El Latino*. See "Se Repitió el Ultraje Hacia los Mexicanos de San Angelo," *En Defensa*, 2: 72-73.

[32]Alonso S. Perales, "Problemas de Nuestra Raza en Estados Unidos," III *En Defensa* 2: 11.

[33]"Discurso Pronunciado Por El Autor de Esta Obra . . . ," Perales, *En Defensa*, 2: 78.

[34]"La Asociación de Padres y Maestros," Perales, *En Defensa*, 1: 71.

[35]"Ecos de la Convención Especial de la 'Lulac' Verificada en Corpus Christi," Perales, *En Defensa* 2: 91.

[36]"A Bill to be Entitled," n.d., AP, Box 4, Folder 1.

[37]Mario T. García, *Católicos: Resistance and Affirmation in Chicano Catholic History* (Austin: University of Texas, 2004), 76.

[38]"Report from the Congress of the Inter-American Bar Federation Held in Mexico City," *Fraternidades*, 1944, 7, AP, Box 14, Folder8.

[39]Letter to His Excellency Franklin Delano Roosevelt, President from Alonso S. Perales, March 31, 1944, Alonso S. Perales, *Are We Good Neighbors?* (San Antonio: Artes Gráficas, 1948), 279.

[40]Perales, *Are We Good Neighbors?* reprint (New York: Arno Press, 1974), 266.

[41]Perales, "Foreword," *Are We*, 7.

[42]See Cristina Beltrán, *The Trouble with Unity: Latino Politics and the Creation of Identity* (Oxford: Oxford University Press, 2010).

[43]"Brother Alonso S. Perales Home Again," *LULAC News*, January 1933, 9, AP, Box 4, Folder 4.

[44]"Mis dignos conciudadanos y hermanos de raza," n.d, AP, Box 8, Folder 10. Eleven speeches in this folder begin with this opening.

[45]Foley, 209.

[46]Ibid, 34.

[47]Brandon H. Mila, "Hermanos de Raza: Alonso S. Perales and the Creation of the Spirit of LULAC," master's thesis, University of North Texas, 2013, 73-74. Original text: "los Nicaragüenses son hermanos de raza nuestros porque ellos, al igual que nosotros los mexicanos, o son de sangre española pura o de sangre india pura o por sus venas circulan ambas. Además, su idioma es el español y sus costumbres e ideología son idénticas a las Nuestras."

[48]Araceli Pérez-Davis, "Marta Pérez de Perales," *El Mesteño* 4: 37 (October 2000), 16.

[49]Perales, *En Defensa* 1: 9. Original text: "Insulto a los representantes oficiales del Gobierno Mexicano y a todas los demás funcionarios diplomáticos hispanoamericanos que residen en Washington, quienes aunque no son mexicanos, resienten tanto como nosotros los ultrajes inferidos a nuestra raza por virtud de los vínculos de sangre e idioma que nos ligan."

[50]Zamora, "Connecting Causes," 296.

[51]Sánchez, 99.

[52]Leigh Ann Wilson, "Fighting Two Devils: Eleuterio Escobar and the School Improvement League's Battle for Mexican and Mexican American Students," Education in the San Antonio, Texas Public Schools from 1934 to 1958," Ph.D. diss., University of Memphis, 2011, 51.

[53]García, *White But Not Equal*, 81.

[54]Ibid, 83.

[55]F. Arturo Rosales book manuscript on Perales, 2017, Chapter 3, 26.

[56]Neal Foley, "Becoming Hispanic: Mexican Americans and the Faustian pact with Whiteness," *Reflexiones: New Directions in Mexican American Studies*, ed. Neil Foley (Austin: Center for Mexican American Studies, University of Texas, 1998), 53-70.

[57]Zamora, *Claiming Rights*, 247-248, fnts 24, 25, and 26 provide a critique of the Foley assertions.

[58]Zamora, "Connecting Causes," 10. María Portillo Saldaña offers a critique of Foley and Lopez. See María Josefina Portillo Saldaña, "'How many Mexicans [is] a horse worth?' The League of United

Latin American Citizens, Desegregation Cases and Chicano Historiography." *South Atlantic Quarterly* 107:4 (Fall 2008): 809-831.

[59]Benjamin H. Johnson, "The Cosmic Race in Texas: Racial Fusion, White Supremacy, and Civil Rights Politics," *Journal of American History* 98:2 (September 2011), 415.

[60]Johnson, 404-419.

[61]Sánchez, 107. (Letter to editor, *El Demócrata*, Oct. 23, 1936)

[62]George A. Martínez, "Alonso S. Perales and the Effort to Establish the Civil Rights of Mexican Americans as Seen Through the lens of Contemporary Critical Legal Theory: Post-racialism, Reality Construction, Interest Convergence, and Other Critical Themes," *In Defense*, 136.

[63]Alonso S. Perales, "Problemas de Nuestra Raza en los Estados Unidos," III, *En Defensa,* 12-13.

[64]Virginia Marie Raymond, "Faithful Dissident: Alonso S. Perales, Discrimination, and the Catholic Church," *In Defense*, 201.

[65]Testimony of Alonso S. Perales, House, Committee on Immigration, Hearings on Western Hemisphere Immigration, 71st Congress, 2nd Session, 1930, 183.

[66]Letter to White Man's Union Association of Wharton County from Alonso S. Perales, July 5, 1937, *En Defensa* 2: 93-94.

[67]Mario T. García, "Mexican Americans the Politics of Citizenship: The Case of El Paso, 1936," *New Mexico Historical Review* 59:2 (April 1984), 187-204; Carlos Kevin Blanton, "George I. Sanchez, Ideology, and Whiteness in the Making of the Mexican American Civil Rights Movement, 1930-1960," *Journal of Southern History* 72:3 (August 2006): 569-604; and Foley, *Quest for Equality.*

[68]Letter to White Man's Union, Wharton, Texas," July 5, 1937 in Perales, *En Defensa* 2: 94.

[69]Lupe S. Salinas, "Legally White, Socially Brown: Alonso S. Perales and His Crusade for Justice for La Raza," *In Defense*, 91.

[70]Letter to Hon. John W. Brown, M.D., State Health Officer from Alonso S. Perales, Nov. 28, 1936, AP, Box 4, Folder 9.

[71]"A Bill," attachment to Letter to Dr. Carlos E. Castañeda from Alonso S. Perales, Feb. 23, 1951, Carlos Eduardo Castañeda Papers

(hereafter CC), Benson Latin American Collection (hereafter BLAC), University of Texas at Austin, Box 34, Folder 3.

[72]Márquez, "In Defense," *In Defense*, 35. See Alonso S. Perales to Carlos Castañeda, December 9, 1944, CC, Box 34, Folder 1.

[73]Laura E. Cannon, "Situational Solidarity: LULAC's Civil Rights Strategy and the Challenge of the Mexican American Worker, 1934-1946," Ph.D. diss., Texas Tech University, 2016, Chapter 1.

[74]García, *White but Not Equal*, 77.

[75]Benjamín Márquez, "In Defense," *In Defense*, 34.

[76]Ibid.

[77]Foley, *Quest*, 42.

[78]F. Arturo Rosales, "Writing a Biography of Alonso Sandoval Perales," *In Defense*, 276.

[79]Brian D. Behnken, *Fighting their Own Battles: Mexican Americans, African Americans, and the Struggle for Civil Rights in Texas* (Chapel Hill: University of North Carolina Press, 2014).

[80]Rosales, *In Defense*, 276.

[81]Letter from Frank J. Galvan, Jr. LULAC National President to "Notice to All LULAC Councils," Oct. 8, 1936, AP, Box 4, Folder 20.

[82]Sánchez, 107. The letter was from Gregory R. Salinas to Louis Wilmot, August 13, 1936. Salinas was a LULAC Council 16 leader from San Antonio.

[83]Thomas Kreneck, *Mexican American Odyssey, Felix Tijerina, Entrepreneur and Civic Leader, 1905-1965* (College Station: Texas A&M University, 2001), 108.

[84]Foley, *Quest*, 69.

[85]Ibid, 41.

[86]Letter to Mr. Alonso S. Perales from Carlos E. Castañeda, February 26, 1947, CC, Box 34, Folder 2.

[87]Letter to Mr. Alonso S. Perales from Dr. Carlos E. Castañeda, April 11, 1947, CC, Box 34, Folder 2.

[88]Zamora, *Claiming Rights*, 10.

[89]Raymond, ftnt. 20, 217.

[90]Emma Tenayuca and Homer Brooks, "The Mexican Question in the Southwest," *The Communist* (March 1939), 265-266.

[91]Quoted in Gabriela González, *Redeeming La Raza, Transborder Modernity, Race, Respectability, and Rights* (Oxford: Oxford University Press, 2018), 167.

[92]Ibid.

[93]"Report from the Congress of the Inter-American Bar Federation Held in Mexico City," AP, Box 14, Folder 8.

[94]Mario T. García, *Católicos: Resistance and Affirmation in Chicano Catholic History* (Austin: University of Texas, 2004), 64.

[95]Ibid, 66.

[96]Alonso S. Perales, "Al Margen de Proyectos de Ley que Muy Importantes son Para Nuestra Raza," *La Prensa*, February 13, 1937, AP, Box 1, Folder 10.

[97]Márquez, "In Defense," *In Defense*, 47.

[98]Richard A. Garcia, *Rise of the Mexican American Middle Class, San Antonio 1929-1941* (College Station: Texas A&M University, 1991), 271.

[99]"Toma Ímpetu el Movimiento de los Lulacs en Pro de Aumento de Jornales Para los Mexicanos," AP, Box 3, Folder 39. Original text: "Para remedir la situación de nuestra gente es indispensable que a les pague lo que vale su trabajo."

[100]David Montejano, *Anglos and Mexicans in the Making of Texas* (Austin: University of Texas, 1990), 244.

[101]Laura Cannon, "Situational Solidarity," Chapter 1.

[102]Zamora, *Claiming Rights*, 101.

[103]Guglielmo, 1219.

[104]Zaragoza Vargas, *Labor Rights Are Civil Rights: Mexican American Workers in Twentieth-Century America* (Princeton: Princeton University Press, 2005), 63.

[105]Márquez, *LULAC*, 66.

[106]Zamora, *Claiming Rights*, 205.

[107]Montejano, 234.

[108]González, 6-8.

[109]No author, "Our Aim: Good Citizenship," *La Verdad* (Falfurrias), June 1, 1935, 2, AP, Box 11, Folder 23.

[110]Alonso S. Perales, "Lo Que Significa Para Nosotros las Escuelas Para Adultos," *En Defensa* 2: 21. Original text: "...una nueva era

en la evolución de los latinoamericanos de esta ciudad y de este Estado."

[111]Alonso S. Perales, "My Message to United Latin American Citizens," ca. Spring 1928, AP, Box 3, Folder 41.

[112]"Report from the Congress of the Inter-American Bar Federation Held in Mexico City," AP, Box 14, Folder 8.

[113]F. Arturo Rosales book manuscript on Perales (2017), Chapter 1, 16.

[114]Letter to Carlos E. Castañeda from Alonso S. Perales, 1957, CC, Box 34, Folder 3. Here Perales made a distinction between "high" culture and popular culture, the former considered more educational and valuable by those with a higher class standing.

[115]Márquez, *LULAC*, 10.

[116]Márquez, "In Defense," 30.

[117]Garcia, *Rise*, 254.

[118]Vargas, 81.

[119]Joseph Orbock Medina, "The Trials of Unity: Rethinking the Mexican-American Generation in Texas, 1948-1960," *In Defense*, 56.

[120]Orbock Medina, 56.

[121]Richard A. Garcia, "Alonso S. Perales," *Leaders of the Mexican American Generation, Biographical Essays*, ed. Anthony Quiroz (Denver: University of Colorado, 2015)," 101.

[122]"Memorandum, Subject: Conditions in San Antonio, Texas, February 23, 1939," AP, Box 3, Folder 42.

[123]"Arrangement Completed for Huge Americanism Meeting," n.d. (ca. late 1930s), AP, Box 3, Folder 36; "Conditions in San Antonio," 2.

[124]Márquez, *LULAC*, 30.

[125]Lupe S. Salinas, "Legally White, Socially Brown: Alonso S. Perales and His Crusade for Justice for La Raza," *In Defense*, 93.

[126]Márquez, "In Defense," 41.

[127] Ibid.

[128]Sister Frances Jerome Woods, "Mexican Ethnic Leadership in San Antonio," Ph.D. diss., Catholic University, Washington DC, 1947 reprint (New York: Arno Press,1974), 91.

[129] Adela Sloss-Vento, *Alonso S. Perales: His Struggle for the Rights of Mexican Americans* (San Antonio: Artes Gráficas, 1977), 16.

[130] Foley, *Quest*, 90.

[131] Brandon H. Mila, "Alonso S. Perales and the Spirit of LULAC," master's thesis, University of North Texas, 2013, 89.

[132] Matthew Gritter, *Mexican Inclusion: The Origins of Anti-Discrimination Policy in Texas and the Southwest* (College Station: Texas A&M University, 2012), 7.

[133] Márquez, "In Defense," 32.

[134] Ibid.

[135] "Una presentación teatral que no hace justicia al pueblo Mexicano," May 14, 1923, *La Prensa*, AP, Box 12, Folder 2.

[136] Letter to Srita. Alberta Besch from Alonso S. Perales, July 6, 1937, *En Defensa* 2: 95-97.

[137] Márquez, "In Defense," 33.

[138] Alonso S. Perales, "Nuestro pueblo puede ayudarse a si mismo," *La Prensa*, November 20, 1948, AP, Box 9, Folder 10.

[139] Julie Leininger Pycior, *Democratic Renewal and the Mutual Aid Legacy of US Mexicans* (College Station: Texas A&M University Press, 2014).

[140] Garcia, "Alonso S. Perales," 87.

[141] Letter to Carlos E. Castañeda from Alonso S. Perales, May 30, 1940, CECP, Box 33, Folder 12.

[142] Garcia, *Rise*, 253.

[143] Ibid, 260.

[144] Garcia, "Alonso S. Perales," 99.

[145] "Problemas de Nuestra Raza en Estados Unidos," III, *En Defensa* 2:7. Original text: "no somos fundamentalmente inferiores."

[146] García, *Católicos*, 71-72.

[147] Márquez, 32.

[148] Alonso S. Perales, "Problemas de Nuestra Raza en Estados Unidos," II, *En Defensa* 2: 6.

[149] Salinas, 92-93; editorial, AP, Box 8, Folder 12.

[150] Alonso S. Perales, "Un Decidido Defensor de Nuestra Raza en Texas en 1859," (Arquitectos de Nuestros Propios Destinos), no date, *La Prensa*, José de la Luz Sáenz Papers, BLAC, Box 5, Fol-

der 17. Original text: "un ciudadano integro y una verdadero campeón de la justicia y defensor de los mexicanos en Texas." Juan Cortina used violence.

[151]"Mr. President," Flyer, Convention Hall, Edinburg, May 4, 1931, AP, Box 3, Folder 40.

[152]Quoted in John-Michael Rivera, *Emergence of Mexican America: Recovering Stories of Mexican Peoplehood in U.S. Culture* (New York: New York University Press, 2006), 159.

[153]Chávez, 113.

[154]Garcia, *Rise*, 181.

[155]Priscilla Falcón, "Public Intellectuals and Historical Memory," *Confluencia: Revista Hispánica de Cultura y Literatura*, 30:1 (Fall 2014): 190-191.

[156]José Angel Gutiérrez, *Albert Pena Jr., the Dean of Chicano Politics* (East Lansing: Michigan State University, 2017), 48.

[157]Garcia, *Rise*, 289.

CHAPTER 24

[1]Email to Cynthia Orozco from Marta Carmen Perales Carrizales, November 19, 2018.

[2]Adela Sloss-Vento, "Alonso S. Perales-Precursor and Founder of the LULAC," 1977, Alonso S. Perales (hereafter AP), M.D. Ander-son Library, University of Houston, Box 10, Folder 10.

[3]Adela Sloss Vento, "Alonso S. Perales," (letter to Edgewood School Board, ca. November 1974), AP, Box 10, Folder 10. See Cynthia E. Orozco, *Agent of Change, Adela Sloss-Vento, Mexican American Civil Rights Activist and Texas Feminist* (Austin: University of Texas, 2020) and Arnoldo Carlos Vento, *Adela Sloss-Vento, Writer, Political Activist, and Civil Rights Pioneer* (Lanham: Hamilton Books, 2017).

[4]Letter to Alonso S. Perales from M.C. Gonzales, March 21, 1952, AP, Box 12, Folder 1.

[5]Letter to Mrs. Alonso Perales Sr. from Henry Cisneros, May 12, 1979, AP, Box 10, Folder 1.

[6]Michael A. Olivas, "Introduction, Alonso S. Perales, The Rule of Law and the Development of Mexican-American Public Intellectuals," *In Defense of My People, Alonso S. Perales and the Development of Mexican-American Public Intellectuals*, ed. Michael A. Olivas (Houston: Arte Público Press, 2012), x.

[7]*In Defense*, viii.

[8]Michael A. Olivas, "Are We Good Neighbors? Academic Duty and Public Service," https://www.aals.org/services/presidents-messages/ good-neighbors/. Accessed on March 2, 2018.

[9]Hector Saldana, "Unsung Hero of Civil Rights," *San Antonio Express News*, September 14, 2003.

[10]Al Kaufman, "The Birth of Latino Rights Organizations," *300Years of San Antonio & Bexar County*, ed. Claudia R. Guerra and Char Miller (San Antonio: Maverick Books, Trinity University Press, 2018), 218-219. The sidebar of the article features Gus Garcia.

[11]Cynthia E. Orozco, "William C. Velásquez," *New Handbook of Texas*, ed. Ronnie C. Tyler, Douglas E. Barnett, and Roy R. Barkley 6 (Austin: Texas State Historical Association, 1996), 720; Juan A. Sepúlveda Jr., *The Life and Times of Willie Velásquez, Su Voto es Su Voz* (Houston: Arte Publico Press, 2014); see Hector Galan's film "Willie Velasquez: Your Vote is Your Voice," PBS, Voces, 2016

[12]Adela Sloss-Vento, *Alonso S. Perales, His Struggle for the Rights of Mexican-Americans* (San Antonio: Arte Público Press, 1977), 95. She included San Antonio Judge Joe Bernal's comments who incorrectly attributed the quote to President John F. Kennedy.

[13]*La Calavera*, November 2, 1942, AP, Box 10, Folder 30.